"Colored Men"
AND
"Hombres Aquí"

Hernandez v. Texas and the Emergence
of Mexican-American Lawyering

"Colored Men"
AND
"Hombres Aquí"

Hernandez v. Texas and the Emergence
of Mexican-American Lawyering

Michael A. Olivas, Ed.
Foreword by Mark Tushnet

Arte Público Press
Houston, Texas

This volume is made possible through grants from the City of Houston through The Cultural Arts Council of Houston, Harris County and the Exemplar Program, a program of Americans for the Arts in collaboration with the LarsonAllen Public Services Group, funded by the Ford Foundation.

Recovering the past, creating the future

Arte Público Press
University of Houston
452 Cullen Performance Hall
Houston, Texas 77204-2004

Cotton Picker document, located in University of Texas-Permian Basin, Dungan Library, Archives / Special Collections, in personal library of John Bell Shepperd. Reprinted with permission.

Cover design by James Brisson

"Colored Men" and "Hombres Aquí": *Hernandez v. Texas* and the Emergence of Mexican-American Lawyering / edited by Michael A. Olivas.
    p. cm.
  ISBN-10: 1-55885-476-2 (alk. paper)
  ISBN-13: 978-1-55885-476-5
    1. Hernandez, Pete—Trials, litigation, etc. 2. Jackson County (Tex.)
—Trials, litigation, etc. 3. Trials (Murder)—Texas—Jackson County.
4. Race discrimination—Texas—Jackson County. 5. Jury selection
—United States. I. Olivas, Michael A.
  KF224.H468C65   2006

                                            2006040240

6 7 8 9 0 1 2 3 4 5   10 9 8 7 6 5 4 3 2 1

"The petitioner's initial burden in substantiating his charge of group discrimination was to prove that persons of Mexican descent constitute a separate class in Jackson County, distinct from 'whites.' One method by which this may be demonstrated is by showing the attitude of the community. Here the testimony of responsible officials and citizens contained the admission that residents of the community distinguished between 'white' and 'Mexican.' The participation of persons of Mexican descent in business and community groups was shown to be slight. Until very recent times, children of Mexican descent were required to attend a segregated school for the first four grades. At least one restaurant in town prominently displayed a sign announcing 'No Mexicans Served.' On the courthouse grounds at the time of the hearing, there were two men's toilets, one unmarked, and the other marked 'Colored Men' and 'Hombres Aqui' ('Men Here'). No substantial evidence was offered to rebut the logical inference to be drawn from these facts, and it must be concluded that petitioner succeeded in his proof."

Hernandez v. Texas, 347 U.S. 475, 479-80 (1954) (footnotes and references omitted)

Dedication

To the attorneys who brought this case and worked so hard on behalf of our community: Gus Garcia, Carlos Cadena, Johh J. Herrera, and James de Anda. They leaned against power when it was dangerous to do so, and left the trail clearer for those who followed so long after. All Latino and Latina lawyers and advocates stand on these shoulders, even if they do not realize it.

CP

Table of Contents

Foreword

The so-called New Western Historians have shown us how to write cultural and social history from West and Southwest to East, in contrast to the traditional narrative written from East—the Pilgrims and all that—to West and Southwest. Writing political history from West and Southwest to East is more difficult, though perhaps possible. Writing constitutional history in that direction seems impossible, because of the central role African slavery played in the creation and early development of the Constitution. As this collection of articles on *Hernandez v. Texas* shows, the situation is different for contemporary constitutional law. The West and Southwest can become central to our understanding of the constitutional law of the twentieth and twenty-first century.

Constitutional law in the nineteenth century did confront the West and Southwest, but the issues implicated in those confrontations reflected the centrality of slavery in the constitutional law of the era. This is true of both the adjudicated Constitution and the non-adjudicated one. The Cherokee Removal cases presented a conflict among three national institutions—the national government, state governments, and the Supreme Court—in the course of implementing a national policy aimed at separating indigenous Americans from an area white Americans hoped to control. The Supreme Court's constitutional cases, though, were about the role of states and the Supreme Court in implementing that policy. That is, they were federalism cases in the ordinary mold. (*Johnson v. MacIntosh*, a non-constitutional case, did deal with fundamental questions about how the encounter between indigenous Americans and newcomers would develop.)

The Louisiana Purchase opened the way for migration from the East to what was then described as the West, and later to what we now call the West and Southwest. And there were constitutional issues connected to the Louisiana Purchase, though none reached the courts. The basic issue was whether the national government had the power to acquire territory by purchase. None of the powers enumerated in Article I—and nothing obviously inherent in the executive power of Article II—seemed to authorize permanent expansion by purchase. Note, though, that the question of whether an action fell within the enumerated powers was understood at the time to be fundamentally a question of states' rights. That is, the national government's power was limited so as to ensure that states would continue to control matters of particularly local concern, the most important of which was slavery in the South.

It would be relatively easy to write the constitutional history of the nineteenth century with slavery and its post-1865 legacy at its heart. And, I think, scholars of constitutional law continue to see slavery's legacy as central to the development of constitutional law in the twentieth century. In the standard story, for example, *Brown*

ix

v. Board of Education lies at the core of twentieth century constitutional history. Harry Kalven wrote *The Negro and the First Amendment*, showing how cases arising out of the civil rights movement of the 1960s transformed free speech law. The Warren Court's revolution in constitutional criminal procedure is often described as an effort by the Supreme Court to regularize the law arising out of routine interactions between African Americans and the police in the nation's cities.

Yet, this collection shows how the standard narrative can be displaced. Accidental facts indicate the opening: that *Hernandez* was decided just a week before *Brown*; that two central cases in the criminal procedure revolution—*Escobedo v. Illinois* and *Miranda v. Arizona*—involved not African American but Latino defendants and one arose in the Southwest. In some ways, the question is, How wide an opening does the perspective from the West and Southwest provide?

Without intending to disparage the insights on constitutional criminal procedure we can get by looking from the West and Southwest, I will focus here on equal protection law, moving from some relatively narrow doctrinal points to a broader vision of the nation's self-understanding. We can begin by noting the transformation of the subject matter of the equal protection clause from "African Americans" to "race." The Supreme Court suggested in the *Slaughterhouse Cases* that the clause was not likely to be invoked successfully on behalf of any class other than African Americans. That observation seems at best quaint today. Partly because of a deep universalism in U.S. constitutionalism, the litany, "race, religion, and national origin" rapidly became embedded in our understanding of equality's concerns, later to be expanded to include gender, sexual orientation, age, and more.

What, though, is "race"? How do we know when people are discriminating on the basis of race? As several essays here demonstrate, *Hernandez* can be seen as the origin of, and perhaps the best justification for, the view that race discrimination consists of a socially constructed process of subordination, and so as the origin and justification for a view of the equal protection clause in severe tension with the now prevailing view that the clause aims at practices that are not neutral with respect to race. The anti-subordination interpretation of the equal protection clause carries with it important doctrinal consequences, such as the near-automatic validation of genuine affirmative action programs.

The view from the West and Southwest illuminates issues even from within the race-neutrality interpretation of the equal protection clause. A persistent issue within that interpretation is what to do about practices, neutral on their face, that have a racially disparate impact. Again, the account of the facts in *Hernandez*, and the Court's explanation for its holding that those facts demonstrated an equal protection violation, show both why disparate impacts should be constitutionally troubling, and how to identify practices with such impacts. A less common issue that *Hernandez v. Texas* brings to the surface is the one directly confronted, and decided wrongly, in *Hernandez v. New York*: What is the constitutional status of a practice expressly grounded on a racially neutral criterion that is closely correlated with race? This question differs from that of disparate impact, because disparate effects can arise from the use of racially neutral criteria that are only loosely correlated with race (but are correlated with other facts, such as poverty, that are correlated with race). Few cases involving African Americans raise the "correlated with race" issue in as clear a form as *Hernandez v. New York* does. The *Hernandez* cases make it clear that the "correlated trait" cases cannot sensibly be resolved without paying attention to the social construction of race.

The view from the West and Southwest brings into clearer view some even broader questions. With slavery and its legacy at the center of the narrative of constitutional law, it is possible to pose the constitutional choice open to the United States as one between binationalism and integration. The black-white racial binary might be used to describe segregation, or a world in which institutions are truly separate and equal, or the world envisioned by some black nationalists. The universalist alternative is integrationism. Some of the essays in this collection show precisely how the view from the West and Southwest came to complicate the narrative. In the first instance, the question was, Given the black-white racial binary, where can law locate Mexican-Americans in the two-category system of racial hierarchy? The background and litigation posture of *Hernandez v. Texas* show how that question came to seem badly posed. Mexican-Americans were, from one angle, neither black nor white, and from another, were both black and white.

The next step was conceptually simple, though difficult to take in practice. The racial binary was replaced by a multi-tiered system of racial hierarchy, still with whites at the top. One might say that multinationalism replaced binationalism. And that replacement transforms quite dramatically the way we can think about race. Sustaining a vision of a binationalism of equals was enormously difficult given the history of racial subordination in the United States. Sustaining a vision of a multi-nationalism of equals was substantially easier—and even easier once multinationalism became understood anew as multiculturalism. The integrationist alternative did not disappear, of course, but the competition between multiculturalism and integrationism as visions of a society of equals occurred on terms much more favorable to the multicultural alternative than had characterized the position of binationalism in its competition with integrationism.

I have sketched out how the view from the West and Southwest can modify the presently prevailing modes of understanding equal protection law. A question for future research is the extent to which that view might have similar effects on the modes of understanding other parts of constitutional law. It seems clear to me that the view from the West and Southwest could affect the presently prevailing mode of understanding the constitutional organization of foreign affairs, for example, by making the Insular Cases as important as the Steel Seizure Case, and by treating cases involving national power over immigration as foundational cases—equivalent in importance to the cases involving national power over the economy.

What of other areas of constitutional law? Can the view from the West and Southwest change the way students of constitutional law understand the First Amendment? Questions of federalism? The essays in this collection of course do not offer answers to those questions. What they do, though, is make it possible to ask them. Over the next decades, we may come to see how the view from the West and Southwest helps us see the entire Constitution differently.

Mark Tushnet
Georgetown University Law Center

Acknowledgements

As with so many other things in life, nothing gets done alone or by one's self. A project like this had many parents, and it took a village. The actual idea came from a number of discussions I had with my Houston attorney friend J. Michael Solar, whose firm had been joined by Judge James de Anda. He and I wanted to take the Judge's light out from underneath the bushel basket, and to honor him for his many accomplishments. We were joined at lunch one day by Nicolás Kanellos, fellow UH professor and publisher of Arte Público Press, whose Board I had chaired for over ten years. He wanted to launch a Latino Civil Rights Series, and had already lined up an author to undertake a volume on the GI Forum, the Mexican American veteran's group that had been founded by Dr. Hector P. García, a Corpus Christi physician and civil rights veteran who had been a friend of James de Anda when he practiced in that city. These unfocused ideas converged into a conference on the fast-approaching fiftieth anniversary of the *Hernandez v. Texas* case, and we all took note of how many *Brown v. Board* conferences and commemorations were being held. All of us took note that there were scheduled to be over fifty *Brown* symposia in its fifty year celebration, and a national commission established to spur reconsideration of that important case. Yet this was the only *Hernandez* symposium to lead to publication. It was a scene straight out of a Mickey Rooney movie of the 1940's: hey, let's put on a conference!

It was natural that the University of Houston Law Center would host this conference, as it was Houston lawyers who took the cases that led to *Hernandez*, and it is the nearest law school to Jackson County, Texas. In 1951, when Pete Hernandez shot Joe Espinosa, the lawyers feared for their safety in that town where the case was being tried, so two drove back to Houston each night (James de Anda and Johnny Herrera), while the two from San Antonio (Carlos Cadena and Gus Garcia) returned to their homes there.

Of course, I thank the wonderful scholars who participated in this project: Laura Gómez, Ian Haney López, Clare Sheridan, Sandra Guerra Thompson, Neil Foley, Kevin Johnson, and Steven Wilson. Juan Perea delivered a paper at the conference, but did not include it in the earlier *Chicano-Latino Law Review* volume; I appreciate his submitting it for this larger book project. In addition, Professors Amilcar Shabazz, George Martinez, and Richard Delgado presented talks at the conference which were not submitted for either volume. Earlier work by virtually all these scholars had suggested *Hernandez*'s importance, and I was very pleased that we were able to attract such fresh and nuanced scholarship from so many accomplished authors. Overall research assistance was provided by UHLC students Ryan T. Miller and Eric L. Munoz, while additional assistance was provided by University of Chicago undergraduate student Alejandro Flores, a Houston native. The UCLA Chicano-Latino Law Review staff provided superb legal research and editorial assistance, particularly Isabel Cesanto and Caryn Mandelbaum. From Arte Público Press, I acknowledge Nicolás Kanellos, Marina Tristán, and Gabriela Baeza Ventura. At UHLC, many colleagues helped out, but I single out Deborah Jones, Nancy Rapoport, Leah Gross, Ruth Shauberger, Sam Barker, Waqar Jamil, and Augustina Reyes. My New Mexico grade school classmate Paul Espinosa showed us his brilliant film The Lemon Grove Incident and inspired all the conference participants. I also acknowledge the generosity of the J. Michael and Patricia Solar Fund of the Greater Houston Community Foundation, the Mexican American Bar Association of Houston, the Hispanic Bar Association of Houston, the Hispanic National Bar Association, Perry & Haas, LLP, Prudential Financial, Belo Corp., and KHOU-TV. In particular, I acknowledge the support of Philip Shelton and Kent Lollis of the Law School Admissions Council and Rafael Magallan of the College Board.

Michael A. Olivas
University of Houston Law Center

Chronology in *Hernandez v. Texas*

APRIL 23, 1950: Aniceto Sanchez commits murder in Richmond, Ft. Bend County, TX; defended by John Herrera, A.D. Azios, and James de Anda.

MAY 1, 1950: Sanchez indicted by grand jury.

FALL 1950: Attorneys move to quash indictment, charging that all white grand jury and petit jury violated Equal Protection; denied by District Court.

MARCH 19, 1951: Attorneys file exception, appeal decision not to quash indictment, citing Ft. Bend demography; brief written by James de Anda.

MARCH 20, 1951: Aniceto Sanchez goes to trial.

APRIL 7, 1951: Sanchez sentenced to not less than 2 years and not more than 10 years.

APRIL 20, 1951: Sanchez appeals to Texas Court of Criminal Appeals.

AUGUST 4, 1951: 24 year old service station attendant Pedro (Pete) Hernandez shoots and kills tenant farmer Joe Espinosa in Chinco Sanchez's Tavern, Sprung's Grocery, Edna, Jackson County, TX.

AUGUST 4, 1951: Indicted by all white grand jury and petit jury panel for murder.

AUGUST 8, 1951: Hernandez denied bail.

SEPTEMBER 1951: San Antonio attorneys Gustavo Garcia and Carlos Cadena join defense team to challenge Texas jury practices.

OCTOBER 4, 1951: District court refuses to quash indictment; attorneys use Aniceto Sanchez brief, edited for Jackson County demographics; de Anda sends materials to Cadena, who re-drafts with updated data.

OCTOBER 8-11, 1951: Tried by all white jury (actual trial on October 11: charge read 1:15 pm; jury reviews case 4:30 pm; verdict received 8:00 pm).

OCTOBER 11, 1951: Convicted of murder with malice aforethought by all white jury.

OCTOBER 11, 1951: Sentenced to 99 years.

NOVEMBER 21, 1951: *Aniceto Sanchez v. State* decided by Texas Court of Criminal Appeals.

JUNE 18, 1952: Texas Court of Criminal Appeals affirms judgment.

OCTOBER 22, 1952: Texas Court of Criminal Appeals refuses rehearing.

JANUARY 21, 1953: Petition for writ of certiorari filed with U. S. Supreme Court.

OCTOBER 12, 1953: Certiorari granted by U.S. Supreme Court, 346 U.S. 811 (1953).

OCTOBER 1953: Marshall Trust donates $5000 for civil rights trials; funds disbursed by George I. Sanchez; local LULAC councils donate funds for printing, filing costs.

JANUARY 11, 1954: Gus Garcia and Carlos Cadena argue *Hernandez*; Garcia given 12 minutes more than usually allowed for oral arguments.

MAY 3, 1954: Supreme Court issues *Hernandez v. Texas*, 347 U.S. 475 (1954).

MAY 7, 1954: TX Prison System notifies Jackson County Sheriff that Pete Hernandez (No. 124147) is to be handed over to Jackson County.

JUNE 10, 1954: Case remanded to TX Court of Criminal Appeals.

JUNE 14, 1954: Remanded case filed in TX Court of Criminal Appeals.

SEPTEMBER 28, 1954: Hernandez re-indicted.

OCTOBER 16, 1954: Gus Garcia files change of venue motion; retrial moved to Refugio County.

NOVEMBER 15, 1954: Second trial held.

NOVEMBER 1954: Jury finds Pete Hernandez guilty, sentences him to 20 years; he serves sentence in Harlem State Prison Farm, inmate No. 136125.

JUNE 7, 1960: Recommended for parole by TX Board of Pardons and Paroles.

JUNE 8, 1960: Paroled and released by order of Gov. Price Daniel.

Introduction
Commemorating the 50th Anniversary of *Hernandez v. Texas*
Michael A. Olivas

Like most of the readers of this volume, I never studied the *Hernandez v. Texas*[1] case in law school, and never heard of it in civics class or in regular civilian life. As I pursued my career as a law professor and legal scholar, I saw tantalizing references to the case, and looked it up one day in the law library, pulling out the U.S. Supreme Court Reporter volume. The law librarian who helped me knew exactly where the volume was, as many people had requested her help to read the *Brown v. Board of Education* decision.[2] There it was, just before *Brown*.

As were others who are writing in this book, I was riveted by the Court's decision, which sketches 1950s Texas justice, the role of Mexican Americans, and the symbolic signage of the Jackson County Courthouse bathrooms that struck the justices so clearly.[3] I grew up in 1950s and 1960s New Mexico, and my people were from Tierra Amarilla. My cousin, Eulogio Salazar, was shot in the famous 1967 Tierra Amarilla, New Mexico courthouse raid led by Reies López Tijerina,[4] so I knew that Mexican Americans were not accorded full status, but I never knew the extent of these historical facts. Even after I moved to Houston and became friends with Judge James de Anda, one of the trial attorneys in the original *Hernandez* case, I never thought of it as a Houston case with my modest friend as one of its architects. After today, with all the papers written for this project, I expect this wrong to be righted.

---

[1]347 U.S. 475 (1954).

[2]347 U.S. 483 (1954).

[3]"The petitioner's initial burden in substantiating his charge of group discrimination was to prove that persons of Mexican descent constitute a separate class in Jackson County, distinct from 'whites.' One method by which this may be demonstrated is by showing the attitude of the community. Here the testimony of responsible officials and citizens contained the admission that residents of the community distinguished between 'white' and 'Mexican.' The participation of persons of Mexican descent in business and community groups was shown to be slight. Until very recent times, children of Mexican descent were required to attend a segregated school for the first four grades. At least one restaurant in town prominently displayed a sign announcing 'No Mexicans Served.' On the courthouse grounds at the time of the hearing, there were two men's toilets, one unmarked, and the other marked 'Colored Men' and 'Hombres Aqui' ('Men Here'). No substantial evidence was offered to rebut the logical inference to be drawn from these facts, and it must be concluded that petitioner succeeded in his proof." *Hernandez v. Texas*, 347 U.S. 475, 479-80 (1954) (footnotes and references omitted).

[4]REIES LÓPEZ TIJERINA, THEY CALLED ME "KING TIGER" 80-81, 99-100 (José Angel Gutiérrez trans. & ed., 2000).

The racial question in the case of Mexican Americans may seem quaint to some observers in today's artificially "race-neutral" era, but it has been an issue with real consequence for this community over time, virtually always to the detriment and exclusion of Mexican-origin people. History is replete with such racial calculations concerning Mexicans, even if traditional histories do not recount this version of American apartheid.[5] One of the Californio signers of the 1849 California Constitution, Manuel Dominguez, was dismissed as a witness in a court proceeding, as he had "Indian blood," and thus was not deemed to be a reliable witness; Dominguez was a relatively privileged landholder and elected official, indicating that the caste system even extended to landowning elites.[6] Pete Hernandez and his lawyers knew he was not Anglo, in Jackson County, Texas or elsewhere, but it took the U.S. Supreme Court to acknowledge the sociology of Texas rural life and parse the criminal justice implications of this racial ascription. The quotidian details of bathroom and restaurant signage and the recitation of the town's social divide prompted this terse acknowledgement by the Court, almost hidden in the case's dry civil procedure: "No substantial evidence was offered to rebut the logical inference to be drawn from these facts, and it must be concluded that petitioner succeeded in his proof."[7] And the Court could count, noting, "it taxes our credulity to say that mere chance resulted in there being no Mexican-Americans among the over six thousand jurors called in the past 25 years."[8]

Years later, Professor Charles L. Black, Jr. referred to the veil of ignorance that was cast over Jim Crow practices, where Anglos would be so inured to the practices, and benefit so substantially from this system that they did not even recognize it. Although he was speaking specifically of the condition of Blacks, he noted:

> [I]f a whole race of people finds itself confined within a system which is set up and continued for the very purpose of keeping it in an inferior station, and if the question is then solemnly propounded whether such a race is being treated "equally," I think we ought to exercise one of the sovereign prerogatives of philosophers—that of laughter. The only question remaining (after we get our laughter under control) is whether the segregation system answers to this description. Here, I must confess to a tendency to start laughing all over again. I was raised in the South, in a Texas city where the pattern of segregation was firmly fixed. I am sure it never occurred to anyone, white or colored, to question its meaning.[9]

---

[5]For example, in a widely-used textbook that accompanied the PBS series of the same name, one paragraph is devoted to the case, and it is not even cited in the footnoted text. See F. ARTURO ROSALES, CHICANO!: THE HISTORY OF THE MEXICAN AMERICAN CIVIL RIGHTS MOVEMENT 108 (1997). As of 2005, there is no full-length book on the case, or on any of the lawyers involved, in contrast to the hundreds of texts and thousands of articles on *Brown* and its lawyers.

[6]LEONARD PITT, THE DECLINE OF THE CALIFORNIOS: A SOCIAL HISTORY OF THE SPANISH-SPEAKING CALIFORNIANS, 1846-1890, at 202 (1966). See also Ricardo Romo, Southern California and the Origins of Latino Civil-Rights Activism, 3 WEST. LEG. HIST. 379, 380 n.3 (1990).

[7]Hernandez v. Texas, 347 U.S. 475, 480 (1954).

[8]*Id.* at 481.

[9]CHARLES L. BLACK, JR. THE LAWFULNESS OF THE SEGREGATION DECISIONS, 69 YALE L.J. 421, 424 (1961). See also GERALD TORRES, THE EVOLUTION OF EQUALITY IN AMERICAN LAW, HASTINGS CONST. L.Q. 613 (2003) (citing Black's conclusions).

Interestingly, he did not allude to the similar caste status accorded Mexican Americans such as was evident in Jackson County, Texas society and juryboxes, and he was surely wrong that subjugated African Americans did not "question its meaning." By the time of the *Hernandez* case, surely Texas lawmakers and decisionmakers were on notice by *Sweatt v. Painter*[10] that the terrain was shifting on its racial tectonic plates and that people of color in Texas were questioning segregation's meaning.

A recent Houston Chronicle story reminded us that women, including white women, were not allowed to be seated on Houston juries until November 1954—several months and many jury panels after the *Hernandez* and *Brown* decisions.[11] Yet it is clear that the demography and social norms have changed to the extent that it is inconceivable that women or African Americans or Mexican Americans can be held back or excluded. The Houston Independent School District, with nearly a quarter of a million schoolchildren is less than ten percent white.[12] *Hopwood*[13] has been overturned by *Grutter*,[14] and it may only be a matter of time before jury trials,[15] voting,[16] school attendance patterns,[17] and all the other racial and gender practices that divide us will be eliminated.

[10]339 U.S. 629 (1950) (striking down a separate Texas public law school for Blacks, citing it as unequal).

[11]Roma Khanna, Legal Strides for Women Came with Time: 50 Years ago, Houstonian was the First Female Juror to Lawfully Sit on Texas Panel, HOUS. CHRON., Sept. 26, 2004, at B1.

[12]For Houston Independent School District data see http:// www.houstonisd.org (last visited Nov. 20, 2004). For studies of the Houston Independent School District, which gave birth to the Houston College for Negroes, later Texas Southern University (1935), the Houston Junior College, later the University of Houston (1927), and the Houston Community College System (1989), see WILLIAM H. KELLAR, MAKE HASTE SLOWLY: MODERATES, CONSERVATIVES AND SCHOOL DESEGREGATION IN HOUSTON (1999); GUADALUPE SAN MIGUEL, BROWN, NOT WHITE: SCHOOL INTEGRATION AND THE CHICANO MOVEMENT IN HOUSTON (2001); ANGELA VALENZUELA, SUBTRACTIVE SCHOOLING: U.S.-MEXICAN YOUTH AND THE POLITICS OF CARING (1999). For a more personal, less-objective narrative of the Houston Independent School District see DONALD R. MCADAMS, FIGHTING TO SAVE OUR URBAN SCHOOLS—AND WINNING!: LESSONS FROM HOUSTON (2000). The "win" in Houston has been quite contested, especially considering how dropout data and "zero tolerance" policies have evolved. See Jason Spencer, Assistant Principal Files Whistleblower Suit, HOUS. CHRON., Apr. 17, 2004, at 29A (discussing data fraud in Houston Independent School District dropout records); Rachel Graves, Backlash Growing Over Zero Tolerance, HOUS. CHRON, Apr. 18, 2004, at 1A (reviewing inconsistencies in discipline policies); Jason Spencer, HISD Focuses on Achievement Gap, HOUS. CHRON., May 16, 2004, at 1A (discussing racial isolation in Houston Independent School District schools).

[13]Hopwood v. Texas, 236 F 3d 256 (5th Cir. 2000), cert. denied, 533 U.S. 929 (2001).

[14]Grutter v. Bollinger, 539 U.S. 306 (2003) (upholding the use of race in college admissions to establish a "critical mass"); see also Gratz v. Bollinger, 539 U.S. 244 (2003) (striking down college admissions practice of allocating points on racial basis).

[15]McClesky v. Kemp, 481 U.S. 279 (1987) (racial sentencing disparities). See also Angela J. Davis, Prosecution and Race: The Power and Privilege of Discretion, 67 FORDHAM L. REV. 13 (1998); RANDALL KENNEDY, RACE, CRIME, AND THE LAW (1997). Texas, especially the Houston-area Harris County, has been engaged in an extraordinary tug of war with the U.S. Supreme Court, regarding the racial composition of juries. See Patty Reinert, High Court, 5th Circuit Battling Over Death Row, HOUS. CHRON., Dec. 5, 2004, at A1; Linda Greenhouse, Justices Give Second Hearing in a Texas Death Row Case, N.Y. TIMES, Dec. 7, 2004, at A1. See the chapters by Thompson and Sheridan, repectively, in this volume.

[16]Pamela S. Karlan, The Fire Next Time: Reapportionment After the 2000 Census, 50 STAN. L. REV. 731 (1998); Pamela S. Karlan, Just Politics? Five Not So Easy Pieces of the 1995 Term, 34 HOUS. L. REV. 289 (1997).

[17]Nancy A. Denton, The Persistence of Segregation: Links Between Residential Segregation and School Segregation, 80 MINN. L. REV. 795 (1996). For the postsecondary counterpart, including an analysis of college admissions based in part upon residency issues see Michael A. Olivas, Brown and the Desegregative Ideal: Higher Education, Location, and Racial College Attendance Policies, 90 CORNELL L. REV. 391 (2005).

At least that is what we hope for, perhaps against all logic and odds. Within weeks of the death of the first Mexican-American federal judge, Reynaldo Garza, asked by then-President Carter to be his Attorney General,[18] Houstonian Alberto Gonzales was named to the post, completing an arc of many years.[19] The Houston City Attorney is Mexican American,[20] as is the new school superintendent.[21] However, Professors Guerra Thompson's and Sheridan's contributions to this volume reveal that race still matters a great deal in the criminal justice system, in Texas and elsewhere.[22] A recent Houston study revealed the extent to which jury selection remains predominantly white: only nine percent of Harris County's grand jurors were Latino, far less than the demographics would dictate in a county where over a third of the residents are Latino.[23] Equally troubling was the evidence that a very high percentage of the grand jurors are employees of law enforcement agencies or closely related to law enforcement officials, suggesting a less-than-arm's length relationship with police or court officials.[24]

Recent events in Arizona and other states where anti-alien animus is so evident,[25] even when courts have struck down such official scapegoating,[26] continue to provide evidence that Latinos, especially Mexican-origin communities, have a great deal to struggle against. Mexicans and Mexican Americans are still subject to excessive police force, as in the Harris County cases of Jose Campos Torres, who was thrown into Buffalo Bayou by police and drowned while in their custody in Houston,[27] and Luis Torres, who was strangled by police on a street in Baytown,[28] yet the

---

[18]See LOUISE ANN FISCH, ALL RISE: REYNALDO G. GARZA, THE FIRST MEXICAN AMERICAN FEDERAL JUDGE (1996). Garza died on September 14, 2004. Laura B. Martinez, Judge Garza dead at 89, Nation's first Mexican-American District Judge Dies of Pneumonia, BROWNSVILLE HERALD, Sept. 15, 2004, at A1. For a critique of the poor record of such appointments, see Kevin R. Johnson and Luis Fuentes-Rohwer, A Principled Approach to the Quest for Racial Diversity on the Judiciary, 10 MICH. J. of RACE & L. 5 (2004)

[19]Eric Lichtblau, Broad Influence for Justice Dept. Choice, N.Y. TIMES, Nov. 21, 2004, at A30.

[20]Kristen Mack, Mayor Appoints City Attorney to Staff, HOUS. CHRON., Feb. 18, 2004, at A18.

[21]Jason Spencer, Just the Standard Perks, Please, HOUS. CHRON., Dec. 5, 2004, at B1 (reporting on the appointment of Abe Saavedra to be Houston Independent School District Superintendent and salary negotiations).

[22]Clare Sheridan, Peremptory Challenges: Lessons from Hernandez v. Texas, 25 CHICANO-LATINO L. REV. 77 (2005); Sandra Guerra Thompson, The Non-Discrimination Ideal of Hernandez v. Texas Confronts a "Culture" of Discrimination: The Amazing Story of Miller El v. Texas, 25 CHICANO-LATINO L. REV. 97 (2005).

[23]Steve McVicker, Are Judges Taking a Narrow View of Justice, HOUS. CHRON., Nov. 14, 2004, at A18 (citing study of jury composition in Harris County).

[24]Id. (showing that many if not most of the grand jury commissioners were employees or former employees of courts or law enforcement agencies).

[25]Susan Carroll, Elvia Diaz & Yvonne Wingett, Prop. 200: Federal Judge will Hear Constitutional Issues Dec. 22, THE ARIZ. REPUBLIC, Dec. 1, 2004, at A1 (Temporary restraining order on public referendum concerning undocumented aliens and state presence).

[26]Kevin R. Johnson, An Essay on Immigration Politics, Popular Democracy and California's Proposition 187: The Political Relevance and Legal Irrelevance of Race, 70 WASH. L. REV. 629 (1995); Kevin R. Johnson, Public Benefits and Immigration: The Intersection of Immigration Status, Ethnicity, Gender, and Class, 42 UCLA L. REV. 1509 (1995).

[27]Jose Campos Torres was thrown into a Houston bayou by police officers, where he drowned in May 1977; see http://www.tdcj.state.tx.us/stat/porterhenrylast.htm (last visited Apr. 14, 2005).

[28]Luis Torres was choked to death by Baytown, Texas police officers while their police car video was running. For the story on the death, see Jake Bernstein, Are you Experienced? Video of a Police Killing Produces Shockwaves in Baytown, TEX. OBSERVER, Mar. 29, 2002, at 3. To review the actual police video, see http://www.texasobserver.org/showTOC.asp?IssueID=55 (last visited May 3, 2005).

perpetrators were never punished. And no Mexican American represents the city in Congress or sits on the Southern District federal bench in Houston,[29] the country's fourth largest city. Controversy swirling around the racial character of twenty-first-century designer medicines and the conundrum presented by genetic markers and racial ascriptions[30] remind us that racism and racial privilege are eddies and flows, seeking their own path and deeply etching the landscape.

Authors in this volume have noted these currents throughout their writings over the years; indeed, my own knowledge of *Hernandez* arose in large part due to the earlier efforts of several of these authors.[31] Writing in another venue, Kevin Johnson noted:

> Unfortunate as it may be, uncivil times for civil rights has been a recurrent theme in U.S. history. Ebbs and flows of racism and nativism have deeply affected racial and other minorities in the country. Importantly, in the struggle for social justice, minority groups must appreciate the relationship between the various subordinations. Backlashes against the groups often are related in a complex matrix.[32]

But today, we take note of one substantial change—the *Hernandez* case is a clear example of how a people took control of their own fate, and with persistence and sheer talent, prevailed. The larger Anglo society may not have heeded the message or behaved properly, then or now, but these courageous lawyers raised their voices and prevailed in our highest court, on behalf of their client and their community. Judge James de Anda's remarks, delivered in his quiet and unassuming manner at the November 2004 conference that spawned these chapters, cannot disguise the extraordinary challenge these lawyers faced in mid-century Texas, where they did not even feel safe enough to stay the night in Edna, Texas, and as a result, retreated

---

[29]Judge de Anda, who left the bench in 1992 for private practice, was the last Mexican American to serve in the Houston federal judiciary.

[30]MICHAEL OMI & HOWARD WINANT, RACIAL FORMATION IN THE UNITED STATES: FROM THE 1960s TO THE 1990s (1994). For a recent review of issues concerning "racial designer drugs" see January W. Payne, A Cure for a Race? Heart Drug Findings Set off Ethics Debate, WASH. POST, Nov. 16, 2004, at HE-1. While it is clear that race is a social construct and a function of sociology, there are also clear biological and physiological features as well. These racial characteristics are often at odds with the sociology of race. For the long arc of this topic see Ariela J. Gross, Litigating Whiteness: Trials of Racial Determination in the Nineteenth Century South, 108 YALE L. J. 109 (1998); Tanya Kateri Hernandez, Multiracial Discourse: Racial Classifications in an Era of Color-Blind Jurisprudence, 57 MD. L. REV. 97 (1998); Rachel L. Swarns, Hispanics Debate Census Plan to Change Racial Grouping, N.Y. TIMES, Oct. 24, 2004, § 1, at 21.

[31]See, e.g., George A. Martínez, Legal Indeterminacy, Judicial Discretion and the Mexican-American Litigation Experience, 1930-1980, 27 U.C. DAVIS L. REV. 555 (1994); George A. Martínez, The Legal Construction of Race: Mexican-Americans and Whiteness, 2 HARV. LATINO L. REV. 321 (1997); JUAN PEREA ET AL., RACE AND RACISM: CASES AND RESOURCES FOR A DIVERSE AMERICA 517 (2000) (casebook including *Hernandez* case and commentary); Ian Haney López, RACISM ON TRIAL: THE CHICANO FIGHT FOR JUSTICE (2003); Steven Wilson, Brown Over "Other White": Mexican Americans' Legal Arguments and Litigation Strategy in School Desegregation Lawsuits, 21 LAW & HIST. REV. 145 (2003); Clare Sheridan, "Another White Race": Mexican Americans and the Paradoxes of Whiteness in Jury Selection, 21 LAW & HIST. REV. 109 (2003); NEIL FOLEY, THE WHITE SCOURGE: MEXICANS, BLACKS, AND POOR WHITES IN TEXAS COTTON CULTURE (1997); Kevin R. Johnson, "Melting Pot" or "Ring of Fire"?: Assimilation and the Mexican-American Experience, 85 CAL. L. REV. 1259 (1997).

[32]Kevin R. Johnson, Immigration, Civil Rights, and Coalitions for Social Justice, 1 HASTINGS RACE AND POVERTY L.J. 181, 200 (2003).

every night to their homes in Houston and San Antonio.[33] Many of these same lawyers learned the lesson from Thurgood Marshall and the NAACP Legal Defense lawyers, and with LDF assistance, established the Mexican American Legal Defense and Educational Fund (MALDEF) in Texas in 1968.[34] MALDEF has since exceeded the modest expectations of its founders, and has evolved to become the major organizational legal force on behalf of Latino communities.[35]

In its fiftieth year anniversary in 2004, all of America has remembered the towering *Brown v. Board* decision, and assessed its impact.[36] Others have remembered the occasion of a young white Tupelo, Mississippi truckdriver, Elvis Presley, wandering into a Memphis, Tennessee recording studio the same year, and changing the world in another racially significant manner.[37] However, this is the only major scholarly occasion devoted to this fascinating Texas case, decided within days of *Brown*, and which signaled the start of Mexican-American lawyering. That development is still in progress, and the scholarship evident here is in the tradition of George I. Sánchez and the others who provided the intellectual foundation of this movement.[38] I thank all the authors who contributed to this volume and to the conference that led to this discussion.

I welcome all of you to *Hernandez*.

---

[33]James de Anda, Nov. 2004 Remarks, at pp. 229-239 in this volume. See also GUSTAVO GARCIA, A COTTON-PICKER FINDS JUSTICE, THE SAGA OF THE HERNANDEZ CASE (Ruben Munguia ed., 1954). This fascinating pamphlet was published by the San Antonio printer Ruben Munguia in June, 1954, following the announcement of the decision a month earlier. Few copies exist, and I consulted the one from the Special Collection of the Library at the University of Texas, Permian Basin. I placed the public domain document on the Hernandez at 50 conference website at http://www.law.uh.edu/hernandez50 (last visited May 3, 2005), and it is reprinted in the Appendix of this volume.

[34]GUADALUPE SAN MIGUEL, "LET ALL OF THEM TAKE HEED": MEXICAN AMERICANS AND THE CAMPAIGN FOR EDUCATIONAL EQUALITY IN TEXAS, 1910-1981 (1987).

[35]*Id*. To review MALDEF's range of litigation efforts see http://www.maldef.org (last visited May 3, 2005) (listing recent cases filed in civil rights actions).

[36]Many law schools and organizations have celebrated the decision with commemorations and special law review issues. For a listing of several such activities see http://www.brownat50.org/index.html (last visited May 3, 2005).

[37]PETER GURALNICK, LAST TRAIN TO MEMPHIS: THE RISE OF ELVIS PRESLEY (1994).

[38]George I. Sánchez was one of the first Mexican-American scholars, and served on the University of Texas Education faculty for many years, until his death in 1972. See, e.g., George I. Sánchez, Group Differences and Spanish-Speaking Children: A Critical Review, 16 J. APPLIED PSYCHOL. 5 (1932); GEORGE I. SÁNCHEZ, FORGOTTEN PEOPLE: A STUDY OF NEW MEXICANS (1940). For a volume that reviewed his career and scholarship see HUMANIDAD: ESSAYS IN HONOR OF GEORGE I. SÁNCHEZ (Americo Paredes ed., 1977).

Off-White in an Age of White Supremacy: Mexican Elites and the Rights of Indians and Blacks in Nineteenth-Century New Mexico

Laura E. Gómez*

Introduction

In their studies of mid-twentieth century civil rights litigation involving Chicanos, several scholars have reached the conclusion that, in this era, Mexican Americans occupied an ambivalent racial niche, being neither black nor white.[1] The Supreme Court case *Hernandez v. Texas*,[2] decided in 1954 during the same term as *Brown v. Board of Education*,[3] is cited as evidence for that proposition because it reveals tensions among members of the bench and bar involved with the case regarding claims to whiteness, claims to protected status under the Constitution, and the social reality of 1950s Texas for Chicanos, especially working class Chicanos such as Pedro "Pete" Hernandez. Hernandez was a 24-year-old cotton picker who was convicted by an all-white jury of murdering 40-year-old Joe Espinosa, a tenant farmer, outside a bar one Saturday afternoon.

Hernandez's lawyers, who would come to include one of the first Mexican Americans appointed to the federal bench in Texas and the first Mexican American law professor, appealed Hernandez's conviction and sentence of life imprisonment.[4]

*Professor of Law & American Studies, University of New Mexico. Ph.D. Stanford (1994), J.D. Stanford (1992), M.A. Stanford (1988), A.B. Harvard (1986). The author thanks the following individuals for their input: Rick Abel, Kip Bobroff, Tobias Duran, Lawrence Friedman, Carole Goldberg, Gillian Lester, Joel Handler, Ian Haney Lopez, Antonio Gómez, Michael Olivas, Estevan Rael-Gálvez, Leti Volpp, as well as audiences at the School of American Research and the "Hernandez at 50" Conference at the University of Houston Law Center. I am also indebted to the extraordinary library staffs at the UCLA School of Law, the UNM School of Law, and the School of American Research. Research for this chapter was supported by the UCLA School of Law Dean's Fund and the Weatherhead Foundation (supporting my tenure as a resident scholar at the School of American Research, 2004-05).

[1] See George Martinez, The Legal Construction of Race: Mexican-Americans and Whiteness, 2 HARV. LATINO L. REV. 321, 326-29 (1997); George Martinez, Legal Indeterminacy, Judicial Discretion and the Mexican-American Litigation Experience: 1930-1980, 27 U.C. DAVIS L. REV. 555 (1994); Ian Haney López, Retaining Race: LatCrit Theory and Mexican American Identity in Hernandez v. Texas, 1 Harv. Latino L. Rev. 297 (1997); Steven H. Wilson, Brown Over "Other White": Mexican Americans' Legal Arguments and Litigation Strategy in School Desegregation, 21 LAW & HIST. REV. 145 (2003); Clare Sheridan, "Another White Race:" Mexican Americans and the Paradox of Whiteness in Jury Selection, 21 LAW & HIST. REV. 109 (2003); See also, Ariela Gross, Texas Mexicans and the Politics of Whiteness, 21 LAW & HIST. REV. 195 (2003).

[2] Hernandez v. Texas, 347 U.S. 475, 482 (1954).

[3] Brown v. Board of Education, 347 U.S. 483, 496 (1954).

[4] The four lawyers who worked on the Hernandez appeal were Gus García, John J. Herrera, Carlos C. Cadena (the first Mexican American law professor, who taught at St. Mary's Law School), and James DeAnda (one of the first Mexican Americans appointed to the federal bench in Texas).

1

They argued that their client's constitutional right to equal protection under the law had been violated because, despite being 16 percent of the Jackson County population, no Mexican American had ever been summoned for service as jury commissioner, grand juror or petit juror in the county in 25 years. One of the deep ironies in the case was the reasoning used by the Texas appellate court in 1952 to conclude that Mr. Hernandez's rights had not been violated: "Mexicans are white people . . . The grand jury that indicted appellant, and the petit jury that tried him being composed of members of his race, it cannot be said, in the absence of proof of actual discrimination, that appellant has been discriminated against . . ."[5] The Supreme Court overturned the Texas appellate court, concluding that Mr. Hernandez's constitutional rights had been violated and, for the first time, broadening the equal protection clause to cover Mexican Americans.

I share the view of scholars who have identified the mid-twentieth century as a formative period in the formation of Chicanos' racial identity and position in the U.S. racial order as an "in-between" racial group that was neither Black nor fully white. At the same time, I join other scholars in arguing that this racial ambivalence had its origins a century earlier, by virtue of the American occupation of Mexico's northern territories.[6] In part due to unique demographics, the 60,000 Mexicans then living in New Mexico,[7] existed both as a racially subordinate group in the U.S. racial hierarchy and as a group that at times successfully claimed white status (and, thereby, a dominant position relative to other racial minority groups).[8] Armed with this

---

[5]*Hernandez v. State*, 251 S.W.2d 531, 536 (Tex. Crim. App. 1952), rev'd sub nom. *Hernandez v. Texas*, 347 U.S. 475 (1954).

[6]See, e.g., DAVID MONTEJANO, ANGLOS AND MEXICANS IN THE MAKING OF TEXAS 1836-1986 (1987); NEIL FOLEY, THE WHITE SCOURGE: MEXICANS, BLACKS AND POOR WHITES IN TEXAS COTTON CULTURE (1997); JOHN M. NIETO-PHILLIPS, THE LANGUAGE OF BLOOD: THE MAKING OF SPANISH-AMERICAN IDENTITY IN NEW MEXICO 1880S-1930S (2004); and CHARLES H. MONTGOMERY, THE SPANISH REDEMPTION: HERITAGE, POWER, AND LOSS ON NEW MEXICO'S UPPER RIO GRANDE (2002). An increasing subset of studies explores how groups change status from "white" to "non-white" or from "non-white" to white. See THEODORE W. ALLEN, INVENTION OF THE WHITE RACE (1994); DAVID R. ROEDIGER, WAGES OF WHITENESS: RACE AND THE MAKING OF THE AMERICAN WORKING CLASS (1999); MATTHEW F. JACOBSON, WHITENESS OF A DIFFERENT COLOR: EUROPEAN IMMIGRANTS AND THE ALCHEMY OF RACE (1999); KAREN BRODKIN SACKS, HOW JEWS BECAME WHITE FOLKS AND WHAT THAT SAYS ABOUT RACE IN AMERICA (1998); RUTH FRANKENBERG, WHITE WOMEN, RACE MATTERS: THE SOCIAL CONSTRUCTION OF WHITENESS (1993) ; NOEL IGNATIEV, HOW THE IRISH BECAME WHITE (1995); MICHELLE FINE, ET AL., OFF WHITE: READINGS ON POWER, PRIVILEGE AND SOCIETY (2004).

[7]As the northern Mexican region, New Mexico was an expansive geographic area that included all of present-day New Mexico, present-day Arizona, as well as parts of present-day Colorado, Nevada, Utah and Wyoming. In all, with the end of the war with the U.S., Mexico ceded around one million square miles or half its territory, if you include Texas (which Mexico had continued to claim during the war). GENE M. BRACK, MEXICO VIEWS MANIFEST DESTINY, 1821-1846: AN ESSAY ON THE ORIGINS OF THE MEXICAN WAR, 2, 54, 135 (1975).

[8]In this paper, I use the term "Mexican" as an ethno-racial category distinct from Euro-American whites, blacks, Pueblo Indians and other Indians. I include in that category Mexicans regardless of their status as Mexican nationals or U.S. citizens (this is especially important given that in the first 20 years of the American occupation it was not always clear whether Mexicans had elected to maintain their Mexican citizenship or become U.S. citizens). In the contemporary literature of the period (whether newspapers, court records, government documents, or private papers), "Mexican" (or "Mexicano" in Spanish) was used almost exclusively to refer to the former Mexican citizens of the region whose ancestry was mestizo (Spanish and Indian). Variants of "Spanish," "Hispano" and the like did not become widespread in the region until the late 19th and early 20th centuries—partly as a result of some of the racial formation processes I describe in this study. For analyses that consider that latter process, see NIETO-PHILLIPS, supra note 6; MONTGOMERY, supra note 6; PHILLIP B. GONZALES, FORCED SACRIFICE AS ETHNIC PROTEST: THE HISPANO CAUSE IN NEW MEXICO AND THE RACIAL ATTITUDE CONFRONTATION OF 1933 (2001); A. GABRIEL MELENDEZ, SO ALL IS NOT LOST: THE POETICS OF PRINT IN NUEVOMEXICANO COMMUNITIES, 1834-1958 (1997); DORIS MEYER, SPEAKING FOR THEMSELVES: NEOMEXICANO CULTURAL IDENTITY AND THE SPANISH-LANGUAGE PRESS, 1880-1920 (1996).

nineteenth-century historical reality, mid-twentieth-century civil rights litigation such as Hernandez is easier to comprehend and, in fact, to have predicted.

In this chapter, I use Mexicans' "off-white" racial status in nineteenth-century New Mexico as a point of departure for exploring four themes. The first theme concerns the extent to which we can and should understand the transition from Spanish-Mexican to Anglo-American control of the Southwest as a key period that shaped American race relations both in the Southwest and nationally. Mexicans' status as an off-white or wedge racial group is crucial for understanding that period as well as for understanding the twentieth and even the twenty-first century trajectories of Latinos in the U.S. A second theme is how the study of Mexican American political agency in New Mexico opens up a range of nationally important nineteenth-century debates. For example, studying Mexicans' status under the Treaty of Guadalupe Hidalgo (as well as the status of Pueblo Indians under that law) prompts questions about the nature of citizenship, the links between race and citizenship, and the parameters of federal as compared to state citizenship. Similarly, studying New Mexico politics yields new insights and raises new questions about slavery of Blacks in the South and comparisons with the enslavement of Indians in the Southwest.

A third theme is how Mexicans' position in nineteenth-century New Mexico functioned simultaneously to challenge and buttress white supremacy. Mexicans' sometimes successful claims to whiteness challenged white supremacy by forcing a rupture in categories. At the same time, Mexicans' claim to whiteness was fragile and continually contested; as a result, Mexican elites sought to subordinate non-white groups lower on the racial hierarchy, including Pueblo Indians, Blacks (free and enslaved), and other communities of Indians. The fourth and final theme concerns the way in which Mexicans' second-class citizenship interacted with their precarious white status to produce conditions under which Mexicans sought to continually distance themselves from other non-white groups. Mexicans' citizenship was circumscribed in ways both symbolic and real by their non-white racial status; at the same time, Mexicans had certain citizenship rights precisely because they could sometimes successfully claim they were white. Both conditions provided incentives for emphasizing their whiteness, when it was possible to do so, and for distancing themselves from other non-white groups by excluding them as full citizens and rights-holders.

This chapter is organized into five remaining parts.[9] Part II provides background about the Spanish-Mexican and Anglo-American racial orders at mid-nineteenth-century and the socio-political context. In the subsequent three sections of the paper, Parts III-V, I examine laws passed by majority-Mexican legislatures that affected the rights of Pueblo Indians, free and enslaved African-Americans, and other, non-Pueblo Indians in the region (including Navajo, Apache, Comanche, and Ute). In

---

[9]This chapter is part of a forthcoming book that focuses on the first 45 years of the American occupation of the Southwest, from 1846 to 1890. Tentatively titled, MANIFEST DESTINIES: LAW AND RACE IN THE NINETEENTH-CENTURY SOUTHWEST, the book is under advance contract with New York University Press. For related, already published work, see Laura Gómez, Race, Colonialism and Criminal Law: Mexicans and the American Criminal Justice System in Territorial New Mexico, 34 LAW & SOC'Y. REV. 1129 (2000) and Laura Gómez, Race Mattered: Racial Formation and the Politics of Crime in Territorial New Mexico, 49 UCLA L. REV. 1395 (2002). Due to space limitations, I have necessarily had to simplify and sometimes omit discussions of important events and processes.

each of those three parts, I argue that Mexican elites (who were the majority of territorial legislators) enacted legislation in order to reinforce their fragile claim to
whiteness. In Part VI of the chapter, I conclude by reflecting on the significance of
these dynamics for understanding our nation's legacy of racial inequality and the
emerging twentieth-century racial order. I argue that Mexican American political
agency in nineteenth-century New Mexico functioned simultaneously to challenge
white supremacy (with the insistence of the expansion of the white category to
include Mexicans under certain conditions) and to buttress white supremacy (with
Mexicans themselves functioning as a wedge racial group that reproduced the subordination of Pueblo Indians, Blacks, and nomadic Indians).

Conflict in New Mexico at Mid-Century

The American military occupation of New Mexico in 1846 and Congress's subsequent designation of the region as a federal territory resulted in an ambiguous
political status that evoked both a colonial legacy and the promise of eventual annexation as a state.[10] Against the backdrop of vigorous congressional and press debate
about the propriety of U.S. military aggression against Mexico, it was not at all clear
what would become of New Mexico's 60,000 ethnic Mexicans, 60,000 nomadic and
semi-nomadic Indians (including members of the Navajo, Apache, Comanche, Ute,
and Kiowa Tribes), 15,000 Pueblo Indians, and 1,000 Euro-Americans.[11] Despite
their differences, the pro-war (mostly Democrats) and anti-war (mostly Whigs) fac-
tions in Congress were united in their fears about incorporating New Mexico's population of Mexicans and Indians, which both camps deemed racially inferior and
unworthy of citizenship.[12] This was in sharp contrast with congressional views
toward California, which by 1848 had a majority of Anglo-American settlers in the
San Francisco region and, it was presumed by all, would quickly be admitted to the
Union.

In many ways, New Mexico was merely an annoying obstacle to reaching the
Pacific Coast.[13] As is often the case, however, the law of unintended consequences
was at work. Unfolding events in the war and its conclusion in 1848 with the Treaty

---

[10]With 1700 troops following the Santa Fe Trail (and what would become, 30 years later, the route of the
Atchison, Topeka, and Santa Fe Railroad), Colonel Stephen W. Kearny asserted American control of New
Mexico at Las Vegas on August 14, 1846, moving to take the capital at Santa Fe four days later. Over the
next month, Kearny supervised construction of Fort Marcy in Santa Fe, the compilation of a code of laws
known as "The Kearny Code" (drawn substantially from the laws of Missouri and Texas), and appointed a
civilian government. Kearny was promoted to Brigadier-General for this successful invasion, and then on
Sept. 25 led his troops to California. Eventually moving south to fight the war in Mexico's interior, he died
in Veracruz, Mexico in October 1848. In October 1846, Kearny's troops were replaced by 1800 men under
the command of Colonel Price. HUBERT HOWE BANCROFT, HISTORY OF THE PACIFIC STATES OF
NORTH AMERICA, ARIZONA AND NEW MEXICO, 1530-1888, VOL. XII, 408-421 (1888); RALPH EMER-
SON TWITCHELL, THE LEADING FACTS OF NEW MEXICAN HISTORY, VOL. II 200 n.138, 205 (1912).
[11]HOWARD R. LAMAR, FAR SOUTHWEST, 1846-1912: A TERRITORIAL HISTORY 92 (1966).
[12]On arguments of Mexicans' racial inferiority in Congress and the American press, see REGINALD HORS-
MAN, RACE AND MANIFEST DESTINY: THE ORIGINS OF RACIAL ANGLO-SAXONISM, 210-217, 229-
260, 276-278 (1981); ROGERS M. SMITH, CIVIC IDEALS, 198, 204-209 (1997); FREDERICK MERK,
MANIFEST DESTINY AND MISSION IN AMERICAN HISTORY: A REINTERPRETATION, 29-40, 157-169
(1963); ANDERS STEPHANSON, MANIFEST DESTINY: AMERICAN EXPANSION AND THE EMPIRE OF
RIGHT, 46-49, 55-57 (1995); THOMAS R. HIETALA, MANIFEST DESIGN: ANXIOUS AGGRANDIZEMENT
IN LATE JACKSONIAN AMERICA 133-34, 152-66 (1985).
[13]BANCROFT, supra note 10, at 408.

of Guadalupe Hidalgo, as well as the unique circumstances of the region, made New Mexico more of a problem for the U.S. than had been anticipated. In particular, the U.S., feeling its way as a colonial power for the first time in New Mexico, was unprepared for the relatively unusual dynamics of what I term "double colonization." The U.S. colonization of the 19th century was grafted onto a previous European colonization of the region—the Spanish colonization of the 17th and 18th centuries. For our purposes, one of the most significant features of double colonization was that American military and civil authorities encountered an entrenched set of European-origin political and social institutions that were operated by a largely non-European population consisting of small, widely dispersed mestizo (mixed Spanish and indigenous) and Pueblo Indian communities.[14] For example, Americans encountered a fully developed Spanish-Mexican legal system, as well as an entrenched system of canon law in the Catholic Church.[15] This was, of course, a new scenario for the Americans, since they had previously encountered Indian communities living under circumstances, which from their Euro-centric worldview, did not evoke established societies with institutions.

An important dimension of the Spanish colonization of the region was a system of racial inequality grounded in white supremacy that resulted in a hierarchy of castes based on racial mixture among Spaniards, Indians, Africans, and the various mestizo combinations resulting from those categories. While specific categorizations were complex and localized, the general hierarchy placed Spaniards at the top, Indian/Spanish mestizos in the middle, and Indians and Blacks at the bottom, with a detailed system of rights and privileges structuring property relations, occupational entry, and family relationships according to position in the hierarchy.[16] In Mexico, demographics overwhelmed the system, causing it to collapse of its own weight: consider that in 1646 Mexico's population contained roughly equal numbers of those claiming Spanish descent (most of whom were born in Mexico) and Black descent, but ten times as many mestizos and Indians as either of those groups, so that an inevitable mestizo population resulted in later centuries.[17]

---

[14]Writing with no small trace of sarcasm, one historian evoked the dilemma of double colonization for the U.S. in more colorful terms: "But Mexico—there was a problem. Eight million human beings, rooted in soil of their own, covered by a veneer of civilization, and professing the Christian religion!" MERK, supra note 12, at 34.

[15]See GÓMEZ, supra note 9, at 1145-46.

[16]See generally MARTHA MENCHACA, RECOVERING HISTORY, CONSTRUCTING RACE: THE INDIAN, BLACK, AND WHITE ROOTS OF MEXICAN AMERICANS 49-66 (2001). Alonso describes the Spanish racial order as follows:
In this pigmentocratic 'regime of castes' (regimen de castas), somatic distinctions in skin color, eye shape, hair quality, and the like became the visible indexes of what were construed as natural inequalities of social being. Ontological differences, constructed in terms of a series of homologous oppositions in which pure-impure was a core distinction, underpinned the honor of Spanish conquerors and the infamy of conquered Indians and enslaved blacks. A hermeneutics of descent, based on a calculus of types and mixtures of pure and impure blood, specified the quality (calidad) of social subjects and endowed them with a differential value that defined their place in society. Religion, color, blood, and descent became fused in the calculation of status and in the determination of class membership . . .[T]hrough this logic of racial difference, power was personified and embodied; relations of domination and exploitation were produced, naturalized, and legitimated. . .
ANA MARÍA ALONSO, THREAD OF BLOOD: COLONIALISM, REVOLUTION, AND GENDER ON MEXICO'S NORTHERN FRONTIER 53-54 (1995).

[17]MENCHACA, supra note 16, at 61; see also, ALAN KNIGHT, RACISM, REVOLUTION, AND INDIGENISMO: MEXICO, 1900-1940, in THE IDEA OF RACE IN LATIN AMERICA, 1870-1940, 72 (Richard Graham ed., 1990).

While it is difficult to document with precision, it appears that the late 18th and early 19th centuries were periods in which the Spanish racial legacy was softening, so that some mestizos were able to successfully claim entitlement to the privileges of whiteness formerly limited to Spaniards. This was a phenomenon well-recognized throughout the former Spanish colonies, so that in Latin America, white skin, money and other attributes of social mobility were perceived as being able to "whiten" otherwise disadvantaged mestizos.[18] Moreover, it appears that the Spanish racial order was especially susceptible to challenge (and so was breaking down) in frontier areas, such as New Mexico.[19] In frontier settings, after all, even those with "impure blood" (meaning, indigenous ancestry) could transform themselves into "civilized" persons in the context of a presumed uncivilized, majority Indian region.[20]

By the early nineteenth-century, the Spanish racial order was facing tremendous pressure due to the growth of the mestizo and Indian populations, relative to persons of Spanish descent.[21] Motivated largely by the need to culturally and economically incorporate the majority of Mexicans, the Spanish legislature in 1810 initiated a variety of changes to improve the position of mestizos and Indians.[22] Two years later, the Spanish legislature enacted the Law of Cadiz, which abolished the racial castes and promised formal equality regardless of racial status.[23] Additional liberalization policies occurred after Mexican independence in 1821, with the Plan de Iguala declaring all persons equal citizens of the new republic without regard to race.[24]

Despite substantial support for the abolition of slavery at the time of Mexican independence, the Mexican legislature opted instead to institute what they considered a more "progressive" slave code: it banned the future importation of slaves from Africa and mandated that current slaves would be free after an additional ten years of servitude.[25] In practice, the only northern Mexico region affected by the slave code was Texas, where by 1831 American immigrants outnumbered Mexicans.[26] The major cause of the breaking away of Texas (by then economically, if not politically, dominated by settlers from the southern U.S.) and formation of the Texas Republic in 1836 was the slavery question, with the central Mexican government insisting that its prohibition of slavery extended to its northeastern frontier and the American immigrants insisting they had the right to hold African slaves in the region. Texas

[18]ALONSO, supra note 16, at 67; PETER WADE, BLACKNESS AND RACE MIXTURE: THE DYNAMICS OF RACIAL IDENTITY IN COLOMBIA 10-11, 297 (1993).

[19]Anthropologist Martha Menchaca asserts that, over the centuries, "Blatant racial disparities became painfully intolerable to the non-White population and generated the conditions for their movement toward the northern frontier, where the racial order was relaxed and people of color had the opportunity to own land and enter most occupations." MENCHACA, supra note 16, at 66. In her study of northern Mexico, Alonso reaches a similar conclusion. See ALONSO, supra note 16, at 54, 65-67.

[20]ALONSO, supra note 16, at 54.

[21]MENCHACA, supra note 16, at 158 (noting that by 1810 80% of Mexico's population was either mestizo or Indian).

[22]Ibid. These changes included lifting occupational restrictions, releasing Indians from paying tribute to the crown, and making Indians liable for taxation like other subjects.

[23]Ibid.

[24]Id. at 161.

[25]Id. at 163.

[26]NEIL FOLEY supra note 6, 18. Although most Euro-American immigration to Texas resulted from liberalization of Mexican immigration laws, historian Richard White estimates that as much as 40 percent of Euro-Americans in Texas were in violation of Mexican laws or were, according to him, "illegal aliens." White, "IT'S YOUR MISFORTUNE AND NONE MY OWN": A NEW HISTORY OF THE AMERICAN WEST, at 65 (1991).

later became the target of additional anti-slavery laws enacted in the 1820s by both the Mexican legislature and the Coahuila state legislature—laws that culminated in Mexico's abolition of African slavery in 1829.[27] Texas entered the Union of states nine years later as a slave state.[28]

One of the benefits of using the concept of double colonization is to bring into focus the impact of two successive, white supremacist racial orders with the Spanish and then American colonization of New Mexico. The Anglo-American racial order at mid-century rested on the legacy of European colonialism of North America that was openly and forcefully justified by a doctrine that defined the native Indian people as racially inferior—as both an entirely separate, sub-human category that was undeserving of humane treatment, worthy of extermination, and, for the long-term, incapable of incorporation into the newly formed American polity (so long as they maintained political allegiance and cultural affiliations to their tribes).[29] Another key dimension of the U.S. racial order was the legalized enslavement of African peoples on the basis of race, justified with claims of Blacks' racial inferiority to whites. Beginning with the first arrival at the port of Jamestown in 1619 of a ship carrying Africans, "slavery developed quickly into a regular institution, into the normal labor relations of [B]lacks to whites in the New World."[30] Even in those states in which slavery was not legal (and even among most abolitionists), the idea of Black inferiority was unchallenged, whether speaking of slaves or free Blacks.[31]

A central feature of the 19th century U.S. racial order was the primacy of science to justify the racial subordination of non-white people; scientific racism was crucial because it "explained why some [races] succeeded while others failed, seemed to make clear the reasons for contemporary realities in international relations, and justified the dominance domestically of the few (whites) over the many (colored)."[32] Three tenets of "scientific racism" as it was preached in the nineteenth-century heavily shaped later policies and popular attitudes about race. First, there was the core idea "that outer physical characteristics were but markers of inner intellectual, moral, or tempermental qualities." Second, it was believed that such traits were inherited. And, third, was the idea that these traits were fixed and unchangeable.[33]

[27]Menchaca, supra note 16, 165-66. The legislation that emancipated Mexico's African slaves was signed into law by President Vicente Guerrero, who was an Afro-mestizo. Id. At 166 and 322 (n. 6).

[28]On the war for Texas and its annexation, see HORSMAN, supra note 12, at 213-15, 216-19; HIETALA, supra note 12, at 10-54.

[29]STEPHEN CORNELL AND DOUGLAS HARTMANN, ETHNICITY AND RACE: MAKING IDENTITIES IN A CHANGING WORLD, 110 (1998); GEORGE FREDERICKSON, RACISM: A SHORT HISTORY, 68-69 (2002). Sociologist Eduardo Bonilla-Silva argues persuasively that the roots of a global racial structure lie in European colonialism and concludes that "racialized social systems, or white supremacy for short, became global and affected all societies where Europeans extended their reach." EDUARDO BONILLA-SILVA RACISM WITHOUT RACISTS: COLOR-BLIND RACISM AND THE PERSISTENCE OF INEQUALITY IN THE UNITED STATES 9 (2003).

[30]HOWARD ZINN, A PEOPLE'S HISTORY OF THE UNITED STATES: 1492-PRESENT, 23 (1995).

[31]FREDERICKSON, supra note 29, at 80-81.

[32]FREDERICKSON, supra note 29, at 56-58. On scientific racism, see also, HORSMAN, supra note 12, at 139-157; RICHARD GRAHAM, ED., THE IDEA OF RACE IN LATIN AMERICA, 1870-1940, 2-3; and SMITH, supra note 12, at 203-205 (emphasizing the portrayal of scientific racism in the U.S. popular press of the mid and late 19th century).

[33]JACOBSON, supra note 6, 32.

Overall, the American racial hierarchy placed whites at the top (with relevant ethnic distinctions remaining in the 19th century) and Indians and Blacks at the bottom. Given the encounter of American settlers and traders with Mexican mestizos in the early and, especially, middle 19th century, it was by no means clear where Mexicans would fit within this hierarchy. Contemporary commentaries were split (sometimes seemingly within the mind of the same commentator) between the views that Mexicans were "really Indians" (because they were more Indian than Spanish in ancestry) or more comparable to Blacks in color, custom, and overall depravity.[34] Given that, in either case, the outcome of exclusion from the rights and privileges accorded whites, treating Mexicans as "like Indians" or "like Blacks" in the American context may have been inconsequential. On the other hand, it was precisely the ambiguity of Mexicans' racial status that positioned them to play a role as an off-white or intermediate white group in the context of the Southwest.

Congressional debate about ratification of the Treaty of Guadalupe Hidalgo reflected racist concerns about incorporating New Mexico's population that echoed those heard at the start of the war with Mexico. A major concern during these debates was how to get the most land from Mexico with the smallest number of Mexicans.[35] Debate over whether and precisely how to incorporate Mexico's former citizens was not unique for its emphasis on race. The American racial hierarchy (and a patriarchal gender order) had heavily shaped American citizenship laws throughout the nation's history. In his comprehensive study of federal legislation and judicial decisions on citizenship,[36] political scientist Rogers Smith concludes:

> [W]hen restrictions on voting rights, naturalization, and immigration are taken into account, it turns out that for over 80 percent of U.S. history, American laws declared most people in the world legally ineligible to become full U.S. citizens solely because of their race, original nationality, or gender. For at least two-thirds of American history, the majority of the domestic adult population was also ineligible for full citizenship for the same reasons. Those racial, ethnic, and gender restrictions were blatant, not "latent."[37]

What was meant by "citizenship," moreover, was not self-evident.[38] Smith notes that the Constitution "did not define or describe citizenship, discuss criteria for inclusion or exclusion, or address the sensitive relationship between state and national citizenship."[39] One of the central tensions was how broadly we conceive of "citi-

---

[34]In particular, southerners were ambivalent about the nation's expansion to Mexico because they considered "the Mexican race" a suspect, colored race "but little removed above the Negro." MERK, supra note 12, at 38-39 n.25; See also, supra note 12.

[35]For example, see MERK, supra note 12, at 151-52 (quoting editorials in the Louisville Democrat and the Washington Union).

[36]Smith surveyed all proposed and enacted federal legislation in these areas and more than 2,500 appellate cases decided between 1798 and 1912. SMITH, supra note 12.

[37]SMITH, supra note 12, at 15.

[38]For thoughtful discussions of how race shapes the meaning of citizenship in other contexts, see Leti Volpp, "The Citizen and the Terrorist," 49 UCLA Law Rev. 1575 (2002) and Leti Volpp, ""Obnoxious to Their Very Nature": Asian Americans and Constitutional Citizenship," 5 Citizenship Studies 57 (2001).

[39]SMITH, supra note 12, at 115. He goes further with respect to the latter: "Issues of state versus national identity and slavery, especially, were so explosive that the framers avoided raising them whenever possible and left them largely unresolved." SMITH, supra note 12, at 116.

zenship." We can conceive of citizenship as involving a bundle of rights positioned along a continuum. In a narrow sense, American citizenship refers to national identity and the right to carry an American passport (for example, every American, native-born or naturalized, adult or child, retains this right). At the other end of the spectrum, we can think of "citizenship" as entailing full political rights, including voting, office-holding, and jury service (many American citizens do not have that full bundle of political rights, including children, for example).[40] In between the two, are such rights as the right to sue in federal court, the right to own and alienate property—a bundle of rights seen as economic more than political, but seen as related to being a member of the polity, and hence a citizen. In the remaining sections of the paper, one of the major themes is the various combinations of rights that were accorded racially subordinated groups in New Mexico: Mexicans, accorded rights by Congress; Pueblo Indians as accorded such rights by Congress and the Mexican elite; Blacks as accorded rights by Mexican elites and federal actors; and non-Pueblo Indians, as accorded rights by federal actors and the Mexican elite.

In the end Congress compromised on the Mexican question, ratifying the Treaty of Guadalupe Hidalgo to achieve two ends: a cession by Mexico of the maximum possible amount of land, coupled with the barest (and most legally vague) guarantees regarding the citizenship rights of the former Mexican citizens living in the ceded lands, the majority of whom lived in New Mexico. For instance, Article VIII of the Treaty refers to the rights of Mexican citizens to become "citizens of the United States," but no where specifies what being a "citizen" means.[41] In Article IX, the Senate rejected the citizenship provisions negotiated in Mexico City, choosing instead substitution language that made it clear that the Mexican citizens residing in New Mexico were not endowed with full rights, since they were not, at the time of ratification or necessarily at any set time in the future, assured of status as citizens of a state within the Union.[42] Reading the provisions together, we can conclude that the former Mexican citizens had been accorded limited American citizenship. For the purposes of nation-

---

[40]Free Blacks, who numbered around half a million in the U.S. in 1860 (divided almost evenly between the North and the South), likewise, had an ambiguous political status. According to Smith, southern courts "tended to deny [free] black citizenship altogether"; while "[n]orthern courts generally acknowledged [free] black citizenship formally while rejecting democratic notions of the political privileges inherent in that status." SMITH, supra note 12, at 255-58.

[41]Article VIII of the Treaty of Guadalupe Hidalgo contains three references to U.S. citizenship: "[T]hose who shall prefer to remain in the said territories, may either retain title and rights of Mexican citizens, or acquire those of citizens of the United States . . . and those who shall remain in the said territories, after the expiration of that year . . . shall be considered to have elected to become citizens of the United States. [T]he present owners, the heirs of these, and all Mexicans who may hereafter acquire said property by contract, shall enjoy with respect to it, guaranties equally ample as if the same belonged to citizens of the United States." RICHARD GRISWOLD DEL CASTILLO, THE TREATY OF GUADALUPE HIDALGO: A LEGACY OF CONFLICT, 189-90 (1990) (emphasis added).

[42]Article IX of the Treaty of Guadalupe Hidalgo reads as follows:
The Mexicans who, in the territories aforesaid, shall not preserve the character of citizens of the Mexican Republic, conformably with what is stipulated in the preceding article, shall be incorporated into the Union of the United States and be admitted, at the proper time (to be judged of by the Congress of the United States) to the enjoyment of all the rights of citizens of the United States according to the principles of the Constitution; and in the mean time shall be maintained and protected in the free enjoyment of their liberty and property, and secured in the free exercise of religion without restriction.
GRISWOLD DEL CASTILLO, supra note 33, at 190. This phrase implies that full citizenship was linked to being a citizen of a state—a condition to be determined by Congress under Article IX of the Treaty. Americans who were citizens of federal territories, as opposed to states, by definition were second-class citizens.

ality (for example, obtaining a passport) and in terms of relations with nationals of other nation-states, the former Mexican citizens were citizens of the U.S. On the other hand, the second provision made it clear that they were not citizens of any state (and would not necessarily become state citizens), and, within the context of the meaning of citizenship in the mid-19th century, they therefore had a kind of second-class citizenship.[43]

Compared to Texas and California, New Mexico's population had three distinguishing features. First, by virtue of the Treaty ending the war, the majority of its native population (60,000 Mexicans and 15,000 Pueblo Indians) had at least some claim to citizenship (whether these claims would extend to full citizenship or some kind of second or third class citizenship was not known in 1848, of course). Second, New Mexico's multi-racial demographics were unique among the other former Mexican territories. Neither California or Texas had as large and as diverse an Indian population as New Mexico.[44] New Mexico's Indian population was divided between the more numerous nomadic and semi-nomadic tribes who were openly hostile to the U.S. (just as they had been hostile to the Spanish and Mexican governments), on the one hand, and the various Pueblo Indian communities who were open to U.S. authority in the region (at least in part as a way to gain protection from raids by the nomadic tribes), on the other hand. In this multi-group, multi-racial context, Mexicans could and would position themselves as a wedge racial group between Euro-Americans above them and Indians below them. A third key feature of New Mexico's racial demographics was the tiny number of Euro-American settlers in the region at the time of the American conquest. Unlike in California and Texas, Euro-American settlers were vastly outnumbered by native Mexicans and Indians in New Mexico, with fewer than 1,000 in the region at the time of the American military occupation.

Given this unique racial context, I will examine how majority-Mexican legislatures responded to Pueblo Indians, Blacks (free and enslaved), and nomadic Indians during the first 25 years of the American occupation (1846-1869). I use the term "Mexican elite" to refer to Mexican men who were the majority of elected officials at the county and territorial levels in New Mexico during this period. During most of the 19th century, New Mexico constitutional conventions and legislatures were conducted in Spanish, and legislative acts were proposed and adopted in Spanish, translated into English, and then officially printed in both Spanish and English. Mexican men were the majority of all legislative bodies and elected political conventions in New Mexico during this time period, ranging from a low of 55% to a high of 95%

---

[43]This interpretation is consistent with the Supreme Court's 1828 ruling in American Insurance Co. v. 356 Bales of Cotton, concluding that residents of an acquired U.S. territory (whether acquired "by conquest or by treaty") automatically become U.S. citizens, but not state citizens. American Insurance Co. v. 356 Bales of Cotton, 26 U.S. 511 (1828) (discussed in SMITH, supra note 12, at 192). Speaking about the 1829-1856 period, Smith concludes that "At the federal level, the Jacksonian [period] story was one of minimizing the importance of national as opposed to state citizenship, along with yet more explicit recognition of gender and racial restrictions on full civic membership." SMITH, supra note 12, at 220.

[44]It should be noted that this distinction resulted both from a more completely executed genocidal policy in California and Texas and also from the enslavement of so-called "Mission Indians" in the two regions. The point I am making here is that, at the time American settlers and armies occupied the three regions, they encountered different demographics and accompanying social dynamics in New Mexico, as compared to California and Texas.

of the membership of these elected bodies.[45] Thus, the laws and other actions and pronouncements of these bodies were the voice and will of elite Mexican men as a group self-defined and defined by others as distinct both from Euro-Americans and the various Indian communities in New Mexico. Treating Mexican elites as agents with a powerful voice and role in creating their own destinies, even after the imposition of U.S. military and civil rule in the region, is a significant departure from past historic scholarship, which has tended to treat Mexican political elites as mere pawns of the small cadre of Euro-American elites who lived in the region or the small numbers of federally appointed officials sent from outside New Mexico.[46]

Despite the significant ways in which Mexican men had bona fide claims to full American citizenship (though these claims rarely went uncontested), there were several respects in which their agency as political actors was circumscribed. The earliest legislatures and conventions (which convened before Congress had formally declared New Mexico a federal territory in 1850) and the later territorial legislatures existed as less than fully autonomous bodies in two respects. First, for at least the first three decades of the U.S. occupation, military rule trumped civilian rule, meaning that power was, first and foremost, in the hands of military commanders rather than either presidentially appointed officials or elected officials. Second, under the federal statutes that created New Mexico and other western territories, Congress had the power to nullify any act of the territorial legislature.[47]

In addition to these fundamental constraints, there were three additional ways in which Mexican elites' agency was circumscribed. First, the President appointed (with senatorial confirmation) the most powerful positions in civil government for the territory, including governor, secretary and three justices of the Territorial Supreme Court. In the first 15 years of territorial status, these appointees were virtually all Euro-Americans and most had never set foot in New Mexico prior to their appointments. Second, the design and implementation of the Treaty of Guadalupe Hidalgo operated to over-represent the Euro-American population and under-represent the Mexican population.

The Treaty gave the 60,000 Mexicans in New Mexico three options.[48] First, they could choose to leave their homes to relocate in Mexico, south of the newly estab-

---

[45]These percentages are my own estimates, based on surname (and, in some cases, first and last name) of legislators for the various legislatures and constitutional conventions between 1846 and 1870. William Gillett Ritch (Secretary of the Territory), NEW MEXICO BLUE BOOK FOR 1882 (Legislative Directory), which includes legislative membership going back to 1847. For secondary sources, see also BANCROFT, supra note 10; ROBERT W. LARSON, NEW MEXICO'S QUEST FOR STATEHOOD, 1846-1912 (1968); LAMAR, supra note 11.

[46]Even as I take this position, however, I am wary of overstating the extent to which Mexican elites "controlled" New Mexico's political sector, much less its legal system and economy. In my forthcoming book, I treat Mexican elites' role as central, but also devote considerable analysis to the role played by Euro-American outsiders who dominated New Mexico's bench and bar throughout the territorial period. Many of these men, including lawyers Thomas Catron and LeBaron Bradford Prince were among the wealthiest men in the territory, in addition to serving variously as New Mexico's first senator and its governor and supreme court chief justice, respectively. For general works on New Mexico history that feature these and other prominent Euro-Americans, see LARSON, supra note 37; LAMAR, supra note 11; PORTER A. STRATTON, THE TERRITORIAL PRESS OF NEW MEXICO, 1834-1912 (1969). For a perspective on the territorial period that focuses on Spanish-Mexican actors, see DURAN, infra note 55.

[47]In this sense, status as a federal territory was substantially different than status as a state. This was especially true during the 19th century, when the notion and operation of federalism were much different than they are today, such that states had comparatively more power.

[48]See GRISWOLD DEL CASTILLO, supra note 33, at 62-72.

lished border with the U.S.; an estimated 4,000 people chose this option, an astounding number given the trauma and cost such moves must have entailed at that time.[49] A second option for the former Mexican citizens was to remain in their homes in New Mexico and formally elect Mexican citizenship before a county official (usually a probate judge), which substantial numbers appear to have done.[50] The third option was by default: if the former Mexican citizens living in New Mexico remained in their homes and did not formally move to retain their Mexican citizenship, after a year they would be presumed to be U.S. citizens. The first two options functioned to under-represent the Mexican majority that was effectively enfranchised by the third option, since they decreased the proportion of Mexican citizens relative to the proportion of Euro-American citizens. A third important way in which the Treaty's grant of citizenship was in some sense hollow was that it granted federal citizenship at a time when the most important rights came through state citizenship.[51]

Mexican Elites and Pueblo Indians

By 1850, when Congress declared New Mexico a federal territory, New Mexico's 60,000 mestizo villagers and 15,000 Pueblo Indians had lived through two colonizations by European nations, making this a double colonization context.[52] As Ramón Gutiérrez has noted, one sees parallels in the centrality of race and racism in the two colonial projects: "the Spanish rhetoric of colonialism, particularly the racist tenets that were advanced to describe and justify the vanquishment and enslavement of New Mexico's various Indian groups" was matched by "a very similar discourse

---

[49]Samuel E. Sisneros, "Los Emigrantes Nuevomexicanos: The 1849 Repatriation to Guadalupe and San Ignacio, Chihuahua, Mexico," (2001) (unpublished M.A. thesis, Univ. of Texas at El Paso) (on file with author). Writing as a roughly contemporary historian, Bancroft notes the absence of any "very definite records on the subject," but concludes that "about 1,200" New Mexicans moved south in 1848-49 to leave the newly established U.S. and also that, in 1850, "a considerable number of wealthy hacendados moved south to Mexico." BANCROFT, supra note 10, at 472. Twitchell puts the number significantly lower than Sisneros, at 1500-2000, but it is likely he was referring only to heads of households (he does not provide any sources for his estimate but the surrounding text suggests he based it on Bancroft's estimate). TWITCHELL, supra note 10, at 290.

[50]Twitchell reports that "a large number" took this option and that that number included "many names of prominent men," but he is not more specific. TWITCHELL, supra note 10, at 65. Griswold estimates 2,000 Mexican men took this route, but does not provide sources for his conclusion. GRISWOLD DEL CASTILLO, supra note 33, at 65. Given conflicts during the early 1850s about who was eligible to vote and hold office, it appears that substantial numbers of Mexican elites elected to maintain their Mexican citizenship in the period immediately following treaty ratification. In one instance in 1853, 40 Mexicans were indicted for falsely swearing that they were U.S. citizens in order to vote. When the U.S. Attorney produced record books showing these men had elected to retain their Mexican citizenship, the judge ruled the records unreliable, invalidated the process (in 1849) established by the military commander for so electing, and dismissed all cases. See TWITCHELL, supra note 10, at 291 n.216; and W.W.H. DAVIS, EL GRINGO: NEW MEXICO AND HER PEOPLE 331-332 (2004).

[51]See discussion, supra note 33 and 34.

[52]A large part of my objective with this study is to make visible both moments of colonization, as well as uncover the ways in which both left a racial legacy that continues to affect us today. In his study of the enslavement of Indians by New Mexico's Spanish/Mexican people, Estevan Rael-Gálvez notes the importance of "cycles of conquest through which nuevomexicanos have passed": "It is the overlapping of empires and the imperial transitions that have occurred that have exacerbated this invisibility [of Indian slavery] . . . these subjects are not just heirs to the more contemporary influence of racial slavery in the U.S., but certainly more intimately to that of the impact of Spain's peopling and dis-peopling practices along the banks of the Rio Grande." Estevan Rael-Gálvez, Identifying Captivity and Capturing Identity: Narratives of American Indian Slavery, Colorado and New Mexico, 1776-1934, 372-373 (2002) (unpublished Ph.D. dissertation, University. of Michigan) (on file with author).

being articulated" by the American colonizers.[53] For the mestizo villagers especially, the two colonizations could not have been more different. In the first colonization, they were colonists—"settlers" in the colonial enterprise (and so the subjects of the colonial project); in the second colonization, however, they were "natives" (and so effectively the objects of the colonial project). A central goal of the American colonization became the co-optation of Mexicans, so that they would not resist the colonization as natives (and, particularly, as natives allied with the other numerically large native social groups).[54]

An important form of psychological inducement was allowing Mexicans to claim, publicly and formally, white status.[55] Mexicans received a kind of collective psychological boost by being allowed to claim whiteness within the American context of white supremacy. Consider that, however, in order for the boost to be meaningful, Indians had to be excluded from it. The assertion that members of the Navajo, Apache, Comanche, Ute and other nomadic and semi-nomadic tribes were not "white" was not in the least controversial. From the Euro-American perspective, these Indian tribes looked like the Indian tribes whom they had been battling, slaughtering, and gradually pushing west from the time of the first New England settlements. But, as noted Pueblo scholar Alfonso Ortiz has said, Pueblo Indians "posed a paradox for American policymakers."[56] "[American] officials in New Mexico were quick to point out the contrasts between such "savage" tribes as the Apaches, Utes, Navajos, Comanches, Cayugas, Cheyennes, and Arapahos, and the "civilized" Pueblos . . . "[57]

In short, New Mexico's Pueblo Indians puzzled Euro-Americans because they did not correspond to their racist notion of how Indians lived. An additional complication, for the American colonizers, was that Pueblo Indians and Mexicans seemed to share much in common. As historian Marc Simmons has noted, the Americans encountered distinct Pueblo Indian and Mexican communities with many overlapping similarities:

> When Anglo-Americans assumed control of the Southwest, they discovered in the upper Rio Grande Valley [of New Mexico] two distinct village culture types: one, an archaic Spanish rural culture, heavily overlaid with Indian elements; the other, the Pueblo, preserving the underpinnings of its indigenous

---

[53] RAMÓN A. GUTIÉRREZ, WHEN JESUS CAME, THE CORN MOTHERS WENT AWAY: MARRIAGE, SEXUALITY, AND POWER IN NEW MEXICO, 1500-1846, 338 (1991).

[54] In discussing Mexicans as a social group in this way, I am purposefully minimizing other important dimensions of social differentiation. In particular, class and status distinctions (themselves embedded in racial origins) among the region's Mexicans were extremely important. In many ways, the American objective was to co-opt elite Mexicans, rather than all Mexicans. At the same time, my argument is that a racialized collective identity formed during this period of colonial contact, precisely because Americans viewed the native mestizos as racially inferior "Mexicans," often undifferentiated in terms of status, wealth, and regional differences that had been extremely important prior to the American conquest.

[55] By using the phrase "psychological inducement" in this context, I am borrowing from and building on W.E.B. DuBois's concept of "the psychological wages of whiteness." In his monumental Black Reconstruction in America, DuBois argued that white workers earned, in effect "a sort of public and psychological wage" in the form of "public deference and titles of courtesy because they were white," which proved a palatable substitute for lower wages that had been undercut by capitalist employers' reliance on black labor made cheaper by the currency of racism. W.E.B. DUBOIS, BLACK RECONSTRUCTION IN AMERICA, 1860-1880, 701 (1962); see also DAVID R. ROEDIGER, supra note 6.

[56] ALFONSO ORTIZ, THE PUEBLO (from the series: Indians of North America) (1994), 90.

[57] Ibid.

culture, yet showing to a significant degree the assimilation of Hispanic folkways. This situation required an adjustment in Anglo thinking, which then was firmly attached to stereotypes drawn from contact with Indians in the eastern United States and the Mississippi Valley.[58]

Moreover, given the political changes of the late Spanish and especially Mexican independence period, Pueblo Indians were formally recognized as Mexican citizens.[59] It was, precisely, the region's prior colonization by Spain that had produced these commonalities between Mexicans and Pueblo Indians.[60]

In turn, these commonalities greatly influenced the shape of the second, American-led colonization of the region, such that one of its central aims was to divide Pueblos and Mexicans, as two of the major native social groups. White racial status proved a useful wedge. For whiteness to be a sufficient psychological inducement for Mexicans, it had to be denied to Pueblo Indians. The result was a regional racial hierarchy with four tiers (omitting Blacks, who officially numbered only a handful in the region):[61] Euro-Americans at the top; followed by Mexicans, as a "native" group with a formal claim to white status; followed by Pueblo Indians as a buffer group between Mexicans and non-Pueblo Indians; with nomadic and semi-nomadic Indians at the bottom. It was precisely the tenuousness of Mexicans' claim to whiteness, moreover, that accentuated the need to distinguish themselves from Pueblo Indians and that ultimately drove Mexican elites to follow Euro-Americans' lead in disenfranchising Pueblo men.

Ironically, it was both Mexicans' ability to claim whiteness and the inherent instability of that very claim that stemmed from their mestizo ancestry, as a people that resulted from the sexual and social mixture of Spanish colonizers and indigenous peoples. Precisely because of this mestizo heritage, Mexicans could at least make out a claim of whiteness grounded in their European ancestry and, especially, European culture. And for precisely the same reason—that is, because of their collective mixed Spanish/indigenous ancestry—Mexicans' whiteness was inherently fragile and subject to challenge. These dynamics were further strained by the fact that Mexican elites, although almost always mestizos (rather than pure Spaniards), tended to have more European ancestry (and hence less indigenous ancestry) than

---

[58]MARC SIMMONS, "History of the Pueblos Since 1821," in HANDBOOK OF NORTH AMERICAN INDIANS, Vol. 9, SOUTHWEST (ed. Alfonso Ortiz) (1979), at 209 (emphasis added). See also, JOE S. SANDO, PUEBLO NATIONS: EIGHT CENTURIES OF PUEBLO INDIAN HISTORY (1992), 9 (noting the influence of "Hispanic traditions" on Pueblo life); ORTIZ, supra note 56, 79 (noting that, beginning in the early 19th century Spanish settlers, became heavily dependent on Pueblo communities).

[59]Some historians have argued that these liberalization policies amounted to equality in form, but not in substance, but Emlan Hall and David Weber caution that the evidence "suggests a greater change in the legal status of Pueblos under independent Mexico than most historians have acknowledged" in the direction of equal rights for Pueblo Indians. G. EMLEN HALL and DAVID J. WEBER, MEXICAN LIBERALS AND THE PUEBLO INDIANS, 1821-1829, 59 NEW MEXICO HIST. REV. 1, 19 (1984).

[60]I do not intend to overstate the extent to which multiple, diverse Pueblo societies resembled Mexican village society in the region. I agree that "[t]he two societies coexisted but were separate in many ways. Since 1598, when Spanish-Mexicans first began to settle among them, the Pueblos had borrowed new kinds of animals, foods, technology, and ideas from their neighbors, but they had borrowed selectively. The essentials of Pueblo culture—language, religion, society—had remained intact." HALL, supra note 59, at 5. An additional, important point is the extent to which Pueblos resisted Hispanicization; these resistance strategies were violent and overt in the Pueblo Revolt against the Spanish in 1680, but they existed in myriad other ways both before and after that time. On the Pueblo Revolt, see GUTIÉRREZ, supra note 53, at 130-140; see also, SANDO, supra note 58. My objective here is merely to emphasize that the new, American colonizers would have seen certain significant similarities between Pueblo Indians and Mexicans and, at the same time, substantial differences between Pueblo Indians and non-Pueblo Indians.

[61]For example, New Mexico's 1850 census included only 22 Blacks. RAEL-GALVEZ, supra note 52, 197.

the majority of Mexicans, whose indigenous ancestry far outweighed their European blood. If we imagine New Mexico's Mexican society as a triangle, with elites at the top, we see that, as one moves down to the base of the triangle, one encounters decreasing Spanish ancestry and increasing indigenous ancestry. One of the trademarks of Spanish colonialism was precisely this indigenous-heavy mestizaje combined with intensive cultural assimilation such that most mestizos did not have, even in the mid-nineteenth century, a connection with their indigenous cultures of origin; thus, over the full spectrum of the triangle, Spanish cultural patterns predominated over indigenous cultural patterns.

The American colonizers had multiple reasons for seeking to divide Mexicans and Pueblos. As I have argued, a major reason was the need to make meaningful the admittance of Mexicans (especially Mexican elites) into the white community; the value of whiteness as a psychological inducement that tempered the American conquest was increased because Pueblo Indians were excluded from whiteness. An additional incentive to divide Pueblos and Mexicans was to disrupt the Pueblo/Mexican alliance that actively resisted the American military occupation in its early years. The U.S. occupation of New Mexico has long been touted as "bloodless" and occurring "without a single gunshot."[62] It is true that the Mexican army did not engage American forces, having received advance notice of their arrival and, apparently, a bribe to abandon Santa Fe.[63]

There are, however, three ways in which the U.S. conquest of New Mexico is quite appropriately thought of as "bloody" (rather than "bloodless"), as an essentially violent conquest. First, the U.S. occupation of New Mexico led directly to one of the most violent, brutal assault on the non-Pueblo Indian tribes of the region (between 1850 and 1870).[64] Second, it makes eminent good sense to describe the

---

[62]This portrayal of the American invasion has withstood the test of time, embraced by chroniclers spanning from Bancroft's monumental history of New Mexico published in 1888 ("Thus was the capital of New Mexico occupied without the shedding of blood." BANCROFT, supra note 10, at 416), to the official 2004 brochure published by the New Mexico Tourism Department ("Not a single shot was fired [in Las Vegas] and Kearny's army went on to occupy Santa Fe . . . " NEW MEXICO TOURISM DEPARTMENT, OFFICIAL 2004 BROCHURE 26 [2004]). In what is probably the most respected modern chronicle of the invasion of New Mexico, historian Howard Lamar downplays the military's role, instead emphasizing the notion of a presumably non-violent "conquest by merchants." LAMAR, supra note 11, at 51-70.

[63]TWITCHELL, supra note 10, 203-204. See also, BANCROFT, supra note 10, 415-416.

[64]During the first full decade of the occupation, the 1850s, the American army conducted a series of genocidal raids on the nomadic and semi-nomadic tribes living in the New Mexico region. In his 1912 history, New Mexico lawyer and history Ralph Emerson Twitchell is unabashedly racist (referring repeatedly, for example, to the nomadic and semi-nomadic Indians as "savages"; he nonetheless provides a catalogue of the American military's deadly raids (which he portrays as purely defensive in nature) against the Jicarilla Apaches (1854), the Utes (1855), the Mescalero Apaches (1853-57), the Gila Apaches (1852-53), the Mogollon Apaches (1857), the Mimbres Apaches (1855); and the Navajos (of whom Twitchell says, "They caused the military more trouble between 1850 and 1860 than all the other New Mexico Indians combined." See Twitchell, supra, note 10, at 200, 299-300, 301 n.225, 302, 302-303, 303-304. For their part, native Mexicans in the region complained repeatedly of the increase in violence against them by the nomadic and semi-nomadic tribes, blaming the Americans for the increased hostilities. In a resolution passed by the first Territorial Legislature in 1851, lawmakers declared that "since the entrance of the American army under General Kearny this Territory has been a continual scene of outrage, robbery and violence carried on by the savage nations by which it is surrounded; that citizens daily are massacred, stock stolen, our wives and daughters violated and our children carried into captivity." TWITCHELL, supra note 10, at 292. Anthropologist Ana María Alonso has argued that the American occupation of northern Mexico produced a political economy in which Apache and Comanche warriors responded to encroachments on their territory by increasing violent raids on mestizo and Euro-American settlements and, at the same time, found such raiding to be more lucrative given the availability of weapons, horses and livestock that could be subsequently traded. ALONSO, supra note 16, at 25-26. Very likely, Pueblo communities also experienced an increase in attacks from nomadic and semi-nomadic tribes during this time period, and Indians from six Pueblos formed the Pueblo Volunteer Militia that participated in the U.S. Army's campaign against the Navajos in 1849. FRANK MCNITT, ED., NAVAHO EXPEDITION: JOURNAL OF A MILITARY RECONNAISSANCE FROM SANTA FE, NEW MEXICO, TO THE NAVAHO COUNTRY MADE IN 1849 xxix (1964).

conquest and subsequent land takings from Mexicans and Indians in the region as violent and accomplished only with the threat of military action (even when it was not exercised).[65] A third way in which the American conquest of the region was far from "bloodless" centers around a series of armed revolts carried out by an alliance of Mexican and Pueblo men in several northern New Mexico villages and pueblos during the first year of the occupation.[66]

With the capitulation of the Mexican army, New Mexico's mestizo and Pueblo Indian communities had to plot their resistance methodically, over a period of months in order to assemble the cache of weapons needed to launch a multi-village resistance against the American occupiers. There were a number of armed revolts in late 1846 and early 1847, about six months after the initial American occupation. The most successful and well coordinated of these revolts was the January 1847 attack in Taos which resulted in the be-heading of the Euro-American civil governor (a Taos merchant named Charles Bent), the murder of several other American-appointed officials, and the murder of some members of the governor's household.[67] The attack on the Americans was well-planned and carried out by a coalition of Taos Pueblo men and Mexican men from villages in the Taos area.[68] Within a few days, U.S. military forces moving to contain the rebels had encountered an Indian/Mexican force of 1500 men.[69] Within a few weeks, American forces had killed several dozen rebels in skirmishes and 150 who had barricaded themselves in the church at Taos Pueblo. Taos Pueblo felt the brunt of the crushing defeat by the American army: its church was destroyed in two days of bombing and large numbers of Taos men, women and children died in the conflict. Some fifty male survivors of the raid on Taos Pueblo were arrested and several were tried on murder and treason charges; eight Mexican and Taos Pueblo men were eventually hanged after their convictions.[70]

A central figure in New Mexico politics during the Mexican period and the early decades of the American occupation was Antonio Jose Martinez, who served as the

---

[65]At Las Vegas, Santa Fe and other locales, Kearny and later military commanders of New Mexico repeatedly warned the native population that they had superior military power and untruthfully said that additional troops were on their way to New Mexico. TWITCHELL, supra note 10, at 206, 211 n.148; see also TOBIAS DURAN, WE COME AS FRIENDS: VIOLENT SOCIAL CONFLICT IN NEW MEXICO, 1810-1910, 40, 46-47 (1985) (unpublished Ph.D. dissertation, University of New Mexico) (on file with author).

[66]See DURAN, supra note 65, at 3, 48-65; ROBERT J. TORREZ, CRIME AND PUNISHMENT IN SPANISH COLONIAL NEW MEXICO, Research Paper No. 34, Center for Land Grant Studies 1-2 (1990).

[67]In addition to Bent (the civil governor of New Mexico appointed by Kearny, who had been prominent in the region as a trader and who was married to a Mexican woman), others assassinated included the Euro-American sheriff and prosecutor, two Mexicans identified as allies of the Americans (one because he was an appointed official and one because he was Bent's brother-in-law), and the young, mixed-race son of a prominent Euro-American trader (who had been appointed a judge) and Mexican woman. See TWITCHELL, supra note 10, at 233-35 n.170; BANCROFT, supra note 10, at 432 n.27.

[68]Twitchell reports that "the lower order of Mexicans of the Taos valley [sic] and of the small towns in the vicinity rose en masse and joined with the Pueblo Indians in the work of pillage and murder." TWITCHELL, supra note 10, at 236.

[69]DURAN, supra note 65, at 59.

[70]See BANCROFT, supra note 10, at 432-436; TWITCHELL, supra note 10, at 248-261. There are numerous ways in which the trial—the first American criminal trial held in the Southwest—did not meet the fundamental, constitutionally guaranteed protections for criminal defendants. My forthcoming book discusses the trials in detail.

Taos priest from 1826-1856.[71] Although he was not among those prosecuted for the 1847 Taos revolt, Martinez is credited by some as one of its major organizers.[72] It is likely that he had both a direct and indirect leadership role, the latter via the large network of youths and young adults who were or had been under his tutelage at the only school in the Taos Valley during the Mexican period.[73] Martinez was born in 1804 into one of the most land-rich families of the region.[74] As a young man, he witnessed and partook in the ideological republican movement that spawned Mexico's independence from Spain.[75] As a middle-aged man, he both actively resisted the U.S. occupation and later held leadership roles in the American territorial government.[76]

Martinez was a complex figure who in many ways epitomized the dilemmas of Mexican elites. On the one hand, he subscribed to the liberal ideology that resulted in a Mexican Constitution that proclaimed all Mexicans equal under the law, without regard to their racial status, and specifically sought to incorporate "civilized" Indians (including Pueblos) and heavily indigenous mestizos into the Mexican polity. He also worked closely with the Taos Pueblo community, as their priest and, at times, advocate before various Spanish and Mexican officials. At the same time, Martinez was a social and economic elite who owned Indian slaves and who, at times, may have grossly abused the trust placed in him by members of Taos Pueblo.[77]

But Martinez's dilemma reflected a long-standing janus-like quality in Mexican policy toward "civilized" Indians such as the Pueblo peoples of New Mexico. As I have discussed in Part II, supra, the Mexican Constitution promised equality without regard to Indian versus non-Indian status. Several caveats are worth bearing in mind, however, when considering the citizenship status of Pueblo Indians under Mexican law. First, while the law on the books granted "civilized Indians" (including Pueblo

---

[71]Martinez eventually resigned his position over conflict with then-newly appointed Archbishop Lamy, who initiated an overt campaign to replace New Mexico's Mexican priests with French, Italian and Spanish priests. Some time after his resignation as parish priest (and replacement by Spanish-born Damaso Talarid), Lamy formally suspended Martinez, forbidding him to perform church rites under any circumstances. TWITCHELL, supra note 10, at 337-339. I rely on Twitchell's account with some hesitation, as I believe he had an anti-Martinez and pro-Lamy bias (e.g., he describes Lamy's suspension of Martinez thusly: "No alternative was left to Bishop Lamy, after all sorts of fatherly advice and admonitions had been unheeded, but to suspend Father Martinez from the exercise of every priestly function," and he describes Martinez as "very crafty" and motivated to oppose the U.S. occupation because it "was a death blow to his power and prestige"). Father Martinez also was the model for the arrogant protagonist in the novel DEATH COMES FOR THE ARCH-BISHOP by WILLA CATHER. On the roots of anti-Catholic sentiment as it affected the U.S. conquest of New Mexico, see DURAN, supra note 65, 30-35.

[72]TWITCHELL, supra note 10, 337-38 n.264 (singling out the leadership of Father Martinez).

[73]Martinez also owned the only printing press in the region during the Mexican period (and through the first few decades of the American period), which he used to published textbooks for his pupils, a short-lived newspaper, and the many treatises he wrote. TWITCHELL, supra note 10, at 337-338 n.264.

[74]RAEL-GÁLVEZ, supra note 52, at 105-106; LAMAR, supra note 11, at 34-36 [Lamar erroneously gives Martinez's year of birth as 1793 and misidentifies his name throughout his work as "Jose Antonio Martinez" rather than Antonio Jose Martinez.]

[75]In the 1830s, Martinez served three terms in the Mexican legislature. RAEL-GÁLVEZ, supra note 52, at 109; see also, BANCROFT, supra note 10, at 311 n.3.

[76]As early as 1843, Martinez wrote a manifesto warning of the encroachments of Euro-Americans and portending the future invasion of northern Mexico. RAEL-GALVEZ, supra note 52, 109-112 (noting also that Marintez harbored special enmity for Charles Bent, the American governor assassinated in the 1847 rebellion).

[77]Although I have been unable to find any secondary references to it, a 20th century Taos Pueblo leader, Governor Porfirio Mirabel, alleged before Congress that Father Martinez had reneged on a promise to obtain leniency for some of the Taos Pueblo men tried for the 1847 uprising. Martinez allegedly took and kept pueblo land in exchange for the assistance, which he either failed to extend at all or tried but failed to achieve. Hearings of the Committee on Indian Affairs, House of Representatives (printed by the Government Printing Office, 1920, as "Indians of the United States: Investigation of the Field Service") p. 599-602.

Indians) full citizenship rights, the law in practice likely recognized differences among Pueblo Indians, mestizos and other racial groups—differences that are difficult to discern in official government documents.[78] Second, it is very likely that at least one motivation for the liberalization toward Indians was the plan to strip them of protections on their land grants and, thus, facilitate the dispossession of Indian lands into Mexican hands. As Pueblo historian Joe Sando puts it, "The doctrine of equal rights . . . soon became the right for all equally to take Pueblo land."[79] At the same time, a third important dimension of the liberalism that characterized the transition from Spanish monarchy to Mexican republic was the anti-clerical bent that led to greater religious autonomy for New Mexico's Pueblo nations.

> Though the Mexican law regarding land ownership proved not always beneficial to the Pueblos, the Mexican neglect of the Spanish missionary system helped strengthen the Pueblo religion. The liberal spirit that inspired Mexico's independence movement was often anticlerical, and after independence the Mexican government showed little interest in rebuilding the mission system. By the 1830s, only five missionaries were assigned to the [New Mexico pueblos].[80]

Beyond reflecting the ambivalence Mexico felt toward its "civilized" Indians, Martinez's views also represent the dilemma Mexican elites faced with respect to their Pueblo brethren. As the majority of legislators in the post-war period, Mexicans held in their hands the fate of Pueblo Indians, and their actions revealed a deep ambivalence. Martinez was involved in all the early conventions and legislatures, frequently holding a leadership position. He was elected president of the first constitutional convention (organized in 1850 before Congress had officially declared New Mexico a federal territory), in which a majority-Mexican body proposed a state constitution for New Mexico that enfranchised Pueblo, Mexican and Euro-American men over 21 who had lived in New Mexico for at least six months.[81] In the same section, Mexican elites denied the franchise to Blacks and afro-mestizos ("africanos o descendientes de africanos") and nomadic and semi-nomadic Indians ("indios bárbaros"). Given liberalization toward Pueblo Indians under Mexican independence, this is perhaps unsurprising, but it is interesting that Mexican elites' liberalism did not extend to Blacks and afro-mestizos, despite similar liberalization aimed at them under Mexican rule.

But prior to the 1850 convention, the majority-Mexican legislature in 1849 (operating under a military regime, since Congress had yet to grant New Mexico federal territorial status) limited the franchise to "free white male inhabitants," intending to exclude Pueblo Indians. As part of the Compromise of 1850 establishing New

---

[78]DEBORAH A. ROSEN, "PUEBLO INDIANS AND CITIZENSHIP IN TERRITORIAL NEW MEXICO," 78 NEW MEXICO HISTORICAL REVIEW (2003), 21 n.1 But cf. Hall and Weber, supra note 59, 8, 19 ("Liberalism, then, with its most immediate antecedents in the legislation of the Spanish Cortes, dramatically altered the legal status of Pueblo Indians in theory and in practice.").

[79]SANDO, supra note 58, 83; see also, HALL AND WEBER, supra note 59, 20-21 ("By defining the Pueblos as citizens, and by removing government restrictions that gave the Indians special protection, the liberals left the way open for Pueblos to sell parcels of real estate" and also discussing the legality of squatting on Pueblo land by Mexicans.)

[80]ORTIZ, supra note 56, 80.

[81]Article VII of the proposed New Mexico State Constitution of 1850.

Mexico as a federal territory, Congress restricted the right of suffrage to "free white males".[82] Even after Congress and successive territorial legislatures excluded Pueblo men from the franchise, however, evidence suggests that these laws may have been laxly enforced in elections, with local variation existing such that in some communities Pueblo Indian men voted and otherwise participated in the territorial polity. According to the chief justice of the territorial supreme court, in the early years of the American occupation, Pueblo Indians "not only voted, but held both civil and military offices. In many localities, they, by their numerical strength, controlled the political destinies of [towns and counties]."[83]

Indeed, Pueblo electoral participation spawned its own cycle of protest and politics. In 1853 a committee of the territorial legislature considered a complaint that more than 100 Pueblo Indians had voted illegally. The contest at issue was critical in that it involved the most important elected position in the Territory (for nonvoting delegate to Congress) and pit against each other candidates that were racially polarizing. The race pit the native, monolingual-Spanish priest, Jose Manuel Gallegos, against a Missouri politician, William Carr Lane, who prior to a presidential appointment had never set foot in New Mexico and could not speak Spanish.[84] Gallegos won, but Lane contested the results, alleging that Pueblo men had illegally voted and that, in some precincts, votes for Lane had been destroyed.[85] The territorial legislative committee had to decide whether to follow the 1850 constitutional convention's extension of voting rights to Pueblo men or Congress' 1850 restriction of voting to white males (including Mexicans). Not surprisingly (given that all their acts were subject to congressional nullification), they chose to follow the congressional mandate, an outcome affirmed by Congress in the following year. Still, even with the disputed Pueblo votes removed, Gallegos was declared the winner.[86]

During the early years of the American occupation, Mexican elites took a variety of positions toward Pueblo Indians—from working with Pueblo men to actively combat the American colonizers (in the Taos revolt), to disenfranchising Pueblo men. These positions undoubtedly reflected deep material conflicts between the groups (as when Mexican settlers encroached on Pueblo lands) but also reflected, at least in part, the efforts of Mexican elites to negotiate their position in the new, post-occupation racial order. In terms of the latter, Mexicans sought to differentiate themselves from Pueblos by claiming whiteness and, relatedly, the bundle of full citizenship rights reserved for white males in American society (including voting and holding office). In this way, Mexicans insured their position as second-from-the-top

---

[82]Senate Bill 225, Thirty-first Congress, 1st Session, May 8, 1850 ("A Bill to admit California as a State into the Union; to establish Territorial Governments for Utah and New Mexico, etc.).

[83]U.S. v. Lucero, 1 N.M. 422, 456 (1869).

[84]BANCROFT, supra note 10, at 650-651. Like Father Martinez, Gallegos was among the fiercely nationalist Mexican priests who butted heads with Archbishop Lamy.

[85]Laguna Pueblo and Taos Pueblo men voted in the election. BANCROFT, supra note 10, at 650, n.23.

[86]TWITCHELL , supra note 10, at 309; LOOMIS GANAWAY, NEW MEXICO AND THE SECTIONAL CONTROVERSY, 1846-1861, 61 (1944) (citing original congressional report). Gallegos' election travails were not at an end, however. When he was up for reelection in 1855, Gallegos faced Miguel Antonio Otero; rather than support their fellow, Mexican priest, newly appointed French and Italian priests backed Otero. Gallegos won the election by 99 votes, but Otero appealed, this time alleging that 1400 Mexicans who had retained their Mexican citizenship had voted illegally. Congress sided with Otero and he was seated as delegate. See BANCROFT, supra note 10, at 650-651.

in a four-group racial hierarchy. What ultimately became an anti-Pueblo project of Mexican elites played into the hands of the American colonizers, who sought to divide Mexicans and Pueblos in order to disrupt a potentially powerful native resistance.

These dynamics are illustrated by how the question of Pueblo Indian citizenship played out in the judiciary, legislative and executive branches. Pueblo Indians entered the U.S. only by virtue of the Treaty of Guadalupe Hidalgo, which ended the Mexican war in 1848.[87] What followed was a long period of contestation among the three branches (and within them, in some cases) about the place of Pueblos in the American polity. There were two central questions, which both ultimately led to the question of how Pueblo lands would be treated and, specifically, whether they could be transferred to non-Pueblo buyers, whether they be Mexican or Euro-American. One question was whether Pueblo Indians were federal citizens, like Mexicans, under the Treaty of Guadalupe Hidalgo. The second question was whether, in essence, Pueblo Indians were like other Indians and, hence, subject to federal legislation such as the Trade and Intercourse Act of 1834 (which prohibited the sale of Indian lands).[88]

These issues were at the center of a land dispute regarding Mexican settlers and Cochiti Pueblo, which is located south of Santa Fe.[89] U.S. Attorney Stephen B. Elkins initiated the case against the Mexicans under the Indian Trade and Intercourse Act of 1834, seeking to eject and fine them $1,000.[90] Testifying to the precedent-setting nature of the case and its potential impact on land sales, lawyer Kirby Benedict and his partner represented the Mexican defendants. Only recently returned to private practice after having served a total of 17 years on the territorial supreme court (first as associate justice then as chief justice), Benedict was one of the most influential lawyers in the state.[91] As was the case throughout the territorial period, New Mexico's judicial system consisted of a two-tiered federal court (one court hearing cases under the laws of the territory, one under federal laws), with the same judges filling the roles of both trial judges riding circuit and sitting en banc as an appellate court.[92] In this case, both Chief Justice Slough, the trial judge who first decided the case, and Chief Justice Watts, who wrote the appellate decision, sided with the defendants, finding that the federal legislation did not apply to Pueblo Indians.[93]

Both opinions rested on the twin conclusions that: (1) Pueblo Indians held Mexican citizenship and so, under the Treaty of Guadalupe Hidalgo, became federal citizens of the U.S., and so they occupied a distinctive position with respect to other

---

[87]U.S. v. Lucero, 1 NM 422, 425 (1869).

[88]25 U.S.C. § 180 (1983).

[89]See U.S. v. Lucero, 1 N.M. 422, 425 (1869) (quoting the full text of the unpublished trial court opinion, U.S. v. Ortiz (1867)).

[90]The records do not state whether Elkins acted independently or at the behest of Cochiti Pueblo.

[91]It has been noted that three of seven lawyers for the defendants (who sought Indian lands as squatters or purchasers) were former New Mexico Supreme Court justices. ROSEN, supra note 78, 25, n. 31. While it is not known what kind of fee arrangement Benedict and his partner had with his Mexican clients, it was common for lawyers in land dispute cases to receive a portion of the land in question as a fee. LAMAR, supra note 11, at 131 (noting that lawyers were generally paid in land in real estate cases).

[92]GÓMEZ (2000), supra note 9, 1147, n. 39 (on trial judges serving as part of their court of appellate review).

[93]Slough's ruling was issued in 1867; by the time Watt's opinion was published in 1869, Slough had been killed and replaced by Watts as chief justice. Arie Poldervaart, Black-Robed Justice (1948 [1999 reprint]), 72 On the duel with a legislator that led to Slough's death, see, Id., 71.

Indians; and, (2) Congress did not intend to treat Pueblo Indians like they did other Indians. The first conclusion was grounded in Mexico's extension of citizenship rights to "civilized" Indians and the citizenship provisions of Article IX of the Treaty.[94] The courts' rulings on the second question embroiled them in a multi-decade battle with Indian agents in the executive branch (who advocated treating Pueblo Indians like other Indians, in terms of assigning federal agents, making their land inalienable, and in other respects), Congress (which took various actions regarding Pueblo Indians, culminating in 1910 legislation specifying that "Indian country" included Pueblo lands), and the U.S. Supreme Court (which ruled, first, to uphold Lucero and, later, to overrule it).[95]

In essence, the Lucero court argued that Congress did not intend to treat Pueblo Indians like other Indians because they had, on the whole, not done so in the past. The Lucero court emphasized the Congress had not ratified treaties with any Pueblo nations, had not appointed Indian agents to the Pueblos, and had not specifically mentioned Pueblo Indians in legislation other than that confirming the titles of Spanish land grants to 17 Pueblos in New Mexico.[96] Perhaps reflecting its author's former status as a legislator (he had been New Mexico's congressional delegate), the opinion dared Congress to act, if it saw things differently: "If such destiny is in store for a large number of the most law-abiding, sober, and industrious people of New Mexico, it must be the result of the direct legislation of congress [sic] or the mandate of the supreme court [sic]."[97] At one level, the Lucero opinion reflects a tension between Euro-American outsiders to New Mexico in Congress and the executive branch and Euro-American insiders (that is, those within New Mexico), who asserted a personal knowledge of Pueblo Indians and sought to vouch for their distinctiveness from other Indians.[98]

The New Mexico-based Euro-American judges, in the Lucero opinion, made two related moves in reaching their conclusion that the Trade and Intercourse Act did not apply to Pueblo Indians (and, as a result, that their property could be bought and sold). First, as illustrated above, they portrayed Pueblo Indians in a positive light, emphasizing that they were citizens equal to the "one thousand best Americans" and "one thousand best Mexicans" in New Mexico in terms of their "virtue, honesty and industry."[99] The more dominant strand of reasoning in the Lucero opinion, however, was the drawing of a hard classificatory line between Pueblo Indians, as "civilized,"

---

[94]"But as a race, we think it impossible to deny that, under the [Mexican] constitution and the laws of the country [of Mexico], no distinction was made as to the rights of citizenship and the privileges belonging to it, between this ["civilized" Indian] and European or Spanish blood." U.S. v. Lucero, 1 N.M. 422, 429, 431-432, 434, 454-457 (1869) (quoting the lower court decision).

[95]See generally, ROSEN, supra note 78.

[96]See generally, U.S. v. Lucero, 1 N.M. 422(1869). On December 22, 1858, Congress confirmed the titles of Spanish land grants to 17 Pueblos in New Mexico. U.S. v. Lucero, 1 N.M. 422, 435 (1869).

[97]Id. at 441.

[98]As I have noted, the chief justice quoted the full opinion of the trial judge, Chief Justice Slough, who had died by the time of the release of the Lucero opinion. As to the other two appellate judges, the chief justice specifically alluded to their familiarity with New Mexico's Pueblo Indians in order to bolster their authority, stating that the court had known "the conduct and habits of these Indians for eighteen or twenty years" and that Associate Justice Joab Houghton had been a judge and lawyer in New Mexico for the same period, during which time "not twenty pueblo [sic] Indians have been brought before the courts in all New Mexico, accused of violation of the criminal laws of this territory." Id.

[99]Id. at 442.

and other Indians, as "savage." The court repeatedly asserted that Congress had passed the 1834 legislation to govern the class of Indians who were "wandering savages, given to murder, robbery, and theft, living on the game of the mountains, the forest, and the plains, unaccustomed to the cultivation of the soil, and unwilling to follow the pursuits of civilized man."[100] In contrast, the court found the Pueblos to be "a peaceful, quiet, and industrious people, residing in villages for their protection against the wild Indians, and living by the cultivation of the soil."[101]

Beyond creating a sharp divide between Pueblos and other Indians, the Lucero court braided an additional strand into its racial narrative of the territory recently ceded from Mexico. In what was a preview of public efforts by Euro-Americans to create and enshrine a "Spanish" identity and heritage among New Mexico's mestizo villagers in the late nineteenth-century,[102] Chief Justice Watts signaled his admiration for "the true Spanish adventurers," whom, he emphasized, had begun colonizing Mexico (and what would become the American Southwest) long before "our timid forefathers, who peeped out into the wilderness from their colony of Plymouth."[103] The region's first European colonizers were credited for bringing "civilization" and, especially, the Catholic religion to the Pueblos, but, simultaneously, criticized for their "cruelty," "cupidity," and "despotic rule" over the Pueblo Indians.[104] The final trope in this racial narrative was the juxtaposition of Spanish despotism with Pueblo victimhood, expressed as "this condition of domineering on the part of the Spaniards, and meek obedience on the part of the pueblo [sic] Indians."[105] A similar narrative had appeared in an opinion by Chief Justice Benedict more than a decade earlier, when he sided with Acoma Pueblo and against Mexicans accused of encroaching on their lands. Benedict called Mexicans "the better-instructed and more civilized race" compared to Pueblo Indians and admonished them for trying to take advantage of Pueblos. He saw the role of the American courts as evening the playing field: "It is gratifying to us to be the judicial agents . . . affirming the rights of Pueblo Indians."[106]

My analysis is not meant to lessen the devastating material impact of the Lucero decision, which allowed Pueblo lands to be freely alienated in the marketplace, thereby leading directly to the transfer of Pueblo lands to Mexicans and Euro-Americans. Yet my primary interest in the opinion is as a racial narrative that makes several key moves. Even as with one hand the Euro-American judges annointed Pueblo Indians as "civilized," and therefore racially superior to non-Pueblo Indians, with the other hand, they reinforced the divide between Pueblos and Mexicans, emphasizing the Spanish dominance of the former (rather than, for example, the mestizo character of the latter). At the same time, the representation of Mexicans as possessing Spanish ancestry (even within the context of the demonization of Spanish cruelty to

---

[100]*Id.* at 425-426.
[101]*Id.* at 427.
[102]See generally, MONTGOMERY, supra note 6; and NIETO-PHILLIPS, supra note 6.
[103]U.S. v. Lucero, 1 N.M. 422, 427 (1869)
[104]*Id.* at 427
[105]*Id.*
[106]De La O v. Acoma, 1 NM 226 (1857). It was, of course, Benedict who later represented the Mexican squatters against Cochiti Pueblo in the Lucero case.

Indians) fostered the basis Mexicans' claim to whiteness, while Pueblos' exclusion from whiteness was taken for granted such that it was not subject to challenge.

From the vantage point of the American colonizers, this move was a predictable divide-and-conquer strategy: by allowing Mexican men to claim white status (and therefore vote and hold elected office), but denying such opportunity to Pueblo Indian men, they achieved multiple goals. This strategy allowed for the operation of a civilian government (in the dark shadow of military rule) that could not have functioned without natives (given the paucity of Euro-American settlers in the region prior to the occupation). Neither could it have functioned without the interruption of the mestizo Mexican/Pueblo Indian coalition that had resisted the American occupation at Taos and elsewhere. Consider the racial positioning that occurred. Vis a vis Mexicans, the Americans positioned themselves as racially generous, allowing Mexicans to take a position under the white tent. This occurred against a reality in which American writers, newspapermen, and politicians had denounced Mexicans as racially inferior and unfit to govern themselves or join the Union.[107] Mexicans mobilized their Indo-hispano mestizo heritage in a way that emphasized their European roots (hence, whiteness), despite the fact that their racial stock, overall, was much more indigenous than European. In ways that likely were akin to moves under the Spanish-Mexican racial system, mestizos sought to distance themselves from Pueblo Indians, even as they shared much in common with these communities.

Mexican Elites and Blacks, Free and Enslaved

In 1829, Miguel Antonio Otero was born into a wealthy ranching family in Valencia County, New Mexico.[108] He would have been 17 years old when the Americans claimed control of the region, and, hence, among the first generation to come of age under American rule. He spoke English fluently, which at that time was rare even among Mexican elites of Otero's generation.[109] Otero attended college in St. Louis and New York, studied law in Missouri, and returned to New Mexico in his early twenties. He quickly ascended to a political career, first as a representative of Valencia County in the 1852 and 1853 Territorial Legislatures (where he was among the youngest legislators) and then as New Mexico's nonvoting delegate to Congress from 1855-1859 (winning election to two consecutive two-year terms).[110]

---

[107]See the sources cited in note 12, infra.

[108]Some reports claim that his parents, Gertrudis Aragon and Vicente Otero, were born in Spain. See e.g., TWITCHELL, supra note 10, at 309 n.234. If this was the case, they would have been among a very elite population indeed. Out of 13,204 people legally married in the region between 1693 (the date of the Spanish reconquest after the Pueblo Revolt of 1680) and 1846, a mere 10 persons listed their parents' birthplace as Spain. GUTIÉRREZ, supra note 53, at 149. More likely is that Otero and his parents claimed "Spanish" heritage in a less strictly ancestral sense, a phenomenon that became popular in New Mexico in the late 19th and early 20th centuries. Twitchell's often romanticized history of this period, written in 1912, reflects a desire to designate elite Mexicans as "Spanish" that was common among some Euro-American elites. On Otero's biography, see, TWITCHELL, supra note 10, at 309-310 n.234; RAEL-GÁLVEZ, supra note 52, at 192.

[109]The first Mexican generation with a sizable segment of bilingual Spanish-English speakers came of age in the 1880s and 1890s. See GÓMEZ, supra note 9, at 1144 n.31.

[110]See discussion, supra note 87, regarding Otero's first run for delegate, against Father Gallegos.

He was an outspoken Democrat during his years as delegate, aligning himself politically and socially with southerners.[111] During his third year serving in Washington, D.C., Otero married Mary Blackwood of Charleston, South Carolina, whose father was a slaveholder.[112] In the years before the Civil War, Otero took a strong pro-slavery stand and used his influence to persuade New Mexico legislators to enact a slave code in 1859.[113] After secession, however, Otero did not openly advocate that New Mexico join the fledgling Confederacy. In an 1861 letter written early in the Lincoln administration and published in the Santa Fe Weekly Gazette, Otero seemed genuinely wrought over the question and recommended siding with California and Oregon.

> If a dissolution of this country should take place, we of New Mexico will be expected to take sides with one of the two or three or four of the Republics into which it would be divided. What will be the determination of the people of New Mexico if such deplorable consequences should come to pass, I cannot say. My own opinion and my counsel to them would be, in that event, a union with the Pacific free states, west of the great prairies. If California and Oregon declare their independence of this Government I am for joining them.[114]

On the other hand, Otero may simply have been preserving his options with a Republican administration; Lincoln appointed him Secretary of the Territory in 1861.[115]

Whereas Mexicans and Pueblo Indians lived near each other, shared some common cultural and other practices, and regularly clashed over material resources such as land and water, Mexicans had little interaction or resource competition with African Americans. When New Mexico became a U.S. territory in 1850, the Census recorded 22 Blacks living in New Mexico; ten years later, there were 64 Blacks.[116]

---

[111]LAMAR, supra note 11, 91 (describing Otero's many "Southern connections" in politics and noting that Otero's brother-in-law William Blackwood was appointed to the Territorial Supreme Court).

[112]TWITCHELL, supra note 10, at 309-310 n.234; and RAEL-GÁLVEZ, supra note 52, at 192. Providing a glimpse into the extent of Euro-American historians' unwillingness to credit even elite Mexicans with agency and self-determination, Loomis Ganaway, writing in 1944, claimed Otero did not have an opinion on slavery until marriage and attributed his pro-slavery views to his wife's influence. Ganaway, supra note 86, at 61, 90. In contrast, one does not find in the literature on the prominent Euro-American settlers of New Mexico who married native Mexican women a corresponding tendency to attribute their views or actions to their Mexican wives.

[113]LAMAR, supra note 11, 91.

[114]GANAWAY, supra note 86, at 89. On the other hand, Bancroft refers to contemporary references to an 1861 speech by Otero "which incited the New Mexicans to rebellion," but states that he (Bancroft) had not been able to confirm such reports. BANCROFT, supra note 10, at 684 n.9. According to Twitchell, the Southern cause was largely rejected in New Mexico, "the masses favoring the union cause, and furnishing five or six thousand troops, volunteers, and militia, to resist the [Confederate] invasion" and "without avail, most of the wealthy and influential families being pronounced union men." Id. at 684.

[115]TWITCHELL, supra note 10, 310, n. 234.

[116]RAEL-GALVEZ, supra note 52, 197. Brooks speculates about the Blacks in New Mexico in the two censuses, suggesting that most of those in the 1860 census were servants of army officers. JAMES F. BROOKS, CAPTIVES AND COUSINS: SLAVERY, KINSHIP, AND COMMUNITY IN THE SOUTHWEST BORDERLANDS 309-310 (2002). Given the history of anti-Black racism, it is likely that the official records of all types undercounted afro-mestizo Mexicans who could pass for Spanish/Indian mestizos. There is, however, little data that allows us to draw a more precise conclusion than this about New Mexico's afro-mestizo populations. For an analysis of African and Indian racial mixture in Mexico and the Southwest. See generally, MENCHACA, supra note 16.

The census records did not distinguish, so we do not know whether New Mexico's Blacks were slaves or free persons, but the tiny numbers relative to the population suggest that New Mexico's legislative politics around slavery and the rights of free Blacks fall into the category of symbolic politics. Rather than reflecting resource competition with other social groups and/or their material interests, or even some reflection of interests and symbolism, we should read Mexican elites's actions regarding Blacks as primarily representative of other struggles and conflicts in the mid-nineteenth-century.

The conventional interpretation is to link the shift from an anti-slavery to a pro-slavery position to the politics of statehood. Virtually continuously from the end of the war in 1848 until 1911, when Congress passed a resolution recommending statehood for New Mexico and Arizona, a significant segment of elites (both Mexican and Euro-American, but probably predominantly Euro-American) had pushed, within New Mexico and at the congressional level, for statehood.[117] According to the stock story, New Mexico elites took an anti-slavery position when they felt their chances of being admitted to the Union would be best as a free state, and then shifted to a pro-slavery position when they felt their odds improved as a slave state. The argument is rarely made with respect to the majority of legislators and convention delegates who were Mexican, but is instead attributed to Euro-American elites in New Mexico and in Congress. For example, Ganaway claims that anti-Black legislative acts

> [r]eflected the growing influence of southerners in territorial politics. During the next three or four years, their control was tightened by the alignment of Miguel Otero, territorial delegate from 1855-1861, with southern political leaders and institutions.[118]

Ganaway's use of the passive voice to discuss Otero is consistent with his attribution of important political shifts in New Mexico politics to Euro-American political actors (in New Mexico and nationally) and to national issues.

Absent from this approach is serious attention to the ways in which Mexican elites constructed their interests, in either symbolic or material terms. A recent exception is offered by Estevan Rael-Gálvez, who provides an analysis that takes seriously the interests and strategies of Mexican political elites. He argues that Mexican legislators enacted a slave code that legalized Black chattel slavery in order to better protect their actual interest in slavery—the enslavement of Indians taken captive from nomadic tribes and sold into Mexican households.[119] Rael-Gálvez cites a letter written by Territorial Secretary Alexander Jackson (the likely author of the 1859 Slave Code) in which he states, "we have assured the Mexicans that [passage of a slave code] would protect their own system of peonage."[120] Both the conventional interpretation related to statehood politics and Rael-Gálvez's argument link-

---

[117]The most complete analysis is provided by LARSON (supra note 45). In asking the question why it took almost 64 years from the ratification of the Treaty of Guadalupe Hidalgo for New Mexico to become a U.S. state, Larson concludes that the best explanation has to do with the distinctive racial character of New Mexico's population. *Id.* at 303-04.

[118]GANAWAY, supra note 86, at 59.

[119]In the section on Mexican elites' relationship with non-Pueblo Indian groups, I discuss the issue of Indian slavery in part V, infra.

[120]RAEL-GÁLVEZ, supra note 52, at 198. See also, BROOKS, supra note 114, at 329 (quoting the same letter).

ing a pro-slavery position and Mexicans' interest in maintaining Indian slavery are important explanations, but I do not believe they exhaust the range of possibilities.

Given the fragility of Mexicans' claim to whiteness, an additional interpretative angle is to view Mexican elites' acts regarding African Americans as means of distancing themselves from the group undeniably at the bottom of the American racial order. Mexicans would have been well-aware of Euro-Americans' presumptions of racial superiority and concomitant Mexican inferiority at the time of the occupation; in the following decade, Mexican elites essentially were allowed to claim white status in the political sphere,[121] while inequality remained entrenched in the social sphere. The questions that plagued Congress and the rest of America at the outset and conclusion of the war with Mexico still remained: Where do Mexicans fit? Are they more like Blacks or Indians? Mexican elites, too, were well aware of these questions, and Euro-America's potential answers to them helped shape their position on the question of slavery.

In early actions, majority-Mexican bodies took anti-slavery positions. In the first Constitutional convention (held in October 1848, only a few months after Congress had ratified the Treaty of Guadalupe Hidalgo), Father Martinez presided over a majority-Mexican body that strongly opposed slavery.[122] The resolution issued by the convention stated the following: "We do not desire to have domestic slavery within our borders; and, until the time shall arrive for admission into the union of states, we desire to be protected by Congress against the introduction of slaves into the territory."[123] In 1850, the proposed New Mexico state constitution said that New Mexico would join the Union as a free state; in a popular vote on that constitution, 6,771 New Mexican men voted in favor, with only 39 voting against it.[124] In the first meeting of the New Mexico legislature (which occurred in 1848, after ratification of the Treaty of Guadalupe Hidalgo but well before Congress declared New Mexico a federal territory in 1850), a majority-Mexican legislature, with Father Martinez as president, banned African slavery. This anti-slavery sentiment likely reflected Mexico's historic opposition to African slavery, as well as ongoing hostilities with Texas.[125] Between 1845 when Texas joined the Union as a slave state and 1850, Texas actively claimed that its western border extended into New Mexico, going so far as to claim Santa Fe within its boundaries.[126] Hostilities between New Mexico and

---

[121]See GÓMEZ, supra note 9, at 1140-1144.

[122]Of 13 delegates to the convention, 10 were Mexican. GANAWAY, supra note 86, 40.

[123]Congressional Globe, 30th Congress, 2nd Session, Tues., Dec. 19, 1848. See also, GANAWAY, supra note 86, 40-41.

[124]GANAWAY, supra note 86, at 49-52.

[125]For example, in the 1848 Resolution to Congress, the clause immediately preceding the anti-slavery clause read as follows: "We respectfully but firmly protest against the dismemberment of our territory in favor of Texas or from any other cause." Id. At 40-41.

[126]Texas relinquished its claim on New Mexico only when Congress paid it $10 million to drop its claims against New Mexico. As part of the same legislative package known as the Compromise of 1850, Congress admitted California as a free state; established New Mexico and Utah as federal territories (with the proviso that the slavery issue would be determined in the future by "popular sovereignty" in those territories); abolished the slave trade but kept slavery legal in the District of Columbia; and enacted the Fugitive Slave Act to protect slaveholder's property across state and territorial boundaries. White, supra note 26, 159. See also, SMITH, supra note 12, at 262 (referring to the Fugitive Slave Act as "horrifically Kafkaesque"); and ROBERT COVER, JUSTICE ACCUSED: ANTISLAVERY AND THE JUDICIAL PROCESS 175 (1975) (describing the Fugitive Slave Act and concluding it significantly modified the Act of 1793).

Texas remained intense for decades (and persist in some quarters into the present), and some historians have credited animosity toward Texans as fueling volunteer participation in Civil War militias.[127]

Seen in this historical light, the early anti-slavery positions by the majority-Mexican conventions and legislatures could have been anticipated, but the shift to a pro-slavery position in the late 1850s would not have been. In 1857, the territorial legislature enacted a law severely restricting the rights of free Blacks.[128] The heart of the law was the restriction to 30 days of the presence of free Blacks and mulattos in New Mexico, with a violation punishable, in the first offense, by fine and imprisonment and increasing in severity to "hard labor" if the free Black person refused to leave New Mexico after serving their sentence. The law also required free Blacks and mulattos already in New Mexico to "give bond for their good conduct and behaviour . . . with two or more honorable securities." Finally, the law banned marriage and cohabitation between Black men and white women, and we can presume that Mexican men would have intended to include Mexican women within the category of "white women."[129] The latter move is especially interesting given the widespread, historic marriage, cohabitation and/or reproduction between Indians from various tribes and descendants of the Spanish. In other words, "miscegenation" between Mexicans and Indians was widespread and in fact implicitly condoned by the movement of descendants of Indian-Spanish unions into the general mestizo category. This provision also supports the claim that these laws were primarily symbolic in intent: given the small numbers of Blacks, it was feasible to prohibit Black/white sexual unions in a way that was impossible for other inter-racial unions.[130]

In 1859, two years after the law targeting free Blacks, a nearly unanimous legislative body composed of 34 Mexicans and three Euro-Americans enacted a slave code.[131] Entitled "An Act to Provide for the Protection of Property in Slaves in this Territory," the law imposed stiff criminal penalties for stealing slaves, assisting slaves in escape, or otherwise inducing them to leave their masters. It also made it illegal for free persons to gamble with slaves, to sell or give them weapons, and to trade or do business with them. New Mexico's slave code included provisions for private individuals and public officials to deal with runaway slaves, constituting a mini version of a fugitive slave law within the slave code. Like many slave codes of the era, the law imposed more severe and different sentences on slaves convicted of crimes than provided for by the general penal code; for example, it imposed the penalty of hang-

---

[127]BANCROFT, supra note 10, at 684, 686; DURAN, supra note 65, at 22-23.

[128]"An Act Concerning Free Negroes," New Mexico Laws, 1857. The law appears typical of other, contemporaneous so-called "Black Codes" passed by states that banned slavery. Legislators in such states were motivated by the racist fear that they would be "overrun" by Blacks from the South, whether they were illegally fleeing their owners or had been manumitted. For a discussion of these laws, see EUGENE H. BERWANGER, THE FRONTIER AGAINST SLAVERY: WESTERN ANTI-NEGRO PREJUDICE AND THE SLAVERY EXTENSION CONTROVERSY 118-19 (1967); see also, *Id.* at 18-32.

[129]Offending Black males were punished more harshly than offending white females, with male violators subject to 2-3 years at hard labor and female violators subject to a fine of $100-$200.

[130]For studies that focus on inter-racial intimacy in New Mexico, see GUTIERREZ, supra note 53, and BROOKS, supra note 114. For a legal history of miscegenation laws involving various racial groups, see Rachel Moran, INTER-RACIAL INTIMACY: THE REGULATION OF RACE AND ROMANCE (2001).

[131]Chap. XXVI, Laws of NM (1859). New Mexico's slave code never became law as such because it was repealed by Congress in May 1860. H.R. Res. 64, 36th Cong. (1st Sess. 1860). Recall that under federal territorial status, the New Mexico legislature's acts were subject to review and approval by Congress.

ing for the rape or attempted rape of a white woman by a slave or free Black or mulatto. Like the Black Codes enacted three years earlier, the slave code banned marriage between "white persons" and Blacks, free or slave (but, this time, did so without regard to gender, e.g., it criminalized Black women and white men along with Black men and white women, as the earlier law had done). In the first provision of its kind in New Mexico, the law prohibited Blacks, free and slave, from testifying "against a free white person" in any court of law.[132] Perhaps most significantly, the New Mexico slave code ended with a declaration that the law applied only to "the African race" and did not affect the question of Indian slavery.[133]

Within a decade, Mexican elites went from supporting abolition to enacting a harsh and comprehensive slave code. They went from little concern for Blacks, one way or the other, to enacting a "Black code" that severely restricted the rights of free Blacks, aiming to lock them out of the Territory. The laws are as harsh as those of the southern states (in the case of the slave code) and "the early old northwest states" (Illinois, Indiana, Ohio), who enacted Black Codes to deal with increases in their free Black populations.[134] The irony here is that while, for example, Illinois enacted a Black Code in reaction to a 258% increase in its population of free Blacks between 1820 and 1830,[135] the New Mexico legislature enacted its law when there were fewer than 100 Blacks in a geographic area that spanned all of present-day New Mexico and Arizona. Rather than being motivated by fear of being overrun by free Blacks or labor or land competition with free Blacks, something else was at work. The laws reflected the preoccupation with degrading and separating the races; for instance, both contained miscegenation clauses that protected the "white" daughters and sisters of Mexican elites (although the Black Code also punished transgressing "white"/Mexican women). The Slave Code banned Blacks' testimony against "whites" at a time when Mexicans controlled the grand jury and petit juries. In these ways, the laws served to harden the line between Mexicans as whites and Blacks.

In 1857 the U.S. Supreme Court issued its infamous Dred Scott opinion, deciding that neither free Negroes or slaves had federal citizenship and, therefore, the right to file suit in federal courts.[136] At one level, here was another opportunity for

---

[132]While statutes restricting the right of Blacks, Indians and Asians were common in other jurisdictions (e.g., California), no such practices had existed in New Mexico regarding Indians or others. On California's statute, see People v. Hall, 4 Cal. 399 (1854); on the rights of Chinese persons in California, see generally, CHARLES J. MCCLAIN, IN SEARCH OF EQUALITY: THE CHINESE STRUGGLE AGAINST DISCRIMINATION IN NINETEENTH-CENTURY AMERICA (1994).

[133]Section 30, the last substantive section of the act, states: ". . . this act shall in no manner apply to relation[s] between masters and contracted servants in this Territory, but the word "slave" shall only apply to the African race." In Part III, I discuss the issue of Indian slavery in New Mexico.

[134]BERWANGER, supra note 126, at 30-59.

[135]Id., at 31.

[136]60 U.S. 393 (1856). Historian James Kettner has described the broad holding of the case as follows: "Taney's majority opinion denied that Sdott or any other black man could be a citizen of the United States within the meaning of the Constitution." Kettner, The Development of American Citizenship, 1608-1870 (1978), 326. Dred Scott has been called "the most famous of all American judicial decisions," and a voluminous literature on it exists, but a thorough discussion of the case is beyond the scope of this article. Don E. Fehrenbacher, The Dred Scott Case: Its Significance in American Law and Politics (1978), vii. Fehrenbacher's discussion of the division in the contemporary popular reaction to the case is important to keep in mind. He distinguishes "three major streams of opinion": "most conspicuous by far was the roar of anger and defiance from antislavery voices throughout the North . . . From southerners, in contrast, came expressions of satisfaction and renewed sectional confidence at this overdue vindication . . . Meanwhile, northern Democrats and certain other conservatives were . . . [relieved] at the settlement of a dangerous issue and [delivered] pious lectures on the duty of every citizen to accept the wise judgment of the Court." Id., at 3.

Mexicans to distinguish themselves from Blacks, for they were, under the Treaty of Guadalupe Hidalgo, federal citizens. Otero, then New Mexico's congressional delegate and as previously noted a slavery proponent, wrote a series of letters about the Dred Scott opinion. In one letter, written to the territorial secretary Alexander Jackson in 1858, Otero writes:

> I know that the laws of the United States, the Constitution, and the decision of the Supreme Court in the Dred Scott case, establishes property in slaves in the Territories, but I think something should be done on the part of our Legislature to protect it. You will perceive at once the advantages that will result from the passage of such a law for our Territory, and I expect you will take good care to procure its passage. Immediately after its passage, you will dispatch copies to all the principal newspapers in the Southern States for publication, and also a copy to the New York Herald "very quick."[137]

It is difficult to gauge Mexican elites' reactions to the case—other than this pointed example from Otero who was in Washington, D.C. at the time the case was decided. However, a legislative committee consisting of five Mexican elites wrote, shortly after passage of the 1859 slave code, a report inviting whites to migrate to New Mexico and identifying the Dred Scott decision as one of the factors that convinced New Mexico legislators of the need to act to support slavery.[138] My review of surviving newspapers of that time, for instance, did not uncover any mention of the Dred Scott case in the English or Spanish language press of New Mexico.

Otero's letter provides support for the conventional analysis. A Supreme Court decision widely viewed as pro-South and pro-slavery, indicated the direction of the political winds (and, in many scholars' opinions, was one of the catalysts for succession and the Civil War). Otero's letter speaks of benefits to New Mexico, which could be interpreted to mean the potential for Congress's grant of statehood as a slave state. On the other hand, for those who had been genuinely committed to an anti-slavery position, the Supreme Court's opinion must have given them great pause. It was a resounding statement of the official exclusion of Blacks (free and slave) from the polity and from all but the minimum sense of citizenship. In this climate, one can imagine Mexican elites wanting to distinguish themselves from this pariah group, and enacting the Slave Code to do just that. In addition, we need not rule out the importance of the link between African slavery and Indian slavery, noted by Rael-Gálvez. Very likely, all three things were working together to motivate Mexican elites to switch from an abolitionist to a pro-slavery position.

Mexican Elites and Indian Slavery

The decade of the 1860s witnessed the election of Lincoln, the formation and secession of the Confederacy, the Civil War, and the passage by a largely northern, Republican Congress of the most sweeping civil rights laws ever in the form of the

---

[137]GANAWAY, supra note 86, at 68. Otero's letter became widely available when an abolition organization reprinted it in a pamphlet that was published in both English and Spanish and widely distributed in Washington and New Mexico. *Id.* at 68 n.29 (noting that "[w]hen this letter was made public, Otero did not deny its authenticity, although he had an opportunity of doing so in a number of public letters which he issued early in 1861.").
[138]*Id.* at 73-74.

Thirteenth, Fourteenth, and Fifteenth Amendments to the Constitution. In 1862, Lincoln issued the Emancipation Proclamation freeing all Black slaves and, three years later, Johnson issued the "Special Proclamation" seeking the same result with respect to Indians in New Mexico.[139] That presidential act and federal legislation in 1867 that made it illegal to hold Indian slaves brought the national preoccupation with slavery to New Mexico in more than symbolic terms, as had the enactment in 1859 of the slave code.

In 1868, nearly three hundred New Mexicans were served with arrest warrants charging them with the crime of holding Indian slaves or peons, and they were subpoenaed to testify before a federal grand jury (that would decide whether or not to grant indictments in the cases).[140] Among them were many prominent citizens, including elected and appointed officials, priests, and merchants. Those testifying included Juan Jose Santistevan, who at the time was between stints as the elected probate judge of Taos County; later, he would preside over the Taos County Commission and serve in the Territorial Legislature.[141]

Santistevan testified without shame and, apparently, without fear of indictment or conviction—since he implicated his mother as a fellow slaveholder (though she was not one of those initially charged). About the Indians in his own and his mother's households, he said:

> They are there of their own free will. I don't know that they are paid especially . . . I know as long as I can remember that the Indians have been as servants, that campaigns have been made against Indian tribes [Navajos] and the captives brought back and sold into slavery by parties making a campaign. In this way most of the Indians held and now living in the territory were obtained. In years past the Pah Utahs [Paiutes] before the American conquest used to sell and trade their children to the citizens of New Mexico as slaves. The descendants of these slaves or servants now live in the families of the people.[142]

Even in such a brief excerpt, Santistevan succinctly catalogues the various justifications for Indian slavery. He presents the "custom" of holding Indian slaves as a product of military conflict and as historically rooted. And, like southern slaveholders, his justification of the practice ("they are here of their own free will") is belied by his own description (they were not paid, they were captured and sold into slavery). He speaks about the history and mechanics of slavery in a detached way (for example, Indian slaves "were obtained" rather than purchased by himself or his ancestors), as if he is not personally implicated, despite the fact that he has been charged with being a slaveholder. Moreover, Santistevan's description presents a system of slavery that includes inter-generational transmission of slave status—the children and grandchildren of the slaves originally purchased or traded remain as

---

[139]BROOKS, supra note 114, at 346 n.63 (citing June 9, 1865 proclamation by President Andrew Johnson).
[140]RAEL-GÁLVEZ, supra note 52, at 292-93.
[141]Id., at 312-313 n. 597.
[142]Id. at 294-295 (quoting from Santistevan's grand jury testimony); see also, BROOKS, supra note 114, at 352.

"slaves or servants" within the households of the original owners and their descendants.[143]

In the end, the grand jury refused to return indictments against any of those charged with Indian slavery. This is not surprising, given that the grand jury likely was composed of Mexican men who knew or knew of Santistevan.[144] If Santistevan's experience is any guide, there was no lasting stigma in being charged with this crime, in either the community of Mexican elites to which he belonged or among Euro-American elites. In the decade following his indictment as a slaveholder, Santistevan played an active role as a layperson in the American court in Taos County.[145] On four occasions, three different Chief Justices of the Territorial Supreme Court (all Euro-American) appointed Santistevan as one of three lay jury commissioners, whose task was to select grand jury and petit jury venires for the following court session (along with the Chief Justice and the elected county Probate Judge). Several chief justices, who also served as presiding judges riding circuit in the first judicial district that included Taos County, named Santistevan interpreter to the grand jury seven times during the 1870s, a position for which he was paid $3/day. During the Sept. 1875 term of court, Chief Justice Palen selected Santistevan foreman of the grand jury.[146] In short, Santistevan was a model citizen—and an elite Mexican who owned Indian slaves.

There is a kind of cognitive dissonance that radiates from all sides of the post-Civil War efforts by American officials to contain Indian slavery in New Mexico. In this section of the paper, my aim is to analyze the multiple, cross-cutting ways in which these efforts shaped relations among the various racial groups in the region during the first decades of the American colonization. As a point of entry, let me briefly describe the parameters of Indian slavery in the region.[147] Despite the formal prohibition of Indian slavery under Spanish law, enslavement of Indians by Spanish and mestizo settlers in New Mexico occurred throughout the 17th and 18th and well into the 19th centuries. Gutiérrez describes slaves captured directly from nomadic tribes and those purchased from middle-man captors (other nomadic tribes) as crucial to the frontier economy: "Slaves were a medium of exchange and were pieces

[143]For a defense of Indian slavery by another Mexican elite that raises similar themes, see BROOKS, supra note 114, at 346-47 (quoting Felipe Delgado, New Mexico Superintendent of Indian Affairs in 1865).

[144]The federal grand jury empaneled to hear these charges in 1868 would have been similar in racial composition to grand jury and petit jury venires at the county-level, territorial district court. In the Taos County District Court in the 1860s and 1870s, grand jury and petit jury venires had no more than three Euro-Americans and many venires in that period had no Euro-Americans. Taos County Record Book AA (1863-1877), Taos County Record Book (1877-1884), Taos County District Court Records, New Mexico State Records Center and Archives.

[145]Taos County, like other northern New Mexico counties, only began to have a substantial caseload—and hence a routinely functioning court apparatus—in the 1870s. Prior to that time, it is likely that disputes were settled informally or in lower courts such as the justice of the peace courts or the probate court. See GÓMEZ, supra note 9, at 1136 n.10, 1153-58.

[146]During the 1870s, Santistevan was appointed jury commissioner during the Apr. 1871, Sept. 1874, Mar. 1877, and Sept. 1879 terms of court. He served as grand jury interpreter in the Apr. 1873, Apr. 1875, Sept. 1875, Mar. 1876, Sept. 1876, Mar. 1877, and Apr. 1879 terms. I have compiled Santistevan's record of court participation as a layperson from the following: Taos County Record Book AA (1863-1877), Taos County Record Book (1877-1884), Taos County District Court Records, New Mexico State Records Center and Archives.

[147]Given space limitations, my description cannot do justice to the richness and complexity of the situation. Interested readers should see generally BROOKS, supra note 114, and RAEL-GÁLVEZ, supra note 52.

of movable wealth."[148] Using a quantitative analysis of baptisms in New Mexico of nomadic Indians between 1700 and 1849, Gutiérrez shows that the number of Navajo, Apache, Ute and Comanche Indians baptized correlated strongly with the number of deaths of Spanish/Mexican settlers, revealing the links between slavery and cyclical armed conflict between settlers and nomadic tribes.[149]

In a comprehensive study of slavery in the Southwest, Brooks describes the complex political economy of exchange in humans that included both captivity of Spanish-Mexican settlers by nomadic and semi-nomadic tribes and captivity and enslavement of Indians by the settlers.[150] This political economy was gradually transformed and eventually destroyed with the American conquest of the region.[151] In the short term, however, the effect of the transition from a Mexican to an American sovereign in the region was to greatly increase hostilities between the non-Pueblo Indian tribes and both Americans and Mexicans. Using a slave census taken in 1865 by an Indian agent in southern Colorado and northern New Mexico, Rael-Gálvez concludes that the vast majority of Indian slaves were Navajo (others were Utahs, Utes, Pi-Utes, as described in the document) and that almost three-fifths had been sold to Mexican households by Mexican middle-men, while two-fifths having been sold to Mexican households by members of other nomadic tribes.[152]

For our purposes, perhaps the most striking fact was that conflict with nomadic Indians increased dramatically in the first two decades of the American occupation, likely leading to a correspondingly dramatic increase in the number of Indian slaves held in mestizo households. Even after the Civil War, when American military and civil officials were charged with eliminating Indian slavery and peonage from New Mexico, evidence suggests that campaigns to do so sometimes resulted in the production of more captives who were then sold into slavery.[153] Ironies abound. After emancipation and the Civil War, the U.S. government participated in the transfer of Indian captives into slavery in New Mexico. While anti-peonage initiatives were underway in Washington, the army was, literally, engaged in a war against the same peoples who were the objects of the peonage legislation (the nomadic and semi-nomadic tribes). In effect, the U.S. was simultaneously warring against Indians and warring against Indian slavery.

---

[148]GUTIÉRREZ, supra note 53, at 152.

[149]Id. at 153-54; see BROOKS, supra note 114, at 124 [arguing that a regional exchange in people (especially women and children) of different nomadic Indian tribes predated the Spanish conquest].

[150]Brooks concludes that Mexican captives "continued to face a range of possible fates from full cultural assimilation through subordinate labor status to resale among the expectant capitalists of American Texas." BROOKS, supra note 114, at 324. He also describes the experience José Andrés Martínez, a mestizo who was taken captive by Mescalero Apaches as a ten-year-old in 1866: after being renamed Andali, he grew up with the Apaches, returned to his birth family as an adult, only to decide to return to live permanently with the Apaches, where he eventually played a role as a translator and spokesman for a Kiowa, Apache and Comanche delegation to Washington, D.C. in the 1880s. Id. at 356.

[151]Id. at 327, 331-337. Ultimately, the American campaign to pacify Indians and the fight against slavery intertwined to destroy the system, though not in ways that necessarily improved conditions for Indians: "This campaign involved eliminating the use of livestock and captives as exchangeable resources in the system, placing Indians on reservations to disrupt their exchange economy, and replacing kin-based subjectivity with state-sponsored individual autonomy—all to clear the way for a capitalist system." Id. 331.

[152]RAEL-GÁLVEZ, supra note 52, at 249.

[153]For example, Kit Carson's First New Mexico Volunteers conducted campaigns against the Navajos, in an effort to limit their raids and captive-taking, but rewarded his Mexican militiamen and Ute scouts with Navajo captives! BROOKS, supra note 114, at 331-32.

At the federal level, a number of Reconstruction-era initiatives were directed at ending the so-called "custom" of Indian slavery in New Mexico. President Johnson's "Special Proclamation of 1865" indicated that Emancipation Proclamation extended to Indian slaves in the federal territories.[154] In 1867, multiple bills were introduced in Congress on the subject, culminating in the passage of the so-called Peon Law whose purpose was "to abolish and forever prohibit the system of peonage in the Territory of New Mexico. . . ."[155] There is little evidence to suggest, however, that change resulted from either of these federal initiatives, as neither contained enforcement provisions.[156]

My concern is with the symbolic politics of these debates, even against a backdrop that suggests little change for either slaves or slaveholders. Indian slavery emerges, then, as a site for multiple conflicts among racial groups—between Indian slaves and their Mexican masters, between Mexican and Euro-American elites, and even as a dramatic status difference between Pueblo Indians and other Indians in New Mexico. Americans' efforts to dislodge Indian slavery can be read in multiple ways. On the one hand, they are consistent with the principles of equality and liberty and with the abolition of slavery and eventual Emancipation of enslaved Blacks after the Civil War. At the same time, Euro-Americans' advocacy of Indian slaves can be read as an effort to further entrench American hegemony against the interests of Mexican elites. Whether conscious or not, the war against Indian slavery (concomitant, as noted above, with the war against Indians) also became a political war against Mexican elites who held Indian slaves.

Some evidence against the notion that the Euro-Americans fighting Indian slavery comes from the fact that Euro-Americans themselves kept Indian slaves. Writing almost contemporaneously and speaking of Euro-American elites in New Mexico, Bancroft wrote that "[t]here were few military or civil officials who did not own captive slaves, and they were found even in the service of the Indian agents."[157] Lafayette Head, the former New Mexico Territorial legislator and Indian Agent charged specifically with identifying and liberating Indian slaves, held multiple Indian slaves in his southern Colorado household in the mid-1860s.[158] Indeed, Head justified his slaveholding in a manner resonant with Santistevan's testimony before the grand jury, saying they "enjoy the full privilege of returning to their people whenever they have the inclination or disposition to do so," but failing to note that they were children who had been taken in raids and whose family's whereabouts where both distant and unknown.[159] Rael-Gálvez documents that, although the majority of those prosecuted in 1868 for holding Indian slaves were native New Mexico Mexicans, they included, as well, significant numbers of Euro-Americans.[160]

---

[154]RAEL-GÁLVEZ, supra note 52, at 277, 279. .

[155]RAEL-GALVEZ, supra note 52, 286-87.

[156]*Id.*, 288 (noting that few Indians were liberated and "the system continued, as did the baptisms of captives").

[157]BANCROFT, supra note 10, at 681. Like the majority of Euro-American and Mexican elites whose history he chronicles, Bancroft conceives of Indian slavery as benign, noting that "in most instances" slavery had improved the living conditions of the slaves. *Id.* at 681.

[158]RAEL-GALVEZ, supra note 52, 274.

[159]*Id.*, 276.

[160]*Id.* 301, 306-309 (noting, as well, that those charged with holding slaves including numerous Mexican women married to Euro-American men).

For Mexican elites, holding Indian slaves marked them as both economically and racially privileged. While it is difficult to determine with accuracy, it appears that slaveholding occurred primarily in elite families. Brooks reports that 288 households in Taos County were identified by American authorities in 1868 as having Indian slaves or peons out of a total of 2,820 households in the county.[161] Extrapolating from these numbers, this would mean that just over six percent of Taos County households included Indian slaves or peons, and even if we reasonably assumed this number to be a substantial undercount, even doubling the numbers would bring us only to 12 percent of households.[162] Brooks also shows that, typically, households with Indian slaves held only one or two such persons: 87 percent of those holding Indian slaves held only one such person and 85 percent of those holding Indian peons held only one or two such persons.[163] This provides another contrast with the South: in New Mexico, Indian slaves provided mostly household labor (perhaps because they were predominantly captive women and children), rather than labor of a capitalist nature.

Mexican families with Indian servants were not restricted to the very richest native New Mexicans, but they were an indication of wealth and, perhaps more so, past status under the Spanish and Mexican governments. Within the context of American colonization and the intensifying debates over Black slavery, the holding of Indian slaves may have become a different kind of status marker, one which marked white racial privilege in addition to wealth. From this perspective, Mexican elites' defense of the system of Indian slavery constituted resistance to American hegemony. One sees this in the strained dance between three sets of actors in the legal system: Mexican justices of the peace, Mexican legislators, and Euro-American judges (who, it is recalled served both as justices of the territorial supreme court and trial judges riding circuit in one of three judicial districts). Over the course of the first two full decades of the American occupation of New Mexico, these three sets of actors engaged each other in a series of legal battles that reveal the contestation and ultimate negotiation of a new racial order.

Often, these disputes entered the legal system at the level of justice of the peace courts, where Indian slaves complained of unfair or mis-treatment by their Mexican masters or where Mexican slaveholders sought to regain control of an Indian slave who had been stolen or who had run away. Because these forums were not courts of record, we have relatively little data about how these disputes typically proceeded. In what we can assume is a small number of special cases, however, the losing party in the justice of the peace court appealed to the district court, presided over by one of the territorial supreme court justices (appointed, you will recall, by the President); and, in an even smaller number of cases, the loser in this second litigation forum pursued an additional appeal to the territorial supreme court. The pattern in these cases was for justices of the peace—who were overwhelmingly native Mexicans during

---

[161]BROOKS, supra note 114, at 403 app. C.
[162]*Id.* at 351-52.
[163]Ibid.

the 1850s and 1860s—to rule in favor of slaveholders and for Euro-American judges to rule against Mexican slaveholders.[164]

Two additional patterns can be teased out. First, majority-Mexican legislatures continually sought legislative solutions to what they perceived as an activist judiciary composed exclusively of Euro-Americans. They formalized the ownership of Indian slaves by other names—under the rubric of an expanding master-servant law, drawing heavily on Anglo-American common law traditions.[165] As Brooks notes, this meant that "after 1851, peonage and slavery became densely interwoven" and, he concludes, virtually merged."[166] Even as this route was increasingly stymied by Euro-American judges, Mexican slaveholders turned to county probate courts to use the guardianship system to essentially disguise the master-slave relationship in euphemistic familial language.[167] By taking the guardianship route, Mexican slaveholders accomplished two things simultaneously: first, establishing their forum as probate court (rather than either the justice of the peace courts or the Euro-American controlled district courts), and, second, cloaking the practice of slavery in familial terms (such that they were rescuing "orphaned" Indian children).[168] Like justices of the peace, probate judges (like Juan Santistevan) were elected officials and in this era were virtually all Mexicans.[169]

Euro-American judges responded in two ways that substantially curtailed the power of Mexican elites. First, they overturned or narrowly construed master-servant legislation in the interests of litigants who were Indian slaves.[170] Second, and more comprehensively, they sought over a period of decades to curtail the power of the justice of the peace courts, with the effect of gradually emasculating these largely Mexican-controlled courts of first resort.[171] Eventually, Euro-American elites appealed to higher authority—not in the form of the U.S. Supreme Court, but in the form of the Congress, which, as the reader will recall, had the authority to nullify any act of the territorial legislature. Frustrated by unsuccessful attempts to use general slavery and

---

[164]For example, Rael-Galvez traces the case of Tomas Heredia, who sued Jose Maria Garcia, who fled Garcia's residence, arguing that the peonage contract under which he worked was illegal. Multiple justices of the peace in Dona Ana County sided with Garcia, ordering Heredia to return to him. On a habeas corpus petition to the Territorial Supreme Court, the justices reasoned that "peonage must be as illegal as Negro slavery" and ordered Heredia freed. RAEL-GALVEZ, supra note 52, 284-85 (citing records of the New Mexico Supreme Court [no published opinion exists]).

[165]The first master-servant law was enacted by the territorial legislature in 1851, and was expanded in a variety of ways over the 1850s and 1860s. RAEL-GALVEZ, supra note 52, 188 (citing the various pieces of legislation). The legislature formally abolished peonage in 1867, but the practice apparently continued well into the next decade, according to Brooks. BROOKS, supra note 114, at 349 n.70.

[166]BROOKS, supra note 114, at 348.

[167]RAEL-GALVEZ, supra note 52, at 200 (citing legislation enacted in 1859).

[168]Rael-Galvez powerfully observes: "While terms such as "genizaro" and "criado," were much more common, "guardianship" may also have begun to be used in similar ways. As is true with all these euphemisms, however, what this reveals is precisely what it attempts to hid: a continually constructed ideology of a legally mandated benevolence, which while read outside of slavery, was in fact constitutive of an uniquely situated colonial paternalism, hierarchy and racism." Id., 201.

[169]GÓMEZ (2000), supra note 9, at 1156, n. 65 (describing probate judges and the probate court).

[170]For example, see, Jaramillo v. Romero (1857).

[171]GÓMEZ (2000), supra note 9, at 1158 (noting that the Territorial Supreme Court curtailed the power of justices of the peace in several cases in the 1860s). In my forthcoming book, I analyze how these various conflicts in the legal sphere challenged Mexican men's masculinity and power and ultimately reinforced Euro-American men's masculinity and power.

peonage prohibitions to address Indian slavery in New Mexico, in 1867 Congress directly prohibited Indian slavery and the practice of Indian peonage.[172]

One way to read these actions on the part of Euro-American judges and federal legislators is to view them as champions of civil rights and, in particular, advocates of the extension of recently won Black civil rights to Indians. In order to fully understand these dynamics, however, we must consider the constellation of racial groups, racial ideologies, and the new racial order that was in formation. From the actions of Mexican elites in the first 25 years of American colonization, it is clear that they perceived it in their interest to defend and elaborate the practice of Indian slavery. It also is clear that Euro-Americans, especially judges, were increasingly critical of the practice euphemistically labeled peonage. What were the motivations of each group? What do the debates between Mexican elites and Euro-Americans over Indian slavery reveal about the deeper, highly racialized conflict in this colonial moment?

The broader historic context is extremely important because, at this same point in history, the American military was engaged in its most intense "Indian wars" against the nomadic tribes of New Mexico.[173] The culmination was Kit Carson's forced march of 8,000 Navajo men, women and children over 300 miles from their homeland to the Bosque Redondo Reservation, where they were held as captives of the U.S. from 1864-68. Historian Richard White's description provides additional context:

> The "Long Walk" became an event seared into the Navajo memory, a lasting reminder of the power and ruthlessness of the federal government. It would be four years before the Dine, as the Navajos call themselves, returned to their own country . . . These were four years of humiliation, suffering, death, and near starvation."[174]

Against this context, consider what "choices" a hypothetical Navajo woman enslaved in a Mexican household would have had in 1868, the year of the indictment against Santistevan and the other slaveholders. Griffin described how he liberated the Indian slaves and peons in 1868:

> Upon the examination of each [of the] persons charged as aforesaid and finding the charges true, I at once had the Indians so held as slaves brought before me, and informed them that under the laws of the United States and the holding of the Supreme Court of New Mexico thereunder, they were strictly and absolutely free to live where and work for whom they desired, and were at perfect liberty to go where and when they pleased . . . that slavery could not exist in the United States and if they should prefer changing their homes, and go to the Navajo Country . . . they could do so . . . [175]

---

[172]RAEL-GALVEZ, supra note 52, 286-87.

[173]One result of the American-led Indian wars of the 1860s was the largest number of baptisms of nomadic Indians ever recorded in Catholic records. RAEL-GÁLVEZ, supra note 52, at 215. As Rael-Gálvez notes, these military campaigns revealed a shift "from the wars against slavery to the wars against Indians." *Id.* at 211. Admittedly, Mexicans, as army volunteers and in other support capacities, supported this assault on Navajos and other nomadic tribes. See *Id.* at 203 n.387 (citing an 1860 proclamation exhorting Mexican men to join up to "create a force of 1,000 men" to fight the "savage" Navajos.)

[174]WHITE, supra not 26, at 100.

[175]RAEL-GÁLVEZ, supra note 52, at 292. Oddly, Griffin's emancipations apparently occurred at the time he issued arrest warrants and subpoenas of the alleged slaveholders, but before the federal grand jury had opportunity to consider (and, in these cases, reject) indictments.

Had the hypothetical Navajo slave in a Mexican household sought emancipation and return to her people, she would have been forcibly removed to Bosque Redondo.[176] To say this is not to in any way justify Indian slavery, but instead to point out the disingenuousness of American liberation efforts.

Instead, I read Americans' actions here as part of a larger project of institution-building for the purpose of extending and preserving American material and ideological interests in this newest colony. From this perspective, the Mexican/Euro-American conflict over Indian slavery represented both a power struggle between colonizer and native and between dominant (Euro-American) and subordinate (Mexican) racial groups. Mexican elites attempted to resist American hegemony by, literally, holding on to one of their most valuable assets (even as their land holdings plummeted during the 19th century). At another level, Mexican elites sought to maintain their honor and status, which under the Spanish and Mexican periods had been deeply connected to making raids, taking captives, and holding Indian slaves in their households. This tradition surely resonated with the transfer of power to the Americans, who, after all, understood both the traffic in human beings and its justification on the basis of racial inferiority. In the context of American racial hierarchy, then, we must also read Mexican elites' fierce battle to maintain Indian slavery as an effort to legitimize (and, thus, fortify) their ever-tenuous claim to whiteness.

Conclusion

Racism and the ideology of white supremacy were bound up with colonialism in New Mexico. The American colonizers needed a native governing elite, both because they had insufficient numbers of Euro-American settlers in the region and in order to legitimize the military occupation. The latter was especially important given extensive Whig criticism of the war with Mexico and of imperialism more generally. Americans did not want to see themselves as a colonial power. One of the striking features of the standard American history of this period—of the Mexican War and the subsequent annexation of more than half Mexico's territory—is the sheer absence of colonialism as a topic or theme. In the national mythmaking constituted by this conventional history, this encounter of peoples is not presented as one of conquest and colonialism. Instead, most histories of U.S. imperialism begin in 1898, with the end of the Spanish-American War and the acquisition by the U.S. of Puerto Rico, Guam, and the Philippines, and with the annexation of Hawaii.[177] But we cannot fully understand the second imperial moment of the 1890s without understanding what occurred in the first imperial moment in the 1840s, in what is today the American Southwest.

---

[176]Rael-Galvez similarly observes: "The irony here is profound, since the Dine [the Navajo] were also just then being held captive by the United States government, removed from their homeland and bound within military control." *Id.*, 270.

[177]Reliance on 1898 as the beginning of U.S. imperialism cuts across the political spectrum, with even left-leaning scholars evoking that year as the start of "the New American Empire." SMITH, supra note 12, at 429. See also RUBIN FRANCIS WESTON, RACISM IN U.S. IMPERIALISM (1973) (arguing that American imperialism begins in 1893 with efforts to annex Hawaii). Recent legal scholarship on U.S. imperialism in Puerto Rico includes PEDRO MALAVET, AMERICA'S COLONY: THE POLITICAL AND CULTURAL CONFLICT BETWEEN THE UNITED STATES AND PUERTO RICO (2004) and EDIBERTO ROMAN, AMERICAN COLONIES: EXAMINATION OF U.S. ISLAND CONQUESTS (2005).

Even as American colonizers tapped a native elite to govern in a region with far more Euro-American soldiers than civilians, they also needed to keep Mexicans and Indians in their racial place. For Mexicans incorporated as the native elite in the colony, the distinction between political and social equality became paramount, if not always openly discussed. Though Euro-American men ceded formal political equality to Mexican men, this did not translate into social equality between Euro-Americans and Mexicans. An essential element of the colonial strategy hinged on breaking up the military alliance and cultural affinity between Mexicans and Pueblo Indians. The lure of whiteness proved an ideal tool; with it, the American colonizers could, in one move, co-opt Mexicans willing to trade on their mestizo, part-European heritage and divide Mexicans from their Pueblo Indian neighbors.

Ultimately, the power of racism is ideological, achieving its apex when racially subordinated groups themselves help to reproduce racism. I have shown how this worked by describing situations in which Mexicans gained the upper-hand over non-white groups lower on the racial hierarchy, including Pueblo Indians, free and enslaved Blacks, and nomadic Indians. Despite evidence of ambivalence in both the law on the books and the law in action during the early years of the American occupation, Mexican men disenfranchised their Pueblo brothers to the extent that the latter were virtually excluded from the new, American polity in the region. Acting in symbolic terms because of the tiny numbers of Blacks in the region, Mexican elites sided with pro-slavery and scientific racism to enact a draconian Black Code and Slave Code in the 1850s. Partly in order to affirm their whiteness, Mexican elites actively sought to continue the enslavement of nomadic Indians during the first 25 years of the American occupation.

Mexicans took up the American racial project by claiming whiteness for themselves and seeking to distance themselves from non-white groups including Pueblo Indians, free and enslaved Blacks, and Indians from the nomadic tribes. But Mexicans paid a price for the legal fiction that they were "white," and, therefore, that their men were eligible to vote and hold office; they ultimately were co-opted by the American colonizers. By the end of the 19th century, we begin to see shifts in the political system reflective of Euro-Americans' ascendancy in the region and the end of the period of power-sharing with Mexican elites. At the same time, in all of these contexts, the divisions between Mexicans and other subordinated groups gave tremendous power to the American colonizers, increasing divisions among potential allies in an anti-American campaign, legitimizing the American presence as "protector" of Indians, and entrenching the American legal system as a neutral, fair forum for dispute resolution and punishment.

At the same time, conquest was not a totalizing experience. At the edges of a system of co-optation and colonial authority, Mexican elites exercised more self-determination than other non-white racial groups in New Mexico and, perhaps, anywhere in the U.S. at the time. Given their control of lower court forums such as the justices of the peace and probate courts, Mexican men exercised considerable control over disputes among themselves, disputes with Euro-American merchants and ranchers, and disputes with members of various Indian communities. Although these victories were sometimes literally overruled by the higher, Euro-American controlled district courts, Mexicans held the balance of power even in those forums, where they were the majority of grand jurors checking the power of Euro-American prosecutors and the majority of petit jurors checking the power of Euro-American judges.

Mexicans' status as a middle-man or wedge racial group simultaneously buttressed and challenged white supremacy. Mexicans' sometimes successful claims to whiteness challenged white supremacist ideology by forcing a rupture in categories; what was "whiteness" if it was a permeable rather than a closed category? At the same time, race relations in New Mexico served to buttress white supremacy. Mexicans' claim to whiteness was fragile because, while they were formally recognized as whites, they were informally treated as non-white, as racially inferior to Euro-Americans. As a result, Mexican elites vigorously sought to distance themselves from non-white groups lower on the racial hierarchy, including Blacks (free and slave) and Pueblo and nomadic Indians. In this way, they played a leading role in reproducing the American racial hierarchy in the Southwest and, ultimately, in the nation.

In this chapter, I have frequently emphasized the agency of Mexican elites and the extent to which they exercised rights under the banner of claims to whiteness. In so doing, it is easy to overstate the extent to which Mexicans' racial subordination—even as elites—impacted them on a daily basis. An important reminder of this comes from the Mexican American elites who represented Mr. Hernandez in his appeal to the Supreme Court. Although the lawyers and various members of the bench involved in the case debated in both formal and informal venues the extent to which Mexican Americans were "white" or not, there never really was any doubt about the daily, pernicious ways in which Mexicans were subordinate to whites, whether or not they were allowed to officially claim white status.

One of the lawyers, John J. Herrera, made the point in a letter to the editor of the Houston Chronicle he penned twenty years after the *Hernandez* decision. Writing in 1974 in response to an article on discrimination against Blacks, Herrera recalled his memories of a Jim Crow Texas that singled out both African Americans and Chicanos:

> The story brought back many memories to me. The signs in West Texas cafes: NO CHILI! "They mean us, son. Don't go in there," dad would admonish me. The rest of Texas was no better. Seguin [Texas]: a public park with the sign, Negros y Mexicanos Afuera! In a Houston personnel office: "No Mexicans hired." On Washington Ave.: "No Mexicans Allowed in Dance Hall." In a refinery, all water fountains were painted white, black, or brown. You know where I had to drink.[178]

Herrera did not mention here but recalled in many other instances the signs in the county courthouse where Pete Hernandez was tried and convicted of murder, where men's bathrooms were separately marked for "Colored Men" and "Hombres

---

[178]JOHN J. HERRERA, Editorial, HOUSTON CHRON, May 31, 1974, § 1, at 27 (emphasis in original). I am indebted to University of Houston Law Center Professor Michael A. Olivas for bringing this letter to my attention.

Aquí." The fact that Herrera was one of the most elite Mexican Americans in Texas did not change the fact that he was required to use a segregated washroom in 1950s Texas. The fact that Herrera was a lawyer (even one who would soon argue before the U.S. Supreme Court) was secondary; first and foremost, he was a Mexican.

Race and Colorblindness after *Hernandez* and *Brown*[+]

Ian Haney López[*]

The fiftieth anniversary of *Brown v. Board of Education*[1] has been widely commemorated, but has also occasioned concern regarding the persistence of racism and racial inequality. *Brown* stands for some as the shining moment when the United States finally and fully committed itself to treating its citizens equally without regard to race; for others, it represents a failed promise, a moment of important but only partial transition when the United States moved from Jim Crow, not to equality, but only to a new, less overt, but hardly less oppressive or pervasive racism. Despite this disagreement, however, almost all view *Brown* as the first case in which Chief Justice Earl Warren unified the Supreme Court to begin dismantling Jim Crow. This quality of being "the first case" adds to *Brown's* prominence, whether that's understood as representing a complete rupture or heralding instead only a shift in racial practices.

But *Brown* is not the first case. Instead, that distinction belongs to a jury exclusion case decided two weeks earlier, *Hernandez v. Texas.*[2] *Hernandez* deserves our attention, not least for reasons of historical accuracy. The Mexican American community has long been an active participant in the struggle for racial justice in the United States, and *Hernandez* brings this fact to the fore. *Hernandez* also has contemporary relevance because it represents the first extension of constitutional protection to Latinos as a class, no small matter now that Hispanics constitute the largest minority group in the United States. But I concentrate on *Hernandez* here for yet another reason: because it comes much closer than *Brown* to explaining when and why the Constitution should concern itself with race. *Hernandez* unambiguously insists, in a way that *Brown* does not, that it is race as subordination, rather than race per se, that demands constitutional intervention.

[+]This is a slightly different version of a paper of the same title which I presented at the American Anthropological Association's Conference on Race and Human Variation held in Alexandria, Virginia, in September 2004. The Association has kindly granted permission for the use of this paper.

[*]Professor of Law, Boalt Hall, University of California, Berkeley. My thanks to Professor Michael A. Olivas for his dedicated efforts to raise *Hernandez v. Texas* to its proper place in legal history as well as in the pantheon of great constitutional cases.

[1]Brown v. Bd. of Educ., 347 U.S. 483 (1954).
[2]Hernandez v. Texas, 347 U.S. 475 (1954). For an earlier article on *Hernandez v. Texas*, see IAN HANEY LÓPEZ, RACE, ETHNICITY, ERASURE: THE SALIENCE OF RACE TO LATCRIT THEORY, 85 CAL. L. REV. 1143 (1998); see also IAN HANEY LÓPEZ, HERNANDEZ VS. BROWN, N.Y. TIMES, May 21, 2004, A2.

In the first half of this paper, I bring *Hernandez v. Texas* out from behind the shadow of *Brown*. The second half then uses the lessons of *Hernandez* to critique the colorblind racial ideology that now dominates the constitutional jurisprudence of race.

Hernandez and Race

Hernandez represents the first effort by the newly constituted Warren Court to dismantle Jim Crow segregation. And yet, this presents a paradox, for the opinion, written by Chief Justice Warren himself, disclaims race as a basis for its analysis. *Hernandez v. Texas* centers on Jim Crow practices, and yet it is not explicitly a race case.

After a two day trial and less than three hours of deliberation, an all white jury in Jackson County, Texas, in 1951, convicted Pete Hernandez of murder and sentenced him to life in prison. The jury's racial composition was not an aberration. The county stipulated at trial that no person with a Spanish surname had served on a trial or grand jury in more than a quarter century; more than six thousand jurors had been seated, but in a county over fifteen percent Mexican American, none had been from that group.

In deciding whether impermissible discrimination occurred, the Court considered a veritable catalog of Jim Crow oppressions. The Court noted that a restaurant in the county seat prominently displayed a sign saying "No Mexicans Served." In addition, Jackson County residents routinely distinguished between "whites" and "Mexicans." Business and civic groups almost entirely excluded Mexican American members. The schools were segregated, at least through the fourth grade, after which almost all Mexican Americans were forced out of school altogether. Finally, the opinion also recorded that on the Jackson County courthouse grounds, there were two men's bathrooms. One was unmarked. The other said "Colored Men" and "Hombres Aquí," meaning, "Men Here."

Consider more fully the underlying claim of jury exclusion. The League of United Latin American Citizens, or LULAC, then the most prominent Mexican American civil rights group in the country, agreed to argue Pete Hernandez's case as part of a larger legal strategy to attack three pernicious practices: school segregation, racially restrictive covenants, and jury exclusion. What ranked jury exclusion with school and residential segregation? To be sure, all-white juries imperiled Mexican American defendants who, like Pete Hernandez himself, risked conviction by hostile and biased juries. Moreover, the Mexican American community suffered because white juries rarely and reluctantly convicted whites for depredations against Mexican Americans. But LULAC's determined opposition to jury exclusion arose first and foremost because of its symbolism.[3] Trial by jury rests on the idea of peers judging and being judged by peers. In the context of Texas race politics, however, to put Mexican Americans on juries was tantamount to elevating them to equal status with whites. The idea that "Mexicans" might judge whites deeply violated Texas' racial

---

[3]CLARE SHERIDAN, "ANOTHER WHITE RACE"; MEXICAN AMERICANS AND THE PARADOX OF WHITE-NESS IN JURY SELECTION, 21 LAW & HIST. REV. 109, 138-39 (2003).

caste system. LULAC hoped *Hernandez* would help to topple a key pillar of Jim Crow: the belief that whites should judge all, but be judged by none but themselves.

Hernandez v. Texas challenged a Jim Crow practice. Yet, the Supreme Court did not decide *Hernandez* as a race case. At the outset of his opinion, Chief Justice Warren observed that while the Constitution's Fourteenth Amendment primarily protected groups marked by "differences in race and color,"[4] he also noted that "the exclusion of a class of persons from jury service on grounds *other* than race or color may also deprive a defendant who is a member of that class of the constitutional guarantee of equal protection of the laws."[5] Why did Warren say that this case concerned something *other* than race or color? The answer is simple, though perhaps startling: every party in *Hernandez* argued that Mexican Americans were white.

As the evidence in *Hernandez* demonstrates, Anglos in Texas in the 1950s considered Mexicans an inferior race. This belief originated during the Anglo expansion into the Southwest in the early to mid-1800s that culminated in the expropriation of the northern half of Mexico.[6] During this era, a consensus emerged among Anglos that Mexicans were "mongrels," a degenerate mixture of Spanish and indigenous American ancestry. Applying established prejudices regarding miscegenation and dark skin to Mexicans, Anglos denigrated that group as dark, filthy, lazy, cowardly, and criminal—with each of these calumnies informing the most common anti-Mexican epithet, "dirty greaser." Needless to say, in articulating an inferior racial identity for Mexicans, Anglos concomitantly elaborated a superior identity for themselves. It was Anglo expansion into the Southwest that most directly gave rise to the racial ideology of Manifest Destiny.[7]

Mexicans in the United States, or at least the community's leaders, initially resisted their racial subordination by constructing themselves as Mexican nationals and by envisioning an eventual return to Mexico. Rather than directly challenging the racial logic that depicted them as inferiors, they sought to evade it by holding themselves apart from American society. In the 1920s and 1930s, however, broad swaths of the U.S. Mexican community came to see themselves as Americans. During this epoch, Mexican community leaders embraced an assimilationist ideology; indeed, the label "Mexican American" emerged from this period and encapsulated the effort to both retain pride in the community's Mexican cultural origins and to express an American national identity. Inseparable from this new assimilationist identity, however, was an engagement with American racial logic. On this score, the community leaders were certain: Mexican Americans were white.

Not all U.S. Mexicans embraced a white racial identity. The elite's ability to claim a white identity partly reflected their elevated class standing and their relatively fair features, attributes that stemmed from race politics not only in the Southwest but also in Mexico. Those who were poor or who had dark features were much less likely to insist they were white. Similarly, recent immigrants were more likely to

---

[4]Hernandez, 347 U.S. at 478.

[5]*Id.* at 477 (emphasis added).

[6]I discuss the early racialization of Mexicans at length in IAN HANEY LÓPEZ, RACISM ON TRIAL: THE CHICANO FIGHT FOR JUSTICE (2003).

[7]See REGINALD HORSMAN, RACE AND MANIFEST DESTINY: THE ORIGINS OF AMERICAN RACIAL ANGLO-SAXONISM (1981).

identify in cultural or national, rather than racial, terms. No homogenous racial identity existed within the U.S. Mexican community. Nevertheless, whiteness formed a central component of elite Mexican identity in the Southwest at mid-century.

The emergence of a white identity among Mexican Americans appears rooted in the development of a notion of "ethnicity" in the early twentieth-century, as well as a concomitant expansion in the popular conception regarding who counted as white. Ethnicity arose as a term of group difference in the early 1900s, when it emerged as a form of identity that would allow expressions of group pride while avoiding the hierarchy central to racial thinking. Ethnicity developed, particularly among Zionists, as a way of capturing what was thought to be "good" about race—a sense of group identity, transmitted by descent, and worthy of loyalty and pride—while eschewing the "bad," the ordering of races and their super- and subordination.[8] Mexican leaders embraced a version of ethnicity in proclaiming at once that they were racially white and so deserved to be free from discrimination, but simultaneously Mexican as a matter of group culture, pride, and political mobilization.

These ideas found clear expression in LULAC's arguments in *Hernandez v. Texas*. As in other cases, LULAC followed what it termed its "other white" legal strategy, protesting not segregation itself, but the inappropriate segregation of Mexican Americans as a white racial group.[9] Thus, LULAC objected in its brief to the Supreme Court that, "while legally white," in Jackson County "frequently the term white excludes the Mexicans and is reserved for the rest of the non-Negro population."[10] Hernandez's lawyers did not argue principally that segregation was legally wrong, but that Mexican Americans were legally white. In this, as one of the lead attorneys in the case explained to the Mexican American public, Mexicans were in no different position than other white ethnic groups that had overcome prejudice:

> We are not passing through anything different from that endured at one time or another by other unassimilated population groups: the Irish in Boston (damned micks, they were derisively called); the Polish in the Detroit area (their designation was bohunks and polackers); the Italians in New York (referred to as stinking little wops, dagoes and guineas); the Germans in many sections of the country (call dumb square-heads and krauts); and our much maligned friends of the Jewish faith, who have been persecuted even here, in the land of the free, because to the bigoted they were just "lousy kikes."[11]

The notion of a white ethnic, as opposed to a nonwhite racial, identity was at the root of LULAC's legal challenge to Mexican jury exclusion in Texas.

---

[8]See generally THEORIES OF ETHNICITY: A CLASSICAL READER (Werner Sollors ed., 1996); MATHEW FRYE JACOBSON, WHITENESS OF A DIFFERENT COLOR: EUROPEAN IMMIGRANTS AND THE ALCHEMY OF RACE (1998).

[9]On the "other white" legal strategy, see Steven H. Wilson, Brown over "Other White": Mexican Americans' Legal Arguments and Litigation Strategy in School Desegregation Lawsuits, 21 LAW & HIST. REV. 145 (2003).

[10]Brief for Petitioner at 38, Hernandez v. Texas, 347 U.S. 475 (1954) (No. 406). See also Neil Foley, Becoming Hispanic: Mexican Americans and the Faustian Pact with Whiteness, in REFLEXIONES 1997: NEW DIRECTIONS IN MEXICAN AMERICAN STUDIES 53 (Neil Foley ed., 1997).

[11]Gustavo C. García, An Informal Report to the People, in A COTTON PICKER FINDS JUSTICE: THE SAGA OF THE HERNANDEZ CASE (Ruben Munguia ed., 1954), in Appendix.

Texas, meanwhile, also adopted the claim that Mexican Americans were white—though to preserve segregation. Beginning in 1931, LULAC and others had brought at least seven challenges to jury exclusion in Texas before *Hernandez*. In the initial cases, Texas courts had upheld the all-white juries after accepting evidence that no Mexican Americans qualified for jury service. For example, one court quoted a jury commissioner as saying that "he did not consider the Mexicans . . . as being intelligent enough to make good jurors, so that [he] just disregarded the whole Mexican list and did not consider any of them."[12] The court cited this as showing that "there was no evidence that there was any Mexican in the County who possessed the statutory qualifications of a juror," and thus concluded that there had been no discrimination "against the Mexican race." [13]

Eventually, this approach proved troubling for the Texas courts, as their evidence regarding the lack of qualified Mexican Americans seemed to demonstrate rather the prevalence of racial prejudice. By the late 1940s, the Texas courts shifted to a new basis for excluding Mexican Americans: they would accept the claim that Mexican Americans were white, but hold that since so too were all of the jurors, there was no discrimination. As the decision under appeal in *Hernandez* reasoned, "Mexicans are white people . . . . The grand jury that indicted [Hernandez] and the petit jury that tried him being composed of members of his race, it cannot be said . . . that appellant has been discriminated against in the organization of such juries."[14]

Confronted with contending parties who nevertheless agreed that Mexican Americans were white, how did the Supreme Court react? Immediately, it jettisoned an explicitly racial analysis. The case, Warren said, did not turn on "race or color." But Warren did not then attempt to decide the case in terms of some other form of difference, for instance national origin, ancestry or ethnicity. Rather, the Court approached this case as concerning group subordination generally. "Community prejudices are not static," Warren wrote, "and from time to time other differences from the community norm may define other groups which need the same [constitutional] protection. Whether such a group exists within a community is a question of fact." In this context, Warren reasoned, Hernandez's "initial burden in substantiating his charge of group discrimination was to prove that persons of Mexican descent constitute a separate class in Jackson County, distinct from 'whites.' One method by which this may be demonstrated is by showing the attitude of the community."[15]

Hernandez articulated a simple test for when a class deserves constitutional protection: In the context of the local situation, was the group mistreated? To answer this question, the Court catalogued the Jim Crow system that defined race relations in Jackson County. *Hernandez* struck down jury discrimination against Mexican Americans not because Mexican Americans were nominally a race, but because in the context of mid-century Texas they were a subordinated group.

There's a wonderful irony to *Hernandez v. Texas*: All parties sought to avoid a racial analysis, and the Court claimed to decide the case as if race was not an issue;

---

[12]Ramirez v. State, 40 S.W.2d 138, 138 (Tex. Crim. App. 1931).
[13]*Id.* at 139-40.
[14]Hernandez v. State, 251 S.W.2d 531, 536 (Tex. Crim. App. 1951), *rev'd*, 347 U.S. 475 (1954).
[15]Hernandez v. Texas, 347 U.S. 475, 478-79 (1954).

and yet the case's holding is perhaps the single most insightful Supreme Court opinion on race ever handed down. *Hernandez* understands (even if Chief Justice Warren as the opinion's author did not quite) that race is ultimately a question of community norms and practices—that is, a social construction. No Supreme Court opinion before or since has come so close to this understanding, nor perceived so clearly that subordination should be the touchstone for invoking constitutional intervention when a state distinguishes between groups.

From *Hernandez*, we can extract three fundamental points about race. First, race is constituted through ideas. By asking about community norms in Jackson County, the Court correctly directed attention to how people thought about race and identity. In this regard, though, note that the Court did not confine itself to seeking expressions of clear prejudice; the Court's examination of community norms did not reduce to a search for intentional animus. Instead, the Court found to be relevant seemingly non-hierarchical norms, such as the fact that community members routinely distinguished between whites and Mexicans. Though the Court did not make this point, it should be clear that racial ideas often form part of an overarching ideology about group difference and social hierarchy. Racial ideas are not limited to a few discrete misconceptions, but form part of a web of beliefs. Moreover, large components of racial ideology operate not consciously but as background beliefs that people take for granted.[16] The vast majority of Anglos in Jackson County probably accepted without considered examination most of the ideas swirling around the bromide that they were white and Mexicans were inferior.

The second point *Hernandez* drives home is that racial ideas produce and then are strengthened by settled practices and material reality. Consider Jackson County's segregated school system: although not mandated by state law, from the turn of the century, Texas school boards customarily segregated Mexican American children because they were, in the words of one school superintendent, "an inferior race."[17] This routine practice translated into a hard reality for Mexican students in Jackson County. According to the testimony of one frustrated mother, the "Latin American school" noted by the Court was a decaying one-room wooden building that flooded repeatedly during the rains, with only a wood stove for heat and outside bathroom facilities, and with but one teacher for the four grades taught there.[18] Segregation's material consequences extended to the Mexican American population as a whole. Among the 645 Mexican American adults in Jackson County, only five had completed college, while 245 had no better than a fourth grade education, fully 175 had received no formal education whatsoever, and the median number of school years hovered at a dismal 3.2 years.[19]

[16]HANEY LÓPEZ, supra note 6, esp. chap. 5.

[17]GUADALUPE SAN MIGUEL, JR., "LET THEM ALL TAKE HEED": MEXICAN AMERICANS AND THE CAMPAIGN FOR EDUCATIONAL EQUALITY IN TEXAS, 1910-1981, at 32 (1987).

[18]Transcript of Hearing on Motion to Quash Jury Panel and Motion to Quash the Indictment at 84-87, State v. Hernandez (Dist. Ct. Jackson Co., Oct. 4, 1951) (No. 2091), *reprinted in* Transcript of Record at 74-75, Hernandez v. Texas, 347 U.S. 475 (1954) (No. 406). This testimony relates to experiences with the school in the early 1940s. By 1948, there were apparently two teachers and two rooms in the district's "Latin American school." *Id.* at 51. The Court relies on these latter figures. *Hernandez*, 347 U.S. at 479 n.10.

[19]Brief for Petitioner at 19, Hernandez v. Texas, 347 U.S. 475 (1954) (No. 406); U.S. BUREAU OF THE CENSUS, U.S. CENSUS OF POPULATION: 1950, VOLUME IV: SPECIAL REPORTS: PERSONS OF SPANISH SURNAMES, at 3C-67 (1953).

down school segregation because it oppressed blacks. But *Brown* did
and unambiguously ground its decision on an anti-subordination ration-
rtcoming opened the door to the misreading of *Brown* that now domi-
utional race law: *Brown*, the contemporary Court insists, stands for the
hat the Constitution prohibits, not subordination, but explicit state invo-
ce.

tional race law as it stands now is a disaster. On one side, the Court
n the most egregious instances of discrimination. *McCleskey v. Kemp*
en though Georgia sentenced to death blacks who murdered whites at
imes the rate it mandated death for blacks who killed blacks, there was
onal harm absent the identification of a particular biased actor.[22] On the
ourt wields the Constitution to strike down almost every effort to ame-
n's legacy. Thus, *Richmond v. Croson* told us that, when the former cap-
onfederacy adopted an affirmative action program to steer some of its
 dollars to minority owned firms, this was impermissible discrimina-
vhen, without the program, less than two-thirds of one percent of those
to minorities in a city over fifty percent African American.[23] It is not too
 that the current Court uses the Constitution to protect the racial status
ipally condones discrimination against minorities, and virtually always
fforts to achieve greater racial equality.

reme Court justifies much of its current racial jurisprudence in terms of
s as "colorblindness." Invoking the formal antiracism of the early civil
ment, colorblindness calls for a principled refusal to recognize race in
et, in practice, colorblindness advances an abstracted conception of race
he Court to be aggressive, not in fighting racism, but in preserving the
quo. The colorblind Court refuses to stop discrimination against racial
vhile it relentlessly condemns efforts to directly remedy racial inequali-
dness as an ideology is committed to protecting racial inequality; its
heart, however, is not a theory of racial inferiority, but of race as an
aningless category.

reme Court recently handed down a second jury discrimination case
atinos, this one too entitled *Hernandez*.[24] *Hernandez v. New York*, in
to cases like *McCleskey* and *Croson*, is a minor case, but it puts into
 the understanding of race that undergirds the Court's contemporary
udence. In *Hernandez v. New York*, the prosecutor peremptorily struck
 every Latino in a case involving a Hispanic defendant and the use of a
guage translator. He did so, he said, because he believed these potential
 not" set aside their familiarity with Spanish. The phrase "could not,"
would not," is significant, for while the latter term suggests concern
dual temperament, the former invokes a sense of group disability. Also
he prosecutor questioned only Hispanic potential jurors about their abil-
Spanish.

Kemp, 481 U.S. 279 (1987).
.A. Croson Co., 488 U.S. 469 (1989).
New York, 500 U.S. 352 (1991).

It is not just that racial ideas have real con
tions in turn buttress racial ideas. The stereoty
enough to serve on juries surely found suppo
Mexican Americans in Jackson County. More g
ulation's low educational level conjoined with
dination, such as their general status as manua
regated and impoverished enclaves, to confirm
practices that immiserated them but rather the s
inferiority. Racial ideas and practices create a
that world serve immediately as the surest evid

Finally, *Hernandez* tells us also that race i
inseparably bound up with social structures—th
privileges they confer, and the miseries they imp
son County, Anglo racial ideas cannot be unders
secure material and symbolic advantage, and to
ization they wreaked on others. Similarly, the
identity reflected an effort to use racial ideas
and to secure the privileges of whiteness. In T
both outside and within that community, stem
material advantage.[20] I do not claim that race i
as class conflict, or that race is *always* consciou
al actors. Race is not only shaped by but shape
and racial ideas have a self-sustaining, taken-fo
is also true that race is functional: people enga
own interests. Put more concretely, racial ine
groups, and they will fight to preserve their priv

Colorblindness

Compare *Hernandez* to *Brown v. Board o*
was whether the Fourteenth Amendment prote
their exclusion from juries was clearly prohibite
forms of segregation struck down by the Recor
Court could not rely on race per se, it was fo
deserved constitutional protection, and thereby
rather than the nature of group identity as the co
obvious that the Constitution protected African
was whether it prohibited school segregation. Bl
beneficiaries of the Fourteenth Amendment, an
particular justification. In contrast, segregated so
hesitated to condemn such practices in strong te
lash. Hence, the Court equivocated. Any fair rea

[20]NEIL FOLEY, THE WHITE SCOURGE: MEXICANS, BLACK
CULTURE (1997); DAVID MONTEJANO, ANGLOS AND ME
1986 (1987).
[21]Strauder v. West Virginia, 100 U.S. 303 (1879).

Court struck
not strongly
ale. That sh
nates consti
proposition
cations of ra

Constit
upholds eve
held that ev
twenty-two
no constitut
other, the C
liorate racis
ital of the C
construction
tion—even
dollars went
strong to sa
quo: it prin
condemns e

The Su
what it exto
rights move
public life.
that allows
racial status
minorities,
ty. Colorbli
intellectual
abstract, me

The Su
involving L
comparison
sharp relief
racial jurisp
from the ju
Spanish-lan
jurors "cou
rather than
about indiv
of concern,
ity to speak

[22]McCleskey v.
[23]Richmond v.
[24]Hernandez v.

Nevertheless, the Court upheld the exclusion, finding no bias on the part of the prosecutor. Justice O'Connor's rationale, offered in a concurring opinion, is particularly revealing. O'Connor thought it irrelevant that the basis for exclusion correlated closely to Hispanic identity and operated to exclude all and only Latinos. Because the strikes were not explicitly justified in racial terms, O'Connor reasoned, no basis existed for constitutional intervention. The strikes "may have acted like strikes based on race," O'Connor conceded, "but they were *not* based on race. *No matter how closely tied or significantly correlated to race* the explanation for a peremptory strike may be, the strike does not implicate the Equal Protection Clause unless it is based on race."[25] According to O'Connor, race is not at issue until and unless someone utters that term. Race exists in this conception almost as a magic word: say it, and race suddenly springs into being, but not otherwise. This magic word formalism strips race of all social meaning; more, it disconnects race from social practices of group conflict and subordination. This ethereal understanding of race provides the cornerstone of the Court's colorblind jurisprudence.

Consider the current requirement that intentional discrimination be shown, exemplified in the *McCleskey* case. Since slavery, Georgia has run a dual system of crime and punishment, incarcerating and executing blacks at far greater rates than whites. When Warren McCleskey challenged his death sentence, he drew on one of the most extensive and sophisticated statistical analyses of capital punishment ever conducted to show that persons like himself, blacks who killed whites, were *twenty-two* times more likely to be condemned to die than blacks who killed blacks.[26] The Supreme Court assumed that the study's findings were accurate, but nevertheless upheld his death sentence because he failed to prove intentional discrimination. According to the Court, the study was "clearly insufficient to support an inference that any of the decisionmakers in McCleskey's case acted with discriminatory purpose."[27]

But what of the study's uncontroverted showing that racial disparities pervaded Georgia's death penalty system? The study clearly demonstrated, for instance, that race was as powerful a variable in predicting who would live or die in Georgia's death machinery as a prior murder conviction or acting as the principal planner of a homicide.[28] "At most," the Court said, "the . . . study indicates a discrepancy that appears to correlate with race. Apparent disparities in sentencing are an inevitable part of our criminal justice system."[29] In dismissing McCleskey's challenge, the Court stated emphatically: "we decline to assume that what is unexplained is invidious."[30] For the Court, the uncontroverted fact that McCleskey was twenty-two times more likely to be executed because his victim had been white rather than black constituted no more than a mere "discrepancy," an "apparent disparity," something "unexplained" which it refused to assume was somehow "invidious."

---

[25]*Id.* at 375 (O'Connor, J., concurring) (emphasis added).
[26]*McCleskey*, 481 U.S. at 327.
[27]*Id.* at 297.
[28]*Id.* at 326.
[29]*Id.* at 312.
[30]*Id.* at 312-13.

The intent test and the Court's resistance to connecting disparate treatment to racial discrimination tie back to the Court's narrow conception of race. If race reduces to a question of mere physical difference unconnected in any way to social hierarchy or history, then mistreatment on any basis not explicitly tied to physical difference or descent by definition is not racial discrimination. In this context, an intent test makes sense. Race becomes the basis for discrimination only when a party intends that result; otherwise, there is no discrimination, only the "discrepancies" of social life.

In *Hernandez*, Chief Justice Warren emphatically held that constitutional harm could be demonstrated absent a showing of intentional discrimination. Responding to the state's contention that no purposeful racism could be shown, Warren retorted "it taxes our credulity to say that mere chance resulted in their being no members of [the Mexican group] among the over six thousand jurors called in the past twenty-five years. The result bespeaks discrimination, whether or not it was a conscious decision on the part of any individual jury commissioner."[31] Cannot we say the same? Does it not tax our credulity to say that the racial disparities in Georgia's death penalty system resulted from mere chance? Race is not merely a word or skin pigment, it is a social identity deeply connected to history and power, privilege and disadvantage. It makes a travesty of the Fourteenth Amendment to refuse to see McCleskey's case as rooted in the context of a Georgia penal system steeped in racial oppression.

If the Court's pinched conception of race lends support to an intent test, it also allows the Court to equate race conscious responses to racial inequality with racism. Under colorblindness, there is no difference between racism and affirmative action, between Jim Crow and racial remediation. As Justice Clarence Thomas declares, "there is a 'moral [and] constitutional equivalence' between laws designed to subjugate a race and those that distribute benefits on the basis of race in order to foster some current notion of equality."[32] How can affirmative action be the equivalent of the segregated juries, schools, restaurants, and bathrooms in Jackson County, Texas? The answer again lies in the colorblind Court's conception of race as just skin color. When race is abstracted from social context and group conflict, then the harm of racism is reduced to a violation of liberal norms. Under this conception, to treat someone differently on the basis of race is to treat them in an arbitrary manner unrelated to anything meaningful about them. This is, to be sure, a potential issue with affirmative action, as it is with a wide range of distinctions our society commonly makes. But it is hard to imagine a more impoverished understanding of the harms of Jim Crow. The lawyers for Hernandez drove 100 miles every morning to the Jackson County seat to argue the case; they left every evening, for lack of accommodations available to Mexican Americans and because they feared for their safety should they remain.[33] As *Hernandez* emphatically demonstrates, the principal harm of racism is violent subordination, not the transgression of meritocratic norms usually honored only in the breach.

---

[31]Hernandez v. Texas, 347 U.S. 475, 482 (1954).
[32]Adarand Constructors, Inc. v. Pena, 515 U.S. 200, 240 (1995) (Thomas, J., concurring).
[33]García, supra note 11.

Today's Court gets racism backwards: it claims that racism amounts to any use of race, when in fact efforts to counteract racial oppression's extensive harms have no choice but to reference race. And it denies there is racism no matter how stark the impact if race is not specifically invoked by a state actor, even though most racism now occurs through institutionalized practices.[34] This misunderstanding of racism is anchored by a narrow, no-context conception of race. It is race-as-a-word-that-must-be-uttered-for-it-to-exist, race-as-skin-disconnected-from-social-practice-or-national-history, which undergirds colorblindness. This is no innocent error. Colorblindness is a new racial ideology geared to the preservation of racial inequality. It does so not by openly embracing white supremacy; on the contrary, it seeks legitimacy by vociferously decrying old-style racism. Rather, colorblindness rests—as all racial ideologies ultimately do—on a particular, consequential conception of race.

Anti-Categorical Politics

Colorblindness usually presents race as merely blood or skin color to justify its regressive understanding of race as lacking any social meaning. One might suppose, then, that colorblindness can be attacked by showing that race is not a matter of physical differences, but instead a social construction. This tactic will fail, however, unless one emphasizes not the made-up nature of race, but race's continued vitality in structuring inequality in our society.

Colorblindness already contains within it an anti-categorical element, a drive to bring into doubt racial taxonomies. This politics has been most pronounced with respect to the existence of a white category, where it follows from the effort to distance race from the dynamics of group conflict. At least since 1978, the Court has reasoned as if whites do not exist as a race—except as victims of racism. In the *Bakke* affirmative action case, Justice Powell addressed whether the Court should defer when the state discriminated in favor of, rather than against, minorities. He began by acknowledging that the Fourteenth Amendment was originally crafted to protect African Americans. But, Powell averred, by the time of *Brown*, "the United States had become a Nation of minorities. Each had to struggle—and to some extent struggles still—to overcome the prejudices not of a monolithic majority, but of a 'majority' composed of various minority groups of whom it was said—perhaps unfairly in many cases—that a shared characteristic was a willingness to disadvantage other groups." Insisting that "the concepts of 'majority' and 'minority' necessarily reflect temporary arrangements and political judgments," Justice Powell asserted that "the white 'majority' itself is composed of various minority groups, most of which can lay claim to a history of prior discrimination at the hands of the State and private individuals. Not all of these groups can receive preferential treatment and corresponding judicial tolerance of distinctions drawn in terms of race and nationality, for then the only 'majority' left would be a new minority of white Anglo-Saxon Protestants."[35] In a few short paragraphs, Justice Powell erased whites as a

---

[34]Ian F. Haney López, *Institutional Racism: Judicial Conduct and a New Theory of Racial Discrimination*, 109 YALE L.J. 1717 (2000).

[35]Regents of Univ. of Cal. v. Bakke, 438 U.S. 265, 292, 295-96 (1978).

dominant group—and conjured instead whites as potential victims in the brave new world of civil rights and racial remediation.

To be sure, this anti-categorical politics has not been in evidence with respect to most minorities. As you might expect where race is viewed as a matter of skin color, the Court's colorblind jurisprudence has largely reasoned as if black, yellow, and red are unproblematic categories. Consider, for instance, Chief Justice Rehnquist, who consistently took positions against Native American interests in federal Indian law cases—in one opinion, he approvingly quoted a description of Indians as "fine physical specimens" who "lived only for the day, recognized no rights of property, robbed or killed anyone if they thought they could get away with it, inflicted cruelty without a qualm, and endured torture without flinching."[36] This is not exactly the language of someone deeply skeptical about the existence of races.

Nevertheless, the Court's selective hostility to racial categories has been a prominent component of its colorblind jurisprudence, one that I suspect will gain in response to the spreading recognition that race is socially constructed. Constructionist arguments challenge the sort of physically wbased reasoning that has been common on the Court. But directed merely at the contingent nature of racial ideas, such arguments will not topple colorblindness. The linchpin of colorblindness is not the claim that race reduces to physical differences, but that race is divorced from social meaning. Rather than recoil from constructionist arguments, the Court and colorblindness proponents generally will most likely seize on them to buttress their attacks on racial categories. Already, the colorblind refrain is shifting from the claim that race amounts to superficial differences to the notion that racial categories are egregious errors. Colorblindness is assisted rather than opposed by arguments that race lacks coherent meaning.

Not all who attack racial categories as contingent inventions aim to promote colorblind politics. Indeed, revealing the made-up nature of racial ideas is fundamental to counteracting regnant racial ideology. Nevertheless, we should be careful not to assume that deconstructing racial categories will necessarily disestablish race. Efforts to deconstruct racial categories, without more, lose sight of the fact that race is much more than a set of ideas; it is an on-going set of social practices and structures. We best oppose colorblind politics by insisting on the deep connection between ideas of race and social inequality. This, perhaps, is the single most important insight of *Hernandez v. Texas*. The core issue was not whether race was invoked directly, as the current Court would require, nor was it whether Mexican Americans did or did not constitute a race, as someone concerned with categorical coherence might ask. The core question for the Court was, and should be again: do social practices subordinate groups based upon ideas of racial difference? Then and now, the answer remains a tragic but resounding yes.

---

[36]United States 371, 436-37 (1980) (Rehnquist, J.)

Hernandez v. Texas: Legacies of Justice and Injustice

Kevin R. Johnson*

---

*Associate Dean for Academic Affairs, School of Law, and Mabie-Apallas Professor of Public Interest Law, School of Law, and Chicana/o Studies, University of California at Davis; A.B., University of California, Berkeley; J.D., Harvard University. Thanks to Michael Olivas for inviting me to participate in the important conference commemorating the 50th anniversary of Hernandez v. Texas, 347 U.S. 475 (1954) at the University of Houston Law Center in November 2004. Participants in the conference, especially Richard Delgado, Ian Haney López, and Juan Perea, offered helpful comments. Olivas' generous support and mentorship throughout my professional career have been invaluable to me. Conversations with George A. Martínez helped my thinking on the issues raised in this paper. The expert staff of the U.C. Davis Law Library, especially Peg Durkin, Susan Llano, Aaron Dailey, and Elizabeth McKechnie, was extraordinarily helpful in patiently locating historical documents and other materials for this paper. The able research and editorial assistance of law student Jeff Finucane is much appreciated. Michael Olivas, Ralph Armbruster-Sandoval, Miroslava Chavez-Garcia, Mary Romero, and Nancy Marder offered insightful comments on a draft of this paper. I also received helpful feedback from participants, especially John R. Chavez and David Gutiérrez, in a discussion of this paper at the Western History Association 2004 annual conference.

INTRODUCTION

The Supreme Court's 1954 decision in *Hernandez v. Texas*[1] was a legal land-mark[2] for Mexican Americans in the United States. In that decision, the nation's highest court ruled that the systematic exclusion of persons of Mexican ancestry from juries in Jackson County, Texas violated the Constitution. Even though Mexicans comprised more than ten percent of the adult population, no person of Mexican ancestry had served on a jury in that county in the previous twenty-five years.[3] That discrimination against Mexican Americans existed in the United States was no surprise to the greater Mexican community in 1954, which had long been relegated to second class citizenship in much of the Southwest.[4] Housing and job segregation was common.[5] Mexican Americans as a group were well aware that the United States had conquered Mexico's northern territories in a war of aggression,[6] that persons of Mexican ancestry had suffered mass deportations during the Great Depression,[7] that Mexican Americans were beaten on the streets of Los Angeles by members of the armed forces in the infamous "Zoot Suit" riots during World War II,[8] that Mexican immigrants experienced exploitation and abuse through the Bracero Program that brought temporary workers from Mexico to the United States from the 1940s to the 1960s,[9] and that they lived through

---

[1] 347 U.S. 475 (1954).

[2] To characterize the decision as a landmark does not mean to suggest that the promise of the case has been fully realized. See infra text accompanying notes 160-251. At the same time, however, *Hernandez v. Texas* is an important case that has been the subject of considerable attention. See, e.g., JUAN F. PEREA ET AL., RACE AND RACES: CASES AND RESOURCES FOR A DIVERSE AMERICA 517 (2000) (excerpting decision in chapter on race and developing notions of equality); Richard Delgado & Vicky Palacios, *Mexican Americans as a Legally Cognizable Class Under Rule 23 and the Equal Protection Clause*, 50 NOTRE DAME L. REV. 393 (1975) (analyzing *Hernandez v. Texas* and its implications on civil rights class actions).

[3] See *infra* text accompanying notes 107-39.

[4] See, e.g., RODOLFO ACUÑA, OCCUPIED AMERICA: A HISTORY OF CHICANOS (3D ED. 1988); TOMÁS ALMAGUER, RACIAL FAULT LINES: THE HISTORICAL ORIGINS OF WHITE SUPREMACY IN CALIFORNIA (1994); MARIO BARRERA, RACE AND CLASS IN THE SOUTHWEST: A THEORY OF RACIAL INEQUALITY (1979); LEONARD PITT, THE DECLINE OF THE CALIFORNIOS: A SOCIAL HISTORY OF THE SPANISH-SPEAKING CALIFORNIANS, 1846-1890 (1966).

[5] See *Hernandez*, 347 U.S. at 471, 481.

[6] See REGINALD HORSMAN, RACE AND MANIFEST DESTINY: THE ORIGINS OF AMERICAN RACIAL ANGLO-SAXONISM 208-14 (1981).

[7] See FRANCISCO E. BALDERRAMA & FRANCISCO RODRÍGUEZ, DECADE OF BETRAYAL: MEXICAN REPATRIATION IN THE 1930S (1995); CAMILLE GUERIN-GONZALES, MEXICAN WORKERS AND THE AMERICAN DREAM: IMMIGRATION, REPATRIATION, AND CALIFORNIA FARM LABOR, 1900-1939 (1994); ABRAHAM HOFFMAN, UNWANTED MEXICAN AMERICANS IN THE GREAT DEPRESSION: REPATRIATION PRESSURES, 1929-1939 (1974); EDWIN J. ESCOBAR, RACE, POLICE, AND THE MAKING OF A POLITICAL IDENTITY: MEXICAN AMERICANS AND THE LOS ANGELES POLICE DEPARTMENT, 1900-1945, at 84-90 (1999).

[8] See ESCOBAR, supra note 7, at 233-55; *infra* text accompanying notes 68-82.

[9] See KITTY CALAVITA, INSIDE THE STATE: THE BRACERO PROGRAM, IMMIGRATION AND THE I.N.S. (1992); ERNESTO GALARZA, MERCHANTS OF LABOR: THE MEXICAN BRACERO STORY, AN ACCOUNT OF THE MANAGED MIGRATION OF MEXICAN FARM WORKERS IN CALIFORNIA, 1942-1960 (1964).

raids and mass deportations in "Operation Wetback" in 1954,[10] the very same year that *Hernandez* was decided.[11]

Although not alone among the states in discriminating against persons of Mexican ancestry, Texas earned a reputation for its multiracial caste system.[12] Indeed, in negotiating the agreements with the United States creating the Bracero Program, the Mexican government initially insisted on barring temporary workers from employment in Texas because of the notorious discrimination against persons of Mexican ancestry in the Lone Star state.[13]

With *Hernandez v. Texas*, the law began to recognize the social reality of Mexican Americans in the United States, a development that occurred somewhat later than it did for other minority groups.[14] A unanimous Supreme Court, in an opinion by Chief Justice Earl Warren, who also authored the unanimous opinion in *Brown v. Board of Education*,[15] ruled that the Equal Protection Clause of the Fourteenth Amendment barred the systematic exclusion of persons of Mexican ancestry from juries, one of the institutions often identified as exemplifying the United States' commitment to democracy.[16] As a legal matter, the Court held only that Mexican

---

[10]See generally JUAN RAMON GARCÍA, OPERATION WETBACK: THE MASS DEPORTATION OF MEXI-CAN UNDOCUMENTED WORKERS IN 1954 (1980) (analyzing federal government's deportation campaign directed at immigrants from Mexico).

[11]Moreover, Mexican immigrants long have suffered from violence along the U.S./Mexico border at the hands of immigration enforcement authorities. See, e.g., ALFREDO MIRANDÉ, GRINGO JUSTICE (1987); AMNESTY INT'L, UNITED STATES OF AMERICA: HUMAN RIGHTS CONCERNS IN THE BORDER REGION WITH MEXICO (1998); AMERICAN FRIENDS SERVICE COMM., HUMAN AND CIVIL RIGHTS VIOLATIONS ON THE U.S. MEXICO BORDER 1995-97 (1998). For analysis of the impacts of the dramatic increase in border enforcement operations along the United State's southern border with Mexico in the 1990s, which has resulted in the deaths of thousands of Mexican nationals, see Wayne A. Cornelius, *Death at the Border: Efficacy and Unintended Consequences of US Immigration Control Policy*, 27 POPULATION & DEV. REV. 661 (2001); Karl Eschbach et al., *Death at the Border*, 33 INT'L MIGRATION REV. 430 (1999); Bill Ong Hing, *The Dark Side of Operation Gatekeeper*, 7 U.C. DAVIS J. INT'L L. & POL'Y 121 (2001). Personal accounts of the deaths of migrants caused by the enforcement operations can be found in KEN ELLINGWOOD, HARD LINE: LIFE AND DEATH ON THE U.S.-MEXICO BORDER (2004); LUIS ALBERTO URREA, THE DEVIL'S HIGHWAY: A TRUE STORY (2004).

[12]See generally NEIL FOLEY, THE WHITE SCOURGE: MEXICANS, BLACKS AND POOR WHITES IN TEXAS COTTON CULTURE (1997) (analyzing discrimination against different groups in Texas); DAVID MONTEJANO, ANGLOS AND MEXICANS IN THE MAKING OF TEXAS, 1836-1986 (1987) (documenting a history of discrimination against persons of Mexican ancestry in Texas); ARNOLDO DE LEÓN, THEY CALL THEM GREASERS: ANGLO ATTITUDES TOWARD MEXICANS IN TEXAS, 1821-1900 (1983) (reviewing a history of negative attitudes toward Mexican Americans by Anglos); GUADALUPE SAN MIGUEL, JR., "LET ALL OF THEM TAKE HEED": MEXICAN AMERICANS AND THE CAMPAIGN FOR EDUCATIONAL EQUALITY IN TEXAS, 1910-1981 (1987) (analyzing the Mexican American fight for educational equity in Texas); Thomas D. Russell, *Law School Affirmative Action: An Empirical Study—The Shape of the Michigan River as Viewed from the Land of* Sweatt v. Painter *and* Hopwood, 25 LAW & SOC. INQUIRY 507 (2000) (studying affirmative action from the perspective of a history of racial discrimination in Texas); *The Texas Assessment of Academic Skills Exit Test—"Driver of Equity" or "Ticket to Nowhere?"*, 2 THE SCHOLAR: ST. MARY'S REVIEW ON MINORITY ISSUES 187, 193, 195-96 (2000) (Report of Professor Amilcar Shabazz) (summarizing racial discrimination in Texas education); Jorge Rangel & Carlos M. Alcala, *DeJure Segregation of Chicanos in Texas Schools*, 7 HARV. C.R.-C.L. L. REV. 307 (1972) (reviewing segregation of students of Mexican ancestry in Texas public schools); Gary A. Greenfield & Don B. Kates, Jr., *Mexican Americans, Racial Discrimination, and the Civil Rights Act of 1866*, 63 CAL. L. REV. 662 (1975) (discussing racial discrimination against Mexican Americans).

[13]See CALAVITA, supra note 9, at 20, 23-24

[14]See, e.g., Yick Wo v. Hopkins, 118 U.S. 356 (1886); Plessy v. Ferguson, 163 U.S. 537 (1896).

[15]347 U.S. 483 (1954).

[16]See, e.g., ALEXIS DE TOCQUEVILLE, DEMOCRACY IN AMERICA 252 (Jacob P. Mayer ed., George Lawrence trans., 1st Perennial Library ed. 1969).

American citizens could not be barred as a group from jury service. However, the Court's decision meant much more than that.

This paper highlights two important legacies of *Hernandez v. Texas*. First, as other commentators have observed, the Court's decision represented a critical inroad into the commonly-understood view that the Equal Protection Clause of the Fourteenth Amendment only protected African Americans.[17] Until 1954, this narrow understanding had worked to the detriment of Mexican Americans seeking to vindicate their constitutional rights.[18] The legal challenge to the Black/white paradigm of civil rights ultimately triumphed, with the Equal Protection guarantee now protecting all (including whites), not just some, races from invidious discrimination.[19] The Court in *Hernandez v. Texas* thus continued the gradual expansion of the Equal Protection Clause.

Although this important aspect of *Hernandez v. Texas* is well recognized, not much attention has been paid to why the Supreme Court made such an important ruling at this time in U.S. history. The author of the opinion for the Court, Chief Justice Earl Warren, a native son of California, knew well from personal and professional experience of the discrimination against Mexican Americans in the Golden State.[20] Indeed, the World War II period—when Earl Warren was California's Attorney General and later Governor—was one of the most concentrated and well-publicized periods of anti-Mexican violence in California in the entire twentieth-century.[21] The Mexican American community reacted with outrage to what it perceived as a racially biased law enforcement and criminal justice system. Earl Warren's experience with the Mexican American civil rights struggle undoubtedly contributed to the timing of the Court's decision in *Hernandez v. Texas*.

Appointed as Chief Justice of the Supreme Court in 1953, Earl Warren previously had served as Attorney General and Governor of California, a racially diverse state that had experienced more than its share of racial tensions during his life. His experience as a political leader at the center of several high profile racial controversies no doubt allowed him to have a better fundamental understanding of the complexities, as well as the political repercussions, of racial discrimination against Mexican Americans. This experience helps explain how Chief Justice Earl Warren could write an informed opinion like *Hernandez v. Texas*.[22]

---

[17]See *infra* text accompanying notes 88-106.

[18]See *infra* text accompanying notes 98-102, 112-14.

[19]See *infra* text accompanying notes 88-106.

[20]See *infra* text accompanying notes 33-87. Commentators have contended that Cold War foreign policy concerns may have converged with African American interests to culminate in Brown v. Board of Education, 347 U.S. 483 (1954). See MARY L. DUDZIAK, RACE AND THE IMAGE OF AMERICAN DEMOCRACY (2002); Derrick Bell, Brown v. Board of Education *and the Interest Convergence Dilemma*," 93 HARV. L. REV. 518 (1980). One possibility, not squarely addressed in this paper, is that the Supreme Court's decision in *Hernandez v. Texas* was the product of a similar interest convergence with the United States feeling pressure from the Mexican government to more fairly treat persons of Mexican ancestry in the United States.

[21]See *infra* text accompanying notes 33-87.

[22]The impact of Earl Warren on the Supreme Court's decisions suggests the importance to the judicial process of judges with diverse life experiences. See THERESA M. BEINER, THE ELUSIVE (BUT WORTHWHILE) QUEST FOR A DIVERSE BENCH IN THE NEW MILLENNIUM, 36 U.C. DAVIS L. REV. 597 (2003). For analysis of the importance of racial diversity in the judiciary, see Kevin R. Johnson & Luis Fuentes-Rohwer, *A Principled Approach to the Quest for Racial Diversity on the Judiciary*, 10 MICH. J. RACE & L. 5 (2004).

Second, this paper analyzes *Hernandez v. Texas*'s important unfinished business. The Supreme Court concluded that the systematic exclusion of Mexican Americans from petit and grand juries violated the Equal Protection Clause of the Fourteenth Amendment, which logically extended previous case law dating back to the nineteenth-century that prohibited the exclusion of African Americans from juries.[23]

The jury systems in place throughout the United States, however, include a variety of color-blind—and, to this point, entirely legal—mechanisms that operate to limit the number of Latina/o jurors and ensure that juries in localities across the country fail to represent a cross-section of the community.[24] Citizenship and English language requirements for jury service, as well as the disqualification of felons, bar disproportionate numbers of Latina/os from serving on juries.[25] In addition, the Supreme Court has sanctioned the use of peremptory challenges to strike bilingual jurors, thus allowing parties to remove bilingual Latina/os from juries on ostensibly race neutral grounds.[26]

The end result is that Latina/os are significantly underrepresented on juries. Racially skewed juries undermine the perceived impartiality of the justice system and, at the most fundamental level, the rule of law. Cynicism about the law and its enforcement, already a problem among Latina/os and other minority communities, creates the potential for domestic unrest. The violence following the Rodney King verdict in May 1992 in South Central Los Angeles exemplifies the potentially explosive impacts of a justice system viewed by minorities as racially-biased.[27]

In sum, the promise of full representation of Mexican Americans on juries in *Hernandez v. Texas* has yet to be realized.[28] The legacy of *Hernandez v. Texas* resembles that of *Brown v. Board of Education*,[29] perhaps the most heralded Supreme Court decision of the twentieth-century, in that the mandate in both path-breaking cases remains to be achieved because racially disparate results continue despite the legal prohibition against de jure discrimination.

I. LEGACY OF JUSTICE: RECOGNITION OF THE MEXICAN "RACE"

The Equal Protection Clause of the Fourteenth Amendment long has been the protector of African American civil rights, which makes sense given that it was ratified as part of the package of Reconstruction Amendments that ended the institution of slavery.[30] Over the last few decades, critical theorists have contended that this Black/white paradigm of civil rights must be expanded to account for the status of

---

[23]See *infra* text accompanying notes 160-251.

[24]See *infra* text accompanying notes 160-251.

[25]See *infra* text accompanying notes 182-223.

[26]See *infra* text accompanying notes 224-38.

[27]See *infra* text accompanying notes 239-51.

[28]See *infra* text accompanying notes 160-251.

[29]347 U.S. 483 (1954). By some accounts, public schools remain just as segregated today as they were in 1954. See Gary Orfield & John T. Yun, *Resegregation in American Schools* (1999), *available at* http://www.civilrightsproject.harvard.edu/research/deseg/Resegregation_American_Schools99.pdf (June 1999); GARY ORFIELD & SUSAN E. EATON, DISMANTLING DESEGREGATION: THE QUIET REVERSAL OF BROWN V. BOARD OF EDUCATION (1996).

[30]See The Slaughterhouse Cases, 83 U.S. 36, 67-78 (1873); JACOBUS TENBROEK, THE ANTI-SLAVERY ORIGINS OF THE FOURTEENTH AMENDMENT (1951).

other racial minority groups to allow for a fuller understanding of race relations and civil rights in the United States.[31] The growing awareness of an increasingly multiracial America required this shift in the view of civil rights law.[32]

This section demonstrates how *Hernandez v. Texas* came to the U.S. Supreme Court at an opportune time for civil rights advocates, just one year after Chief Justice Earl Warren—who was familiar with the discrimination against Mexican Americans in California—had been confirmed. Moreover, the Court already had held in several cases that various non-African American racial minorities were protected by the U.S. Constitution. The section then analyzes the Court's treatment of Mexicans as a discrete and insular minority in Texas and the Supreme Court's subsequent general acceptance of the racialization of Latina/os to a point where today the group identity of, and discrimination against, Latina/os is assumed without much question or inquiry.

A. California's Native Son: Earl Warren

California has had a rich, if not altogether laudatory, racial history.[33] The state championed exclusion of Chinese immigrants in the late 1800s[34] and the "alien" land laws restricting ownership of land by noncitizens, which targeted Japanese immigrants in the early 1900s.[35] Although California may not have been the center of the civil rights struggle of African Americans, other racial minorities have sought for generations to vindicate their rights in the state.[36]

Against this historical backdrop, Chief Justice Earl Warren could not have been ignorant of the many different minorities besides African Americans subject to discrimination in American social life. In fact, as we will see, he was an active participant in what turned out to be one of the most regrettable chapters of racial discrimination in modern U.S. history.[37]

---

[31]See, e.g., Richard Delgado, *Rodrigo's Fifteenth Chronicle: Racial Mixture, Latino-Critical Scholarship, and the Black-White Binary*, 75 TEX. L. REV. 1181 (1997) (book review); Juan F. Perea, *The Black/White Binary Paradigm of Race: The "Normal Science" of American Racial Thought*, 85 CAL. L. REV. 1213 (1997).

[32]See Kevin R. Johnson, *The End of "Civil Rights" as We Know It?: Immigration and Civil Rights in the New Millennium*, 49 UCLA L. REV. 1481, 1491-1510 (2002).

[33]See generally ALMAGUER, supra note 4 (analyzing history of discrimination against different racial minority groups in California); Richard Delgado & Jean Stefancic, *California's Racial History and Constitutional Rationales for Race-Conscious Decision Making in Higher Education*, 47 UCLA L. REV. 1521 (2000) (summarizing California's history of discrimination against racial minorities and attempting to use it to justify remedial affirmative action in higher education).

[34]See, e.g., The Chinese Exclusion Case (Chae Chan Ping v. United States), 130 U.S. 581 (1889) (upholding one of a series of laws designed to bar immigration of Chinese to the United States). See generally LUCY E. SALYER, LAWS HARSH AS TIGERS: CHINESE IMMIGRANTS AND THE SHAPING OF MODERN IMMIGRATION LAW (1995) (analyzing the impact of Chinese exclusion laws on development of U.S. immigration law); BILL ONG HING, MAKING AND REMAKING ASIAN AMERICA THROUGH IMMIGRATION POLICY, 1850-1990 (1993) (documenting how U.S. immigration law and policy shaped the formation of Asian American communities).

[35]See Keith Aoki, *No Right to Own?: The Early Twentieth Century "Alien Land Laws" as a Prelude to Internment*, 40 B.C. L. REV. 37 (1998); see, e.g., Oyama v. California, 332 U.S. 633 (1948); Cockrill v. California, 268 U.S. 258 (1925); Frick v. Webb, 263 U.S. 326 (1923); Webb v. O'Brien, 263 U.S. 313 (1923); Porterfield v. Webb, 263 U.S. 225 (1923).

[36]See Neil Gotanda, *"Other Non-Whites" in American Legal History: A Review of Justice at War*, 85 COLUM. L. REV. 1186 (1985) (book review); see, e.g., CHARLES J. MCCLAIN, IN SEARCH OF EQUALITY: THE CHINESE STRUGGLE AGAINST DISCRIMINATION IN NINETEENTH CENTURY CALIFORNIA (1994).

[37]See *infra* text accompanying notes 49-53.

Born in Los Angeles,[38] Earl Warren's personal and professional life had been deeply immersed in the "sticky mess of race"[39] of a rapidly changing United States. Growing up in a working class family in Bakersfield, California, Warren had lived in a rural town that segregated Chinese workers[40] and saw "minority groups brought into the country for cheap labor paid a dollar a day for ten hours of work only to be fleeced out of much of that at the company store where they were obliged to trade."[41]

As a District Attorney in Northern California, Warren had encountered the Ku Klux Klan in law enforcement, grand juries, and the judiciary.[42] He thus knew of the racism that influenced the justice system, and this knowledge influenced his public decisions. As Governor, Warren commuted a death sentence to life imprisonment in the case of an African American defendant when convinced, after consulting with the trial judge and having the jury interviewed, that the defendant would not have been sentenced to death if he were white.[43]

Politics—the lifeblood of any politician—shaped Warren's stance on civil rights before his appointment to the Supreme Court. As Attorney General of California in the early 1940s, he supported the internment of persons of Japanese ancestry.[44] The Attorney General's office under his leadership advocated against the rights of Latino criminal defendants.[45]

Earl Warren was familiar with discrimination against persons of Mexican ancestry. He was a young attorney when state and local officials in Los Angeles County had assisted in the "repatriation" of thousands of persons of Mexican ancestry—U.S. citizens and immigrants—to reduce the welfare rolls and "save" jobs for Americans.[46] "The raids [during this deportation campaign] fostered an anti-immigrant fervor in Los Angeles that makes the days of Proposition 187 in the 1990s seem like a marathon Cinco de Mayo dance."[47] The repatriation laid the groundwork for the

---

[38]In his autobiography, Warren waxed fondly about the Mexican and Spanish influences on Los Angeles. See EARL WARREN, THE MEMOIRS OF EARL WARREN 11 (1977).

[39]This phrase is borrowed from Leslie Espinoza & Angela P. Harris, *Afterward: Embracing the Tar-Baby—LatCrit Theory and the Sticky Mess of Race*, 85 CAL. L. REV. 1585 (1997).

[40]See WARREN, supra note 38, at 17; see also *id.* at 55 (noting that Warren learned in the Alameda County District Attorney's office that "there were many people in California who were anti-Oriental and who looked with favor on any restrictions upon the Chinese. The resurgence of the Ku Klux Klan contributed greatly to this spirit, and the Legislature itself gave evidence of condoning it."); *Id.* at 147-48 (mentioning anti-Japanese sentiment in California that grew in the wake of the attack on Pearl Harbor).

[41]*Id.* at 30.

[42]See WARREN, supra note 38, at 85, 87, 99, 100-01.

[43]See *id.* at 212.

[44]See *id.* at 153-55.

[45]See, e.g., People v. Gonzalez, 20 Cal. 2d 165 (1942) (rejecting exclusionary rule in case of improper search), *cert. denied*, 317 U.S. 657 (1942); People v. Chavez, 41 Cal. App. 2d 428 (1940) (affirming conviction of Latino in robbery case).

[46]See supra note 7.

[47]Antonio Olivo, *Ghosts of a 1931 Raid*, L.A. TIMES, Feb. 25, 2001, at B1. Proposition 187 was an anti-immigrant law passed overwhelmingly by the California voters in 1994, over the opposition of the vast majority of Latina/o voters, after a bitter racially divisive campaign. See Kevin R. Johnson, *An Essay on Immigration Politics, Popular Democracy, and California's Proposition 187: The Political Relevance and Legal Irrelevance of Race*, 70 WASH. L. REV. 629 (1995); Ruben J. García, Comment, *Critical Race Theory and Proposition 187: The Racial Politics of Immigration Law*, 17 CHICANO-LATINO L. REV. 118 (1995).

anti-Mexican hysteria that later gripped Southern California during World War II and attracted the attention of the entire nation.[48]

1. Japanese Internment

A critical period during Earl Warren's early professional career had long term consequences on the nation and his view of race and racial discrimination. As Attorney General of California and a gubernatorial candidate, Warren played a central role in advocating for the internment of persons of Japanese ancestry during World War II. Indeed, he was no less than an anti-Japanese agitator during this time, working closely with the Native Sons of the Golden West, a fraternal society of which he was a member.[49] This regrettable period of Warren's professional life, which has been overshadowed by his civil rights landmark decision of *Brown v. Board of Education*, has been ably analyzed by Professor Sumi Cho.[50] The gravity of the mistake was understood shortly after the Supreme Court's upholding of the internment,[51] with sharp criticism immediately following the decision.[52]

Years later, Warren admitted remorse about his important role in the internment:

I have since deeply regretted the removal order and my own testimony advocating it, because it was not in keeping with our American concept of freedom and the rights of citizens. Whenever I thought of the innocent little children who were torn from home, school friends, and congenial surroundings, I was conscience-stricken. It was wrong to react so impulsively, without positive evidence of disloyalty, even though we felt we had a good motive in the security of our state. It demonstrates the cruelty of war when fear, get tough military psychology, propaganda, and racial antagonism combine with one's responsibility for public security to produce such acts. I have always believed that I had no prejudice against the Japanese as such, except that directly spawned by Pearl Harbor and its aftermath.[53]

---

[48]See *infra* text accompanying notes 54-87.

[49]For a critical analysis of Earl Warren's involvement as California Attorney General in supporting Japanese internment, see Sumi Cho, *Redeeming Whiteness in the Shadow of Internment: Earl Warren, Brown, and a Theory of Racial Redemption*, 40 B.C. L. REV. 73 (1998). Professor Cho contends that Warren's later civil rights decisions on the Supreme Court amounted to an effort at "racial redemption" for his discriminatory past. This rationale might help explain *Hernandez v. Texas*, as well as many of the Warren Court's civil rights decisions.

[50]See Cho, supra note 49.

[51]See Korematsu v. United States, 323 U.S. 214 (1944).

[52]See Eugene V. Rostow, *The Japanese American Cases—A Disaster*, 54 YALE L.J. 489 (1945).

[53]WARREN, supra note 38, at 149. In many respects, the United States government's mindset in its treatment of Arabs and Muslims after the tragic events of September 11, 2001, is reminiscent of Warren's concerns with the anti-Japanese hysteria that swept California after Pearl Harbor. See, e.g., Susan M. Akram & Kevin R. Johnson, *Race, Civil Rights, and Immigration Law after September 11, 2001: The Targeting of Arabs and Muslims*, 48 ANN. SURV. AM. L. 377, 351-55 (2002); David Cole, *Enemy Aliens*, 54 STAN. L. REV. 953 (2002); Thomas W. Joo, *Presumed Disloyal: Executive Power, Judicial Deference, and the Construction of Race Before and After September 11*, 34 COLUM. HUM. RTS L. REV. 1 (2002). See generally MIGRATION POLICY INSTITUTE, AMERICA'S CHALLENGE: DOMESTIC SECURITY, CIVIL LIBERTIES, AND NATIONAL UNITY AFTER SEPTEMBER 11 (2003) (documenting civil rights abuses by federal government); U.S. OFFICE OF THE INSPECTOR GENERAL, THE SEPTEMBER 11 DETAINEES: A REVIEW OF THE TREATMENT OF ALIENS HELD ON IMMIGRATION CHARGES IN CONNECTION WITH THE INVESTIGATION OF THE SEPTEMBER 11 ATTACKS (2003) (same); U.S. OFFICE OF THE INSPECTOR GENERAL, REPORT TO CONGRESS ON IMPLEMENTATION OF SECTION 1001 OF THE USA PATRIOT ACT (2003) (same). *But see* MICHELLE MALKIN, IN DEFENSE OF INTERNMENT: THE CASE FOR "RACIAL PROFILING" IN WORLD WAR II AND THE WAR ON TERROR (2004) (defending the decision to intern persons of Japanese ancestry during World War II and racial profiling in the war on terror).

2. The Sleepy Lagoon Murder Case

The internment of the Japanese was just the beginning of the racial turmoil in California during World War II. A series of nationally publicized events gripped the nation and revealed the depth of racial discrimination against persons of Mexican ancestry.[54]

Long before World War II, the Los Angeles Police Department had a history of discriminating against persons of Mexican ancestry.[55] Mexican Americans, who often were unfairly blamed for crime and membership in gangs, feared the police. That fear grew substantially after the Sleepy Lagoon murder case.

In August 1942, a young Mexican American man was found dead at a local Los Angeles lake known as Sleepy Lagoon. In response, Los Angeles police rounded up hundreds of Mexican American youth. The dragnet produced scores of arrests and beatings, and ultimately resulted in the wrongful conviction of a group of Mexican Americans.[56]

The judicial proceedings were flawed from the outset. A Los Angeles County Sheriff, with his superior's written concurrence, testified before a special session of the Los Angeles County Grand Jury (which in all likelihood failed to include many, if any, persons of Mexican ancestry),[57] about the biological propensity of Mexicans toward crime, which caused the "Mexican gang" problem.[58] A representative of the Los Angeles Sheriff's office stated succinctly that, because of their Indian roots, Mexicans had a "total disregard for human life [that] has always been universal throughout the Americas among the Indian population, which of course is well known to everyone";[59] this character flaw could not be remedied because "*one cannot change the spots of a leopard.*"[60] Not surprisingly, the grand jury indicted a group of Mexican American youths for the Sleepy Lagoon murder.

Even given their alleged criminal propensity, the Sheriff's office acknowledged that persons of Mexican ancestry suffered discrimination in Los Angeles County:

> Discrimination and segregation as evidenced by public signs and rules such as appear in certain restaurants, public swimming plunges, public parks, theatres and even in schools, causes resentment among the Mexican people. There are certain parks in the state in which a Mexican may not appear, or

---

[54]For a discussion on the Sleepy Lagoon case and subsequent events during that era of Southern California history as Mexican Americans resisted violations of their civil rights, see Ricardo Romo, *Southern California and the Origins of Latino Civil-Rights Activism*, 3 W. LEGAL. HIST. 379 (1990).

[55]See Theodore W. Maya, Comment, *To Serve and Protect or to Betray and Neglect?: The LAPD and Undocumented Immigrants*, 49 UCLA L. REV. 1611, 1614-20 (2002).

[56]See CAREY MCWILLIAMS, NORTH FROM MEXICO: THE SPANISH-SPEAKING PEOPLE OF THE UNITED STATES 227-43 (1948). See generally EDUARDO OBREGÓN PAGÁN, MURDER AT THE SLEEPY LAGOON: ZOOT SUITS, RACE, & RIOT IN WARTIME L.A. (2003) (chronicling the Sleepy Lagoon case and its connection with the subsequent Zoot Suit riots).

[57]See *infra* text accompanying note 175 (discussing underrepresentation of Mexican Americans on Los Angeles County Grand Jury).

[58]See SOLOMON J. JONES, THE GOVERNMENT RIOTS OF LOS ANGELES, JUNE 1943, at 14-15, 85-95 (1969); MCWILLIAMS, supra note 56, at 232-35; Robert S. Chang, *Policing the Criminal Justice System: Los Angeles as a Single-Celled Organism*, 34 LOY. L.A. L. REV. 843, 847-49 (2001).

[59]Foreign Relations Bureau of Los Angeles, Sheriff's Office Statistics, in JONES, supra note 58, at 86.

[60]*Id.* at 87 (emphasis added).

else only on a certain day of the week. There are certain plunges where they are not allowed to swim or else only a certain day of the week, and it is made evident by signs reading to that effect; for instance, "Tuesdays reserved for Negroes and Mexicans." Certain theatres in certain towns either do not allow the Mexicans to enter or else segregate them in a certain section. Some restaurants absolutely refuse to serve them a meal and so state by public signs. The Mexicans take the attitude that they pay taxes for the maintenance of public institutions the same as anyone else. Certain court actions have been brought by them to force the admittance of their children into certain public schools.[61]

Despite this widespread discrimination, the official position of law enforcement was that the cause of the Mexican American crime "problem" was a biological propensity toward criminality.

The Sleepy Lagoon murder trial was later described as "a travesty,"[62] with the courts "outrageously biased" against the Mexican American defendants.[63] The judge had it in for the defendants and refused to allow them to have their hair cut or change their clothes during the lengthy trial because, in his estimation, their appearance and attire was relevant to the determination of their guilt. During the trial, he denied them the right of effective representation by counsel by separating the defendants from their attorneys in the courtroom, which along with other improprieties ultimately resulted in reversal of the convictions.[64]

Some influential Angelenos believed that the defendants had been railroaded. The Sleepy Lagoon Defense Committee built a broad base of political and financial support for release of the Sleepy Lagoon defendants. Supporters included labor and minority groups, and entertainers, such as Orson Wells, Will Rogers, Nat King Cole, Rita Hayworth, Anthony Quinn, Elia Kazan, Vincent Price, Gene Kelly, and Lena Horne.[65] Among other activities, the committee presented a petition to Governor Warren asking him to free the young Mexican American defendants.[66] Although it failed to trigger Warren to act, the petition, and the accompanying political pressure and press attention given the case, put the Governor on notice of claims of racial bias against persons of Mexican ancestry in the criminal justice system.

As in the Sleepy Lagoon murder case, unfairness with the grand jury, and the appearance of a deeply biased, anti-Mexican justice system, was at issue in *Hernandez v. Texas*.[67] The controversy of the much-publicized case necessarily sensitized Governor Warren to the civil right issues facing Mexican Americans.

3. The "Zoot Suit" Race Riots

After the Sleepy Lagoon trial, the stage was set for a more concentrated, and violent, outburst of anti-Mexican sentiment in Southern California. In June 1943,

---

[61]*Id.* at 85.
[62]ESCOBAR, supra note 7, at 225.
[63]KEVIN STARR, EMBATTLED DREAMS: CALIFORNIA IN WAR AND PEACE, 1940-1950, at 102 (2002).
[64]See People v. Zammora, 66 Cal. App. 2d 166 (1944).
[65]See ESCOBAR, supra note 7, at 276-78; PAGÁN, supra note 56, at 205.
[66]See ESCOBAR, supra note 7, at 275-76; see also Chang, supra note 58, at 845-49 (analyzing anti-Mexican frenzy in greater Los Angeles area during time of Zoot Suit riots and Sleepy Lagoon Murder trial).
[67]See *infra* text accompanying notes 107-39.

Los Angeles saw the mass deprivation of civil rights of Mexican Americans as, over a period of days, Anglo servicemen beat Mexican Americans on the city streets while police watched.[68]

The "Zoot Suit" riots were named after the then-fashionable attire worn by Mexican American and African American youth of the time; the clothes were a sign of the jazz counterculture of the day. Despite the naming of the violence after the clothing of the victims, the events, however, were most appropriately classified as race riots, with Anglo serviceman beating and stripping Mexican Americans of their zoot suits in the streets, with police in many instances watching and, if arresting anyone, only arresting the victims. The press sensationalized the threat of the "zoot suiters," further fomenting racial hatred.

The Zoot Suit riots attracted national attention,[69] including that of the nation's First Lady, Eleanor Roosevelt. In a syndicated national column, Roosevelt equated the violence to race riots that had recently occurred across the country, including in Beaumont, Texas and Detroit, Michigan as racial minorities migrated to urban areas to fill jobs in the war industries.[70]

Worried about the impacts of the political controversy on his national political ambitions,[71] Governor Earl Warren quickly appointed a committee to investigate the violence.[72] The report of the California Citizens Committee on Civil Disturbances in Los Angeles, chaired by a Catholic Bishop, Joseph T. McGucken and including Mexican American actor Leo Carrillo, criticized the police, the newspapers, and the climate of anti-Mexican prejudice surrounding the riots.[73] McGucken's cover letter, addressed to Governor Warren, stated that "[t]here are many reported instances of police and sheriff indifference, neglect of duty, and discrimination against members of minority groups"; the committee concluded "that the situation on the East side, where Los Angeles has the largest concentration of persons of Mexican and Negro ancestry, *is a potential powder keg . . . .*"[74]

The committee report observed that nearly a quarter million persons of Mexican ancestry lived in Los Angeles County and that "[l]iving conditions among the majority of these people are far below the general level of the community. *Housing is inadequate; sanitation is bad and made worse by congestion. Recreational facilities for children are very poor; and there is insufficient supervision of the playgrounds, swimming pools and other youth centers.*"[75]

---

[68]See MCWILLIAMS, supra note 56, at 255; STARR, supra note 63, at 104-11. See generally MAURICIO MAZÓN, THE ZOOT-SUIT RIOTS: THE PSYCHOLOGY OF SYMBOLIC ANNIHILATION (1984) (documenting the events giving rise to the Zoot Suit riots and analyzing their meaning).

[69]See ESCOBAR, supra note 7, at 233-53; MCWILLIAMS, supra note 56, at 228-33.

[70]See ESCOBAR, supra note 7, at 245; MCWILLIAMS, supra note 56, at 256.

[71]See STARR, supra note 63, at 111.

[72]See ACUÑA, supra note 4, at 59; Lupe S. Salinas, *Gus Garcia and Thurgood Marshall: Two Legal Giants Fighting for Justice*, 28 T. MARSHALL L. REV. 145, 151-52 (2003).

[73]See ESCOBAR, supra note 7, at 244-45.

[74]Letter from Joseph T. McGucken, Auxiliary Bishop of Los Angeles, to Governor Earl Warren (June 21, 1943) (in Earl Warren Papers—Administrative Files—Department of Justice, Attorney General, Law Enforcement (3640:2624), Sacramento, California) (emphasis added).

[75]Report and Recommendations of the California Citizens Committee on Civil Disturbances in Los Angeles 3 (June 12, 1943) (on file with author) (emphasis added).

The report added that:

> *Most of the persons mistreated during the recent incidents in Los Angeles*
> *were either persons of Mexican descent or Negroes. In undertaking to deal*
> *with the cause of these outbreaks, the existence of race prejudice cannot be*
> *ignored.* . . . Any solution of the problems involves, among other things, an
> educational program throughout the community designed to combat race
> prejudice in all its forms.[76]

The committee made a number of recommendations, including not focusing law
enforcement activities exclusively on minority communities, better police training,
and hiring officers who speak Spanish.[77] To improve the racial sensibilities of the
Los Angeles Police Department, various groups advocated the hiring of more Mexican American police officers, a recommendation that appealed to Governor Warren.[78] Most generally, the committee recommended that *"[d]iscrimination against*
any race in the provision or use of public facilities should be abolished" and that
educational programs "should be undertaken to make the entire community understand the problems and background of the minority group."[79]

The charges of racial discrimination could not have been missed by Earl Warren. Nor was the context in which the violence occurred. In responding to an inquiry
about the riots by U.S. Attorney General Francis Biddle, Governor Warren wrote that
the African American and Mexican American populations had increased dramatically in Los Angeles during the war and that "[t]he housing situation, particularly for
minority groups is deplorable. Recreational facilities are inadequate. Juvenile crime
and delinquency has increased, although not in excess of other sections of the country"; Warren further admitted that the newspapers had incited hatred of "the Mexican boys" and that "[t]here had been bad feeling[s] between some of Los Angeles
police force and youthful Mexicans, and *I am sorry to report that some of the police*
officers were derelict in their duty in failing to stop the rioting promptly."[80]

The violence of those few days of June 1943 remain an important part of the
collective memory of the Mexican American community in Southern California and
has been the subject of a popular play and movie, as well as a documentary.[81] Along
with the deportation campaign of the 1930s, the Zoot Suit riots placed pressure on
the Mexican American community in Southern California to conform to Anglo ways
and have served as a reminder of the outsider status of persons of Mexican ancestry
in the United States.[82]

---

[76]*Id.* at 4 (emphasis added).

[77]See *id.* at 5-6.

[78]See ESCOBAR, supra note 7, at 263.

[79]Report and Recommendations of the California Citizens Committee on Civil Disturbances in Los Angeles,
supra note 75, at 7 (emphasis added).

[80]Letter from Governor Earl Warren, to the Honorable Francis Biddle, Attorney General of the United States (Oct.
14, 1943) (in Earl Warren Papers—Administrative Files—Department of Justice, Attorney General, Law
Enforcement - McGucken Committee (F3640:2627) Sacramento, California) (emphasis added).

[81]See LUIS VALDEZ, ZOOT SUIT AND OTHER PLAYS (1992); Susan King, *A City at War With Itself*, L.A. TIMES,
Feb. 10, 2002, Calendar, at TV 3.

[82]See *infra* text accompanying notes 103-06.

3. Mexican American Desegregation Litigation:
Westminster School District v. Mendez (1947)

A few years after the Zoot Suit riots, national attention focused on a successful Mexican American school desegregation case involving the Westminster School District in Orange County in Southern California.[83] In that case, Thurgood Marshall and Robert Carter, on behalf of the NAACP, filed an *amicus curiae* brief in support of the Mexican American plaintiffs.[84] *Mendez* was a critical milestone on the road to *Brown v. Board of Education* as well as *Hernandez v. Texas*.

In *Mendez*, a federal court of appeals held that the California law in question, which permitted the segregation of Chinese, Japanese, and persons of "Mongolian" ancestry, failed to authorize the segregation of Mexican Americans.[85] Although the court did not find that segregation was per se unconstitutional, it ruled that the segregation of Mexican Americans was invalid in this case because the law failed to authorize it. The court did not address the constitutionality of the segregation of Asians, which the California law in fact authorized.

Rather than amend the law to authorize the segregation of persons of Mexican ancestry, the California legislature repealed the law in its entirety. After being advised that all racial segregation might well be unconstitutional, Governor Warren signed the law repealing the authorization for all racial segregation in the California public schools.[86] This episode helped prepare Warren for his subsequent work on the Supreme Court in *Brown v. Board of Education*.

5. Summary

The tumultuous 1940s had seen much publicized racial tension—marred by sporadic outbursts of violence—between Mexican Americans and Anglos in Cali-

---

[83]See Westminster Sch. Dist. v. Mendez, 161 F.2d 774 (9th Cir. 1947); *infra* text accompanying notes 121-23 (discussing the reliance on the *Mendez* case in *Hernandez v. Texas*). The *Mendez* case attracted national attention. See Note, *Segregation in the Public Schools—A Violation of "Equal Protection of the Laws,"* 56 YALE L.J. 1059 (1947); Note, *Segregation in Schools as a Violation of the XIVth Amendment*, 47 COLUM. L. REV. 325 (1947).

[84]See RICHARD KLUGER, SIMPLE JUSTICE 399-400 (sp. ed. 1994); see also Perea, supra note 31, at 1246-47 (describing how *Mendez* was an important case in NAACP's strategy to dismantle school segregation); George A. Martínez, *Legal Indeterminacy, Judicial Discretion and the Mexican-American Litigation Experience: 1930-1980*, 27 U.C. DAVIS L. REV. 555, 574-78 (1994) (discussing importance of *Mendez*); Margaret E. Montoya, *A Brief History of Chicana/o School Segregation*, 12 LA RAZA L.J. 159, 166-70 (2001) (same). For analysis of the history of the litigation, as well as difficulties that arose in the efforts among groups to formulate a consistent legal strategy, see Toni Robinson & Greg Robinson, Mendez v. Westminster*: Asian-Latino Coalition Triumphant?*, 10 ASIAN L.J. 161 (2003); Charles Wollenberg, Mendez v. Westminster*: Race, Nationality and Segregation in California Schools*, 53 CAL. HIST. Q. 317, 329 (1974).

[85]See *Westminster Sch. Dist v. Mendez*, 161 F.2d at 780-81.

[86]See CHARLES WOLLENBERG, ALL DELIBERATE SPEED: SEGREGATION AND EXCLUSION IN CALIFORNIA SCHOOLS, 1855-1975, at 132-33 (1976); Wollenberg, supra note 84, at 329. (1974). Not long after *Mendez*, the California Supreme Court invalidated the state's anti-miscegenation law that had been enforced to bar the marriage between a Mexican American woman and an African American man. See Perez v. Sharp, 32 Cal. 2d 711 (1948). California law prohibited marriages of white persons with "Negroes, Mongolians, members of the Malay race, or mulattoes." Cal. Civ. Code § 60 (repealed) (quoted in *Perez*, 32 Cal.2d at 712). As in *Mendez*, the law in question enumerated several different races—not just African Americans—as separate, distinct, and inferior from whites. For analysis of *Perez v. Sharp*, see Kevin R. Johnson & Kristina L. Burrows, *Struck by Lightning? Interracial Intimacy and Racial Justice*, 25 HUM. RTS. Q. 528, 531-42 (2003). Almost twenty years later, Chief Justice Warren in an opinion for a unanimous Supreme Court invalidated Virginia's antimiscegenation law in Loving v. Virginia, 388 U.S. 1 (1967).

fornia. Mexican Americans consistently claimed that their civil rights had been violated by law enforcement and the justice system.

High profile events, such as the Sleepy Lagoon Murder Trial, Zoot Suit race riots, and the *Mendez* school desegregation case, all made the national news. Each of these politically charged matters landed on Governor Warren's desk. One simply could not have lived in California during that time—much less have been governor of the state—and not understood the racial tensions between Anglos and Mexican Americans and the prevailing discrimination against persons of Mexican ancestry. Thus, Chief Justice Warren should not be given too much credit for having an appreciation of the civil rights struggles of Mexican Americans that he wrote about in *Hernandez v. Texas*;[87] what he read about in the briefs of the treatment of Mexican Americans in Texas must have resonated with his personal experiences in California and informed the way that he looked at the case.

As the Governor of California, Earl Warren had lived through a momentous time for Mexican Americans. He saw race influence the enforcement of the criminal laws and result in a violent outburst. Warren also had seen how the appearances of a racially biased justice system could poison race relations and contribute to the potential for violence.

B. The Multiracial Equal Protection Clause

As some have acknowledged,[88] the Supreme Court in *Hernandez v. Texas*, decided two weeks before *Brown v. Board of Education*, was ahead of its time in recognizing the discrimination against Mexicans in Texas and moving beyond the Black/white paradigm. However, in many respects, the opinion merely reflects the rich life experiences of its author. Moreover, for the Court to have held otherwise would have been to ignore much recent history about discrimination against persons of Mexican ancestry in the United States and to deviate from the general trajectory of the Court's Equal Protection jurisprudence.

The Supreme Court's 1954 decision in *Brown v. Board of Education* with its focus on the segregation of African Americans, the central issue of dispute in the case, could be read as reinforcing the Black/white paradigm.[89] However, the Court's civil rights opinions of this era must be considered as a whole to gain a full understanding of the Court's understanding of race relations in U.S. social life.

Chief Justice Earl Warren's appreciation of the complexities of race relations in the United States is seen through reading *Brown* in tandem with *Hernandez v. Texas*. Indeed, from his experiences as Governor of California, he had to have been well aware that school segregation and exclusion from juries had been directed at other groups—especially persons of Asian and Mexican ancestry—besides African Americans.[90]

Perhaps more importantly, the time was right for a more inclusive reading of the Equal Protection Clause of the Fourteenth Amendment. By 1954, the Supreme Court

---

[87]See *infra* text accompanying notes 107-39.
[88]See *infra* note 115.
[89]See supra text accompanying notes 17-19.
[90]See supra text accompanying notes 33-87.

had effectively rejected the idea that the Equal Protection Clause only protected African Americans. The Court had found that the Constitution's protections extended to several different minority groups and had proclaimed that it protected all "discrete and insular minorities."

This extension of the Equal Protection Clause in *Hernandez v. Texas* was a culmination of a series of decisions. In the 1886 case of *Yick Wo v. Hopkins*,[91] the Court held that the discriminatory enforcement of a local ordinance against persons of Chinese ancestry violated the Equal Protection Clause of the Fourteenth Amendment. More than fifty years later, in the famous footnote four of *Carolene Products* case, the Court used general language to describe the groups protected by the Equal Protection Clause and famously proclaimed that the Court may have to inquire to determine "whether prejudice against discrete and insular minorities may be a special condition, which tends seriously to curtail the operation of those political processes ordinarily to be relied upon to protect minorities, and which may call for a correspondingly more searching judicial inquiry."[92]

In *Korematsu v. United States*,[93] the Court addressed whether the internment of persons of Japanese ancestry was unconstitutional. Although the Court committed a grave error in finding that military necessity justified the extreme action,[94] it understood that the equal protection guarantee in theory protected persons of Japanese ancestry. The 1954 decision of *Brown v. Board of Education*[95] vindicated the rights of African American school children and held that racial segregation of the public schools was unconstitutional.

Brown, when read in combination with *Yick Wo*, *Carolene Products*, and *Korematsu*, made it clear that the protections of the Fourteenth Amendment extended well beyond African Americans. It was not much of a leap to hold that Mexican Americans deserved the same constitutional protections as other racial minorities, which was the precise question posed by *Hernandez v. Texas*. Indeed, it would have contradicted the general trajectory of the law to hold otherwise. As Earl Warren later explained,

> [a]ll of the various segregation case decisions went hand-in-hand with the principle of *Brown v. Board of Education*. *Those decisions related not only to blacks but equally to all racial groups that were discriminated against.* In fact, I reported a case of jury discrimination against Mexican Americans . . . two weeks before the *Brown* case in *Hernandez v. Texas* . . . . The state

---

[91]118 U.S. 356 (1886); see Thomas Wuil Joo, *New "Conspiracy Theory" of the Fourteenth Amendment: Nineteenth Century Chinese Civil Rights Cases and the Development of Substantive Due Process Jurisprudence*, 29 U.S.F. L. REV. 353 (1995).

[92]United States v. Carolene Products Co., 304 U.S. 144, 153 n.4 (1938) (citations omitted). See generally JOHN HART ELY, DEMOCRACY AND DISTRUST: A THEORY OF JUDICIAL REVIEW (1980) (offering a theory of judicial review based on *Carolene Products*). For analysis on the limitations of *Carolene Products* in addressing modern discrimination, see Bruce A. Ackerman, *Beyond* Carolene Products, 98 HARV. L. REV. 713 (1985).

[93]323 U.S. 214 (1944); supra text accompanying notes 49-53. Before *Korematsu*, the Supreme Court had held that Japanese immigrants were not "white" and thus were not eligible for citizenship under the naturalization laws then in effect. See Ozawa v. United States, 260 U.S. 178 (1922).

[94]See, e.g., ERIC K. YAMAMOTO ET AL., RACE, RIGHTS AND REPARATION: LAW AND THE JAPANESE AMERICAN INTERNMENT (2001); Symposium, *The Long Shadow of* Korematsu, 40 B.C. L. REV. 1 (1998).

[95]347 U.S. 483 (1954).

contended that [the] acts of discrimination did not violate the Constitution because the Fourteenth Amendment bore only on the relationship between blacks and whites. We hold that it applied to "any delineated class" and reversed the conviction. And so it must go with any such cases. *They apply to any class that is singled out for discrimination.* Most of our cases have involved blacks, but that is because there are more of them; they are more widespread and have been the most discriminated against.[96]

However, recognition of Mexican Americans as a group distinct from Anglos and deserving of constitutional protection, which the Court did in *Hernandez v. Texas*, is complicated. Mexican Americans in reality are a complex mixture of biological races, with a great variation of physical appearances. This racial complexity is captured in the Spanish word *mestizaje*.[97]

Nonetheless, Mexican Americans frequently embraced a "white" identity as a way of attempting to avoid social discrimination and, in some cases, as a litigation strategy.[98] Mexican Americans at times claimed to be "white" to avoid the discrimination suffered by African Americans and to accrue the benefits of whiteness secured by law.[99] Before *Hernandez v. Texas*, Mexican American litigants found it difficult to prevail in cases seeking to vindicate their civil rights because of the law's classification of Mexicans as white.[100] Courts often did not know how to classify persons of Mexican ancestry, as a "race" or an ethnic or national origin group[101] and frequently concluded that Mexican Americans were white, not Black, and denied them the protections of the Equal Protection Clause, which were said to be reserved for African Americans.[102]

Because Mexican Americans frequently adopted a white identity defensively,[103] the statement that "[u]ntil the late 1960s, the Mexican community in the United States thought of itself as racially white,"[104] does not fully capture the complex realities of the Mexican American experience. Events long before 1960, including the 1930s repatriation campaign, the Sleepy Lagoon murder case, and the Zoot Suit riots, contributed to the formation of a group identity among persons of Mexican ancestry in Southern California, just as rampant discrimination against persons of

---

[96]WARREN, supra note 38, at 299 (emphasis added).

[97]See CLAUDIO ESTEVA-FABREGAT, MESTIZAJE IN IBERO-AMERICA (1995); JULIAN SAMORA, MESTIZAJE: THE FORMATION OF CHICANOS (1996).

[98]See George A. Martínez, *The Legal Construction of Race: Mexican-Americans and Whiteness*, 2 HARV. LATINO L. REV. 321, 336-39 (1997); Kevin R. Johnson, *"Melting Pot" or "Ring of Fire"?: Assimilation and the Mexican-American Experience*, 85 CAL. L. REV. 1259, 1269-77 (1997). See generally RODOLFO ACUÑA, ANYTHING BUT MEXICAN: CHICANOS IN CONTEMPORARY LOS ANGELES (1995) (analyzing critically, efforts by Mexican Americans to embrace Spanish as opposed to Mexican identity in greater Los Angeles in the twentieth-century).

[99]See *infra* text accompanying notes 100-06.

[100]See generally Martínez, supra note 84 (reviewing Mexican American civil rights litigation over a fifty-year period).

[101]See, e.g., Westminster Sch. Dist. v. Mendez, 161 F.2d 774, 780-81 (9th Cir. 1947) (noting that persons of Mexican descent are not one of the "great races" and that California law did not permit their segregation in public schools).

[102]See Martínez, supra note 98.

[103]See Neil Foley, *Becoming Hispanic: Mexican Americans and the Faustian Pact with Whiteness*, in REFLEXIONES 1997: NEW DIRECTIONS IN MEXICAN AMERICAN STUDIES 53, 53 (Neil Foley ed., 1967).

[104]Ian Haney López, *Protest, Repression, and Race: Legal Violence and the Chicano Movement*, 150 U. PA. L. REV. 205, 205 (2001) (footnote omitted).

Mexican ancestry in much of Texas had.[105] Influential historian Ricardo Romo documented how Mexican Americans in Los Angeles from 1900 to 1930 formed institutions in response to hostility directed toward them by Anglos.[106] Even if not thought of as a "race" in biological terms, Latina/os across the United States have long embraced a non-Anglo group identity. This was true in Jackson County, Texas, where the case of *Hernandez v. Texas* arose.

C. The Racialization of Mexicans in Jackson County, Texas

Within days of *Brown v. Board of Education*, the Supreme Court decided *Hernandez v. Texas*. Both were written by Chief Justice Earl Warren and reflected consistent interpretation of the Equal Protection Clause. At a most fundamental level, the Court in *Hernandez v. Texas* implicitly recognized the unmistakable racialization of Mexicans and the reality that race is socially constructed, changing with place, time, and economic circumstance.[107] As a matter of law, the Court reasoned that the Equal Protection Clause applied to discrimination against all groups suffering discrimination: "The State of Texas would have us hold that there are only two classes—white and Negro—within the contemplation of the Fourteenth Amendment. The decisions of this Court do not support that view."[108] To emphasize its rejection of the state's argument, the Court quoted from *Strauder v. West Virginia*,[109] which held that African Americans could not be excluded from juries: "Nor if a law should be passed excluding all naturalized Celtic Irishmen [from jury service], would there be any doubt of its inconsistency with the spirit of the amendment." Besides obliquely acknowledging that the Irish at one time had been treated as non-white in the United States,[110] this statement suggests an understanding that race is a social construction, and presages the careful interrogation of whites as a race.[111]

The Supreme Court expressly rejected the lower court's holding that Mexicans were white and that, because the Fourteenth Amendment only recognized Blacks

---

[105]See supra text accompanying notes 4-11, 54-87.

[106]See RICARDO ROMO, EAST LOS ANGELES: HISTORY OF A BARRIO 129-62 (1983).

[107]See generally MICHAEL OMI & HOWARD WINANT, RACIAL FORMATION IN THE UNITED STATES (2d ed. 1994) (analyzing the social construction of race in United States); Christine B. Hickman, *The Devil and the One Drop Rule: Racial Categories, African Americans, and the U.S. Census*, 95 MICH. L. REV. 1161 (1997) (studying the impacts of the "one drop" of blood rule in defining African Americans in the United States); Ian F. Haney López, *The Social Construction of Race: Some Observations on Illusion, Fabrication, and Choice*, 29 HARV. C.R.-C.L. L. REV. 1 (1994) (same).

[108]Hernandez v. Texas, 347 U.S. 475, 477-78 n.4 (1954) (footnote citing Truax v. Raich, 239 U.S. 33 (1915)); Takahashi v. Fish & Game Comm'n, 334 U.S. 410 (1948); Hirabayashi v. United States, 320 U.S. 81, 100 (1943); see, e.g., Yick Wo v. Hopkins, 118 U.S. 356 (1886) (holding that discriminatory enforcement of local ordinance against persons of Chinese ancestry violated the Equal Protection Clause).

[109]100 U.S. 303, 308 (1880). *Strauder v. West Virginia* in this way took a color blind approach to the Equal Protection Clause. See *infra* text accompanying note 238. Not long after the case was decided, the Court recognized the existence of races other than African American. See, e.g., The Chinese Exclusion Case (Chae Chan Ping v. United States), 130 U.S. 581, 606-07 (1889) (upholding the exclusion of Chinese immigrants from United States under immigration laws and referring to them as "foreigners of a different race"); Plessy v. Ferguson, 163 U.S. 537, 552, 561 (1896) (Harlan, J., dissenting) (noting different social treatment of African Americans and Chinese); see also supra text accompanying notes 88-106 (discussing Court's recognition of various races).

[110]For an analysis of the transformation of the Irish from non-white to white, see NOEL IGNATIEV, HOW THE IRISH BECAME WHITE (1995); see also Karen Brodkin Sacks, *How Did Jews Become White Folks?*, in RACE 78 (Steven Gregory & Roger Sanjek eds., 1994) (analyzing a similar transformation for Jews).

[111]See, e.g., CRITICAL WHITE STUDIES: LOOKING BEHIND THE MIRROR (Richard Delgado & Jean Stefancic eds., 1997) (collecting readings on the subject of constructing whites as a race).

and whites, Mexicans did not enjoy its protections.[112] The Texas Criminal Appeals Court had emphasized that:

> [I]t is conclusive that, in so far as the question of discrimination in the organization of juries in state courts is concerned, the Equal Protection Clause of the Fourteenth Amendment contemplated and recognized only two classes as coming within that guarantee: the white race . . . , as distinguished from members of the Negro race.[113]

Other Texas cases had reached similar conclusions, which permitted discrimination against Mexicans to go unchecked by the courts.[114]

In the end, the Supreme Court's decision in *Hernandez v. Texas* helped seal the doom of the Black/white paradigm in the Supreme Court's jurisprudence and ensure that the protections of the U.S. Constitution were afforded to Mexican Americans. As might be expected given Chief Justice Warren's experiences in California, his unanimous opinion for the Court reflected an understanding of the variable, sometimes volatile, nature of discrimination:

> Throughout our history differences in race and color have defined easily identifiable groups which have at times required the aid of the courts in securing equal treatment under the laws. *But community prejudices are not static, and from time to time other differences from the community norm may define other groups which need the same protection. Whether such a group exists within a community is a question of fact.* When the existence of a distinct class is demonstrated, and it is further shown that the laws, as written or as applied, single out that class for different treatment not based on some reasonable classification, the guarantees of the Constitution have been violated. *The Fourteenth Amendment is not directed solely against discrimination due to a "two-class theory"—that is, based upon differences between "white" and Negro.*[115]

---

[112]Hernandez v. State, 251 S.W.2d 531, 535 (Tex. Crim. App. 1952); see Martínez, supra note 98, at 328; Leti Volpp, *Righting Wrongs*, 47 UCLA L. REV. 1815, 1823 & n.24 (2000).

[113]*Hernandez*, 251 S.W.2d at 535.

[114]See Sanchez v. State, 243 S.W.2d 700, 701 (Tex. Crim. App. 1951) ("[Mexican people] are not a separate race but are white people of Spanish descent."); Indep. Sch. Dist. v. Salvatierra, 33 S.W.2d 790 (Tex. Civ. App. 1930) (classifying Mexican Americans as "white" for purposes of school segregation litigation and finding that schools with predominantly African American and Mexican American school children were integrated); see also Martínez, supra note 98 (analyzing these and other cases in which courts concluded that persons of Mexican ancestry were "white" to their detriment); In re Rodriguez, 81 F. 337 (W.D. Tex. 1897) (holding that Mexicans were "white" for purposes of naturalization).

[115]Hernandez v. Texas, 347 U.S. 475, 478 (1954) (emphasis added). For analysis of the importance of *Hernandez v. Texas* in recognizing the construction of Mexicans as a race, see Ian F. Haney López, *Race, Ethnicity, Erasure: The Salience of Race to LatCrit Theory*, 85 CAL. L. REV. 1143, 1164-66 (1997); Ian F. Haney López, *Retaining Race: LatCrit Theory and Mexican Identity in* Hernandez v. Texas, 2 HARV. LATINO L. REV. 279 (1997) [hereinafter López, *Retaining Race*]; Perea, supra note 31, at 1248-50; Clare Sheridan, *"Another White Race": Mexican Americans and the Paradox of Whiteness in Jury Selection*, 21 LAW & HIST. REV. 109 (2003); Steven H. Wilson, Brown *Over "Other White": Mexican Americans' Legal Arguments and Litigation Strategy in School Desegregation Lawsuits*, 21 LAW & HIST. REV. 145, 160-64 (2003).

The Court in *Hernandez v. Texas* can be understood as repudiating the "framers' intent" interpretation of the Fourteenth Amendment. See Robert C. Post, *The Supreme Court, 2002 Term: Foreword—Fashioning the Legal Constitution: Culture, Courts, and Law*, 117 HARV. L. REV. 4, 52 (2003) (observing that the Supreme Court found that the Equal Protection Clause barred racial and gender discrimination "not because of changes in the intent of the framers of the Fourteenth Amendment, but because American constitutional culture evolved in such a way as to render these practices intolerable") (footnote omitted). Even assuming that the framers of the Amendment only envisioned African Americans as those protected by its mandate, time has made it clear that a broader scope is necessary to eliminate the scourge of invidious discrimination from U.S. social life. See supra text accompanying note 92 (analyzing the significance of *Carolene Products*).

In recognizing the variability of racial discrimination by time and place, the Court's opinion in *Hernandez v. Texas* has been characterized as "offer[ing] a sophisticated insight into racial formation: whether a racial group exists . . . is a local question that can be answered only in terms of community attitudes. To translate this insight into broader language, race is social, not biological; it is a matter of what people believe, rather than of natural decree."[116] Although the view of racial formation of Mexican Americans may be "sophisticated," it follows almost naturally from what Earl Warren personally saw first hand in California during World War II.[117]

The Court's conclusion was ahead of its time in effectively identifying the fluidity of race and races[118] and acknowledging that "community prejudices are not static," a position hard to dispute in light of the treatment of persons of Japanese ancestry during World War II, as well as the Zoot Suit race riots.[119] The case of discrimination outlined for the Supreme Court in *Hernandez v. Texas* must have resonated in important ways with Earl Warren's experiences in California. He had seen the surge of anti-Japanese animus and anti-Mexican sentiment, as well as the human misery caused by government's swift, harsh responses.[120]

In his brief in *Hernandez v. Texas*, Pete Hernandez relied on *Westminster School District v. Mendez*,[121] the Ninth Circuit decision barring school segregation of Mexican Americans, to contend that Mexican Americans were protected by the Equal Protection Clause.[122] Again, Chief Justice Warren was familiar with *Mendez*, having signed into law the California law responding to the decision and ending de jure segregation in the California public schools.[123]

More generally, the briefing in the case painted a picture of discriminatory treatment of Mexican Americans in Texas that mirrored that which existed in California. In an appendix to the main brief entitled "Status of Persons of Mexican Descent in Texas," a sort of "Brandeis brief" on discrimination against Mexicans in Texas, Hernandez succinctly summarized in five pages the discrimination against Mexican Americans in that state.[124] This discrimination included the segregation of Mexican Americans in the public schools and accommodations and racially restrictive covenants ensuring housing segregation, which tended to establish that Anglos in Texas viewed Mexican Americans as an inferior class of people. This discrimination resembled that facing African Americans,[125] some of which the Court grappled with in *Brown v. Board of Education*, as well as that which Mexican Americans faced in California.[126]

---

[116]López, *Retaining Race*, supra note 115, at 288.

[117]See supra text accompanying notes 33-87.

[118]See supra note 115.

[119]See supra text accompanying notes 68-82.

[120]See supra text accompanying notes 33-87.

[121]161 F.2d 774 (9th Cir. 1947); see supra text accompanying notes 83-86. The *Mendez* case may have influenced Chief Justice Warren's later thinking in Brown v. Bd. of Educ., 347 U.S. 483 (1954).

[122]See Brief for Petitioner at 10, Hernandez v. Texas, 347 U.S. 475 (1954) (No. 406).

[123]See supra text accompanying notes 83-86.

[124]See Brief for Petitioner at 37-41 (Appendix B), Hernandez v. Texas, 347 U.S. 475 (1954) (No. 406).

[125]See, e.g., Brown v. Bd. of Educ., 347 U.S. 483 (1954); Shelley v. Kraemer, 334 U.S. 1 (1948).

[126]See supra text accompanying note 33-87.

Pete Hernandez, charged with the murder of Joe Espinosa, argued that, in Jackson County, Texas, the state had systematically excluded persons of Mexican descent from jury commissions and petit and grand juries.[127] The record showed that, for the county, more than fourteen percent of the population, and eleven percent of the people over age twenty-one, had Spanish surnames.[128] The state of Texas admitted that there were eligible jurors of Mexican ancestry in the community.[129] However, the state conceded that *"for the last twenty-five years* there is no record of *any* person with a Mexican or Latin American name having served on a jury commission, grand jury or petit jury in Jackson County."[130] The Court declared that "it taxes our credulity to say that mere chance resulted in there being no members of this class [Mexicans] among the over six thousand jurors called in the past twenty-five years. The result bespeaks discrimination, *whether or not* it was a conscious decision on the part of any individual jury commissioner."[131]

In analyzing the racial discrimination at work against Mexican Americans, the Supreme Court appreciated the racial dynamics. In this passage, the Court alludes to the possibility that racial discrimination may be intentional or unconscious.[132] *Hernandez v. Texas* thus appears inconsistent with the Court's subsequent decision in *Washington v. Davis*,[133] which held that proof of a "discriminatory intent" was necessary to establish a violation of the Equal Protection Clause.

In considering community attitudes in Jackson County toward persons of Mexican ancestry and the pervasive discrimination against them, the Supreme Court observed:

the testimony of responsible officials and citizens contained the admission that residents of the community distinguished between "white" and "Mexican." The participation of persons of Mexican descent in business and community groups was shown to be slight. *Until very recent times, children of Mexican descent were required to attend a segregated school for the first four grades.* At least one restaurant in town prominently displayed a sign

---

[127]See Hernandez v. Texas, 347 U.S. 475, 476-77 (1954).

[128]See *id.* at 480.

[129]See *id.* at 481.

[130]*Id.* (emphasis added) (footnote omitted).

[131]*Id.* at 482 (emphasis added). The Court later quoted this language and found that the evidence supported the claim that the prosecutor had considered race in exercising peremptory challenges. See Miller-El v. Cockrell, 537 U.S. 322, 346-47 (2003); see *infra* text accompanying notes 224-38 (discussing the prohibition on race-based peremptory challenges).

[132]See, e.g., Charles R. Lawrence III, *The Id, the Ego, and Equal Protection: Reckoning with Unconscious Racism*, 39 STAN. L. REV. 317 (1987); Barbara J. Flagg, *"Was Blind, But Now I See": White Race Consciousness and the Requirement of Discriminatory Intent*, 91 MICH. L. REV. 953 (1993); Sheila Foster, *Intent and Incoherence*, 72 TUL. L. REV. 1065 (1998); Alan D. Freeman, *Legitimizing Racial Discrimination Through Antidiscrimination Law: A Critical Review of Supreme Court Doctrine*, 62 MINN. L. REV. 1049 (1978).

[133]426 U.S. 229 (1976); see, e.g., McCleskey v. Kemp, 481 U.S. 279 (1987) (rejecting overwhelming statistical evidence of the disparate application of the death penalty as establishing an Equal Protection violation); United States v. Armstrong, 517 U.S. 456 (1996) (holding that discovery based on selective prosecution claim could not be required absent a showing that similarly situated whites had not been prosecuted under crack cocaine law, even though African Americans were disproportionately affected by strict criminal penalties for crack cocaine compared to more lenient penalties for powder cocaine).

announcing "No Mexicans Served." On the courthouse grounds at the time of the hearing, there were two men's toilets, one unmarked, and the other marked "Colored Men" and "Hombres Aqui" ("Men Here").[134]

This description again resembles the events in California in the 1940s and is not that different from the description of the conditions of the lives of Mexican Americans in Los Angeles during World War II.[135] Recall the widespread discrimination against persons of Mexican ancestry in Los Angeles and the school desegregation litigation decided by the court of appeals in 1947.[136]

Nor is it any great surprise that the Supreme Court's first recognition of discrimination against Mexican Americans occurred in a case involving Texas, a former slave state with a long history of subordination of African Americans and Mexican Americans, as well as poor whites.[137] Indeed, the state was rather infamous for violating the rights of its minorities, and offers perhaps one of the starkest examples of the racialization of Mexican Americans.

In summary, Chief Justice Earl Warren, often credited with his ability to grow and learn,[138] had learned from his experiences with the discrimination against Mexican Americans in California and could appreciate similar racial animosities in Texas. Moreover, he understood the importance of the appearance of impartial juries in keeping the peace and maintaining public (especially minority) confidence in the justice system. As it was in California in the 1940s, this was an issue in Texas in the 1950s and clearly would remain an issue in the future. The racial composition of juries long had been an issue for African Americans,[139] and there was no reason to think it would be any different for persons of Mexican ancestry.

D. The Court's General Acceptance of *Hernandez v. Texas*'s Racial Teachings

After the breakthrough of *Hernandez v. Texas*, the analysis of Mexicans as a separate and distinct class took hold relatively quickly in the Supreme Court's jurisprudence. This development no doubt was facilitated by the growth of a racial consciousness among Chicana/os and the Chicana/o movement of the 1960s,[140] as well as the growing national awareness of the emerging Latina/o population.

Hernandez v. Texas suggested that whether a group had been the subject of prejudice was a question of fact to be determined on a case-by-case basis.[141] Commen-

---

[134]*Hernandez v. Texas*, 347 U S. at 479-80 (emphasis added) (footnote omitted).
[135]See supra text accompanying notes 33-87.
[136]See supra text accompanying notes 83-86.
[137]See supra text accompanying notes 12-13.
[138]See Carey McWilliams, *The Education of Earl Warren*, NATION, Oct. 12, 1974, at 325-26.
[139]See, e.g., Norris v. Alabama, 294 U.S. 587 (1935); Carter v. Texas, 177 U.S. 442 (1900); Strauder v. West Virginia, 100 U.S. 303, 308 (1880). Warren was well aware of the racial exclusion of African Americans from juries and understood that it remained a problem years after the Supreme Court ruled that such exclusion was unconstitutional. See WARREN, supra note 38, at 292, 295.
[140]See ACUÑA, supra note 4, at 307-62. For analysis of the emergence of the Chicana/o movement, see IGNACIO M. GARCÍA, CHICANISMO: THE FORGING OF A MILITANT ETHOS AMONG MEXICAN AMERICANS (1997).
[141]See Hernandez v. Texas, 347 U.S. 475, 479-80 (1954); supra text accompanying note 115.

tators criticized that suggestion.[142] In later cases, however, the Supreme Court never really required a fact specific analysis to determine whether Latina/os were a separate class for Equal Protection purposes. Rather, the Court simply assumed that they were.[143] For example, less than two decades after the Court decided *Hernandez v. Texas*, in *Keyes v. School District No. 1*, the Court, in a school desegregation case involving the public schools in Denver, stated matter of factly that "Hispanos constitute an identifiable class for purposes of the Fourteenth Amendment." [144]

In 1977, the Court in *Castaneda v. Partida* reviewed another criminal case in which a defendant claimed that Mexican Americans were underrepresented on Texas juries and emphasized that "it is no longer open to dispute that Mexican Americans are a clearly identifiable class." [145] In light of *Hernandez v. Texas*, the Texas Court of Criminal Appeals in *Castaneda v. Partida* could not deny that Mexican Americans were protected by the Equal Protection Clause of the Fourteenth Amendment; rather, the court questioned the statistical evidence of Mexican American underrepresentation on juries in part because it was uncertain how many "were so-called 'wet backs' from the south side of the Rio Grande."[146] Today, reading the epithet "wetbacks" in a judicial opinion is jarring, suggesting the social acceptance of the deep antipathy toward persons of Mexican ancestry in Texas at that time. It also reflects the general presumption that Latina/os are "foreigners" who deserve less in terms of rights than U.S. citizens.[147]

In *Castaneda v. Partida*, the Supreme Court relied upon *Hernandez v. Texas* and *White v. Regester*[148] to support its statement that Mexican Americans were a cognizable group for Equal Protection purposes. In *White v. Regester*, the Court in a voting rights case considered the discrimination against Mexican Americans in the political process in Texas, which included a history of poll taxes and restrictive voter registration practices.[149] By 1991, in the case of *Hernandez v. New York*,[150] the Court simply assumed that Latina/os were protected by the Equal Protection Clause and did not discuss the issue.[151]

---

[142]Delgado & Palacios, supra note 2, at 395-96.

[143]See *id.* at 395; *infra* text accompanying notes 144-59.

[144]413 U.S. 189, 197 (1973) (citing, inter alia, Hernandez v. Texas, 347 U.S. 475 (1954)); see United States v. Texas Educ. Agency, 467 F.2d 848, 861-62 (5th Cir. 1972) (reaching similar conclusion in school desegregation case based on *Hernandez v. Texas*). The transformation of Mexicans into a distinctive class in civil rights litigation did not come about quite as smoothly in the lower federal and state courts. For example, the lower court in the much-publicized decision of Lopez Tijerina v. Henry, 48 F.R.D. 274 (D.N.M. 1969) (per curiam), *appeal dismissed sub nom.* Tijerina v. Henry 398 U.S. 922 (1970), refused to certify a class of Mexican Americans because the members of the class were not readily identifiable, see Tijerina v. Henry, 398 U.S. 922 (1970) (Douglas, J., dissenting from dismissal of appeal). See also United States v. Duran de Amesquita, 582 F. Supp. 1326, 1328-29 (S.D. Fla. 1984) (refusing to recognize Hispanics as a cognizable group because of the great diversity among various Latina/o national origin groups); State v. Alen, 616 So. 2d 452, 455-56 (Fla. 1993) (reversing case law holding that Hispanics were not a recognized class for purposes of jury selection).

[145]430 U.S. 482, 495 (1977); see Garcia v. State, 919 S.W.2d 370, 392-93 (Tex. Crim. App. 1994) (en banc); Hernandez v. State, 24 S.W.3d 846 (Tex. App. 2000); Flores v. State, 783 S.W.2d 793 (Tex. App. 1990).

[146]Partida v. State, 506 S.W.2d 209, 211 (Tex. Crim. App. 1974).

[147]See *infra* text accompanying notes 199-200.

[148]412 U.S. 755 (1973).

[149]See *id.* at 767-71.

[150]500 U.S. 352 (1991).

[151]See *infra* text accompanying notes 228-35 (analyzing *Hernandez v. New York*); see also United States v. Pion, 25 F.3d 18, 22-24 (1st Cir. 1994) (evaluating claim of underrepresentation of Hispanics on jury in Massachusetts); United States v. Espinoza, 641 F.2d 153, 168 (4th Cir. 1981) (addressing claim that Hispanic jurors were excluded from jury pool in West Virginia).

Consequently, *Hernandez v. Texas* represents an important chapter in the transformation of persons of Mexican ancestry, as well as Latina/os generally, into a cognizable "race" for purposes of anti-discrimination law and its enforcement. During the same general period of the twentieth-century, persons of Mexican ancestry organized politically along racial lines in their struggle for equality.[152] The governmental classification of all Latina/os—a heterogeneous group—in the category "Hispanic" for Census purposes helped encourage a pan-Latina/o identity and facilitated group attempts to combat discrimination.[153]

The Supreme Court did not stop with extending the protections of anti-discrimination law to persons of Mexican ancestry. Indeed, the Court later (but well before the United State's recent war in Iraq) held that the civil rights laws barred racial discrimination against Iraqis, even if they are ordinarily classified as white, and recognized that "some, but not all scientists [have] conclude[d] that racial classifications are for the most part sociopolitical, rather than biological, in nature."[154] In *Plyler v. Doe*,[155] the Court held that undocumented immigrant children in Texas, many of whom were of Mexican descent, came within the purview of the Equal Protection Clause and could not constitutionally be barred from the public schools. One influential commentator has contended that the reasoning of *Hernandez v. Texas* justifies a constitutional bar on discrimination against homosexuals.[156]

Interestingly, the slow but steady expansion of the protections of the Fourteenth Amendment, and the embrace of color blindness, resulted in the unexpected consequence of opening the door to subsequent claims of "reverse discrimination" by whites.[157] Ultimately, discrimination came to be understood as something that could happen to whites.[158] In the famous *Bakke* case, Justice Powell relied on *Hernandez v. Texas* for the proposition that the Equal Protection Clause "extended to all ethnic

---

[152]See generally ESCOBAR, supra note 7 (analyzing the emergence of Mexican political and racial identity resulting from the conduct of law enforcement authorities in Los Angeles); IAN F. HANEY LÓPEZ, RACISM ON TRIAL: THE CHICANO FIGHT FOR JUSTICE (2003) (analyzing racial consciousness of Chicana/o activism in the 1960s).

[153]See Kevin R. Johnson, *Some Thoughts on the Future of Latino Legal Scholarship*, 2 HARV. LATINO L. REV. 101, 117-29 (1997). For criticism of the Hispanic classification, see Luis Angel Toro, *"A People Distinct from Others": Race and Identity in Federal Indian Law and the Hispanic Classification in OMB Directive No. 15*, 26 TEX. TECH L. REV. 1219 (1995).

[154]Saint Francis Coll. v. Al-Khazraji, 481 U.S. 604, 610 n.4 (1987) (citations omitted). The Court cited *Hernandez v. Texas* as one of the cases recognizing that discrimination based on "ancestry" violates the Fourteenth Amendment. See *id.* at 613 n.5; see also McCleskey v. Kemp, 481 U.S. 279, 316 n.39 (1987) (citing *Hernandez v. Texas* for the proposition that racial discrimination may be directed at a variety of groups).

[155]457 U.S. 202, 215-23 (1982).

[156]See MICHAEL J. PERRY, WE THE PEOPLE: THE FOURTEENTH AMENDMENT AND THE SUPREME COURT 149-50 (1999); see also Duren v. Missouri, 439 U.S. 357 (1979) (applying fair cross-section of the community requirement to include women); Barber v. Ponte, 772 F.2d 982, 997-1000 (1st Cir. 1985) (addressing claim of exclusion of young people from jury pool).

[157]See *infra* note 158.

[158]See, e.g., Gratz v. Bollinger, 539 U.S. 244 (2003) (evaluating undergraduate affirmative action program challenged by prospective white applicants); Grutter v. Bollinger, 539 U.S. 306 (2003) (same for law school applicants); Adarand Constructors, Inc. v. Peña, 515 U.S. 200 (1995) (holding that all racial classifications, including those in federal program to increase government contracting with minority businesses, are subject to strict scrutiny); City of Richmond v. J.A. Croson Co., 488 U.S. 469 (1989) (to the same effect); Hopwood v. Texas, 78 F.3d 932 (5th Cir. 1996) (invalidating University of Texas law school's race conscious affirmative action admissions system in lawsuit brought by white applicant), *cert. denied sub nom.* Thurgood Marshall Legal Soc'y v. Hopwood, 518 U.S. 1033 (1996); see also Fullilove v. Klutznick, 448 U.S. 448, 522, 526 (1980) (Stewart, J., dissenting) (citing *Hernandez v. Texas* in contending that minority business contracting program violated Equal Protection Clause).

groups" and rejected the claim that Alan Bakke's claim of racial discrimination should be subject to anything less than strict constitutional scrutiny.[159]

Thus, besides serving as an important bridge in ensuring that Mexican Americans, and Latina/os generally, enjoyed protections against racial discrimination, *Hernandez v. Texas* in some ways contributed to a broadening of Equal Protection challenges.

II. LEGACY OF INJUSTICE: THE PERSISTENT UNDERREPRESENTATION OF LATINAS/OS ON JURIES

As *Hernandez v. Texas* exemplifies, discrimination in the selection of petit and grand juries has long plagued Mexican Americans in the United States.[160] Exclusion of Latina/os from jury service historically has denoted the subordinated status of Latina/os in American social life.[161]

Latina/o underrepresentation on juries can be expected to have substantive impacts. In the 1960s, Chicano activist attorney Oscar "Zeta" Acosta challenged the grand jury system in Los Angeles County by defending Chicana/o political activists charged with criminal offenses,[162] just as the lawyers did on behalf of Pete Hernández and Mexican Americans in *Hernandez v. Texas*.[163] The unstated hope was that the inclusion of Latina/os on grand juries would affect the outcomes of cases.[164] At a minimum, the parties sought a more impartial jury that would not hold Mexican ancestry against Mexican defendants.[165]

Hernandez v. Texas was the Supreme Court's first decision to expressly acknowledge discrimination against Mexican Americans. However, it was not the last time that the courts found it necessary to address claims of Latina/o exclusion

---

[159]See Regents of the Univ. of Cal. v. Bakke, 438 U.S. 265, 292-93 (1978) (Powell, J.).

[160]See, e.g., Ian F. Haney López, *Institutional Racism: Judicial Conduct and a New Theory of Racial Discrimination*, 109 YALE L.J. 1717 (2000) (analyzing racial discrimination against Mexican Americans in selecting grand juries in Los Angeles County); Hiroshi Fukurai, *Critical Evaluations of Hispanic Participation on the Grand Jury: Key-Man Selection, Jurymandering, Language, and Representative Quotas*, 5 TEX. HISP. J.L. & POL'Y 7 (2001) [hereinafter Fukurai, *Critical Evaluations*] (studying exclusion of Latina/os from juries); see also Hiroshi Fukurai, *Social De-Construction of Race and Affirmative Action in Jury Selection*, 11 LA RAZA L.J. 17 (1999) [hereinafter Fukurai, *Social De-Construction*] (offering proposals designed to improve representation of racial minorities on juries); Nancy S. Marder, *Juries, Justice & Multiculturalism*, 75 S. CAL. L. REV. 659, 678-701 (2002) (explaining importance of cultural diversity on juries to juror deliberations). See generally HIROSHI FUKURAI, EDGAR W. BUTLER & RICHARD KROOTH, RACE AND THE JURY: RACIAL DISENFRANCHISEMENT AND THE SEARCH FOR JUSTICE (1993) (discussing generally the representation of racial minorities on juries).

[161]See generally KENNETH L. KARST, BELONGING TO AMERICA: EQUAL CITIZENSHIP AND THE CONSTITUTION (1989) (analyzing quest of various groups to achieve full membership in U.S. society).

[162]See LÓPEZ, supra note 152, at 76-77; Montez v. Superior Court, 10 Cal. App. 3d 343 (1970).

[163]See López, supra note 104, at 238-42; Michael A. Olivas, *"Breaking the Law" on Principle: An Essay on Lawyers' Dilemmas, Unpopular Causes, and Legal Remedies*, 52 U. PITT. L. REV. 815, 846-54 (1991).

[164]See Laura E. Gómez, *Race, Colonialism, and Criminal Law: Mexicans and the American Criminal Justice System in Territorial New Mexico*, 34 LAW & SOC'Y REV. 1129 (2000) (analyzing, historically, the role of persons of Mexican ancestry in the criminal justice system, including as jurors, in territorial New Mexico); see also Pugliano v. United States, 315 F. Supp. 2d 197 (D. Conn. 2004) (ruling against admission of expert testimony that a racially diverse jury is less likely to convict a criminal defendant).

[165]See Kim Forde-Mazrui, *Jural Districting: Selecting Impartial Juries Through Community Representation*, 52 VAND. L. REV. 353, 362-64 (1999); Nancy J. King, *The Effects of Race-Conscious Jury Selection on Public Confidence in the Fairness of Jury Proceedings: An Empirical Puzzle*, 31 AM. CRIM. L. REV. 1177 (1994).

from juries. Lower courts regularly rely on *Hernandez v. Texas* to challenge the exclusion of Latina/os, African Americans, and other groups from the jury pool.[166] By removing a bar to Latina/o jury participation and allowing for more racially diverse juries, the Court's decision offers the promise of greater impartiality and provides the appearance of greater legitimacy to juries and the decisions that they reach.[167]

Consistent with this promise, the official policy today is that petit juries should be pulled from a cross-section of the community.[168] In this way, juries symbolize the nation's commitment to democracy in the U.S. justice system and protect against the arbitrary use of judicial power.[169] No racial prerequisites for jury service exist in the United States; racial exclusions are prohibited.

However, just as the segregation of public schools did not end instantly with the ruling in *Brown v. Board of Education*, juries did not immediately become integrated with the Supreme Court's decision in *Hernandez v. Texas*. True, Latina/os served on juries in greater numbers in the years following the Court's decision than before 1954. However, representation of Latina/os on juries continues to lag significantly behind their percentage of the population.[170]

For example, over twenty years after the Court decided *Hernandez v. Texas*, in the 1977 case of *Castaneda v. Partida*,[171] the Supreme Court addressed a case in which Mexican Americans constituted about eighty percent of Hidalgo County—a county in south Texas along the U.S./Mexico border—but from 1962 to 1972, averaged less than forty percent of the grand jurors. As in *Hernandez v. Texas*, a Mexican American criminal defendant, Rodrigo Partida, successfully challenged the constitutionality of the system for impaneling the grand jury.[172]

---

[166]See, e.g., United States v. Raszkiewicz, 169 F.3d 459, 463 (7th Cir. 1999) (reservation Indians); United States v. Pion, 25 F.3d 18, 27 (1st Cir. 1994) (Torruela, J., concurring) (Hispanics); United States v. Chinchilla, 874 F.2d 695, 698 (9th Cir. 1989) (Hispanics); Anaya v. Hansen, 781 F.2d 1, 6-7 (1st Cir. 1986) (blue collar workers, less educated, and young adults); Ciudadanos Unidos de San Juan v. Hidalgo County Grand Jury Comm'r, 622 F.2d 807, 810 (5th Cir. 1980) (Mexican Americans, women, young people, and the poor), *cert. denied*, 450 U.S. 964 (1981); Muniz v. Beto, 434 F.2d 697, 701 (5th Cir. 1970) (Mexican Americans); United States v. Duran de Amesquita, 582 F. Supp. 1326, 1328 (S.D. Fla. 1984) (Hispanics); Dumont v. Estelle, 377 F. Supp. 374, 375-76 (S.D. Tex. 1974) (freeholder or householder), *aff'd*, 513 F.2d 793 (5th Cir. 1975); Bokulich v. Jury Comm'n, 298 F. Supp. 181, 190 n.11 (N.D. Ala. 1968), *aff'd sub nom.* Carter v. Jury Comm'n, 396 U.S. 320 (1970) (African Americans).

[167]See JON M. VAN DYKE, JURY SELECTION PROCEDURES 32, 45 (1977); Forde-Mazrui, supra note 165, at 362-64.

[168]See 28 U.S.C. § 1861 (2000) (declaring policy that juries be "selected at random from a fair cross-section of the community in the district or division wherein the court convenes"); see also Thiel v. S. Pac. Co., 328 U.S. 217, 220 (1946) (emphasizing that "[t]he American tradition of trial by jury . . . necessarily contemplates an impartial jury drawn from a cross-section of the community.") (citations omitted).

[169]See, e.g., R.R. Co. v. Stout, 84 U.S. (17 Wall.) 657, 664 (1873).

[170]See U.S. COMM'N ON CIVIL RIGHTS, MEXICAN AMERICANS AND THE ADMINISTRATION OF JUSTICE 36-46 (1970); Lorenzo Arredondo & Donato Tapia, Comment, *El Chicano y the Constitution: The Legacy of Hernandez v. Texas Grand Jury Discrimination*, 6 U.S.F. L. REV. 129 (1971); Edward A. Villalobos, Comment, *Grand Jury Discrimination and the Mexican American*, 5 LOY. L.A. L. REV. 87 (1972).

[171]430 U.S. 482, 485, 487 & n.7, 495 (1977); see supra text accompanying notes 145-47.

[172]Such underrepresentation of Latina/os exists today on Texas grand juries. See Larry Karson, Choosing Justice: The Implications of a Key-Man System for Selecting a Grand Jury 3 S.W.J.CRIM.J. (forthcoming, 2006) (analyzing grand jury selection process in Harris County, Texas).

In states across the country, challenges to Latina/o jury participation continue to the present.[173] They are not limited to Texas.[174] As Professor Ian Haney López summarized in an article studying legal strategies used by political activists challenging the institutional racism in grand jury selection:

> The number of Mexicans actually seated [in Los Angeles County] as grand jurors [not long after the 1954 decision in *Hernandez v. Texas*] was . . . dismal. Between 1959 and 1969, Mexicans comprised only 4 of 233 grand jurors—no more than 1.7 percent of all grand jurors. If one assumes Mexicans on average constituted 14 percent of Los Angeles County's population during this period, Mexicans were under-represented on Los Angeles grand juries by a ratio of 8 to 1. During the 1960s, Mexicans counted for 1 of every 7 persons in Los Angeles, but only 1 of every 36 nominees and 1 of every 58 grand jurors. Prior to the 1960s the exclusion of Mexicans was no doubt even greater. *A study of Los Angeles grand juries published in 1945 noted that "as far as the writer was able to discover no Mexicans have ever been chosen for jury duty."*[175]

Los Angeles County was not alone in the underrepresentation of Latina/os on juries. In the early 1990s, Santa Cruz County in California, with a large and growing Latina/o population, experienced the underrepresentation of Latina/os on grand juries.[176] There is no reason to believe that Latina/os are underrepresented on juries in only these counties.

Socioeconomic class differences contribute to lower representation on juries by poor and working class people.[177] Latina/os are in the aggregate more likely than Anglos to be in the lower end of the socioeconomic spectrum.[178] Financial consid-

---

[173]See, e.g., Sanders v. Woodford, 373 F.3d 1054, 1068-70 (9th Cir. 2004); United States v. Esquivel, 88 F.3d 722 (9th Cir. 1996); Ciudadanos Unidos de San Juan v. Hidalgo County Grand Jury Comm'r, 622 F.2d 807 (5th Cir. 1980), *cert. denied*, 450 U.S. 964 (1981); United States v. Rodriguez, 588 F.2d 1003 (5th Cir. 1979); *In re* Special Feb. 1975 Grand Jury, 565 F.2d 407 (7th Cir. 1977); Muniz v. Beto, 434 F.2d 697 (5th Cir. 1970); United States ex rel. Martinez v. Hinlsey, 2004 U.S. Dist. LEXIS 11238, *10 to *18 (N.D. Ill. June 21, 2004); Sosa v. Dretke, 2004 U.S. Dist. LEXIS 9143, *146 to *209 (W.D. Tex. May 20, 2004); Anderson v. Hickman, 2004 U.S. Dist. LEXIS 7001, *15 to *32 (N.D. Cal. Apr. 23, 2004); United States v. Gerena, 677 F. Supp. 1266 (D. Conn. 1987); Villafane v. Manson, 504 F. Supp. 78 (D. Conn. 1980); State v. Gibbs, 758 A.2d 327 (Conn. 2000); Hernandez v. State, 24 S.W.3d 846 (Tex. App. 2000); State v. Alen, 616 So.2d 452 (Fla. 1993); People v. Cerrone, 854 P.2d 178 (Colo. 1993).

[174]See, e.g., People v. Morales, 48 Cal. 3d 527, 541-49 (1989), *cert. denied*, 493 U.S. 984 (1989); State v. Villafane, 164 Conn. 637 (1973); State v. Paz, 118 Idaho 542, 547-52 (1990), *cert. denied*, 501 U.S. 1259 (1991); People v. Flores, 193 Ill. App. 3d 501 (1990); State v. Lopez, 182 Kan. 46, 50-51 (1957); People v. Guzman, 60 N.Y.2d 403 (1983), *cert. denied*, 466 U.S. 951 (1984); State v. Esparza, 39 Ohio St. 3d 8, 13 (1988), *cert. denied*, 490 U.S. 1012 (1989); State v. Salinas, 87 Wash. 2d 112 (1976).

[175]See LÓPEZ, supra note 152, at 100-01 (emphasis added) (footnote omitted).

[176]See Fukurai, *Critical Evaluations*, supra note 160, at 25; Hiroshi Fukurai, *Where Did Hispanic Jurors Go? Racial and Ethnic Discrimination in the Grand Jury and the Search for Justice*, 2 W. CRIM. REV. 2 (2000), *available at* http://wcr.sonoma.edu/v2n2/fukurai.html (last visited Apr. 25, 2005).

[177]See Mitchell S. Zuklie, Comment, *Rethinking the Fair Cross-Section Requirement*, 84 CAL. L. REV. 101, 103 n.18 (1996) (citing studies); see also Joanna Sobol, Note, *Hardship Excuses and Occupational Exemptions: The Impairment of the "Fair Cross-Section of the Community,"* 69 S. CAL. L. REV. 155 (1995) (analyzing how excuse of jurors for "hardship" and certain occupational exemptions, render juries less representative of a cross-section of the community).

[178]See Christopher D. Ruiz Cameron, *The Labyrinth of Solidarity: Why the Future of the American Labor Movement Depends on Latino Workers*, 53 U. MIAMI. L. REV. 1089, 1098-03 (1999); Spencer Overton, *Voices From the Past: Race, Privilege, and Campaign Finance*, 79 N.C. L. REV. 1541, 1548-50 (2001).

erations make it more difficult for Latina/os to serve on juries and reduce Latina/o representation, just as they also tend to do with respect to African Americans.[179]

In light of the prohibition of racial exclusions to jury service and the increase in the Latina/o population, the persistence of the low representation of Latina/os on juries at first glance may appear puzzling. Although the Court in *Hernandez v. Texas* barred systematic exclusion of persons of Mexican ancestry, a variety of race neutral mechanisms are employed in the selection of jury pools today that result in the underrepresentation of Mexican Americans, and Latina/os generally, on juries in this country.[180] Citizenship, language requirements, economic circumstances, and selection procedures all contribute to this lack of representation.[181]

A. The Citizenship Requirement

All noncitizens, even those who have lawfully lived in the United States for many years, are excluded from jury service.[182] Courts have upheld this requirement in the face of claims that it denies a criminal defendant the right to an impartial jury.[183] The often-unstated assumption is that noncitizens cannot be expected to be loyal to the United States—and the greater community—in serving on juries.[184]

The citizenship requirement has significant impacts on the pool of eligible jurors in some regions of the country, such as Los Angeles, New York City, San Francisco, Chicago, and Miami.[185] The impacts are not limited to large urban centers, however. Large immigrant populations have emerged, and continue to grow, in suburban and rural parts of the country, including in the South and Midwest.[186]

Given the demographics of the immigrant stream, the citizenship requirement for jury service has racial impacts. According to the 2000 U.S. Census, almost thirty percent of Hispanics in the United States are *not* U.S. citizens,[187] and thus are ineligible for jury service. More than one-third of all residents of Los Angeles County

---

[179]See, e.g., Nancy J. King, *Racial Jurymandering: Cancer or Cure? A Contemporary Review of Affirmative Action in Jury Selection*, 68 N.Y. U. L. REV. 707, 712-19 (1993).

[180]See Berta Esperanza Hernández-Truyol, *Las Olvidadas—Gendered in Justice/Gendered Injustice: Latinas, Fronteras and the Law*, 1 J. GENDER RACE & JUST. 353, 373-74 (1998).

[181]See Fukurai, *Critical Evaluations*, supra note 160, at 32-34.

[182]See Carter v. Jury Comm'n, 396 U.S. 320, 333 (1970) ("Nearly every State requires that its jurors be citizens of the United States") (footnote omitted); see, e.g., 28 U.S.C. § 1865(b)(1) (providing that person who "is not a citizen of the United States" is not eligible for jury service).

[183]See, e.g., United States v. Toner, 728 F.2d 115, 129-30 (2d Cir. 1984); United States v. Avalos, 541 F.2d 1100, 1118 (5th Cir. 1976), cert. denied, 430 U.S. 970 (1977).

[184]See VAN DYKE, supra note 167, 132-33. *But cf.* Peter J. Spiro, *Dual Nationality and the Meaning of Citizenship*, 46 EMORY L.J. 1411 (1997) (rejecting similar concerns as a reason for the refusal to recognize dual nationality).

[185]See *Developments in the Law—Race and the Criminal Process*, 101 HARV. L. REV. 1472, 1564 (1988) ("The citizenship requirement . . . may be unnecessary and inappropriate in areas with large resident alien populations, such as Miami, where at least thirty percent of the population are resident aliens.") (footnote omitted).

[186]See Johnson, supra note 32, at 1492-96 (discussing Mexican diaspora across the United States); Bill Ong Hing, *Answering Challenges of the New Immigrant-Driven Diversity: Considering Integration Strategies*, 40 BRANDEIS L.J. 861, 864-68 (2002) (same); Sylvia R. Lazos Vargas, *"Latina/o-ization" of the Midwest: Cambio de Colores (Change of Colors) as Agromaquilas Expand into the Heartland*, 13 LA RAZA L.J. 343 (2002) (same).

[187]See U.S. Census Bureau, Census 2000, PCT63H. Place of Birth by Citizenship Status (Hispanic or Latino), *available at* http://factfinder.census.gov (last visited Apr. 25, 2005).

were foreign born, including many natives of Mexico who are noncitizens, and thus excluded from the jury pool.[188] Because "[t]he vast majority of today's immigrants are people of color,"[189] immigration status in modern times serves as a rough proxy for race.

The exclusion of immigrants from juries impacts the representativeness of juries and the extent to which they reflect a true cross-section of the community living in a jurisdiction. For several reasons, this has become a more significant issue since *Hernandez v. Texas* was decided in 1954. Since then, the number of immigrants in the United States has increased. This is explained, in part, by Congress's removal of racially exclusionary provisions in the immigration laws in 1965, leading to a substantial increase in the number of immigrants of color coming to the United States.[190]

Put simply, noncitizens have disputes, civil and criminal, resolved in a justice system in which they are not represented among the jurors who will decide their cases.[191] This has not always been the rule in the United States. Until nativism emerged with a vengeance early in the twentieth-century,[192] noncitizens were permitted to vote and serve on juries in many states.[193] Indeed, for centuries, in order to ensure fairness to noncitizens, English law authorized juries *de medietate linguae*— juries of half citizens and half noncitizens—in cases involving a noncitizen.[194] This procedure reflected the understanding of the need for representation of noncitizens on the jury in order to offer the appearance of impartiality.

---

[188]See California Quick Facts (Los Angeles County), U.S. Census Bureau, *available at* http://quickfacts.census.gov/qfd/states/06/06037.html (last visited Apr. 25, 2005).

[189]Johnson, supra note 32, at 1505.

[190]See Gabriel J. Chin, *The Civil Rights Revolution Comes to Immigration Law: A New Look at the Immigration and Nationality Act of 1965*, 75 N.C. L. REV. 273, 276 (1996).

[191]See Vikram D. Amar & Alan Brownstein, *The Hybrid Nature of Political Rights*, 50 STAN. L. REV. 915 (1998) (contending that the right to a jury trial, as well as voting, has group, as well as individual, rights dimension that involve minority representation). Noncitizens in certain circumstances can have their disputes resolved in federal, rather than state, courts, the assumption being that federal courts will less likely be biased against foreigner because the judges have life tenure and are more immune from political pressures than elected state court judges. See 28 U.S.C. § 1332. See generally Kevin R. Johnson, *Why Alienage Jurisdiction? Historical Foundations and Modern Justifications for Federal Jurisdiction Over Disputes Involving Noncitizens*, 21 YALE J. INT'L L. 1 (1996) (analyzing reasons for alienage jurisdiction). However, noncitizens cannot sit on juries in federal court.

[192]See JOHN HIGHAM, STRANGERS IN THE LAND: PATTERNS OF AMERICAN NATIVISM 1860-1925, at 158-330 (3d ed. 1994).

[193]See Jamin B. Raskin, *Legal Aliens, Local Citizens: The Historical, Constitutional and Theoretical Meanings of Alien Suffrage*, 141 U. PA. L. REV. 1391, 1397-17 (1993) (summarizing history of alienage suffrage in the United States); Gerald M. Rosberg, *Aliens and Equal Protection: Why Not the Right to Vote?*, 75 MICH. L. REV. 1092, 1093-1100 (1977) (same); Gabriela Evia, Note, *Consent By All the Governed: Reenfranchising Noncitizens as Partners in America's Democracy*, 77 S. CAL. L. REV. 151 (2003); see also Sandra Guerra, Note, *Voting Rights and the Constitution: The Disenfranchisement of Non-English Speaking Citizens*, 97 YALE L.J. 1419 (1988) (contending that failure to assist non-English proficient speakers in voting in effect disenfranchised them in violation of the law). See generally HIGHAM, supra note 192 (analyzing nativist sentiment at this time in U.S. history).

[194]See Deborah A. Ramirez, *The Mixed Jury and the Ancient Custom of Trial by Jury de Medietate Linguae: A History and A Proposal for Change*, 74 B.U. L. REV. 777 (1994).

A few commentators have advocated the extension of the franchise to noncitizens,[195] which would have a dramatic impact on Latina/o voting power.[196] Along those lines, one could advocate allowing noncitizens, perhaps only those who have fulfilled a residency requirement by living in a jurisdiction for a certain length of time, to serve on juries. This would allow for the possibility of a more representative cross-section of the community, including a larger percentage of Latina/os, to participate. By making juries appear more representative and impartial, noncitizen service on juries would allow decisions to carry more legitimacy with the greater Latina/o community.

By barring a portion of the community from the voting booths and the jury rooms, citizenship requirements deny input from a segment of the community and limit our ability to have political processes that fully represent the larger community. Consequently, at the individual level, noncitizens with criminal or civil disputes must have them decided by a jury *not* of their peers. In this way, the citizenship requirement for jury service tests the nation's true commitment to a trial before a jury pulled from a cross-section of the community. Today, noncitizens in the community are not full members of, or participants in, American society.

The increase in naturalization rates among Latina/os in the 1990s may reduce the underrepresentation of Mexican immigrants on juries.[197] However, because of a variety of considerations, including class, language, and other factors,[198] that development alone is unlikely to increase Latina/o jury participation to a level that would reflect the percentage of Latina/os in the general community.

The citizenship requirement for jury service should be placed in its larger social and political context. Historically, citizenship status often has been used to rationalize discrimination against, and the mistreatment of, Latina/os.[199] The citizen/noncitizen distinction helps legitimate not only the protections afforded Mexican Americans in *Hernandez v. Texas* but also the "repatriation" of Mexican immigrants and U.S. citizens of Mexican ancestry during the Great Depression, the mass deportation campaign that same year directed at persons of Mexican ancestry in Operation "Wetback," and the deadly border enforcement measures pursued by the U.S. government today.[200]

Given the lessons of history, we should be leery of differential treatment of Latina/os based on citizenship status.[201] Ultimately, the social benefits of the citizenship

---

[195]See supra note 193.
[196]See Joaquin Avila, *Political Apartheid in California: Consequences of Excluding a Growing Noncitizen Population* (UCLA Chicano Studies Research Center, Latino Policy and Issues Brief, L.A., Cal.), Dec. 2003, *available at* http://www.chicano.ucla.edu/press/siteart/LPIB_09Dec2003.pdf (last visited Apr. 25, 2005). Recently, immigrants have been pushing for voting rights in local elections and several jurisdictions have been weighing such proposals. See Rachel L. Swarns, *Immigrants Raise Call for Right to Be Voters*, N.Y. TIMES, Aug. 9, 2004, at A13.
[197]See Kevin R. Johnson, *Latina/os and the Political Process: The Need for Critical Inquiry*, 81 OR. L. REV. 917, 930-31 (2002).
[198]See supra text accompanying notes 177-79.
[199]See supra text accompanying notes 145-47.
[200]See supra text accompanying notes 4-11.
[201]*Cf.* Ruben J. García, *Across the Borders: Immigrant Status and Identity in Law and LatCrit Theory*, 55 FLA. L. REV. 511 (2003) (arguing that Congress should amend anti-discrimination laws to prohibit discrimination based on immigration status).

requirement for jury service may outweigh the costs to the perceived impartiality and legitimacy of juries by diminishing Latina/o representation on juries.

B. The English Language Requirement

Under federal law, to be eligible for jury service, a person must be able to read, write, understand and speak English.[202] Many states have similar English language proficiency requirements.[203] In the days before *Hernandez v. Texas*, English language ability had been used to justify the lack of representation of persons of Mexican ancestry on juries[204] even though many Mexican Americans spoke English fluently.

In the modern United States, with its high levels of immigration from non-English speaking nations,[205] English language requirements have disparate racial impacts on jury pools. A substantial percentage of Latina/os in this country are native Spanish speakers.[206] Many Asian immigrants, as well as Native Americans in areas of the country where indigenous languages are the primary languages spoken by significant portions of the local population, also do not speak English as a first language.[207]

In U.S. society today, with large scale immigration and a large immigrant population, language proficiency may serve as a proxy for race. "Given the huge numbers of immigrants who enter this country from Asian and Latin American countries whose citizens are not white and who in most cases do not speak English, criticism of the inability to speak English coincides neatly with race."[208] Language, like citizenship, requirements for jury service have disparate impacts on minority communities, particularly Latin American and Asian immigrant communities. They tend to reduce the representation of significant populations of the community and restrict the degree to which the jury will be pulled from a representative cross-section of the community. Like the citizenship requirement for jury service, English language requirements make juries less, not more, representative of the greater community.

The English language requirement for jury service has predictable impacts on the Latina/o community. It dilutes Latina/o jury service and moves jury pools further away from the ideal of representing a fair cross-section of the community.

If truly committed to juries representing a cross-section of the community, we should re-evaluate whether limiting juror eligibility to English speakers costs more than it benefits the system as a whole. The English language requirement has racial-

---

[202]See 28 U.S.C. § 1865(b)(2), (3) (2000).

[203]See, e.g., ALA. CODE § 12-16-60(a)(2) (1978); N.Y. JUD. CODE § 510(4) (Consol. 1983); COLO. REV. STAT. 13-71-105 (2)(b) (2000).

[204]See, e.g., Lugo v. Texas, 124 S.W. 344, 348 (1938).

[205]See supra text accompanying notes 182-89.

[206]See Christopher D. Ruiz Cameron, *How the García Cousins Lost Their Accents: Understanding the Language of Title VII Decisions Approving English-Only Rules as a Product of Racial Dualism, Latino Invisibility, and Legal Indeterminacy*, 85 CAL. L. REV. 1347, 1364-67 (1997) (analyzing importance of Spanish language to Latina/o identity).

[207]See Allison M. Dussias, *Waging War With Words: Native Americans' Continuing Struggle Against the Suppression of Their Languages*, 60 OHIO ST. L.J. 901 (1999).

[208]Bill Ong Hing, *Beyond the Rhetoric of Assimilation and Cultural Pluralism: Addressing the Tension of Separatism and Conflict in an Immigration-Driven Multiracial Society*, 81 CAL. L. REV. 863, 874 (1993).

ly disparate impacts, especially at a time in U.S. history when immigration has made the nation increasingly diverse, linguistically as well as racially.[209]

Various logistical difficulties obviously would arise if the law was changed to permit non-English speaking persons to serve on juries. The costs of accommodating non-English speakers would not be inconsequential. The translations and interpreters necessary for a mixed language jury would cost money, not a trivial matter because the courts perennially face serious funding problems. An important question would be how jury deliberations might work if all jurors did not speak English.[210] However, the racial impacts of the English language requirement have significant costs to the racial demographics of the jury that deserve consideration and might well outweigh the associated costs.

C. The Exclusion of Felons

Under federal law, convicted felons whose civil rights have not been restored, and persons with felony charges pending, are excluded from jury service.[211] The racially disparate impacts of the criminal justice system in the United States are well-documented,[212] as is the dramatic expansion of the crimes that constitute felonies.[213] Consequently, minority groups are over-represented among those excluded from jury service by the bar on convicted felons.

For example, more than thirty percent of the potentially eligible African American men in Florida and Alabama are denied the right to serve on juries, as well as the right to vote.[214] "Fourteen percent of African-American men are ineligible to vote because of criminal convictions. In seven states, one in four black men are [sic] permanently barred from voting because of their [sic] criminal records."[215] Far smaller percentages of whites are declared ineligible to vote and for jury service by this rule. The end result of the prohibition of felons from jury service is racially

---

[209]See supra text accompanying notes 205-07.

[210]I thank Nancy Marder for bringing this issue to my attention.

[211]See 28 U.S.C. § 1865(b)(5) (2000). The disenfranchisement of convicted felons by the states was most recently upheld by the Supreme Court in Richardson v. Ramirez, 418 U.S. 24 (1974).

[212]See, e.g., DAVID COLE, NO EQUAL JUSTICE: RACE AND CLASS IN THE AMERICAN CRIMINAL JUSTICE SYSTEM (1999); RANDALL KENNEDY, RACE, CRIME AND THE LAW (1998); Cruz Reynoso, *Hispanics and the Criminal Justice System, in* HISPANICS IN THE UNITED STATES: AN AGENDA FOR THE TWENTY-FIRST CENTURY 277 (Pastora San Juan Cafferty & David W. Engstrom eds., 2000); Mary Romero, *State Violence, and the Social and Legal Construction of Latino Criminality: From El Bandido to Gang Member*, 78 DEN. U. L. REV. 1081, 1088-98 (2001).

[213]See William J. Stuntz, *The Pathological Politics of Criminal Law*, 100 MICH. L. REV. 505 (2001).

[214]See John O. Calmore, *Race-Conscious Voting Rights and the New Demography in a Multiracing America*, 79 N.C. L. REV. 1253, 1277-80 & nn.115-16 (2001); see also *Developments in the Law: The Law of Prisons*, 115 HARV. L. REV. 1839, 1845 (2002) ("Florida has disqualified 31.2% of its black voting-age population—the second highest rate in the nation [Alabama's rate was 31.5%]—based on felony convictions.") (footnote omitted).

[215]George P. Fletcher, *Disenfranchisement as Punishment: Reflections on the Racial Uses of Infamia*, 46 UCLA L. REV. 1895, 1900 (1999) (footnotes omitted). For critical analysis of the prohibition of felons from serving on juries, see Brian C. Kalt, *The Exclusion of Felons From Jury Service*, 53 AM. U.L. REV. 65 (2003); see also Alec C. Ewald, *"Civil Death": The Ideological Paradox of Criminal Disenfranchisement Law in the United States*, 2002 WIS. L. REV. 1045 (questioning state laws that bar convicted felons from voting); Carlos M. Portugal, Comment, *Democracy Frozen in Devonian Amber: The Racial Impact of Permanent Felon Disenfranchisement in Florida*, 57 U. MIAMI L. REV. 1317 (2003) (same).

skewed jury pools, which tend to produce juries that deviate substantially from a cross-section of the community.

Like African Americans, Latina/os are disparately affected by the exclusion of felons from juries. Over-represented in the criminal justice system compared to their proportion of the population, Latina/os can be expected to be excluded from jury service in disproportionate numbers by the bar on felons serving as jurors.[216] This is the case in states with large Latina/o populations and large numbers of Latina/os in prison, such as California, Arizona, New York, Florida, and Texas.[217]

In certain circumstances, disenfranchisement laws can be successfully challenged under the Equal Protection Clause of the Fourteenth Amendment.[218] Proving that state laws were enacted with a discriminatory intent is difficult,[219] although possible in certain circumstances.[220] However, a facially neutral explanation exists for the rule that convicted felons cannot be relied upon to uphold the law; it is difficult to prove that this is not the true intent for barring convicts from jury service.[221]

Some convicted felons, as well as those charged with felonies, may be biased against the government, an important consideration in any criminal prosecution. However, it seems appropriate to reconsider the blanket exclusion based on group membership and, as done with respect to other life experiences, allow parties to strike "for cause" jurors on an individual basis in a specific case when they cannot impartially weigh the evidence.

It may seem eminently reasonable to deny persons convicted of serious crimes from jury service. However, the racial overlay to the criminal justice system in the United States strongly suggests that the criminal laws are unevenly enforced.[222] Race-based law enforcement has plagued the nation for centuries and continues to do so, as the recent flap over the phenomenon of "driving while Black" starkly reminds us.[223]

Attention should be given to whether barring felons from jury service continues to make sense in light of what we suspect about unequal operation of the modern criminal justice system. The racially skewed impacts of the criminal justice system have ripple effects on jury service and tends to diminish Latina/o representation on

[216]See Reynoso, supra note 212.

[217]See MARISA J. DEMEO & STEVEN A. OCHOA, MEXICAN AMERICAN LEGAL DEFENSE AND EDUCA-TION FUND, DIMINISHED VOTING POWER IN THE LATINO COMMUNITY: THE IMPACT OF FELONY DISENFRANCHISEMENT LAWS IN TEN TARGETED STATES (2003).

[218]See Washington v. Davis, 426 U.S. 229 (1976).

[219]See Theodore Eisenberg & Sheri Lynn Johnson, *The Effects of Intent: Do We Know How Legal Standards Work?*, 76 CORNELL L. REV. 1151 (1991) (providing empirical data showing difficulties imposed on plaintiffs by discriminatory intent standard); see also supra note 132 (citing authorities criticizing the discriminatory intent requirement).

[220]See, e.g., Hunter v. Underwood, 471 U.S. 222, 223 (1985) (holding that an Alabama constitutional provision that disenfranchised any person convicted of, among other crimes, "any . . . involving moral turpitude," had been adopted with the intent to discriminate against African Americans).

[221]See Fletcher, supra note 215, at 1899; Kalt, supra note 215, at 122-28.

[222]See supra note 212 (citing authorities).

[223]See, e.g., David A. Harris, *The Stories, the Statistics, and the Law: Why "Driving While Black" Matters*, 84 MINN. L. REV. 265, 275-88 (1999); Tracey Maclin, *Race and the Fourth Amendment*, 51 VAND. L. REV. 333, 342-62 (1998); Katheryn K. Russell, *"Driving While Black": Corollary Phenomena and Collateral Consequences*, 40 B.C. L. REV. 717, 718-19 (1999).

civil and criminal juries, thus undermining the legitimacy of the judicial system in the eyes of the Latina/o community.

D. The Use of Peremptory Challenges to Strike Latinas/os by Proxy

The use of peremptory challenges to strike jurors tends to reduce Latina/o representation on juries, although not in as systematic a fashion as certain jury qualifications. This is the case even though the Supreme Court has barred the consideration of race in the exercise of peremptories.[224] Language proficiency, which the Court has permitted parties to rely upon in exercising a peremptory challenge to strike a juror, may serve as a convenient proxy for race.

In 1986, the U.S. Supreme Court held that a prosecutor could not exercise a peremptory challenge on the basis of race to strike African Americans, a practice that previously had been permitted.[225] Reflecting the triumph of *Hernandez v. Texas*,[226] the lower courts extended this bar on the use of peremptory challenges to strike Latina/os from juries.[227] The prohibition protects Latina/os from the most flagrant exclusion from jury service on account of their race.

However, peremptory challenges based on certain so-called race neutral reasons are permitted and can have racially disparate impacts. The Supreme Court expanded such possibilities to the detriment of Latina/os in *Hernandez v. New York*.[228] In that case, the prosecutor, claiming that the prospective jurors might disregard official translations, used peremptory challenges to strike two bilingual Spanish speaking Latina/os in a criminal case involving a Latino defendant.[229] Consistent with *Hernandez v. Texas*, the Court assumed that Hispanics were a racial group deserving the protections of the Equal Protection Clause.[230] Spanish speaking ability, however, was treated as a "race neutral" explanation for the exercise of peremptory challenges

---

[224]See *infra* text accompanying notes 225-27.

[225]See Batson v. Kentucky, 476 U.S. 79 (1986); see also Edmonson v. Leesville Concrete Co., 500 U.S. 614 (1991) (extending *Batson* to civil case); J.E.B. v. Alabama *ex rel.* T.B., 511 U.S. 127 (1994) (holding that exercise of peremptory challenge based on gender violated Constitution); Nancy S. Marder, *Beyond Gender: Peremptory Challenges and the Roles of the Jury*, 73 TEX. L. REV. 1041 (1995) (analyzing continuing usefulness of peremptory challenges after ban on consideration of race and gender in their exercise) In *Batson*, the Court repeatedly relied on *Hernandez v. Texas* and its holding that juries could not be excluded because of their race. See *Batson*, 476 U.S. at 84 n.3, 86 n.5, 86 n.7, 88, 90, 94, 100.

[226]See supra text accompanying notes 107-39.

[227]See, e.g., United States v. Martinez-Salazar, 528 U.S. 304, 315 (2000) ("Under the Equal Protection Clause, a defendant may not exercise a peremptory challenge to remove a potential juror solely on the basis of the juror's gender, ethnic origin, or race.") (citations omitted); Fernandez v. Roe, 286 F.3d 1073, 1077 (9th Cir. 2002) ("Both Hispanics and African-Americans constitute 'cognizable groups' for" purposes of evaluation whether peremptory challenges were based on race."), *cert. denied*, 537 U.S. 1000 (2002); Galarza v. Keane, 252 F.3d 630 (2d Cir. 2001) (applying *Batson* to claim by Hispanic defendant claiming that prosecutor used peremptory challenges to strike Hispanics); United States v. Novaton, 271 F.3d 968, 1000-04 (11th Cir. 2001) (same), *cert. denied*, 535 U.S. 1120 (2002).

[228]500 U.S. 352 (1991).

[229]See People v. Hernandez, 75 N.Y.2d 350, 353 (1990). The dissent in the Court of Appeals for the State of New York observed that "While the people emphasize their interest in excluding Spanish-speaking jurors because of the presence of an interpreter, there is no indication that any other members of the panel were also asked if they spoke Spanish." See *id.* at 363 (Kaye, J., dissenting). For criticism of the Court's decisions on peremptory challenges, see Sandra Guerra Thompson, *The Non-Discrimination Ideal of* Hernandez v. Texas *Confronts a "Culture" of Discrimination: The Amazing Story of* Miller-El v. Texas *and* Clare Sheridan, *Peremptory Challenges: Lessons From* Hernandez v. Texas, in this volume.

[230]See supra text accompanying notes 140-59.

to strike jurors, despite the correlation between language and Latina/o identity.[231] The Court found that, absent a finding of a discriminatory intent, reliance on peremptories to strike bilingual Spanish/English speakers was permissible.[232] *Hernandez v. New York* has been followed in the lower courts to authorize the use of peremptories to strike bilingual Spanish speakers.[233]

The racial impacts of *Hernandez v. New York* bear similarities to the exclusion of Mexican American jurors at issue in *Hernandez v. Texas*. Both involve the exclusion of Latina/os from jury service. In one, the Court looked beyond the denial of discrimination by the state and demanded an explanation.[234] In the other case, the Court reflexively accepted the race neutral explanation, suspect as it was under the circumstances. In certain respects, the Supreme Court in 1954 had a more sophisticated view of the workings of racial discrimination than the 1991 Court.

Because of the overlap between language and race,[235] and increased bilingualism resulting from immigration, the use of peremptories based on language will decrease Latina/o representation on juries. Moreover, because fluency in the Spanish language has been used to strike jurors in cases involving the translation of Spanish, Latina/os are more likely to be stricken in precisely those cases, such as *Hernandez v. New York*, in which Latina/o representation generally is considered to be most necessary.

The bar on the consideration of race in jury selection may adversely affect racial minorities in another, less obvious way. As Justice Clarence Thomas has emphasized,[236] racial minorities may "rue the day" that race was barred from consideration in the use of peremptory challenges. One could see a minority striking white jurors in the hopes of securing a more racially diverse jury, especially given the skewed

---

[231]See supra text accompanying note 208.

[232]See *Hernandez v. New York*, 500 U.S. at 369-70. A plurality of the Court, however, acknowledged the importance of language to personal identity and group membership and that, in certain circumstances (but not those in the case before it), language may be relied on as a pretext for race. See *id.* at 370-72; *cf.* Kevin R. Johnson & George A. Martínez, *Discrimination by Proxy: The Case of Proposition 227 and the Ban on Bilingual Education*, 33 U.C. DAVIS L. REV. 1227 (2000) (contending that a political campaign culminating in the passage of a law ending bilingual education in California employed language as a proxy for race). The Court's holding in *Hernandez v. New York* has been the subject of sustained academic criticism. See, e.g., Jeffrey S. Brand, *The Supreme Court, Equal Protection and Jury Selection: Denying That Race Still Matters*, 1994 WIS. L. REV. 511, 600-05 (1994); Marina Hsieh, *"Language-Qualifying" Juries to Exclude Bilingual Speakers*, 66 BROOK. L. REV. 1181 (2001); Kevin R. Johnson, *Civil Rights and Immigration: Challenges for the Latino Community in the Twenty-First Century*, 8 LA RAZA L.J. 42, 74-76 (1995); Sheri L. Johnson, *The Language and Culture (Not to Say Race) of Peremptory Challenges*, 35 WM. & MARY L. REV. 21, 52-59 (1993); Miguel A. Mendez, *Hernandez: The Wrong Message at the Wrong Time*, 4 STAN. L. & POL'Y REV. 193 (1993); Juan F. Perea, *Hernandez v. New York: Courts, Prosecutor's and the Fear of Spanish*, 21 HOFSTRA L. REV. 1 (1992); Deborah Ramirez, *Excluded Voices: The Disenfranchisement of Ethnic Groups from Jury Service*, 1993 WIS. L. REV. 761 (1993). Over a decade ago, more than twenty states had a bilingual population of more than five percent of their overall population. See *id.* at 807.

[233]See, e.g., Pemberthy v. Beyer, 19 F.3d 857 (3d Cir. 1994), *cert. denied*, 513 U.S. 969 (1994); United States v. Munoz, 15 F.3d 395 (5th Cir. 1994), *cert. denied*, 511 U.S. 1134 (1994); United States v. Changco, 1 F.3d 837 (9th Cir. 1993), *cert. denied*, 510 U.S. 1019 (1993).

[234]See supra text accompanying notes 107-39.

[235]See supra text accompanying note 208.

[236]See Georgia v. McCollum, 505 U.S. 42, 60 (1992) (Thomas, J., concurring in the judgment). For discussion of these issues, see Arielle Siebert, Batson v. Kentucky: *Application to Whites and the Effect on the Peremptory Challenge System*, 32 COLUM. J. L. & SOC. PROBS. 307 (1999); Tanya E. Coke, Note, *Lady Justice May be Blind, But is She a Soul Sister? Race-Neutrality and the Ideal of Representative Juries*, 69 N.Y.U. L. REV. 327 (1994).

pool rendered by the current set of juror eligibility rules.[237] This illustrates the perceived problem with the Supreme Court's "color blind" approach to the interpretation and application of the Equal Protection Clause.[238] Such reasoning may be invoked by the Court to bar a Latina/o from striking white jurors in an effort to impanel a diverse jury.

As we have seen, juror eligibility requirements tend to decrease the racial diversity of the jury pool. Litigants are denied the opportunity to use peremptory challenges or any other device that might allow for the impaneling of a more diverse jury.

E. The Dangers of Racially Skewed Juries in a Multiracial Society

Despite the promise of *Hernandez v. Texas*, Latina/os remain seriously underrepresented on juries. Systematic exclusion has been replaced by facially neutral juror eligibility requirements and other devices. Jury eligibility requirements tend to reduce, not improve, Latina/o representation on juries.

The underrepresentation of Latina/os on grand and petit juries threatens to undermine the impartiality of the jury system, as well as the civil and criminal justice systems as a whole.[239] It dampens the belief among Latina/os in the fairness and impartiality of the justice system and promotes distrust of the system and its outcomes

After an initial increase in representation after the Court decided *Hernandez v. Texas*, Latina/os have become less, not more, represented on juries. Once again, the trajectory of *Hernandez* resembles that of *Brown v. Board of Education*. The "war on drugs" has vastly expanded the number of Latina/os incarcerated and barred an ever-growing percentage of the community from jury service.[240] Immigration has increased as well, with a growing Latina/o immigrant population in the United States.[241] More noncitizens live in the United States today than in 1954; more noncitizens are involved in the criminal and civil justice systems, and more are barred from jury service. Many languages other than English are spoken in this country, with Spanish as the primary language spoken by many Latina/os. As a result, we face a near-crisis with respect to a justice system that denies ever-larger segments of the Latina/o community from jury service and subjects Latina/os to a justice system that appears much like that of Texas before 1954.

This is not simply a theoretical problem of democracy and community membership, but instead may have dramatic practical consequences. Before our eyes, we can see a recipe for mass unrest and violence. Consider that a significant minority community is denied the right to vote[242] and to serve on juries, the two cornerstones

---

[237]See supra text accompanying notes 182-223 (reviewing race-neutral reasons for underrepresentation of Latina/os on juries).

[238]For a more general criticism of the Court's color-blindness jurisprudence, see Neil Gotanda, *A Critique of "Our Constitution is Color-Blind,"* 44 STAN. L. REV. 1 (1991); *cf.* Daria Roithmayr, *Deconstructing the Distinction Between Bias and Merit*, 85 CAL. L. REV. 1449 (1997) (analyzing how a facially neutral concept of "merit" used in law school admissions allows for racial discrimination).

[239]See supra text accompanying notes 160-81 (reviewing the persistent underrepresentation of Latina/os on juries).

[240]See supra text accompanying notes 211-13.

[241]See supra text accompanying notes 185-89.

[242]See supra text accompanying notes 191-96.

of U.S. democracy. This group may question the legitimacy of the political process and the operation of government. The legitimacy of the justice system and the outcomes it produces is fostered by having diverse juries; conversely, the legitimacy of the process is seriously undercut by having homogeneous juries that lack meaningful representation of certain segments of the community:

> The jury system is supposed to establish the legitimacy of the justice rendered—to prevent . . . mistrust and hostility from occurring. But racially connected misconceptions and prejudice can imperil the impartiality of a jury. Only by balancing this prejudice—which jurors of all kinds feel about issues and people—through a jury composed of a cross-section of the community can impartiality be fostered.[243]

Put differently, being locked out of the political process, Latina/os can be expected to lack faith in that process, as well as its outcomes, and to consider political and legal decisions rendered by a non-democratic process as lacking legitimacy. As a result, they may seek relief through means outside the formal processes.

Consider an example. The reaction to a racially-mixed jury's conviction of a minority defendant differs substantially from the public perception of the criminal conviction of an African American by "an all-white jury."[244] Indeed, the mere reference to an "all-white jury" amounts to a strong rebuke of the jury verdict, in no small part because it taps into a notorious history of racism in the criminal justice system in the United States. The riots following the all-white jury's acquittal of the Los Angeles police officers videotaped beating African American Rodney King,[245] serve as a ready reminder of the incendiary potential of such perceptions.

In the Rodney King case, the African American community believed that because the jury did not represent the community as a whole (especially the African American community), its verdict was illegitimate. This widespread perception spurred on, if not justified, the mass uprising that followed the acquittal in May 1992. The teachings of the Rodney King violence have been grimly summarized as follows:

> Many lessons may be learned from the embers of burned homes and storefronts in South Central Los Angeles. Among the most important is that America's failure to include minorities in judicial decisions that affect their lives is a prescription for chaos . . . The lesson is not new. *Violent reactions*

---

[243]VAN DYKE, supra note 167, at 32.

[244]See Albert W. Alschuler, *Racial Quotas and the Jury*, 44 DUKE L.J. 704, 704 (1995) ("Few statements are more likely to evoke disturbing images of American criminal justice than this one: 'The defendant was tried by an all-white jury.'"); James Forman, Jr., *Juries and Race in the Nineteenth Century*, 113 YALE L.J. 895 (2004) (stating that one of the goals of Reconstruction Amendments was "to protect[] black victims from all-white juries"); Coke, supra note 236, at 327-31 (offering examples of controversial verdicts rendered by all-white juries); see also Carter v. Jury Comm'n, 396 U.S. 320, 341, 342-43 (1970) (Douglas, J., dissenting in part) ("[W]here there exists a pattern of discrimination, an all-white or all-black jury commission in these times probably means that the race in power retains authority to control the community's official life, and that no jury will likely be selected that is a true cross-section of the community.").

[245]See generally READING RODNEY KING, READING URBAN UPRISING (Robert Gooding-Williams ed., 1993). In the Rodney King case, the trial was moved from downtown Los Angeles to Simi Valley, a white suburb, with an all-white jury ultimately hearing the case.

> *to miscarriages of justice by white judges and all-white juries are an all-too-common signpost of American history.*[246]

Latina/os participated in the unrest and comprised a large percentage of the people arrested and injured during the violence.[247] As this suggests, social anomie, and deep dissatisfaction with the criminal justice system, is not limited to African Americans. Such distrust continues to this day. Over the last few years, signs of Latina/o resistance have begun to emerge.[248]

Currently, racial minorities see the courts in the United States that are predominantly white, with white lawyers and judges as the norm.[249] "Nonwhites are underrepresented on juries in the vast majority of courts in the country."[250] The decisions meted out by the justice system are viewed as having racially disparate impacts, with "justice" being dispensed, and defined, by white people. This is not healthy for a society that extols its democratic institutions, embraces diversity, and preaches equality under the law.

Hernandez v. Texas promised to improve the operation of the justice system for Latina/os. It ended racial bars on jury participation by Mexican Americans but has yet to fulfill the promise of integrated juries. Reforms must be considered and implemented to ensure that juries do not exclude large portions of certain minority communities, including the Latina/o community. If such steps are not taken, or are not successful, it is only a matter of time until a racially-charged case will cause national controversy and political protest, if not mass violence, like that seen in Los Angeles in May 1992.[251] In sum, the wholesale political disenfranchisement of large segments of the Latina/o community is a recipe for civil unrest and social disaster.

CONCLUSION

Hernandez v. Texas was a momentous decision, whose 50th birthday merits the scholarly attention that it has been given. The Court's decision helped expand the protections of the Fourteenth Amendment to include Latina/os—"neither Black nor White"[252]—and for the first time in a Supreme Court decision recognized the discrimination against Mexican Americans in American social life.

In later cases, the Court made clear that Latina/os in fact were generally protected under the Equal Protection Clause. In addition, the Court's finding in *Hernandez v. Texas* that persons of Mexican ancestry were racialized in Texas was later

---

[246]Jeffrey S. Brand, *The Supreme Court, Equal Protection, and Jury Selection: Denying That Race Still Matters*, 1994 WIS. L. REV. 511, 516 (1994) (emphasis added) (footnote omitted).

[247]See Johnson, supra note 232, at 64-65.

[248]See, e.g., David G. Gutiérrez, *Migration, Emergent Ethnicity, and the "Third Space": The Shifting Politics of Nationalism in Greater Mexico*, 86 J. AM. HIST. 481 (1999) (analyzing significance of mass protests by persons of Mexican ancestry, waving Mexican flags, opposing California's anti-immigrant Proposition 187); Cameron, supra note 178, at 1089-93 (discussing recent efforts of Latina/os to organize into labor unions); Johnson, supra note 197, at 930-31 (noting increase in naturalization of immigrants in wake of anti-immigrant legislation of the 1990s).

[249]See Hernández-Truyol, supra note 180, at 373-75.

[250]VAN DYKE, supra note 167, at 28.

[251]See supra text accompanying notes 54-67 (analyzing Sleepy Lagoon murder case).

[252]Rachel F. Moran, *Neither Black Nor White*, 2 HARV. LATINO L. REV. 61 (1997).

extended to apply to localities across the United States. The decision thus contributed to greater civil rights protections for Latina/os nationwide.

The case came at an opportune time in the nation's history. At the helm of the Supreme Court, Chief Justice Earl Warren had seen first-hand, the discrimination against persons of Mexican ancestry in California and could appreciate the claim of discrimination being made about the justice system in Texas, which was not all that different from that in the Golden State. Racial segregation against African Americans was under scrutiny, as exemplified by *Brown v. Board of Education*, and it was difficult to justify prohibiting discrimination against one victimized group while permitting it against another.

However, the nation has a long way to go before it realizes the promise of *Hernandez v. Texas*. Race neutral requirements for jury service that correlate with race in U.S. society—citizenship and language requirements—as well as the disqualification of felons, have resulted in the serious underrepresentation of Latina/os on juries. Peremptory challenges based on bilingual proficiency also allow certain Latina/os to be struck from juries.

Just as the promise of *Brown v. Board of Education* has yet to be achieved with respect to racially integrated public schools, the promise of *Hernandez v. Texas* has not yet been fulfilled. And just as we have grappled mightily with how to integrate our schools, we will need to struggle to ensure that our juries are in fact representative of U.S. society as a whole.

Mi Profundo Azul: Why Latinos Have a Right to Sing the Blues

Juan Francisco Perea*

In the same sense that Columbus "discovered" America, the United States Supreme Court "discovered" Mexican-Americans in *Hernandez v. Texas*.[1] More precisely, the Court recognized what had been painfully, and long, obvious to Mexican Americans in the lands forcibly stolen from Mexico over a century before: that Mexican-Americans were subject to extreme, overt white racism. Forcefully, the Court decided that the systematic exclusion of Mexican Americans from Texas juries violated the Equal Protection Clause.

In this chapter, I discuss the historical context of Jim Crow segregation deployed against Mexican Americans in the Southwestern United States. I discuss both the pervasive segregation imposed upon Mexican Americans in all areas of life, and then the particular ways and means of segregation in the jury box. Against this historical background, I discuss the Warren Court's decision in *Hernandez v. Texas*. The Court was clearly correct in deciding that Mexican Americans in Texas were subject to racism and deserved Supreme Court enforcement of equal protection principles. Also assessed against this historical background, the contrary decisions of the lower Texas courts in the *Hernandez* case look like profoundly cynical and self-serving endorsements of white racism.

Significantly, the Warren Court's reasoning in *Hernandez v. Texas* contained language suggesting that the understanding of equal protection could be broadened to encompass any group shown to be subject to shifting community prejudices. Accordingly, the decision can be read to promise an equal protection doctrine responsive to our developing understanding of racism and its deployment against different groups of people. A more recent *Hernandez* decision, *Hernandez v. New York*, put that promise of the earlier decision to the test in a remarkably similar context: again, the exclusion of Latino jurors, but this time because of language discrimination against their bilingualism. This Rehnquist Court decision shows that the promise of a broader, progressive equal protection doctrine has not been fulfilled. I

*I'd like to thank the editor, Michael A. Olivas, for his inspiration, perspiration, courage, humor, and patience in organizing the conference that yielded this book. Over the years, Professor Olivas has demonstrated, time and time again, the importance of planting and nurturing seeds of growth and knowledge in his teaching, his writing, his advocacy and his collegiality. Many thanks to you, Michael, from one who has grown through your efforts and example.
[1] Hernandez v. Texas, 347 U.S. 475 (1954).

preface my discussion of the *Hernandez v. New York* case with historical context on language discrimination against Latinos, which, like segregation against Mexican Americans, has a long, demonstrable history with considerable present ramifications. I then discuss *Hernandez v. New York* and its troubling shortcomings. Comparing the two *Hernandez* decisions yields interesting insights into some of the profound differences between the Warren and Rehnquist Courts in their interpretations of equal protection and their respective abilities to recognize discrimination.

I conclude with a few thoughts on why Latinos have a right to sing the blues: given the institutional nature of the Supreme Court and its constituency, the forecast for a meaningful equal protection responsive to Latino particularity is not good.

The Meaning and Historical Context of Segregation against Mexican Americans

I begin by describing the sociological understanding of segregation and providing historical context within which to understand the long deployment of segregation against Mexican Americans in the Southwest. Sociologists define segregation as:

> a system of racial etiquette that keeps the oppressed group separate from the oppressor when both are doing equal tasks, like learning the multiplication tables, but allows intimate closeness when the tasks are hierarchical, like cooking or cleaning for white employers.[2]

The segregation law challenged, and upheld, in the Supreme Court's most famous endorsement of segregation, *Plessy v. Ferguson*,[3] illustrates the definition perfectly. "Louisiana statute required that railroad companies provide Aequal but separate accommodations for the white and colored races," but provided an exception stating that "nothing in this act shall be construed as applying to nurses attending children of the other race."[4] When Whites and Blacks might otherwise share space on equal terms, riding together in the same railroad cars, the statute commanded separation of the races. When the relationship was clearly hierarchical and Blacks were in a subordinate position to Whites, such as when a Black nursemaid was tending to a White child, then the statute allows proximity and even intimate physical contact between the races. Segregation laws attempt to express an idea and to impute it to their nonwhite targets: that nonwhites are unfit to be in proximity to Whites when the nature of the interaction might suggest equality with Whites.

The segregation imposed upon Mexican Americans by whites is quite comparable to, though much less well known, than the segregation suffered by Blacks in the United States. Jim Crow, enforced against Mexican Americans, was a fact of life throughout the Southwest.[5] Carey McWilliams, lawyer and historian of Mexican America, described the pervasive segregation in the California citrus belt:

---

[2]JAMES W. LOEWEN, LIES MY TEACHER TOLD ME 162 (1995).
[3]Plessy v. Ferguson, 163 U.S. 537 (1896).
[4]Statute reproduced in Plessy, 163 U.S. at 540-41.
[5]See, e.g., PAUL SCHUSTER TAYLOR, AN AMERICAN-MEXICAN FRONTIER 226 (1934) ("The segregation of residence according to race, which is common in the rural areas of the United States where numbers of Mexicans live, exists also in the towns of Nueces County[, Texas].");). Professor Laura Gomez's excellent study demonstrates that, due to the unique demographics in New Mexico, Mexican elites there were able to situate themselves as an "off-white" wedge group, subject to white racism but also exercising sufficient agency to oppress other groups such as Indians and Blacks. See Laura E. Gómez, Ph.D., *Off-White in an Age of White Supremacy: Mexican Elites and the Rights of Indians and Blacks in Nineteenth-Century New Mexico*, 25 CHICANO-LATINO L. REV. 9, 21-24, 41-45 (2005).

Throughout the citrus belt, the workers are Spanish-speaking, Catholic, and dark-skinned, the owners are white, Protestant, and English-speaking. The owners occupy the heights, the Mexicans the lowlands. . . . While the towns deny that they practice segregation, nevertheless segregation is the rule. Since the Mexicans all live in jim-town, it has always been easy to effect residential segregation. The omnipresent Mexican school is, of course, an outgrowth of segregated residence. The swimming pools in the towns are usually reserved for "whites," with an insulting exception being noted in the designation of one day in the week as "Mexican Day" . . . Mexicans attend separate schools and churches, occupy the balcony seats in the motion-picture theaters, and frequent separate places of amusement. . . . The whole system of employment, in fact, is perfectly designed to insulate workers from employers in every walk of life, from the cradle to the grave, from the church to the saloon.[6]

By the 1920s, the *de jure* or *de facto* segregation of most public facilities to exclude Mexican Americans was common in California.[7] Throughout the Southwest, segregated schools for Mexican American children were also common.[8]

In Texas, Whites established segregation that was no different in its pervasive isolation of Mexicans and Mexican Americans. This segregation "cut across all spheres of rural life, separation in domicile, separation in politics, and separation in education."[9] One study concluded that 117 Texas towns practiced segregation against Mexican Americans, and most of these towns enacted laws requiring segregation.[10] As described by David Montejano,

The modern [Texas] order framed Mexican-Anglo relations in stark "Jim Crow" segregation. Separate quarters for Mexican and Anglo were to be found in the farm towns. Specific rules defined the proper place of Mexicans and regulated interracial contact. The separation was so complete and seemingly absolute that several observers have described the farm society as "caste-like."[11]

White farm owners, who exerted the greatest influence over rural, agricultural Texas society defined Mexicans as their manual laborers by race, and enforced their status through economic coercion, physical hardship, and the denial of education.[12]

---

[6]CAREY MCWILLIAMS, SOUTHERN CALIFORNIA COUNTRY 219 (1946).

[7]CHARLES M. WOLLENBERG, SEGREGATION AND EXCLUSION IN CALIFORNIA SCHOOLS, 1855-1975, 113 (1978) [hereinafter WOLLENBERG]. See, e.g., Lopez v. Seccombe, 71 F. Supp. 769 (S.D. Cal. 1944) (Mexican American and Puerto Ricans in San Bernardino, Ca., sued successfully for access to a segregated public park).

[8]See CAREY MCWILLIAMS, NORTH FROM MEXICO 272-73 (1949) [hereinafter MCWILLIAMS]; Guadalupe San Miguel, Jr., *The Schooling of Mexicanos in the Southwest*, 1848-1891 *in* THE ELUSIVE QUEST FOR EQUALITY 36-37 (José F. Moreno ed., 1999); Gilbert G. Gonzalez, *Segregation and the Education of Mexican Children*, 1900-1940, *in* THE ELUSIVE QUEST FOR EQUALITY, supra, at 55-58. Jorge C. Rangel & Carlos M. Alcala, *Project Report: De Jure Segregation of Chicanos in Texas Schools*, 7 HARV. C.R.-C.L. L. REV. 307 (1972) [hereinafter Rangel & Alcala]; WOLLENBERG, supra note 8, at 108-35.

[9]DAVID MONTEJANO, ANGLOS AND MEXICANS IN THE MAKING OF TEXAS, 1836-1986 162 (1987) (quoting Paul Taylor).

[10]MARTHA MENCHACA, RECOVERING HISTORY, CONSTRUCTING RACE 287 (U. Texas 2001).

[11]*Id.* At 160 (quoting LEO GREBLER ET AL., THE MEXICAN-AMERICAN PEOPLE 322-25 (1970)).

[12]MONTEJANO, supra note 10, at 191, 197-233.

Residential segregation was enforced through restrictive racial covenants in property deeds, refusals to sell to Mexicans, and White protests when Mexicans attempted to buy in areas reserved for Whites.[13]

The sheer extent of the segregation against Mexican Americans in Texas is painfully clear from the personal recollections of John J. Herrera, one of the lawyers who represented Pete Hernandez in *Hernandez v. Texas*. In a letter published twenty years after the *Hernandez* decision, Herrera recalled:

> The signs in West Texas cafes: NO CHILI! "They mean us, son. Don't go in there," dad would admonish me. The rest of Texas was no better. Seguin [Texas]: a public park with the sign, Negros y Mexicanos Afuera! In a Houston personnel office: "No Mexicans hired." On Washington Ave.: "No Mexicans Allowed in Dance Hall." In a refinery, all water fountains were painted white, black, or brown. You know where I had to drink.[14]

Segregation in the Courtroom: A Historical Overview

Just like segregation in other spheres of life, segregation in the courtroom has a long history. Two of the most significant, visible roles played by the public in the courtroom are the ability to present testimony regarding the events in a trial, and the ability to sit on the jury that determines guilt or innocence. Not surprisingly, given the importance of these responsibilities, racial minority groups have been largely excluded from these public roles in the administration of justice.

The courts became complicit early in skewing the justice system in favor of white defendants and against the interests of victims and defendants of minority races. In *People v. Hall*, decided in 1854, the California Supreme Court interpreted a statute providing that "no Black or Mulatto person, or Indian, shall be allowed to give evidence in favor of, or against a white man."[15] The court decided that this ban on testimony applied to exclude the testimony of Chinese persons against a white defendant, reasoning that the "intention of the [statute] was to throw around the citizen[16] a protection for life and property, which could only be secured by removing him above the corrupting influences of degraded castes."[17] In effect, the ban on the testimony of Blacks, Indians and Chinese left these communities unable to defend themselves against crimes committed against their peoples by Whites when the witnesses were non-white.[18] The ban on the testimony of non-whites was also enforced against Mexican Americans. In 1857, Manuel Dominguez, a delegate to the California Constitutional convention and signer of the California Constitution in 1849, was dismissed as a witness because of his Indian blood and mestizo appearance.[19] Heizer and

---

[13]PAUL SCHUSTER TAYLOR, AN AMERICAN-MEXICAN FRONTIER 226-29 (1934).

[14]John J. Herrera, Letter to the Editor, HOUS. CHRON., May 31, 1974, at 27, quoted in Gómez, supra note 6, at 59.

[15]People v. Hall, 4 Cal. 399 (1854).

[16]"Citizen" should be read "White Person." At the time, the Chinese in California were recent immigrants, and only "free white persons" were allowed to become naturalized citizens.

[17]HALL, 4 Cal. at 403.

[18]See ROBERT F. HEIZER & ALAN F. ALMQUIST, THE OTHER CALIFORNIANS (1971).

[19]HEIZER & ALMQUIST, supra note 19, at 131; LEONARD PITT, DECLINE OF THE CALIFORNIOS 201-02 (1966).

Almquist described the racist rationale for the ban: "it was more desirable to release a Caucasian convicted of murder through the testimony of [non-white] witnesses than it was to permit any deviation in the established policy of white supremacy."[20]

This same policy of white supremacy played out in the exclusion of non-whites from juries. The overt statutory exclusion of Blacks from jury service ended in 1871, when the Supreme Court decided *Strauder v. West Virginia,* which struck down a statute allowing only white males to serve on juries.[21] The *Strauder* Court, however, suggested some of the many other ways that States could exclude Blacks from jury service constitutionally, such as by limiting such service to freeholders, or persons having certain educational qualifications. While this ended de jure segregation on juries, de facto segregation continued for many years afterward. In 1935, the Court decided that the systematic exclusion of qualified Black jurors from juries violated the equal protection clause in *Norris v. Alabama.*[22] Despite these Supreme Court decisions, systematic exclusion of non-white jurors remained persistent.

Mexican Americans were excluded from jury service before, until, and after *Hernandez v. Texas* was decided in 1954. During the 1930s, Mexican Americans in Texas resisted their routine exclusion from jury service, with some success.[23] However, as the *Hernandez* Court recounted, in Jackson County no Mexican American had served on a jury in twenty-five years. This fact bears witness to the resiliency of discriminatory jury selection practices. Even after *Hernandez v. Texas*, Mexican Americans continued to be excluded routinely from juries. A 1970 report by the United States Commission on Civil Rights found "serious and widespread under-representation of Mexican Americans on grand and petit juries in State courts in many areas of the Southwest."[24] The report cited many causes of the underrepresentation studied at that time, some apparently nondiscriminatory, such as limited English-speaking ability (although it is difficult to credit this explanation for otherwise qualified, citizen or resident potential jurors), and hardship posed by jury service for low-income Mexican Americans.[25] The report also cited more credible explanatory factors, including peremptory challenges used to remove Mexican Americans, and selection systems that vested excessive discretion in jury commissioners and judges.[26]

In 1986, the Supreme Court decided that peremptory challenges based explicitly on race violated the Equal Protection Clause in *Batson v. Kentucky.*[27] Accordingly, it might be tempting to think that the Supreme Court has ended the problem of

---

[20]HEIZER & ALMQUIST, supra note 19, at 129.
[21]Strauder v. West Virginia, 100 U.S. 303 (1879).
[22]Norris v. Alabama, 294 U.S. 587 (1935).
[23]Paul S. Taylor describes this resistance in AN AMERICAN-MEXICAN FRONTIER at 246-47 (1934). Taylor reports that requests for Mexican Americans to serve on juries were "acceeded to, and those qualified by knowledge of English, etc., for jury service, have been admitted." *Id.* at 247. Despite such apparent success, this likely did not mean that Mexicans often, or ever, actually served on juries. Through devices such as peremptory challenges, which at the time could be exercised for any reason, including race, Mexicans could easily be excluded from the jury panel actually deciding a case.
[24]UNITED STATES COMMISSION ON CIVIL RIGHTS, MEXICAN AMERICANS AND THE ADMINISTRATION OF JUSTICE IN THE SOUTHWEST 36 (1970) [hereinafter REPORT].
[25]*Id.* at 40-43.
[26]*Id.* at 43-45.
[27]Batson v. Kentucky, 476 U.S. 79 (1986).

discriminatory exclusion of Latinos from jury service. As I will discuss below, however, the exclusion of Latino jurors continues apace today in different guises, including language discrimination.

The *Hernandez v. Texas* decision

In *Hernandez*, the Court considered whether Mexican Americans were a "cognizable class" for equal protection purposes, and, if so, whether the systematic exclusion of Mexican Americans from juries violated the Equal Protection Clause. The Court first rejected the State's theory that the Fourteenth Amendment contemplated only two racial groups, Black and White: "The Fourteenth Amendment is not directed solely against discrimination due to a 'two-class theory' that is, based upon differences between 'white' and 'Negro.'"[28]

The petitioner, Pete Hernandez, had to establish that Mexican Americans in Jackson County were treated as a separate class, distinct from whites and subject to discrimination. The Court described the attitude of the community towards Mexican Americans:

> The testimony of responsible officials and citizens contained the admission that residents of the community distinguished between "white" and "Mexican." The participation of persons of Mexican descent in business and community groups was shown to be slight. Until very recent times, children of Mexican descent were required to attend a segregated school for the first four grades. At least one restaurant in town prominently displayed a sign announcing ANo Mexicans Served." On the courthouse grounds at the time of the hearing, there were two men's toilets, one unmarked, and the other marked "Colored Men" and "Hombres Aquí."[29]

Having recognized the existence of segregated schools for children of Mexican descent, the Court also described the alleged linguistic justification for the segregation: Athe reason given by the school superintendent for this segregation was that these children needed special help in learning English."[30] The Court appeared mistrustful of this explanation, noting that teachers in the school for Mexican American children taught two grades, compared to teachers in the regular school who taught only one grade.[31] The Court concluded that the logical inference from all of these facts was that Mexican Americans were considered a distinct class subject to group discrimination in Jackson County, Texas.

Pete Hernandez then had to prove that discrimination existed in jury selection. According to the Court, Hernandez proved the following facts:

> The petitioner established that 14% of the population of Jackson County were persons with Mexican or Latin surnames, and that 11% of the males over 21 bore such names. The County Tax Assessor testified that 6 or 7 percent of the freeholders on the tax rolls of the County were persons of Mex-

---

[28]Hernandez v. Texas, 347 U.S. 475, 478 (1954).
[29]*Id.* at 479-80.
[30]*Id.* at 479 n.10.
[31]*Id.* at 479 n.10.

ican descent. The State of Texas stipulated that "for the last 25 years there is no record of any person with a Mexican or Latin American name having served on a jury commission, grand jury or petit jury in Jackson County." The parties also stipulated that "there are some male persons of Mexican or Latin American descent in Jackson County who, by virtue of being citizens, freeholders, and having all other legal prerequisites to jury service, are eligible to serve as members of a jury commission, grand jury and/or petit jury."[32]

The state attempted interesting counterarguments throughout the litigation. In lower Texas courts, the State presented two winning arguments. First, the state argued, and the Texas courts accepted, that Mexican-Americans were a "nationality," not a "race," and that the Supreme Court had never treated "nationality" the same as "race" under the equal protection clause.[33] Secondly, the Texas courts had interpreted equal protection to apply only to discrimination between two racial groups, Whites and Blacks.[34] The lower court wrote that "Mexican people * * * are not a separate race but are white people of Spanish descent". In contemplation of the Fourteenth Amendment, Mexicans are therefore members of and within the classification of the white race, as distinguished from members of the "Negro race."[35] Since Mexicans were considered "white" in Texas, the court reasoned that equal protection principles did not apply to distinctions made within the group of "whites."[36] In the alternative, the State also attempted to justify the systematic exclusion of Mexicans. Five jury commissioners testified that they had not discriminated against persons of Mexican descent and that they had merely been trying to select the best qualified jurors.[37]

The Warren Court concluded that Pete Hernandez had proved discrimination in the systematic exclusion of Mexican Americans from the jury:

> [I]t taxes our credulity to say that mere chance resulted in there being no members of this class among the over six thousand jurors called in the past 25 years. The result bespeaks discrimination, whether or not it was a conscious decision on the part of any individual jury commissioner.[38]

The Court held that the fraudulent, racist jury selection system in Jackson County, Texas, a system which had excluded all qualified Mexican-American jurors for over twenty-five years, violated the Equal Protection Clause of the Fourteenth Amendment. And so, for the first time in its history, the Supreme Court recognized that Mexican-Americans victimized by state-sponsored racism were entitled to protection and relief under the Constitution.

---

[32]*Id.* at 480-81 (internal footnotes omitted).
[33]See Hernandez v. State, 251 S.W.2d 531, 533 (1952); see also Sanchez v. State, 181 S.W.2d 87, 90 (1944).
[34]See, e.g., Hernandez v. State, 251 S.W.2d 531 (1952); see also Sanchez v. State, 243 S.W.2d 700 (1951).
[35]Hernandez v. State, 251 S.W.2d at 535.
[36]*Id.* at 535-36.
[37]Hernandez v. Texas, 347 U.S. at 481.
[38]*Id.* at 482.

Assessing the Lower Court Decisions in *Hernandez v. Texas*

The most significant holding in *Hernandez v. Texas* was the Warren Court's conclusion that Mexican-Americans were entitled to protection from government-spon-
sored racism under the Equal Protection Clause. In reaching this holding, as obvious
and correct as it may seem today, the Court reversed decades of precedent from the
Texas courts stating the opposite. The plaintiff had argued that the systematic exclusion of qualified Mexican-American-surnamed jurors from grand and petit juries
over many years should violate the equal protection clause, just as the same exclusion of qualified Black jurors would.[39] Rather than remedy blatant discrimination
against Mexican-Americans in jury selection, the Texas courts concluded that neither the principles of equal protection, nor the Equal Protection Clause itself, applied
to Mexican-Americans.

The Texas courts gave two reasons for these startling conclusions. First, the
courts reasoned that Mexican-Americans were a "nationality," not a "race," and that
the Supreme Court had never treated "nationality" the same as "race" under the
equal protection clause.[40] Secondly, the Texas courts had interpreted equal protection to apply only to discrimination between two racial groups, Whites and Blacks.[41]
I shall consider each of these reasons in turn.

The assertion that discrimination because of "nationality" differs from discrimination because of "race" for purposes of equal protection is interesting, but misleading. To a certain, simple extent, the Texas courts are right. Nationality, or national origin, is not commonly understood to be the same as "race." But the courts'
reasoning is sophistic. It doesn't matter whether Mexican-Americans are named
with a national-origin term rather than a color term like "Black," or "Brown." What
mattered, and what should always matter in present contexts, is that Mexican-
Americans were subject to racism, regardless of nomenclature. Racism in the United States developed as the desire and practice of whites to disadvantage and disparage others who are non-white. It is obvious that Mexican-Americans in Texas constituted a "race" subject to white racism and all the excesses of Jim Crow and
segregation. The Supreme Court recognized the obvious racism at issue in *Hernandez* and responded appropriately to it.

Interestingly, the Texas courts reached the wrong conclusion regarding Mexican-Americans even based on the constitutional law available at that time. Even if
we take seriously the Texas courts' distinction between "nationality" and "race," the
Supreme Court had already suggested that they could be functional equivalents for
equal protection purposes. In *Strauder v. West Virginia*, discussed earlier, the Court's
opinion contained dicta directly relevant to the *Hernandez* case: "Nor if a law should
be passed excluding all naturalized Celtic Irishmen, would there be any doubt of its
inconsistency with the spirit of the [14th] amendment."[42] As early as the *Strauder*

---

[39]See *id.* at 477, 480 (asserting that the Equal Protection Clause had been violated by the exclusion of Mexican-American jurors and relying on Norris v. Alabama, 294 U.S. 587 (1935), which held that "rule of exclusion" can supply evidence of discrimination).

[40]See Hernandez v. State, 251 S.W.2d at 533; Sanchez v. State, 181 S.W.2d 87, 90 (1944).

[41]See, e.g., Hernandez v. State, 251 S.W.2d 531; Sanchez v. State, 243 S.W.2d 700 (1951).

[42]Strauder v. West Virginia, 100 U.S. 303, 308 (1879).

decision, discrimination because of national origin and "race" were understood to be equivalent for equal protection purposes. Later, in *Yick Wo v. Hopkins*, an exceedingly rare victory for the California Chinese, the Supreme Court struck down a San Francisco law that effectively forced only Chinese-owned and operated laundries out of business.[43] Like the classification at issue in *Hernandez*, the targeting of Chinese-owned businesses could be named either "race" or Anational origin" discrimination, or both. In *Hernandez v. Texas*, the Warren Court cited *Strauder* and other opinions to rebut the contention of the Texas courts that equal protection had never been extended beyond binary, Black/White meanings.[44]

The Texas courts found further reason for denying equal protection to Mexican-Americans in the history of the equal protection clause. The lower courts fashioned a fascinating argument that, based on the history of the 14th Amendment, equal protection was meant to apply only to the protection of two groups of people, Whites and Blacks. In part, the courts relied on a kind of framers' intent argument, quoting language in early Supreme Court decisions that described the paramount purpose of the 14th Amendment as securing the rights of the newly freed slaves.[45] In the court's words,

> It is conclusive that, in so far as the question of discrimination in the organization of juries in state courts is concerned, the equal protection clause of the Fourteenth Amendment contemplated and recognized only two classes as coming within that guarantee: the white race, comprising one class, and the Negro race, comprising the other class.[46]

Again, however, an early Supreme Court decision had long ago contradicted the assertions well accepted in the Texas courts. In the *Slaughterhouse Cases,* decided in 1873, the Supreme Court described Mexicans as a distinct "race" and described generality greater than Black/White in the scope of equal protection:

> We do not say that no one else but the negro can share in this protection. . . . Undoubtedly while negro slavery alone was in the mind of the Congress which proposed the thirteenth [amendment], it forbids any other kind of slavery, now or hereafter. If Mexican peonage or the Chinese coolie labor system shall develop slavery of the Mexican or Chinese race within our territory, this amendment may safely be trusted to make it void. And so if other rights are assailed by the States which properly and necessarily fall within the protection of these articles, that protection will apply, though the party interested may not be of African descent.[47]

Defying history, experience, and observation, the Texas courts had decided that "Mexican people . . . are not a separate race but are white people of Spanish descent."[48] Since, according to the courts, Mexican-Americans were white (and

---

43Yick Wo v. Hopkins, 118 U.S. 356 (1886).
44Hernandez v. Texas, 347 U.S. at 477-78, 478 n.4.
45The Slaughterhouse Cases, 83 U.S. (16 Wall.) 36 (1873); *Strauder*, 100 U.S. 303 (1879).
46Hernandez v. State, 251 S.W.2d at 535.
47The Slaughterhouse Cases, 83 U.S. at 72.
48Sanchez v. State, 243 S.W.2d 700, 701 (1951).

since they were not Black), they could not claim rights of equal protection against their fellow white counterparts.[49] One wonders how Texas judges could reach such conclusions while observing the sign on the courthouse grounds designating one bathroom "Colored Men" and "Hombres Aquí."

Assessing the Success of *Hernandez v. Texas*

Though the Warren Court rejected the "two-class" or binary understanding of equal protection in *Hernandez v. Texas*, the Court was still influenced by the history of the equal protection clause with respect to the kind of discrimination that it was able to recognize as race discrimination. In considering the systematic exclusion of Mexican-Americans from Jackson county juries, the Court relied upon its past precedents that recognized the similar exclusion of Black jurors as violations of equal protection.[50] The constellation of facts the Court assembled (the evidence of Jim Crow segregation of Mexican-Americans, the evidence of unequal treatment) was familiar ground. All of the evidence of discrimination mentioned by the Court was discriminatory treatment that the Court had recognized as discriminatory with respect to Blacks.

An interesting question remains. How successfully has the Court expanded its conception of equal protection beyond the "two-class" theory? The Warren Court took a first step (for Latinos) by recognizing that Mexican Americans were entitled to equal protection of the laws. As the Court itself recognized, this was not really a new development; the Court had decided equal protection cases favorably to non-white, non-Black litigants before.

But to what extent can the Court recognize as discriminatory other forms of white racism that are unlike, or less like, the forms of white racism experienced by Blacks? Fifty years after *Hernandez v. Texas*, the Court still lacks understanding and recognition of some of the particular forms of white racism against Latinos even in the same context of discriminatory jury selection. Even though the Court ostensibly broadened the scope of equal protection in *Hernandez*, the binary understanding of "race" as Black/White color still cramps current understandings of race discrimination and robs equal protection of its relevance for Latinos.

Language discrimination against Latinos is an excellent example of the under-inclusive understanding of race discrimination. Language discrimination has a long history as a tool of oppression against Latino people.[51] The history of language discrimination in public education is well documented and I will briefly recount it here.

---

[49]Hernandez v. State, 251 S.W.2d at 535.

[50]Hernandez v. Texas, 347 U.S. 475, 477 n.2, 479 nn.7-8 (1954) (citing Carter v. Texas, 177 U.S. 442 (1900); Smith v. Texas, 311 U.S. 128 (1940); Hill v. Texas, 316 U.S. 400 (1942); Cassell v. Texas, 3339 U.S. 282 (1950)—all of which dealt with the unconstitutional exclusion of Blacks from juries in Texas).

[51]See, e.g., JUAN F. PEREA, BUSCANDO AMERICA: WHY INTEGRATION AND EQUAL PROTECTION FAIL TO PROTECT LATINOS, 117 HARV. L. REV. 1420, 1439-46 (2004).[hereinafter cited as *Buscando America*].

Language Discrimination: Some Historical Context

The segregated, inferior schools provided for Mexican American children in the Southwest were intended to teach inferiority and subservience.[52] One strategy for teaching the lessons of subservience was to attempt to destroy the language and culture of young Mexican American students. As described by Thomas Carter, "the full force of the educational system in the Southwest [was] directed toward the eradication of both the Spanish language and the Spanish-American or Mexican-American cultures."[53]

Teachers employed, and continue to employ, many language-related reasons to justify the segregation of Mexican American children and to deny them equal education. Mexican American children were retained in first grade for two or three years, allegedly because they lacked linguistic competence in English.[54] However, their linguistic competence was often tested hastily and with inconclusive results, if it was tested at all.[55] Schools have responded to their Spanish-speaking students by ignoring the Spanish language, prohibiting it altogether, and by punishing Latino students who spoke their native tongue publicly.[56] Punishments included "Spanish detention," spanking, suspension, expulsion and other physical abuse and public humiliation.[57] Punishments like these were, and continue to be, inflicted in heavily Mexican-populated schools. Very recently in jurisdictions that have repealed bilingual education by referendum, including Massachusetts, Arizona, and California, some educators enforce the new laws in old, discriminatory ways by prohibiting the use of Spanish among students and on school campuses.[58]

Educators persistently devalue bilingualism and language ability in Spanish. Many teachers, perhaps most, see childhood bilingualism as a deficit and impediment to learning.[59] Many teachers also believe that Spanish-speaking or bilingual

---

[52]*Id.* at 1439-40.

[53]THOMAS P. CARTER, MEXICAN AMERICANS IN SCHOOL: A HISTORY OF EDUCATIONAL NEGLECT 96 (1970). [hereinafter cited as EDUCATIONAL NEGLECT].

[54]See BUSCANDO AMERICA, supra note 52, at 1441.

[55]See *id.*; *Mendez v. Westminster*, 64 F. Supp. 544, 550 (S.D. Cal. 1946) ("The [language] tests applied to the beginners are shown to have been generally hasty, superficial, and not reliable.").

[56]MEYER WEINBERG, A CHANCE TO LEARN 152-53 (1977).

[57]EDUCATIONAL NEGLECT, supra note 54, at 98. One writer describes the harsh treatment awaiting Latino olomontary oohool ohildron on thoir firot day of oohool:

Then, suddenly, [the children] were torn from loving arms and put into a room full of strange sounds and harsh voices. Please for help were ignored, and as late as the 1950s children who spoke Spanish in school were made to kneel on upturned bottle caps, forced to hold bricks in outstretched hands in the schoolyard, or told to put their nose in a chalk circle drawn on a blackboard. And this would happen in Texas towns that were 98 percent Spanish-speaking.

THOMAS WEYR, HISPANIC U.S.A.: BREAKING THE MELTING POT 51-52 (1988). See also MEL MELENDEZ, MOLERA BACKS DISTRICT ON ITS SPANISH BAN, ARIZ. REPUBLIC, Aug. 20, 2002, at 1B (Arizona native describing how he "was paddled every time [he] spoke Spanish, and that was the only language he knew.")

[58]See MEL MELENDEZ, NO-SPANISH RULE VEXES STUDENTS, ARIZ. REPUBLIC, Oct. 16, 2003, at 1B; MELENDEZ, MOLERA BACKS DISTRICT ON ITS SPANISH BAN, supra note 58.; MARY BUSTAMANTE, PLAYING EN ESPAÑOL, TUCSON CITIZEN, Aug. 26, 2002, at 1C (A state school chief's support of speaking only English to non-English-proficient students even on playgrounds, in cafeterias and on buses has some local educators concerned.").

[59]EDUCATIONAL NEGLECT, supra note 54, at 51. CARMEN ROLÓN, EDUCATING LATINO STUDENTS, 60 EDUC. LEADERSHIP 40, 41 (2002-2003) ("The deficit view is that [linguistically diverse] students lack English language skills and the sooner they stop speaking their mother tongue and learn English, the sooner they will be able to succeed in school and be better prepared for life. This perspective, pervasive in many school systems, defines Latinos and other linguistically diverse students by what they don't have rather than by what they bring to the school."); CYNTHIA MIGUELEZ, THE NORMALIZATION OF MINORITY LANGUAGES IN SPAIN, IN ROSEANN DUEÑAS GONZÁLEZ & ILDIKÓ MELIS, LANGUAGE IDEOLOGIES 346, 348 (2001); GARCIA, HISPANIC EDUCATION IN THE UNITED STATES 52-57 (2001). See, e.g., AMANDA E. LEWIS, RACE IN THE SCHOOLYARD 82-83 (2003) (negative student and teacher attitudes towards Spanish).

Mexican American children speak no language at all.[60] Regardless of their linguistic abilities, Mexican American children are considered deficient and alingual from the start.[61] It is important to recognize that "no Spanish" rules and disparaging judgments about native Spanish-speakers are part of a whole system of behavioral controls intended to banish manifestations of "Mexicanness" or "Latinoness" from the public schools.[62]

This desire to eradicate Spanish was never limited to the educational system and, in forms both conscious and unconscious, it remains evident today. It is evident in state campaigns to eliminate bilingual education, and in the continuing campaign for Official English.[63] It is also evident in the workplace. The United States Courts of Appeals are currently consistent in holding that Spanish-speaking workers may be fired, without violating Title VII, merely for speaking Spanish in violation of an employer's English-only rule.[64] The degree of judicial bias against native Spanish speakers is evident in the fact that the judges in these cases reject the Equal Employment Opportunity Commission's expert guidelines finding that English-only rules are presumptively invalid and must be justified by employer proof of business necessity.[65]

There have also been notorious incidents of more obvious judicial bias against Spanish speakers. One Texas judge threatened a Mexican-American mother with the loss of her daughter unless she stopped speaking Spanish to her daughter at home:

> [Y]ou're abusing that child and you're relegating her to the position of a housemaid. Now get this straight. You start speaking English to this child

---

[60]EDUCATIONAL NEGLECT, supra note 54, at 52.

[61]Reporting the results of interviews with teachers, Carter writes:
Many interviewees regard Mexican American Spanish as deficient: "The language spoken at home is pocho, 'Tex-Mex,' or 'wetback Spanish,' really nonstandard dialects." Such comments as these were commonly encountered: "Their Spanish is of such an inferior quality that it does not warrant classification as a language." "The child's Spanish provides a meager base for future learning in even that language."
Id. at 52. *Cf.* LENORE CATALOGNA et al., AN EXPLORATORY EXAMINATION OF TEACHERS' PERCEPTIONS OF PUPILS' RACE, J. OF NEGRO EDUC. 370, 379 (1981) ("a significant degree of pro-white and anti-Hispanic prejudice on the part of teachers surfaced in this study.").

[62]EDUCATIONAL NEGLECT, supra note 54, at 98.

[63]See JENNIFER MEDINA, BILINGUAL EDUCATION ON BALLOT IN TWO STATES, N.Y. TIMES, Oct. 9, 2002, at A1 (reporting that Massachusetts and Colorado had ballot initiatives to place non-English speaking students in English immersion classes); ANAND VAISHNAV, DISSECTING BILINGUAL EDUCATION'S POLL DEFEAT MOVEMENT LACKED MONEY, MESSAGE, BOSTON GLOBE, Nov. 10, 2002, at B9 (analyzing the defeat of bilingual education at the polls in Massachusetts and comparing similar initiatives in Arizona, California, and Colorado). See generally RENE GALINDO & JAMI VIGIL, LANGUAGE RESTRICTIONISM REVISITED: THE CASE AGAINST COLORADO'S 2000 ANTI-BILINGUAL EDUCATION INITIATIVE, 7 HARV. LATINO L. REV. 27 (2004) (discussing state initiatives in California, Arizona, Massachusetts, and Colorado); CHARU A. CHANDRASEKHAR, Comment, THE BAY STATE BURIES BILINGUALISM: ADVOCACY LESSONS FROM BILINGUAL EDUCATION'S RECENT DEFEAT IN MASSACHUSETTS, 24 CHICANO-LATINO L. REV. 43 (2003) (examining the Massachusetts initiative to end bilingual education).

[64]See, e.g., Garcia v. Gloor, 618 F.2d 264 (5th Cir. 1980) (holding that a bilingual employee fired for speaking Spanish in public areas does not violate Title VII because the employee was fired for failing to follow store policy not because of impermissible discrimination); Garcia v. Spun Steak, 998 F.2d 1480 (9th Cir. 1993) (reversing summary judgment for an employee in a Title VII lawsuit).

[65]*Spun Steak*, 998 F.2d at 1489-90 (rejecting EEOC guidelines on English-only policies in the workplace). The court rejected the guidelines that had "provide[d] that an employee meets the prima facie case in a disparate impact cause of action merely by proving the existence of the English-only policy." *Id.* (citing 29 C.F.R. § 1606.7 (a), (b) (1991)).

because if she doesn't do good in school, then I can remove her because it's not in her best interest to be ignorant. The child will hear only English.[66]

Similarly, a Nebraska judge threatened to limit a Mexican-American father's rights to visit his daughter if he continued speaking to her in Spanish.[67] Whether at school, at work, at home, or in the courthouse, Latinos face hostility and discriminatory treatment based on their use of Spanish.

Language Discrimination in the Courtroom

And today, despite the seeming promise of *Hernandez v. Texas*, Latinos still face hostility and discrimination in the jury box based on their Spanish language. Although *Batson* eliminated peremptory challenges based overtly on race, *Batson* is easily circumvented. *Batson* and its progeny require only that litigants articulate a "race-neutral" reason for exercising a peremptory challenge. The flaw in the *Batson* framework was recognized early by Justice Thurgood Marshall, who saw that "Any prosecutor can easily assert facially neutral reasons for striking a juror, and trial courts are ill-equipped to second-guess those reasons."[68] Indeed, because of the ease with which litigants can articulate facially neutral reasons, jury selection is almost as discriminatory today as it was before *Batson*.[69] The justifications for discrimination have changed, but the discrimination itself has not.

With respect to Latinos, the Supreme Court encountered, but failed to recognize, a palpable case of language discrimination against prospective Latino jurors in *Hernandez v. New York*, decided in 1991.[70] The case involved many Spanish-speakers: the defendant, several witnesses, the courtroom interpreter, and two bilingual jurors were all Spanish speaking. Because several witnesses were Spanish-speaking, their testimony was interpreted into English for the benefit of the court and monolingual English-speaking jurors. The prosecutor asked the bilingual jurors whether they would be able to accept the interpreter's translated version of the Spanish-language testimony. Despite their assurances that they would accept the interpreter's translation, the prosecutor used peremptory challenges to exclude these bilingual jurors. The defense then raised objections to these peremptory challenges under the *Batson* framework.

Under that framework, the prosecutor had to articulate facially neutral reasons for these peremptory challenges against Latino jurors. Here is what he said:

> my reason for rejecting these two is I feel very uncertain that they would be able to listen and follow the interpreter. . . . We talked to them for a long time; the Court talked to them, I talked to them. I believe that in their heart

---

[66]SAM HOWE VERHOVEK, MOTHER SCOLDED BY JUDGE FOR SPEAKING IN SPANISH, N.Y. TIMES, Aug. 30, 1995, at A12 (quoting judge Samuel C. Kiser).

[67]See DARRYL FEARS, JUDGE ORDERS NEB. FATHER TO NOT SPEAK "HISPANIC", WASH. POST, Oct. 17, 2003, at A3.

[68]Batson v. Kentucky, 476 U.S. 79, 106 (1986) (Marshall, J., concurring).

[69]See KENNETH J. MELILLI, BATSON IN PRACTICE: WHAT WE HAVE LEARNED ABOUT BATSON AND PEREMPTORY CHALLENGES, 71 NOTRE DAME L. REV. 447 (1996) (analyzing *Batson* challenges filed between 1986 and 1993 and arguing for an end to peremptory challenges).

[70]Hernandez v. New York, 500 U.S. 352 (1991).

they will try to follow it, but I felt there was a great deal of uncertainty as to whether they could accept the interpreter as the final arbiter of what was said by each of the witnesses, especially where there were going to be Spanish-speaking witnesses, and I didn't feel, when I asked them whether or not they could accept the interpreter's translation of it, I didn't feel that they could. They each looked away from me and said with some hesitancy that they would try, not that they could but that they would try to follow the interpreter, and I feel that in a case where the interpreter will be for the main witnesses, they would have an undue impact upon the jury. . . . I thought they both indicated that they would have trouble, though their final answer was they could do it. I just felt from the hesitancy in their answers and their lack of eye contact that they would not be able to do it.[71]

Despite the absence of any finding that these potential jurors were not credible, the prosecutor simply felt uncomfortable with the demeanor of the bilingual jurors and dismissed them. The trial court heard the prosecutor's reasons and accepted his explanation as "race-neutral." The Supreme Court, too, agreed that the prosecutor's reasons were "race-neutral" and found that these peremptory challenges did not violate the Equal Protection Clause.

The Supreme Court decided wrongly that language discrimination against bilingual Latinos was not race discrimination. While I have critiqued this decision at length elsewhere, here I will focus on two reasons why the Court was wrong.[72] First, the Court seemed entirely unaware of the history discussed above. Language discrimination has a pervasive past and present in the United States, and there was no reason to assume that the parties peopling the New York courts were immune from what is otherwise a national phenomenon. Although the Court, in an apparent attempt to show sensitivity to the issues raised by language differences, offered citations to sociolinguistic insights on language, its effort was poor and inconsequential.[73]

The bottom line was that the Court didn't "get it." The Court did not understand that language discrimination against bilingual Latinos in the United States is race discrimination. As concluded by Guadalupe Valdes, "in the United States language discrimination against bilingual individuals is not subtle."[74] Professor Valdes's first example of clear language discrimination was the Court's decision in *Hernandez v. New York.*[75]

Another prominent flaw was the consistent judicial decision, in all the courts that considered the case, to validate the prosecutor's personal discomfort with the bilingual jurors as credible and "race-neutral." Given the context of national discrimination on the basis of language and the serious misunderstandings that monolingual persons, including judges and prosecutors, have with respect to bilinguals,

---

[71]*Id.* at 356-57 & n.1.

[72]For a thorough critique of the decision, see JUAN F. PEREA, HERNANDEZ V. NEW YORK: Courts, Prosecutors, and the Fear of Spanish, 21 HOFSTRA L. REV. 1 (1992).

[73]Hernandez v. New York, 500 U.S. at 370-71.

[74]See GUADALUPE VALDES, BILINGUAL INDIVIDUALS AND LANGUAGE-BASED DISCRIMINATION: ADVANCING THE STATE OF THE LAW ON LANGUAGE RIGHTS, IN, 2 LANGUAGE IDEOLOGIES: PERSPECTIVES ON THE OFFICIAL ENGLISH MOVEMENT 140, 142 (Roseann Dueñas Gonzales & Ildiko Melis eds., 2001) [hereinafter cited as Valdes].

[75]See *id.* at 143-47.

reliance on a prosecutor's discomfort is simply too thin a reason to accept in excluding qualified individuals from a jury. As I discuss below, the prosecutor's questions to the bilinguals imposed on them much more difficult conditions than those imposed on monolingual jurors.[76] Although the prosecutor may have appeared credible, he was likely sincere and wrong, misinformed and uncomprehending as most monolinguals are with respect to bilinguals.[77] Or, given the lengthy history of bias against Spanish speakers in the United States, he may have been sincere and unconsciously biased.[78]

In the end, despite some bland, palliative recognition of the harshness and disproportionate impact on Latinos that its decision inflicted,[79] the Supreme Court decided that a prosecutor's "uncertainty" and mistrust of the bilingual jurors justified their peremptory removal. And here is where an interesting arc can be drawn from *Hernandez v. Texas* to *Hernandez v. New York*. Separated by approximately forty years, both cases concerned the exclusion of Latinos from the jury. How much has changed in these forty years, and how much remains to be changed?

One interesting axis along which to compare the cases is to consider the way each decision treated the role of majoritarian discretion in making determinations about fitness or not to serve on juries. Historically, the vesting of excessive discretion in jury commissioners is well understood to produce discriminatory results, whether or not individuals can be proven to have acted with intent to discriminate.[80] This was a pattern proven to be true in Texas. Just such a system was at issue in *Hernandez v. Texas*. Despite formally neutral, egalitarian statutes and qualified Mexican Americans, jury commissioners vested with discretion to decide who they felt was best qualified to serve decided in a way that produced the extraordinary result that no Mexican Americans on a Jackson County jury in twenty-five years. The Warren Court did not flinch from the obvious import of that statistic. As the Court wrote, "it taxes our credulity to say that mere chance resulted in there being no members of this class among the over six thousand jurors called in the past 25 years. The result bespeaks discrimination, whether or not it was a conscious decision on the part of any individual jury commissioner."[81]

Consider now the Court's stance in *Hernandez v. New York* toward similar discretion that yields disproportionately discriminatory results. Under the *Batson* framework, prosecutors have discretion to advance any credible non-discriminatory reason for a peremptory challenge. Our prosecutor's stated reason for excluding the bilingual jurors was that he felt "very uncertain that they would be able to listen and follow the interpreter." The prosecutor's highly subjective "uncertainty" or distrust of the bilingual jurors seems very similar to the judgments of jury commissioners that qualified Mexican American jury candidates were not the best qualified. Unlike the Warren Court, which was suspicious of unbridled discretion

---

[76]*Id.* at 145-47.

[77]*Id.* at 144-47.

[78]On unconscious bias, see CHARLES R. LAWRENCE, III, *The Id, the Ego, and Equal Protection: Reckoning with Unconscious Racism*, 39 STAN. L. REV. 317 (1987).

[79]See HERNANDEZ V. NEW YORK, 500 U.S. 352, 363, 370-72 (1991).

[80]REPORT, supra note 25, at 43-44 (1970).

[81]Hernandez v. Texas, 347 U.S. 475, 482 (1954).

that yielded discriminatory results, here the Rehnquist Court embraces similar discretion with full knowledge of the discriminatory results that will ensue for bilingual Latino jurors. The courts consistently trust the prosecutor's "uncertainty" and credit the trial court's determination that the prosecutor was credible. And the courts credit the prosecutor's "uncertainty" over the uncontradicted and credible testimony of the bilingual jurors themselves, who swore that they would do what the prosecutor asked. Where the history of language discrimination and the pervasive misunderstanding of bilinguals by monolinguals would counsel skepticism with respect to peremptory dismissals of bilingual jurors, today's courts simply endorse prosecutorial discrimination against bilinguals.

Another axis along which to compare these decisions is to consider their treatment of the particular discrimination faced by the Latinos before the Court. The very cynical and self-serving conclusion of the lower Texas courts in *Hernandez v. Texas* was that Mexican Americans were considered whites and therefore were ineligible for relief under the Equal Protection Clause. This conclusion flew in the face of all past and present historical evidence of profound, sustained Jim Crow racism and segregation inflicted upon Mexican Americans in all quarters. Texas judges denied or ignored all the obvious evidence of Jim Crow Latino to produce a self-serving, preemptive legal fiction of Mexican American "whiteness." The Warren Court, at last recognizing the obvious, saw the white racism and understood and dismantled the racist stricture before it. Indeed, the Court first articulated what scholars have developed into a powerful, well-accepted understanding of the socially constructed nature of racism.

In profound contrast, in *Hernandez v. New York*, the Court was entirely unable to understand and respond to the language discrimination against bilingual Latinos that was presented in the case. The Court failed to understand that bilinguals are not the same as monolinguals, nor are they similarly situated with respect to the questions the prosecutor asked of them.[82] The prosecutor's questions imposed much more difficult conditions upon the bilingual jurors than upon monolingual jurors. If the expectation of courts or prosecutors is that bilinguals shut down the portion of their brains that processes one or both of the languages they know, then the expectation is absurd and impossible to fulfill:

> From the perspective of bilingual individuals, however, the [prosecutor's] request itself is absurd if it is understood to mean that they must block or shut down one of their language-processing channels. Research on bilingualism carried out from the psycholinguistic perspective has determined that this is an impossible task.[83]

It is no more possible for a bilingual to not hear what has been heard than it is for a monolingual English speaker to "unhear" something that has already been heard, or to "unread" something that has already been read. How does anyone remove from consciousness something that has already entered? While it may be

---

[82]VALDES, supra note 75, at 145.
[83]*Id.* at 146.

possible to disregard information already heard, as jurors are often instructed to do, it is impossible to "unhear" what one has already heard.

If the expectation of courts and prosecutors is that bilingual jurors set aside their own understanding of testimony in a source language and replace that understanding with the official interpreter's version of the testimony, then bilingual jurors are again being unusually burdened in a way not demanded of monolinguals. The bilingual jurors are asked, in effect, to ignore possible discrepancies between the interpretation and the original and not to use their judgment in evaluating the evidence. Monolinguals, who have no choice but to accept the interpreter's version of the evidence, right or wrong, are not asked to disregard their understanding of the evidence.[84] This expectation is problematic for another reason. Since it is well known that interpretations are often wrong or incorrect, why should any juror be asked to adhere to a version of the evidence which may well be incorrect? By allowing the peremptory removals of bilingual jurors based on the "uncertainty" expressed by the prosecutor, the courts are preferring adherence to an official, and possibly incorrect, version of the evidence rather than allowing the jury to serve its traditional truth-finding function. This is an odd choice of values for courts, including the Supreme Court, to enforce considering that the whole purpose of the trial is to arrive at some understanding of the truth of the events on trial.

It is possible to conclude that, even if wrongly decided, the conclusion in *Hernandez v. New York*, does not do major damage. Although the Court has sanctioned the peremptory removal of bilingual jurors in cases involving interpreted Spanish-language testimony, in fact this is probably a small proportion of cases faced in the courts. And, presumably, bilingual jurors will not be subject to peremptory exclusion because of their bilingualism in every other sort of case. In most cases, then, bilingual jurors will still be able to serve. They can be peremptorily excluded only in cases in which bilingual jurors are bilingual in the same language spoken by witnesses whose testimony will be interpreted.

While these aspects of the Court's decision contain truth, I believe that understanding the case as a relatively innocuous mistake would be a grave error. Here's why. First, our changing national demographics are by now well known, and the principal change is the increasing percentage of Latinos in the population. Corresponding to this change, we can reasonably expect an ever-increasing number of trials involving Spanish-language testimony, and increasing numbers of potential bilingual jurors who can easily be stricken from the jury under the Court's current rules. In some cities and areas of the country, such as Miami, Houston, New York, or Los Angeles, which already contain large numbers of Latinos, it is likely that the situation presented in *Hernandez v. New York* arises regularly. The scope of damage done in *Hernandez v. New York* is not small, and that scope is growing steadily because of demographic factors.

Hernandez v. New York wrought more major damage in the decision's refusal to acknowledge meaningfully the linguistic and racial particularity of the Latino community with respect to jury service. The Court denied the particularity of bilingual

---

[84]See *id.* at 146-47.

Latinos and refused to protect bilingual jurors in the important, public role they can play on juries. Under this decision, bilinguals can easily be excluded from precisely those cases in which they share the language spoken by potential witnesses, defendants and victims of crime. Latino bilinguals can most easily be excluded in cases in which they are most likely to share community affiliations and cultural and racial ties to the parties in a case. These are the cases in which the particular linguistic, racial and community knowledge of bilingual Latino jurors matters the most. But the Court has effectively precluded these jurors' participation in these cases in which their community membership matters most. Unlike the Warren Court, which rejected the possibility that Mexican American jurors could plausibly be excluded from their community, the Rehnquist Court has endorsed just such a result with respect to bilinguals.

When I write that the particular knowledge and experience of bilingual Latino jurors "matters the most" in these cases, I am not describing anything that constitutes "undue influence" of the kind the prosecutor feared. I can illustrate this best with a hypothetical. Suppose we had a criminal trial in a predominantly white, English-speaking, middle-class suburb somewhere in the United States. Further suppose that the jury trying the suburban, white middle class defendant, and evaluating the testimony of the white, middle-class suburban witnesses turned out to be virtually all white, English-speaking suburbanites drawn from the relevant jury-service district. Would there be any concern raised about "undue influence" resulting solely from the shared demographic characteristics of the parties and the jury? I don't think so. Most people would understand this as a proper trial conducted before a jury of one's peers, with a cross-section of the community, as it exists, represented on the jury. *The situation is no different with respect to bilingual jurors hearing Spanish-language testimony.* There is no "undue influence" in simply bringing one's experience and understanding of a community into the jury box. As it is for whites, so should it be for Latinos, bilingual and otherwise.

The greatest damage done in *Hernandez v. New York* is the rejection of the racial and linguistic particularity of bilingual Latino jurors, and the relevance of that particularity, within the justice system in the cases in which that particularity is the most relevant. In cases in which community ties among Spanish-speakers would be the greatest, the Court chose to break those and future ties instead of exercising skepticism about a prosecutor's "uncertainty." The Court effectively decided that the linguistic, racial and cultural particularity of bilingual Latino jurors was either not relevant or, worse, that their particularity was capable of damaging the jury process.

The Rehnquist Court essentially enforced a normative monolingual, English-speaking identity on all jurors. In the future, bilingual jurors will only be allowed to remain on juries on which they will function like monolinguals. Excludable if they understand testimony in a language other than English, bilingual jurors will be entitled to remain only in cases in the testimony is in English or in other languages in which they are not bilingual. In other words, the Constitution will protect their ability to serve as jurors only if they can serve exactly as English-speaking monolinguals. The Court has rejected the relevance of their particularity and has obliterated their ability to represent their community in that famous cross-section of the community that our juries supposedly represent.

Compare the values vindicated in *Hernandez v. New York* with those subverted. The Court vindicated the prosecutor's sense of discomfort with bilingual jurors, a very common discomfort that many people experience in the presence of persons who speak other languages, a discomfort that we could label *prejudice*. The Court vindicated the prosecutor's and the courts' illusory sense of control over the information considered by the jury. On the other hand, the Court subverted the concept of a trial by a jury of one's peers, since all of the defendant's peers were peremptorily removed from the jury. The Court subverted equal protection by not protecting at all the rights of Spanish-speaking jurors to remain on a jury free from state-sponsored prejudice. The Court subverted the equal protection principle that seemed to be vindicated in our celebrated case, *Hernandez v. Texas*, the principle that Latinos subject to community prejudices are entitled to relief from discriminatory practices. Considering this balance sheet, the Court enforced Anglocentric comfort and control and threw equal protection and a jury of one's peers out the window for Latino Spanish-speakers.

The legacy of *Hernandez v. Texas* is paradoxical and remains unfulfilled. The Court explicitly rejected the view that "there are only two classes—white and Negro—within the contemplation of the Fourteenth Amendment."[85] The Warren Court understood, in its time, the shifting nature of community prejudices and notion that discrimination was not static:

> Throughout our history differences in race and color have defined easily identifiable groups which have at times required the aid of the courts in securing equal treatment under the laws. But community prejudices are not static, and from time to time other differences from the community norm may define other groups which need the same protection. Whether such a group exists within a community is a question of fact. When the existence of a distinct class is demonstrated, and it is further shown that the laws, as written or as applied, single out that class for different treatment not based on some reasonable classification, the guarantees of the Constitution have been violated. The Fourteenth Amendment is not directed solely against discrimination due to a 'two class theory' that is, based upon differences between 'white' and Negro.[86]

The "two-class" theory ostensibly rejected in *Hernandez v. Texas* remains alive and well, however, through the refusal to recognize and protect the particularity of Latino bilinguals. The *Hernandez v. New York* Court should have paid attention to the history of language discrimination and to the consistent community prejudices against Spanish speakers and bilinguals. The Court should have used history to inform its understanding of discrimination against bilinguals. The Court should have recognized that language discrimination against Latino bilinguals is race discrimination against Latinos.

---

[85]Hernandez v. Texas, 347 U.S. at 477.
[86]*Id.* at 478.

Why Latinos Have a Right to Sing the Blues

At this writing it is hard to be optimistic regarding the future possibilities of greater justice for Latino people in the United States with regard to language discrimination. Why has the promise of *Hernandez v. Texas*, a promise of meaningful equal protection for Latinos, remained unfulfilled? Some part of the reason lies in the profound differences between the Warren and Rehnquist courts. The Warren Court looked to context, found racism, and corrected it. The Rehnquist Court, in contrast, applied an equal protection devoid of historical context and failed to recognize the language discrimination squarely facing the Court.

Excellent recent writing on the nature of the Supreme Court, and by extension the lower federal courts, also helps provide an answer.[87] The Supreme Court, rather than being countermajoritarian, is nationalist. The Court is most responsive to national political majorities and national elites.[88] A nationalist Court will enforce a nationalist view of American identity as the norm for equal protection. Additionally, as Jack Balkin writes, "Courts tend to protect minorities just about as much as majorities want them to."[89]

With respect to race, this understanding suggests that the Court will enforce a nationalist view of race rooted in slavery and its constitutional corrections, the Reconstruction Amendments. Thus a nationalist view of race corresponds well to the Black/White paradigm, but less well to the particular needs of non-Black communities becoming more numerically prominent as our national demographics change.[90] Rather than protect minority particularity, in our case the particular linguistic traits of bilingual Spanish speakers, the Court enforces the nationally preferred dominance of English and Anglocentric assimilation. There is little evidence of any majoritarian will for the protection of non-English languages. Indeed, the political results in many jurisdictions suggest exactly the opposite, that national majorities may prefer the extinction, or at least the silencing, of Spanish-speakers. While there is ample evidence of majoritarian opposition to linguistic particularity and linguistic equal rights—Official English laws and referenda seeking the abolition of bilingual education are prime examples—there is scant evidence of any equally large countervailing mobilization of advocates favoring linguistic diversity, bilingualism, and linguistic equality. There simply aren't enough of us.

In the end, *Hernandez v. Texas* stands as a distressingly rare moment of Supreme Court acknowledgement of communitarian norms of white racism against Latino people. This now-distant precedential beacon once signaled the enforcement of the possibly majestic, now withered, words of equal protection.

---

[87]See JACK M. BALKIN, WHAT BROWN TEACHES US ABOUT CONSTITUTIONAL THEORY, 90 VA. L. REV. 1537 (2004).

[88]*Id.* at 1538-39.

[89]*Id.* at 1551-58. (capitals removed from quotation).

[90]On the paradigmatic nature of the Black/White understanding of race, see Juan F. Perea, The Black/White Binary Paradigm of Race: the Normal Science of American Racial Thought, 85 CAL. L. REV. 1213 (1997).

Over the Rainbow: *Hernandez v. Texas, Brown v. Board of Education,* and *Black v. Brown*

Neil Foley*

In the aftermath of the 2004 presidential election, many pundits sought to explain why President Bush received over forty percent of the Latino vote compared to only twelve percent of the African American vote. The notion persists that minorities, like African Americans and Latinos, often share similar political views that reflect a similar history of racial discrimination and civil rights struggles against Jim Crow practices. The picture is much more complicated than that, of course, and always has been.

Some of the differences that divide many blacks and Latinos today, such as the dominance of African Americans on school boards and city councils in districts and cities where Latinos greatly outnumber blacks, stand in contrast to the efforts of both groups to find common ground in their earliest civil rights struggles, especially school desegregation cases in California and Texas. In the 1946 Mexican school desegregation case in Orange County, California, *Mendez v. Westminster*,[1] Thurgood Marshall and the NAACP submitted an amicus curiae brief that many legal scholars acknowledge was a dry run for *Brown v. Board of Education.*[2] And in Corpus Christi, in the late 1960s, parents of African American and Mexican American school children brought suit against the school district for busing ethnic Mexicans to predominantly black schools and African Americans to predominantly Mexican schools, while leaving Anglo schools alone.[3] These black-brown collaborations in lawsuits represent high water marks in the relations between African Americans and Mexican Americans.

However, Mexican American commitment to a Caucasian racial identity from the 1930s through the 1950s complicated, and in some ways compromised, what at first appeared to be a promising start to interracial cooperation. African Americans can hardly be faulted for failing to find common ground with a civil rights strategy

---

*Associate Professor of History, University of Texas at Austin.
[1]Mendez v. Westminister Sch. Dist., 64 F. Supp. 544 (D. Cal. 1946), *aff'd*, 161 F.2d 774 (9th Cir. 1947). Although the district court misspells the name of the school district, spelling it incorrectly as "Westminister" instead of "Westminster," I use the correct spelling within the text.

[2]Brown v. Bd. of Educ., 347 U.S. 483 (1954).

[3]*Mendez*, 64 F. Supp. 544 (D. Cal. 1946); Cisneros v. Corpus Christi Indep. Sch. Dist., 324 F. Supp. 599 (S.D. Tex. 1970), *aff'd in part, modified in part*, 467 F.2d 142 (5th Cir. 1972), *cert denied*, 413 U.S. 922 (1973).

based on the premise that Mexican Americans were Caucasians, and whose goal it was to end de facto segregation of Mexicans—not de jure segregation of blacks. Of significant importance in the evolution of this Caucasian identity was the finding of the 1930 U.S. census that for the first time, persons of Mexican descent, born in the United States, outnumbered Mexican immigrants. Second generation Mexican Americans, the so-called Mexican American generation, thought of themselves as "Americans" and stressed their American citizenship as the basis for being treated with equality under the law. The Mexican American generation was quick to learn a fundamental lesson of American life: being white was not just a racial identity; it was a property right that conferred concrete privileges and rights denied to those, like African and Asian Americans, who could not claim a white identity.

The first Mexican American civil rights organizations, both founded in Texas, the League of United Latin American Citizens (LULAC) and the American GI Forum, argued to anyone within earshot that Mexican Americans were white and citizens of the United States. The word "Mexican" does not even appear in the name of these organizations. "Latin American" in the 1940s and 1950s was the politically correct way to refer to Mexican Americans, and was intended to stress their affiliation with other Caucasians, principally Anglo Americans. The word "Mexican," civil rights leaders decided, was too often conflated with Mexican nationality and carried the stigma of racial mixture. In fact, to further cement their place within American society, LULAC and American GI Forum leaders joined forces with working-class Anglos to end the *bracero* program, referring to Mexican farm workers in the United States as "wetbacks" who competed with Americans for jobs and lowered wages in agricultural work.

The Mexican American generation had two decades of success in litigating against school segregation in the courts before 1954, and in all these cases the courts acknowledged, whether implicitly or explicitly, the membership of Mexicans in the Caucasian race. In response to pressure from LULAC to end discrimination against Mexican Americans in Texas and the Mexican government's deep concern over the mistreatment of *braceros*, the Texas state legislature passed the Caucasian Race Resolution in 1943, declaring that "all persons of the Caucasian Race" are entitled to "equal accommodations" and that "whoever denies to any [Caucasian] person" these equal accommodations "shall be considered as violating the good neighbor policy of this state."[4] While the concurrent resolution did not have the force of law, which would have levied fines for discrimination against Mexicans, the resolution did reflect the urgency of reaching an accommodation with the Mexican government to import *braceros* at a critical moment for the United States' involvement in World War II. LULAC took advantage of this emergency farm worker program to press its case for official recognition of their status as Caucasians, much as the courts and the census, with the exception of 1930, had been doing for decades.

With this brief history in mind, African Americans can be forgiven for not always recognizing Mexican Americans as people of color. That is not to imply,

---

[4]NEIL FOLEY, THE WHITE SCOURGE: MEXICANS, BLACKS, AND POOR WHITES IN TEXAS COTTON CULTURE 206 (1997).

however, that blacks were unmindful of discrimination against Mexican Americans, particularly in states like Texas and California where segregation included other groups besides African Americans. Rather, African Americans had to contend with a Supreme Court decision, *Plessy v. Ferguson*,[5] that allowed states to enforce segregated accommodations on public transportation, which became the basis for the separate but equal doctrine in education. Because of *Plessy*, African Americans and the NAACP sought to use the courts to force school districts to provide the same educational facilities, teacher salaries, and per student expenditures for blacks as they did for whites. While Mexican Americans were challenging school segregation in the West during the 1930s and 1940s, African Americans, primarily under the leadership of Thurgood Marshall and the NAACP, were challenging separate and unequal schooling for black children throughout the South. Mexican Americans, however, were segregated by custom rather than law, and they therefore challenged segregation head-on, no matter how equal the facilities, as an unlawful violation of the Fourteenth Amendment. They were white, and whites cannot segregate "other whites."

This strategy could not have worked for blacks, obviously, but when the NAACP decided to attack *Plessy* head-on in the 1940s to argue that separate was inherently unequal, African American litigators began taking a closer look at challenges to segregation made by other groups. And it was to the Mexican American school segregation cases that they turned, just as Gus García and Carlos Cadena turned to black challenges to jury exclusion in arguing the *Hernandez*[6] case.

Let us briefly look at three Mexican American school desegregation cases for the information and ideas that may have been useful to the NAACP in their uphill battle to overturn *Plessy*. The first thing they would have noticed was the relative ease with which the courts ended segregation in school districts where it appeared that Mexicans were being segregated on account of race. Thurgood Marshall wanted to challenge *Plessy* on precisely the ground that segregation based on race was inherently unequal and had damaging effects on those being segregated. At least in legal matters it appeared that African Americans and Mexican Americans had much to learn from each other.

We begin in 1930 when Mexican American parents in Del Rio, Texas, brought the first desegregation suit in Texas, *Independent School District v. Salvatierra*.[7] They charged school officials with enacting policies designed to accomplish "the complete segregation of the school children of Mexican and Spanish descent . . . from the school children of all other white races in the same grade. . . ."[8] The parents did not question the quality of the instruction or the condition of the separate school house; their suit was aimed exclusively at the school district's policy of separating Mexican American children from Anglo children. The district Superintendent argued that the district had a "peculiar situation as regards people of Spanish or Mexican extraction here,"[9] which involved their English language deficiency and the

---

[5]Plessy v. Ferguson, 163 U.S. 537 (1896).
[6]Hernandez v. Texas, 347 U.S. 475, 482 (1954).
[7]Indep. Sch. Dist. v. Salvatierra, 33 S.W.2d 790 (Tex. Civ. App. 1930).
[8]*Id.* at 794.
[9]*Id.* at 792.

fact that they missed a lot of school because most followed the cotton crop during the fall and were therefore "more greatly retarded" than Anglo pupils.[10] He assured the court that separate schooling "was not actuated by any motive of segregation by reason of race or color. . . ."[11] In fact, he continued, Mexican children had teachers specialized in "the matter of teaching them English and American citizenship," revealing that citizenship was something even U.S.-born Mexicans needed to learn.[12] He also told the segregated Parent Teachers Association of the Latin American Association that "Spanish speaking children are unusually gifted in music" and possessed "special facilities" for art and handicrafts, talents he hoped to develop with the hiring of new teachers.[13] Never did the Superintendent mention the word race and was careful to refer to Mexican children as "Latin Americans" or "children of Spanish or Mexican descent."[14]

The Texas Court of Appeals reversed the lower court's ruling and dissolved the injunction against expanding "the Mexican school," but warned that "school authorities have no power to arbitrarily segregate Mexican children, assign them to separate schools, and exclude them from schools maintained for children of other white races, merely or solely because they are Mexicans."[15] The arbitrary exclusion of Mexican American children from "other whites," the court ruled, constituted "unlawful racial discrimination."[16] Segregation, in other words, was unlawful when Anglo whites treated Mexican whites as a separate racial group. The Texas Court of Appeals recognized that Mexicans constituted a distinct "race" distinguished "from all other white races."[17] Almost twenty-five years later, the Supreme Court ruled in *Hernandez* that Mexicans constituted a "distinct class" that had been discriminated against in jury selection.[18] While the *Hernandez* case avoided references to Mexicans as a race, the wording of the *Salvatierra* ruling could have easily been adapted to *Hernandez*: That is, jury commissioners "have no power to exclude" Mexicans from juries, "merely or solely because they are Mexicans."[19] Where cases involving jury exclusion are concerned, one could substitute the word Italian or German or even Negro for Mexicans.

The understanding that Mexicans could not be arbitrarily segregated as a separate race from whites, like blacks in the South or Chinese and Native Americans in California, was affirmed in 1947 when the United States Ninth Circuit Court of Appeals ruled in *Westminster School District v. Mendez* that segregation of Mexican-descent children, in the absence of state law mandating segregation of Mexicans,

---

[10]*Id.*

[11]*Id.*

[12]*Id.*

[13]*Id.*

[14]*Id.*

[15]*Id.* at 795.

[16]*Id.*

[17]The language of the court decision in 1930 was interesting because it made no distinction between "race" and "ethnicity" as has been the general practice since World War II. Thus, the court wrote in the same decision, "Naturally, and in fact, the population of this section is in many communities and counties largely of Spanish and Mexican descent, who may be designated, for convenience of expression in this opinion, as the Mexican race, as distinguished, for like convenience, from all other white races." *Id.* at 794.

[18]Hernandez v. Texas, 347 U.S. 475, 480 (1954).

[19]Indep. Sch. Dist. v. Salvatierra, 33 S.W.2d 790, 795 (Tex. Civ. App. 1930).

deprived them of "liberty and property without due process" and "denied them the equal protection of the laws."[20] Judge Stephens noted that California law authorized segregation of children "belonging to one or another of the great races of mankind," which Stephens identified as Caucasoid, Mongoloid, and Negro.[21] Stephens further noted that California law permitted segregation of Indians and "Asiatics" (as well as blacks), but that no state law authorized the segregation of children "*within*" one of the great races."[22] Although European Americans, or Anglos, rarely regarded Mexican Americans as "within" the white race, in the eyes of the law, Mexican Americans were "Caucasoid" who could not be arbitrarily segregated from "other whites." In other words, the Court of Appeals for the Ninth Circuit ruled in favor of Mexican American children not on the ground that the separate-but-equal provision of *Plessy* was invalid, but that there was no California statute that mandated the segregation of Mexican Americans.

While the Ninth Circuit narrowly tailored its ruling to the illegality of segregation of Mexicans in the absence of state law, the lower district court ruling attacked segregation on much broader grounds. In ruling that segregated education violated the Fourteenth Amendment, Judge McCormick cited the 1943 Supreme Court decision *Hirabayashi v. United States*, which held that singling out citizens of Japanese descent for restriction of movement during curfew hours was constitutional in time of warfare.[23] Nevertheless, the Court did so reluctantly and acknowledged the offensiveness of making distinctions based on race: "Distinctions between citizens solely because of their ancestry are by their very nature odious to a free people whose institutions are founded upon the doctrine of equality."[24] McCormick then stated that:

> "[E]qual protection of the laws" pertaining to . . . California [public schools] is not provided by furnishing in separate schools the same technical facilities, text books and courses of instruction to children of Mexican ancestry. . . . A paramount requisite in the American system of public education is social equality. It must be open to all children by unified school association regardless of lineage.[25]

In other words, a California district court had just ruled that separate but equal was unconstitutional.

Here, the trajectories of Mexican American civil rights intersected with those of African Americans. During the 1940s, after a decade of litigation, the NAACP shifted its strategy of forcing school districts to provide equal facilities for black children to attacking the separate-but-equal doctrine of *Plessy* head-on. In the *Mendez* decision they had found a court willing to rule that segregation based on race was unconstitutional. Thurgood Marshall seized on the language of the *Mendez* lower court ruling to argue in his brief that "separation itself [is] violative of the equal protection of the laws . . . on the grounds that equality cannot be effected under a dual system of

[20]Westminster Sch. Dist. v. Mendez, 161 F.2d 774, 777 (9th Cir. 1947).
[21]*Id.* at 780 & n.7.
[22]*Id.* (emphasis added).
[23]Hirabayashi v. United States, 320 U.S. 81 (1943).
[24]*Id.* at 100.
[25]Mendez v. Westminister Sch. Dist., 64 F. Supp. 544, 549 (D. Cal. 1946), *aff'd*, 161 F.2d 774 (9th Cir. 1947).

education."[26] In that brief, Marshall skillfully combined the goals of African Americans and Latinos, namely, "equality at home" as well as the "equality which we profess to accord Mexico and Latin American nationals in our international relations."[27] For added measure, Marshall reminded the Ninth Circuit Court that the United States had ratified and adopted the Charter of the United Nations in 1945, which states that our government is obligated to promote "[u]niversal respect for . . . human rights and fundamental freedoms for all without distinction as to race. . . ."[28] Seven years later, in *Brown v. Board of Education*, Marshall would hammer home the idea, using social science literature, that segregation was inherently unequal because of the damaging effects of discrimination on black children.[29]

Unfortunately, the Ninth Circuit dismissed Marshall's argument that segregation was unconstitutional. Some of the briefs alluded to the "recent world stirring"—World War II—in the hope that the court would "strike out independently on the whole question of segregation" and re-examine "concepts considered fixed."[30] Instead Judge Stephens wrote, almost disdainfully, "[w]e are not tempted by the siren who calls to us that the sometimes slow and tedious ways of democratic legislation is [sic] no longer respected in a progressive society." [31] While the Ninth Circuit decision in *Mendez* gave Mexican Americans what they wanted, an end to segregated schooling, it gave African Americans little to hope for, since it was not likely that state legislatures throughout the South would enact democratic legislation to end Jim Crow laws in anybody's lifetime. The remedy to racial segregation would have to come from the courts, if it was to come at all. The district court in the *Mendez* case offered African Americans at least a glimmer of hope: American public education, it held, "must be open to all children . . . regardless of lineage," an unambiguous repudiation of *Plessy v. Ferguson*.[32] Judging from the roster of civil rights groups presenting briefs in the case—the American Jewish Congress, the Japanese American Citizenship League, the American Civil Liberties Union, the NAACP, and the Attorney General of California—the *Mendez* case illustrates the possibilities for cooperation and coalition building, particularly between Mexican Americans and African Americans.

The *Mendez* case, for all of its historical and juridical importance, was not cited in *Brown v. Board of Education* principally because *Brown* occurred within the familiar black-white binary. The *Brown* decision was premised on racial segregation, which was not the central issue in the *Mendez* case. The Mexican American claim that they could not be segregated because they were Caucasians and that no state law specifically mandated their segregation was virtually irrelevant to the legal argument being made by Marshall and the NAACP. And of course, the Ninth Circuit Court

---

[26]Motion and Brief of Amicus Curiae NAACP at 9, Westminster Sch. Dist. v. Mendez, 161 F.2d 774 (9th Cir. 1947) (No. 11310).

[27]*Id.*

[28]U.N. CHARTER art. 55, para. c.

[29]Brown v. Bd. of Educ. 347 U.S. 483 (1954).

[30]Westminster Sch. Dist. v. Mendez, 161 F.2d 774, 780 (9th Cir. 1947).

[31]*Id.*

[32]Mendez v. Westminister Sch. Dist., 64 F. Supp. 544, 549 (D. Cal. 1946), *aff'd*, 161 F.2d 774 (9th Cir. 1947).

flatly rejected Judge McCormick's direct attack on the separate-but-equal doctrine of *Plessy*. *Plessy* remained practically immune to constitutional challenges that segregation was a violation of the Fourteenth Amendment. The Fourteenth Amendment, paradoxically, was ratified in 1868 at the very time the U.S. Congress had devised a system of segregated schooling in the District of Columbia. Segregation of blacks and whites was the natural order of things and did not, until 1896, require constitutional approval. The *Brown* decision was based on relatively recent rulings having to do with inequality of professional and graduate education for African Americans in Oklahoma, Texas, and Missouri, as well as on social science literature that made clear the connection between segregated schooling and feelings of racial inferiority fostered by state-mandated segregation.

The influence of the *Mendez* case, however, went beyond California. Thurgood Marshall and other NAACP lawyers were preparing a desegregation case in Hearne, a small town in east Texas, in 1948, while LULAC, Mexican American attorney Gus García, and University of Texas Education Professor, George I. Sánchez, were preparing the first desegregation case in Texas since the 1930 *Salvatierra* case. With financial support from LULAC and the legal assistance of Gus García, Minerva Delgado and twenty parents of Mexican American children from five segregated school districts filed a complaint alleging that the school districts had "prohibited, barred and excluded" children "from attending the certain regular schools and classes . . . [with] other white school children. . . ." and that segregation was "unjust, capricious, and arbitrary and in violation of the Constitution . . . and denies them the equal protection of laws . . . as guaranteed by the Fourteenth Amendment. . . ."[33] Judge Rice ruled on June 15, 1948, that the five school districts named in the suit and the state superintendent of public instruction were "permanently restrained and enjoined from . . . segregating pupils of Mexican or other Latin American descent in separate schools or classes."[34] Two weeks later Professor Sánchez received a letter from Thurgood Marshall asking for access to the case file in preparation for the desegregation case in Hearne, Texas, that was going to trial later that month.[35] Sánchez wrote back that he would be happy to cooperate, but that the affidavits in the case would not be useful "in an issue such as being raised in Hearne." Affidavits in the *Delgado* case, Sánchez wrote, are "pointed specifically towards a denial of the pedagogical soundness of segregation that is based on the 'language handicap'

[33]Complaint to Enjoin Violation of Federal Civil Rights and for Damages, Delgado v. Bastrop Indep. Sch. Dist., Civil Action No. 388 (W.D. Tex. June 15, 1948) (unpublished order).

[34]Final Judgment, Delgado v. Bastrop Indep. Sch. Dist., Civ. No. 388 (W.D. Tex. June 15, 1948) *in* George I. Sánchez Papers, Box 79, Folder 5 (Benson Latin American Collection, General Libraries, University of Texas at Austin). *See also* GUADALUPE SAN MIGUEL, "LET ALL OF THEM TAKE HEED": MEXICAN AMERICANS AND THE CAMPAIGN FOR EDUCATIONAL EQUALITY IN TEXAS, 1910-1981, at 123-26 (1987).

[35]Letter from Thurgood Marshall, to George I. Sánchez (July 1, 1948) *in* George I. Sánchez Papers, Box 24, Folder 8 (Benson Latin American Collection, General Libraries, University of Texas at Austin). Marshall learned about the work of Sánchez in school desegregation cases from a phone conversation with Arthur Wirin, ACLU attorney from Los Angeles, who had filed amicus curiae briefs in numerous court cases involving school desegregation, including Mendez v. Westminster School District, 161 F.2d 774 (9th Cir. 1947) and Gonzales v. Sheely, 96 F. Supp. 1004 (D. Ariz. 1951). Marshall had also filed an amicus brief in the *Mendez* case.

excuse."[36] In other words, the strategy in the *Delgado* case was not to challenge segregation on the grounds that distinctions based on race were odious to a free people, but rather on the grounds that segregation on the basis of a "language handicap" was pedagogically unsound. Sánchez abhorred discrimination of all kinds, but his pedagogical approach to ending segregation did not resonate with Marshall's direct challenge to *Plessy* that separate schooling was inherently unequal.

A few years after the *Mendez* and *Delgado* cases, attorneys chose to challenge the court conviction of Pete Hernandez on the grounds that Mexican Americans had been systematically excluded from jury service in Jackson County, Texas. The details of the case are too well known to bear repetition here. What is important is that they relied heavily on numerous jury discrimination cases brought by African Americans who had won their cases by demonstrating that blacks had been systematically excluded from jury service. So why were Texas courts ignoring these cases (particularly *Norris v. Alabama*)[37] in ruling against Hernandez? Texas courts consistently ruled that the Fourteenth Amendment applied only to the interplay between blacks and whites in discrimination cases. Since Mexican Americans had for two decades argued that they were white, they could not claim discrimination. In their brief, the *Hernandez* lawyers strenuously objected to the appeal court judge's ruling in these words: "If, then, this Court holds that, while such statutes forbid exclusion of Negroes [from jury service], they allow exclusion of persons of Mexican descent because the latter are members of the white race, the Court is in effect saying that the statutes protect only colored men, and allow discrimination against white men."[38] The attorneys concluded their brief in these words: "All of the talk about 'two classes;' all of the verbal pointing with alarm at a 'special class' which seeks 'special privileges' cannot obscure one very simple fact which stands out in bold relief: the Texas law points in one direction for persons of Mexican descent . . . and in another for Negroes."[39] Mexican Americans wanted to be accorded the same treatment as African Americans, at least where the law and the Fourteenth Amendment were concerned.

Two weeks after the *Hernandez* ruling, African Americans won their case in *Brown v. Board of Education*. Mexican Americans wondered if the law applied to them, or if the courts might rule, as the lower courts in Texas had ruled in the *Hernandez* case, that desegregation applied only to black and white schools. Mexican Americans sought the answer twelve years later when busing appeared to be the way

---

[36]Although the plaintiffs won the case before it went to trial, Sánchez offered to share with Marshall the strategies they had developed for winning the case, which he thought might have "some value" to Marshall. Letter from George I. Sánchez, to Thurgood Marshall (July 6, 1948) *in* George I. Sánchez Papers, Box 24, Folder 8 (Benson Latin American Collection, General Libraries, University of Texas at Austin). The only other evidence of contact between the two civil rights leaders, one a lawyer, the other a professor, came in 1955 when Sánchez discussed the merits of enforcing desegregation by using the "discretionary power" of state education commissioners to cancel teacher certificates for teachers in school districts that were not desegregating, and the "disturbing tendency" of using "'free choice' and 'transfer policies' for students who do not wish to attend the school nearest their homes (that is, the 'Negro' school)." Letter from George I. Sánchez, to Thurgood Marshall (Sept. 24, 1955) *in* George I. Sánchez Papers, Box 24, Folder 8 (Benson Latin American Collection, General Libraries, University of Texas at Austin).

[37]Norris v. Alabama, 294 U.S. 587 (1935).

[38]Brief for Appellant at 16, Hernandez v. State, 251 S.W.2d 531 (Tex. Crim. App. 1952) (No. 25816).

[39]Brief for Petitioner at 30, Hernandez v. State, 347 U.S. 475 (1954) (No. 406).

to integrate schools. In 1968 African Americans and Mexican Americans in Corpus Christi joined together in a suit against the practice of busing Mexican children to predominantly black schools to achieve integration, while leaving predominantly white schools alone. School officials used the "other white" argument to justify grouping black and Latino children to achieve integration. But the judge in the case ruled otherwise: As "an identifiable, ethnic-minority group . . . *Brown* can apply to Mexican-American students in public schools."[40] The Corpus Christi desegregation case coincided with the Chicano/a Movement's evocation of "la raza," signifying their rejection of a white racial identity and embracing their mestizo heritage.

So what became of the promise of black-brown cooperation and collaboration in the years after World War II when Mexican Americans and African Americans borrowed from each other's case law to end segregation and jury discrimination? This is a complicated question and there is no easy answer. One is struck by the possibilities for meaningful collaboration and the failed promise of two very different civil rights activists, Thurgood Marshall and George I. Sánchez. They communicated by letter a few times, offered each other support and assistance, but their brief exchange of letters bore little fruit. A. I. Wirin, the activist lawyer from Los Angeles, even suggested to Sánchez that LULAC file an amicus brief in the *Heman Sweatt* case to desegregate the University of Texas Law School. Sánchez wrote back that he "would like to see an amicus brief developed along somewhat different lines from those forwarded by Thurgood Marshall."[41] In fact, however, Sánchez endorsed the logic of Marshall's argument. It's worth quoting in full how Sánchez's thinking had evolved in this 1949 letter to Wirin, a year or two after the *Delgado* and *Mendez* desegregation cases and five years before *Brown v. Board of Education*:

> In the first place, "equal protection" should go far beyond mere comparison of professors-books-buildings in law school. The comparison should be one which involves the *whole* of education that has been made available to the white law-school graduate and the *whole* of education available to the Negro. This would involve comparison of the entire common school program, the preparation of teachers, general college libraries, the pre-law programs, cultural entertainment and lecture programs, etc. Such a comparison would lead to the conclusion that equality would call for duplication all the way along the line—an impossibility since experts (not only in law but in the sciences and arts) cannot be duplicated. Furthermore, the whole idea of dichotomous education implies ostracism—and its whole spirit is based on the concept of inequality.[42]

Dichotomous education—segregation—does indeed imply ostracism, the "badge of inferiority" that *Plessy v. Ferguson* fraudulently claimed was a figment of the African American imagination. However different were their strategies for ending segregation, Mexican Americans and African Americans were determined to

---

[40]Cisneros v. Corpus Christi Indep. Sch. Dist., 324 F. Supp. 599 (S.D. Tex. 1970), *aff'd in part, modified in part*, 467 F.2d 142 (5th Cir. 1972), *cert denied*, 413 U.S. 922 (1973).

[41]Letter from George I. Sánchez, to A. L. Wirin (Nov. 18, 1949) *in* George I. Sánchez Papers, Box 62, Folder 15 (Benson Latin American Collection, General Libraries, University of Texas at Austin).

[42]*Id.* (underlining in original).

make the state acknowledge the badge of inferiority that segregation imposed, and
end it in every town and city of every state.

Perhaps it was the narrow focus on legal strategy that made it improbable that
Marshall and Sánchez, NAACP and LULAC, might work closely with each other.
When Sánchez was told in 1953 that the outcome of the *Brown* case would be influ-
enced by the *Mendez* and *Delgado* decisions, he declared:

> There is no connection! Our cases really were on the "due process" clause
> [that segregation was] ("arbitrary, capricious") much more than on the
> equality ("discrimination") clause—whereas the present [*Brown*] cases
> attack the right of the states to legislate segregation (something which has
> never been done for Mexicans). Does one of the present cases attack Negro
> segregation where there is no law decreeing such segregation? Only in such
> a case would be concerned.[43]

Sánchez was correct in arguing that African Americans were challenging a half-
century old Supreme Court decision that gave states the constitutional right to segregate on the basis of race, whereas Mexican Americans challenged not state laws
but the decisions of school district officials to arbitrarily segregate Mexicans in the
absence of state law. But this legal distinction misses the point that Sánchez himself
made years earlier, that the "whole spirit" of segregation "is based on the concept of
inequality."

Perhaps the single greatest obstacle to black-brown cooperation stemmed from
the Mexican American insistence on a white racial identity. In a letter to Roger Baldwin, the Director of the ACLU, urging continued support for Mexican-American
civil rights activities, George Sánchez wrote in 1958:

> Let us keep in mind that the Mexican-American can easily become *the
> front-line defense* of the civil liberties of ethnic minorities. The racial, cul-
> tural, and historical involvements in his case embrace those of *all . . . other
> minority groups*. Yet, God bless the law, he is "white"! So, the Mexican-
> American can be the wedge for broadening of civil liberties for others (who
> are not so fortunate as to be "white" and "Christian"!).[44]

He concluded, "I am sorry that Thurgood Marshall and the NAACP have not
seen fit to consult with us in these matters."[45] Perhaps Marshall had good reason not
to. Marshall, after all, did not bless the law that granted white privilege to Mexican
Americans but denied it to blacks, nor could he bless a strategy that opposed segregation on the narrow ground that Mexicans could not be segregated from other
whites.

In more recent times the possibilities for collaboration and cooperation between
blacks and Latinos in the political sphere seem remote, though not implausible.

---

[43]Letter from George I. Sánchez, to A. L. Wirin (Oct. 14, 1953) *in* George I. Sánchez Papers, Box 62, Folder
18 (Benson Latin American Collection, General Libraries, University of Texas at Austin).

[44]Letter from George I. Sánchez, to Roger N. Baldwin (Aug. 27, 1958) *in* George I. Sánchez Papers, Box 31,
Folder 8 (Benson Latin American Collection, General Libraries, University of Texas at Austin) (underlining in
original).

[45]*Id.*

African Americans and Mexican Americans often support different political candidates for local and national elections. It is no secret that many African Americas resent the "minority" status of Mexican Americans who, they believe, have not suffered the degree of discrimination and exclusion they have. They also point out that forty-eight percent of all Latinos in the United States chose "white" as their race in the 2000 census. Many Latinos, on the other hand, were troubled when almost half of all African Americans in California voted for Proposition 187 in 1994 to deny undocumented Mexican immigrants basic public services, including education and health care. In many cities, African Americans and Latinos continue to regard each other with mutual suspicion over competition for municipal employment and private sector jobs, representation on school boards and in city councils, and supporting candidates for political office, especially when one of their own is running.

Tensions between blacks and Latinos surfaced in the mayoral election in Los Angeles in 2001 when African Americans joined ranks with Anglos to elect James Hahn over Antonio Villaraigosa, the former speaker of the California state assembly, thus denying Latinos the opportunity to have a Mexican American mayor for the first time since the nineteenth-century. It was an especially bitter loss because Latinos constituted forty-five percent of the population compared to eleven percent for African Americans. Four years later, however, Villaraigosa defeated Hahn decisively, in large part because of Hahn's extreme unpopularity and the ongoing investigation of corruption during his term, but also because Villaraigosa ran in 2005 as a non-ideological pan-ethnic who played down his ethnic roots and won the support of the African American community. It is too early to predict if this election represents a meaningful political re-alignment of Latinos, Anglos, and African Americans in the nation's second largest city.

The 2001 mayoral election in Houston was also a source of conflict between Latinos and blacks when the incumbent African American mayor, Lee Brown, was challenged by a Cuban American Republican, Orlando Sánchez. Of those who voted, seventy-two percent of Latinos voted for Sánchez, while ninety percent of African American voters supported Lee, who won by a few percentage points.[46] Voting for one's own, regardless of party affiliation or political beliefs, may merely be an expression of ethnic or racial pride, but the suspicion nevertheless remains that Latinos do not trust African American politicians to look after their interests any more than African Americans trust Latinos who are in office. Ask any African American or Haitian resident of Miami. Looking back on early black and brown civil rights struggles in Texas, we have to wonder if African Americans and Mexican Americans can find common ground again.

---

[46]On recent tensions between Latinos and African Americans in political contests see NICK CORONA VACA, THE PRESUMED ALLIANCE: THE UNSPOKEN CONFLICT BETWEEN LATINOS AND BLACKS AND WHAT IT MEANS FOR AMERICA.

Some Are Born White, Some Achieve Whiteness, and Some Have Whiteness Thrust Upon Them: Mexican Americans and the Politics of Racial Classification in the Federal Judicial Bureaucracy, Twenty-five Years after *Hernandez v. Texas*

Steven Harmon Wilson*

This paper examines the problem of the racial and ethnic classification of Mexican Americans, and later, Hispanics, in terms of both self- and official identification, during the quarter-century after *Hernandez v. Texas*. The *Hernandez* case was the landmark 1954 decision in which the U.S. Supreme Court condemned the "systematic exclusion of persons of Mexican descent" from state jury pools.[1] Instead of reviewing the judicial rulings in civil rights cases, what follows focuses on efforts by federal judges in the Southern District of Texas to justify their jury selection practices to administrators charged with monitoring the application of various equal protection rules coming into force in the late 1970s.

This topic arises from two curious coincidences. First, in the spring of 1979, James de Anda—who had helped prepare the *Hernandez* case, and who was plaintiffs' attorney in another landmark to be described below, *Cisneros v. Corpus Christi Independent School District*—was nominated to a judgeship in the Southern District of Texas. He was confirmed by the U.S. Senate twenty-five years and one-week after the Court issued its ruling in *Hernandez*. Progress had been slow, as de Anda became only the nation's second Mexican American federal trial judge. He was sworn in by the first, Chief Judge Reynaldo Garza, who had served since 1961. Judge Garza would soon accept an appointment to the U.S. Court of Appeals for the Fifth Circuit, where he would also be breaking new ground for Mexican Americans.

Second, Judge de Anda joined the court at a time when Judge Garza was embroiled in a struggle—fought via administrative memorandum—with a judicial bureaucracy in Washington, D.C., worried about the racial composition of the district's jury pools. The federal Jury Act called for random selection of names, usually derived from local voter registration lists, or from combined voters and drivers lists. Discrimination in juror selection was prohibited under section 1862, which

---

*Assistant Professor of History, Prairie View A&M University.
[1]Hernandez v. Texas, 347 U.S. 475, 475 (1954).

states that, "[n]o citizen shall be excluded from service as a grand or petit juror . . . on account of race, color, religion, sex, national origin, or economic status."[2]

The trouble arose from a conflict regarding the application of this act to Mexican Americans: namely, were they "white" or "non-white," for the purposes of the Southern District's jury wheel (as the tabulation was still known, even after the list was computer-generated)? The references—statutory, scientific, and cultural—were contradictory. This paper will explore this practical quandary through an analysis of the various memoranda exchanged by the concerned parties.

Before discussing these issues, however, it is important to consider the context of the judicial confusion that defined race, color and origin. Throughout the twentieth-century, Mexican Americans saw civil rights claims repeatedly obscured by their muddled position in the black-or-white regime of Jim Crow. This reality continues to bedevil the study of Mexican American civil rights. For example, for fifty years, *Hernandez v. Texas* has been seen as a landmark; yet, until quite recently, there has been little scholarly analysis of the decision, its winning and losing arguments, or its ultimate constitutional legacy.[3]

The *Hernandez* at 50 conference seeks to amend this situation by looking back and taking stock. The initial question to pose is, why the half-century of neglect? One answer might begin this way: perhaps the neglect is only apparent, in that the case has been consistently cited as precedent in subsequent cases. Yes, cited but passed over quickly. Or, this answer: perhaps the silence is proper. This is a milestone erected by pioneers, who left it behind them as they continued the momentous journey towards perfected social justice. However satisfying the image, this answer would be a romantic spin, not analysis. There are at least three other answers, less satisfying, but more revealing.

First, most discussions of the case, including the caption announcement for this conference, will note that *Hernandez v. Texas* has not been given the prominence that it deserves because it arrived in the shadow of a more famous case. The *Hernandez* decision was handed down by the Supreme Court on May 3, 1954, just two weeks before the Court ruled in *Brown v. Board of Education*. The *Hernandez* decision immediately precedes *Brown* in the published U.S. Reports.[4]

---

[2]28 U.S.C. § 1862 (2004).

[3]As Clare Sheridan notes, her *Law and History Review* contribution was the first article to focus attention on *Hernandez*. See Clare Sheridan, *"Another White Race": Mexican Americans and the Paradox of Whiteness in Jury Selection*, 21 LAW & HIST. REV. 109, 122 n.52 (2003).

[4]See, e.g., Brown v. Bd. of Educ., 347 U.S. 483 (1954). The timing of the cases was coincidental. The *Brown* decision joined various "School Cases" from Kansas, South Carolina, Virginia, and Delaware. A federal judge found in 1952 that black schools in the segregated Topeka district were substantially equal to the white schools, and therefore were permissible under the "separate but equal" doctrine established by Plessy v. Ferguson, 163 U.S. 537 (1896). The plaintiffs appealed on the grounds that separation rendered facilities unequal. The Justices heard arguments in the case twice. NAACP attorneys, specifically chief counsel (and future Associate Justice of the U.S. Supreme Court) Thurgood Marshall, first argued the case on December 9, 1952. A re-argument on December 8, 1953, was generally concerned with the historical context of the passage and ratification of the Fourteenth Amendment. In another companion case, Bolling v. Sharpe, 347 U.S. 497 (1954), the Court declared the segregated schools in the federal enclave of the District of Columbia to be unconstitutional. See generally RICHARD KLUGER, SIMPLE JUSTICE: THE HISTORY OF *BROWN V. BOARD OF EDUCATION* AND BLACK AMERICA'S STRUGGLE FOR EQUALITY (2d ed. 1977).

Although the Court did not explicitly link *Hernandez* and *Brown*, the Justices' embrace of an expanded understanding of the equal protection clause in both opinions invites the logical association and constitutional comparison.[5] Yet, it is *Brown* that compelled notice then, riveted attention in the decades since, and continues to be the subject of much analysis during this joint fiftieth anniversary year, during which *Brown* is not necessarily being celebrated.[6]

There are concrete reasons for *Brown's* greater prominence in law, history, and culture. The upheaval associated with court-directed racial desegregation of schools—promising to bring about racial-mixing of children, no less—picked at the oldest scars in American society, while *Hernandez's* declaration that Mexican Americans as a class should not be barred from juries because of their "ancestry or national origin" paled by comparison. The one was fundamental, the other merely administrative, or, it must have seemed that way to the white and black families living under Jim Crow.

Mentioning this fact is not to complain about class being trumped by race in the scholarly literature. Rather, it brings me to a second point about *Hernandez's* half-century of neglect. It must be noted that both the lawyers arguing for Texas and those arguing for Pete Hernandez understood that Mexican Americans were white under the laws of Texas, albeit members of a non-Anglo "other white race." *Hernandez* seemed to prove the efficacy of the so-called "other white" legal strategy. This had significant ramifications on the decision's impact and legacy.

Within a very few years, in part because *Brown* sparked a legal and cultural revolution, *Hernandez's* failure even to question the racist basis of the Jim Crow system appeared short-sighted, perhaps even embarrassing. The "other white" victories committed Mexican American civil rights advocates to an unfruitful constitutional trajectory, based as it was on receiving due process under Jim Crow. In time, it became clear that success in those terms delayed Mexican Americans benefiting from *Brown's* equal protection arguments, which had sought to abolish Jim Crow. Yet, it was more than fifteen years before Mexican American lawyers (notably James de Anda) successfully litigated *Cisneros v. Corpus Christi Independent School District*, the case that established (at least in the Southern District of Texas) that Mexican Americans were an "identifiable ethnic minority."[7] This new landmark revived the forgotten heart of *Hernandez*, and extended it by establishing that Mexican

---

[5]Ian Haney López, Hernandez v. Brown, N.Y. TIMES, May 22, 2004, at A17.

[6]*Brown* has been rightly treated as a landmark case, but recent books about the case have begun to question its long-term benefit to African Americans. For evidence of this revisioning of *Brown* as a limited victory in a long and continuing struggle against inequality see ROBERT J. COTTROL, ET AL., BROWN V. BOARD OF EDUCATION: CASTE, CULTURE, AND THE CONSTITUTION (2003); MICHAEL J. KLARMAN, FROM JIM CROW TO CIVIL RIGHTS: THE SUPREME COURT AND THE STRUGGLE FOR RACIAL EQUALITY (2004); JAMES T. PATTERSON, BROWN V. BOARD OF EDUCATION: A CIVIL RIGHTS MILESTONE AND ITS TROUBLED LEGACY (2001); see *also* KLUGER, supra note 4. The legal histories of Mexican Americans and African Americans are linked at an earlier point, since challenges to the segregation of Mexican students laid some of the groundwork for *Brown v. Board of Education*. In California, for example, Westminster Sch. Dist. v. Mendez, 161 F.2d 774 (9th Cir. 1947) came seven years before *Brown*, and its progress was followed by the NAACP legal team. Yet, this proves the fact of the divide: this case represents the only mention Klarman makes of a Mexican American civil rights tradition (and that mention comes in a footnote). See generally KLARMAN, e.g., at 190 & n.49.

[7]Cisneros v. Corpus Christi Indep. Sch. Dist., 467 F.2d 142, 149 (5th Cir. 1972).

Americans ought to be accorded judicial protection under that other landmark of May 1954: *Brown*.[8]

Mexican Americans had not missed much in the way of court-ordered racial or ethnic progress during the fifteen years since the spring of 1954. This suggests a third explanation for the comparative lack of attention that *Hernandez* has received during the past fifty years. What *Brown* had, and *Hernandez* did not have, was follow-up litigation. The *Brown* decision of 1954 simply marked the beginning of a new phase of litigation, not the end of segregation. Chief Justice Earl Warren set out the basic rationale for the Court's decision—"separate was inherently unequal"—but he declined to broach the contentious question regarding the remedial actions that would be required to restore rights.[9]

In 1955's *Brown II*, the Justices gave local authorities "primary responsibility for elucidating, assessing, and solving" problems of administration that could be expected to delay desegregation. But the Court did not completely leave enforcement to the uncertain consciences of local, usually elected, school boards. In addition to directing (famously or infamously) the administrators to desegregate schools with "all deliberate speed," the Justices charged federal district judges with overseeing the progress of that desegregation. The decision directed judges to bring about "systematic and effective" compliance.[10]

School desegregation did not come deliberately, speedily, systematically, or effectively, because *Brown II* was vague with regard to timing and manner of desegregation. Instead, the Court all but guaranteed that African Americans would not gain the full benefits of the court victory unless and until they had filed and prevailed in many more lawsuits. These *Brown II* lawsuits occupied plaintiffs, lawyers, and federal district judges for decades to come. Progress was much too slow, but, at least the parties were engaged.[11]

---

[8]Steven H. Wilson, Brown *Over "Other White": Mexican Americans' Legal Arguments and Litigation Strategy in School Desegregation Lawsuits*, 21 LAW & HIST. REV. 145 (2003). The article in *Law & History Review* distills the relevant chapters and argument from my book, STEVEN HARMON WILSON, THE RISE OF JUDICIAL MANAGEMENT IN THE U.S. DISTRICT COURT, SOUTHERN DISTRICT OF TEXAS, 1955–2000 (2003). See, e.g., *Cisneros*, 467 F.2d 142. For contemporary legal analysis see Gerald M. Birnberg, Note, Brown v. Board of Education *Applies to Mexican-American Students and Any Other Readily Identifiable Ethnic-Minority Group or Class*, 49 TEX. L. REV. 337, 339 (1971); Betsy Levin & Philip Moise, *School Desegregation Litigation in the Seventies and the Use of Social Science Evidence: An Annotated Guide*, 39 LAW & CONTEMP. PROBS. 50, 76-80 (1975).

[9]See generally LUCAS A. POWE JR., THE WARREN COURT AND AMERICAN POLITICS 50-57 (2000); KLUGER, supra note 4.

[10]Brown v. Bd. of Educ., 349 U.S. 294, 299-301 (1955).

[11]Scholars have pondered the rationale underpinning the Supreme Court's decision to support desegregation in principle, but to abandon it in fact by ordering that segregation be dismantled through individual lawsuits in the district courts. Many critics argue that the timid Court simply passed the buck. Peter Hoffer has argued that *Brown II* was not, as is frequently contended, an instance of cynical compromise of principle in a difficult case. Hoffer noted that, if *Brown* was not "good constitutional law," the compromises it contained were "very good constitutional equity." The *Brown II* order was an equitable solution appropriate to the case. It was misinterpreted, often deliberately, by judges and local school boards choosing to read "all deliberate speed" as permission to delay. But, Hoffer concluded, the Justice's decision to remand to the district courts was not a nod to federalism, a capitulation to states' rights, or a failure of nerve; rather, Hoffer believes, the Court sought to achieve a fair decision that would respect the rights of all, even the segregationists. PETER CHARLES HOFFER, THE LAW'S CONSCIENCE: EQUITABLE CONSTITUTIONALISM IN AMERICA xii, 180-91 (1990). Another scholar has argued, however, that the Justices were concerned that a more "activist" decision would threaten the Court's prestige, already at risk, and that they decided that the federal district courts could "take the heat" of the ruling without undermining faith in the system. STEPHEN C. HALPERN, ON THE LIMITS OF THE LAW: THE IRONIC LEGACY OF TITLE VI OF THE 1964 CIVIL RIGHTS ACT 74 (1995).

There was no *Hernandez II*, which might have required the nation's federal judges to bear the burden of implementing more equitable jury selection rules. As a result, *Hernandez* languished until it was revived briefly and superseded by *Cisneros v. Corpus Christi Independent School District*, which perhaps is the closest thing to a *Hernandez II*. And this point brings us to the main theme.

Even after *Cisneros*, principles of equal protection have been applied very erratically to this "identifiable ethnic minority," mostly because the ethnic identity of Mexican Americans has ever been in the eye of the beholder. Their ethnic identity was rather more fluid than many observers wished to recognize. *Hernandez II* might have clarified the key issues (despite the failure of *Brown II* and its progeny to clarify some issues for African Americans—desegregation or integration, for example). In the absence of follow-up litigation, Mexican American ethnic identity has remained fluid, and, as a result, slippery.

How did this come about? In United States law, history, and culture, race has always been a simple matter of black and white. In 1790, the U.S. Congress limited naturalization to "white" persons. The Founders and Framers left no criteria for "whiteness," and, as F. James Davis reminds us in his book, this begged the basic question: *Who Is Black?* In the South, under the "one-drop rule," the answer was that any "black blood" at all makes a person black.[12] However, in America's multi-racial, multi-ethnic society, it did not always follow that the absence of "black blood" defined a person as "white." Instead, as Professor Haney López has shown, many people could and did claim to be *White by Law*. Haney López tells us that the criteria used to determine whiteness included skin color, facial features, national origin, language, culture, scientific opinion, and popular opinion. These criteria were usually arbitrarily applied, which is taken as proof that "race" is a social construct, reinforced by law.[13] More to the point, this history shows that racial identity was simply in the eye of the beholder.

Throughout the twentieth-century, the beholders included not only judges in courtrooms, but also representatives of varied administrative agencies, all seeking to apply their own interpretation of the latest official racial policy. Often, bureaucrats were forced to contend with individuals about the latter's racial self-identity. In particular, Mexican Americans accepted, and even defended the color line, by staking out legal claims to "whiteness." It was these debates that brought the question before the judges.[14]

These bureaucratic controversies are rooted in a long, familiar history. In a well-known early example, federal District Judge Thomas Maxey took an opportunity to indulge in anthropological speculation, in the 1897 naturalization case *In re Rodriguez*. Maxey noted that "as to color, [the plaintiff] may be classed with the copper-colored or red men. He has dark eyes, straight black hair, and high cheek bones." Judge Maxey noted that, "[I]f the strict scientific classification of the anthropologist should be adopted, he would probably not be classed as white." Yet, despite his

---

[12]F. JAMES DAVIS, WHO IS BLACK? ONE NATION'S DEFINITION 5 (1991).
[13]See generally IAN F. HANEY LÓPEZ, WHITE BY LAW: THE LEGAL CONSTRUCTION OF RACE (1996).
[14]*Id.*; see *also* Cheryl I. Harris, *Whiteness as Property*, 106 HARV. L. REV. 1707, 1753 (1993).

doubts, the judge bowed to Rodriguez's self-identification, namely, that he was not Indian, Spanish, or African, but just "pure blooded Mexican."[15]

The inclusion of Mexican-descended persons (but only if pure-blooded?) in the white race had practical consequences under the Jim Crow regime, which extended beyond the South. The federal Immigration Act of 1924 categorized national or ethnic groups around notions of whiteness, invoking current anthropological theories, contemporary scientific racism known as eugenics, and plain secular bigotry to create new immigration restrictions linked to national origin.[16] Still, this failed to solve the problem of self-identification. Note the conflation and confusion of personal opinion (that is, self-knowledge), with scientific opinion in the letter Secretary of Labor James Davis (a key player in immigration policy) wrote in 1929 to a concerned Congressman:

> [T]he Mexican people are of such a mixed stock and individuals have such a limited knowledge of their racial composition that it would be impossible for the most learned and experienced ethnologist or anthropologist to classify or determine their racial origin. Thus, making an effort to exclude them from admission or citizenship because of their racial status is practically impossible.[17]

Practically impossible, perhaps, but not impossible in practice? Civil servants tried to develop categories that were at once national, geographical, and racial, but which also blurred the personal with scientific opinion. In 1930, the Census Bureau listed Mexicans as a separate race, under an imprecise definition of persons born in Mexico, or with parents born in Mexico, and who were "not definitely white, Negro, Indian, Chinese, or Japanese."[18] Persons of Mexican-descent, and the Mexican government, vigorously protested the creation of this separate racial classification. To lessen international tension, the 1940 Census classified persons of Mexican-descent as "white," if they were "not definitely Indian or of other nonwhite race . . . ."[19]

To be on the safe side, the Census Bureau began to compile statistics on "Spanish speaking persons." In addition, the selective service created the category, "Mexican," during World War II. Such official designations, appealing in some cases to the latest science and in others to plain common knowledge, guided the courts in determinations of whether individuals did or did not belong to the "white" race.[20]

Recognizing that the official and community distinctions on lines of ethnicity, language, and even surname watered down the value of Mexican American "whiteness," the *Hernandez* lawyers appended a report, entitled "Status of Persons of Mex-

---

[15]*In re* Rodriguez, 81 F. 337, 349 (W.D. Tex 1897).

[16]Mae M. Ngai, *The Architecture of Race in American Immigration Law: A Reexamination of the Immigration Act of 1924*, J. AM. HIST. 86, 93 (1999).

[17]*Id.* at 89.

[18]*Id.* at 91.

[19]Ian F. Haney López, *Race, Ethnicity, Erasure: The Salience of Race to LatCrit Theory*, 85 CAL. L. REV. 1143, 1148 n.20, 1170–71, 1179 n.115 (1997). For a more detailed account of the fight by Mexican-descended persons to have the separate category eliminated, and thus be reclassified as white see Mario T. García, *Mexican Americans and the Politics of Citizenship: The Case of El Paso, 1936*, 59 N. M. HIST. REV. 187 (1984).

[20]LÓPEZ, supra note 13, at 205-07.

ican Descent in Texas," to their brief to the Supreme Court. This documented how many "natio-racial distinctions" differentiated Mexican Americans from other whites.[21]

In *Hernandez*, the Justices agreed that such distinctions were evidence that, despite the binary (black-versus-white) Jim Crow laws, Anglo Texans considered Mexican Americans to be a class apart from real "whites." Making a distinction of its own, however, the Court maintained that existence of prejudice did not necessarily require judges to consider Mexican descent as a protected status.[22] Follow-up lawsuits might have clarified this point, but, as previously noted, there was to be no *Hernandez II* until *Cisneros*. During the fifteen years prior to *Cisneros*, clarifications came only from political and bureaucratic efforts. These attempted clarifications left much to be desired.[23]

The civil rights consciousness of the 1960s, sparked in part by *Brown*, produced a variety of new tools that proved useful for refashioning Mexican Americans' bureaucratically approved ethnic identity. The Civil Rights Act (CRA) of 1964, for example, authorized federal officials to withhold funds from states that continued to countenance racial discrimination. Among other things, the 1964 CRA authorized the Department of Health, Education, and Welfare (HEW) to issue goals and guidelines for school desegregation.[24]

Yet, despite the fact that the Act extended its protections to "national origin" minorities, HEW's own Office of Civil Rights (OCR) blocked the value of the 1964

---

[21]See Sheridan, supra note 3, at 125 . Under Texas "Jim Crow" laws, Mexican Americans were members of the "white" race. The terms 'colored race' and 'colored children' encompassed all persons of mixed blood descended from Negro ancestry. TEX. REV. CIV. STAT. ANN., ch. 19, § 2900 (combining former arts. 2897-2898), which provided: "All available public school funds of this state shall be appropriated in each county for the education alike of white and colored children, and impartial provision shall be made for both races. No white child shall attend schools supported for colored children, nor shall colored children attend schools supported for white children." See C. H. JENKINS, 1 THE REVISED CIVIL STATUTES OF TEXAS, 1925, ANNOTATED 1036 (1925).

[22]See Hernandez v. Texas, 347 U.S. 475, 478-79, esp. n.9 (1954).

[23]In general, Mexican American civil rights advocates were inactive in the courts during the 1960s, in part because lawsuits were costly to undertake. Instead, politics consumed the older, established organizations like the League of United Latin American Citizens (LULAC) and the American GI Forum (AGIF), and inspired newer upstarts such as the Political Association of Spanish Speaking Organizations (PASSO). If asked, these organizations continued to maintain that their constituencies represented the "other white." Guadalupe Salinas, Comment, *Mexican-Americans and the Desegregation of Schools in the Southwest*, 8 HOUS. L. REV. 929, 941 (1971); Guadalupe San Miguel, Jr., *Mexican American Organizations and the Changing Politics of School Desegregation in Texas, 1945 to 1980*, 63 SOC. SCI. Q. 701, 708-09 (1982). For the older organization see BENJAMIN MÁRQUEZ, LULAC: THE EVOLUTION OF A MEXICAN AMERICAN POLITICAL ORGANIZATION (1993); CARL ALLSUP, THE AMERICAN G.I. FORUM: ORIGINS AND EVOLUTION (1982); HENRY A.J. RAMOS, THE AMERICAN GI FORUM: IN PURSUIT OF THE DREAM, 1948-1983, at 22, 58-63 (1998). PASSO (or PASO) was founded around 1960, led the campaign in 1962 that resulted in the brief Mexican American domination of the municipal government in Crystal City, Texas. ARMANDO NAVARRO, THE CRISTAL EXPERIMENT: A CHICANO STRUGGLE FOR COMMUNITY CONTROL 17-51 (1998). For later political developments in the same city, in years after the Chicano movement emerged see ARMANDO L. TRUJILLO, CHICANO EMPOWERMENT AND BILINGUAL EDUCATION: MOVIMIENTO POLITICS IN CRYSTAL CITY, TEXAS (1998). See also DAVID MONTEJANO, ANGLOS AND MEXICANS IN THE MAKING OF TEXAS, 1836-1986, at 282-84 (1987).

[24]42 U.S.C. § 2000(a). See Comment, *The Courts, HEW, and Southern School Desegregation*, 77 YALE L.J. 321 (1967); see also Louis Fisher, *The Judge As Manager*, 25 PUB. MANAGER 7 (1996); J. HARVIE WILKINSON III, FROM *BROWN* TO *BAKKE*: THE SUPREME COURT AND SCHOOL INTEGRATION: 1954-1978, at 102-07 (1979).

CRA for Mexican Americans. OCR investigated alleged discrimination, but initially gathered statistics using only black and white categories. HEW began to collect data on Mexican Americans only after physician Hector P. Garcia, the founder of the American G.I. Forum (AGIF) and the first Mexican American member of the U.S. Civil Rights Commission, rebuked OCR for failing to examine Mexican Americans' complaints.[25]

HEW began to publish data on black, white, and "other" in 1967. The "others" now included "any racial or national origin group for which separate schools have in the past been maintained or which are recognized as significant 'minority groups' in the community." Examples HEW offered included: "Indian American, Oriental, Eskimo, Mexican-American, Puerto Rican, Latin, Cuban, etc." Later, HEW published statistics on "Spanish Surnamed Americans," and issued a series of "Mexican-American Studies."[26]

The shift to a newly official "other minority" status, as opposed to the old "other white" status, was resisted by some of those persons affected. Carlos Guerra, a Spanish-surnamed and presumably Mexican-descended student at Texas A&I (now Texas A&M University-Kingsville), wrote a column for the October 1967 issue of the *Texas Observer*, entitled *Discourse by An Other*. Mr. Guerra complained specifically about Washington's misguided attempts—or perhaps it was a too clever ploy—to declare "the second largest minority group in the country non-White."[27] This response suggests that, in addition to complaining about official statements that were effectively setting aside Mexican Americans as a distinct group, Mr. Guerra was at the same time resistant to Chicano activism, which was emerging at Texas A&I around this time. Chicanos rejected the very "white" status fought for by their elders. Instead, Chicanos celebrated a "brown" identity they had constructed for themselves.[28]

Clearly, social forces were working to change the terms of the traditional racial and ethnic discourse. Yet, opposed to the Chicano movement's politics, and HEW's bureaucracy, there were still the old-style armchair racial theorists.[29]

---

[25]See Salinas, supra note 23, at 939; GUADALUPE SAN MIGUEL, JR., "LET ALL OF THEM TAKE HEED": MEXICAN AMERICANS AND THE CAMPAIGN FOR EDUCATIONAL EQUALITY IN TEXAS, 1910-1981, at 175-77 (1987).

[26]Jorge C. Rangel & Carlos M. Alcala, *Project Report: De Jure Segregation of Chicanos in Texas Schools*, 7 HARV. C.R.-C.L. L. REV. 307, 365-66 n.359-60, 366 (1972). See *also* Testimony of Jerold D. Ward (Dec. 11, 1968) *in* U.S. COMM'N ON CIVIL RIGHTS, HEARING HELD IN SAN ANTONIO, TEXAS 331-39 (1968).

[27]Carlos Guerra, *Discourse By An Other*, TEX. OBSERVER, Oct. 27, 1967 at 7, 14.

[28]The literature on the rise of Chicanismo as a political and cultural force is increasing in recent years. The following older sources are still a good place to begin. See MATT S. MEIER & FELICIANO RIBERA, MEXICAN AMERICANS/AMERICAN MEXICANS: FROM CONQUISTADORS TO CHICANOS 211 (rev. ed. 1993); *see also* MONTEJANO, supra note 23, at 262-87 (1987); Walter Elwood Smith, Jr., Mexicano Resistance to Schooled Ethnicity: Ethnic Student Power in South Texas, 1930-1970, at 288-97 (1978) (unpublished Ph.D. dissertation, University of Texas at Austin) (on file with the University of Texas at Austin Library); U.S. COMM'N ON CIVIL RIGHTS, MEXICAN AMERICAN EDUCATIONAL STUDY, REPORT I: ETHNIC ISOLATION OF MEXICAN AMERICAN IN THE PUBLIC SCHOOLS OF THE SOUTHWEST 26 (1971).

[29]The same year, 1967, the Supreme Court ruled in the famous interracial marriage case, *Loving v. Virginia*, effectively overturning the trial judge, who had stated in his original opinion that: "Almighty God created the races white, black, yellow, malay and red . . . . The fact that he separated the races shows that he did not intend for the races to mix." Loving v. Virginia, 388 U.S. 1, 3 (1967). Note that there is not a "brown" category, nor is there an indication that various white races fit this judge's bill.

Seventy years after *In re Rodriguez*, a dozen years after *Hernandez*, and in the midst of a civil rights revolution, Mexican Americans still struggled with official confusion and community division regarding color, race, nationality, ethnicity, or some other construct. These were not academic debates, because Mexican Americans—however ill-defined by judges, bureaucrats, or themselves—continued to suffer from the widespread discrimination that had motivated *Hernandez*.

In October 1967, during hearings in El Paso of the newly established "Inter-Agency Committee on Mexican American Affairs," James de Anda, the long-time legal advisor to the G.I. Forum, testified to lingering discrimination in jury selection, voting, and school enrollment. Because the lack of private resources prevented large-scale private litigation, de Anda proposed that the federal government increase public legal assistance. Noting that the 1964 CRA provided for the judicial award of plaintiffs' attorneys' fees in certain employment discrimination cases, de Anda suggested that a similar compensation scheme would be very appropriate in some voting, jury, and school lawsuits. In addition, de Anda challenged the U.S. Justice Department to recognize and begin fighting discrimination against Mexican Americans with the same vigor it finally was beginning to demonstrate in African Americans' cases.[30]

De Anda's recommendations ultimately were acted upon, but only after several years of official dithering.[31] In the meantime, he and other Mexican Americans resumed their own privately funded civil rights litigation. In that momentous year 1967, for example, San Antonio attorney Pete Tijerina obtained a multi-million, multi-year grant from the Ford Foundation, and founded the Mexican American Legal Defense and Education Fund (originally MALD, but now MALDEF). When the Civil Rights Commission held its December 1968 hearings in San Antonio, Dr. Garcia invited Tijerina to describe his reasons for establishing MALDEF. Tijerina answered that his experience in defending Mexican Americans before all-Anglo

---

[30]James de Anda, *Civil Rights-Need for Executive Branch To Take Positive Steps To Rectify Discrimination in Jury Selection, Voting Eligibility and School Enrollment, in* INTER-AGENCY COMMITTEE ON MEXICAN AMERICAN AFFAIRS, THE MEXICAN AMERICAN: A NEW FOCUS ON OPPORTUNITY 217, 217-21 (1968). President Lyndon B. Johnson created the Inter-Agency Committee in response to Mexican American complaints that his administration had ignored their community's problems. The El Paso meetings became yet another point of contention, however, when the Committee excluded the "militant" Mexican American leaders. See ALLSUP, supra note 23, at 136-41; RAMOS, supra note 23, at 99-106. Fees for counsel were provided in some employment discrimination cases under Title VII of the Civil Rights Act of 1964. 42 U.S.C. § 2000e-5(k) (1964). Congress later enacted provisions similar to those de Anda suggested. These statutes authorize and even encourage the award of attorney's fees to the prevailing parties in school desegregation cases. The case for court-ordered imposition of attorney's fees is particularly strong where the plaintiffs have incurred substantial expense due to the obstinate refusal of a school board to recognize and comply with its legal obligations. See Emergency School Aid Act, 20 U.S.C. § 1617 (1972). On Oct. 19, 1976, Congress enacted the Civil Rights Attorney's Fees Awards Act, 42 U.S.C. § 1988 (1976). This provided for prevailing plaintiffs to recover reasonable attorney's fees in § 1983 actions. The trial judge has discretion to decide what is a "reasonable" fee. 42 U.S.C. § 1988(b) (1976), *amended by* Pub.L. 104-317, Tit. III, § 309(b), 110 Stat. 3853 (119) (describing "attorney's fees."). See generally ALAN HIRSCH & DIANE SHEEHEY, AWARDING ATTORNEYS' FEES AND MANAGING FEE LITIGATION (1994) (pamphlet by Federal Judicial Center). In 1969, Congress established the Committee on Opportunities for Spanish Speaking People to Succeed the Inter Agency Committee. 91 Pub.L. 181, 83 Stat. 838 (1969).

[31]The U.S. Attorney General waited until late 1969 to join in a Mexican American lawsuit. The unreported case was Perez v. Sonora Indep. Sch. Dist., Civ. No. 6-224 (N.D.Tex. 1969) *cited in* Birnberg, supra note 8, at 339 n.10.

juries, more than a decade after *Hernandez*, convinced him that a dedicated legal defense organization was necessary.[32]

By the late-1960s, the most pressing issue for Mexican American civil rights attorneys seemed to be the need to reframe the judicial responses to *Brown's* mandates. Mexican Americans maintained their hard-won "white" status as late as 1966, when de Anda sought to enjoin "ability tracking," a common high school practice which established two "tracks," one for college-bound student and another for "terminal" high school students. De Anda argued, successfully, that an arbitrary testing system ensured that students of Mexican-descent dominated the latter category.[33] As in *Hernandez*, de Anda argued that the arbitrariness of the method denied the due process guaranteed in the Fourteenth Amendment.[34]

But, de Anda was at last ready to abandon the "other white" strategy and base a Mexican American civil rights complaint on an equal protection rationale. If successful, this might yield the expansive court-ordered remedies that *Brown* had made available to African Americans fifteen years earlier. In the path-breaking *Cisneros* case, de Anda complained that Corpus Christi Independent School District, like many Texas districts, had turned the "other white" notion to its own illegitimate purposes. In order to delay the court-ordered desegregation, while at the same time obscuring its slow pace, district officials frequently assigned African and Mexican Americans to the same schools, rather than to white schools, a practice often facilitated by the close proximity of the ghettos to the barrios. The administrators maintained that, because Mexican Americans were "white," the barrio-ghetto schools had been desegregated. Federal judges and HEW—continuing to operate under Jim Crow's black-white binary—accepted this logic.[35] Although de Anda hedged his bets a bit by referring briefly to the "other white" strategy, he focused most on the novel contention that *Brown* should apply to, and so condemn, this systematic segregation of Mexican Americans.[36]

De Anda marshaled evidence from history, sociology, and demography (that is, he used arguments rooted in both scientific opinion and common knowledge) to show that, despite being "white," many Mexican Texans still suffered widespread discrimination at the hands of the Anglos in the majority. De Anda persuaded Southern District Judge Woodrow Seals, who declared that, for the purposes of desegre-

---

[32]Tijerina modeled the new organization on the NAACP's incorporated litigation arm, the Legal Defense Fund (LDF, or the "Inc. Fund"), and intended to imitate LDF's strategy of undertaking "planned" litigation. Karen O'Connor & Lee Epstein, *A Legal Voice for the Chicano Community: The Activities of the Mexican American Legal Defense and Educational Fund, 1968-1982, in* THE MEXICAN AMERICAN EXPERIENCE: AN INTERDISCIPLINARY ANTHOLOGY 281, 284-85 (Rodolfo O. de la Garza et al. eds., 1985). In time, MALDEF supported de Anda's suit against the Corpus Christi Independent School District as amicus curiae.

[33]For the practice of "tracking" see Rangel & Alcala, supra note 26, at 331-33, esp. n.139 (1972). See ALLSUP, supra note 23, at 94-97 (1982); RAMOS, supra note 23, at 22, 58-63 .

[34]See e.g., Chapa v. Odem Indep. Sch. Dist., Civ. No. 66-C-72 (S.D. Tex 1967) (on file in appellate case files for Cisneros v. Corpus Christi Indep. Sch. Dist., Civ. A. No. 68-C-95). However, Judge Woodrow Seals requested additional evidence to support the validity of the ability testing in general. See Rangel & Alcala, supra note 26, at 347-48 & nn.241-45 (1972).

[35]*Id.* at 342-43, n.216, 348-49; Birnberg, supra note 8, at 339; Levin & Moise, supra note 8, at 76-80 (1975); SAN MIGUEL, supra note 25.

[36]Rangel & Alcala, supra note 26, at 342, 359 (1972).

gating public schools, Mexican Americans formed an "identifiable ethnic minority" which deserved, but had been denied, the equal protection of the laws.[37]

Judge Seals' ruling pleased many Mexican Americans, but it remained to be seen whether the court could devise a "tri-ethnic" remedy to desegregate the white, black, and brown schools.[38] There was no guarantee that Seals' judicial colleagues and superiors would accept the ruling. In 1969, for example, Judge Ben C. Connally opened what he called "another chapter" in the long Houston desegregation saga, *Ross v. Houston Independent School District*. Houston Independent School District enrolled 240,000 students of which two-thirds were designated white and one-third black. HEW estimated that 36,000 of these students were "Spanish-surnamed Americans," approximately fifteen percent of the student population. According to standard practice, Judge Connally included the Spanish-surnamed students in the "white" figures, and approved a district plan to combine Mexican Americans with African Americans. In Houston, it was the African American plaintiffs who appealed.[39]

In their August 1970 majority opinion, Fifth Circuit Judges Homer Thornberry and Lewis Morgan affirmed Judge Connally's ruling, in part, praising his "learned, thorough, detailed consideration" of the legal and practical issues.[40] Judge Charles Clark, a usually conservative Nixon appointee and the third member of the Circuit panel,[41] alone voiced any concern that the Spanish-surnamed students were officially ignored in integration plans, yet Mexican American majority schools were to be paired with black schools in order to "integrate" them. Referring to Seals' *Cisneros* ruling, the judge asserted that "it is a mock justice when we 'force' the numbers by pairing disadvantaged Negro students into schools with members of this equally disadvantaged ethnic group." Clark then declared:

> We seem to have forgotten that the equal protection right enforced is a right to education, not statistical integration. Why, on this kind of a theory, we could end our problems by the simple expedient of requiring that in compiling statistics every student in every school be alternately labeled white

---

[37]See e.g., Cisneros v. Corpus Christi Indep. Sch. Dist., 324 F.Supp. 599, 607 (S.D. Tex. 1970).

[38]Salinas, supra note 23, at 951. For the rest of this story see WILSON, supra note 8, at chap. 5.

[39]Ross v. Eckels, 317 F.Supp. 512, 513-14 (S.D. Tex. 1970), *aff'd in part, rev'd in part*, 434 F.2d 1140, 1141 (5th Cir. 1970).

[40]Ross v. Eckels, 434 F.2d 1140, 1146-48 (5th Cir. 1970).

[41]As Nixon's first appointee to the Fifth Circuit, Clark harbored at least some of the President's reservations regarding the pace and direction of recent integration decisions. But Clark was a conservative judge, who argued for caution, not a reactionary who called for the rollback of civil rights. For example, he had also written a dissent in the latest en banc rehearing of the *Singleton* case. See Singleton v. Jackson Mun. Separate Sch. Dist., 425 F.2d 1211, 1217-24 (5th Cir. 1970). Clark was already well-known to his new Fifth Circuit colleagues. And, despite having defended Governor Ross Barnett before the Fifth Circuit during the 1962 desegregation showdown over James Meredith's registration for classes at "Ole Miss," he was well respected. See Meredith v. Fair, 305 F.2d 345 (5th Cir. 1962), *cert. denied*, 371 U.S. 828 (1962). FRANK T. READ & LUCY S. MCGOUGH, LET THEM BE JUDGED: THE JUDICIAL INTEGRATION OF THE DEEP SOUTH 228-32, 346-47, 453-58 (1978). See also JACK BASS, UNLIKELY HEROES 176-77, 312-13, 331 (1990).

and Negro! Then, you see, everything would come out 50-50 and could get our seal of approval once and for all.[42]

After delivering this taunt, Clark "respectfully" dissented. This had no effect on the ruling, but Clark's pointed remarks reflected his, and probably the minority community's, growing frustration with the course of desegregation.

In early 1971, MALDEF attempted to keep the question open, and sought Judge Connally's permission to intervene in the *Ross* litigation. In a brief memorandum opinion denying the motion, Connally noted that the Houston Independent School District and other school districts "always treated Latin-Americans as of the Anglo or White race." In a reference to MALDEF's reliance on the *Cisneros* ruling, Connally declared that, even if Mexican Americans were an identifiable minority group, that did not entitle them "to escape the effects of integration" with African Americans. The judge stood among the many policy-makers of the period who failed to recognize the effect of Mexican Americans' evolving consciousness. Indeed, as suggested by Mr. Guerra's 1967 column, acceptance of this portentous political shift was far from universal, even among younger Mexican Americans. Incredibly, in denying MALDEF's motion, the judge contended that Mexican Americans had never been subject to "state-imposed segregation."[43]

Judge Connally wrestled further with the ambiguities of Mexican American self-identification when he grappled with the old problem of equitable jury selection. In a March 1969 note to Fifth Circuit Judge Walter Gewin, for example, he had to

---

[42]*Ross v. Eckels*, 434 F.2d at 1150-51. For contemporary comments on Judge Clark's dissent see Salinas, supra note 23, at 943, 949-50. No one in Houston was happy with the Ross plan. In late August 1970, the Houston Independent School District board reluctantly prepared to implement the zoning and pairing ordered by the Fifth Circuit. The African American plaintiffs contemplated appealing to the Supreme Court. Several Mexican American civic, political, and religious groups formed an umbrella organization, the Mexican American Education Council (MAEC), to coordinate responses to *Ross*, including a school boycott. The group encouraged parents to keep students out of class on opening-day of the new term. More than 3500 Mexican American students stayed home. The group also roused the Mexican American parents to picket elementary schools, bus stops, and the Houston Independent School District administration building. MAEC organized more than two dozen huelga ("strike") schools staffed by volunteer teachers. Leonel Castillo, who would be named director of the federal Immigration and Naturalization Service (INS) by President Jimmy Carter, was a MAEC leader. He was employed as the community relations director for the Roman Catholic diocese of Galveston and Houston. GUADALUPE SAN MIGUEL, JR., BROWN, NOT WHITE: SCHOOL INTEGRATION AND THE CHICANO MOVEMENT IN HOUSTON 98–103 (2001). Castillo entered mainstream politics in Houston in 1971 and was elected the city controller. See Leonel Castillo, *The Growth of Hispanic Political Power in the Houston Area, in* HISPANICS IN HOUSTON AND HARRIS COUNTY, 1519–1986, at 186-87, 192-93, 198 (Dorothy F. Caram et al. eds., 1989); ARNOLDO DE LEÓN, ETHNICITY IN THE SUNBELT: A HISTORY OF MEXICAN AMERICANS IN HOUSTON 186-87, 192-93 (2001); SAN MIGUEL, supra note 25, at 179; WILLIAM HENRY KELLAR, MAKE HASTE SLOWLY: MODERATES, CONSERVATIVES, AND SCHOOL DESEGREGATION IN HOUSTON 158 (1999). For other attempts in Houston to form multi-ethnic or multi-racial solutions see Ann Dee Quiroz, Black, White, and Brown: The Houston Council on Human Relations and Tri-Racial Relations in Houston 66–82 (1998) (unpublished M.A. thesis, University of Houston) (on file with the University of Houston at Austin Library). At a school board meeting during this period, fourteen people were arrested for inciting a riot. Most of those arrested were not members of MAEC, but members of two militant groups, the Mexican-American Youth Organization and the Chicano Student Committee. Guadalupe San Miguel, Jr., *A Struggle In Vain; Ignoring Ethnicity is a Slap in the Face Of All Colors by HISD*, HOUS. CHRON., Sept. 28, 1997, at Outlook 1. As originally published this article indicated that 1400 people were arrested at the board meeting. The editors printed a correction changing the number to fourteen arrested protesters two days later. See HOUS. CHRON., Sept. 30, 1997.
[43]Rangel & Alcala, supra note 26, at 349.

explain the recently reported racial imbalance of the jury pools in the Southern District of Texas. His position was consistent with his declaration in the school case. "I reiterate," Connally wrote to his administrative superior, "that during my long and close association with the Laredo Division, and long though less close association with Brownsville, there is not and has never been any discrimination against Latins."[44]

The report in question was part of a program established by the Judicial Conference Committee on the Operation of the Jury System, conceived for monitoring the compliance with the Jury Selection and Service Act of 1968, which required that jury pools reflect a 'fair cross section'[45] of the local community. Judge Connally argued that, especially in the Brownsville and Laredo Divisions, the large population of Mexican Americans complicated the statistics. The Administrative Office of the U.S. Courts, following the lead of many other federal agencies, admitted only the old binary racial categories. Mexican Americans often self-identified in ways that did not satisfy the Administrative Office. Connally wrote Gewin to present "an accurate tabulation."[46]

The figures were based on questionnaires, Connally wrote, and some of the potential jurors were "of racially-mixed Anglo-Latin blood," and "simply refer to themselves as 'White' rather than as either Anglo or Latin." From his own observations, the judge estimated that juries were composed of "50 to 75% of persons bearing Latin surnames or who are obviously of Latin extraction in whole or in part."[47]

As a result of the choice being left to the prospective jurors, there were varied and ambiguous answers to Question 16, which inquired into the "race" of prospective jurors.[48] Judge Connally suggested that the Administrative Office consider changing the questionnaire, so the juror should have only certain categories in which to answer, rather than a blank line to fill. The Southern District clerks saw 'Spanish,' 'German extraction,' and other idiosyncratic responses, which required them to exercise a discretion that the judge believed "should be avoided."[49]

But, the data was in the report as it was tabulated, and Connally sought to allow the administrators "properly to understand [and] interpret it." As his example, the judge noted that in the Laredo Division, of the 755 prospective jurors who answered Question 16, 725 answered "Anglo;" 30 answered "Latin;" and no one answered "Negro" or "Other."[50]

This left the impression that the Laredo juries were disproportionately white. Not so, said Connally. "Whether of common knowledge or not," the judge wrote, "it is a fact by my personal knowledge and observation that there is no discrimination

---

[44]Memorandum from Chief Judge Connally, to Judge Walter Gewin (Mar. 7, 1969) (Clerk's files of Chief Judge Ben C. Connally, folder 2) (on file with the Office of the Clerk of the Court, U.S. District Court, Southern District of Texas).

[45]Jury Selection and Service Act, 28 U.S.C.S. § 1861 (1968).

[46]See Memorandum from Chief Judge Connally, supra note 44.

[47]Id.

[40]Id.

[49]Id.

[50]Memorandum from Chief Judge Connally, Addendum to 'Tabulation by Race and Sex of Prospective Jurors, to Judge Walter Gewin 1 (Mar. 7, 1969) (Clerk's files of Chief Judge Ben C. Connally, folder 2) (on file with the Office of the Clerk of the Court, U.S. District Court, Southern District of Texas).

directed at those of Latin ancestry. There is a complete mixing and mingling of the races in all spheres of business and society. There is and always has been a high incidence of intermarriage between the races. There is scarcely a family which has lived in the area for a matter of several generations which is not of mixed Anglo-Latin blood." Bearing this in mind, the judge concluded, the report of "'Anglo . . . 725' and 'Latin . . . 30' [was] not a true reflection of the situation as it exists."[51] Indeed, a recount of the questionnaires showed the following: "'White . . . 640,' 'Anglo . . . 13,' 'Caucasian . . . 72,' 'Latin' or 'Mexican . . . 30.'" It was apparent, to the judge, that a great majority of those prospective jurors of "Latin-Anglo extraction" answered "'White' or 'Caucasian.'"[52]

To confirm this suspicion, Connally examined the lists of petit and grand jurors who appeared in Laredo during 1968. Of these, by his count, 111 had Latin surnames, and 168 had Anglo surnames. The judge contended that even this, however, was not an accurate reflection of the ratio of the races, "in that a great many of those with Anglo surnames are the product of a mixed marriage and are of Latin-Anglo blood."[53]

With regard to the Brownsville Division, where the racial composition was essentially the same as in Laredo, the data showed that, of the 1687 prospective jurors who replied to Question 16 (and, it should be noted that 385 prospectives did not answer), there were reportedly "Anglo . . . 696, Latin . . . 987, Negro . . . 4, Other . . . 0."[54] On the surface, this would appear to be a reasonably accurate ratio, but a judicial recount showed the following: "Unanswered . . . 518, Anglo . . . 73, Latin . . . 63, Negro . . . 4, White . . . 1293, Caucasian . . . 121, Human . . . 2, $1.60 per hour . . . 1."[55] The discrepancies between the second count and the first arose because the deputy clerk in Brownsville, misunderstanding the instructions, used her own judgment in classifying the prospective juror as either Latin or Anglo, based on surname, if Question 16 was left blank. Additionally, there were a number of cases where the answer was ambiguous. As had been done in Laredo, the judge surmised, a majority of those replying "White" were "entirely or partly of Latin blood."[56]

Given these recurring mistaken tabulations, Judge Connally suggested that Question 16 should be eliminated from the questionnaire. In addition, he believed that some of these answers showed resentment on the part of several prospective jurors that the question had been asked, even though they were instructed that they could omit the answer if desired. The attitude seemed to be that, on the question of jury service in a federal court, "race should not matter and should not be inquired into." Perhaps the judge was projecting his own feelings. He closed his memorandum noting that, "Personally, I share those sentiments."[57]

The questions continued, and the myriad ambiguities of the "Anglo-Latin," "Latin," or even "Spanish surname" continued as well. Within a few years, this was

[51]*Id.* at 2.
[52]*Id.*
[53]*Id.*
[54]*Id.* at 3.
[55]*Id.*
[56]*Id.*
[57]See supra note 44.

no longer Connally's concern. In December 1974, he reached the age of sixty-five years, and took semi-retirement as a "senior judge."[58] His replacement on the bench was Laredo attorney Robert O'Conor Jr., whose own background seemed to prove Connally's point about the ambiguities of ethnic identity. Although Judge O'Conor had a Mexican-descended grandmother, he was clearly an Anglo, not the newest Mexican American federal judge.[59]

As Chief Judge, Connally was succeeded by Brownsville's own Reynaldo Garza, who was the first (and, until 1979, only) Mexican American federal judge in the Southern District. In the late 1970s, Judge Garza was still attempting to square self-identified racial status with the approved judicial-legislative-administrative distinctions.[60]

In 1977, in response to policy requirements, the federal Office of Management and Budget (OMB) issued Statistical Policy Directive Number 15, *Race and Ethnic Standards for Federal Statistics and Administrative Reporting*. Now, four racial categories were established: (1) American Indian or Alaskan Native; (2) Asian or Pacific Islander; (3) Black; and (4) White. In addition, however, two ethnic categories were established: "Hispanic origin;" and "Not of Hispanic origin." Although the Census Bureau traditionally had used more categories than these for the decennial census, they now collapsed into the same four racial categories used by OMB, plus, of course, the category "some other race."[61]

The Census Bureau published the following to explain its latest attempts to clarify racial reporting: "The category 'white' includes persons who indicated their race as white, as well as persons who did not classify themselves in one of the specific race categories on the questionnaire[,] but entered Mexican, Puerto Rican, or a response suggesting Indo-European stock."[62] Thus, "white" was to be the default designation in cases of questionable self-identification.

---

[58]Judges were eligible for this status at seventy-years of age (after ten years of service), or sixty-five-years of age (after fifteen). Senior Judges retained their judgeship but carried a reduced docket, and continued to draw a salary. They could be called back to assist the court if the judge wished to serve temporarily. 28 U.S.C. § 371 (2004). Senior Judge Connally suffered a heart attack on December 2, 1975, while hunting on a ranch near Falfurrias, Texas. He was accompanied on the trip—and then to the Brooks County Hospital, where he died—by his wife, by Chief Judge Garza, and by Judge Cox. *Judge Ben Connally Dies of Heart Attack*, HOUS. POST, Dec. 3, 1975 at 1A, 19A; *Judge Ben C. Connally, Who Presided Over Houston's School Integration Battles*, N.Y. TIMES, Dec. 4, 1975, at 44.

[59]President Gerald R. Ford appointed Robert O'Conor, Jr. in April 1975. O'Conor was born on June 22, 1934, in Los Angeles, California, where his Texas-born father worked as a stuntman and extra in westerns. Eventually, the family returned to Texas, where O'Conor attended UT as an undergraduate, earning his B.A. in 1956, and as a law student, earning his LL.B. in 1957. He entered private general legal practice in Laredo as soon as he graduated. O'Conor was the first Southern District judge in a generation to have missed service during wartime, but he was a U.S. Army Reserve Captain in the Judge Advocate General Corps from 1957 to 1964. O'Conor was not particularly active in local politics. Perhaps, in the aftermath of the Watergate crisis, the disgrace and resignation of President Nixon, and accession of President Ford, O'Conor's basic neutrality in partisan matters was a benefit. Interview with Robert J. O'Conor Jr., U.S. District Judge, Southern District of Texas, in Houston, Tex. (Jan. 2, 1998).

[60]Memorandum from Chief Judge Reynaldo Garza, to John Shapard (June 5, 1978) (Clerk's files of Chief Judge Reynaldo G. Garza, folder 4) (on file with the Office of the Clerk of the Court, U.S. District Court, Southern District of Texas).

[61]U.S. CENSUS BUREAU, RACIAL AND ETHNIC CLASSIFICATIONS USED IN CENSUS 2000 AND BEYOND *available at* http://www.census.gov/population/www/socdemo/race/racefactcb.html (last revised Apr. 12, 2000).

[62]Recall that in the 1930 Census reports, Mexicans were classified in the 'other' race category, the bureau also confirmed that the 1930 data had been revised to include Mexicans in the white population, as in the census reports in subsequent years. Memorandum from John Shapard, to "All Clerks of Court" (Feb. 4. 1977) (Clerk's files of Chief Judge Reynaldo G. Garza, folder 4) (on file with the Office of the Clerk of the Court, U.S. District Court, Southern District of Texas).

John Shapard, of the Research Division of the Federal Judicial Center (FJC), wrote to court clerks in February 1977, to instruct them how the evolution of the Census and OMB rules would affect their future tabulation of local jury composition, required by the Judicial Conference to be reported on Form JS-12. Shapard wrote that any prospective jurors whose questionnaires "show race as Mexican, Puerto Rican, or similar Latin or Spanish races, should be counted as WHITE." The reason for this "odd-seeming requirement," he added, was that the Census Bureau now classified race in the same fashion. That mattered because the purpose of the JS-12 (which also recorded sex) was to permit a comparison of jury wheels to the population eligible for jury service, and Census reporting was regarded as the only source of reliable population data. Shapard particularly worried that if JS-12 reports did not include "Indo-European" in "white" totals, statistical analysis "may falsely indicate racial imbalance in . . . jury wheels." Shapard invited the clerks to call him directly if they had questions.[63]

In April 1978, Carl H. Imlay, the Administrative Office's General Counsel, wrote to all District Court Chief Judges. Imlay enclosed the most recent statistical reports derived from returned JS-12 forms. Noting that the report "involved complex data gathering that presented many opportunities for the introduction of error," Imlay sent the preliminary report in order to afford judges an opportunity to review the results prior to the submission to the Jury Committee. Imlay invited any judge suspecting erroneous or misleading results to share these concerns with the Research Division of the FJC, which analyzed the JS-12s.[64]

The racial distribution reported among prospective jurors for Houston, and several others of the court's divisions, fell within the proportions suggested by the 1970 Census of population distribution. Some initially disturbing numbers could be explained away as computer errors. The report did raise several red flags, however, particularly with regard to Brownsville and Laredo, where the distribution indicated a disproportionate representation vis-à-vis the 1970 Census tally. Clearly, not everyone involved in the jury selection process had received, read, or understood the memorandum explaining the new rules. Some of the Southern District's clerks' continued to designate Mexican American jurors as "non-white," which, as Shapard feared would occur, resulted in the "drastic overrepresentation" of non-whites.[65]

Roughly, the reported ratios were: Brownsville, 3 whites to 1 non-white; Laredo, 7 to 1; Corpus Christi, 30 to 1; Houston 4.5 to 1; Galveston, 5.5 to 1; Victoria, more than 20 to 1.[66] Note how the grounds of the debate shifted: two decades after *Hernandez*, jury pools in Texas federal courts that feature a 3-to-1 ratio were not white enough, because the 1970 Census predicted much higher ratios.

[63]Memorandum from John Shapard, to "All Clerks of Court" (Feb. 4. 1977) (Clerk's files of Chief Judge Reynaldo G. Garza, folder 4) (on file with the Office of the Clerk of the Court, U.S. District Court, Southern District of Texas).

[64]Memorandum from Carl H. Imlay, to "Chief Judges, United States District Courts" (Apr. 12, 1978) (Clerk's files of Chief Judge Reynaldo G. Garza, folder 4) (on file with the Office of the Clerk of the Court, U.S. District Court, Southern District of Texas.)

[65]Memorandum from David B. Coe, to Jesse Clark, Chief Deputy Clerk (May 3, 1978) (Clerk's files of Chief Judge Reynaldo G. Garza, folder 4) (on file with the Office of the Clerk of the Court, U.S. District Court, Southern District of Texas).

No one involved in the analysis believed these numbers to reflect reality, although the "reality" one accepted would, naturally, be in the eye of the beholder. The problem, once again, arose from the perennial tension between the strict official rules and the vagaries of self-identification. The latest questionnaires mailed to prospective jurors had listed five racial categories, the four noted above plus "other." There was no designated box for "Spanish" or "Mexican-American." This apparently led some respondents to check the fifth box, labeled "other." Next to the box, many respondents then wrote the phrase "Mexican-American." Under JS-12 tabulation rules, people marking "other" were counted as non-whites, leading to the overrepresentation of "non-white" in the analysis.[67]

David Coe, another judicial statistician in Washington, D.C., corresponded with Jesse E. Clark, then the Southern District's chief deputy clerk (later to become chief clerk), seeking to resolve the concerns. Coe noted that the FJC analysis posed "several perplexing problems." He realized that a certain percentage of registered voters in the Southern District were of "Spanish-Latin" origin, and that there was some debate whether "people with Spanish surnames" ought to be counted as white or non-white. That debate notwithstanding, Coe wrote, for the statistical purposes of the JS-12, the Judicial Research Jury Committee had concluded that people of "Spanish-Latin" descent were not a separate race, and should be counted as white.[68]

The Southern District clerks were not resistant to change so much as confused by it. Clark had investigated and found that, even though they were aware that people with Spanish surnames were to be counted as white, some of the deputy clerks who worked with the jury questionnaires invariably counted them as "non-white" when the "other" category was marked. This accidental mistake accounted for most of the discrepancies within the Laredo and Brownsville Divisions. Coe admitted that this was an error caused by the terminology, and that the Southern District should not be criticized for selecting disproportionately non-white juries in Laredo and Brownsville. He promised to send a letter to Chief Judge Garza reassuring him that these two divisions were not "disproportionately represented."[69]

Although Coe and Clark resolved this issue to their own satisfaction, John Shapard nevertheless wrote Chief Judge Garza, to offer his analysis of the JS-12 problems in the Southern District. Shapard admitted that his analysis was "based primarily on educated guesses, with the education being that derived from reviewing several hundred of these reports and discussing them with at least twenty-five of the

---

[66]The reported ratio of white versus non-white prospective jurors, according to the court division, are as follows: Brownsville (255/70); Laredo (168/23); Corpus Christi (301/10); Houston (253/57); Galveston (174/32); and Victoria (143/6). Derived from: JS-12 [Jury Selection Form] for Southern District of Texas, submitted Nov. 29, 1977 from Brownsville Division, submitted Nov. 15, 1977 from Laredo Division, submitted Nov. 10, 1977 from Corpus Christi Division, submitted Oct. 18, 1977 from Houston Division, submitted Nov. 2, 1977 from Galveston Division, submitted Nov. 2, 1977 from Victoria Division, all attached with Memorandum from Jesse E. Clark, to Judge Reynaldo Garza (May 11, 1978) *enclosure to* Memorandum from Chief Judge Reynaldo Garza, to John Shapard (June 5, 1978) (Clerk's files of Chief Judge Reynaldo G. Garza, folder 4) (on file with the Office of the Clerk of the Court, U.S. District Court, Southern District of Texas).

[67]See Coe, supra note 65.

[68]*Id.*

[69]*Id.* at 1, 3.

ninety-four clerks of court."[70] Like Coe, Shapard acknowledged the depiction of
Brownsville and Laredo as suffering from a drastic over-representation of non-white
juries. He stipulated that this was undoubtedly a problem with the data, not with the
jury selection in those divisions. He assumed that the deputy clerks who prepared the
JS-12s simply failed to follow the instructions that persons indicating their race as
Mexican, Spanish, brown, Latin, and the like, should be counted as white. Shapard
concluded that the substantial effort needed to correct the data—sending new questionnaires, for example—would yield little benefit. According to the 1970 Census,
the non-white population of the border divisions represented only 0.5% of the population. The researcher simply worried that judiciary was left with no useful analysis of the race or ethnic balance of those juries.[71]

Chief Judge Garza replied to Shapard's letter, and found himself defending his
districts' jury practices in terms only slightly different from his predecessor Connally. Garza sought to reassure Shapard that the Southern District of Texas complied
with the Jury Selection Act, and "there [was] no indication that any group is being
discriminated against in the composition of our jury panels." The judge attached the
correspondence explaining the problems with the Southern District's data, and said
he would appreciate it if Shapard presented this along with his report to the Committee on the Operation of the Jury System.[72]

Nearly twenty-five years after *Hernandez*, and almost ten years after *Cisneros*,
the federal judicial bureaucracy and other institutions continued to fall into the trap
of the black-white binary. But, change appeared to be in the wind.

James de Anda's legal career in the twenty-five years after *Hernandez* is among
the legacies of that landmark decision. By the late 1970s, minority activists, including Mexican Americans, began to complain that President Carter had not fulfilled a
campaign promise to appoint women and minorities to the judiciary.[73] Carter's opportunity to make good on his pledge came when Congress resolved to increase the number of federal judgeships. The Omnibus Judgeship Act of 1978 opened 150 positions
on the federal district and circuit benches. The growth was especially significant in

---

[70]Memorandum from John Shapard, to Judge Reynaldo Garza 1 (May 11, 1978) (Clerk's files of Chief Judge
Reynaldo G. Garza, folder 4) (on file with the Office of the Clerk of the Court, U.S. District Court, Southern
District of Texas).

[71]*Id.* Shapard was also concerned that the Brownsville, Corpus Christi, and Victoria juries showed some
underrepresentation of females. He suggested that moderate underrepresentation of females was common
in federal jury wheels, due to a lower incidence of voter registration, as well as a higher incidence of excuse
of exemption from jury service, among females. The largest underrepresentation is probably attributable to
two excuses: (a) the excuse for the persons responsible for the care of young children, and (b) the excuse
for persons older than some specified age (Shapard noted that roughly sixty percent of those over seventy-years of age were female). Of course, correction of sex imbalance in the wheel would compete with the
policy considerations behind the normal excuses, and Shapard concluded that he was "glad that resolution
of such policy conflicts is [Garza's] responsibility, and not mine." *Id.* at 2.

[72]Memorandum from Chief Judge Reynaldo Garza, to John Shapard 2 (June 5, 1978) *enclosing* Memorandum
from Jesse E. Clark, to Judge Reynaldo Garza (May 11, 1978) (Clerk's files of Chief Judge Reynaldo G. Garza,
folder 4) (on file with the Office of the Clerk of the Court, U.S. District Court, Southern District of Texas).

[73]Approximately ninety-percent of Mexican Americans in Texas who voted in 1976 voted for President Carter,
which gave him his thin margin of victory in the state. *Swift Indictments in Torres Case Could Aid Carter-
Hispanic Relations*, HOUS. POST, Oct. 23, 1977, at D4.

the Southern District of Texas, because the Act increased the number of judges there from eight to thirteen.[74]

The language of the 1978 Act explicitly invited the President to make a revolution in the judiciary. Section 8 of the Act, for example, stated that Congress: "(1) takes notice of the fact that only one percent of Federal judges are women and only four percent are blacks; and (2) suggests that the President, in selecting individuals for nomination to Federal judgeships created by this Act, give due consideration to qualified individuals regardless of race, color, sex, religion, or national origin."[75] Carter seized the opportunity. During his single term, more than fifteen percent of his judicial appointees were female, and more than twenty-one percent were minorities.[76]

In due course, President Carter appointed James de Anda to the Southern District of Texas, where he became the second Mexican American judge in its history. But, did that mean he was the new white, "other white," "Latin," "Spanish-surnamed," or "Hispanic" judge? By May 11, 1979, the day the Senate confirmed the judge, the answer was not yet clear.[77]

Unfortunately, another twenty-five years have passed and the tension between administrative judgments regarding race and ethnicity, and self-identification by minority groups has yet to be resolved. Complicating the issue is the fact that the racial and ethnic makeup of the United States has changed greatly since 1977, when OMB established the definitions discussed above. The OMB initiated a review in the late 1990s, which included public hearings, references to the National Academy of Science, and an "Interagency Committee for the Review of Racial and Ethnic Standards."[78]

Currently, the OMB's categories for race are: (1) American Indian or Alaska Native; (2) Asian; (3) Black or African American; (4) Native Hawaiian or Other Pacific Islander; and (5) White. With OMB's approval, the Census Bureau's 2000 questionnaires included a sixth racial category: "some other race." There are also two categories for ethnicity, namely, "Hispanic or Latino" and "not Hispanic or Latino." This accepts a consensus that Hispanics and Latinos may be of any race. Instead of a new "multiracial" category, as suggested in public and congressional hearings, the OMB adopted the Interagency Committee's recommendation that people be

---

[74]The Omnibus Judgeship Act of 1978, Pub. L. 95-486, 92 Stat. 1629 (revising number of judgeships allocated in 28 U.S.C. § 133 (2004)). For the legislative history of this act see U.S. CODE CONGRESSIONAL AND ADMINISTRATIVE NEWS 3569 (1978). The Act also increased the number of federal appellate judges on the Fifth Circuit from fifteen to twenty-six judges. See also House OKs More Courts, 12 in Texas, HOUS. POST, Feb. 8, 1978, at 7A.

[75]Id.

[76]CHRISTOPHER E. SMITH, COURTS, POLITICS, AND THE JUDICIAL PROCESS 113-14 (1993). President Carter was a proponent of reform by other means, as well. He created nominating committees to vet judicial candidates. On November 8, 1978, he signed Exec. Order No. 12,097. 43 Fed. Reg. 52,455 (Nov. 8, 1978), calling for the establishment of standards and guidelines for the merit selection of U.S. District Judges.

[77]He was one of the five new federal district judges. All five were confirmed by the Senate on the same day. Senate Confirms 5 Federal Judges for Southern District of Texas, HOUS. POST, May 11, 1979, at A16; Judge James de Anda: Graduate Blazed Trails in Texas Civil Rights, TOWNES HALL NOTES, Fall 2000, at 74–77. Barbara Brooker, Bell to Take Part in Judicial Post Nominee Selection, HOUS. POST, February 20, 1977, at 5B.

[78]U.S. CENSUS BUREAU, RACIAL AND ETHNIC CLASSIFICATIONS USED IN CENSUS 2000 AND BEYOND available at http://www.census.gov/population/www/socdemo/race/racefactcb.html (last revised Apr. 12, 2000).

allowed to select more than one race when they self-identify. There were fifteen boxes to choose from, and three write-in blanks on the Census 2000 questionnaire (as compared with sixteen box categories and two write-in areas in 1990). Finally, there is the category "some other race," which also has a write-in blank. This is intended to allow responses from people identifying as Mulatto, Creole, and Mestizo. Reportedly, there are sixty-three possible combinations of the six basic racial categories, including six categories for those who report exactly one race, and fifty-seven categories for those who report two or more races.[79]

Still unresolved is the basic question, what race should Hispanics check on this form? Apparently to encourage more useful responses, the question on Hispanic origin appears immediately before the question on race, as if to remind the respondents that, in the federal statistical system, ethnic origin and race are separate concepts. This subtle point continues to run up against self-identification. The National Latino Political Survey, for example, found that three of four respondents preferred to be labeled by their country of origin rather than by "pan-ethnic" terms such as Hispanic or Latino. Indeed, on the 2000 Census, 47.9% of Hispanics identified their race as "white," and 42.2% declined to provide any racial categorization at all.[80]

And so the debate continues. Recently, the *New York Times* reported on the Census Bureau's struggle to find a "racial" home for "ethnic" Hispanics. The major stumbling block is, as it always has been, the vagaries of self-identification. The large number of Hispanics checking "some other race" has made it the fastest growing racial category. Census officials are hoping to eliminate this option from the 2010 questionnaires, once more hoping to encourage Hispanics to choose one or more of the five standard racial categories.[81] If the contested fifty year history of self-identification since *Hernandez v. Texas* is any guide at all, the keepers of the official categories will still not like the results.

---

[79]*Id.*

[80]Changes to the questions on race and Hispanic origin that have occurred for the Census 2000 conform to the revisions of the standards for the classification of federal data on race and ethnicity promulgated by the OMB in October 1997. *Id.*

[81]Rachel L. Swarns, Hispanic Debate Census Plan to Change Racial Groupings, N.Y. Times, Oct. 24, 2004, §1, at 21.

Peremptory Challenges: Lessons from *Hernandez v. Texas*

Clare Sheridan*

"The inherent potential of peremptory challenges to distort the jury process by permitting the exclusion of jurors on racial grounds should ideally lead the Court to ban them entirely from the criminal justice system."[1]

Justice Thurgood Marshall

I. Introduction

What insights can *Hernandez v. Texas*[2] contribute to current debates about the use of peremptory challenges to strike non-whites from venires? In light of the Supreme Court's recent ruling in *Miller-El v. Dretke*[3] and *Hernandez v. New York*,[4] analysis of the reasoning in *Hernandez v. Texas* as well as analysis of the evolution in the Court's understanding of the concept of "race," pre- and post-*Hernandez*, is warranted.

In *Miller-El*, the Court held that the defendant should have been issued a certificate of appealability to review the denial of his habeas appeal. The district and circuit courts had denied it, deferring to the trial court's acceptance of the prosecutor's justifications for using peremptory strikes against African American prospective jurors. In reversing, the Supreme Court held that the evidence he presented demonstrating that the prosecutor's peremptory challenges were based on race was convincing. In some ways, the Court stepped back to 1935 when, in *Norris v. Alabama*,[5] it rejected the common practice of accepting jury commissioners' assertions that they did not intend to discriminate as evidence of non-discrimination. Instead, the Court ruled that discrimination could be shown through a pattern of absence of blacks from juries. That is, they ruled on the result of selection procedures, even if the procedures, themselves, were facially neutral. In subsequent decisions[6] the spir-

---

*Clare Sheridan is an independent scholar. She can be contacted at clare_s@berkeley.edu.
[1]Batson v. Kentucky, 476 U.S. 79, 107 (1986).
[2]Hernandez v. Texas, 347 U.S. 475 (1954).
[3]Miller-El v. Dretke, 125 S.Ct 2317 (2005). Please note that the bulk of this chapter was written prior to the Supreme Court's final 2005 decision. I use the full case name, Miller-El v. Dretke when quoting from the ultimate decision. Other citations using the shorthand "Miller-El" come from the Supreme Court's prior decision, Miller-El v. Cockrell, 537 U.S. 322 (2003).
[4]Hernandez v. New York, 500 U.S. 352 (1991).
[5]Norris v. Alabama, 294 U.S. 587 (1935).
[6]See generally Swain v. Alabama, 380 U.S. 202 (1965).

it of *Norris* was ignored. It was not until *Batson v. Kentucky*, that the Court developed more reasonable criteria for determining whether peremptory challenges were used unconstitutionally. Thus, if the defendant is part of a recognizable group and can make a prima facie case that jurors were struck for race-based reasons, then the burden of proof shifts to the prosecution to provide a race-neutral explanation. Yet, in case after case, appeals courts assumed that lower courts made the correct determination in balancing evidence of discrimination against prosecutorial explanations. In essence, *Batson* often operates to return us to the pre-*Norris* era, when a prosecutor's word that he did not intend to discriminate was trusted. The *Miller-El* case both clarifies and enforces *Batson*. However, two key questions remain.

First, the question raised in *Hernandez*—whether race and nationality can be construed similarly under the auspices of the Equal Protection Clause—remains salient. In 1991, in *Hernandez v. New York*, the Court ruled that peremptory challenges may be used to strike bilingual venirepersons so long as the action was not based on race.[7] Yet it evaded the opportunity to define the term race, while insisting that the Equal Protection Clause protected only racial discrimination.[8] Here, *Hernandez v. Texas* is instructive. The lawyers in *Hernandez* struggled with the relationship between race and ethnicity, as well as with their applicability to the Fourteenth Amendment. They offered nuanced arguments that should be revisited by the Court, today, in considering *Batson* claims.

Second, what if there is no evidence of prosecutorial malfeasance and yet a pattern of exclusion can be demonstrated? Again, *Hernandez v. Texas* can inform the debate. Although it dealt with people who were not black, prejudicial attitudes influenced the seating of Mexican Americans on juries. Such attitudes were based on things "other than race," but that served as proxies for race. How can we justify allowing peremptory challenges based on subjective judgments that may be consciously or unconsciously racially rooted?[9] How do the rules governing drawing jury pools determine outcomes that are continually unrepresentative of the community? How could this be remedied? These issues raise the larger question of whether systems allowing peremptory challenges are so flawed as to interfere with the delivery of justice.

Our two concerns—that discriminatory effects can occur without conscious intent and that the courts have based their decisions on a limited, and not clearly articulated conception of race, are intertwined. While the technical legal issues faced by the Court in *Hernandez v. Texas*, *Hernandez v. New York* and *Miller-El* are different the issues they deal with are remarkably and unfortunately enduring. What is race and what serves as a proxy for race? Should unrepresentative juries be recognized as discriminatory even if no intentional discrimination can be identified as causing the underrepresentation? Is the traditional deference accorded to prosecutors

---

[7]Hernandez v. New York, 500 U.S. at 370.

[8]In a recent 2003 case, Rico v. Leftridge-Byrd, 340 F.3d 178, 185 (3d Cir. 2003), the defendant asserted a *Batson* claim based on presumed ethnicity (Italian). The lower courts accepted the claim, but the key question was not decided, as the state supreme court upheld the trial court's factual determination that discrimination was not a factor and the circuit court agreed.

[9]Here, the Sixth Amendment guarantee of an impartial jury drawn from a fair cross-section of the community may be an alternative to the Equal Protection Clause to defend fairness in the jury system.

and trial courts' reasoning for excluding certain jurors, part of systemic discrimination against minorities' participation? In what other ways is the system of justice inflected by common sense notions of racial import?

In this chapter, I discuss two contemporary jury discrimination cases, *Hernandez v. New York* and *Miller-El*, in light of the landmark *Hernandez v. Texas* case. In Part II, I focus on the debate over whether intent to discriminate is more probative of discrimination than the result of an unrepresentative jury. I then turn, in Part III, to the question of how to assess the credibility of prosecutors' reasons for striking jurors and the role of deference to trial courts in evaluating their credibility. In Part IV, I address the import of jury selection rules in creating systemic discrimination. In Part V, I discuss the significance and limitations of the definition of race implicit in the Court's decisions. This discussion is an attempt to think beyond precedence and legal tradition. It is not meant to be a roadmap to legal change—it is far too impractical for that. Rather, it simply aims to provide a critique of the Court's jurisprudence and a view of legal doctrine from outside of the discipline and to suggest alternative pathways for conceiving of rights and fairness in jury selection. The lawyers for *Hernandez* persuasively articulated one alternative fifty years ago. Their voices can illuminate contemporary problems with confidence in the jury selection system.

II. The Question of Intent

The intent of the prosecutor or jury commissioner has long been the acid test in jury discrimination cases. In 1935, in *Norris v. Alabama*, the Supreme Court reviewed the evidence and judged the lower court's findings for the first time in a jury bias case.[10] The Court declared that prima facie discrimination could be shown through a pattern of the absence of blacks from petit juries, not just jury pools. Once this was established, the burden shifted to the state to provide a convincing explanation for the underrepresentation of blacks. Evidence of systematic exclusion was the standard for scrutiny (e.g., no names of African Americans on jury rolls). In contrast to past cases, declarations that jury commissioners did not intend to discriminate were not accepted as proving nondiscrimination. The Court ruled on the results of the process, rather than the stated intent of the prosecutors and jury commissioners.

In 1965, in the next landmark case on jury bias, *Swain v. Alabama* recognized the use of peremptory challenges to exclude African Americans as unconstitutional. However, it held that petitioners must prove a pattern of systematic exclusion, not only discrimination in their particular case.[11] *Batson v. Kentucky* remedied this by ruling that defendants only had to show that discrimination was a factor in their own trial, rather than having to prove a history of systemic discrimination by shifting the evidentiary burden to the prosecution once the defendant established a prima face case of bias.[12]

Batson developed criteria for determining whether peremptory challenges were used unconstitutionally. First, the defendant must make a prima facie case that dis-

---

[10]*Norris*, 294 U.S. 587 (1935).
[11]*Swain*, 380 U.S. 202 (1965).
[12]Batson v. Kentucky, 476 U.S. 79 (1986).

crimination was possible. The prosecution then must offer racially neutral explanations for their strikes. Finally, the judge must decide whether any discrimination is purposeful. That is, the judge must evaluate the persuasiveness of the prosecution's reasons for striking venire members. Yet in case after case, appeals courts assumed that lower courts made the correct determination in balancing evidence of discrimination against prosecutorial explanations. In essence, court decisions were thrown back to the late 1920s and early 1930s when the prosecutor's word that he or she did not intend to discriminate was trusted.

The prosecutor in *Hernandez v. New York* offered a "neutral" explanation for the challenged strike—that the potential juror's ability to understand testimony in Spanish may undermine his or her ability to abide by the interpreter's version of the testimony. The prosecutor noted that the jurors in question looked away from him and answered hesitantly that they would try to abide by the official interpretation. The Court accepted this reason, noting that the prosecutor divided the jurors into two categories: those who convinced him they would accept the translator's version and those who would not, and that both categories could include Latinos and non-Latinos. This argument is reminiscent of earlier arguments that there are qualified and non-qualified venirepersons and that Mexican Americans on the venire just happened not to be qualified. For instance, in *Lugo v. Texas* (decided three years after *Norris*) the sheriff testified, "I know as a fact of my own knowledge that the majority of the Mexican population of this county are unable to speak intelligently in English and are unable to read and write the English language."[13] Based on this subjective judgment, the Texas Court of Criminal Appeals refused to overturn the trial court's finding of fact.[14]

The Court has long focused on the prosecutors' and other state officials' "demeanor" and "state of mind." Returning to *Hernandez v. New York*, the Court noted that the prosecutor offered a reason for his challenges without being prompted to do so, which seemed to demonstrate his good will in the Court's eyes. Could it conversely have demonstrated his heightened awareness of race? If this standard had been applied by the Court in *Hernandez v. Texas*, the testimony of the jury commissioners that they did not intend to discriminate but rather chose the most qualified jurors would be considered race-neutral.

The defense suggested that this standard could exclude *all* bilingual people from serving on juries. Even if this were true, the Court countered, this would not be enough to trigger an Equal Protection issue because "[a]n argument relating to the impact of a classification does not alone show its purpose. . . . Equal protection analysis turns on the intended consequences of government classification."[15] This is precisely the Achilles' heel of the way *Batson* has been interpreted. *Any* explanation by the prosecutor, as long as it does not specifically mention race, is deemed race-neutral.

In its decision the Court quoted *Arlington Heights v. Metropolitan Housing Development Corporation* as authoritative: "Proof of racially discriminatory intent

---

[13]Lugo v. Texas, 124 S.W.2d 344, 348 (Tex. Crim. App. 1939).
[14]*Id.*
[15]Hernandez v. New York, 500 U.S. 352, 361 (1991).

or purpose is required to show a violation of the Equal Protection Clause."[16] But how does one gauge intention? At one point the prosecutor in *Hernandez* said that he was not even certain whether the jurors in question were Hispanic and did not notice how many Hispanics were on the venire. This appears disingenuous, considering the context of his claim. He stated:

> Your honor, my reason for rejecting the—these two jurors [sic]—I'm not certain as to whether they're Hispanics. I did not notice how many Hispanics had been called to the panel, but my reason for rejecting these two is I feel very uncertain that they would be able to listen and follow the interpreter.[17]

He invoked their ethnicity while simultaneously denying knowledge of it. It could be argued that the prosecutor offered race-neutral reasons for his strikes because of his heightened awareness of the role that race could play in the trial.

In an attempt to deny the possibility that he had predisposed ideas that Hispanics would be less likely to convict, a common perception, he further claimed that since the defendant and the witnesses were Hispanic, he would have no motive to exclude Hispanics from the jury.[18] This misapplies *Batson* and its progeny in two ways. First, in focusing on the defendant, it glosses over whether the right of the potential jurors not to be excluded from the opportunity to serve on a jury has been improperly denied. As Kenneth Melilli argues, *Batson* is often overlooked in the fact that it shifted the focus of efforts to secure rights from the defendant to prospective jurors.[19] Second, it ignores subsequent decisions that expand *Batson,* including *Powers v. Ohio,*[20] which allows third parties to lodge *Batson* claims on behalf of allegedly excluded jurors. His invocation of the race of the parties involved suggests that he does, indeed, take race into consideration. It means that race matters. In essence, because *Batson* realigns our concern with the juror, rather than the defendant, the prosecutor's explanation of motive is moot.

The Court concluded that the challenges:

> May have acted like strikes based on race, but they were not based on race. No matter how closely tied or significantly correlated to race the explanation for a peremptory strike may be, the strike does not implicate the Equal Protection Clause unless it is based on race. That is the distinction between disproportionate effect, which is not sufficient to constitute an equal protection violation, and intentional discrimination, which is.[21]

Yet, the Court in *Batson* noted "[c]ircumstantial evidence of invidious intent may include proof of disproportionate impact. . . . We have observed that under some circumstances proof of discriminatory impact 'may for all practical purposes

---

[16]*Id.* at 360 (quoting Arlington Heights v. Metro. Hous. Dev. Corp., 429 U.S. 252, 264-65 (1977)). It is interesting to note that the Court depended on reasoning in a case decided *prior* to *Batson.*

[17]*Id.* at 356.

[18]*Id.* at 357.

[19]Kenneth Melilli, Batson *in Practice: What We Have Learned About Batson and Peremptory Challenges*, 71 NOTRE DAME L. REV. 447, 453 (1996).

[20]Powers v. Ohio, 499 U.S. 400 (1991).

[21]*Hernandez v. New York*, 500 U.S. at 375.

demonstrate unconstitutionality because in various circumstances the discrimination is very difficult to explain on nonracial grounds.'"[22] Despite *Batson's* stand on race-based peremptory challenges in its interpretation, courts have returned to the pre-*Batson* era in subsequent cases.

Justice Stevens differs with the Court's interpretation of *Batson*. In his dissent, he counters, "[i]f any explanation, no matter how insubstantial and no matter how great its disparate impact, could rebut a prima facie inference of discrimination provided only that the explanation itself was not facially discriminatory, 'the Equal Protection Clause would be but a vain and illusory requirement.'"[23] He argues that once a prima facie case is made, "unless the explanation provided by the prosecutor is sufficiently powerful to rebut the prima facie proof of discriminatory purpose," the fact of discrimination rests.[24] That is, he places a greater burden on the prosecution to provide a convincing explanation. He continues, "the Court has imposed on the defendant the added requirement that he generate evidence of the prosecutor's actual subjective intent to discriminate. Neither *Batson* nor our other equal protection holdings demand such a heightened quantum of proof."[25]

The Court did, however, admit that disproportionate impact is relevant to the identification of the prosecution's discriminatory intent. Moreover, they admitted that language ability could be a pretext for race-based challenges and that in an area with a large Latino population this could exclude a large percentage of jurors. They even noted that there could be less-impacting alternatives, such as permitting Spanish-speaking jurors "to advise the judge in a discreet way of any concerns with the translation. . . ."[26]

The test of whether there are alternatives to striking a juror is worthy of consideration. In his dissent, Justice Stevens firmly stated, "[a]n explanation based on a concern that can easily be accommodated by means less drastic than excluding the challenged venireperson from the petit jury will also generally not qualify as a legitimate reason. . . ."[27] In this case, he suggests simultaneous translation as an easy fix. Yet despite the Court's admissions, they still conclude that "in the absence of exceptional circumstances, we would defer to state-court factual findings. . . ."[28]

III. Questions of Credibility and Deference

This tradition of deference to trial courts, combined with the ways in which the Court evaluates the prosecutor's credibility, has severely limited the success of *Batson* challenges. Yet, as Justice Kennedy, writing for the majority in *Miller-El* noted, "[d]eference does not imply abandonment or abdication of judicial review."[29]

In *Hernandez v. New York*, the Court once again accorded deference to the stated intent of the prosecutor. "Unless a discriminatory intent is inherent in the prose-

---

[22]Batson v. Kentucky, 476 U.S. 79, 93 (1986) (quoting Washington v. Davis, 426 U.S. 229, 242 (1976)).
[23]*Hernandez v. New York*, 500 U.S. at 377 (Stevens, J., dissenting) (quotes omitted).
[24]*Id.* at 378.
[25]*Id.*
[26]*Id.* at 364.
[27]*Id.* at 376.
[28]*Id.* at 366.
[29]Miller-El v. Cockrell, 537 U.S. 322, 340 (2003).

cutor's explanation, the reason offered will be deemed race neutral."[30] The Court depends on the subjective impression the prosecutor has of the potential juror. They note:

> In the typical peremptory challenge inquiry, the decisive question will be whether counsel's race-neutral explanation for a peremptory challenge should be believed. There will seldom be much evidence bearing on that issue, and the best evidence often will be the demeanor of the attorney who exercises the challenge. As with the state of mind of a juror, evaluation of the prosecutor's state of mind based on demeanor and credibility lies 'peculiarly within a trial judge's province.'[31]

Why is this the "best evidence?" Are lawyers not paid to convince judges and juries of the truth of their argument? A good lawyer must be persuasive. In many senses, lawyering is a type of acting—so a prosecutor's demeanor may be the least helpful piece of evidence in evaluating the truth of his claims. In his dissent, Justice Stevens argues that the best evidence of discrimination is "what actually happened," that is, the outcome of jury selection—the composition of the jury versus the composition of the venire.[32]

In *Miller-El*, the Court reviewed its decision in *Hernandez v. New York* and then conducted a lengthy discussion of step three of *Batson's* framework. Quoting *Purkett v. Elem*, they note: At this stage, "implausible or fantastic justifications may (and probably will) be found to be pretexts for purposeful discrimination."[33] The *Purkett v. Elem* standard makes a successful *Batson* claim a virtual impossibility. Based on the standard that pretexts are identified only when "fantastic," it is very unlikely that any savvy prosecutor will provide such reasoning. The "fantastic" standard excludes the possibility that race and class are articulated and that class-based reasons, such as neighborhood residence or employment status can operate to disproportionately exclude racial minorities. Similarly, having a personal relationship with someone who was convicted for a felony can disproportionately exclude minorities, given their overrepresentation in the nation's prisons. For example, two of the *Batson*-challenged venirepersons in *Miller-El*, Joe Warren and Billy Jean Fields, had relatives who had been convicted of crimes. In his dissent Justice Thomas argues that this is a legitimate reason for the prosecution to exercise a peremptory challenge.[34] Yet the majority notes that the prosecution "never questioned Warren about his errant relative at all; as with Fields's brother, the failure to ask undermines the persuasiveness of the claimed concern."[35] Furthermore, they argue that there were white jurors seated who had relatives convicted of crimes.

In its final decision, the *Miller-El* majority recognized the impossibility of the *Purkett* standard and attempted to outline methods for assessing the reasons for

---

[30]*Hernandez v. New York*, 500 U.S. at 360.

[31]*Id.* at 365.

[32]*Id.* at 377 (Stevens, J., dissenting). See Melilli, supra note 19 (similarly suggesting that this is the most convincing method used to establish a *prima facie* case of discrimination).

[33]*Miller-El*, 537 U.S. at 339 (quoting Purkett v. Elem, 514 U.S. 765, 768 (1995)).

[34]*Miller-El v. Dretke*, 125 S.Ct 2317 at 2352.

[35]*Id.*, note 8 at 2330-31.

peremptory strikes. They state, "Credibility can be measured by, among other factors, the prosecutor's demeanor; by how reasonable, or how improbable, the explanations are; and by whether the proffered rationale has some basis in accepted trial strategy."[36] But this stance still cedes the ground of truth to the intuition of prosecutors and lower court judges. Unless there is direct evidence of invidious use of the strike, their explanation can be weak and still be accepted. Since appellate judges usually accept lower courts' findings of "fact," it is rare that prosecutorial credibility will be reassessed. Despite Miller-El's significant body of evidence, multiple courts ruled against him. After the Supreme Court remanded the case to the Fifth Circuit to reassess the evidence, and were essentially ignored, they took the extraordinary step of examining *voir dire* transcripts themselves. The fact that three justices dissented demonstrates the difficulty of determining how reasonable explanations are and assessing credibility years later on appeal.

For instance, in *Miller-El* the prosecutors claimed that many of the African American venirepersons who they eliminated through peremptory challenges were struck because of their lack of support for the death penalty. White jurors did not express such hesitancy. The Texas Court of Criminal Appeals noted that the main reason for the strikes was their "reservations concerning the imposition of the death penalty."[37] This seems, on its face, like a valid explanation. However, the defense countered that the prosecutor engaged in a suspect strategy of disparate questioning that led African American venirepersons to be more reticent about applying the law. The prosecutor accomplished this by using a "graphic script" describing in detail the process of administering the death penalty when questioning African Americans, while asking of whites a more general question about how they feel about the death penalty and whether they could serve on a jury that would have to make a decision about sentencing someone to death. Fifty-three percent of African Americans were led through the graphic script, while only six percent of white venirepersons were. The Supreme Court was impressed by this difference, quoting the appeal extensively.[38] Justice Thomas, writing for the dissent, vigorously demurred. He parses the jury questionnaires at great length and comes to a different conclusion from the majority—that the disparate questioning was directly related to inconsistencies on the answers given regarding the death penalty.[39]

In another example of the justices' differing views of the import of disparate questioning, the majority concluded that the way in which the prosecution questioned one African American juror led him to respond that the law was not severe enough in applying the death penalty and that the prosecution used this as an excuse to strike him. The majority goes so far as to call this strategy "trickery."[40] In the dissent's view, this was "beside the point." Rather, it was his ambivalence about *when* he would impose the ultimate penalty and when he would prefer lesser types of punishment.[41]

---

[36]*Miller-El*, 537 U.S. at 339.
[37]*Id.* at 329.
[38]*Id.* at 332.
[39]*Miller-El v. Dretke* at 2357-2360.
[40]*Id.,* at 2337.
[41]*Id.,* at 2352

The dissent also insists that in comparing jurors, similarly situated jurors must be similar in *all* respects.[42] That is, if the prosecution objected to a particular venireperson along three lines, the defense can not assert that a white juror who was seated was similar unless they shared all three circumstances. The majority counters, "A *per se* rule that a defendant cannot win a *Batson* claim unless there is an exactly identical white juror would leave *Batson* inoperable."[43] Justice Breyer succinctly sums up *Batson's* Achilles' heel: ". . .at step three, *Batson* asks judges to engage in the awkward, sometime hopeless, task of second-guessing a prosecutor's instinctive judgment—the underlying basis for which may be invisible even to the prosecutor exercising the challenge."[44]

The majority, however, fails to aggregate their objections to the ways in which *Batson* has been applied and promulgate a new rule that would put teeth in *Batson* and apply to other cases. They take refuge in their faith that credibility can by assessed and measured by appellate judges, and they mainly confine their disagreement with the dissent to footnotes. As such, they miss an opportunity to significantly impact discrimination in jury selection. They have identified a problem, but have not provided a satisfactory solution.

The combination of disparate questioning, the dubious (though legal in Texas) practice of "jury shuffling," that is, reordering the venire, and the use of peremptory challenges had resulted in one African American juror out of twenty prospective African American jurors and 108 of those interviewed. That is, African Americans made up over eighteen percent of those interviewed and comprised less than one percent of those selected for the jury. The Court finds that:

> Nine (African Americans) were excused for cause or by agreement of the parties. Of the 11 African American jurors remaining, however, all but one were excluded by peremptory strikes exercised by the prosecutors. In contrast, the prosecutors used their peremptory strikes against just 13% (4 out of 31) of the eligible nonblack prospective jurors qualified to serve.[45]

Were these strikes "race-neutral," if the result was so starkly racially divided?[46]

Some seemingly race-neutral explanations for strikes appeal to "common sense." But often this conventional wisdom is racially inflected.[47] It is possible that the prosecution and judges do *not* intentionally discriminate but make discriminatory judgments reflecting social "common sense." In his concurrence in *Batson*, Justice Marshall argues,

> A prosecutor's own conscious or unconscious racism may lead him easily to the conclusion that a prospective black juror is "sullen," or "distant," a

---

[42]*Id.*, at 2354.

[43]*Id.*, note 6 at 2329.

[44]*Id.*, at 2341.

[45]*Miller-El*, 537 U.S. at 331.

[46]While the Court has insisted in Holland v. Illinois, 493 U.S. 474 (1990), that a defendant is not entitled to proportional representation of his or her racial group on the jury, but only that there is a fair cross-section of the community represented on the lists from which the jury is drawn, it did hold in Castañeda v. Partida, 430 U.S. 483 (1977), that a significant statistical disparity raises the inference of a prima facie case of discrimination.

[47]See generally Charles Lawrence III, *The Id, the Ego and Equal Protection: Reckoning with Unconscious Racism*, 39 STAN. L. REV. 317 (1987).

characterization that would not have come to his mind if a white juror had acted identically. A judge's own conscious or unconscious racism may lead him to accept such an explanation as well supported.[48]

In support of this supposition, Juan F. Perea cites a recent example of a case in which the prosecutor struck a venireperson who had a heavy accent because he did not think he would be able to understand the proceedings.[49]

In *Hernandez v. New York*, Justice Stevens similarly points out, "[t]he Court overlooks, however, the fact that the 'discriminatory purpose' which characterizes violations of the Equal Protection Clause can sometimes be established by objective evidence that is consistent with a decisionmaker's honest belief that his motive was entirely benign."[50] "[S]eat-of-the-pants instincts," in Justice Marshall's words, are often based on conventional wisdom inflected by social prejudices.[51]

Whether or not the prosecutor intends to stack the jury, the result of an unbalanced jury is to undermine confidence in the outcome of the trial and the legal system.[52] There are decades of cases where deference was shown to prosecutors' explanations, resulting in either the wholesale exclusion of minorities or only nominal inclusion.

IV. Systemic Questions

Justices Marshall and Stevens highlight the possibility that discrimination can result without invidious intent. Discriminatory notions ingrained in society can produce systemic structures of discrimination. These structures continue to produce unrepresentative juries long after the initial invidious intent has been forgotten. For example, real estate covenants are now illegal, but America's neighborhoods largely remain segregated along racial lines.[53]

In *Hernandez v. Texas*, the Court declared, "[b]ut it taxes our credulity to say that mere chance resulted in there being no members of this class among the over six thousand jurors called in the past 25 years."[54] However, the absence of minorities can *seem* to be mere chance, or at least not the result of purposeful discrimination, because the way the system is structured militates against a representative petit jury. Focusing on the intent of the prosecutor helps to construe discrimination as a tort, rather than as unconscious or systemic.[55] It delegitimates a focus on the rules for

---

[48]Batson v. Kentucky, 476 U.S. 79, 106 (1986) (Marshall, J., concurring).

[49]See Juan F. Perea, Hernandez v. New York: *Courts, Prosecutors, and the Fear of Spanish*, 21 HOFSTRA L. REV. 1, 17-18 (1992). Perea offers several examples of recent cases where other ostensibly race-neutral reasons were given for striking Latino venirepersons that acted suspiciously like strikes based on race. These included the prospective juror's Catholicism and ironically, the idea that having a Hispanic surname does not mean that the venireperson necessarily was Latino.

[50]Hernandez v. New York, 500 U.S. 352, 377 (1991) (Stevens, J., dissenting).

[51]*Batson*, 476 U.S. 79 at 138 (quoting Justice Rehnquist).

[52]HIROSHI FUKURAI ET AL., RACE AND THE JURY: RACIAL DISENFRANCHISEMENT AND THE SEARCH FOR JUSTICE (1993).

[53]See generally THOMAS SUGRUE, THE ORIGINS OF THE URBAN CRISIS: RACE AND INEQUALITY IN POSTWAR DETROIT (1996) (for an excellent analysis of the impact of racial covenants on continuing inequality).

[54]Hernandez v. Texas, 347 U.S. 475, 482 (1954).

[55]See Lawrence, supra note 38.

juror selection. Yet rules are never neutral; they always advantage some and disadvantage others. In redistricting, for example, districts are drawn by legislatures and usually advantage the incumbents—the very people responsible for setting the rules. Even apart from invidious intent, rules unintentionally still create winners and losers and can have disproportionate impact on certain groups.

Fukurai and Krooth examine every stage leading up to the seating of a jury and detail the ways in which the system misses or dismisses potential jurors who are minorities.[56] This includes the use of voting rolls instead of lists that would encompass a wider range of citizens, the granting of hardship deferments, which disproportionately affects minority participation, and minorities' lower response rate to juror summonses and lack of follow-up by the state, jury qualification processes, and voir dire itself, all of which may not be purposeful but result from historical economic and educational disenfranchisement and conspire to skew the racial makeup of the jury. The practice of jury shuffling used in *Miller-El* certainly falls into this category. Given the fact that African Americans are a minority, it is easy to shuffle the panel, resulting in a dearth of African Americans at the front, thereby guaranteeing a jury comprised mainly of whites. In *Miller-El v. Dretke*, Justice Thomas calls the majority's assertion that jury shuffling smacks of overt discrimination "pure speculation." He does so partly because Miller-El's attorneys did not raise this as an issue during his *Batson* hearing. But more importantly, he objects because "Miller-El should not be asking this Court to draw 'inference[s]'; he should be asking it to examine clear and convincing proof."[57] This illustrates a fundamental difference between the majority and the dissent on the standard of proof. Moreover, it highlights blindness to systemic inequities. Not even the fact that prosecutors noted the race of venirepersons on their juror cards gives the dissent pause. "We have no idea. . . whether this was done merely for identification purposes or for some more nefarious reason."[58] The dissent imagines a world where identifying someone racially holds no meaning. They ignore both the conscious and unconscious operation of systemic structures of discrimination.

Even a seemingly benign practice can have discriminatory results. For example, in *Hernandez v. New York* the Court accepted the prosecution's reason for striking bilingual jurors as legitimate because it has been an accepted practice to allow striking people with knowledge beyond what is presented as evidence. Applying this practice to bilingual jurors, however, serves to eliminate diversity from the jury and to create a racially unbalanced jury. It also casts doubt on the ability of bilingual speakers to exercise good judgment, while at the same time assuming that monolingual jurors hearing testimony given in English will not make errors in interpreting the information. It presumes that English speakers will make more reliable jurors and that the interpretation of the non-Spanish speaking majority is the neutral standard by which to judge. Given that most people who are bilingual in English and Spanish are Latino, it casts doubt on their ability to responsibly exercise the rights

---

[56]See FUKURAI ET AL., *supra* note 43, at 141-62.
[57]*Miller-El v. Dretke* at 2362.
[58]*Id.,* at 2363.

of citizenship. Finally, it upholds the status quo by reinforcing the underrepresentation of Latinos on juries.

The Court has not recognized that language ability maps race because they refuse to admit that Latinos often experience discrimination very similar to racial discrimination based on the fact that they are seen by the majority as part of a subordinate group. Therefore, the exclusion of bilingual venirepersons can appear neutral. In fact, judges have been reluctant to extend the umbrella of the Equal Protection Clause to groups other than African Americans and women. While they often distinguish cognizable groups (as in *Hernandez v. Texas*), they do not require heightened scrutiny to be applied to them beyond the limits of a particular case. In this way, the system protects white dominance by appealing to "neutral" principles. Underlying the Court's confidence in the prosecutors' statements and demeanor is the assumption that he or she will not even unconsciously be discriminatory. It also assumes that a majority-white jury will be able to comprehend the life experiences of defendants and victims who may be very different from them. Finally, it presumes that the selection procedures that produced the jury are neutral.[59] It camouflages white dominance of the system by presenting white people's assumptions, experience and the distinctions they use to structure the rules as unbiased.

Prosecutors in *Hernandez v. Texas* claimed to have race-neutral reasons for excluding Mexican Americans. Yet the Court concluded that the result—an all-white jury pool—"bespeaks discrimination, whether or not it was a conscious decision on the part of any individual jury commissioner."[60] When dealing with discrimination that is invisible because it is ingrained in the system of rules, only the composition of the jury should qualify as evidence of a fair system.

V. Questions of Race

In *Hernandez v. New York*, the Court stated, "[i]n holding that a race-neutral reason for a peremptory challenge means a reason other than race, we do not resolve the more difficult question of the breadth with which the concept of race should be defined for equal protection purposes."[61] Here, they admit the complexity and imprecision of race, but refuse to engage in a substantive discussion of it. This evasion is a serious abdication of responsibility. How can judges make decisions about the neutrality of explanations for strikes when the very terms they are judging are not defined?

I would argue that language ability is frequently used as a proxy for race.[62] The Court notes that language constitutes "membership in a community," that is, that Spanish-speakers could be construed as a cognizable group, fulfilling the first test of a *Batson* claim.[63] Further, they admit, "It may well be, for certain ethnic groups and

---

[59]See JEFFREY ABRAMSON, WE, THE JURY: THE JURY SYSTEM AND THE IDEAL OF DEMOCRACY (1994); *see* generally FUKURAI, ET AL., supra note 43, at ch. 13.

[60]*Hernandez v. Texas*, 347 U.S. at 482.

[61]Hernandez v. New York, 500 U.S. 352, 371 (1991).

[62]See Kevin R. Johnson & George A. Martinez, *Discrimination by Proxy: The Case of Proposition 227 and the Ban on Bilingual Education*, 33 U.C. DAVIS L. REV. 1227 (2000). I thank Kevin Johnson for bringing his work to my attention.

[63]*Hernandez v. New York*, 500 U.S. at 370.

in some communities, that proficiency in a particular language, like skin color, should be treated as a surrogate for race under an equal protection analysis."[64] Yet they conclude, "But that case is not before us."[65] Given other discrimination cases regarding the use of Spanish in the workplace, this is a flagrant omission.

A deeper discussion of "race" would include speaking a foreign language when that language is a primary language as a marker of difference and would examine when that difference creates a situation of *de facto* discrimination.[66] In *Hernandez v. Texas*, the Supreme Court presaged *Batson* by agreeing with defense attorney Carlos Cadena that exclusion on the basis of distinctions other than race can deprive a group of equal protection, and acknowledged that community prejudices change, as do the groups needing protection. Chief Justice Warren explained that, "When the existence of a distinct class is demonstrated, and it is further shown that the laws, as written or as applied, single out that class for different treatment not based on some reasonable classification, the guarantees of the Constitution have been violated."[67] The justices accepted the evidence Cadena offered that people of Mexican descent were treated as a distinct class.

One way to determine whether a group is treated differently is to study the social order of the community. In *Hernandez v. Texas*, attorney Carlos Cadena did just this. Cadena found that "persons of his national origin" were "intentionally, arbitrarily and systematically" excluded from jury selection. He used the phrase "national origin" in lieu of race because only "black" and "white" were recognized as races, but he showed that "national origin" operated to exclude in the same way as race. For example, people frequently contrasted "Mexicans and whites," but not "Germans and whites" suggesting that the distinction was rooted in race, not ancestry. He also provided evidence that the state and federal governments distinguished "Mexicans" from "Negroes" and "whites," and differentiated people of Mexican descent from other whites. The federal census bureau compiled statistics on "Spanish speaking persons," the category "Mexican" was used by the Selective Service in World War II, and the Texas Department of Health distinguished them in a separate category from whites. He also showed that Mexicans experienced *de facto* segregation in schools, restaurants, public swimming pools and even in the bathrooms in the very courthouse in Jackson County in which the case was originally tried. [68]

If the *Hernandez v. New York* Court was to model itself after its predecessor in *Hernandez v. Texas*, it would consider such sociological evidence to determine whether language use is melded with notions of race. For example, they could engage in a discussion of the role of continual immigration to the United States from Latin America in fueling discrimination against Spanish-speaking people. Or they could consult experts on the sociopolitical aspects of bilingualism.[69] They would note and puzzle over the fact that the federal census includes a separate, non-racial

---

[64]*Id.* at 371.

[65]*Id.* at 372.

[66]See Perea, supra note 40, at 17-18.

[67]Hernandez v. Texas, 347 U.S. 475, 478 (1954).

[68]Brief for Petitioner at 38-40, Hernandez v. Texas, 347 U.S. 475 (1954) (No. 406).

[69]See RONALD SCHMIDT, LANGUAGE POLICY AND IDENTITY POLITICS IN THE UNITED STATES (2000).

category for "Hispanics," the only such category, and try to determine its import. Although today there is greater recognition of the complexity of race, enduring notions of Latinos' racial difference is betrayed by the curious category "non-Hispanic whites" in many governmental and sociological studies.

In one way, however, both Courts were similar. They both deferred the central question: whether Latinos constitute a racial group. Although the Court's decision in *Hernandez v. Texas* was based on the recognition that people of Mexican descent were a distinct class, it declined to rule on whether they constituted a race. While the case has been interpreted to extend the Equal Protection Clause to national origin groups, the Court insisted on using the term "class" (meaning "category"), rather than "race," to refer to this cognizable group. Thus, it did not extend the mantle of protection to all Latinos. Instead, it returned them to a time in which each defendant must prove that he is part of a cognizable group that experienced discrimination. While it did say that the Equal Protection Clause could cover groups that have "other differences from the community norm," it fostered an erasure of race that continues to affect the prospects for Latinos' participation on juries, today. Indeed, in the post-*Batson* era, it can be very difficult for Latinos to prove discrimination in jury selection. Because the racism they encounter is bound up with cultural difference, it seems less invidious than discrimination based solely on skin color. Its complexity makes it harder to prove.

Scholars have shown that race is a social construction and that its contours constantly change.[70] I have argued elsewhere that "Latino" is a racialized ethnic group.[71] This category includes cultural artifacts such as language and religion and encompasses people of many national origins and colors. While a Latino who was born in the United States and looks white may be less likely to experience discrimination, they can instantly become racialized when speaking Spanish. Just as race and ethnicity were once joined for non-whites,[72] today, language is often a significant marker of racial difference. Because Latinos are "in-between" black and white, they often experience discrimination based on race, but that experience is not recognized as discrimination due to the traditional conception of "race" meaning either black or white. Since their experience of discrimination as a group is not recognized as racial discrimination, their claims are treated on the individual level. In *Hernandez v. New York*, the Court reflects this common understanding by pointing to the particular circumstances of the trial. The legal system sanctions what types of discrimination are deemed permissible and impermissible. While the system reflects the social order, it also helps to define and legitimate it. Thus, once it recognized that a cognizable group is treated differently, a responsible Court *would* tackle the larger issue of what constitutes race.

---

[70]See MICHAEL OMI & HOWARD WINANT, RACIAL FORMATION IN THE UNITED STATES (1994).

[71]See Clare Sheridan, "'A Foreign, Alien Race': Racialization and the Political Rights of Mexican Americans in Progressive Era Texas," *in* A Genealogy of Citizenship: Mexican Americans, Race and National Identity (1999) (unpublished dissertation, Department of Government, University of Texas, Austin) (on file with the University of Texas, Austin).

[72]See Mae M. Ngai, *The Architecture of Race in American Immigration Law: A Reexamination of the Immigration Act of 1924*, 86 J. AM. HIST. 67 (1999).

VI. Conclusion

In the majority's decision in *Miller-El*, the Court noted that "even though the prosecution's reasons for striking African-American members of the venire appear race neutral, the application of these rationales to the venire might have been selective and based on racial consideration."[73] One can imagine many explanations that appear neutral but are selectively applied. In a thorough review of all cases raising *Batson* inquiries between 1986 and 1993, Kenneth Melilli analyzed the reasons given and found that the majority of them are stereotypes of people in cognizable groups. "Indeed" he notes that "evaluating people on the basis of stereotypes is an inherent aspect of the peremptory challenge system."[74] Moreover, most would be allowed as challenges for cause. Thus, he argues, using peremptory strikes for such people should be disallowed.[75] In his dissent in *Hernandez v. New York*, Justice Stevens concurs. "If the prosecutor's concern was valid and substantiated by the record, it would have supported a challenge for cause." He continues, arguing for a significant change in the system of challenges. "The fact that the prosecutor did not make any such challenge . . . should disqualify him from advancing the concern as a justification for a peremptory challenge."[76] Melilli concludes that retaining a system with peremptory challenges is antithetical to outlawing racial discrimination in jury selection.

Melilli found that in seventy-eight percent of the cases in which a prima facie case was made, the prosecutor's explanation for exercising the strike was accepted as race-neutral.[77] Only seventeen percent of blacks and thirteen percent of Hispanics making *Batson* claims were successful despite the fact that sixty-two percent of blacks and sixty-six percent of Hispanics were able to make prima facie cases that they may have been discriminated against. To echo the *Hernandez v. Texas* Court, the gap between the *prima facie* case and their ability to prove it is too large to be "mere chance."[78]

Melilli details 49 cases (of 191) in which prosecutor's explanations were rejected because they were based on stereotypes of other groups that the potential jurors belonged to.[79] Several of these, such as residence in a high crime area, could be proxies for race. In looking at the entire set of cases, he found that over fifty-two percent were based on group stereotypes and close to four percent on the subjective judgments of prosecutors. The remaining forty-three percent could be addressed by challenges for cause.[80] He objects to those based on group stereotypes because they deny individuals the right to participate on juries. The system of peremptory challenges operates, he argues, to seat favorable jurors. But the role of the state should be to create fair and impartial juries, not juries that tend to be favorable to one or the

---

[73]Miller-El v. Cockrell, 537 U.S. 322, 343 (2003).
[74]See Melilli, supra note 19, at 447.
[75]*Id.*
[76]Hernandez v. New York, 500 U.S. 352, 379 (1991) (Stevens, J., dissenting).
[77]See Melilli, supra note 19, at 461 Table D-1.
[78]*Id.* at 463, Tables E-2 and E-3.
[79]*Id.* at 482, Table H-2.
[80]*Id.* at 497, Table III-R.

other side.[81] Melilli concludes that a system in which challenges for cause were the only option, making them more meaningful, would capture the legitimate concerns of both parties and would eliminate pretextual ones based on group stereotypes or subjective assessments by the prosecution.[82]

Justice Marshall also strongly advocated eliminating peremptory challenges. He declared in his concurring opinion in *Batson*, "The decision today will not end the racial discrimination that peremptories inject into the jury-selection process. That goal can be accomplished only by eliminating peremptory challenges entirely."[83] Marshall noted that often, *prima facie* cases are not even made unless the challenges are "flagrant."[84] Moreover, even when a defendant is able to establish a *prima facie* case, it is difficult for trial courts to rebut facially neutral reasons for the strikes. He noted that reasons such as a juror seeming uncommunicative or having a son the same age as the defendant were accepted at face value. He prophetically warns, "If such easily generated explanations are sufficient to discharge the prosecutor's obligation to justify his strikes on nonracial groups, then the protection erected by the Court today may be illusory."[85]

In the final decision in Miller-El's case, Justice Breyer picks up the cause. He notes that, just as Justice Marshall feared, it is too difficult to prove subjective intent. In his concurring opinion he points out the conflict between a prosecutor's duty to his or her client to seat the most favorable jury and the stereotypes rooted in making such determinations. He notes that there is an entire industry dedicated to helping lawyers select jurors who they think would be preferable. He concludes, "the outcome in terms of jury selection is the same as it would be were the motive less benign. And as long as that is so, the law's antidiscrimination command and a peremptory jury-selection system that permits or encourages the use of stereotypes work at cross-purposes."[86]

The most promising grounds for eliminating peremptory challenges may be the Sixth Amendment, rather than the Equal Protection Clause. The Sixth Amendment guarantees that "the accused shall enjoy the right to a speedy and public trial, by an impartial jury."[87] The term "impartial" has subsequently been interpreted to refer to a "fair cross-section" of the community, though the Court noted in *Holland v. Illinois* that it does not require the actual composition of the petit jury to be representative of different groups in the community.[88] Despite this ruling, it seems that a focus on the rights of potential jurors, rather than defendants, requires a reexamination of the Sixth Amendment guarantee. One year after the decision in *Holland*, the Court held in *Powers v. Ohio* that *Batson* did, indeed, apply to the right of jurors not to be excluded from the possibility of serving on a jury.[89] It further held that the

---

[81]*Id.* at 499.
[82]*Id.* at 487-96.
[83]Batson v. Kentucky, 476 U.S. 79, 102-103 (1986) (Marshall, J., concurring).
[84]*Id.* at 105.
[85]*Id.* at 106.
[86]*Miller-El v. Dretke* at 2343.
[87]U.S. CONST. amend. VI.
[88]Holland v. Illinois, 493 U.S. 474, 496 (1990).
[89]Powers v. Ohio, 499 U.S. 400, 429 (1991).

defendant could make a *Batson* claim regarding the exclusion of black members of the venire even though the defendant, himself, was white.[90] Melilli argues that *Batson* caused a largely unrecognized sea-change in focusing on the right of prospective jurors to serve, rather than on the rights of the defendant. He offers *Powers v. Ohio* as evidence that the logical conclusion flowing from *Batson* is the right of potential jurors to have a genuine opportunity to serve on a jury.[91]

Indeed, a case could be made that over history, the Court has progressively expanded its understanding of bias in jury selection. It has extended its reach at each stage, recognizing different forms of bias and methods of exclusion. If Melilli's argument that *Batson* has shifted the focus from the Equal Protection rights of defendants to the Sixth Amendment rights of prospective jurors is correct, than a rethinking of the Court's current position is in order. To some extent, the Court has recognized that it has made this shift in focus, yet it repeatedly returns to language of intent and Equal Protection vis-à-vis defendants.

A focus on the rights of potential jurors, however, requires a more thorough analysis of methods of exclusion and creative thinking about ways to ameliorate non-representative juries. As notions of race evolve, it also requires a rethinking of what constitutes racial discrimination. Finally, as the focus shifts from the defendant to the juror, the terrain of the debate must move from purposeful discriminatory intent to disproportionate effect. Reflecting our discussion of systemic bias, Justice Stevens concludes, "[t]he line between discriminatory purpose and discriminatory impact is neither as bright nor as critical as the Court appears to believe."[92]

The Court objects that allowing examination of disproportionate effect would flood the system with *Batson* claims, causing chaos and undermining the purpose of the peremptory challenge. In their concurrence, Justices O'Connor and Scalia insist,

> [a]bsent intentional discrimination violative of the Equal Protection Clause, parties should be free to exercise their peremptory strikes for any reason, or no reason at all. The peremptory challenge is, "as Blackstone says, an arbitrary and capricious right; and it must be exercised with full freedom, or it fails of its full purpose."[93]

This is precisely where the peremptory challenge fails. The Court has chosen to limit its usage only on the grounds of race and gender. It has created a system where challenges to it are frequent, but has made it nearly impossible for defendants to prove their *Batson* claims. As Melilli concludes, "[a] system which . . . seeks to accommodate both the inherent aspects of the peremptory challenge and the scrutiny of anti-discrimination laws is one which seeks a middle ground which either does not exist or is impossible to locate."[94] The two purposes simply cannot coexist.

In his decision in *Batson*, Justice Powell worries that confidence in the justice system has been undermined. Indeed, the legitimacy of a democratic system of justice rests on the confidence of its citizens in its fairness. In recent years, that confi-

---

[90]*Id.*
[91]See Melilli, supra note 19, at 453.
[92]Hernandez v. New York, 500 U.S. 352, 377-78 (1991) (Stevens, J., dissenting).
[93]*Id.* at 374 (quoting Lewis v. United States, 146 U.S. 370 (1892).
[94]See Melilli, supra note 19, at 483.

dence has eroded along racial lines. The use of peremptory challenges plays a large role in this perception. Most importantly, as Justice Breyer notes, "the right to a jury free of discriminatory taint is constitutionally protected—the right to use peremptory challenges is not."[95] The opportunities to both serve on a jury and to be judged by a jury that has been chosen fairly may improve citizens' confidence in the system, but only if we recognize that discrimination can take many forms and is accomplished through many methods. The current crisis of legitimacy in the judicial system around racially charged cases suggests that we need to have a national conversation about bias recognizing that non-representative juries are inimical to justice.

In many respects, *Miller-El* has restored the promise of *Hernandez v. Texas*. Ironically, this promise was derailed by the ways in which *Batson* has been applied. The ruling in *Hernandez v. New York* is an example of this regression. The *Hernandez v. Texas* Court recognized that some people can be singled out for different treatment as a "distinct class" based on "other differences from the community norm." The existence of this class can be demonstrated through social context. Whether this difference in treatment is based on a "reasonable" classification is a key question. It would seem that Spanish-speaking people not only have historically experienced discrimination, but also that this discrimination has been superimposed on racial stereotypes. Yet, mirroring the case law following *Batson,* the *Hernandez v. New York* court did not find the use of peremptory challenges to strike Spanish-speaking jurors problematic. *Miller-El* rectifies this interpretation, restores the spirit of *Hernandez v. Texas,* and realizes the intent of the justices in *Batson*.

As in *Hernandez v. Texas,* the Justices in *Miller-El* focused on the outcome—a jury panel that was unrepresentative of the venire. They then examined the state's reasons for using its peremptory strikes to eliminate most of the African-Americans empaneled. That is, they did not accept the stated intent of the prosecution and challenged facially neutral reasons for strikes. Moreover, as in *Hernandez v. Texas,* the Justices grappled with the reach of racial discrimination in society and arrived at a nuanced understanding of its operation. Similarly, they concluded that even if there is no evidence of invidious intent in the use of peremptory strikes, such rationales can disproportionately affect African-Americans, acting as proxies for race.

Unfortunately, the two Courts share a similar tendency—neither goes out on a limb and fundamentally changes the structures that permit discrimination in jury selection. While they both serve as correctives to prior cases—*Swain v. Alabama* and *Batson v. Kentucky*, they do not promulgate new procedures guaranteeing substantive change. Given the nature of peremptory challenges and their incompatibility with a non-discriminatory ideal, it is doubtful that *Miller-El* will have immediate impact. The arguments in both cases illuminate one reason for the contemporary crisis of confidence in the justice system. One can only hope that the extraordinary circumstances of *Miller-El's* case history and Justice Breyer's dissent will result an its legacy being realized.

---

[95]Miller-El v. Dretke at 2344.

The Non-Discrimination Ideal of *Hernandez v. Texas* Confronts a "Culture" of Discrimination: The Amazing Story of *Miller-El v. Texas*[1]

Sandra Guerra Thompson*

"If [the trial jury's] composition is a sham, the judgment is a sham."

President Lyndon B. Johnson[2]

Introduction

The history of race discrimination in jury selection dates back to the founding of our nation, but it was not until after Reconstruction that the Supreme Court recognized the right of African Americans to participate in the jury process. The Court struck down exclusionary statutes[3] and disapproved of discriminatory practices.[4] Congress also provided criminal sanctions for any person who excluded African Americans from jury service on the basis of race.[5] Thus, no longer can African Americans be totally excluded from jury lists by statute, nor can they be totally excluded by the discriminatory application of facially neutral statutes.[6]

The Supreme Court has likewise vindicated the constitutional rights of other groups who have been excluded from service on juries. In the 1954 case of *Hernan-*

---

[1]Throughout this chapter, the author refers to the case as "*Miller-El v. Texas*," which was the way the case was originally styled. See Miller-El v. Texas, 748 S.W.2d 459 (Tex. Crim. App. 1988). The case recently decided by the United States Supreme Court is actually styled "Miller-El v. Dretke," 125 S.Ct. 2317 (2005), and was previously also styled "Miller-El v. Cockrell," 537 U.S. 322 (2003), and "Miller-El v. Johnson," 330 F.3d 690 (5th Cir. 2003). The original style is chosen because it more clearly identifies the identity of the true respondent, the State of Texas.

*UH Law Foundation Professor of Law, University of Houston Law Center. The author owes a debt of gratitude to Jacqueline Kelly (University of Houston Law Center J.D. 2004) for her research assistance. The author also thanks the University of Houston Law Foundation for its support.

[2]See Douglas L. Colbert, *Challenging the Challenger: Thirteenth Amendment As a Prohibition Against The Racial Use of Peremptory Challenges*, 76 CORNELL L. REV. 1, 88 (1990) (quoting President Johnson's statement published in N.Y. TIMES, Nov. 17, 1965, at 1).

[3]See, e.g., Neal v. Delaware, 103 U.S. (13 Otto) 370 (1881) (state excluded African Americans from jury service on account of race); Strauder v. West Virginia, 100 U.S. (10 Otto) 303 (1880) (state statute limiting jury service to white males violates equal protection rights of African Americans).

[4]See *infra* notes 31-39 and accompanying text (regarding color-coded cards and discriminatory application of juror qualifications).

[5]See *Ex Parte Virginia*, 100 U.S. (10 Otto) 339 (1880) (upholding federal statute criminalizing a state's exclusion of African Americans from jury service because of their race as a reasonable means of enforcing the Equal Protection Clause).

[6]See, e.g., cases cited *infra* note 40; Hernandez v. Texas, 347 U.S. 475 (1954) (total exclusion of Mexican-Americans from grand jury service).

dez v. Texas, the Court first articulated the universality of the non-discrimination mandate that it had set forth in numerous previous opinions spanning over a century.[7] The Court found that persons of Mexican descent constituted a "separate" and "distinct" class, and, as such, the State of Texas could not discriminate against the group in jury selection.[8] Following *Hernandez*, the Court proceeded to acknowledge the right of women not to be excluded on the basis of their gender.[9] The Court has also held that the right against discrimination belongs to the excluded juror. Thus, it matters not whether the discrimination is practiced by the prosecutor or defense,[10] whether the case is criminal or civil,[11] or whether the defendant in a criminal case is African American, Latino, or white.[12]

In another line of cases, the Supreme Court extended the non-discrimination rule further than simply prohibiting the systematic exclusion of all people of a distinct group. The Court went so far as to require that groups should be "fairly represented" on jury lists according to population statistics for minority groups in a particular jurisdiction.[13] This right emanates from the Sixth Amendment right to a jury trial, rather than from the Equal Protection Clause.[14] Nonetheless, it is an important component of the jurisprudence on non-discrimination in jury selection.

Despite these successes in the Supreme Court for the principal of non-discrimination in jury selection, discrimination continues in many old and new forms. While the Court vigorously rejected total exclusion of a particular racial group from jury lists and even requires fair representation for distinct groups on jury lists, it has never affirmatively required proportionate representation on juries. Instead, the Court continues to allow the exercise of peremptory strikes during jury selection, a practice that has the potential to be used to eliminate all or virtually all of the available minority jurors, and is often used in just that way.[15] Thus, rather than proportionate inclusion on juries, the old practice of total exclusion has been transformed to proportionate inclusion at the front end (jury lists) and, all too often, exclusion or token inclusion at the back end (seated juries).

Such was the state of jury selection practices in 1986 in Dallas County, Texas, when Thomas Joe Miller-El was arrested for murder. When jury selection began in Miller-El's trial, there were twenty African Americans on his jury venire. Nine of them were excused for cause or by agreement of the parties. During the course of jury selection, the prosecutor exercised ten of his fourteen peremptory strikes to remove ten of the eleven remaining African Americans from the jury, leaving only

---

[7]Hernandez v. Texas, 347 U.S. 475, 478-79 (1954).

[8]*Id.* at 482.

[9]J.E.B. v. Alabama *ex rel.* T.B., 511 U.S. 127, 130-31 (1994).

[10]Edmonson v. Leesville Concrete Co., 500 U.S. 614 (1991).

[11]Georgia v. McCollum, 505 U.S. 42 (1992) (criminal defendants do not have the right to racially discriminate against potential jurors and State has standing to raise claims on behalf of potential jurors).

[12]Hernandez v. New York, 500 U.S. 352 (1991) (discrimination against venire persons on basis of ethnic origin is prohibited by *Batson* principles); Powers v. Ohio, 499 U.S. 400 (1991) (white defendant has right to bring third-party equal protection claims on behalf of excluded black venire person); Peters v. Kiff, 407 U.S. 493 (1972) (white defendant's due process rights violated by total exclusion of African Americans on his grand jury and petit jury).

[13]See cases cited *infra* notes 82-84 and accompanying text.

[14]*Id.*

[15]See *infra* notes 85-134 and accompanying text.

one African American who served on the jury.[16] Miller-El challenged the prosecutor's use of its peremptory strikes as racially discriminatory along with other practices during jury selection.[17]

The Supreme Court heard Miller-El's habeas petition twice, first rejecting the Fifth Circuit's denial of a certificate of appealability and then reversing the Fifth Circuit's ruling rejecting the petition on the merits. In June of 2005, the six-justice majority, in no uncertain terms, found that the prosecutors in Miller-El's case had not only discriminated on the basis of race, but that they had lied to the courts about it.
[18] The majority faults prosecutors for using a combination of trick questions, racially disparate questioning, and a constitutionally dubious practice known as the "jury shuffle" to weed out all but one African American venire person. Further evidence was cited of a history of blatant discrimination in jury selection practiced by the Dallas County prosecutors. The Court also took the Fifth Circuit to task for rejecting Miller-El's claims despite what the Court considered clear evidence of discrimination. Thus, Miller-El was granted a new trial, eighteen years after the conclusion of the first.

What the Supreme Court did not do was to announce a new rule or new application of the existing *Batson* rule so as to provide a more effective deterrent to racial discrimination in jury selection. Indeed, it is hard to imagine a rule that could both preserve the litigator's right to rely on gut instincts to discriminate between potential jurors in jury selection, while at the same time effectively guarding against discrimination on improper grounds. This inherent conflict between the stated purpose and principal evil in the exercise of peremptory challenges leads this author to add another voice to the body of literature calling for the abolition of the use of peremptory strikes in order for racial discrimination in jury selection to be eradicated.[19] The chapter begins in Part I with a brief review of the history of racial discrimination in

---

[16]Miller-El v. Cockrell, 537 U.S. 322, 331 (2003).

[17]See *infra* notes 135-56 and accompanying text.

[18]Miller-El v. Dretke, 125 S.Ct. 2317, 2325-32 (2005) (noting that prosecutor "mischaracterized" a juror's testimony, finding evidence of "pretext" in stated reasons for peremptory strikes, and concluding that the stated reasons for a juror's strike were "implausible"). For a discussion of the paucity of decisions finding *Batson* violations, see *infra* notes 107-34 and accompanying text.

[19]Justice Breyer, citing Justice Marshall's earlier calls for abolition of peremptory strikes, issued a concurring opinion in *Miller-El*, calling for a reconsideration of *Batson*'s test and the continued viability of the peremptory system as a whole. *Miller-El*, 125 S.Ct. at 2340-44. In addition, many scholars have likewise taken the view that peremptory challenges should be abolished. See, e.g., Morris B. Hoffman, *Peremptory Challenges Should be Abolished: A Trial Judge's Perspective*, 64 U. CHI. L. REV. 809, 821-22 (1997); Kenneth J. Melilli, Batson *in Practice: What We Have Learned About* Batson *and Peremptory Challenges*, 71 NOTRE DAME L. REV. 447, 502-03, 484 n.109 (listing citations); Vivien Toomey Montz & Craig Lee Montz, *The Peremptory Challenge: Should It Still Exist?: An Examination of Federal and Florida Law*, 54 U. MIAMI L. REV. 451 (2000). Many others have offered solutions short of eliminating the peremptory challenge. See, e.g., Jeb C. Griebat, *Peremptory Challenge by Blind Questionnaire: The Most Practical Solution for Ending the Problem of Racial and Gender Discrimination in Kansas Courts While Preserving the Necessary Function of the Peremptory Challenge*, 12 KAN. J. L. & PUB. POL'Y 323, 343 (2003) (proposing blind questionnaires for use of peremptories); Leonard L. Cavise, *The Batson Doctrine: The Supreme Court's Utter Failure to Meet The Challenge of Discrimination in Jury Selection*, 1999 WIS. L. REV. 501, 505 (1999) (arguing that all peremptories should have some rational basis to pass constitutional muster); Charles J. Ogletree, *Just Say No!: A Proposal to Eliminate Racially Discriminatory Uses of Peremptory Challenges*, 31 AM. CRIM. L. REV. 1099, 1110 (1994) (recommending a number of reforms); Colbert, supra note 2, at 101 (arguing for use of the Thirteenth Amendment to prohibit use of peremptory challenges to exclude African Americans); Sheri Lynn Johnson, *Black Innocence and the White Jury*, 83 MICH. L. REV. 1611, 1698-99 (1985) (proposing that a minimum of three black jurors is necessary to guarantee a fair jury verdict when the accused is black).

jury selection from the nineteenth-century to the 1950s. It traces the development of the Supreme Court's non-discrimination principle as applied in cases in which African Americans were systematically excluded from jury service.

Part II of the Article highlights the importance of *Hernandez v. Texas* as the first case to broaden the non-discrimination concept to include all identifiable groups. This part describes the evolution of the Court's non-discrimination jurisprudence as it extended its reach to include ethnic minorities and women. The constitutional protections against discrimination in jury selection even include a "fair cross-section" requirement, but this requirement only applies to the creation of jury lists and does not place any limits on the use of peremptory challenges in selecting actual jurors. The last section of Part II provides an empirical analysis of appellate case law reviewing claims of discrimination to determine whether *Batson's* three-part rule appears to provide an effective remedy for discrimination in the use of peremptory strikes.

In Part III, the Article tells the amazing story of *Miller-El v. Texas*, a case that amply illustrates the extreme difficulty of prevailing under *Batson*, even when the facts overwhelmingly suggest discrimination.

I. A Thumbnail Sketch of Discrimination in Jury Selection and the Focus on Exclusion of African Americans

At the founding of our country, juries were racist, sexist and elitist in composition.[20] Juries were comprised exclusively of men in all states.[21] With the exception of Vermont, jury service was also restricted to property owners or taxpayers.[22] Three states had statutes permitting only whites to serve on juries, and the state of Maryland disqualified atheists.[23] Over the course of the nineteenth-century, property qualifications for eligibility to *vote* began to disappear and the country moved toward universal suffrage for white males.[24] But the reform of jury eligibility criteria seemed to lag behind the reform of voting requirements.[25]

Interestingly, Alschuler and Deiss note that nineteenth-century juries were faulted more for their incompetence than their elitism. They write, "As early as 1803, St. George Tucker's influential American edition of *Blackstone's Commentaries* reported that, 'after the first day or two,' juries hearing civil lawsuits in the rural areas of Virginia were 'made up, generally, of idle loiterers about the court, . . . the most unfit persons to decide upon the controversies of suitors."[26] Similar complaints were made in other parts of the country as well, and there were complaints that jurors (of such low qualifications) were easily subject to corruption and bribery.[27]

---

[20]See Albert W. Alschuler & Andrew G. Deiss, *A Brief History of the Criminal Jury in the United States,* 61 U. CHI. L. REV. 867, 876 (1994).

[21]*Id.*

[22]*Id.*

[23]*Id.*

[24]*Id.* at 878.

[25]*Id.*

[26]*Id.* at 880 (quoting 3 WILLIAM BLACKSTONE, COMMENTARIES APP. 64 (St. George Tucker, ed., Birch and Small 1803)).

[27]*Id.* at 881-82.

Statistics on racial inclusion have never been available as such. Any historical description is thus necessarily pieced together from available information gathered from various sources. Alschuler and Deiss report that the first African Americans known to serve on a jury did so in Massachusetts in 1860.[28] By all accounts, however, jury service was a right exercised by a few African Americans at this time in a few jurisdictions. Alschuler and Deiss provide examples of integrated juries from two jurisdictions:

> In 1867, the military commander of South Carolina declared every taxpayer or registered voter to be eligible for jury service. Since the military itself had registered virtually every adult African American male, integrated juries became common in this district. Two years later, the South Carolina legislature mandated not only that grand and petit juries be integrated but also that their racial composition duplicates the composition of the counties in which they sat.[29]

> Almost one-third of the citizens called for grand jury service in New Orleans between 1872 and 1878 were African Americans—a percentage that matched the percentage of African Americans in the population of Orleans Parish generally.[30]

Still in most jurisdictions, African Americans and other minority groups were excluded by means of a number of practices. In most states, "jury commissioners" were (and still are in some states) members of the community who were charged with compiling lists of potential jurors. Cases showed that state courts tended to appoint all-white jury commissioners who applied subjective criteria to create jury lists that tended to include primarily, if not exclusively, white prospective jurors.[31] In some cases, States defended their exclusionary practices by arguing that no African Americans met the qualifications for jury service. For example, in *Neal v. Delaware*, the Court rejected the State's argument that no African American had been called to jury service because "the great body of black men residing in [the] State are utterly unqualified by want of intelligence, experience, or moral integrity to sit on juries."[32] In *Neal*, the Supreme Court rejected this proposition with strong language that it would repeat in several cases over the decades:

> It was, we think, under all the circumstances, *a violent presumption* which the State court indulged, that such uniform exclusion of that race from juries, during a period of many years, was solely because, in the judgment of those officers, fairly exercised, the black race in Delaware were utterly

---

[28]*Id.* at 886.
[29]*Id.*
[30]*Id.*
[31]Carter v. Jury Comm'n. of Greene County, 396 U.S. 320 (1970) (in class action by potential African American jurors substantially underrepresented in jury service, Court holds that excluded class has a cognizable claim); Turner v. Fouche, 396 U.S. 346 (1970) (jury commissioners used juror qualifications in unconstitutional manner such that African Americans were substantially underrepresented).
[32]Neal v. Delaware, 103 U.S. 370, 402 (1880).

disqualified, by want of intelligence, experience, or moral integrity, to sit on juries.[33]

In places in which more diverse jury lists were compiled, trial courts employed other means to exclude African Americans. In one case, the court used different colored tickets for African Americans and whites which were drawn by a judge, ostensibly at random, from a box.[34] It so happened that no African American had ever been selected to serve on a jury.[35] A concurring opinion notes that "the aperture in the box was sufficiently wide to make open to view the color of slips."[36] Moreover, the concurring justice expresses the concern that the "opportunity for working of a discriminatory system exists whenever the mechanism for jury selection has a component part, such as the slips here, that differentiates between white and colored." [37] The practice of distinguishing jurors by race on cards would continue in some places into modern times.[38] In another case, the State argued that the jury lists included African Americans. The evidence, however, suggested that lists may not have included African Americans, but that the names of African American may have been added later after the claim of discrimination had been lodged.[39]

Thus, the Supreme Court encountered many forms of discrimination, and in case after case found equal protection violations resulting from the total exclusion of African Americans from jury lists.[40] In the first seventy-four years of its jury discrimination jurisprudence, the Court had occasion to consider only claims brought by African Americans. The extent of similar protection for other groups was not

---

[33]*Id.* at 397 (emphasis added); see *also* Hill v. Texas, 316 U.S. 400, 405 (1942) (quoting "violent presumption" language); Norris v. Alabama, 294 U.S. 587, 599 (1935) (same).

[34]Avery v. Georgia, 345 U.S. 559, 560-61 (1953); see *also* Alexander v. Louisiana, 405 U.S. 625 (1972) (racial designation on both questionnaire and information card established that jury selection procedures were not racially neutral); Whitus v. Georgia, 385 U.S. 545 (1967) (jurors selected from one-volume tax digest divided into separate sections of "Negroes" and "whites"); Arnold v. North Carolina, 376 U.S. 773 (1964) (grand jurors selected from tax records of county in which "Negroes" and "whites" are listed separately).

[35]*Avery*, 345 U.S. at 561.

[36]*Id.* at 564 (Frankfurter, J., concurring).

[37]*Id.*

[38]See, e.g., Ford v. Kentucky, 469 U.S. 984, 984 (1984) (Marshall, J., dissenting) (defendant claimed selection system for grand jurors not facially neutral, for the voter registration list from which grand jurors selected in county contained information on gender, race, and date of birth); Alexander v. Louisiana, 405 U.S. 625 (1972) (racial designation on both questionnaire and information card established that jury selection procedures were not racially neutral). Indeed, the Supreme Court has suggested that jury selection procedures are never racially neutral with respect to Latinos, finding that "Spanish surnames are just as easily identifiable as race was from the questionnaires in *Alexander* or the notations and card colors in *Whitus v. Georgia,* and in *Avery v. Georgia.*" Castañeda v. Partida, 430 U.S. 482, 495 (1977).

[39]See Norris v. Alabama, 294 U.S. 587, 592-93 (1935).

[40]See, e.g., Coleman v. Alabama, 389 U.S. 22 (1967) (no African American had ever served on a grand jury and few, if any, had served on petit juries in the county); Arnold v. North Carolina, 376 U.S. 773 (1964) (only one African American had served on a grand jury in previous twenty-four years); Eubanks v. Louisiana, 356 U.S. 584 (1958) (uniform and long-continued exclusion of African Americans from grand jury service); Reece v. Georgia, 350 U.S. 85 (1955) (no African American had ever been called to serve on grand jury); Patton v. Mississippi, 332 U.S. 463 (1947) (no African American had served on grand or petit criminal court juries for thirty years or more); Hill v. Texas, 316 U.S. 400 (1942) (no African American had ever been called to grand jury service); Norris v. Alabama, 294 U.S. 587 (1935) (continuous and systematic exclusion of African Americans from grand and petit juries); Neal v. Delaware, 103 U.S. 370, 397 (1880) ("no colored citizen had ever been summoned as a juror in the courts of the State").

determined until the earliest days of the civil rights movement when the Court decided *Hernandez v. Texas* in 1954.[41]

II. The Universal Non-Discrimination Ideal of *Hernandez v. Texas*: Jury Venires and Peremptory Strikes

Whereas the nineteenth-century cases to arrive before the Supreme Court involved the total exclusion of African Americans from jury lists or venires, the twentieth-century would bring a wider variety of claims and claimants. The Court's landmark decision in *Hernandez v. Texas* recognized the rights of *all* identifiable groups to be free from discrimination in the creation of jury venires, or lists—the first stage in the jury selection process. The final stage in jury selection—the exercise of peremptory strikes during voir dire—would present a different set of obstacles for parties claiming discrimination. Ultimately, the Court attempted in *Batson v. Kentucky* and its progeny to provide a remedy for discrimination in the use of peremptory strikes. Unfortunately, *Batson* has not proved to be an effective remedy, and the problem of discriminatory strikes by litigants continues virtually unabated.[42]

The following sections trace the Supreme Court's jurisprudence from *Hernandez* to *Batson* and provides a backdrop for a discussion of the pending case of *Miller-El v. Texas,* a case that ultimately proves the ineffectiveness of the *Batson* remedy.

A. *Hernandez v. Texas* Extends Equal Protection Against Exclusion From Jury Venires to "Identifiable Groups"

Pete Hernandez was indicted for murder in Jackson County, Texas. He moved timely to quash his indictment on the ground that persons of Mexican descent were systematically excluded from service as jury commissioners, grand jurors, and petit jurors although a substantial number of qualified persons of Mexican descent resided in the county.[43]

As a preliminary matter, the Court would have to determine whether the Equal Protection Clause even applied to persons of "Mexican descent." The State of Texas argued that the Fourteenth Amendment protected only African Americans against discrimination by whites.[44] The Court found that such a view was not supported either by its own prior case law or that of the courts of Texas. However, since the United States Supreme Court had never considered a similar claim brought by Latinos, it could not rely on its own prior precedent in defining the class of persons belonging to the group. The Court determined that Hernandez had the initial burden of showing that "persons of Mexican descent constitute a separate class in Jackson County, distinct from 'whites.'"[45] The Court relied on testimony about the disparate

---

[41]347 U.S. 475 (1954).
[42]See *infra* notes 107-34 and accompanying text.
[43]*Hernandez*, 347 U.S. at 476-77.
[44]*Id.* at 477.
[45]*Id.* at 479.

and inferior treatment of Latinos in the community as proof that the "attitude of the community" recognized a distinct class.[46]

The Court turned to the question of whether Hernandez had proved that Mexican Americans had been excluded from jury service as a result of discrimination. Typically, the Court considered the percentage of people of different races in the population from which jury lists are drawn. In the case of Latinos, even this can be a tricky thing. In order to determine the percentage of persons of Mexican descent, the Court relied on census data for the county identifying the numbers of people with "Mexican or Latin American surnames," as well as data indicating how many of these persons were native born American citizens and how many were naturalized citizens.[47] The State challenged the reliance on surnames as a method for determining which members of the community were of Mexican descent.[48] The Court found that relying on surnames was a satisfactory method for calculating the relative size of the community, finding that "just as persons of a different race are distinguished by color, these Spanish names provide ready identification of the members of this class."[49]

Based on the census data, the Court concluded that fourteen of the population of the county and eleven percent of the males over twenty-one bore Spanish surnames.[50] The tax rolls of the county showed that six or seven percent of the freeholders were persons of Mexican descent. At the same time, the State stipulated that "for the last twenty-five years there is no record of any person with a Mexican or Latin American name having served on a jury commission, grand jury, or petit jury in Jackson County."[51] Based on this evidence, the Court held that Hernandez had met the burden of proof of making a strong prima facie case of the denial of equal protection.[52] The State offered only the testimony of five jury commissioners who stated that they did not discriminate against persons of Mexican or Latin American descent. This testimony was not enough to overcome the petitioner's case.[53]

The true significance of *Hernandez* is in the Court's recognition that any "separate" and "distinct" class of persons who may be excluded from jury service by

---

[46]The Court recounts testimony provided by the petitioner:

Here the testimony of responsible officials and citizens contained the admission that residents of the community distinguished between 'white' and 'Mexican.' The participation of persons of Mexican descent in business and community groups was shown to be slight. Until very recent times, children of Mexican descent were required to attend a segregated school for the first four grades. At least one restaurant in town prominently displayed a sign announcing 'No Mexicans Served.' On the courthouse grounds at the time of the hearing, there were two men's toilets, one unmarked, and the other marked 'Colored Men' and 'Hombres Aqui' ('Men Here').

Id. at 479-80 (citations omitted).

[47]*Id.* at 480-81 n.12. By relying on "Latin American surnames" the Court was presumably willing to include persons whose lineage might be traceable to other Latin American countries such as Peru or Guatemala, although the defendant's claim was that persons of Mexican descent were the "distinct" class. Given the testimony provided at the hearing, it is likely that the community would have treated all persons of Latin American descent as "Mexican."

[48]*Id.*

[49]*Id.*

[50]*Id.* at 480.

[51]*Id.* at 481.

[52]*Id.*

[53]*Id.*

invidious discrimination can rely on the Equal Protection Clause to vindicate their rights. Following *Hernandez,* cases involving the total exclusion of particular groups dwindled as jurisdictions expanded their jury lists to include both minorities and, eventually, women.[54]

B. The Supreme Court Upholds Requirement of "Substantial Underrepresentation" on Jury Lists

Having struck definitive blows against the blatantly discriminatory practices that led to the total exclusion of minorities from jury selection in many jurisdictions, the Court next considered whether groups had a right to "fair representation" on jury lists. In a series of cases, the Court compared census data showing the percentage of the group claiming discrimination in a jurisdiction to the information showing the percentage on grand jury lists.[55]

In the 1965 decision of *Swain v. Alabama,* the Court rejected the contention that African Americans have a right to fair representation on jury lists. The Court refused to find a prima facie case of discrimination based on statistics showing a consistent underrepresentation of African Americans on grand and petit jury panels.[56] The Court acknowledged that African Americans were "unquestionably" included in smaller proportions than members of the white community. Yet, the Court stated that "a defendant in a criminal case is not constitutionally entitled to demand a proportionate number of his race on the jury which tries him *nor on the venire or jury roll from which petit jurors are drawn.*"[57]

The Court seemed to accept as evidence rebutting the allegation of purposeful discrimination the testimony of jury commissioners that racial considerations did not play a part in their selections.[58] The Court also appears to have placed the burden on the petitioner to prove that different standards of juror qualifications were applied to African Americans and to whites or that African Americans satisfied the standards

---

[54]As late as the late 1960s, however, the Court was addressing cases of total exclusion of African Americans. See Coleman v. Alabama, 389 U.S. 22 (1967) (defendant established prima facie case of denial of equal protection by evidence that no African American served on the grand or petit jury in his case and that no African American had served on a grand jury and few, if any, had served on petit juries in the county).

[55]Turner v. Fouche, 396 U.S. 346 (1970) (60% African Americans in general population, 37% on grand jury lists); Whitus v. Georgia, 385 U.S. 545 (1967) (27.1% of taxpayers, 9.1% on grand jury lists); Sims v. Georgia, 389 U.S. 404 (1967) (24.4% of tax lists, 4.7% of grand jury lists); Jones v. Georgia, 389 U.S. 24 (1967) (19.7% of tax lists, 5% of jury list).

[56]380 U.S. 202, 205-09 (1965). The defendant established the following evidence of discrimination in the creation of jury panels and the selection of juries:
The evidence was that while Negro males over 21 constitute 26% of all males in the county in this age group, only 10 to 15% of the grand and petit jury panels drawn from the jury box since 1953 have been Negroes, there having been only one case in which the percentage was as high as 23%. In this period of time, Negroes served on 80% of the grand juries selected, the number ranging from one to three. There were four or five Negroes on the grand jury panel of about 33 in this case, out of which two served on the grand jury which indicted petitioner. Although there has been an average of six to seven Negroes on petit jury venires in criminal cases, no Negro has actually served on a petit jury since 1950. In this case, there were eight Negroes on the petit jury venire but none actually served, two being exempt and six being struck by the prosecutor in the process of selecting the jury.
Id. at 205.

[57]*Id.* at 208.

[58]*Id.* at 209.

in the same proportion as whites.[59] The Court's treatment of the evidence presented in this case by both parties stands in marked contrast to its treatment in earlier cases of total exclusion. In those cases, the Court had given little to no weight to the testimony of jury commissioners who denied practicing racial discrimination[60] and had categorically refused to accept the proposition that no African Americans met the qualifications to serve on juries, calling it a "violent presumption."[61] One might have expected the Court to have similarly demanded that the State prove that African Americans were proportionately less qualified than whites and not place the burden on the defense to prove otherwise.

In a 1977 case, the Court took a different path and found that significant "mathematical disparities" would be enough to make out a prima facie case of discrimination.[62] In *Castañeda v. Partida*, a criminal defendant, Rodrigo Partida, challenged the grand jury selection process that produced the Hidalgo County, Texas, grand jury that indicted him, claiming that Mexican-Americans were not fairly represented on the grand jury.

The Court had previously considered the selection procedures for grand jury service in Texas in *Castañeda* and other cases.[63] Unlike other cases, however, this case did not present a claim of total exclusion. The evidence presented on behalf of the petitioner showed that according to the 1970 Census statistics, "the population of the county was 79.1% Mexican-American, but that, over an eleven-year period, only thirty-nine percent of the persons summoned for grand jury service were Mexican-American," a disparity of forty percent.[64] The State did not dispute this evidence. The Court found this mathematical disparity sufficient to establish a prima facie case of purposeful discrimination against Mexican-Americans in Hidalgo County, Texas.[65]

The State also failed to produce evidence to rebut the prima facie case of discrimination. The jury commissioners were not called to testify.[66] Thus, it was "impossible to draw any inference about literacy, sound mind and moral character, and criminal record from the statistics about the population as a whole" so as to determine what percentage of Mexican Americans qualified for jury service.[67] As

---

[59]*Id.*

[60]See, e.g., Alexander v. Louisiana, 405 U.S. 625, 632 (1972); Hernandez v. Texas, 347 U.S. 475, 481 (1954); Norris v. Alabama, 294 U.S. 587, 598 (1935); *cf.* Castañeda v. Partida, 430 U.S. 482, 498 n.19 (1977).

[61]See supra notes 32-33 and accompanying text (quoting Neal v. Delaware, 103 U.S. 370, 393-94 (1880)).

[62]*Castañeda*, 430 U.S. at 496.

[63]*Id.* at 484.

[64]*Id.* at 495.

[65]*Id.* at 496.

[66]*Id.* The Court notes, however:

This is not to say, of course, that a simple protestation from a commissioner that racial considerations played no part in the selection would be enough. This kind of testimony has been found insufficient on several occasions. Neither is the State entitled to rely on a presumption that the officials discharged their sworn duties to rebut the case of discrimination.

Id. at 499 n.19 (citations omitted).

[67]*Id.* at 498-99.

Result, the Court held that the petitioner had proved his claim of unconstitutional discrimination.[68]

In some ways, the more interesting aspect of the *Castañeda* case was the Court's position on the "governing majority" theory on which the District Court had relied in rejecting the petitioner's claim.[69] In fact, both the Texas Court of Criminal Appeals and the Federal District Court had found it impossible to believe that Mexican Americans, who held a "governing majority," would discriminate against themselves. In this case, the Supreme Court notes the Texas high court's findings:

> [T]hat the foreman of the grand jury that indicted respondent was Mexican-American, and that 10 of the 20 summoned to serve had Spanish surnames. Seven of the 12 members of the petit jury that convicted him were Mexican-American. In addition, the state judge who presided over the trial was Mexican-American, as were a number of other elected officials in the county.[70]

The District Court had concluded that this theory filled the evidentiary gap in the State's case.[71] The Supreme Court rejected this without much explanation, "Because of the many facets of human motivation, it would be unwise to presume as a matter of law that human beings of one definable group will not discriminate against other members of the group."[72]

While the Court would uphold the rights of minorities to be fairly represented on jury lists, it maintained its long-held position that there is no right to proportion-

---

[68]The *Castañeda* "test" for proving substantial underrepresentation was later outlined in *Rose v. Mitchell*, 443 U.S. 545 (1979):

The first step is to establish that the group is one that is a recognizable, distinct class, singled out for different treatment under the laws, as written or as applied. . . . Next, the degree of underrepresentation must be proved, by comparing the proportion of the group in the total population to the proportion called to serve as [foremen], over a significant period of time. . . . This method of proof, sometimes called the 'rule of exclusion,' has been held to be available as a method of proving discrimination in jury selection against a delineated class. . . . Finally . . . a selection procedure that is susceptible of abuse or is not racially neutral supports the presumption of discrimination raised by the statistical showing.

Id. at 565.

[69]Interestingly, the Fifth Circuit had reversed the District Court's decision, finding that the State had not rebutted the respondent's prima facie case and that the "governing majority" theory added little to the State's case in the absence of specific proof to explain the disparity. *Castañeda*, 430 U.S. at 492. The Court nonetheless granted certiorari to consider "whether the existence of a 'governing majority' in itself can rebut a prima facie case of discrimination in grand jury selection, and, if not, whether the State otherwise met its burden of proof." *Id.*

[70]*Id.* at 490 n.9.

[71]*Id.* at 499.

[72]*Id.* The Court added that the evidence in the record was insufficient to establish a "governing majority" theory in any case. *Id.* at 500.

Justice Marshall's concurring opinion cites social science research showing that, "[M]embers of minority groups frequently respond to discrimination and prejudice by attempting to disassociate themselves from the group, even to the point of adopting the majority's negative attitudes towards the minority. Such behavior occurs with particular frequency among members of minority groups who have achieved some measure of economic or political success and thereby have gained some acceptability among the dominant group." *Id.* at 503 (Marshall, J., concurring).

al representation on actual jury panels.[73] The next phase of the challenge in obtaining fair representation in jury service would be to confront the discretionary means employed to severely restrict the number of minorities who actually serve on juries. The following section demonstrates how the Court's jurisprudence requiring that jury lists be representative of a cross-section of the community accomplished little in terms of diversifying juries in this country. Instead, by affirming the constitutionality of the use of peremptory strikes in *Swain v. Alabama*,[74] *Batson v. Kentucky*,[75] and beyond, the Court's century-long battle to end discrimination in jury selection effectively came to an end.

C. "Fair Cross-Section" Requirement Applies Only to Jury Lists, Not to Actual Juries

As the Court's jurisprudence on discrimination in jury selection evolved, claims of discrimination became more varied in terms of the parties claiming a right to be free from discrimination, the type of discrimination claimed, and the constitutional bases for the claims being made. Ultimately, the Court would rely on various constitutional grounds to uphold the rights of all persons to challenge the systematic exclusion of any large and identifiable segment of the community from the jury *lists* from which grand and petit juries are drawn.

The first expansion of the standing to challenge the exclusion of minorities from a grand jury venire came in a 1972 case. In *Peters v. Kiff*, the Court addressed the claim of a white defendant who alleged that his due process right to a fair trial was violated by the systematic exclusion of African Americans from his grand jury venire.[76] The Court relied on dicta in its earlier cases in which it had spoken of the injury to potential jurors who are denied the "privilege of participating equally . . . in the administration of justice."[77] It also relied on a more recent line of cases identifying a Sixth Amendment right to a jury trial in which the jury venire, panel, or list represents a "fair cross-section of the community."[78] Finding that all criminal defendants have a right to a jury drawn from a fair cross-section of the community, the Court found that a white defendant does have standing to raise a due process claim based on the systematic exclusion of potential African American jurors.[79] The Court

---

[73]Since the days of Reconstruction, the Court had clearly stated that the Equal Protection Clause gave African Americans a right not to be excluded from jury service on account of race, but the Court also made clear that it did *not* grant them a right to fair representation on any particular jury:

[W]hile a colored citizen, party to a trial involving his life, liberty, or property, cannot claim, as a matter of right, that his race shall have a representation on the jury, and while a mixed jury, in a particular case, is not within the meaning of the Constitution, always or absolutely necessary to the equal protection of the laws, it is a right to which he is entitled, "that in the selection of jurors to pass upon his life, liberty, or property, there shall be no exclusion of his race, and no discrimination against them, because of their color."

Neal v. Delaware, 103 U.S. (13 Otto) 370, 394 (1881). The Court would repeat this position numerous times over the years. See, e.g., Swain v. Alabama, 380 U.S. 202, 208 (1965) ("[A] defendant in a criminal case is not constitutionally entitled to demand a proportionate number of his race on the jury which tries him nor on the venire or jury roll from which petit jurors are drawn.").

[74]*Swain*, 380 U.S. at 205-09.

[75]Batson v. Kentucky, 476 U.S. 79, 89 (1986).

[76]407 U.S. 493 (1972).

[77]*Id*. at 499.

[78]*Id*. at 500.

[79]*Id*. at 505.

refused to assume that the exclusion of African Americans had relevance only for issues involving race. Instead, the Court reasoned: "When any large and identifiable segment of the community is excluded from jury service, the effect is to remove from the jury room qualities of human nature and varieties of human experience, the range of which is unknown and perhaps unknowable."[80] Since the possible harms caused by the exclusion of a large segment of the community are impossible to discern, the Court determined that "any doubt should be resolved in favor of giving the opportunity to challenge the jury to too many defendants, rather than to too few."[81] Thus, the Court both recognized the right of a white defendant to challenge the discrimination against African Americans on his jury venire, but also recognized that the due process right to a fair trial prohibits discrimination in jury selection.

The Court also expanded the constitutional bases for requiring that jury venires be representative of the community. In addition to the traditional equal protection rights of minorities not to be substantially underrepresented on jury venires, the Court also found that the Sixth Amendment right to a jury trial[82] encompasses the right of all criminal defendants to have a "fair cross-section" of the community on the jury venire, panel or list from which their petit juries are drawn.[83] This right to a "fair cross-section" was announced in two cases brought by male defendants who claimed that they had been denied their Sixth Amendment rights by the systematic exclusion of women. The Court found violations of the fair cross-section requirement in the systematic exclusion of women from jury lists. Women were being underrepresented due to the operation of state statutes providing automatic exclusions of women unless they either requested to serve or upon their request for exclusion.[84] Thus, the Court broadened the right to challenge the systematic exclusion or underrepresentation of identifiable groups so as to permit all criminal defendants to demand a representative venire or list.

D. Voir Dire Evades Fair Cross-Section Requirement

In applying the fair cross-section requirement of the Equal Protection Clause, the Supreme Court repeatedly has drawn a firm line at jury *lists*.[85] The actual jury seated, on the other hand, is the product of both strikes for cause and peremptory strikes exercised by both parties. Under such a system, it is, of course, impossible to require that the jury represent a fair cross-section of the community, and the Court has refused to eliminate the rights of the parties to exercise peremptory strikes in

---

[80]*Id.* at 503.

[81]*Id.* at 504. *But* see Ford v. Kentucky, 469 U.S. 984, 985-86 (1984) (Marshall, J., dissenting) (noting that *Peters* opinion on standing had not garnered a majority and that it had spawned confusion in the lower courts).

[82]Duncan v. Louisiana, 391 U.S. 145 (1968).

[83]Taylor v. Louisiana, 419 U.S. 522, 529 (1975).

[84]*Id.* at 531 (women excluded unless submitted a request to serve); Duren v. Missouri, 439 U.S. 357, 366-67 (1979) (women automatically excluded upon request).

[85]See Holland v. Illinois, 493 U.S. 474, 482-83 (1990) (Sixth Amendment grants right to a jury venire that represents a fair cross section of community, but not that the jury itself must be representative); *cf.* Lockhart v. McCree, 476 U.S. 162, 173 (1986) ("We have never invoked the fair-cross-section principle to invalidate the use of either for-cause or peremptory challenges to prospective jurors, or to require petit juries, as opposed to jury panels or venires, to reflect the composition of the community at large.").

selecting a jury.[86] Such a system may produce juries that are totally or nearly mono-chromatic once both sides have exercised their peremptory strikes.

The challenge for the Court was to find a way to regulate the use of peremptory strikes so as to prohibit discriminatory practices without changing the "arbitrary" nature of the strike. The Court took one approach in *Swain v. Alabama*,[87] but then changed course in *Batson v. Kentucky.*

In *Swain,* the Court's first foray into policing the use of peremptory strikes, the defendant showed that there had never been an African American on a petit jury in either a civil or criminal case in the county and that in criminal cases, he claimed, prosecutors had "consistently and systematically exercised their strikes to prevent any and all [African Americans] on petit jury venires from serving on the petit jury itself."[88] The Court rejected the defendant's claim on the ground that he had not shown that *the same prosecutor* had systematically used his peremptory challenges to strike African Americans *over a period of time.*[89] The majority emphasized that unlike the production of the jury venire which is purely a product of state officers, the selection of the petit jury is a product of both a prosecutor's and defense counsel's use of strikes.[90] The majority concluded that the record was insufficient to prove that the prosecutor in the defendant's case—and not defense attorneys—was responsible for removing African Americans from juries in case after case.

Further, the majority opinion in *Swain* goes to great lengths to extol the virtues and long history of the peremptory strike system in the United States. The Court concludes that "[t]he function of the challenge is not only to eliminate extremes of partiality on both sides, but to assure the parties that the jurors before whom they try the case will decide on the basis of the evidence placed before them, and not otherwise."[91] In order for the peremptory challenge to function properly, it must be allowed to be "exercised without a reason stated, without inquiry and without being subject to the court's control."[92] Moreover, the decision recognizes a *presumption* that "in any particular case . . . the prosecutor is using the State's challenges to obtain a fair and impartial jury to try the case before the court," and that presumption could not be overcome by subjecting the prosecutor to examination on his or her motives.[93]

In a passage that would be highly criticized (as was the entire *Swain* decision),[94] the Court explains the types of "sudden impressions and unaccountable prejudices" that may provoke a peremptory strike:

---

[86]See *Holland*, 493 U.S. at 484 ("We have acknowledged that that device [the peremptory strike] occupies 'an important position in our trial procedures,' . . . and has indeed been considered 'a necessary part of trial by jury.'") (citations omitted); *accord* Batson v. Kentucky, 476 U.S. 79, 98 (1986); Swain v. Alabama, 380 U.S. 202, 219 (1965).

[87]380 U.S. at 209.

[88]*Id.* at 223.

[89]*Id.* at 227.

[90]*Id.* at 226-27.

[91]*Id.* at 219.

[92]*Id.* at 220.

[93]*Id.* at 222.

[94]See, e.g., Thompson v. United States, 469 U.S. 1024, 1025 (1984) (Marshall, J., dissenting); McCray v. New York, 461 U.S. 961, 965 (1983) (Marshall, J., dissenting) (listing citations); see *also* Melilli, supra note 19, at 449-50.

It [the peremptory strike] is no less frequently exercised on grounds normally thought irrelevant to legal proceedings or official action, namely, the race, religion, nationality, occupation or affiliations of people summoned for jury duty. For the question a prosecutor or defense counsel must decide is not whether a juror of a particular race or nationality is in fact partial, but whether one from a different group is less likely to be. . . . Hence veniremen are not always judged solely as individuals for the purpose of exercising peremptory challenges. Rather they are challenged in light of the limited knowledge counsel has of them, which may include their group affiliations, in the context of the case to be tried.[95]

This passage appears to suggest that it is not objectionable, and indeed is to be expected, that prosecutors (and defense counsel) may evaluate a juror on the basis of group affiliation (e.g., race) and decide to exclude that juror on the ground that a juror of a different race may be less partial to one's opponent.

It took twenty-one years for the Supreme Court to overrule the *Swain* rule requiring proof of a systematic pattern of discrimination by the prosecutors in a defendant's case. In *Batson v. Kentucky*, the prosecutor used his peremptory strikes to eliminate all four black persons on the venire, resulting in a jury comprised only of white persons.[96] The defendant argued that this use of peremptory challenges showed a pattern of purposeful discrimination. The Court found that the Equal Protection Clause extends its protection against discriminatory practices by the State in the exercise of peremptory challenges.[97] In contrast to the dicta in *Swain*, the Court in *Batson* expressly condemned the use of peremptory strikes by prosecutors to exclude potential jurors "solely on account of their race or on the assumption that black jurors as a group will be unable impartially to consider the State's case against a black defendant."[98]

The decision overruled the "crippling" evidentiary burden placed on defendants by the *Swain* rule that required them to prove a pattern of discriminatory strikes, in cases other than their own, by the prosecutors in their cases.[99] Instead, the defendant may establish a prima facie case of purposeful discrimination based "solely on evidence concerning the prosecutor's exercise of peremptory challenges at the defendant's trial."[100] The showing of a "pattern" of strikes against black jurors, as well as "questions or statements during voir dire" may give rise to an "inference of discrimination" sufficient to make a prima facie showing.[101] Upon making a prima facie showing of purposeful discrimination, "the burden shifts to the State to come forward with a race-neutral explanation for challenging black jurors," and that reason should be "related to the particular case to be tried."[102]

---

[95]*Id.* at 220-21 (citations omitted).
[96]Batson v. Kentucky, 476 U.S. 79, 89 (1986).
[97]*Id.*
[98]*Id.*
[99]*Id.* at 92-93.
[100]*Id.* at 96.
[101]*Id.* at 96-97.
[102]*Id.* at 97-99.

The *Batson* rule has since been broadened to prohibit gender discrimination in jury selection,[103] as well as discrimination by defense counsel,[104] and the non-discrimination rule now applies to civil cases as well.[105] Still, because the evidence required to prove discriminatory intent is ordinarily very difficult or impossible to obtain, the vast majority of claims of discrimination made over the past twenty-four years since *Batson* was decided have been rejected by the courts. The Court has made it very easy for litigants to skirt the non-discrimination prohibition of *Batson* by holding that any race-neutral explanation satisfies step two of *Batson*, even if the reason is not specific, trial-related, or even plausible or reasonable.[106]

E. The Viability of Claims of Jury Selection Discrimination Today

There is a sad repetitiveness in most jury discrimination cases today. Prosecutors in hundreds of reported cases over the years continue to exclude minorities from jury venires by means of the peremptory strike and other techniques.[107] The numbers are staggering if one considers that jury trials are a rare event in the criminal justice systems in this country.[108] Proving that the exclusion is the product of intentional discrimination is a real challenge for defendants. In the first 100 years of jury discrimination cases, claimants were able to show that for many years—decades if not the entire history of the jurisdiction—minority groups had been excluded from jury lists. Based on this type of evidence, the Supreme Court usually upheld claims of intentional discrimination, typically reversing lower court decisions to the contrary.[109] States were prohibited from totally excluding minorities from jury lists, and the Court went so far as to require fair representation on jury lists.[110] One might have expected that the juries actually seated to try cases would be greatly diversified by these changes. Unfortunately, this has not been so. Juries have continued to be, to a large extent, comprised mostly, if not exclusively, of white persons largely because prosecutors in modern times rely heavily on their peremptory strikes to exclude a large number of minorities from juries.[111]

Today persons claiming intentional discrimination in the use of peremptory challenges must prove their claims under the *Batson* rule.[112] In Kenneth Melilli's important study of *Batson* challenges, he examined 1156 published decisions of federal and state courts between April 30, 1986 (the date of the *Batson* decision) and the

---

[103]J.E.B. v. Alabama *ex rel.* T.B., 511 U.S. 127, 130-31 (1994).

[104]Georgia v. McCollum, 505 U.S. 42 (1992) (criminal defendants do not have right to racially discriminate against potential jurors and State has standing to raise claims on behalf of potential jurors).

[105]Edmonson v. Leesville Concrete Co., 500 U.S. 614 (1991).

[106]Purkett v. Elem, 514 U.S. 765 (1995) (prosecutor's race-neutral reason—that potential juror had long, unkempt hair and facial hair—need not be reasonable, plausible, specific, or trial-related; it must only be non-discriminatory to satisfy step two).

[107]See *infra* notes 113-15 and accompanying text (number of *Batson* claims) and notes 135-45 (techniques other than peremptory strikes).

[108]Most experts estimate the percentage of cases tried to a jury to be less than ten percent. See, e.g., W. R. LAFAVE, MODERN CRIMINAL LAW 14 (3d ed. 2001).

[109]See supra note 40 and accompanying text.

[110]See supra notes 82-84 and accompanying text.

[111]See, e.g., HIROSHI FUKURAI & RICHARD KROOTH, RACE IN THE JURY BOX: AFFIRMATIVE ACTION IN JURY SELECTION (2003).

[112]See supra notes 96-106 and accompanying text.

end of calendar year 1993.[113] Significantly, he found that the vast majority of claims (approximately 88%) were made by criminal defendants, as opposed to prosecutors or civil claimants.[114] Melilli also showed that blacks are the alleged target of discriminatory peremptory challenges in the vast majority of cases (87.38%), with Hispanics being a very distant second (6.73%).[115] In a few jurisdictions parties do not get very far with their claims because they encounter a high barrier to making out even a prima facie case.[116] In most places, however, *Batson* challenges are typically defended on the grounds that the peremptory strikes were motivated by "race-neutral" reasons. Melilli found that prosecutors succeeded in providing neutral explanations for their challenges in 79.93% of cases.[117] Thus, the vast majority of these claims are brought against prosecutors who, almost always have used their peremptory challenges to exclude blacks, and most courts applying the *Batson* rule—both trial and appellate—usually reject claims of discrimination in the use of peremptory challenges.

Despite the starkness of the statistics gathered by Professor Melilli, one might yet wonder whether there is any credence to the concern that the challenged peremptory strikes were discriminatory. It is possible, for instance, that criminal defendants tend to challenge *any* strikes against minority venire persons. Unfortunately, a brief review of randomly-selected case law from 2004 reveals that the reasons given often correlate with race, even if they are technically "race neutral" (thus, giving rise to suspicions of pretext), or the reasons are simply specious, yet accepted as valid race-neutral reasons by the courts.[118]

The examples of reasons that may correlate with race include having a connection to someone who has been involved in the criminal justice system, socio-economic factors such as unemployment, education, income, and living or working in a high crime area. African Americans are often struck by prosecutors because they have had family members or friends who have been prosecuted by the prosecutor's office, even if the venire person states that the person was treated fairly and/or that the venire person would be able to impose the harshest punishment, or even if the family member is only distantly-related.[119] In one case reviewed by this author, the prosecutor cited the fact that his office had prosecuted people with the same last names (Nance, Randle, Led-

---

[113]Melilli, supra note 19, at 456.

[114]*Id.* at 457-58. The Supreme Court did not extend *Batson* to civil cases until June 3, 1991 and did not extend the obligations to comply with *Batson* to the criminal defense until June 18, 1992. Thus, the study could only provide data for the first year and a half (January 19, 1992—December 31, 1993) that claims could be made against criminal defense as well as by civil parties. The eighty-eight percent figure may therefore have fallen since 1993 as litigants gained greater awareness of the process of making *Batson* challenges.

[115]*Id.* at 462.

[116]In Louisiana, for example, only sixteen of forty-nine complainants succeeded in establishing a prima facie case, as compared to eighty-one of ninety-six in Texas. *Id.* at 470.

[117]*Id.* at 461.

[118]This author reviewed fifty randomly-selected published cases from various federal and state jurisdictions that were decided in 2004.

[119]See, e.g., State v. Strong, 142 S.W.3d 702 (Mo. 2004) (Black juror excused because juror was employed as assistant dean of seminary and distant cousin incarcerated for murder, despite juror statement that he could impose death sentence). See also Melilli, supra note 19, at 487 (finding that in 17.88% of cases reviewed parties (most of whom are prosecutors) cited prior involvement with criminal conduct or litigation as reason for striking venire persons and 53.95% of those cases the venire person had a close friend or relative who had prior criminal activity).

better, and Hairston) in using all four of its strikes to exclude African Americans, without necessarily ascertaining whether those other people were actually related to the venire persons.[120] The high rate of involvement by African Americans in the criminal justice system means that this reason will correlate strongly with race.[121] A natural corollary of this fact is that predominantly African American neighborhoods will be considered "high-crime" neighborhoods, another factor cited as a race-neutral reason.[122] Since African Americans as a group have disproportionately low levels of education and income, which in turn cause high levels of unemployment, reasons related to lower socioeconomic status will tend to eliminate more African Americans than other groups, and the cases bear this out.[123]

In about seven percent of the cases reviewed by Melilli, demeanor, appearance, and facial hair were cited as race-neutral factors.[124] This author's review of cases decided in 2004 discovered many specific appearance-related reasons that give cause to suspect the application of group stereotypes or that the reasons are simply specious. In one case, the prosecutor cited the chewing of gum by two African American jurors as evidence of a "lackadaisical attitude for court procedures" and a failure to show "proper respect."[125] The prosecutor had stricken all four of the African Americans on the venire. In another, the prosecutor thought the venire person's baggy shirt made him look like a gang member and cited his "overly relaxed, lackadaisical" attitude as well.[126]

The "race neutral" reasons given by prosecutors might be scrutinized closely by the courts if there were a requirement that the reasons be reasonable or persuasive, but there is not. Arguably, the Supreme Court has mandated that courts should accept even silly, but race-neutral reasons for peremptory strikes. In *Purkett v. Elem*, the Supreme Court rejected a reading of *Batson* that would have required the proponent of a strike to give a "clear and reasonably specific" explanation of his "legitimate reasons" for exercising the challenges" and that the "reason must be 'related to the particular case to be tried.'"[127] The Court stated: "What it [*Batson*] means by a 'legitimate reason' is not a reason that makes sense, but a reason that does not deny equal protection."[128] In this case, the prosecutor had stricken an African American male on account of his facial hair and long, "unkempt" hairstyle.[129] Finding that this charac-

---

[120]Clay v. State, 881 So.2d 354 (Miss. Ct. App. 2004).

[121]See Eric Schlosser, *The Prison Industrial Complex* (1998) *available at* http://www.pinellasfla.com/prison.htm (last visited Apr. 15, 2005). "[A]bout half the inmates in the United States are African American. One out of every fourteen black men is now in prison or jail. One out of every four black men is likely to be imprisoned at some point during his lifetime." *Id.*

[122]Melilli, supra note 19, at 493 (living or working in a high-crime area was cited in approximately 2.8% of the cases reviewed (32 of 1156)).

[123]Economic factors such as unemployment of venire person or a family member, short or sporadic employment history, low income, renter, welfare recipient, and financial troubles accounted for nineteen percent of the cases reviewed (223 of 1156). *Id.* at 492. Relatedly, educational factors such as insufficient education, errors on juror form, inability to understand basic legal terms or the evidence, and illiteracy also tend disproportionately to correlate with lower economic status, and, thus, disproportionately affects African Americans. Prosecutors gave such reasons for peremptory strikes in twelve percent of the cases. *Id.*

[124]Melilli, supra note 19, at 494 (appearance or demeanor accounted for 79 of 1156 of the cases and facial hair accounted for 7 of 1156, for a total of 85 of 1156 or 7.35%).

[125]Sykes v. Dretke, No. 3:02-CV-0784-G, 2004 WL 1856826, at *7 (N.D. Tex. Aug. 19, 2004).

[126]People v. Johnson, No. B169144, 2004 WL 1879888, at *2 (Cal. Ct. App. Aug. 24, 2004).

[127]Purkett v. Elem, 514 U.S. 765, 768-69 (1995).

[128]*Id.* at 769.

[129]*Id.*

teristic is not "peculiar to any race," the Court upheld the state court finding that the prosecutor was not motivated by discriminatory intent.[130] Thus, even a reason that does not "make sense" and is not related to the case to be tried in any way may suffice as long as it is "race neutral."

The Court has also rejected the notion that reasons that disproportionately affect a particular group, even if technically race neutral, should not be allowed. In *Hernandez v. New York,* the Court upheld strikes of bilingual Hispanic jurors who were hesitant to agree that they could rely on the translation of testimony by a court translator.[131] The Court concludes with the following statements:

> It may well be, for certain ethnic groups and in some communities, that proficiency in a particular language, like skin color, should be treated as a surrogate for race under an equal protection analysis. And, as we make clear, a policy of striking all who speak a given language, without regard to the particular circumstances of the trial or the individual responses of the jurors, may be found by the trial judge to be a pretext for racial discrimination. But that is not the case before us.[132]

In so deciding the case in *Hernandez v. New York*, the Court effectively approves of race-neutral reasons that disproportionately affect a particular race or ethnic group. It is understandable that bilingual venire persons would express hesitancy to fully accept a court translator's translation of testimony if the would-be juror speaks the second language and may foresee that the translation could be inaccurate. What bilingual person would *not* hesitate to give full credit to a translation that he or she knows to be wrong or not quite right? It stands to reason then that Hispanics and other ethnic groups with large populations of bilingual persons will be disproportionately affected by a rule that allows them to be struck on this ground. Nonetheless, the Supreme Court found no mistake in the trial court's finding that the strikes were not discriminatory.[133]

In short, the combined holdings of *Purkett v. Elem* and *Hernandez v. Texas* mandate that the lower courts accept as race neutral any reasons that are technically "race neutral," even if those reasons do not "make sense" or relate to the case to be tried, and even if they disproportionately affect a particular race or ethnic group. Thus, it stands to reason that most *Batson* challenges are rejected by the courts[134] and that the practice of excluding most African Americans from criminal juries proceeds full force.

III. The Amazing Case of *Miller-El v. Texas*: Old-Fashioned Discrimination in Modern Practice

The case of *Miller-El v. Texas* illustrates *Batson's* failings in ways that make the case quite fascinating. It is fascinating because it took the courts so long to litigate

---

[130]*Id.*

[131]Hernandez v. New York, 500 U.S. 352, 361-62 (1991).

[132]*Id.* at 371-72 (citations omitted).

[133]*Id.* at 370.

[134]Melilli's research shows that 84.13% of criminal defendants fail to prove their *Batson* claims. See Melilli, supra note 19, at 459.

his *Batson* claim—fully eighteen years. It is even more fascinating because prosecutors used multiple methods for ultimately excluding all but one of the African Americans on the jury. Finally, the strikingly divergent interpretations of the evidence expressed by the Supreme Court and every other state and federal court that reviewed the case, resulting in *two* Supreme Court reviews, makes it one of the most remarkable *Batson* cases ever.

A. The Jury Selection Process in *Miller-El*

Perhaps the most amazing aspect of *Miller-El* is that it is a modern case, tried in 1986 in Dallas County, Texas, yet the description of the jury selection process reads like an early nineteenth-century case. Like cases of an earlier era, prosecutors used the jury selection tools at their disposal to eliminate almost all African Americans from the jury venire. Unlike the nineteenth-century cases, however, the prosecutors used a combination of several unique techniques to exclude African Americans— jury shuffling, disparate use of questioning tactics, and peremptory strikes.

The first technique, amazing in its blatant applicability as a tool of racial discrimination, is the "jury shuffle," a practice allowed only in the State of Texas.[135] The United States Supreme Court described it as such:

> This practice permits parties to rearrange the order in which members of the venire are examined so as to increase the likelihood that *visually preferable* venire members will be moved forward and empaneled. *With no information about the prospective jurors other than their appearance,* the party requesting the procedure literally shuffles the juror cards, and the venire members are then reseated in the new order.[136]

The Court also explains why practice of jury shuffling affects the composition of the jury:

> [A]ny prospective jurors not questioned during voir dire are dismissed at the end of the week, and a new panel of jurors appears the following week. So jurors who are shuffled to the back of the panel are less likely to be questioned or to serve.[137]

In the *Miller-El* case, the prosecutors availed themselves of the ability to employ jury shuffling as a tool of racial discrimination. The Supreme Court writes,

> On at least two occasions the prosecution requested shuffles when there were a predominant number of African Americans in the front of the panel. On yet another occasion the prosecutors complained about the purported inadequacy of the card shuffle by the defense lawyer but lodged a formal objection only after the postshuffle panel composition revealed that African American prospective jurors had been moved forward.[138]

---

[135]TEX. CRIM. PROC. CODE ANN., Art. 35.11 (Vernon 1989 & Supp. 2004-05).
[136]Miller-El v. Cockrell, 537 U.S. 322, 333-34 (2003) (emphasis added).
[137]*Id.* at 334.
[138]*Id.*

A second tactic was to use a different manner of questioning for most African Americans designed to elicit negative opinions on the imposition of the death penalty, as well as on the subject of the willingness to impose the minimum sentence. The Supreme Court explains:

Most African Americans (53%, or 8 out of 15) were first given a detailed description of the mechanics of an execution in Texas:

> [I]f those three [sentencing] questions are answered yes, at some point[,] Thomas Joe Miller-El will be taken to Huntsville, Texas. He will be placed on death row and at some time will be taken to the death house where he will be strapped on a gurney, an IV put into his arm and he will be injected with a substance that will cause his death . . . as the result of the verdict in this case if those three questions are answered yes.[139]

It was only after being read this "graphic script" (as the defense dubbed it) that the majority of African Americans were asked whether they could render a decision that would lead to a death sentence.[140] In contrast,

> Very few prospective white jurors (6%, or 3 out of 49) were given this preface prior to being asked for their views on capital punishment. Rather, all but three were questioned in vague terms: "Would you share with us . . . your personal feelings, if you could, in your own words how you do feel about the death penalty and capital punishment and secondly, do you feel you could serve on this type of a jury and actually render a decision that would result in the death of the Defendant in this case based on the evidence?"[141]

The Supreme Court notes an even more "pronounced difference, on the apparent basis of race, in the manner the prosecutors questioned members of the venire about their willingness to impose the minimum sentence for murder."[142] This second line of questioning was pursued as a means of identifying jurors who might be unwilling to impose the minimum sentence, which under Texas law at the time warranted removal of the juror for cause.[143] Ironically, as the Court notes, this tactic is often used by the defense to weed out pro state members of the venire. Here, the prosecution appears to have used it to weed out African Americans. Otherwise, it makes no sense for a prosecutor to go out of his or her way to seek out jurors who are reluctant to impose a minimum sentence.

When questioning thirty-four of thirty-six (94%) of white venire members, the prosecutor first informed them that the minimum sentence was five years' imprisonment, and only then asked: "'If you hear a case, to your way of thinking [that] calls for and warrants and justifies five years, you'll give it?'"[144] In this manner, the prosecutor gently led virtually all of the white venire members to state that they would

---

[139]*Id.* at 332 (quoting Miller-El v. Dretke, 361 F.3d 849, 852 (2003)).

[140]*Id.* at 364.

[141]*Id.*

[142]*Id.* at 332.

[143]*Id.* at 332-33 (citing Huffman v. State, 450 S.W.2d 858, 861 (Tex. Crim. App. 1970), *vacated in part*, 408 U.S. 936 (1972)).

[144]*Id.* at 333 (quoting App. 509).

be willing to impose the minimum sentence. For only one of the eight (12.5%) African American venire members did the prosecutor use this approach. In contrast, for the other seven of eight African Americans (87.5%), the typical questioning proceeded as follows:

> [Prosecutor]: Now, the maximum sentence for [murder] . . . is life under the law. Can you give me an idea of just your personal feelings what you feel a minimum sentence should be for the offense of murder the way I've set it out for you?
> [Juror]: Well, to me that's almost like it's premeditated. But you said they don't have a premeditated statute here in Texas.
> [Prosecutor]: Again, we're not talking about self-defense or accident or insanity or killing in the heat of passion or anything like that. We're talking about knowing—
> [Juror]: I know you said the minimum. The minimum amount that I would say would be at least twenty years.[145]

Again, one has to wonder why a prosecutor would *ever* lead a venire member in this type of questioning that is so clearly designed to elicit an answer that will likely disqualify the venire member for being inclined to impose a *harsher punishment* than that which the law allows. Obviously, the prosecutor is trying to remove the potential juror for some other reason.

The ultimate tool for eliminating minority jurors from a jury venire today is the peremptory strike. The numbers alone paint a compelling case of racial discrimination:

> Of the 108 possible jurors reviewed by the prosecution and defense, 20 were African American. Nine of them were excused for cause or by agreement of the parties. Of the 11 African American jurors remaining, however, all but 1 were excluded by peremptory strikes exercised by the prosecutors . . . . In contrast, the prosecutors used their peremptory strikes against just 13% (4 out of 31) of the eligible nonblack prospective jurors qualified to serve on [Miller-El's] jury.[146]

In this manner, the prosecutors in *Miller-El* exercised their preemptory strikes so as to remove all but one African American on the jury. Defense counsel timely objected, and by so doing began what has now been Miller-El's eighteen-year struggle to obtain relief in the courts for his claim of discrimination. In the meantime, the jury convicted Miller-El of murder and ultimately sentenced him to death.

B. *Miller-El's* Eighteen Years in the Appellate Courts

1. The Trial Court Hearings

At the conclusion of jury selection, Miller-El moved to strike the jury on the grounds that the prosecution had violated the Equal Protection Clause of the Four-

---

[145]*Id.* (quoting App. 226-27).
[146]*Id.* at 331.

teenth Amendment.[147] The timing of the trial in the *Miller-El* case was such that the rules relating to the type of evidence required to prove a claim of race discrimination in the use of peremptory strikes changed mid-course. The trial occurred in 1986 when *Swain v. Alabama*[148] provided the governing rule and just before the rule change in *Batson v. Kentucky*.[149]

In accord with the *Swain* rule, Miller-El presented proof at his pre-trial *Swain* hearing of a history of race discrimination in jury selection by the Dallas County District Attorney's Office. The evidence took the form of testimony given by "a number of current and former Dallas County assistant district attorneys, judges, and others who had observed the prosecution's conduct during jury selection over a number of years."[150] Not surprisingly, most of the witnesses denied that the prosecutors followed a systematic policy to exclude African Americans from juries, but, remarkably, others stated otherwise:

> A Dallas County district judge testified that, when he had served in the District Attorney's Office from the late-1950's to early-1960's, his superior warned him that he would be fired if he permitted any African Americans to serve on a jury. Similarly, another Dallas County district judge and former assistant district attorney from 1976 to 1978 testified that he believed the office had a systematic policy of excluding African Americans from juries.[151]

The Supreme Court recently considered it to be of "more importance" that the defense also presented evidence that "the District Attorney's Office had adopted a formal policy to exclude minorities from jury service."[152] Miller-El's attorneys offered a 1963 circular by the District Attorney's Office that "instructed its prosecutors to exercise peremptory strikes against minorities: 'Do not take Jews, Negroes, Dagos, Mexicans or a member of any minority race on a jury, no matter how rich or how well educated.'"[153] In addition, a manual entitled "Jury Selection in a Criminal Case" was issued to prosecutors in the office. The manual included an article written by a former prosecutor (who later became a judge) that outlined the reasons for excluding minorities from jury service.[154] The Court notes that "Although the manual was written in 1968, it remained in circulation until 1976, if not later, and was available at least to one of the prosecutors in Miller-El's trial."[155]

The State argued that these practices had been discontinued prior to Miller-El's trail. Some of the testimony offered by the defense, however, cast doubt on the State's claim:

---

[147]See Miller-El v. Dretke, 361 F.3d 849, 852 (5th Cir. 2004).
[148]Swain v. Alabama, 380 U.S. 202 (1965).
[149]Batson v. Kentucky, 476 U.S. 79 (1986).
[150]Miller-El v. Cockrell, 537 U.S. 322, 334 (2003).
[151]*Id.*
[152]*Id.*
[153]*Id.* at 335.
[154]*Id.*
[155]*Id.*

For example, a judge testified that, in 1985, he had to exclude a prosecutor from trying cases in his courtroom for race-based discrimination in jury selection. Other testimony indicated that the State, by its own admission, once requested a jury shuffle in order to reduce the number of African Americans in the venire. Concerns over the exclusion of African Americans by the District Attorney's Office were echoed by Dallas County's Chief Public Defender.[156]

The trial court considered Miller-El's evidence of a history and culture in the Dallas County District Attorney's Office of racial discrimination against minorities in jury selection. "The trial judge, however, found 'no evidence . . . that indicated any systematic exclusion of blacks as a matter of policy by the District Attorney's office; while it may have been done by individual prosecutors in individual cases.'"[157] Thus, the trial court rejected Miller-El's motion to strike the jury.

2. The State High Court Finds an Inference of Discrimination and Remands for Hearing Under New *Batson* Rule

After trial, Miller-El appealed to the Texas Court of Criminal Appeals. During the pendency of Miller-El's appeal, the Supreme Court issued its 1986 opinion in *Batson v. Kentucky,* establishing a three-part process for evaluating claims that a prosecutor used peremptory challenges in a racially discriminatory manner in violation of the Equal Protection Clause.[158] Rather than requiring a defendant to prove a history of race discrimination in the voir dire process by the prosecutors in his case, *Batson* now required the defendant to put forth evidence that establishes an inference of discrimination in his or her own voir dire. The Texas Court of Criminal Appeals, finding that Miller-El had established an inference of purposeful discrimination, remanded the case for an evidentiary hearing pursuant to *Batson*.[159]

3. Trial Court Finds "No Inference of Discrimination" and State High Court Affirms

The *Batson* hearing was held on May 10, 1988, at which Miller-El presented all of the evidence presented at the *Swain* hearing, as well as the evidence regarding the evidence of differential questioning of African American venire members regarding their views on the death penalty and their willingness to impose the minimum sentence for murder.[160] Miller-El also presented the statistics regarding the prosecutor's use of peremptory strikes against African American venire members as compared to white venire members.[161]

---

[156]*Id.* (citation omitted).

[157]*Id.* at 328.

[158]First, a defendant must make a prima facie showing that a preemptory challenge has been exercised on the basis of race. Second, if that showing is made, the prosecution must offer a race-neutral basis for striking the juror in question. Third, the trial court must determine whether the defendant has shown purposeful discrimination. Batson v. Kentucky, 476 U.S. 79, 96-99 (1986). See cases cited supra notes 96-106 and accompanying text.

[159]Miller-El v. State, 748 S.W.2d 459, 460-61 (Tex. Crim. App. 1988) (en banc).

[160]See supra notes 139-45 and accompanying text.

[161]See supra note 146 and accompanying text.

Eight months later, on January 13, 1989, the trial court concluded that Miller-El's evidence had failed to satisfy the first step of the *Batson* test, finding it "'did not even raise an inference of racial motivation in the use of the state's peremptory challenges'" to support a prima facie case.[162] Note that the trial court made this finding after the Texas Court of Criminal Appeals had explicitly found that Miller-El *had* established an inference of discrimination.[163] Moreover, the trial court also expressed the opinion that even if Miller-El had raised such an inference, "'the state would have prevailed on steps two and three because the prosecutors had offered credible, race-neutral explanations for each black venire member excluded.'"[164] The trial court also rejected the claim that the prosecutors had engaged in disparate questioning in order to develop grounds for excluding African American venire members, finding that "'the primary reasons for the exercise of challenges against each of the venire [members] in question [was] their reluctance to assess or reservations concerning the imposition of the death penalty.'"[165]

The Texas Court of Criminal Appeals denied Miller-El's appeal. Again, note that the appellate court affirms the finding that Miller-El had not proved an inference of discrimination after it had previously found to the contrary. The United States Supreme Court denied his petition for certiorari on direct appeal in 1993.[166] His state habeas petitions fared no better, and the Texas Court of Criminal Appeals again denied him relief.[167] Miller-El then filed a petition for writ of habeas corpus in Federal District Court for the Northern District of Texas.

4. Federal District and Circuit Courts Reject Miller-El's Claims

The federal magistrate judge who reviewed the merits of Miller-El's habeas petition was troubled by some of the evidence adduced in the state-court proceedings.[168] Nonetheless, citing the deference that federal courts are required to show to state courts' acceptance of the prosecutors' race-neutral reasons for challenging potential jurors, the Magistrate recommended that Miller-El's petition be denied.[169] In 2000, the district court then found that "[t]he Magistrate Judge properly deferred to the experience of the trial court judge in evaluating the demeanor of each juror and the prosecutor in determining purposeful discrimination."[170] Miller-El sought a certificate of appealability (COA) from the district court, which it denied.

He then renewed his request for a COA in the Fifth Circuit, and this request was also denied in 2001. The standards for granting a COA then became the focus of the review in the court of appeals. The Fifth Circuit noted that a COA should issue "'only if the applicant has made a substantial showing of the denial of a constitu-

---

[162]See *Miller-El v. Cockrell*, 537 U.S., at 329.
[163]*Miller-El v. State*, 748 S.W.2d at 461.
[164]*Id.*
[165]*Id.*
[166]Miller-El v. Texas, 510 U.S. 831 (1993).
[167]*Miller-El v. Cockrell*, 537 U.S. at 329.
[168]*Id.* at 329-30.
[169]*Id.* at 330.
[170]Miller-El v. Johnson, No. 3:96-CV-1992-H, 2000 U.S. Dist. LEXIS 7763, at *6 (N.D. Tex. June 5, 2000).

tional right.'"[171] The court also applied the requirements of 28 U.S.C. § 2254 into the COA determination:

> As an appellate court reviewing a federal habeas petition, we are required by § 2254(d)(2) to presume the state court findings correct unless we determine that the findings result in a decision which is unreasonable in light of the evidence presented. And the unreasonableness, if any, must be established by clear and convincing evidence.[172]

The court of appeals applied this framework in reviewing Miller-El's application and concluded "that the state court's findings are not unreasonable and that Miller-El has failed to present clear and convincing evidence to the contrary."[173] The court, rejecting Miller-El's request for a COA, also determined that "the state court's adjudication neither resulted in a decision that was unreasonable in light of the evidence presented nor resulted in a decision contrary to clearly established federal law as determined by the Supreme Court."[174]

5. The Supreme Court Reverses

The Supreme Court granted certiorari[175] and then in 2003—in another amazing twist—reversed the Fifth Circuit's denial of a COA in an eight to one decision, with only Justice Thomas dissenting.[176] The Court reiterated the standard it had previously announced for assessing requests for COAs: "'The petitioner must demonstrate that reasonable jurists would find the district court's assessment of the constitutional claims debatable or wrong.'"[177]

The majority then proceeded to assess whether Miller-El's claim was debatable. Of course, the state trial court had found that his proof did not satisfy the first of *Batson*'s three-step test as it did not even raise an inference of discrimination. Before the Supreme Court, however, the State now conceded that he indeed had satisfied step one.[178] Miller-El also conceded that the State had satisfied the second step by offering race-neutral reasons for the strikes.[179] The "critical question," therefore, was whether Miller-El had proved purposeful discrimination by showing that the prosecutor's proffered reasons were actually pretextual.[180] The Court expresses concern, both with the district court's and Fifth Circuit's exercise of "deference" in reviewing Miller-El's habeas petition and his request for a COA. The Court writes:

> Even in the context of federal habeas, deference does not imply abandonment or abdication of judicial review. Deference does not by definition preclude relief. A federal court can disagree with a state court's credibility

---

[171]Miller-El v. Johnson, 261 F.3d 445, 449 (2001) (quoting 28 U.S.C. § 2253(c)(2)).

[172]*Id.* at 451.

[173]*Id.* at 452.

[174]*Id.*

[175]Miller-El v. Cockrell, 534 U.S. 1122 (2002).

[176]Miller-El v. Cockrell, 537 U.S. 322 (2003).

[177]*Id.* at 338 (quoting Slack v. McDaniel, 529 U.S. 473, 484 (2000)).

[178]*Id.* at 338.

[179]*Id.*

[180]*Id.* at 338-39.

determination and, when guided by AEDPA, conclude the decision was unreasonable or that the factual premise was incorrect by clear and convincing evidence.[181]

Applying a less rigorous standard of review to the evidence presented by Miller-El, the Court, thus, concluded that it had "no difficulty concluding that a COA should have issued." First, the Court found that the district court had erred:

> We conclude, on our review of the record at this stage, that the District Court did not give full consideration to the substantial evidence petitioner put forth in support of the prima facie case. Instead, it accepted without question the state court's evaluation of the demeanor of the prosecutors and jurors in petitioner's trial.[182]

The Court also rejected the Fifth Circuit's COA decision as having imposed a burden of proof that is higher than what the law imposes and as having erroneously ruled on the merits of the claim, rather than on the debatability of the claim:

> In ruling that petitioner's claim lacked sufficient merit to justify appellate proceedings, the Court of Appeals recited the requirements for granting a writ under § 2254, which it interpreted as requiring petitioner to prove that the state court decision was objectively unreasonable by clear and convincing evidence.

> This was too demanding a standard on more than one level . . . . The clear and convincing evidence standard . . . pertains only to state-court determinations of factual issues, rather than decisions.

> The Court of Appeals, moreover, was incorrect for an even more fundamental reason. Before the issuance of a COA, the Court of Appeals had no jurisdiction to resolve the merits of petitioner's constitutional claims. . . . [A] COA determination is a separate proceeding, one distinct from the underlying merits . . . . The question is the debatability of the underlying constitutional claim, not the resolution of that debate.[183]

What is quite striking about the Court's opinion is the extent to which the Court seems to evaluate the merits of the claim itself and appears to conclude that Miller-El may have presented a meritorious claim. The Court is equivocal in discussing the state's use of peremptory challenges, concluding that "even though the prosecution's reasons for striking African American members of the venire appear race neutral, the application of these rationales to the venire might have been selective and based on racial considerations." However, in evaluating the claim of disparate questioning, the Court comes closer to addressing the merits of this issue:

> We question the Court of Appeals' and state trial court's dismissive and strained interpretation of petitioner's evidence of disparate questioning . . . . Disparate questioning did occur. . . . It follows that, if the use of disparate

---

[181]*Id.* at 340.
[182]*Id.* at 341.
[183]*Id.* at 341-42.

questioning is determined by race at the outset, it is likely a justification for a strike based on the resulting divergent views would be pretextual. In this context the differences in the questions posed by the prosecutors are some evidence of purposeful discrimination.[184]

On the issue of the Texas "jury shuffle" practice, the Court agreed with Miller-El that:

[T]he prosecution's decision to seek a jury shuffle when a predominate number of African Americans were seated in the front of the panel, along with its decision to delay a formal objection to the defense's shuffle until after the new racial composition was revealed, raise a suspicion that the State sought to exclude African Americans from the jury.[185]

This evidence, the Court found, "tends to erode the credibility of the prosecution's assertion that race was not a motivating factor in the jury selection."[186]

The Court also "accord[ed] some weight to petitioner's historical evidence of racial discrimination by the District Attorney's Office."[187] Miller-El had presented evidence at the earlier *Swain* hearing that persuaded the Supreme Court that "African Americans almost categorically were excluded from jury service" and "that the culture of the District Attorney's Office in the past was suffused with bias against African Americans in jury selection."[188] With regard to the prosecutors in Miller-El's case, the Court found it relevant that "[b]oth prosecutors joined the District Attorney's Office when assistant district attorneys received formal training in excluding minorities from juries."[189] Reminiscent of the nineteenth-century cases of systematic exclusion of African Americans from jury lists, the prosecutors here also raised suspicions that race played a factor in jury selection because they "marked the race of each prospective juror on their juror cards."[190]

Finally, the majority, after having reviewed all the evidence presented by Miller-El, returns again to the state court's rather incredible finding that Miller-El had not raised even an inference of discrimination to support a prima facie case. The Court notes that, "In resolving the equal protection claim against petitioner, the state courts made no mention of either the jury shuffle or the historical record of purposeful discrimination."[191] Acknowledging that detailed factual findings are not required, the Court expresses concerns that the courts might have simply ignored the evidence in "somehow" finding that Miller-El had not raised even an inference of discrimination. This, the Court concludes, was "clear error, and the State declines to defend this particular ruling."[192] Perhaps alluding to the prosecution's "general assertions" that race played no part in jury selection, the Court somewhat cryptically sums up with the

---

[184] *Id.* at 344.
[185] *Id.* at 346.
[186] *Id.*
[187] *Id.*
[188] *Id.* at 346-47.
[189] *Id.*
[190] *Id.* at 347.
[191] *Id.*
[192] *Id.*

following quotation from *Batson*: "If these general assertions were accepted as rebutting a defendant's prima facie case, the Equal Protection Clause 'would be but a vain and illusory requirement.'"[193]

6. Justice Thomas Dissents

What would make the Miller-El case a harder case to win on the merits is that the State's arguments regarding the race-neutral reasons for striking the African American venire members in question is not easily refuted. Justice Thomas dissents from the majority's decision in part based on his divergent view about the correct standard of review and in part based on his assessment of the ultimate issue in the case—whether the prosecution has shown race-neutral reasons for the peremptory strikes against African Americans.

In Justice Thomas's view, the court of appeals properly required the petitioner to provide "clear and convincing" evidence of purposeful discrimination in order to obtain a COA.[194] His opinion, thus, applying the clear and convincing evidence standard, assesses whether Miller-El has refuted the State's evidence of race-neutral reasons for its strikes by clear and convincing evidence. In contrast, the majority's opinion found only that the question whether Miller-El's evidence supports his claim of discrimination is "debatable."

Interestingly, Justice Thomas quickly dispenses with the historical evidence of discrimination in jury selection by the Dallas County District Attorney's Office, as well as the prosecution's use of the jury shuffle technique to eliminate African Americans. He writes:

> The "historical" evidence is entirely circumstantial, so much so that the majority can only bring itself to say it 'casts doubt on the State's claim that [discriminatory] practices had been discontinued before petitioner's trial. And the evidence that the prosecution used jury shuffles no more proves intentional discrimination than it forces petitioner to admit that he sought to eliminate whites from the jury, given that he employed the tactic even more than the prosecution did. Ultimately, these two categories of evidence do very little for petitioner, because they do not address the genuineness of prosecutors' proffered race-neutral reasons for making peremptory strikes of these particular jurors.[195]

Justice Thomas then takes issue with Miller-El's evidence of disparate treatment of African American venire members as compared to similarly-situated white venire members. He states that the white veniremen to whom Miller-El compares the African American veniremen were not "similarly situated" because they had only expressed one factor of concern to the State, whereas the African Americans had made two statements of concern to the prosecution. Thus, he concludes that the prosecution has given race-neutral reasons for challenging those African American

---

[193]*Id.* (quoting Batson v. Kentucky, 476 U.S. 79, 98 (1986), in turn quoting Norris v. Alabama, 294 U.S. 587, 598 (1935)).

[194]*Id.* at 359 (Thomas, J., dissenting).

[195]*Id.* at 360 (Thomas, J., dissenting) (citations omitted).

veniremen, reasons that do not apply to the whites who only mentioned one item of concern. He concludes, "'Similarly situated' does not mean matching any one of several reasons the prosecution gave for striking a potential juror—it means matching *all* of them."[196]

Finally, he also rejects Miller-El's evidence of disparate questioning, concluding that "it amount[s] to little of substance."[197] Justice Thomas notes that the prosecution counters the complaint about the "graphic script" by arguing that this depiction was used only with those potential jurors who "'expressed reservations about the death penalty in their juror questionnaires.'"[198] While the majority does not address the State's arguments, finding them beyond the scope of a request for a COA, Justice Thomas's view is that petitioner should have refuted this argument since "petitioner bears the burden of showing purposeful discrimination by clear and convincing evidence."[199] With regard to the white jurors who Miller-El claims the State should also have questioned using the graphic script, Justice Thomas explains that:

> [T]he eight white veniremen . . . were so emphatically opposed to the death penalty that such a description would have served no purpose in clarifying their position on the issue . . . . The strategy pursued by the prosecution makes perfect sense: When it was necessary to draw out a venireman's feelings about the death penalty they would use the graphic script, but when it was overkill they would not. The record demonstrates that six of these eight white veniremen were so opposed to the death penalty that they were stricken for cause without the need for the prosecution to spend a peremptory challenge.[200]

He sums up by calculating the correlation between questionnaire answers and the use of the graphic script, finding that this correlation to be "far stronger" than the correlation with race. He states:

> Sixteen veniremen clearly indicated on the questionnaires their feelings on the death penalty, and 14 of them did not receive the graphic script. Eight veniremen gave unclear answers and those eight veniremen got the graphic script. In other words, for 23 out of 24, or 96%, of the veniremen for whom questionnaire information is available, the answers given accurately predict whether they got the graphic script. Petitioner's theory that race determined whether a venireman got the graphic script produces a race-to-script correlation of only 74%—far worse.[201]

Similarly, Justice Thomas rejects the claim that the prosecution used a "manipulative" script regarding minimum sentences in order to weed out African American veniremen. The State's position is that it used the questions about the minimum sen-

---

[196]*Id.* at 362 (Thomas, J., dissenting).

[197]*Id.* at 363 (Thomas, J., dissenting).

[198] *Id.* at 364 (Thomas, J., dissenting) (quoting Brief for Respondent at 17, Miller-El v. Cockrell, 537 U.S. 322 (2003) (No. 01-7662)).

[199]*Id.* at 364 (Thomas, J., dissenting).

[200]*Id.*

[201]*Id.* at 368 (Thomas, J., dissenting).

tence with veniremen who were ambivalent on the death penalty so as to get them excused for cause. Justice Thomas briefly reviews the evidence of potential jurors views on the death penalty and whether the "manipulative" script was used. He finds that Miller-El has not rebutted the State's explanation, finding:

> Unless a venireman indicated he would be a poor State's juror (using the criteria that respondent has identified here) *and would not otherwise be struck for cause or by agreement*, there was no reason to use the 'manipulative' script. Thus, when petitioner points to the 'State's failure to use its manipulative method with the vast majority of white veniremembers who expressed reservations about the death penalty,' he ignores the fact that of the 10 whites who expressed opposition to the death penalty, 8 were struck for cause or by agreement, *meaning no 'manipulative' script was necessary to get them removed*. The other two whites were both given the 'manipulative' script *and* peremptorily struck, just like [the African American veniremembers.][202]

Unlike Justice Thomas, in deciding the COA issue, the majority confined itself to the threshold issue of whether Miller-El's claim was "debatable" and explicitly *not* whether he should prevail on the merits. For the time being, the Supreme Court had only remanded the case to the court of appeals for its consideration of Miller-El's habeas appeal.

7. Fifth Circuit Rejects Miller-El's Petition on the Merits

On February 26, 2004, the Fifth Circuit, having now granted the COA consistent with the Supreme Court's instructions, rejected Miller-El's appeal on the merits.[203] In addressing Miller-El's *Batson* claim, the court noted that there was no longer any dispute that he had satisfied *Batson*'s first step. Nor was there any dispute that the prosecution had presented facially race-neutral reasons for each of its peremptory strikes. Thus, "[t]he only issue is Miller-El's disagreement with the trial court's determination at *Batson*'s third step that Miller-El failed to show that the prosecution's reasons for exercising the challenged peremptory strikes were not credible and Miller-El had not demonstrated that purposeful discrimination had occurred."[204]

Since the case was before the court on habeas review, the appellate court applied the review scheme of the Antiterrorism and Effective Death Penalty Act of 1996 (AEDPA) which requires that appellate courts "presume" the state court's findings of fact "to be correct" unless the petitioner rebuts those findings by clear and convincing evidence.[205]

The Fifth Circuit's opinion proceeds to address each of the four types of evidence that Miller-El presented at his *Batson* hearing: (1) the historical evidence of discrimination in jury selection in the Dallas County District Attorney's Office; (2)

---

[202]*Id.* at 369-70 (Thomas, J., dissenting) (emphasis in original).
[203]Miller-El v. Dretke, 361 F.3d 849 (5th Cir. 2004).
[204]*Id.* at 853-54.
[205]*Id.* at 854.

the use of the "jury shuffle" tactic by the prosecution; (3) the alleged similarity between white venire persons who were not struck by the prosecution and six African Americans who were struck; and (4) evidence of so-called disparate questioning with respect to venire member's views on the death penalty and their ability to impose the minimum punishment.[206] It then proceeds to assess each type and renders a judgment as to whether each type of evidence proves by clear and convincing evidence that the state court's finding of the absence of purposeful discrimination in Miller-El's jury selection was incorrect.

Interestingly, the Fifth Circuit opinion closely tracks Justice Thomas's dissenting opinion in the Supreme Court's decision reversing the Circuit's denial of a COA.[207] With regard to the evidence of the history of discrimination in the District Attorney's Office, the opinion refers to the "culture of discrimination" as both "disturbing" and "deplorable." Unlike Justice Thomas who simply dismissed the evidence as "entirely circumstantial," the court of appeals acknowledges that it is "relevant to the extent that it could undermine the credibility of the prosecutors' race-neutral reasons."[208] Nonetheless, showing deference to the factual findings of the state court, the opinion concludes: "Under our standard of review, we must presume this specific determination [finding the prosecutors' race-neutral reasons to be genuine] is correct and accordingly the general historical evidence does not prove by clear and convincing evidence that the state court's finding of the absence of purposeful discrimination . . . was incorrect."[209]

The court adopts Justice Thomas's reasoning with respect to the jury shuffle tactic, concluding that it likewise does not "overcome the race-neutral reasons . . . and accepted by the state court who observed the *voir dire* process including the jury shuffles."[210] The reasoning is puzzling, however. Like Justice Thomas, the Fifth Circuit discounts the jury shuffle claim on the ground that the record shows that Miller-El also shuffled the jury, and, indeed, that the defense shuffled five times while the prosecutors only shuffled twice. This reasoning is puzzling because it does not address whether the prosecutors' shuffles were race-based, as Miller-El argues. It likewise does not say whether Miller-El's shuffles were shown to be race-based. Even assuming that both the defense and prosecution shuffles were motivated by race, it is not clear why a discriminatory act by the defense would cancel out a discriminatory act by the prosecution.

The court next examines the claim that six African Americans venire members were stricken by the prosecution and similarly situated white venire members were not. The opinion provides detailed findings with respect to each venire member in question. Like Justice Thomas, the court of appeals concludes that the African American venire members were stricken for more than one reason, while the white venire members cited by Miller-El had only one pro-defense factor in common with the

---

[206]*Id.* at 854-55.

[207]Indeed, the decision both borrows verbatim and paraphrases heavily (both without attribution) from Justice Thomas's opinion. *Compare Miller-El*, 361 F.3d at 861-62 *and* Miller-El v. Cockrell, 537 U.S. 322, 366-67, 369 (2003).

[208]*Miller-El*, 361 F.3d at 855.

[209]*Id.*

[210]*Id.*

stricken African American venire members. Thus, the white venire members who were not stricken were not "similarly situated" with the stricken African American venire members. Thus, the court concludes that based on the record "there were no unchallenged non-black venire members similarly situated, such that their treatment by the prosecution would indicate the reasons for striking the black members were not genuine."[211]

Finally, the court rejects Miller-El's argument that the prosecution engaged in disparate questioning based on race. Like Justice Thomas, the court finds that the record "reveals that the disparate questioning of venire members depended on the member's views on capital punishment and not race."[212] The Fifth Circuit's opinion provides the same analysis of the record as does Justice Thomas in rejecting the claims of disparate questioning on the death penalty as well as on the ability to impose the minimum punishment.

A troubling aspect of the treatment Miller-El's evidence, and especially of both the historical evidence as well as the jury shuffle claim, is that the court takes the approach of requiring that each individual type of evidence must—by itself—prove by clear and convincing evidence that the prosecutors' proffered race-neutral reasons for the strikes were pretextual.[213] Arguably, the court should have considered whether Miller-El's evidence—viewed in combination—proved the race-neutral reasons were pretextual. The court appears to take this issue into account in the last paragraph of the opinion, which states: "In summary, none of the four areas of evidence Miller-El based his appeal on indicate, *either collectively or separately*, by clear and convincing evidence that the state court erred."[214] Yet none of the analysis in the opinion gives any indication that the court viewed the evidence in its totality, and the treatment of the jury shuffle and evidence of discrimination in the District Attorney's Office raises some concern that it rejected the evidence for failing on its own to satisfy the burden of proof.

8. A Final Appeal is Heard: The Supreme Court Reverses Miller-El's Conviction

On June 13, 2005, the Supreme Court issued a second opinion in the *Miller-El* case, this time ruling on the merits of the habeas petition. Justice Souter, writing for the six Justices in the majority, begins with a brief history of the Court's jury discrimination jurisprudence.[215] He notes that the present *Batson* rule improves on the previous rule of the *Swain* case, which required a defendant to prove a longstanding pattern of discrimination in order to make out a prima facie case. The *Batson* rule instead requires that a defendant show that the prosecutor in his particular case had acted in a racially discriminatory manner.[216] In language that may signal a turning point in the Court's jurisprudence, the Court acknowledges the weakness of the *Bat-*

[211]*Id.* at 856
[212]*Id.* at 860
[213]See supra notes 208-11 and accompanying text.
[214]*Miller-El*, 361 F.3d at 862.
[215]*Miller-El v Dretke*, 125 S.Ct. 2317, 2324-25 (2005).
[216]*Id.* at 2325.

son rule which provides no relief from actual discrimination if courts accept racially neutral, but false, reasons that might be given by prosecutors to overcome a *Batson* challenge:

> Although the move from *Swain* to *Batson* left a defendant free to challenge
> the prosecution without having to cast *Swain's* wide net, the net was not
> entirely consigned to history, for *Batson's* individualized focus came with
> a weakness of its own owing to its very emphasis on the particular reasons
> a prosecutor might give. If any facially neutral reason sufficed to answer a
> *Batson* challenge, then *Batson* would not amount to much more than *Swain*.
> Some stated reasons are false, and although some false reasons are shown
> up within the four corners of a given case, sometimes a court may not be
> sure unless it looks beyond the case at hand.[217]

Thus, the court emphasizes the need for courts to rely on "all relevant circumstances" to raise an inference of purposeful discrimination, as *Batson* requires.[218]

The opinion quotes from its previous decision (finding that Miller-El should
have been granted a certificate of appealability) in which it articulated a more strin-
gent rule for evaluating the credibility of a reason for exercising a peremptory strike:
"the credibility of reasons given can be measured by 'how reasonable, or how
improbable, the explanations are; and by whether the proffered rationale has some
basis in accepted trial strategy.'"[219] This standard for measuring the ultimate credibility of a proffered reason signals a departure from its earlier decision in *Purkett v.
Elem* in which the Court had indicated that a race-neutral reason need not be reasonable, probable or related to the trial to suffice for purposes of satisfying *step two*
of the *Batson* test.[220] *Miller-El* now makes clear that such a reason, while satisfying
the prosecution's burden to put forth a race-neutral reason will not ultimately be
found to be credible so as to prevail at *step three* of the *Batson* analysis.[221]

In reviewing the evidence presented by Miller-El, the Court begins with the
"remarkable" statistics:

> Out of 20 black members of the 108-person venire panel for Miller-El's trial,
> only 1 served. Although 9 were excused for cause or by agreement, 10 were
> peremptorily struck by the prosecution. 'The prosecutors used their peremp-
> tory strikes to exclude 91% of the eligible African American venire members
> . . . Happenstance is unlikely to produce this disparity.'[222]

---

[217]*Id.*

[218]*Id.*

[219]*Id.* at 2329 (quoting Miller-El v. Cockrell, 537 U.S. 322, 339 (2003)).

[220]Purkett v. Elem, 514 U.S. 765 (1995) (prosecutor's race-neutral reason—that potential juror had long,
unkempt hair and facial hair—need not be reasonable, plausible, specific, or trial-related; it must only be
non-discriminatory to satisfy step two).

[221]The Court further explains:
It is true that peremptories are often the subjects of instinct, . . . and it can sometime be hard to say what
the reason is. But when illegitimate grounds like race are in issue, a prosecutor simply has got to state his
reasons as best he can and stand or fall on the plausibility of the reasons he gives. A *Batson* challenge
does not call for a mere exercise in thinking up any rational basis.
Id. at 2332.

[222]*Id.* at 2325 (quoting Miller-El v. Cockrell, 537 U.S., at 342).

Next the opinion provides detailed analysis of the questioning of individual jurors to provide"side-by-side comparisons of some black venire panelists who were struck and white panelists allowed to serve."[223] This comparison is done to determine whether a reason proffered for striking a black panelist applies as well to an otherwise-similar nonblack person who is permitted to serve, which would be evidence of purposeful discrimination. As to one black panelist, Billy Jean Fields, the majority found that the prosecutor "simply mischaracterized [his] testimony" in offering a race-neutral reason, and the Court also determined that the same proffered reason would have applied equally well to a white venire panelist allowed to serve.[224] The Court found that prosecutor James Nelson "represented that Fields said he would not vote for death if rehabilitation was possible, whereas Fields unequivocally stated that he could impose the death penalty regardless of the possibility of rehabilitation."[225] The Court acknowledges the possibility that the prosecutor misunderstood Fields's testimony, but determines that it is more likely he had an "ulterior reason" for proceeding to peremptorily striking Fields.[226] Given Fields's "outspoken support" for the death penalty, the Court would have "expect[ed] the prosecutor to have cleared up any misunderstanding by asking further questions before getting to the point of exercising a strike."[227]

The majority compares the reason stated for striking Fields and concludes that thoughts on rehabilitation should have caused worry about several white panel members who were accepted with no apparent reservations. For example, Sandra Hearn said that she believes in the death penalty "'if a criminal cannot be rehabilitated and continues to commit the same type of crime.'"[228] She also said that "[p]eople change," making it hard to determine the degree of a person's future dangerousness.[229] She concludes, in language that should give a prosecutor pause: "The evidence would have to be awful strong.'"[230] The prosecutor raised no objection to Hearn serving on the jury. Likewise, white panelist Mary Witt and Latino panelist Fernando Gutierrez both indicated that they would consider the possibility of rehabilitation at the penalty phase of the trial, yet the prosecutor did not ask either of them any further question on the subject and accepted them both as jurors.[231]

---

[223]*Id.* at 2325.

[224]*Id.* at 2326-28.

[225]*Miller-El v. Dretke*, 125 S.Ct. at 2327. Panelist Billy Jean Fields is a black man "who expressed unwavering support for the death penalty" and stated "without apparent hesitation[] that he could sit on Miller-El's jury and make a decision to impose this penalty."*Id.* at 2326. He also stated that while he believed anyone could be rehabilitated, this belief would not preclude him from imposing the death penalty. Nonetheless, prosecutor Nelson is quoted as stating that he peremptorily struck Mr. Fields out of concern that "he said that he could only give death if he thought a person could not be rehabilitated and he later made the comment that any person could be rehabilitated if they find God or are introduced to God and the fact that we have a concern that his religious feelings may affect his jury service in this case." *Id.* (citing App. at 197).

[226]*Id.* at 2327.

[227]*Id.*

[228]*Id.* (quoting App. at 429).

[229]*Id.* (quoting App. at 440).

[230]*Id.*

[231]*Id.*at 2327-28 (citing 6 Record of Voir Dire 2433, 2464-65). "Witt ultimately did not serve because she was peremptorily struck by the defense," a fact that the Court did not find to be of consequence to its side-by-side comparison of how prosecutors questioned black and nonblack panelists. *Id.* at 2328 n. 3. The Court also notes that the prosecution did peremptorily strike two other nonblack panelists who expressed views about rehabilitation similar to those of Witt and Gutierrez. *Id.* at 2328 n.5.

The majority found it unlikely that Fields's position on rehabilitation had "any-thing to do" with his being peremptorily struck, citing the prosecutor's response when the defense attorney pointed out that Fields had not testified as the prosecution asserted. Rather than defend his version of the testimony or withdrawing the strike, the prosecutor instead "suddenly came up with Field's brother's prior conviction as another reason for the strike."[232] The Court states that this new explanation "reeks of afterthought" and indicates "pretextual timing."[233] In unequivocal language, the Court concludes that "[t]here is no good reason to doubt that the State's afterthought about Fields's brother was anything but makeweight."[234]

The decision also takes issue with the Fifth Circuit's interpretation of the voir dire evidence. As to the peremptory strike used against Fields, the Supreme Court refers to the Court of Appeals' judgment as "unsupportable," for "failing to note that Fields affirmed that he could give the death penalty if the law and evidence called for it" and for "making no mention of the fact that the prosecution mischaracterized Fields as saying he could not give death if rehabilitation were possible."[235] Without going so far as explicitly saying that the Fifth Circuit was disingenuous in its por-trayal of the evidence, the Supreme Court's opinion certainly implies it.

The Court also takes issue with all the trial and appellate judges who had ruled against Miller-El. The majority objects to the perceived practice of judges discover-ing acceptable reasons for a peremptory strike, even if those reasons were not actu-ally put forth by the prosecutors themselves. The Court explains: "If the stated rea-son [for a peremptory strike] does not hold up [as being plausible], its pretextual significance does not fade because a trial judge, or an appeals court, can imagine a reason that might not have been shown up as false. The Court of Appeals' and the dissent's substitution of a reason for eliminating Warren [one of the black panelists] does nothing to satisfy the prosecutors' burden of stating a racially neutral explana-tion for their own actions."[236]

In addition, the Court reviewed Miller-El's other evidence of alleged discrimi-natory practices by prosecutors—the prosecution's shuffling of the venire panel, and alleged disparate question of venire panelists on their views of the death penalty and about minimum acceptable sentences—and found that "all indicate decisions prob-ably based on race."[237] If any further evidence of discriminatory intent was needed, the Court found it in the evidence that "the Dallas County office had followed a spe-cific policy of systematically excluding blacks from juries."[238] The Court also noted

---

[232]*Id.* at 2328. The prosecutor had questioned Fields about a brother of his who had a criminal history. Fields stated that he did not know much about the criminal proceedings, but acknowledged that his brother had been convicted and served time. He responded "no" when asked whether his brother's conviction would in any way interfere with his service on the jury. *Id.* at 2327.

[233]*Id.* at 2328.

[234]*Id.* In similar fashion, the Court proceeds to a second side-by-side comparison of a black panelist peremp-torily struck by the prosecutor, Paul Macaluso, and other nonblack panelists that the prosecution did not strike. Again, the Court found "evidence of pretext." See *id.* at 2330-31.

[235]*Id.* at 2329.

[236]*Id.* at 2332.

[237]*Id.* at 2332-38. For a discussion of the practices of jury shuffles and disparate questioning, see also supra notes 184-187 and accompanying text.

[238]*Id.* at 2328. See also supra notes 187-90 and accompanying text.

that the prosecutors' own notes indicating the race of each venire panelist further indicates that race continued to be an important factor in their selection practice.[239]

Justice Breyer issued a concurring opinion in which he took up Justice Marshall's earlier call in *Batson* for an end to the practice of peremptory challenges as the only effective means for eliminating racial discrimination in jury selection.[240] He addresses the difficulty of making the subjective judgments in deciding whether a litigant has misused a peremptory strike and the studies and anecdotal reports that indicate a persistent problem of race discrimination.[241] He also notes that professional legal journals tend to promote discrimination on improper grounds as a means of fulfilling a lawyer's obligation to help his or her client's case.[242] His opinion concludes with the suggestion that if a choice had to be made between the right to a jury chosen without regard to impermissible factors and the right to challenge peremptorily, "the Constitution compels a choice of the former."[243] Thus, he concurs with the qualification that he also believes "the *Batson* test and the peremptory challenge system as a whole" should be reconsidered.[244]

Justice Thomas, with whom Chief Justice Rehnquist and Justice Scalia joined, filed a dissenting opinion. The dissenters disagreed with the majority's reliance on evidence that had not been presented before the state trial court, ostensibly in violation of the rules governing writs of habeas corpus found in the Antiterrorism and Effective Death Penalty Act of 1996.[245] Additionally, the dissenting opinion concludes that Miller-El's evidence "does not come remotely close to clearly and convincingly establishing that the state court's factual finding was unreasonable."[246] Taking issue with the majority's assessment of Miller-El's evidence, Justice Thomas determines that none of it meets the high standard of proof—not the side-by-side comparisons, the evidence of alleged disparate questioning, or the jury shuffles.[247] Even the evidence of a history of race discrimination by the District Attorney's office does not support Miller-El's cause, according to Justice Thomas, who dismisses it as "nothing more than guilt by association that is unsupported by the record."[248] The marking of the juror cards with each panelist's race is also not indicative of discrimination: "We have no idea . . .whether this was done merely for identification purposes or for some more nefarious reason. The reason we have no idea is that the juror cards were never introduced before the state courts, and thus prosecutors were never questioned about their use of them."[249]

Conclusion

Prior to *Miller-El*, the courts had not enforced *Batson* in such a way as to vindicate the rights of minorities to serve on juries, and the resulting lack of diversity

---

[239] *Id.* at 2340.
[240] *Id.* at 2340 (Breyer, J., concurring) (quoting Batson, 476 U.S., at 102-103 (Marshall, J., concurring)).
[241] *Id.* at 2341.
[242] *Id.* at 2343.
[243] *Id.* at 2344 (quoting Swain 380 U.S., at 244).
[244] *Id.* at 2344.
[245] *Id.* at 2344-45 (Thomas, J., dissenting).
[246] *Id.* at 2351.
[247] *Id.* at 2351-62.
[248] *Id.* at 2362-63.
[249] *Id.* at 2363.

has made an important difference on the ability of a criminal jury to ascertain the truth.[250] The decision in *Miller-El* gives some glimmer of hope that lower courts may begin to scrutinize litigants' race-neutral reasons for peremptory strikes in a more exacting manner. No longer should any "race neutral" explanation justify a peremptory strike, even if it is unreasonable, improbable and not related to the trial. On the contrary, *Miller-El* calls upon courts to measure the credibility of a stated reason by the extent to which it is reasonable, probable and related to accepted trial strategy. Time will tell whether this new emphasis will be sufficient to end the widely-perceived practice of race discrimination by trial litigants. And in the fifty years since *Hernandez v. Texas*, the clear and total exclusion of minority jurors has given way to more sophisticated state practices; this will require increasingly sophisticated responses. The Supreme Court's experience of over 100 years of efforts to eradicate racial discrimination in jury selection suggests that *Miller-El* will not fully succeed. The only sure way to end the abhorrent practice of racial exclusion is to declare the *Batson* test a failed experiment and do away with peremptory challenges altogether.

---

[250]For a review of the empirical research of juror race on jury decisions, see Nancy J. King, *Postconviction Review of Jury Discrimination: Measuring the Effects of Juror Race on Jury Decisions*, 92 MICH. L. REV. 63 (1993).

Hernandez at Fifty, A Personal History*

James de Anda

Thank you very much. I want to thank Professor Olivas for his introduction, his comments, and his speech, which was a great honor for me. And I feel indebted to all of you here this evening.

I thank you again— and for all the comments that I heard and I only wish that some of the old lawyers that you talked about during the course of the day were here this evening with us—Gus [Garcia], Carlos [Cadena], Johnny [Herrera]—these men who fought together in this case and for civil rights in general.

And I'm especially indebted—indebted to John Herrera as has been said because I told him when I got my license in December of 1950, I came back home to Houston and started looking for a job and after talking to about half the Bar and still looking for a job, I got to wondering if, you know, I should change suits, shoes, or something.

But I hit John's office and he called me. So, the benefit I got from all of that is I did not know a single lawyer when I came—when I started out and when I finished, I had an acquaintance with at least one partner in every law firm in Houston because I called them and because I saw the other guys who were out there scrambling for themselves. So, it wasn't a futile exercise and—and I'm especially indebted to John Herrera.

It's nice to see Mike and John [Herrera (John's sons)] here this evening on this occasion. John and I became very close friends, and our relationship has lasted through many years and when I first moved to Corpus Christi, we still saw each other frequently off and on.

And when I joined Johnny, the first day at work, he assigned a case to me which—well, it was *Aniceto Sanchez v. The State of Texas*. It wasn't the *Hernandez* case, but it was one like it. And he asked me if I would research the case. It was out of Fort Bend County. And so, the significance of the case is—and what I'd like to do this evening is maybe is go back to the beginnings and tell you—I know you've heard all about—about Pete Hernandez' case today and discussed it forwards, back-wards, sideways, inside and out.

---

*(Remarks given as the 2004 George I. Sánchez Lecture, Institute for Higher Education Law & Governance, University of Houston Law Center, November, 2004). Transcribed from the videotape by Michelle Erickson and edited by Michael A. Olivas. The presentation was a dinner speech, and was edited in its conversational style.

So, but I do want to tell you how—how this happened, how it started, and quite frankly, we've heard a lot of things here, but the person that was responsible ultimately for the Pete Hernandez case and getting to the Supreme Court was John Herrera. He's the one that really saw the significance through the *Sanchez* case and he asked me—the *Sanchez* case was based out of Fort Bend County, out of Richmond.

At that time, we traveled to the countryside about 20 minutes to get to Richmond out of Houston and he had noticed—John tried a few cases in Fort Bend County and noticed he'd never seen a Hispanic on the jury in any case he'd ever tried. And he said, "You know, it's"—he said, "I want you to look into the records over there and see why I've never seen a Chicano on the jury while I'm all over town."

And I said, "Well, I don't know why you haven't seen anybody."

I went over and I started checking the records and sure enough, there—there were not any—any Hispanic names on the venire lists on the actual juries to try the lawsuits, on the grand jury panels, nor the grand jury commissioners. And I came back real excited and said, "Johnny, I think we got grounds for filing a motion here and see if we can't get this indictment knocked out or—and do some work—some good work for the folks."

So, John's next assignment to me was to go ahead and prepare some appropriate motions and challenge what happened in Fort Bend County and in the Aniceto Sanchez case as a vehicle to put these matters to the Court.

And as a consequence, we filed a motion to quash the indictment in Sanchez and I explained to him after doing an awful lot of research that if we were going to do it, that I thought we had because of the rulings of the Court of Appeals of Texas at the time that we were going to have to establish a theory of identifiable minority and based on that the Mexicanos were being discriminated against because of the Court of Criminal Appeals' cases which turned on the issue—there weren't that many. There were two or three or four that said, Well, Mexicans are Caucasians and there were Caucasians on the jury. So, what are you fussing about?

And to put an end to it, that was the position of the Court of Criminal Appeals took for many years in trying the validity of the equal protection of the Fourteenth Amendment and essentially just said it did not apply to Hispanics regardless because they were Caucasians.

They were Caucasians.

And so that was—that was the end of that. And so we resumed the matter and we developed, I think in a very fine fashion, in Fort Bend County that the Hispanics were a minority and it was a recognized minority.

And I recall we had one grand jury commissioner on the stand.

John was a real fine cross-examiner and this particular fellow was a barber and had been on the grand jury commission and had been very emphatic about how very well he considered everybody and tried to pick the best people for the grand jury and said he had Mexican friends, et cetera, ate at Mexican restaurants and so forth. And finally John says, "Well, how long have you been a foreman?"

Well, the guy says, "20 years."

I don't recall. It was a long time, he said. Then John said, "Have you ever cut a Mexican's head—haircut? Have you ever given a Mexican a haircut?"

He said, "Not on your life."

So, it went that way. But the bottom line was the judge would—I think the judge either helped him find jurors or precedents that existed at the time, denied our motion to try the lawsuit.

Mr. Sanchez got ten years in the penitentiary in a murder case.

And we appealed to the Court of Criminal Appeals, and the Court of Criminal Appeals handed down one paragraph. It went to something else and denied our claim. We had talked about appealing further.

We just didn't have the funds to do it.

Furthermore, Mr. Sanchez was somewhat reluctant to be a guinea pig because he didn't think that ten years was too bad of a deal. All things considered, he was quite a character. He had 18 children in the courtroom. It was helpful getting ten years instead of more.

But be that as it may, we decided not to appeal on the decision of the Court of Criminal Appeals and that case went by the courts. Within six or seven months, John got the *Hernandez* case out of Jackson County.

And then—incidentally, before I get to the *Hernandez* case—I'm trying to show you that Mexicans were an identifiable group in Fort Bend County, which the District Attorney denied.

You may recall the Garcia case, some of you may remember Sgt. Macario Garcia. He won the Congressional Medal of Honor in World War Two in Europe, a very brave man, for extraordinary acts of heroism, and he lived at that time, I think, in Fort Bend County. He came back from serving in the war and went to a restaurant over there in Sugar Land, as I remember, or Richmond—I don't know the name of the place—and they wouldn't serve him because he was Hispanic even though he was wearing his Congressional Medal at the time. And somebody said, "You're going to have to leave."

And as he did, he tipped a glass of water over on the table and there were two deputy sheriffs sitting in the restaurant at the time, and they took him outside and just beat the hell out of him and filed on him for assaulting an officer.

And the case drew considerable publicity throughout the nation.

In fact, Walter Winchell, I remember, referred to Sugar Land as the dirtiest little town in Texas. And so that wasn't a very fond memory. [The case was in 1945. Ed.]

I think some of you remember better.

I think the case was dismissed, if I recall correctly. I know that Jimmy Allred who was a former Federal judge represented Sgt. Garcia on the case and I know that he probably never suffered any consequences regarding the beating.

But the reason I mention the story because I think it kind of sets the more or less the tone of what was happening here in those days. Things were not good at all and that area between Fort Bend County, Wharton County, Jackson County, really, has a very poor area—a very poor track record as it relates to Hispanics in that area.

I remember Wharton had a theater where the Mexicans had to sit in the balcony. There was always something. It was always some problem that occurs.

So, the Pete Hernandez case comes along. John decided—he said, "This time, Jimmy, we're really going to get after it. You know, we've done the work. All we have to do is change the names. We've got the bill ready to move forward," which we did.

In the meantime, he also asked his good friend, Gus Garcia—I didn't know Gus at the time—this is how I met Gus—to come into the case and help me. And because we knew it was going to be a long haul. And at that time, Gus and Carlos were partners in San Antonio and so Gus came into the case and I and Gus and John tried the case and there were two instances that I thought were very significant. One of which, as Michael [Olivas] already mentioned to you, one about the door, the restroom door.

There were several restaurants that had "No Mexicans Allowed" signs on their windows and so forth but the sheriff went around when there was—everybody got wind of the case, why, they went around and took all the signs down. And so, but later on, the guy 'fessed up and admitted—he had went around to get the signs taken down in the case.

And—but the other two things that happened—one you've heard about from Michael—and the way that came out was sort of strange because I don't know which—we were out there kind of investigating and talking around the courthouse and somebody wanted to use the restroom but for some reason or another that day, the talk turned to some worker there asking him where the restroom was and he told us in Spanish, "Well, go downstairs." He said, "There's some restrooms down there. You can use those."

And so, we went down to the basement of the courthouse and that's where we found, much to Gus' delight, the sign that everyone refers to and which the Supreme Court referred to as well because it was taken aback because it had it right in the courthouse. It was really horrible for the State to discover because it was—it was devastating.

And—but apart from that, when we were examining one of the—we had a witness, a man named Rosas, who testified that—I have to show again discrimination, well, against Hispanics and also the—as an identifiable group—and he testified in this—at this hearing that he had told us about this school that had recently been closed but it was an elementary school exclusively for Mexican children. And there was a nice brick school that the Anglo children went to where everything was nice and then there was this building, this wooden building, that they used for Grades 1 through 4 for Mexican children and then when they had, according to our witness, there was just one teacher for all lower grades in this school and they didn't even have any inside plumbing. It had an outhouse. So that was a pretty terrible thing to see, anyway.

And Mr. Rosas apparently had a young son who was six-years old and he was going to enroll in the white school and so that he could do that, he forbid this young man to speak Spanish. He spoke only English to him, and he couldn't speak Spanish. But when he went over to the school, they said, "That's immaterial and irrelevant. And you're going to the Mexican school because you're Mexican, and you'll have to learn Spanish."

You know, so Mr. Rosas took his child to Victoria, which is about 25 miles away, and enrolled in the Catholic school; and that's where the young man then went to school. And since this happened to this young man's siblings, a sister and a brother, in turn, they all went to school in Victoria because they did not want to go to the Mexican school.

Just as a coincidence, I was trying to find out a few days ago before I came up here whatever happened to Pete Hernandez because I had been asked that question in Austin one evening; and I was embarrassed because I didn't want know what happened to him. And that's what happens to you because you—because your case becomes famous but you don't.

So, I called over there. I called the District Attorney's office. I talked—Michael Solar suggested. I said, "Who the heck do I call?"

He says, "Call the D.A. You know, the guy was in jail."

So, I called over there and I found this young lady, very helpful, and she said, "Well, I don't know. The only person I can think of that might help you is Mr. Rosas."

And I said, "Rosas?"

And she said, "Yes." She said, "Yes, he's here in the city housing."

So, I called Mr. Rosas and asked him and he told me that Pete Hernandez was dead and had been dead for several years and had never gotten married, was a single man. He was crippled. He was miserably crippled. He walked with a very pronounced limp, just generally in bad health. Anyway, he told me that Pete Hernandez had died, and there were no other relatives except possibly a brother who was somewhere—who was no longer there.

So, anyway, I give you that information. If anybody has anything different, I'd appreciate hearing from you.

But—and then it turned out that the man I was talking to was the boy who did not go to the Mexican school. He went to Victoria. That was his father that testified for us in the case—in the case proper.

So, these little things happen some time when you're investigating and I thought it was quite a coincidence and made a very interesting story and, in fact, I asked him for permission to tell you this story and he said, "Sure. You go right ahead and tell them." So, I'm telling you the story.

The bottom line is that we went ahead and tried the case of Pete Hernandez and, of course, he was convicted and got a life sentence and as they say on the radio, you know the rest of the story. But the bottom line is that he is no longer with us and that's the way the case came out.

In the course of my research—and what's really inspired me in the Hernandez case was another Sanchez case I read about—The State versus another Sanchez. [Serapio Sanchez—ED.]

And I tell you, this is relevant because I think it's interesting because I think it shows you—I think it shows the significance of not having jurors —of not getting a fair deal on your jury.

Somewhere between Alpine, Texas and El Paso in West Texas and that —that was a murder case in which Mr. Sanchez was an 18-year-old boy who had been in—this happened in 1944. He had been inducted—well, he'd been called by his Board, been drafted into the Army. It turned out he had an I.Q. of about a 7-year-old and apart from that, he was blind. He couldn't see the fingers of his hand if it was put 18 inches away from him. That's what the doctor testified to at the trial. He was the defendant in the case.

And what happened to him is his father worked for a farmer there and they'd worked on a Saturday night for about 12 hours or so. And after he'd left to work, instead of going home, went into town and threw a good one on and he was supposed to work on Sunday irrigating. And his employer was looking for him on Sunday, as was his wife; and she sent their son, the defendant, to find Daddy.

In the meantime, the employer found Daddy first and was trying to get him to come to work and the man wouldn't do it. So, by the time the son got there, the employer decided to take matters into his own hands, and he just beat the guy—beat him up pretty good.

And the son came running over to intervene and drew out a knife, a pocketknife. The employer said that they both hit each other and they kind of fussed about it. And the employer finally told the son, "Well, you take him on home and"—he said, "I'll—we'll take care of this later on."

Now, as the boy was getting ready to walk away with his dad, a car drove up. The deceased comes out of the car, running over to the employer, and says, "You got any problems with these Mexicans?" He says, "I can help you out."

The guy says, "No, everything's fine. You just"—and he's going, "I'm taking him home."

Whereupon, the deceased turns around and just clobbers—the big guy clobbers the heck out of the father, knocks him down, and when the boy tries to intervene, knocks the boy down, where he just jumps up, gets his knife, and unfortunately, with just one stroke of the knife, he got the jugular vein and the deceased died, became the deceased.

Well, there was a motion filed to transfer the case and also a motion to quash the grand jury because they never had any Mexicans on the juries, all of which were denied and the jury gave this poor boy 35 years in the penitentiary. He had never in his life been in jail or in trouble and those facts had gotten him 35 years.

Well, those were—those were the kind of things that were happening in those days, and that's why we thought it appropriate to do what we did in the Hernandez case. And fortunately, the case turned out well for us.

We—Gus Garcia—I'd like to mention—and Carlos Cadena, they both made arguments to the case. I helped with the briefs. I had done the work before. Carlos wrote some tremendous briefs for the case. It was just marvelous.

And the case—as you know, John was the first one to Washington. There was some other lawyers that we mentioned that were helpful in the matter but primarily these were the lawyers that worked hard on the case but—I had to stay back, No. 1, because they didn't have any money there, No. 2 because I had to send money. As money that came into the office from various plaintiffs, clients to keep these guys out of trouble and really we were short on funds.

But I was getting reports from Gus and from John primarily about the case and I heard, as Michael told you, it was one of the rare instances where the Court allows additional time to a person to present their case.

While a Supreme Court—when they tell you to sit down or when the light comes on, you sit down. You can be in mid-sentence or mid-word, but you're through unless they tell you for some reason they'll let you finish whatever you're saying but—but anyway, the Court, of course, wrote this very wonderful opinion that saved the people an awful lot of time.

Pete never did have to go to the penitentiary, by the way, because—I think I may have heard something differently, Michael—but my understanding was that they didn't want him in there because he was—he was crippled and I know he spent all the time during the appeal he was in county jail there in Jackson County. But it may be that—I know he remained because the authorities at the penitentiary didn't want him.

But, anyway, that's why and so that's more or less the history of the case—the lawyers involved are very interesting.

I know that Doug and Michael and Mike and Mickey mind me telling the story because John told me a thousand times. You know, John Herrera took the Bar either six or seven times. How many times was it?

Okay. He was very proud of that. Well, when he finally passed the Bar, he got this letter from the Bar examiners—never done that before—all signed by all the members of the Bar congratulating him on passing the Bar, and he very prominently displayed that in his office.

And, of course, everybody thought he was something exceptional that the Board members were writing him this letter. But the truth was—and they were very proper and political. They said, "We respect you for your determination and tenacity."

So, he had this letter. John also had a—for a number of years he was a —he told me a story. He worked for the Sanitation Department in the City of Houston, I mean, pick and shovel, and he had this big picture of his crew of all these guys holding shovels and picks and wearing these rubber boots, these high rubber boots. They'd just come out of the sewer system, and they took this picture. John had this picture with him in the middle just plastered all over the place.

So, he was really a man of the people. He'd been a cab driver for—also in his time and he told me that the guys over at the Sanitation Department called him the ragpicker, rags, teasing him because he was going to law school and never could get out of law school and was working his way, they kind of ribbed him as Mexicans are prone to do.

Johnny was a criminal lawyer and he was a great, good trial lawyer, very effective in the courtroom because he knew people so well. He read people so well. I've never met a person that could tell you—he read the body language. This guy knew more about body language than any person I've ever known.

He was very effective in his criminal practice and was a very successful lawyer.

Gus, I did not know Gus until this case came up but after that, Gus and I became good friends and as a matter of fact, I believe it's called the George Sánchez series.

Dr. Sánchez was my witness in my first school desegregation case and I tried
that in 1956 in Corpus Christi Independent School District case very similar to the
situations that we've been talking about. In that case, the school district had a policy that all Hispanic children had to stay three years in the first grade so they could
learn English.

And this applied even though there was a gentlemen and his wife who decided
they didn't want their daughter to be subjected to this so they wouldn't let her speak
English—I mean, they wouldn't let her speak Spanish in the home and, of course,
all the other Hispanic families made fun of them and laughed at them but they said
well, we don't want our child to spend three years in the first grade. So, this child
could not speak a word of Spanish when she went into school but whenever she got
to the school, why, in she went with her fellow Mexicans.

And so, they wound up in my office in Corpus Christi and Dr. Garcia and Victor Garcia and some other Mexicanos referred the case to me and the father sued
them in Federal court in Corpus Christi and I had contacted Dr. Sanchez to be a witness in the case because he was the foremost expert in the world in educational matters and minority problems in education and he had a chair at the University of
Texas. And he agreed to—he didn't know me, but he said he knew about me and he
said he would be glad to help me and he could. Again, I think he got a little nervous
because I was still a fairly young lawyer and he said, "Oh, why don't you get some
a little older to help you in this case?" So, I was a little indignant about it; but I said,
"Fine. Who do you suggest it?

He said, "Well, Gus Garcia."

I said, "Well, I know Gus, too." And I said, "Well, you give him a call; and we'll
see."

So, anyway, he called Gus, and Gus and I talked about it and he said, "Yeah, I'll
second chair you on the case."

So, he came down and worked the case. Dr. Sánchez made a remark. I wanted
to tell you a little Dr. Sánchez story. Dr. Sánchez testified in that case as my expert
and the lawyer on the other side was a man named Davis, Constant Davis, who later
became—old Constant became Federal judge of Corpus Christi—but at the time he
and Allen Davis were partners. Allen was a very astute lawyer, a very capable lawyer
and he had heard that Dr. Sánchez—so he went out and he got a copy of every work
that Dr. Sánchez had ever written. I mean, the stack—a big, long stack of paper,
books, and pamphlets, and whatever it was and I don't know when he had the time
to write them all and he looked—I had put Dr. Sánchez on the stand.

And after I examined him and I turned him over for cross-examination, I think
Allen was trying to upset the doctor, but I don't know what he had in mind. He didn't
know Dr. Sánchez. So, he said, "Dr. Sánchez, I want you to know that this is all the
material you've ever written."

And Dr. Sánchez says, "My, that is impressive. I didn't know."

He said, "I read every book that you have ever written and here they are and I'm
going to ask you some questions about the statements you made in those books."

He said, "I'm so sorry." And Dr. Sánchez said, "Mr. Davis, I'm so sorry. I wish
you had told me you were doing that because there's nothing in those books that

makes any sense." He said, "I wrote most of that stuff when I was young, and over the years I've changed my mind. I tell you that everything I say here today is contrary to something I wrote on the topic. I'll save you the trouble."

I thought the judge was going to fall out of his chair.

James Allred was the judge. He was a former governor of Texas and a wonderful man. And I'll tell you one more story, he was a federal judge during the New Deal when Franklin D. Roosevelt was president and there was a senator from Texas, Patrick Daniel, who hated Roosevelt and was against everything Roosevelt did. So, Roosevelt hated him. And so, President Roosevelt talked to Judge Allred into running against Patrick Daniel and so, he had to resign his judgeship.

And unfortunately, Patrick beat Judge Allred and so, Judge Allred was out of a job and wasn't a state senator. And then Roosevelt tried to reappoint him federal judge. Well, of course, the senator blocked the appointment. And so, he didn't get back, he did not get back on the bench until Patrick Daniel was gone and Truman became president after President Roosevelt died and President Truman reappointed Judge Allred to the bench. So, he got back on the bench.

That's just a really fast story about Judge Allred so you can tell what person he was by the history. Allred enjoyed the trial immensely. After the case was over, he remained on the case—Dr. Sánchez called me and by this time, he had a little more confidence in me. And he congratulated me for a good job and he said, "I got to tell you this story, Jimmy." He said, "I got back to Austin." He said, "my dean called me in." He said, "Yeah, I'm going to give you the blow-by-blow description."

He said—he was outraged, a very conservative man and didn't like the idea of Dr. Sánchez testifying, especially for the plaintiffs in a case of that type. And he said, "Dr. Sánchez, I read this story. I want you to know I didn't like it."

Dr. Sánchez's response was, "Well, I want you to know I didn't write that story."

He said, "Well, that's not what I'm getting at. That's what they quote you as saying." He said, "First of all, you went to the courthouse without even consulting with us, you went to the court."

Dr. Sánchez said, "Well, I hate to tell you this, but I got a subpoena from the court. If I didn't go there, I was in trouble. So, I went because of the subpoena. Is there something wrong with that?"

"Well, no, that's not wrong. Well, why did you testify and say this, and this, and this?"

"Well, I did say that because it's the truth."

And so he said the dean just glared at him and said that's all and walked out. The poor man was purple, he was so mad.

And Dr. Sánchez was really a great, great man. And he helped me immensely in several cases that I had involving educational issues and I am forever in his debt. He's also passed away.

Gus I'm sad to say, has been gone a long time; I think he died four or five years ago, Carlos passed away so I stand here before you this evening. John died in 1988, he passed away.

I'll tell you one more John Herrera story. His last wish was that the funeral entourage circle the courthouse three times. And so, they wouldn't go for that. As I understand it, they did let the hearse go around because John said he wanted to make one last trip to the courthouse before they put him away. So, he made his last trip to the courthouse. So, that's a trial lawyer for you. I promised my wife, who always asks me when I'm going to retire, I promise you I will not make that last trip.

And I thank all of you very much. I appreciate your attention.

Hernandez v. Texas: A Litigation History

Michael A. Olivas

The case of *Hernandez v Texas* was tried in 1951, in Edna, Jackson County, Texas, but that was not where it began. The legal strategy for *Hernandez*—that Mexican Americans tried by juries on criminal charges should be entitled to a "jury of their peers," including other Mexican Americans—actually arose in a different setting in Texas, in an earlier case tried by some of the lawyers who took the *Hernandez* case all the way to the U.S. Supreme Court, and beyond. That case is quite interesting, not only for its offspring, which became more well known and more important, but because it encapsulates the way that mid-twentieth Century Texas worked, how Jim Crow had metasticized in the State, and how the nascent minority of Mexican Americans would organize themselves for their larger, communal good. It also began with a love song.

"Singing a Song in Mexican"

Ft. Bend County was, in the 1950's, an essentially rural setting, an hour Southwest of Houston, and was dominated by sugar plantations and other agricultural production, particularly rice. The town of Sugar Land dominated the area, later made famous by the early Stephen Spielberg movie about a caravan that led to Sugar Land.[1] In 1945, the nearby town of Richmond became known as the home of the Richmond Drive-In Restaurant, where World War II hero Sgt. Macario Garcia had been refused service, occasioning a major dustup, until the case was dropped after national attention to the matter was prompted by Walter Winchell.[2] The attorneys in

---

[1] THE SUGARLAND EXPRESS (Universal Pictures 1974).

[2] After he was refused service at this restaurant, Garcia was said to have trashed the establishment and was charged with the crime. He was defended by Johnny Herrera and others for the charges stemming from this Richmond incident. The case attracted national publicity when columnist Walter Winchell became outraged and drew attention to it in one of his columns. See Marie Theresa Hernandez, Reconditioning History: Adapting Knowledge from the Past into the Realities of the Present: A Mexican-American Graveyard, 3 RETHINKING HISTORY 289, 292-93 (1999) (history of San Isidro Cemetery, Richmond, Texas, by daughter of the man [Jose F. Hernandez] who served as translator for Aniceto Sanchez trial); Marie Theresa Hernandez, Cemeteries of Ambivalent Desire (forthcoming) (Ch. V, "A Warrior" [study of Sgt. Macario Garcia and Ft. Bend County]). One source erroneously indicates that Herrera and Gus Garcia tried the case and that he was acquitted, but Herrera was joined at different stages of the matter not by Gustavo Garcia but rather by Phillip Montalbo and James Allred, and the matter never actually came to trial. See Handbook of Texas Online, [Maria Cristina Garcia] Garcia, Macario, http://www.tsha.utexas.edu/handbook/online/articles/GG/fga76.html (last visited Nov. 12, 2005). A search of Fort Bend felony records from September 1, 1945 through 1972, when Macario Garcia died, revealed no record of the case having been tried. In research files, the authors have a notarized letter from the Ft. Bend County clerk verifying that there were no felony criminal cases on file against Garcia. (February 26, 2006 Letter on file with Michael A. Olivas). See also Alonso S. Perales, ARE WE GOOD NEIGHBORS? (1948) at 156 [notarized statements of Macario Garcia and witnesses].

the Macario Garcia case were Johnny Herrera, Phillip Montalbo, and James Allred. On May 4, 1953 the U.S. Supreme Court decided *Terry v. Adams*, which struck down the Ft. Bend County practice of using a racist surrogate party, the Jaybird Party, to thwart African American voting in the Democratic Party. It was, in other words, the Deep Jim Crow South but with Mexicans also occupying the bottom rungs of the ladder along with Blacks.[3]

Histories of the area reveal that the Kempner family established the area in the early 1900's as a town that would inculcate a "company culture," one that provided a stable and dependent workforce, sharply stratified by race and class, with Blacks, Mexican Americans, and state prisoners of all races as the laborers and an Anglo managerial elite.[4] Until 1914, the Texas Department of Corrections contracted prison labor with Imperial Sugar and other area companies.[5] After that time, the companies recruited and maintained their own workforces, using a traditional Southern corporate racial strategy of separate housing and occupational segregation, complete with ethnic churches, separate graveyards, company stores, and scrip rather than currency—all of which combined to accentuate the different racial groupings and to maintain the subordinate status of minority workers and their families.[6] Harold Hyman's classic study of the area, *Oleander Odyssey*, is somewhat critical of a number of the practices employed by the companies, but appears tone-deaf when it came to one new manager's removal of the shacks in the Mexican part of town: when the new foreman demolished "the noisome shanties of 'Mexico' [as that part of town was dubbed]," there were no "known complaints by the unsalubrious residents" of the barrio.[7]

This scenario appears in *Aniceto Sanchez v. State of Texas*, where the Court pithily summarizes the setting:

> The appellant was convicted for murder and assessed a penalty of ten years in the penitentiary.

> The evidence discloses that appellant, a Mexican, was a farm worker and lived on a large plantation in a cottage within a few feet of that occupied by the deceased. On the night of the tragedy [April 23, 1950], shortly after twelve o'clock, the deceased came up to the residence of appellant where he was engaged with others in drinking beer. He was singing a song in Mexican which, interpreted, is entitled 'You, Only You' and is said to be a Mexican love song. Apparently this incensed appellant who, without any words, went into his house, got his gun, came out and shot, killing the

---

[3]345 U.S. 461 (1953). See Hernandez, supra note 59, at 292-294. See also HAROLD HYMAN, OLEANDER ODYSSEY: THE KEMPNERS OF GALVESTON, TEXAS, 1854–1980s (1990); RANDOLPH B. CAMPBELL, AN EMPIRE FOR SLAVERY: THE PECULIAR INSTITUTION IN TEXAS, 1821–1865, at 57–58 (1991). See generally DAVID MONTEJANO, ANGLOS AND MEXICANS IN THE MAKING OF TEXAS, 1836-1986 (1987); ARNOLDO DE LEON, THEY CALLED THEM GREASERS: ANGLO ATTITUDES TOWARD MEXICANS IN TEXAS, 1821–1900 (1983).
[4]Hernandez, supra note 59, at 291-292; Hyman, supra note 60, at 305.
[5]Hernandez, supra note 59, at 3.
[6]*Id.*
[7]Hyman, supra note 60, at 305.

deceased a short distance from his front door steps. About this there is no controversy.[8]

Aniceto Sanchez had shot Hylario Smershy, whose Czech surname hid his Mexican ancestry.[9] Sanchez and Smershy worked side by side in the Imperial Sugar fields, plowing fields with large mules. Because they lived in shanties near each other in the part of the company town that its residents called "El Gran Centro," they knew each other well and drank together after work, when Semershy would play guitar and sing love songs such as "Tú Sólo Tú," the popular Felipe Valdez Leal song (later recorded by the popular singer Selena, also shot dead in Texas).[10] Sanchez apparently felt that Smershy was acting inappropriately to his wife and trying to woo her, as the song portrays a drunken and passionate man lusting after a woman ("borracho y apasionado nomás por tu amor").[11]

After the indictment, his family hired the only experienced Mexican American lawyer in the Houston area, Johnny Herrera, to defend him. Herrera had graduated from the South Texas College of Law, a freestanding law school in Houston, and at the time the only law school in the State's largest city.[12] He had worked a number of jobs, had gone to law school at night, and had driven a cab until he became licensed in 1943. He had carved out a general civil practice, but increasingly had taken on criminal clients in large part because there was such a need and there were so few Mexican American lawyers in Texas. The Houston area at the time had fewer than a half dozen Mexican American attorneys, and Herrera took two of them into his firm, James de Anda and Arnulfo (A.D.) Azios. Attorney de Anda had graduated from Texas A&M University and the University of Texas Law School, where he later indicated that he had been able to do because he was "güero" (i.e., light-skinned) and because the school officials had likely thought he was Italian.[13] When law firms and city offices found out he was Mexican, he had been unable to secure employment in Houston, so he had accepted the offer to hang out his shingle with Herrera, and later with Azios as well. He had just received his license to practice law when the Sanchez

---

[8]Sanchez v. Texas, 243 S.W.2d 700 (1951).

[9]Hernandez, supra note 59, at 298-299. Otherwise quite accurate, she mistakenly reverses the parties: "A man named Hylario Smershy had killed another man, Aniceto Sanchez." *Id.* at 298. Hernandez's father had been employed as a translator by the court, as Sanchez, born in Mexico, was a monolingual Spanish-speaker.

[10]SELENA, Tú Sólo Tú, on DREAMING OF YOU (EMI International 1995). The album was released three months after her murder in 1995. See Richard Harrington, Número Uno, Slain Tejano Singer's Album Tops Pop Chart, WASH. POST, July 26, 1995, at D1 (reporting on the record sales of the posthumous album).

[11]"Woman, look how I am, due to your loving/ I am drunk and passionate due to your love/ Look how I am given over to drunkenness and perdition" (trans. Michael A. Olivas).

[12]Although Herrera graduated from law school in 1940, it took him several attempts to pass the Texas bar examination, so he did not receive his license to practice law until 1943. See Handbook of Texas, Herrera, John J., http://www.tsha.utexas.edu/handbook/online/articles/HH/fhe63.html (providing a biography of Herrera) (last visited Nov. 12, 2005); Statement of Judge James deAnda, in Marcos Guerra, ed. Symposium: Hernandez v. Texas: A 50th Anniversary Celebration, 11 TEX HISP. J.L. & POL'Y 11, 28 (2005).

[13]Discussion with James de Anda (Nov., 2005). See also Steven H. Wilson, Brown Over "Other White": Mexican Americans' Legal Arguments and Litigation Strategy in School Desegregation Lawsuits, 21 LAW & HIST. REV. 145, 149-150 (2003) (reviewing deAnda's role in Hernandez).

case came to the firm. Within a week of the shooting on April 23, 1950, Sanchez was indicted by an all-Anglo jury on May 1.[14]

By this time, Herrera had tried a number of cases before juries, for whom he had a genuine feel, and he and de Anda discussed the fact that no Mexican-origin jurors had been called at the grand jury or the petit jury stages.[15] While Herrera prepared his larger, overarching defense, de Anda began to gather available data on the demographics of Texas and the Ft. Bend County area.[16] He went to the area's public libraries, inquired of state and local government agencies, and read available studies and newspapers to prepare an assault upon jury selection practices. His research was contained in a six page brief filed with the court on March 19, 1951, as the lawyers moved to quash the indictment, charging that their client's all-white grand jury and petit jury had violated his Equal Protection rights.[17]

The brief argued that there had been a rush to indict Sanchez, that he spoke no English and did not understand any rights he might have asserted, and that he had been in shock ("under severe mental strain").[18] In Part III of the Brief, de Anda and Herrera argued "[that] there has prevailed in Fort Bend County, Texas for a period of over thirty-five years, a systematic, continual and un-interrupted practice of discrimination against Mexican-Americans as a race, and people of Mexican extraction and ancestry as a class separate from other white Americans, a class to which this Defendant belongs, in the selection of Grand Jury Commissioners and Grand Jurors solely because of membership within that class. . . ."[19] They also noted to the court

---

[14]Bill of Exception No. 1, in "COLORED MEN" AND "HOMBRES AQUI": HERNANDEZ V. TEXAS AND THE EMERGENCE OF MEXICAN AMERICAN LAWYERING (Michael A. Olivas ed., 2006) [hereinafter OLIVAS, COLORED MEN] at App. II, p. 1.

[15]Discussion with James deAnda, November 2005. See generally James deAnda, "Hernandez at Fifty, A Personal History," in "COLORED MEN" AND "HOMBRES AQUI": HERNANDEZ V. TEXAS AND THE EMERGENCE OF MEXICAN-AMERICAN LAWYERING 229 (Michael A. Olivas ed., 2006) [hereinafter OLIVAS, COLORED MEN] (oral history of Hernandez lawsuit). They familiarized themselves with earlier Texas cases involving similar issues: Ramirez v. Texas, 40 S.W.2d 138 (1931); Carrasco v. Texas, 95 S.W.2d 433 (1936); Lugo v. Texas, 124 S.W.2d 344 (1939); Sanchez v. Texas, 181 S.W.2d 87 (1944); Terrell Wells Swimming Pool v. Rodriguez, 182 S.W.2d 824 (1944); Salazar v. Texas, 193 S.W.2d 211 (1946); Bustillos v. Texas, 213 S.W.2d 837 (1948); Clifton v. Puente, 218 S.W.2d 272 (1949). See generally IAN F. HANEY LÓPEZ, WHITE BY LAW: THE LEGAL CONSTRUCTION OF RACE (1996); George A. Martinez, Legal Indeterminacy, Judicial Discretion and the Mexican-American Litigation Experience: 1930-1980, 27 U.C. DAVIS L. REV. 555 (1994); Jorge C. Rangel & Carlos M. Alcala, Project Report, De Jure Segregation of Chicanos in Texas Schools, 7 HARV. C.R.-C.L. L. REV. 307 (1972); Ricardo Romo, Southern California and the Origins of Latino Civil-Rights Activism, 3 W. LEGAL HIST. 379 (1990); Guadalupe Salinas, Mexican Americans and the Desegregation of Schools in the Southwest, 8 HOUS. L. REV. 929 (1971); Clare Sheridan, "Another White Race": Mexican Americans and the Paradox of Whiteness in Jury Selection, 21 LAW & HIST. REV. 109 (2003).

[16]James de Anda did the research in part because he had not yet tried a case, having just received his bar membership in December, 1950, and in part because the two of them decided that Herrera would try their cases until de Anda had more experience observing trials. They decided to use to use the tack taken in the Serapio Sanchez case, tried in El Paso in 1944 by attorney A. L. Carlton, which they felt had the most promise, as its facts were most consistent with their own case. Because El Paso was a border community, it also had similar demographic characteristics of jury exclusion. In November, 2005, de Anda indicated in a series of conversations that this case was chosen as an exemplar for their "test-case" [his term] also due to Carlton's willingness to share his case files, copies of which were lost in a fire in the Houston federal courthouse when de Anda was a federal judge. All his personal and professional papers were lost in the accident. Sanchez v. Texas, 181 S.W.2d 87 (1944).

[17]Bill of Exception No. 1, reprinted in Olivas, COLORED MEN, at App. II, p. 1-6.

[18]*Id.*, Olivas, COLORED MEN, at App. II, p. 2.

[19]*Id.*, Olivas, COLORED MEN, at App. II, pp. 2-4.

that in the past thirty five years, no Mexican-American had ever been called to jury duty in any capacity in the County, where the population was approximately one-quarter Mexican American and that in any given year that population numbered over 6,400 members.[20] On March 20, 1951, the jury deliberated and convicted Sanchez of murder.[21] During the closing arguments to the jury, the State's Attorney raised the issue of whether they might be inclined to excuse the shooting because of an unwritten rule that a man could avenge an adulterous affair, even though Sanchez's attorneys had never offered such a defense and even though there was no evidence that Smershy and Mrs. Sanchez had ever had such a relationship.[22] Herrera and de Anda objected to this general line of argumentation, and indicated in their bill of exception that this summation and "argument by Counsel for the State tended to confuse and mislead the jury to believe that the Court did not consider the defendant's testimony [to be] true, and that said argument was therefore prejudicial and harmfully affected the weight given to defendant's testimony establishing provocation."[23] Additional bills of exceptions concerning technical jury instructions were also filed, and denied by the judge.[24] On April 7, 1951, Sanchez was sentenced to not less than two years and no more than 10 years in prison.[25] On November 21, 1951, *Aniceto Sanchez v. State* was decided by the Texas Court of Criminal Appeals, the highest court in Texas for criminal matters, and affirmed the trial decision and sentence; Sanchez would not let his lawyers appeal his case any further, on the theory that had done it and could only fare worse in any re-trial.[26]

Chinco Sanchez's Tavern, Sprung's Grocery, Edna, Jackson County, TX

In the meantime, during the pendency of the Sanchez trial and appeals, on August 4, 1951, 24-year old service station attendant Pedro (Pete) Hernandez shot and killed tenant farmer Joe Espinosa in Chinco Sanchez's Tavern, Sprung's Grocery, Edna, Jackson County, TX.[27] Within 24 hours, Hernandez was indicted by an all-white grand jury and petit jury panel for murder.[28] On August 8, he was denied bail.[29] During this period of time, Herrera and de Anda were retained as counsel for Hernandez. Jackson County, Texas was even further from Houston than was Ft.

---

[20]*Id.,* Olivas, COLORED MEN, at App. II, p. 5.

[21]Sanchez v. State, 243 S.W. 2d 700 (1951).

[22]Theresa Hernandez's father, many years later, told her that he had believed that Herrera and de Anda had made this up in order to confuse the jury. Hernandez, supra note 59, at 292. The pleadings show that the more likely reason for addressing the issue was that the prosecutor raised it preemptively, anticipating that the defense would use it as a justification defense of "an honor killing." Bill of Exception, Olivas, COLORED MEN, at pp. 8-9.

[23]Bill of Exception, in Olivas, COLORED MEN, at App. II, p. 8.

[24]Copy of Sentence, No. 7103, in Olivas, COLORED MEN, at App. II, p.10; Sanchez v. State, 243 S.W. 2d 700, 701 (1951).

[25]Copy of Sentence, No. 7103, in Olivas, COLORED MEN, at App. II, p. 7.

[26]Sanchez v. State, 243 S.W.2d 700 (1951).

[27]The facts of the case are spelled out in the various published opinions, while the entire trial record (Case No. 2091) is available in microfilm in the District Clerk Office, Jackson County, Edna, Texas; reprinted in Transcript of Record, in Olivas, COLORED MEN, App. VI. Additional facts about the arrest and trial are taken from the contemporary news stories, all on p.1 of The Edna Herald: Bond Is Denied Edna Youth Charged in Rifle Slaying, August 5, 1951; Jury to Get Hernandez Case Today, October 11, 1951; Hernandez Life Term Appealed, October 18, 1951.

[28]Discussions with James deAnda, Nov., 2005.

[29]Bond Is Denied Edna Youth Charged in Rifle Slaying, The Edna Herald , August 5, 1951, p. 1.

Bend County, well over an hour's trip on the highway. Although they had not prevailed in the Sanchez trial, the attorneys were encouraged by others with whom they discussed this case, such as Maury Maverick, a progressive San Antonio lawyer and legislator, to press on with the jury selection challenges.[30] In September 1951, San Antonio attorneys Gustavo Garcia and Carlos Cadena joined the defense team in order to challenge Texas jury practices.[31] Garcia and Herrera had known each other through LULAC circles and other community interconnections, but had not maintained close ties, as each was struggling to establish their law practices. In 1950, there were fewer than two dozen Mexican American lawyers in all of Texas, and they came to know each other generally through their membership in LULAC, the American Council of Spanish Speaking People, or the American GI Forum, but they were too geographically isolated from each other and too busy to interact on a regular basis. For example, Johnny Herrera had literally hundreds of criminal and civil cases, stretching from Galveston to Jackson County, and was known as one of the few Mexican American trial lawyers in the Gulf Coast region. It was for this reason that the Hernandez family sought his services when Pete was arrested for the Espinosa murder.

On October 4, 1951, the district court refused to quash the Hernandez indictment,[32] not unexpectedly, and de Anda sent his research materials to Cadena in San Antonio, who re-drafted the Aniceto Sanchez brief, edited for Jackson County demographics and updated data he obtained with the assistance of Dr. George I. Sánchez, a University of Texas professor of Education.[33] Although not an attorney, Sánchez, a native of New Mexico had been an expert witness and general resource for Mexican American lawyers in Texas cases, particularly those involving desegregation, housing, and K-12 schooling issues; he also oversaw some general support funds, which he used to support litigation.[34] As Neil Foley has written, Dr. Sánchez

---

[30]Discussions with James de Anda (Nov. 2005). Maverick signed the brief that was eventually filed with the U.S. Supreme Court, and died a month after the case was decided. See generally RICHARD B. HENDERSON, MAURY MAVERICK: A POLITICAL BIOGRAPHY (1970). Cristobal (Chris) Aldrete, a 1951 STCL graduate, also signed the brief as being Of Counsel; he was a Del Rio, Texas, lawyer whose family had been involved in the 1930 case against the Del Rio school district. See Handbook of Texas, Aldrete, Cristóbal, http://www.tsha.utexas.edu/handbook/online/articles/AA/falwl.html (biography of Aldrete) (last visited Nov. 12, 2005). Herrera and de Anda also signed as being Of Counsel, while Garcia and Cadena were listed as the Attorneys of Record. It is this formal arrangement and the divisions of labor that evolved in the course of this matter that have led many observers to characterize the case as solely the efforts of the more flamboyant Garcia and the more scholarly Cadena.

[31]It is estimated that there were fewer than two dozen Mexican American lawyers in Texas at the time, and they knew each other out of professional courtesy and solidarity. Some, but not all, participated in the various ethnic organizations that were situated in Texas, such as LULAC and the American GI Forum.

[32]Memorandum denying motion to quash indictments, October 4, 1951, Case No. 2091, 24th District Court, Jackson County, Texas, reprinted in Olivas, COLORED MEN, at App. III.

[33]George I. Sánchez had been active in the Delgado case, which Cadena and García tried, and he encouraged the lawyers to mount the same systematic attack on the segregation and caste status of Mexican Americans in Texas that the NAACP Legal Defense Fund was mounting on a national basis for African Americans. Neil Foley, Over the Rainbow: Hernandez v. Texas, Brown v. Board of Education, and Black v. Brown, 25 CHICANO-LATINO L. REV. 139, 146–148 (2005).

[34]For an appraisal of Sanchez's record in his native New Mexico, see PHILLIP B. GONZALES, FORCED SACRIFICE AS ETHNIC PROTEST: THE HISPANO CAUSE IN NEW MEXICO & THE RACIAL ATTITUDE CONFRONTATION OF 1933, at 174–80 (2001) (recounting University of New Mexico protest involving Sanchez and others). See also HUMANIDAD: ESSAYS IN HONOR OF GEORGE I. SANCHEZ (Americo Paredes ed., 1977).

even entered into correspondence with Thurgood Marshall as both Mexican American and African American legal strategies were progressing on parallel tracks.[35] The time was such that several prominent NAACP Legal Defense Fund victories had clearly begun to erode the American apartheid system in higher education and college admissions, such as requiring the University of Texas and Oklahoma State University to admit Black applicants.[36]

On October 8-11, 1951, Pete Hernandez was tried by all-white jury, and at the end of the trial was convicted of murder with malice aforethought and on October 11, was sentenced to life imprisonment.[37] On June 18, 1952, the Texas Court of Criminal Appeals affirmed the judgment.[38] On October 22, 1952, that Court refused a rehearing on the jury selection issue.[39] After discussions with local League of United Latin American Citizens (LULAC) councils and community members, the attorneys decided to reach for the brass ring. While the actual fact pattern in *Sanchez* would have presented a better case than did this particular murder case, a variety of factors had come together and persuaded the attorneys that they should take the case to the next level, the U.S. Supreme Court. At that time, no Mexican American lawyer had ever pleaded a case before that Court.

They had no objective reason to think that the Court would accept their petition for certiorari or that they would prevail, although there was a general feeling that things were slowly getting better. For example, they had watched with great interest as the University of Texas was forced to open itself to Heman Sweatt, striking down the inadequate alternative law school that the State had hurriedly fashioned to accommodate Negro students on the grounds that it was not substantially equal.[40] Three of the team of four had themselves attended the UT Law School, in whatever

---

[35]Foley, supra note 47, at 146–48. See generally GUADALUPE SAN MIGUEL, "LET ALL OF THEM TAKE HEED": MEXICAN AMERICANS AND THE CAMPAIGN FOR EDUCATIONAL EQUALITY IN TEXAS, 1910–1981 (1987); RUBEN DONATO, THE OTHER STRUGGLE FOR EQUAL SCHOOLS: MEXICAN AMERICANS IN THE CIVIL RIGHTS ERA (1997). For an interesting comparison of Gustavo Garcia and Thurgood Marshall, as well as information on the Sgt. Macario Garcia case, see Lupe S. Salinas, Gus Garcia and Thurgood Marshall: Two Legal Giants Fighting for Justice, 28 THUR. M. L. REV. 145 (2003). He notes that Garcia also had a general commercial practice in San Antonio. *Id.* at 146, at fn. 8.

[36]McLaurin v. Bd. of Regents, 339 U.S. 637 (1950); Sweatt v. Painter, 339 U.S. 629 (1950). See generally Michael A. Olivas, Brown and the Desegregative Ideal: Higher Education, Location, and Racial College Identity, 90 CORNELL L. REV. 101 (2005) (reviewing higher education cases leading to Brown). There are literally dozens of works detailing the history of Brown. Some of the best include: Richard Kluger, Simple Justice: The History of Brown v. Board of Education and Black America's Struggle for Equality (1976); Bernard Schwartz, Super Chief: Earl Warren and His Supreme Court— A Judicial Biography (1983); Mark V. Tushnet, The NAACP's Legal Strategy Against Segregated Education, 1925-1950 (1987); Mark V. Tushnet, Making Civil Rights Law: Thurgood Marshall and the Supreme Court, 1936-1961 (1994); Robert J. Cottrol, Raymond T. Diamond, and Leland B. Ware, Brown v. Board of Education: Caste, Culture, and the Constitution (2003); Dennis J. Hutchinson, Unanimity and Desegregation: Decisionmaking in the Supreme Court, 1948-1958, 68 Geo. L.J. 1 (1979); Bernard Schwartz, Chief Justice Rehnquist, Justice Jackson, and the Brown Case, 1988 Sup. Ct. Rev. 245; Mark Tushnet, with Katya Lezin, What Really Happened in Brown v. Board of Education, 91 Colum. L. Rev. 1867 (1991); Kenneth W. Mack, Rethinking Civil Rights Lawyering and Politics in the Era before Brown, 115 YALE L. J. 256 (2005). None of these meticulous studies mentions Hernandez, except in passing.

[37]251 S.W. 2d 531 (1952).

[38]*Id.*

[39]Reprinted in Olivas, COLORED MEN, at App. XXX.

[40]Sweatt, 339 U.S. 629. See AMILCAR SHABAZZ, ADVANCING DEMOCRACY: AFRICAN AMERICANS AND THE STRUGGLE FOR ACCESS AND EQUITY IN HIGHER EDUCATION IN TEXAS (2004).

fashion, and its doors were being ordered fully opened.[41] Gus Garcia in particular was anxious to take the case further. Although he had developed a serious problem with alcoholism and was very feisty, he was a brilliant orator and eager to push this issue as far as they could take it. They felt that the Sanchez case and its appeals had been good practice, and that they were sharpening their tools. They had taken notice of the bathroom signage in the Jackson County Courthouse, and knew that the government attorneys had noticed, and vowed to include the facts in their briefs.[42] Local LULAC councils and other groups in the community promised to raise money for the effort. For example, Albert Armendariz, one of the few Mexican American lawyers in El Paso, offered to use LULAC funds to help with the effort.[43] They knew that it would take thousands of dollars they did not have at their disposal to file and prepare this case. None of them were even admitted to the Supreme Court bar, so they had to find a member to sponsor them for membership.[44]

By the end of the year 1952, they had made the collective decision to appeal the case beyond the State, and on January 21, 1953, they filed a petition for writ of certiorari with U.S. Supreme Court, including the $900 filing fee.[45] As they waited to hear whether they would be allowed to argue their appeal, all the lawyers went about their business, continuing to represent civil and criminal clients in courts across the State of Texas. They knew that if the case were held over for argument, it would be on a fast track and would require their full attention. In October, 1953, the philan-

---

[41]Gus Garcia had graduated from the UT Law School in 1938; Carlos Cadena in 1940 (summa cum laude, with what was at the time the highest grade point average ever accumulated there); and James de Anda in 1950. For a review of the UT Law School experience for Mexican Americans at the time, see Lisa Lizette Barrera, Minorities and the University of Texas Law School (1950-1980), 4 Tex. Hisp. J. of L. & Pol. 99 (1998) (noting that fewer than 20 Mexicans Americans graduated from UTLS before 1950, including the first two in 1932).

[42]As the attorneys took breaks during the trial, the white State's attorneys used the white restrooms, marked "Men," while the Hernandez attorneys went to the basement and used the bathroom marked "Colored Men and Hombres Aqui [Men Here]." Hernandez v. Texas, 347 U.S. 475, 479–80 (1954).

[43]Discussion with Albert Armendariz (Sept., 2004). The various files of the attorneys in this case contain many references to the fundraising. For one representative example, John Herrera wrote to a national LULAC official recounting various costs and quotidian details of the case and its preparation. Letter from John Herrera to Luciano Santoscoy (May 15, 1954) (on file at Houston Metropolitan Research Center, John J. Herrera papers, Box 2, Folder 24). Carlos Cadena and George Sanchez also corresponded about this issue, as Cadena had arranged to get the briefs filed and the court costs paid, with money from the Marshall Trust. Letter from George I. Sanchez to Carlos Cadena (Oct. 2, 1953) (on file at University of Texas Benson Latin American Collection, George I. Sanchez papers, Box 9, folder 2); Letter from Carlos Cadena to George I. Sanchez (May 6, 1954) (on file at University of Texas Benson Latin American Collection, George I. Sanchez papers, Box 9, folder 2).

[44]Letter from James de Anda to Clerk, U.S. Supreme Court (Dec. 1, 1953) (on file at Houston Metropolitan Research Center, John J. Herrera papers, Box 2, Folder 24). Herrera wrote of it being "a very proud moment" when he was sworn in, having been sponsored by then-Sen. Price Daniel. Letter from John Herrera to J.C. Machuca (Jan. 19, 1954) (on file at Houston Metropolitan Research Center, John J. Herrera papers, Box 2, Folder 24); Letter from John Herrera to J.C. Machuca (May 15, 1954) (on file at Houston Metropolitan Research Center, John J. Herrera papers, Box 2, Folder 24); Letter from John Herrera to Luciano Santoscoy (May 15, 1954) (on file at Houston Metropolitan Research Center, John J. Herrera papers, Box 2, Folder 24).

[45]Letter from George I. Sánchez to Carlos Cadena (Oct. 2, 1953) (on file at Houston Metropolitan Research Center, John J. Herrera papers, Box 2, Folder 24); Letter from Carlos Cadena to George I. Sánchez (May 6, 1954) (on file at Houston Metropolitan Research Center, John J. Herrera papers, Box 2, Folder 24).

thropic Marshall Trust donated $5000 for civil rights trials; the funds were to be disbursed by George I. Sánchez, according to his discretion.[46] Various local LULAC councils and individuals donated funds for printing, and filing costs, in the event that the case was chosen. The lawyers also discussed other such test cases, in the event that this one did not get chosen, although they could not imagine a better set of facts on which to challenge jury selction. While there was moral support and some financial support from Latino organizations, the case was not an organization-driven initiative, such as those being carefully chosen by the Legal Defense Fund as systemic assaults upon segregation. A drunken barroom brawl and club-footed murderer were not the poster children or symbolic choices for such a strategy; Norman Rockwell would not be painting pictures of Pete Hernandez. This was a bread and butter murder trial that through accidents of timing and opportunity ripened into the extraordinary. Moreover, LULAC was a very decentralized organization with no central office and no official capacity to hire lawyers, bring lawsuits, or undertake legal actions.[47]

Their patience and preparation were rewarded when on October 12, 1953, certiorari was granted for the case to be heard that term.[48] The Court also granted cert on the well-known school desegregation cases, which had been consolidated and styled *Brown v. Board of Education*, and which were being reargued after the death of Chief Justice Fred Vinson.[49] Brown was the first case in alphabetical order, and national and international attention were focused on that set of cases, which had been carefully selected and prepared for the final assault on segregation. To an extent, the case of Pete Hernandez flew under the radar, not attracting the massive attention accorded *Brown* and the Legal Defense Fund's longstanding and meticulous agenda.[50]

When it came time to go to D.C. for the arguments, the Hernandez team only had funds to send Garcia, Cadena, and Herrera; as the junior partner, de Anda

---

[46]Letter from George I. Sánchez to Carlos Cadena (May 13, 1954) (on file at University of Texas Benson Latin American Collection, George I. Sanchez papers, Box 9, folder 2) (conveying check for $500).

[47]*Id.* Because the records from this era are incomplete and because almost all the parties have died without leaving fuller oral histories, there are discrepancies in the narratives regarding the extent to which this was a "LULAC case." Neil Foley, a careful scholar who has consulted the archival materials surrounding the case has suggested that "two Mexican American civil rights organizations, LULAC (League of United Latin American Citizens) and the American GI Forum, challenged lower court rulings", while Benjamin Marquez, who has written the authoritative history of LULAC, characterized the case as having been brought by "LULAC lawyers" who "volunteered their time and effort for LULAC". My reading of the litigation record is that this was not a LULAC or an AGIF case, even though it was litigated by lawyers with varying degrees of LULAC (and to an even lesser extent, AGIF) involvement. See Neil Foley, Ch. 16, Straddling the Color Line: The Legal Construction of Hispanic Identity in Texas, in NANCY FONER AND GEORGE M. FREDERICKSON, EDS. NOT JUST BLACK AND WHITE (2005) AT 345; BENJAMIN MARQUEZ, LULAC, THE EVOLUTION OF A MEXICAN AMERICAN ORGANIZATION (1993), AT 55. GUADALUPE SAN MIGUEL, JR., IN LET ALL OF THEM TAKE HEED": MEXICAN AMERICANS AND THE CAMPAIGN FOR EDUCATION EQUALITY IN TEXAS, 1910-1981 (1987) makes a compelling argument that LULAC and other Mexican American organizations did play a more formal role in bringing education cases generally, but the evidence does not make Hernandez part of this tradition.

[48]Hernandez v. Texas, 346 U.S. 811 (1953) (granting certiorari).

[49]In 1952, the Court had accepted and consolidated the various appeals in the school desegregation cases, and invited the attorneys in Bolling v. Sharpe, 347 U.S. 497 (1954) to expedite direct appeal to the Court. The first arguments were heard in December, 1952, and in June, 1953 were restored to the docket for rehearing. Brown v. U.S., 347 U.S. 483 (1954).

[50]For a review of the publicity, see, e.g., Cottroll, Ware, Diamond, supra note 93, at 101-118.

remained in Texas to mind the store and continue the trials that were still ongoing. In a later pamphlet designed to publicize the case, Garcia wrote about that time:

> The following country bumpkins went to Washington: Attorneys (1) Cadena, (2) Herrera and (3) Garcia participated in this case before the Supreme Court of the U. S. Messrs. Cadena and Garcia presented the oral arguments, and Mr. Herrera, sitting at counsel table, assisted in the organization of the arguments and the preparation of the notes, made suggestions and rendered memoes as the case progressed before the Court. (4) Mr. Abel Cisneros, courageous radio commentator of Wharton, Texas, who went along because the substantial sum contributed by his home town was conditioned upon his accompanying Mr. Herrera. He took copious notes and, after he came home, rendered a lengthy report over the radio to the people of East Texas. (5) Mr. Manuel B. Lopez of San Antonio, a graduate attorney, who is at present serving his hitch in the Army in Virginia, was very helpful to us, guiding us around Washington, and faithfully carrying out all the duties of an all-round "leg man." (6) Mr. Anthony (Tony) Garcia, Director of Municipal Markets of San Antonio, attended as an observer for the Lulacs, on his vacation time and at his own personal expense. His moral support, his encouragement, and his timely suggestions were invaluable to us. (7) Mr. Chris Aldrete, Chairman of the American G. I. Forum. Though too recent a law graduate to be presented to the Court, he, too, was very helpful. We all stayed at the Mayflower Hotel, which is neither higher nor cheaper than any other first class hospice in Washington. The average rate per person is $10.00 a day. After Tony Garcia, Johnny Herrera, and Abel Cisneros arrived, the writer moved into a suite with them, which cost us $36.00 per day. The undersigned slept on a couch in the living room, which, however, was far more comfortable and luxurious than many a bed in which he has slept in his day. Tony Garcia stretched out his hefty frame on a roll-away bed. By obtaining this suite, we actually saved at least a dollar per person per day and at the same time had a decent place to hold meetings among ourselves, with members of the press, and with some friends from Washington, who guided us and assisted us, and who deserve our sincerest thanks.[51]

On January 11, 1954, Gus Garcia and Carlos Cadena argued Hernandez; in what was unprecedented at the time, Garcia was given 12 minutes more than was usually allowed for oral arguments. According to observers, he was brilliant in his oratory.[52] Two weeks later, *Brown* was argued before the same Court by Thurgood Marshall, with a much larger audience and international attention devoted to his efforts. On May 3, 1954, Justice Warren delivered the unanimous opinion of the Court, overturning the trial result and the Texas Court of Criminal Appeals decision.[53]

---

[51]A Cotton Picker Finds Justice!, reprinted in Olivas, COLORED MEN, at App. VIII.

[52]Letter to the Editor, Houston Post, Feb. 22, 1972, John J. Herrera [setting out many details of the case] (on file at Houston Metropolitan Research Center, John J. Herrera papers, Box 2, Folder 24). At the Supreme Court hearing, Herrera served as timekeeper for Cadena and Garcia. Only the three of them were at the Hernandez table.

[53]Hernandez v. Texas, 347 U.S. 475 (1954).

On May 7, 1954, Texas Department of Corrections notified the Jackson County Sheriff that Pete Hernandez (No. 124147) was to be handed over to Jackson County for the re-trial.[54] Because he had a disability (a severely clubbed foot), Hernandez had never been handed over to a state prison or put into a general population; instead, he had been sequestered in the Jackson County jail all that period of time. On June 10, 1954, the case was formally remanded to the Texas Court of Criminal Appeals, and on June 14, 1954, the remanded case was filed in the Texas Court of Criminal Appeals.[55] In the meantime, Texas juries were being reconstituted to select Mexican American jurors, although this was met with considerable foot-dragging in many jurisdictions. On September 28, 1954, Hernandez was re-indicted, and on October 16, Gus Garcia filed a change of venue motion; the retrial was moved to Refugio County, near Corpus Christi.[56] On November 15, 1954, the second trial was held, with Gus Garcia arguing the case.[57] Even with a more representative jury, Pete Hernandez was again found guilty, and was sentenced to 20 years, although there is evidence that this was a "pickup-jury" trial, where the jury was aware of the arrangement to reduce the sentence, for show.[58] He served the sentence in Harlem State Prison Farm, as inmate No. 136125.

Flash forward five years and all the parties had moved on to other matters. Cadena had become the first Mexican American law professor, joining the St. Mary's law faculty in San Antonio, and then becoming that city's City Attorney. In 1964, he would also argue another case before the Supreme Court, in a case involving a Puerto Rican, *Lopez v. Texas.*[59] Johnny Herrera and James de Anda returned to their practice in Houston, and then de Anda moved to Corpus Christi, in January 1955, where he established a very successful civil practice.[60] Gus Garcia fell on hard times, but

---

[54]Pete Hernandez is Re-Indicted By Jury, The Edna Herald, September 28, 1954, p. 1.

[55]Pete Hernandez is Re-Indicted By Jury, The Edna Herald, September 28, 1954, p. 1.

[56]Garcia Will Ask For Venue Change in Pete Hernandez Trial, The Edna Herald, May 27, 1954, p. 1; Pete Hernandez is Re-Indicted By Jury, The Edna Herald, September 28, 1954, p. 1. The article lists all the indictments handed down by that grand jury, which included 12 persons, two of them apparently Latinas (Ysabel Barron and Sesoria Rodriguez). See also, Murder Trial May Be Nov. 15, The Edna Herald, October 21, 1954, p. 1. Refugio County is near Corpus Christi, and has a long history of anti-Mexican prejudice. See generally HOBART HUSON, REFUGIO: A COMPREHENSIVE HISTORY OF REFUGIO COUNTY FROM ABORIGINAL TIMES TO 1953 (2 vols., 1953 & 1955).

[57]Hernandez Due Parole, [San Antonio] La Prensa, June 15, 1960, p. 1.

[58]Hernandez Due Parole, June 15, 1960, p. 1. In a 1977 interview, Herrera was quoted as saying that Hernandez had received a 10 year sentence and that he had only served eight months of the sentence. Richard Vara, Dedicated Defendant,Lawyers Made Constitutional History, Houston Post, 27 November 1977, at 9. The parole correspondence records reveal that Hernandez was in prison until 1960. James de Anda characterized the 1954 re-trial as a "pickup-jury," one designed to effectuate a plea bargain. Inasmuch as the U.S. Supreme Court had ordered the defendant tried by a more-representative jury, state officials were likely more conscientious in this re-trial than would have ordinarily been the case. Conversation with James de Anda, February 2006.

[59]In Lopez v. Texas, 378 U.S. 567 (1964) Cadena was the attorney for the petitioner, while in Congregation of Sisters of Charity v. San Antonio, 372 U.S. 967 (1963), he was co-counsel for the respondent, and the Supreme Court denied certiorari.

[60]James de Anda and Gus Garcia later tried an important school desegregation case together, Herminia Hernandez v. Driscoll Cons. ISD, 2 Race Rel. L. Rep. 329 (1957) [unpublished opinion, S. D. Tex. Civ. No. 1384]. Ironically, the Judge in the case was James Allred, who had served as Macario Garcia's lawyer a dozen years earlier in the final stages of his Richmond restaurant matter. Garcia so antagonized the federal judge in this case that he was not allowed to speak in court, so James de Anda made objections on the record; the formal filings also listed Richard Casillas and Albert Pena, Jr. as co-counsel. 2 Race Rel. L. Rep. 34 (1957) de Anda later was appointed to serve as a federal judge, becoming the second such Mexican American appointment in the United States (after Reynaldo Garza) and the first who rose to become chief judge (in the Southern District of Texas, Houston offices). In his 80s, he remains in private practice in Houston.

maintained his practice in San Antonio and other cities, including Houston for a short time, as he partnered with Herrera in the late 1950's. Apparently his conscience provoked him, as in 1960 he began to track down the whereabouts of Pete Hernandez, who was still serving his term. He lobbied the State parole authorities and organized efforts to write letters on behalf of his former client.[61] He succeeded on June 7, 1960, when Hernandez was recommended for parole by TX Board of Pardons and Paroles. The next day, he was paroled and released by order of Gov. Price Daniel.[62] On that day, Garcia wrote a letter to Hernandez, urging him, "We all make mistakes in this life, Pete, and yours was a terrible one. But I do not want you to think of the past. You are still young and your whole life is ahead of you . . . More than anything else, I want you to hold that temper of yours in check. If you feel that you are starting to get mad, just think of all those long years in jail and in prison and RUN, don't walk, away from trouble."[63]

On June 3, 1964, Garcia was found dead in a San Antonio market bench, where he had been unnoticed for several hours.[64] Pete Hernandez is even more obscure, and

---

[61]For example, on February 1, 1960, he wrote John Herrera, "Particularly, I would like to know when Hernandez was released and what he is doing now. Don't put this off, John . . . ." Letter from Gus Garcia to John J. Herrera (Feb. 1, 1960) (on file at Houston Metropolitan Research Center, John J. Herrera papers, Box 2, Folder 24). Upon discovering that Hernandez had been in the Harlem State Prison Farm since the second trial, Garcia wrote to the head of the State Board of Pardons and Paroles, on February 12, 1960, "I feel really conscience-stricken, Jack [Ross], about this matter, and I would like to do everything possible within my power to gain freedom for this boy who was willing to risk a possible death sentence upon the second trial of his case in order to help us establish a very important principle of law and civil rights for Latin Americans everywhere." Letter from Gus Garcia to State Board of Pardons and Paroles (Feb. 12, 1960) (on file at Houston Metropolitan Research Center, John J. Herrera papers, Box 2, Folder 24). After the Board acted, he wrote many parties on June 8, 1960, "While I do not wish to claim credit for the final conclusion of our historical issue, I have pestered Jack Ross for several months now via letters, long distance calls, and two personal visits in Austin. I can now truthfully say that my conscience is clear in this matter." Letters from Gus Garcia (on file at Houston Metropolitan Research Center, John J. Herrera papers, Box 2, Folder 24).

[62]Letter to the Editor, Houston Post, Feb. 22, 1972, John J. Herrera [setting out many details of the case] (on file at Houston Metropolitan Research Center, John J. Herrera papers, Box 2, Folder 24). Before he became Texas Governor, U.S. Senator Price Daniel had sponsored several of the Hernandez attorneys for membership to the Supreme Court bar. Carlos Cadena had been sponsored by U.S. Rep. Paul Kilday. Group Seeks Latins on Jury, San Antonio Light, Jan. 5, 1954, p. 6.

[63]He also offered to assist should he get into trouble, and provided his home and office phone numbers to him. Letter from Gus Garcia to Pete Hernandez (June 8, 1960) (on file at Houston Metropolitan Research Center, John J. Herrera papers, Box 2, Folder 24). (Emphasis in original).

[64]Reading the various materials concerning Gus Garcia's alcoholism is a sad task. For example, in a heartbreaking letter to Dr. George Sánchez, Cadena writes in early December, 1953, "Gus is apparently on the wagon, at least for the time being. He told me that he was not going to touch a drop until after January 4 [the day of the Supreme Court arguments] . . . Some time back I had a long talk with Nora [Garcia, Gus Garcia's then-wife]. That was during the time that Gus was off on a toot, and she was quite worried about him. Anyway, somebody gave him a little lecture, because he told me of his plan to stay sober, he mentioned that things had reach[ed] a horrible state when your own family was afraid that you would make a jackass out of yourself before the Supreme Court. Of course, I don't know how long he will continue in his present frame of mind." Letter from Carlos Cadena to George I. Sánchez (Dec., 1953) (on file at University of Texas Benson Latin American Collection, George I. Sánchez papers, Box 9, folder 2). In what may have been among his final letters to Herrera, he wrote, "This is the final turning point in my life, and whether I choose the right road or end up in the gutter or a suicide depends largely on the few friends I have left . . . " Letter from Gus Garcia to John Herrera (January 28, 1963) (on file at Houston Metropolitan Research Center, John J. Herrera papers, Box 2, folder 20). He was later hospitalized in Waco, lost his law license, and died unnoticed for hours on a bench in a San Antonio market. He was 48. Paul Thompson, San Antonio Evening News, June 14, 1964, 2A.

if he died, he did so without public notice of his passing.[65] Much as the case itself was hidden by the bright light of the more famous *Brown*, so it remained obscure for many years.

Conclusion

Unlike its more well-known companion case, *Brown v. Board of Education, Hernandez v. Texas* had more pedestrian, more campesino roots: a drunken barroom brawl and a club-footed murder suspect. Its arc was a shooting in Ft. Bend to a shooting in Edna, Texas. The Aniceto Sánchez trial became a test-case, a run-up, as the lawyers decided to attack the jury system itself, as the only possible way to ensure a fair trial for their clients. The lawyers who took and argued the cases were not long-time collaborators, but general practitioners in a system that rendered them and their largely Mexican origin clients few opportunities. They had few ties before they came together to try this case, and they never tried a major case together again afterwards. While there was some financial and political support from Latino organizations, these organizations were not situated in a manner that provided concerted legal support, and they had never rallied behind a murder trial. The courts were so hostile that Mexicans were not called for juries, and the rural towns were so inhospitable that the lawyers trying a murder case could not safely find housing in the county seat. The State of Texas had fewer than two dozen Mexican-American lawyers in active practice when the crime was committed, and no true legal services network to assist in trying such complex cases. There was local press coverage, but none that rallied to the side of the cause of jury composition. No Mexican-American lawyers had ever tried a case before the United States Supreme Court, and the lawyers were not even sworn into the Supreme Court bar. It would be fifteen years before these same lawyers and others rallied to establish the Mexican American Legal Defense and Educational Fund in 1968—modeled on the LDF/Inc. Fund[66]—an organization that would later provide the structure and resources for strategic litigation on behalf of the larger Latino community, including a 1982 Supreme Court victory for MALDEF client undocumented children, a case that bore all the earmarks of a strategic organizational effort.[67]

There had been earlier efforts to diversify juries, reaching back at least to the trial of Gregorio Cortez in 1901, and there would be later efforts to strike down unrepresentative juries, including efforts by the legendary Oscar Zeta Acosta in Los

---

[65]Tad Walch, Anti-Bias Ruling Hailed, DESERET MORNING NEWS, May 3, 2004 (interview with author of forthcoming Hernandez biography, noting that no authoritative record exists of his death). He was to move to Port LaVaca, Texas after the release from prison. Letter from Gus Garcia to Pete Hernandez (June 8, 1960) (on file at Houston Metropolitan Research Center, John J. Herrera papers, Box 2, Folder 24). James de Anda heard from Jackson County residents that Hernandez became a prison barber, and practiced this trade after his release, and that he had died in the 1970's. Discussions with James de Anda (Nov. 2005).

[66]For a brief history of the founding of MALDEF, see San Miguel, supra note 47, at pp. 169-172.

[67]For a detailed study of the litigation history of this case, see Michael A. Olivas, Plyler v. Doe, the Education of Undocumented Children, and the Polity, in David A. Martin and Peter H. Schuck, eds. IMMIGRATION STORIES 197-220 (2005).

Angeles in the 1960s,[68] and by 2005, there was clear evidence that Latino participation in the Texas jury system was still substantially unrepresentative of the growing population.[69] But in a brief and shining moment in 1954, Mexican American lawyers prevailed in a system that accorded their community no legal status and no respect. Through sheer tenacity, brilliance, and some luck, they showed that it is possible to tilt against windmills and to slay the dragon.

These stories are not a part of the collective consciousness, and although there are very detailed histories of Jim Crow Texas and Mexican Jim Crow Texas, the details of the *Hernandez* case have not made their way into scholarly discourse or public lore. As I write in late 2005, there is not in print a single full length book on any of these extraordinary lawyers, or of this case. The work is drawn from a variety of sources, as noted in the voluminous footnotes, but I acknowledge that a full understanding and situating of this case is still in the early stages. I am hopeful that the occasion of fifty years passing will correct this sad record.

---

[68]As early as 1901, the lawyer for Gregorio Cortez called attention to the jury pool in this famous case. See "Gregorio Cortez's Trial. Motion for a Change of Venue Being Heard," DALLAS MORN. NEWS, 5 Oct. 1901 [App. IX]; Richard J. Mertz, "No One Can Arrest Me," The Story of Gregorio Cortez, 1 J. of SOUTH TEX. 1 (1974). For studies of the series of 1960s jury cases, see Ian Haney Lopez, RACISM ON TRIAL: THE CHICANO FIGHT FOR JUSTICE (2003) and Michael A. Olivas, Breaking the Law on Principle: An Essay on Lawyers' Dilemmas, Unpopular Causes, and Legal Regimes, 52 U. PITT. L. REV. 570 (1992).

[69]For a recent study of Houston-area juries and the problems of underrepresentation, see Larry Karson, The Implications of a Key-Man System for Selecting a Grand Jury: An Exploratory Study, 3 SW J. of CRIM. JUST. (forthcoming, 2006).

APPENDICES

Appendix I

Aniceto Sanchez v. State
156 Tex.Crim. 468, 243 S.W.2d 700 (1951)

Nov. 21, 1951

Aniceto Sanchez was convicted in the District Court, Fort Bend County, T. M. Gupton, J., of murder and defendant appealed. The Court of Criminal Appeals, Beauchamp, J., held that bill of exception which did not certify that argument of prosecuting attorney was not in reply to improper argument made by defendant's counsel was fatally defective.

Affirmed.

John J. Herrera, James De Anda, Houston, for appellant.

George P. Blackburn, State's Atty., of Austin, for the State.

BEAUCHAMP, Judge.

The appellant was convicted for murder and assessed a penalty of ten years in the penitentiary.

The evidence discloses that appellant, a Mexican, was a farm worker and lived on a large plantation in a cottage within a few feet of that occupied by the deceased. On the night of the tragedy, shortly after twelve o'clock, the deceased came up to the residence of appellant where he was engaged with others in drinking beer. He was singing a song in Mexican which, interpreted, is entitled 'You, Only You' and is said to be a Mexican love song. Apparently this incensed appellant who, without any words, went into his house, got his gun, came out and shot, killing the deceased a short distance from his front door steps. About this there is no controversy.

Appellant testified in his own behalf but we find no complaint about the submission of any issue raised by his testimony.

[1] The case is submitted on three bills of exception. The first, upon which reliance seems to be had, complains that there was violation of the due process clause in that there was a systematic, continual and uninterrupted practice in Fort Bend County of discriminating against the Mexican-Americans as a race, and people of Mexican extraction and ancestry as a class, in the selection of grand jury commissioners and grand jurors.

Appellant has filed quite an exhaustive brief on the subject in which he discusses decisions of other jurisdictions which, either intentionally or loosely, refer to Mexican people as a different race. They are not a separate race but are white people of Spanish descent, as has often been said by this court. We find no ground for discussing the question further and the complaint raised by this bill will not be sustained.

Appellant concedes that Bill of Exception No. 2, as qualified by the court, does not show error.

[2] Bill No. 3 complains of argument of the prosecuting attorney. This bill is fatally defective in that it does not certify that the argument was not in reply to argument made by defendant's counsel. The statement made is that it 'was not made in reply to any improper argument of counsel for the defendant.'

This may be taken to concede that it was in reply to argument and, if so, it is immaterial as to whether it was in reply to proper or improper argument, unless it should be shown that the argument itself was improper. This is not done by the bill under consideration.

[3] We think, too, that the interpretation of the argument is incorrect in that it is contended that the argument amounted to unsworn testimony by the state's attorney. He was commenting on the things that transpired in the witness box in the presence of the jury, in the proper conduct of the trial of the case, and sought to draw a conclusion which was not satisfactory to appellant's counsel. The jury had viewed the things which counsel was discussing and he was asking them to see it as he did. We do not interpret this to be evidence on his part as to what happened. We see no error.

Finding no reversible error the judgment of the trial court is affirmed.

Appendix II

Aniceto Sanchez Briefs

NO. 7103

STATE OF TEXAS	)	IN THE DISTRICT COURT OF
	)	
VS.	)	FORT BEND COUNTY
	)	
ANICETO SANCHEZ	)	23rd JUDICIAL DISTRICT
		_____TERM, A. D., 1951

BILL OF EXCEPTION NO. 1

BE IT REMEMBERED that on the 19th day of March, 1951, in advance of the calling of the above numbered and entitled cause for trial, and before pleading to the indictment therein, the Defendant, by counsel, filed the following verified motion to quash the indictment, to-wit:

NO. 7103

STATE OF TEXAS	)	IN THE DISTRICT COURT OF
	)	
VS.	)	FORT BEND COUNTY
	)	
ANICETO SANCHEZ	)	23rd JUDICIAL DISTRICT

TO THE HONORABLE JUDGE OF SAID COURT:

Comes now ANICETO SANCHEZ, Defendant in the above numbered and entitled cause, and in open court, before said cause is called for trial, and before said Defendant has pleaded to the indictment herein in his own proper person, and files this, his MOTION TO QUASH the indictment herein, and, in support of and as a ground for said motion, would respectfully show this Honorable Court the following:

I

That this Defendant, an American citizen, is a member of a class known as Mexican-Americans, that is, an American citizen of Mexican descent or Mexican extraction.

II

That the offense charged in the indictment herein is alleged to have been committed by the Defendant on the 23rd day of April, 1950: that the Grand Jury which returned said indictment was empaneled on the 1st day of May, 1950, and that a period of only eight days elapsed from the occurrence of the alleged offense until the empaneling of said jury. That during said period of time from the

227

-2-

alleged commission of the offense, to and subsequent to the empaneling
of said Grand Jury, the Defendant herein who is uneducated and speaks
little English, was suffering from severe mental shock and was under
severe mental strain and that as a result the condition of said Defendant's mind was such as to render him incapable of protecting, asserting, requesting or demanding any legal right which might have accrued
to him during said period. That as a result of said state of mind the
Defendant herein made no effort and was incapable of making any effort
to obtain an attorney to act in his behalf and consequently said Defen-
had no legal counsel until subsequent to the empaneling of the Grand
Jury which indicted him. That due to the above causes said Defendant
had no opportunity to challenge the array of said Grand Jury at the
time it was empaneled.

III

That there has prevailed in Fort Bend County, Texas, for
a period of over thirty-five years, a systematic, continual and un-
interrupted practice of discrimination against Mexican-Americans as a
race, and people of Mexican extraction and ancestry as a class separate
from other white Americans, a class to which this Defendant belongs, in
the selection of Grand Jury Commissioners and Grand Jurors solely because of membership within that class, as follows:

1. That at no time within the past thirty-five years,
through and including the year in which this Defendant was indicted,
has a member of the Mexican-American class or an American of Mexican
descent, been appointed as a Grand Jury Commissioner in the Judicial
District of Fort Bend County of the State of Texas, and no member of
the said class has participated in the selection of any Grand Jury
in Fort Bend County during the said period; that this exclusion has
prevailed despite the fact that there have been members of that class
in said county at all times during this said thirty-five year period
capable of qualifying, and willing to serve as such Grand Jury
Commissioners under the laws of the State of Texas.

-3-

2. That at no time withint the past thirty-five years, through and including the year in which this Defendant was indicted, has a Mexican-American, an American citizen of Mexican descent, served on the Grand Jury of Fort Bend County, Texas; That no member of said class, to which this Defendant belongs, served on the Grand Jury which returned the indictment in this cause against this Defendant; That this continual and uniterrupted practice of excluding members of the Mexican-American class or American citizens of Mexican extraction was due only because said citizens were members of that class, and that this said practice during the said thirty-five year period has persisted despite the fact that approximately one-fourth of the population of Fort Bend County is of Mexican extraction or descent, that members of said class within said County number over 6,500 and have so numbered for many years; that during the entire thirty-five years period there have been many male citizens within said class in Fort Bend County, Texas which were domiciled in said County, were qualified voters therein, and were and are able to read and write the English language and are of good reputation, and were and are able to qualify and to meet all of the requirements regulating Grand Jurors under the laws and statutes of the State of Texas; and the said members of said class have been arbitrarily and systematically and deliberately excluded and ignored in the selection of Grand Jurors, and that this failure to include any members of said racial class, of which this Defendant is a member, as Grand Jury Commissioners to select Grand Jurors, and the repeated practice of failing to include any members of the Mexican-American class as Grand Jurors over this said period of time, and the exclusion of members of said class on the Grand Jury which indicted the Defendant, and said exclusions being motivated solely by the reason that said citizens were members of the Mexican-American class, said exclusions and practices are contrary to, and avoid and evade the equal protection clause of the Fourteenth Amendment of the Constitution of the United States and of the stautes of the State of Texas enacted pursuant thereto. That as well as being repugnant to the said Fourteenth Amendment, these said exclusions are contrary to the rulings of the Supreme Court of

-4-

the United States in Pierre v Louisiana, 306 U.S. 354, and Neal v State
of Delaware, 103 U.S. 370.

That the aforesaid acts, jointly and severally, and the
exclusion of Mexican-Americans or American citizens of Mexican descent
as alleged aforesaid, due solely to the fact that said citizens are
members of said class is a denial to the Affiant, the Defendant herein,
of the equal protection of the laws guaranteed to him by the Constitution of the United States, all of which this Affiant is ready to verify.

WHEREFORE, aforesaid premises considered, Affiant,
the Defendant herein, prays that the Court grant him a prompt hearing
hereon and that he be granted permission to introduce evidence, and that
upon said hearing that this MOTION TO QUASH the indictment herein be
sustained and that he be discharged with his costs, as he, in duty bound
will ever pray.

s/ John J. Herrera and James De Anda
Attorneys for Defendant

I, ANICETO SANCHEZ, Defendant in the above numbered
and entitled cause, hereby swear and affirm that the allegations contained in the foregoing MOTION TO QUASH are true and correct; so help
me God.

s/ Aniceto Sanchez
ANICETO SANCHEZ

Sworn and subscribed to befoe me, the undersigned authority at
Richmond, Fort Bend County, Texas, this the 19th day of March, A. D.,
1951.

s/ Aline Roane
District Clerk, Fort Bend County, Texas

Be it further remembered that the Defendant introduced
evidence and testimony in support of said motion. Be it further remembered that the State stipulated that said Defendant was of Mexican
descent.

Be it further remembered that the testimony established
that no American citizen of Mexican descent had served on a grand jury
in Fort Bend County, the County in which the indictment herein was re-

-5-

turned, within the memory of the witnesses who testified, and that said
witnesses had lived in the said County for periods ranging from twenty-
six years to fifty-one years.

Be it further remembered that the testimony of the Grand
Jury Commissioners which selected the grand jury which indicted the
Defendant herein, established that no American citizens of Mexican descent,
same being also called Latin-Americans, served on said grand jury,

Be it further remembered that W. L. Ansel, a witness
for the defendant and one of the Grand Jury Commissioners who selected
the grand jury which indicted the defendant herein, testified that people
of Mexican descent could be distinguished from other people merely by
looking at them; that Joe Hernandez, a witness for the defendant that
the Chamber of Commerce of Fort Bend County Report on population divided
said population of Fort Bend County into three groups, to-wit, one fifth
of the population was colored, one-fifth Latin-American and the other
three-fifths was placed in a third group. That said witness further testified that he was an undertaker and that his clientele was exclusively
Latin-American. It is the contention of the defendant herein that said
testimony establishes that American citizens of Mexican descent, same also
being referred to as Latin-Americans or "Mexicans", though members of the
white race, said class is not so considered in Fort Bend County.

Be it further remembered that testimony established during
said period when no Americans of Mexican descent served on the grand
juries in Fort Bend County, that said class or race made up from 15 per
cent to 20 per cent of the population of said county; that said total
population was about 32,500 of which 6400 were Latin-Americans. And that
testimony established that there were members of said class or race who
were qualified to serve as grand jurors and who were willing to serve
as same during this said period.

It is the contention of the Defendant herein that the
aforementioned testimony shows an exclusion of the class or race to which
the defendant blongs from service on the grand juries in Fort Bend County,
including the grand jury which returned the indictment in this cause against
said defendant, and that said exclusion is a denial to this Defendant of the
equal protection of the laws as guaranteed to him by the 14th Amendment of
the Constitution of the United States.

-6-

Be it further remembered that after hearing said testimony the Court overruled said motion to quash the indictment, to which ruling the Defendant, through his counsel, duly excepted, and tenders this bill of exception, and asks that the same be signed and filed as a part of the record in this case.

_____
Attorney for Defendant

The foregoing bill of exception No. 1 having been reduced to writing by counsel for defendant, and having been presented to the undersigned presiding judge of said court for allowance and signature within 80 days from the overruling of defendant's motion for new trial, and notice of appeal, said defendant having been granted an extension of time for the filing of the statement of facts and his bills of exception, and same being filed within the period prescribed in said extension of time, and within the time prescribed by law, and having been by me submitted to counsel for the State of Texas and found by him to be correct, and having been by me found to be correct, is hereby allowed, approved and ordered filed by the clerk of this court as a part of the record in such cause, this _22nd_ day of _June_____,
A. D., 1951.

B-27

No. ____7103_____

IN DISTRICT COURT.

_____Fort Bend_____County, Texas.

COPY OF SENTENCE

THE STATE OF TEXAS

vs.

_____Aniceto Sanchez_____

Crime_____Murder_____

    Not Less than two nor
Term__more than 10_____years.

Date sentenced__April 7,_____19 51

Plea____"Not Guilty"_____

2-39-1m

NO.   7103

THE STATE OF TEXAS	)	IN THE DISTRICT COURT OF
VS	)	FORT BEND COUNTY, TEXAS
ANICETO SANCHEZ	)	23rd JUDICIAL DISTRICT

BE IT REMEMBERED, that on the 29th day of March, 1951,
during the argument of counsel in the above numbered and entitled cause,
Counsel for the State made the following statement to the jury in his
closing argument:

"The attorney asked each one of you, and told each one
of you, said the Judge is going to charge you that a man has got a
right to kill another if he catches his wife with another man in adultery.
The Judge didn't charge you that, because it is not in this case. There
is a law that if you do catch a man right in the act and kill him before
he leaves there, that you would be justified. There is no intimation..."

At this point Counsel for Defendant objected to the said
argument on the ground that it was improper for Counsel for the State to
discuss an element of law that was not in the charge and defendant's
Counsel and requested the Court to instruct the jury to disregard the
said statement. The Court overruled the objection, and refused to so
instruct the jury, to which ruling counsel for defendant duly excepted.

Be it further remembered that immediately subsequent to
the overruling of said objection, counsel for the State continued as
follows:

"This attorney argued all of the way through that his
client had a right to kill Semersky because Semersky had caught him
under the bed. If that was the law, the Judge would have given it to
you in this charge and it is not in this charge; and, therefore, it is
not the law."

At this point counsel for Defendant again objected and
requested that the Court instruct the jury to disregard the statement,
said request was overruled, to which ruling Defendant's counsel duly
excepted.

Be it further remembered that Counsel for the State
was, in the aforementioned arguments, discussing law that was neither

-2-

in the evidence nor in the charge submitted by the Court to the jury;
that Defendant's counsel at no time during the trial argued that the Defendant had a right to kill Semersky. That the sole reference made by
Counsel for the Defendant to the law of justifiable homicide as pertains
to a man discovering his wife in an act of adultery with another occurred
during the examination of the special venire. Each juror was examined
and qualified on this element of the law of justifiable homicide. That
no evidence was presented during the course of the trial to justify
said defense, and no further reference was made to said element of the
law of justifiable homicide by the defense at any stage of the trial;
that no reference was made to said element of the law of justifiable
homicide by the State at any stage of the trial except in the aforementioned
argument to the jury.

Be it further remembered that said argument by Counsel
for the State was not made in rebuttal to improper argument by Defendant's
Counsel.

Be it further remembered that Defendant was entitled
to a charge of murder without malice, and that said charge was submitted
to the jury. That the only evidence on which the Defendant could rely to
establish the adequate provocation necessary to reduce the offense to
murder without malice was his own testimony that he, the Defendant, had
found his wife with the deceased under circumstances which would justify
a reasonable man under similar conditions to believe that his wife had
been engaged in an act of adultery with the deceased.

It is the contention of the defendant that aforesaid
argument by Counsel for the State tended to confuse and mislead the
jury to believe that the Court did not consider the defendant's testimony
true, and that said argument was therefore prejudicial and harmfully
affected the weight given to defendant's testimony establishing provocation.

Wherefore, Defendant, through his consel tenders this
bill of exception and asks that the same be signed and filed as a part
of the record in this case.

_James D. _____
Attorney for Defendant

B 37—COPY OF SENTENCE—CLASS 4   (Chapter 212, Acts of 40th Legislature)   Clarke & Courts, Houston-Dallas-Galveston

THE STATE OF TEXAS,

No. 7103   vs.

Aniceto Sanchez

IN THE DISTRICT COURT OF

Fort Bend ....County, Texas

Nov.-April
Term 19 51   April 7 19 51

This day this cause being again called, the State appeared by her District Attorney, and the
defendant Aniceto Sanchez

was brought into open Court in person, in

charge of the Sheriff, for the purpose of having the sentence of the law pronounced in accordance with the verdict
and judgment herein rendered and entered against him on a former day of this term. And thereupon the
defendant Aniceto Sanchez was asked by the Court whether he had any-
thing to say why said sentence should not be pronounced against him and he answered nothing in
bar thereof. Whereupon the Court proceeded, in the presence of the said defendant Aniceto Sanchez
to pronounce sentence against him as follows: It is the order of the Court that the defendant
Aniceto Sanchez who has been adjudged to be guilty of Murder

be delivered by the Sheriff of Fort Bend County, Texas, immediately to the Manager
of the Prison System of the State of Texas, or other person legally authorized to receive such convicts, and the
said Aniceto Sanchez shall be confined in said penitentiary for a term of
not less than 2 nor more than ten years in accordance with the provisions of the law governing the penitentiaries and the Prison System of the State. And the said Aniceto Sanchez
is hereby remanded to jail until said Sheriff can obey the directions of this sentence. To which defendant
then and there excepted and in open court gave notice of Appeal to the
Court of Criminal Appeals for the State of Texas. Further execution of
the Sentence is stayed until the court of criminal appeals have rendered
final judgment in this case.

THE STATE OF TEXAS.

County of Fort Bend

I, Aline C. Roane Clerk of the District Court
in and for the County of Fort Bend, State of Texas, hereby certify that the above is a true and
correct copy of the sentence in the above entitled cause, as appears of record in the Criminal Minutes of said Court,
in Vol. "C", page 623

WITNESS my hand and seal of office at Richmond, Texas this 16th. day
of April 19 51

Aline C. Roane

Clerk District Court, Fort Bend County, Texas.

By Bud C. Harwood Deputy.

ANICETO SANCHEZ, Appellant |

No. 25,496 | Appeal from Fort Bend County.

THE STATE OF TEXAS, Appellee |

O P I N I O N

The appellant was convicted for murder and assessed a penalty of ten years in the penitentiary.

The evidence discloses that appellant, a Mexican, was a farm worker and lived on a large plantation in a cottage within a few feet of that occupied by the deceased. On the night of the tragedy, shortly after twelve o'clock, the deceased came up to the residence of appellant where he was engaged with others in drinking beer. He was singing a song in Mexican which interpreted, is entitled "You, Only You" and is said to be a Mexican love song. Apparently this incensed appellant who, without any words, went into his house, got his gun, came out and shot, killing the deceased a short distance from his front door steps. About this there is no controversy.

Appellant testified in his own behalf but we find no complaint about the submission of any issue raised by his testimony.

The case is submitted on three bills of exception. The first, upon which reliance seems to be had, complains that there was violation of the due process clause in that there was a systematic, continual and uninterrupted practice in Fort Bend County of discriminating against the Mexican-Americans as a race, and people of Mexican extraction and ancestry as a class, in the selection of grand jury commissioners and grand jurors.

Appellant has filed quite an exhaustive brief on the subject in which he discusses decisions of other jurisdictions which, either intentionally or loosely, refer to Mexican people as a different race. They are not a separate race but are white people of Spanish descent, as has often been said by this court.

Sanchez
-2

We find no ground for discussing the question further and the complaint raised by this bill will not be sustained.

Appellant concedes that Bill of Exception No. 2, as qualified by the court, does not show error.

Bill No. 3 complains of argument of the prosecuting attorney. This bill is fatally defective in that it does not certify that the argument was not in reply to argument made by defendant's counsel. The statement made is that it "was not made in reply to any improper argument of counsel for the defendant." This may be taken to concede that it was in reply to argument and, if so, it is immaterial as to whether it was in reply to proper or improper argument, unless it should be shown that the argument itself was improper. This is not done by the bill under consideration.

We think, too, that the interpretation of the argument is incorrect in that it is contended that the argument amounted to unsworn testimony by the state's attorney. He was commenting on the things that transpired in the witness box in the presence of the jury, in the proper conduct of the trial of the case, and sought to draw a conclusion which was not satisfactory to appellant's counsel. The jury had viewed the things which counsel was discussing and he was asking them to see it as he did. We do not interpret this to be evidence on his part as to what happened. We see no error.

Finding no reversible error the judgment of the trial court is affirmed.

Beauchamp, Judge

(Delivered November 21, 1951.)

APPROVED, with the following qualifications:

I

The defendant placed several witnesses on the
stand who had served as Grand Jury Commissioners, and
each of them testified that the Grand Jury Commissioners
did not deliberately descriminate against the Latin-American
people in selecting their Grand Juries; that they selected
the Grand Jurors regardless of ancestry, race or color.

II

The defendant did not place anyone on the stand
who swore that there had not been Latin-Americans on the
Grand Juries in Fort Bend County, Texas; however, they did
place a witness on the stand who did testify that on the
Grand Jury that indicted this defendant that there was no
Latin-American on said Grand Jury.

Judge Presiding.

Defendant's Bill of Exception

APPROVED, with the following qualifications:

I

Defendant's counsel asked every man who was selected on the jury if he believed a man had a right to kill another man if he caught said man in the act of adultry; with his wife; and, further, told each juror that the Judge would give him that in his Charge, and it was this that State's counsel was alluding to when he made the statement to which the defense objected.

II

Defendant's counsel argued that his client had the right to kill Semersky because Semersky had been caught by him under his bed, and State's counsel argued to the jury that that was not the law, for had it been the law, the Judge would have so charged.

_____
                    Judge Presiding

Appendix III

Hernandez v. State of Texas
160 Tex.Crim. 72, 251 S.W.2d 531(1952)
[State decision]

June 18, 1952.

Rehearing Denied Oct. 22, 1952.

Defendant was convicted of murder. The District Court, Jackson County, Frank W. Martin, J., overruled defendant's motions to quash indictment and petit jury panel on grounds of denial of equal protection of the law, and defendant appealed. The Court of Criminal Appeals, Davidson, J., held that discrimination against defendant was not shown in organization of grand and petit juries.

Judgment affirmed.

Carlos C. Cadena, Gus C. Garcia, San Antonio, for appellant.

George P. Blackburn, State's Atty., Austin, for the State.

DAVIDSON, Commissioner.

Murder is the offense, with punishment assessed at life imprisonment in the penitentiary.

Appellant is a Mexican, or Latin American. He claims that he was discriminated against upon the trial of this case because members of the Mexican nationality were deliberately, systematically, and wilfully excluded from the grand jury that found and returned the indictment in this case and from the petit jury panel from which was selected the petit jury that tried the case. He sought, for said reasons, to quash the indictment and petit jury panel, claiming he had thereby been deprived of equal protection.

The action of the court in overruling the two motions presents the sole question for review.

In support of his contention, appellant relies upon the so-called rule of exclusion as announced by the Supreme Court of the United States—that is, that the long and continued failure to call members of the Negro race for jury service, where it is shown that members of that race were available and qualified for jury service, grand or petit, constitutes a violation of due process and equal protection against members of that race.

The rule appears to have been first announced in *Norris v. Alabama*, 294 U.S. 587, 55 S.Ct. 579, 79 L.Ed. 1074, and since then followed. See Smith v. Texas, 311 U.S. 128, 61 S.Ct. 164, 85 L.Ed. 84; Hill v. Texas, 316 U.S. 400, 62 S.Ct. 1159, 86 L.Ed.

241

1559; Cassell v. Texas, 339 U.S. 282, 70 S.Ct. 629, 94 L.Ed. 839; and Ross v. Texas, 341 U.S. 918, 71 S.Ct. 742, 95 L.Ed. 1352.

Appellant would have the above rule to extend to and apply to members of different nationalities—particularly to Mexicans.

Much testimony was introduced by which appellant sought to show the systematic exclusion of Mexicans from jury service and that there were members of that nationality qualified and available for such service in Jackson County. The facts proven, however, were of no greater probative force than those stipulated by the state and the appellant, which we quote as follows:

'The State will stipulate that for the last twenty-five years there is no record of any person with a Mexican or Latin American name having served on a jury commission, grand jury or petit jury in Jackson County.'

'It is stipulated by counsel for the State and counsel for the defendant that there are some male persons of Mexican or Latin American descent in Jackson County who, by virtue of being citizens, householders, or freeholders, and having all other legal prerequisites to jury service, are eligible to serve as members of a jury commission, grand jury and/or petit jury.'

With reference to the petit jury, we quote the following:

'It is stipulated by counsel for the State and counsel for defendant that there is no person of Mexican or other Latin American descent or blood on the list of talesmen.' These stipulations of necessity included the ability to read and speak the English language.

It was shown that Jackson County had a population of approximately 18,000, 15% of which—a witness estimated as a 'wild guess'—were Mexicans. The same witness also testified as a 'rough estimate' that 6 or 7% of that 15% were freeholders upon the tax rolls of the county. It was shown, also, that the population of Jackson County, was composed also of Bohemians, Germans, Anglo-Americans, and Negroes. The relative percentages of these, however, were not estimated.

It may be said, therefore, that the facts relied upon by the appellant to bring this case within the rule of systematic exclusion are that at the time the grand jury was selected and at the time of the trial of this case there were 'some male persons of Mexican or Latin American descent in Jackson County' who possessed the qualifications requisite to service as grand or petit jurors, and that no Mexican had been called for jury service in that county for a period of twenty-five years.

There is an absence of any testimony here suggesting express or factual discrimination against appellant or other Mexicans in the selection, organization, or empaneling of the grand or petit jury in this case. To sustain his claim of discrimination, appellant relies only upon an application of the rule of exclusion mentioned.

[1] In so far as this court is concerned, the question here presented was determined adversely to appellant's contention in the case of *Sanchez v. State*, 147 Tex.Cr.R. 436, 181 S.W.2d 87, 90, [1952] where we said: 'In the absence of a holding by the Supreme Court of the United States that nationality and race bear the same relation, within the meaning of the constitutional provision (Fourteenth Amendment) mentioned, we shall continue to hold that the statute law of this State furnishes the guide for the selection of juries in this State, and that, in the absence of proof showing express discrimination by administrators of the law, a jury so selected in accordance therewith is valid.' (Parentheses supplied.)

Within our knowledge, no decision of the Supreme Court of the United States has been rendered which would change the conclusion just expressed.

The validity of laws of this state providing for the selection of grand or petit jurors, arts. 333-350, C.C.P., Vernon's Ann.C.C.P. arts. 333-350, has never been seriously challenged. Indeed, the Supreme Court of the United States, in *Smith v. Texas*, 311 U.S. 128, 61 S.Ct. 164, 165, 85 L.Ed. 84, recognized the validity thereof when it said: 'Here, the Texas statutory scheme is not in itself unfair; it is capable of being carried out with no racial discrimination whatsoever.'

It was with this statement in mind that we said, in effect, that, in the absence of express discrimination, a jury, grand or petit, drawn in accordance with the statute law of this state was valid.

Appellant challenges the correctness of our conclusion and charges that by such holding we have extended special benefits to members of the Negro race which are denied to Mexicans, thereby violating equal protection to them. Such contention calls, of necessity, for a construction of the equal protection clause of the Fourteenth Amendment to the Federal Constitution with reference to the selection of juries in state court trials and the decisions of the Supreme Court of the United States relative thereto.

The Fourteenth Amendment to the Federal Constitution in relation to equal protection [FN1] was adopted to secure to members of the Negro race, then recently emancipated, the full enjoyment of their freedom. *Nixon v. Herndon*, 273 U.S. 536, 47 S.Ct. 446, 71 L.Ed. 579; *Buchanan v. Warley*, 245 U.S. 60, 38 S.Ct. 16, 62 L.Ed. 149; *Neal v. Delaware*, 103 U.S. 370, 26 L.Ed. 567; *Strauder v. West Virginia*, 100 U.S. 303, 25 L.Ed. 664; *In re Slaughter-House cases*, 16 Wall. 36, 21 L.Ed. 394.

FN1. 'Section 1. All persons born or naturalized in the United States, and subject to the jurisdiction thereof, are citizens of the United States and of the State wherein they reside. No State shall make or enforce any law which shall abridge the privileges or immunities of citizens of the United States; nor shall any State deprive any person of life, liberty, or property, without due process of law; nor deny to any person within its jurisdiction the equal protection of the laws.'

While the Supreme Court of the United States had before it the question of race discrimination under the Fourteenth Amendment in the Slaughter-House cases, it appears that it was not until the case of Strauder v. West Virginia that the court had occasion to determine that race discrimination in jury organization was prohibited by the Fourteenth Amendment. In the latter case a statute of West Virginia limited jury service to white male persons. This statute was held as discriminatory against members of the Negro race and, therefore, violative of equal protection.

Following the Strauder case, the question of race discrimination in the selection of juries was before the court upon several occasions.

[2] In Carter v. Texas, 177 U.S. 442, 20 S.Ct. 687, 689, 44 L.Ed. 839, the rule was stated as follows: 'Whenever by any action of a State, whether through its legislature, through its courts, or through its executive or administrative officers, all persons of the African race are excluded, solely because of their race or color, from serving as grand jurors in the criminal prosecution of a person of the African race, the equal protection of the laws is denied to him, contrary to the Fourteenth Amendment of the Constitution of the United States. *Strauder v. West Virginia*, 100 U.S. 303, 25 L.Ed. 664; *Neal v. Delaware*, 103 U.S. 370, 397, 26 L.Ed. 567, 574; *Gibson v. Mississippi*, 162 U.S. 565, 16 S.Ct. 904, 40 L.Ed. 1075.' The rule, as thus established, applies equally to petit jury selection.

For a time, and until the case of *Norris v. Alabama*, 294 U.S. 587, 55 S.Ct. 579, 582, 79 L.Ed. 1074, establishment of discrimination rested upon facts showing actual or express discrimination against members of the Negro race. In the Norris case, however, the so-called rule of exclusion was announced in the following language, viz.: 'We think that the evidence that for a generation or longer no Negro had been called for service on any jury in Jackson County, that there were Negroes qualified for jury service, that according to the practice of the jury commission their names would normally appear on the preliminary list of male citizens of the requisite age but that no names of Negroes were placed on the jury roll, and the testimony with respect to the lack of appropriate consideration of the qualifications of Negroes, established the discrimination which the Constitution forbids.'

In succeeding cases this rule of exclusion was followed or adverted to in the cases of *Smith v. Texas*, 311 U.S. 128, 61 S.Ct. 164, 85 L.Ed. 84, *Hill v. Texas*, 316 U.S. 400, 62 S.Ct. 1159, 86 L.Ed. 1559 and *Akins v. Texas*, 325 U.S. 398, 65 S.Ct. 1276, 89 L.Ed. 1692.

The effect of the rule of exclusion is to furnish means by which proof of discrimination may be accomplished.

In the Akins case, the idea of proportional representation of races on a jury as a constitutional requisite was rejected. The basis of such rejection was pointed out in *Cassell v. Texas*, 339 U.S. 282, 70 S.Ct. 629, 631, 94 L.Ed.839, as follows: 'We have recently written why proportional representation of races on a jury is not a constitutional requisite. Succinctly stated, our reason was that the Constitution requires only a fair jury selected without regard to race. Obviously the number of races and nationalities appearing in the ancestry of our citizens would make it impossible to meet a requirement of proportional representation.'

The conclusion of race discrimination expressed in the *Cassell* case, which is one of the latest expressions by the Supreme Court of the United States upon the subject, appears not to have been based upon the so-called rule of exclusion above mentioned but upon the conclusion that the jury commissioners appointed to select the list of names from which the grand jury was to be selected did not 'familiarize themselves fairly with the qualifications of the eligible jurors of the county without regard to race and color. They did not do so here, and the result has been racial discrimination.'

In addition to that conclusion, the Cassell case also announced the rule that discrimination may be shown by inclusion as well as exclusion, on account of race, in jury selection.

[3] To our minds, it is conclusive that, in so far as the question of   discrimination in the organization of juries in state courts is concerned, the equal protection clause of the Fourteenth Amendment contemplated and recognized only two classes as coming within that guarantee: the white race, comprising one class, and the Negro race, comprising the other class.

We said in *Sanchez v. State,* Tex.Cr.App., 243 S.W.2d 700, 701, that 'Mexican people * * * are not a separate race but are white people of Spanish descent'. In contemplation of the Fourteenth Amendment, Mexicans are therefore members of and within the classification of the white race, as distinguished from members of the Negro race. In so far as we are advised, no member of the Mexican nationality challenges that statement. Appellant does not here do so.

It is apparent, therefore, that appellant seeks to have this court recognize and classify Mexicans as a special class within the white race and to recognize that special class as entitled to special privileges in the organization of grand and petit juries in this state.

[4] To so hold would constitute a violation of equal protection, because it would be extending to members of a class special privileges not accorded to all others of that class similarly situated. Moreover, it must be remembered that no man, or set of men, has the right to require that a member of his race be a member of the grand jury that indicts him or of the petit jury that tries him. All that the Constitution, State or Federal, guarantees in that connection is that in the organization of such juries he be not discriminated against by reason of his race or color. *Thomas v. Texas*, 212 U.S. 278, 29 S.Ct. 393, 53 L.Ed. 512; *Martin v. Texas*, 200 U.S. 316, 26 S.Ct. 338, 50 L.Ed. 497; *Carter v. Texas*, 177 U.S. 442, 20 S.Ct. 687, 44 L.Ed. 839.

To say that members of the various nationalities and groups composing the white race must be represented upon grand and petit juries would destroy our jury system, for it would be impossible to meet such requirement. Such, also, would destroy the rule above stated and would be tantamount to authorizing an accused to demand that a member of his nationality be upon the jury that indicts and tries him. In addition, to so hold would write into the equal protection clause proportional representation not only of races but of nationalities, which the Supreme Court of the United States has expressly rejected.

[5] Mexicans are white people, and are entitled at the hands of the state to all the rights, privileges, and immunities guaranteed under the Fourteenth Amendment. So long as they are so treated, the guarantee of equal protection has been accorded to them.

[6] The grand jury that indicted appellant and the petit jury that tried him being composed of members of his race, it cannot be said, in the absence of proof of actual discrimination, that appellant has been discriminated against in the organization of such juries and thereby denied equal protection of the laws.

The judgment is affirmed.

Opinion approved by the court.

Appendix IV

Hernandez v. Texas
347 U.S. 475 (1954)

January 11, 1954, Argued

May 3, 1954, Decided

COUNSEL:

Carlos C. Cadena and Gus C. Garcia argued the cause for petitioner.

With them on the brief were Maury Maverick, Sr. and John J. Herrera.

Horace Wimberly, Assistant Attorney General of Texas, argued the cause for respondent. With him on the brief were John Ben Shepperd, Attorney General, and Rudy G. Rice, Milton Richardson and Wayne L. Hartman, Assistant Attorneys General, for respondent.

JUSTICES:

Warren, Black, Reed, Frankfurter, Douglas, Jackson, Burton, Clark, Minton

MR. CHIEF JUSTICE WARREN delivered the opinion of the Court.

The petitioner, Pete Hernandez, was indicted for the murder of one Joe Espinosa by a grand jury in Jackson County, Texas. He was convicted and sentenced to life imprisonment. The Texas Court of Criminal Appeals affirmed the judgment of the trial court. Tex. Cr. R., 251 S.W. 2d 531. Prior to the trial, the petitioner, by his counsel, offered timely motions to quash the indictment and the jury panel. He alleged that persons of Mexican descent were systematically excluded from service as jury commissioners,[1] grand jurors, and petit jurors, although there were such persons fully qualified to serve residing in Jackson County. The petitioner asserted that exclusion of this class deprived him, as a member of the class, of the equal protection of the laws guaranteed by the Fourteenth Amendment of the Constitution. After a hearing, the trial court denied the motions.

At the trial, the motions were renewed, further evidence taken, and the motions again denied. An allegation that the trial court erred in denying the motions was the sole basis of petitioner's appeal. In affirming the judgment of the trial court, the Texas Court of Criminal Appeals considered and passed upon the substantial federal ques-

---

[1]Texas law provides that at each term of court, the judge shall appoint three to five jury commissioners. The judge instructs these commissioners as to their duties. After taking an oath that they will not knowingly select a grand juror they believe unfit or unqualified, the commissioners retire to a room in the courthouse where they select from the county assessment roll the names of 16 grand jurors from different parts of the county. These names are placed in a sealed envelope and delivered to the clerk. Thirty days before court meets, the clerk delivers a copy of the list to the sheriff who summons the jurors. Vernon's Tex. Code Crim. Proc., 1948, Arts. 333-350. The general jury panel is also selected by the jury commission. Vernon's Tex. Rev. Civ. Stat., 1948, Art. 2107. In capital cases, a special venire may be selected from the list furnished by the commissioners. Vernon's Tex. Code Crim. Proc., 1948, Art. 592.

tion raised by the petitioner. We granted a writ of certiorari to review that decision. 346 U.S. 811.

In numerous decisions, this Court has held that it is a denial of the equal protection of the laws to try a defendant of a particular race or color under an indictment issued by a grand jury, or before a petit jury, from which all persons of his race or color have, solely because of that race or color, been excluded by the State, whether acting through its legislature, its courts, or its executive or administrative officers.[2] Although the Court has had little occasion to rule on the question directly, it has been recognized since *Strauder v. West Virginia*, 100 U.S. 303, that the exclusion of a class of persons from jury service on grounds other than race or color may also deprive a defendant who is a member of that class of the constitutional guarantee of equal protection of the laws.[3] The State of Texas would have us hold that there are only two classes—white and Negro—within the contemplation of the Fourteenth Amendment.

The decisions of this Court do not support that view.[4] And, except where the question presented involves the exclusion of persons of Mexican descent from juries,[5] Texas courts have taken a broader view of the scope of the equal protection clause.[6]

Throughout our history differences in race and color have defined easily identifiable groups which have at times required the aid of the courts in securing equal treatment under the laws. But community prejudices are not static, and from time to time other differences from the community norm may define other groups which need the same protection. Whether such a group exists within a community is a question of fact. When the existence of a distinct class is demonstrated, and it is further shown that the laws, as written or as applied, single out that class for different treatment not based on some reasonable classification, the guarantees of the Constitution have been violated. The Fourteenth Amendment is not directed solely against discrimination due to a "two-class theory"—that is, based upon differences between "white" and Negro.

As the petitioner acknowledges, the Texas system of selecting grand and petit jurors by the use of jury commissions is fair on its face and capable of being utilized without discrimination.[7] But as this Court has held, the system is susceptible to abuse and can be employed in a discriminatory manner.[8] The exclusion of otherwise eligible

---

[2]See *Carter v. Texas*, 177 U.S. 442, 447.

[3]"Nor if a law should be passed excluding all naturalized Celtic Irishmen [from jury service], would there be any doubt of its inconsistency with the spirit of the amendment." 100 U.S., at 308. Cf. American Sugar *Refining Co. v. Louisiana*, 179 U.S. 89, 92.

[4]See *Truax v. Raich*, 239 U.S. 33; *Takahashi v. Fish & Game Commission*, 334 U.S. 410. Cf. *Hirabayashi v. United States*, 320 U.S. 81, 100: "Distinctions between citizens solely because of their ancestry are by their very nature odious to a free people whose institutions are founded upon the doctrine of equality."

[5]*Sanchez v. State*, 147 Tex. Cr. R. 436, 181 S. W. 2d 87; *Salazar v. State*, 149 Tex. Cr. R. 260, 193 S. W. 2d 211; *Sanchez v. State*, 243 S.W. 2d 700.

[6]In *Juarez v. State*, 102 Tex. Cr. R. 297, 277 S. W. 1091, the Texas court held that the systematic exclusion of Roman Catholics from juries was barred by the Fourteenth Amendment. In *Clifton v. Puente*, 218 S. W. 2d 272, the Texas court ruled that restrictive covenants prohibiting the sale of land to persons of Mexican descent were unenforceable.

[7]*Smith v. Texas*, 311 U.S. 128, 130.

[8]*Smith v. Texas*, supra, note 7; *Hill v. Texas*, 316 U.S. 400; *Cassell v. Texas*, 339 U.S. 282; *Ross v. Texas*, 341 U.S. 918.

persons from jury service solely because of their ancestry or national origin is discrimination prohibited by the Fourteenth Amendment. The Texas statute makes no such discrimination, but the petitioner alleges that those administering the law do.

The petitioner's initial burden in substantiating his charge of group discrimination was to prove that persons of Mexican descent constitute a separate class in Jackson County, distinct from "whites."[9] One method by which this may be demonstrated is by showing the attitude of the community. Here the testimony of responsible officials and citizens contained the admission that residents of the community distinguished between "white" and "Mexican." The participation of persons of Mexican descent in business and community groups was shown to be slight. Until very recent times, children of Mexican descent were required to attend a segregated school for the first four grades.[10] At least one restaurant in town prominently displayed a sign announcing "No Mexicans Served." On the courthouse grounds at the time of the hearing, there were two men's toilets, one unmarked, and the other marked "Colored Men" and "Hombres Aqui" ("Men Here"). No substantial evidence was offered to rebut the logical inference to be drawn from these facts, and it must be concluded that petitioner succeeded in his proof.

Having established the existence of a class, petitioner was then charged with the burden of proving discrimination. To do so, he relied on the pattern of proof established by *Norris v. Alabama*, 294 U.S. 587. In that case, proof that Negroes constituted a substantial segment of the population of the jurisdiction, that some Negroes were qualified to serve as jurors, and that none had been called for jury service over an extended period of time, was held to constitute prima facie proof of the systematic exclusion of Negroes from jury service. This holding, sometimes called the "rule of exclusion," has been applied in other cases,[11] and it is available in supplying proof of discrimination against any delineated class.

The petitioner established that 14% of the population of Jackson County were persons with Mexican or Latin-American surnames, and that 11% of the males over 21 bore such names.[12] The County Tax Assessor testified that 6 or 7 percent of the freeholders on the tax rolls of the County were persons of Mexican descent. The State of Texas stipulated that "for the last twenty-five years there is no record of any person with a Mexican or Latin American name having served on a jury commission,

---

[9]We do not have before us the question whether or not the Court might take judicial notice that persons of Mexican descent are there considered as a separate class. See Marden, Minorities in American Society; McDonagh & Richards, Ethnic Relations in the United States.

[10]The reason given by the school superintendent for this segregation was that these children needed special help in learning English. In this special school, however, each teacher taught two grades, while in the regular school each taught only one in most instances. Most of the children of Mexican descent left school by the fifth or sixth grade.

[11]See note 8, supra.

[12]The 1950 census report shows that of the 12,916 residents of Jackson County, 1,865, or about 14%, had Mexican or Latin-American surnames. U.S. Census of Population, 1950, Vol. II, pt. 43, p. 180; id., Vol. IV, pt. 3, c. C, p 45. Of these 1,865, 1,738 were native-born American citizens and 65 were naturalized citizens. Id., Vol. IV, pt. 3, c. C, p. 45. Of the 3,754 males over 21 years of age in the County, 408, or about 11%, had Spanish surnames. Id., Vol. II, pt. 43, p. 180; id., Vol. IV, pt. 3, c. C, p. 67. The State challenges any reliance on names as showing the descent of persons in the County. However, just as persons of a different race are distinguished by color, these Spanish names provide ready identification of the members of this class. In selecting jurors, the jury commissioners work from a list of names.

grand jury or petit jury in Jackson County."[13] The parties also stipulated that "there are some male persons of Mexican or Latin American descent in Jackson County who, by virtue of being citizens, householders, or freeholders, and having all other legal prerequisites to jury service, are eligible to serve as members of a jury commission, grand jury and/or petit jury."[14]

The petitioner met the burden of proof imposed in *Norris v. Alabama*, supra. To rebut the strong prima facie case of the denial of the equal protection of the laws guaranteed by the Constitution thus established, the State offered the testimony of five jury commissioners that they had not discriminated against persons of Mexican or Latin-American descent in selecting jurors. They stated that their only objective had been to select those whom they thought were best qualified. This testimony is not enough to overcome the petitioner's case. As the Court said in *Norris v. Alabama*:

"That showing as to the long-continued exclusion of negroes from jury service, and as to the many negroes qualified for that service, could not be met by mere generalities. If, in the presence of such testimony as defendant adduced, the mere general assertions by officials of their performance of duty were to be accepted as an adequate justification for the complete exclusion of negroes from jury service, the constitutional provision . . . would be but a vain and illusory requirement."[15]

The same reasoning is applicable to these facts.

Circumstances or chance may well dictate that no persons in a certain class will serve on a particular jury or during some particular period. But it taxes our credulity to say that mere chance resulted in there being no members of this class among the over six thousand jurors called in the past 25 years. The result bespeaks discrimination, whether or not it was a conscious decision on the part of any individual jury commissioner. The judgment of conviction must be reversed.

To say that this decision revives the rejected contention that the Fourteenth Amendment requires proportional representation of all the component ethnic groups of the community on every jury[16] ignores the facts. The petitioner did not seek proportional representation, nor did he claim a right to have persons of Mexican descent sit on the particular juries which he faced.[17] His only claim is the right to be indicted and tried by juries from which all members of his class are not systematically excluded—juries selected from among all qualified persons regardless of national origin or descent. To this much, he is entitled by the Constitution.

Reversed.

---

[13]R. 34.

[14]R. 55. The parties also stipulated that there were no persons of Mexican or Latin-American descent on the list of talesmen. R. 83. Each item of each stipulation was amply supported by the testimony adduced at the hearing.

[15]294 U.S., at 598.

[16]See *Akins v. Texas*, 325 U.S. 398, 403; *Cassell v. Texas*, 339 U.S. 282, 286-287.

[17]See *Akins v. Texas*, 325 U.S. 398, 403; *Cassell v. Texas*

Appendix V

TRANSCRIPT OF RECORD
SUPREME COURT OF THE UNITED STATES
OCTOBER TERM, 1953
No. 406
PETE HERNANDEZ, PETITIONER
VS.
THE STATES OF TEXAS

SUPREME COURT OF THE UNITED STATES
OCTOBER TERM, 1953
No. 406
PETE HERNANDEZ, PETITIONER
VS.
THE STATES OF TEXAS

. . .

INDEX

INDEX

Record from the 24th District court Jackson County State of Texas—Continued

?

[fols. 1-3] [Caption omitted]

IN THE 24TH DISTRICT COURT, JACKSON COUNTY
STATE OF TEXAS

THE STATE OF TEXAS
vs.
PETE HERNANDEZ
Charge - Murder
No. 2091
Indictment - filed September 20, 1951
In the Name and by the Authority of the State of Texas:
The Grand Jurors, for the County of Jackson State aforesaid, duty selected, organized, sworn and empaneled as such at the Fall Term. A. D. 1951, of the District Court for said County, upon their oaths in said Court present that Pete Hernandez on or about the 4th day of August. A.D. one thousand nine hundred and fifty one and anterior to the presentment of this Indictment, in the County of Jackson and State of Texas, did then and there unlawfully and voluntarily and with malice aforethought kill Joe Espinosa by shooting him with a gun, against the peace and dignity of the State.
W.F. Germer. Foreman of the Grand Jury.

[fol. 4] A True Bill—W.P. Germer. Foreman of Grand Jury. Names of Witnesses: Mannel Laureles—Jesse Nava   John Tristan—Mike Pena—J. B. Arroyos—E . Sanchez—Manuel Garza—Alex Garza—Henry Cruz.
(File endorsement omitted.)
. . . In District Court of Jackson County
[Title Omitted]
Motion to Quash Indictment—filed October 4, 1951
To the Honorable Judge of Said Court: Now comes Pete Hernandez, Defendant and moves the Court to set aside the Indictment in the above-styled and numbered cause for the following reasons: 1. In the selection of the Grand Jury Commissioners who subsequently appointed the Grand Jurors who returned this Indictment, Defendant was deprived of his Constitutional rights and denied the equal protection of the law as guaranteed by the Fourteenth Amendment to the Constitution of the United States. 2. In the selection of the Grand Jurors who returned this Indictment defendant was likewise deprived of his Constitutional rights and the equal protection of the law as guaranteed by the Fourteenth Amendment to the Constitution of the United States.

In substantiation of the foregoing grounds, Defendant embodies in this Motion the allegations heretofore set out in his motion to Quash the Jury Panel, a copy of which is attached hereto and made a part hereof. 3. Defendant further states that there are persons permanently residing in Jackson County, Texas listed on the Tax rolls and Poll Tax rolls of said County for the year 1951 who are qualified for Jury Commission and Grand Jury Service. 4. Defendant further states that approximately twenty—five per cent (25 per cent) of the population of Jackson County consists of persons of Mexican decent who are members of Defendant's class and of the same national origin and who are considered as members of a separate race by the other residents and citizens of said Jackson County. 5. Defendant further states that this is the first opportunity that he has had to raise the issue of his Constitutional rights to the selection of the members of Jury Commission and the members of the Grand Jury because both the Jury Commissioners and said Grand Jury have been selected prior to the Commission of the alleged offense averred in this Indictment. Gus C. Garcia, Attorney for Defendant.

Overruled, 10-4-51 - Frank W. Martin. Deft Excepts.

(File endorsement omitted.)

[fol. 7] IN THE DISTRICT COURT OF JACKSON COUNTY, TEXAS MOTION TO QUASH JURY PANEL - Filed October 4, 1951.

Now comes Pete Hernandez Defendant in the above-styled and numbered cause and files this his motion to quash the entire panel of petit jurors selected by the Jury Commissioners for the following reasons:

I

The said panel was improperly selected in that from said Grand Jury Commissioners all persons were excluded who are of Mexican or Latin American descent or belonging to a class known as "Mexicans". That the Defendant herein is of Mexican descent and that persons of his national origin or class have been systematically, intentionally and deliberately excluded from Jury Commissioners and Grand Juries. That there are persons of the Defendant's national origin or class who are citizens of Jackson, County, Texas and are qualified to serve as Jury Commissioners but they have been given an opportunity to do so and that the Defendant has been denied and is being denied the equal protection of the laws.

II

In support of the foregoing Defendant would show the Court that people of his national origin or class are, on the whole, of a low economic level and considered members of a distinct race, separate and apart from the other citizens of Jackson County and that by reason of this fact Defendant is not afforded a trial by jury of his peers, and is deprived of his constitutional rights guaranteed by the Fourteenth Amendment to the Federal Constitution.

III

Defendant would further show the Court that not only are persons of Mexican descent excluded from the Jury Commission but that they are otherwise treated as members of an inferior race, are denied service in many public places in Jackson County and for many years [fol. 8] children of said national origin or class were segregated in the public schools of Jackson County, just as if they were members of a different race.

IV

Defendant would further show the Court that he has not heretofore had an opportunity to challenge the selection of the Jury Commissioners or the Jury Panel by them selected because said Commissioner and the Jury Panel were named anterior to the Commission of the alleged offense charged in the Indictment.

Gus C. Garcia. Attorney for Defendant. 433 International Building. San Antonio, Texas

ORDER OVERRULING MOTION TO QUASH JURY PANEL

On this the 24th day of September, A.D. 1951 came on to be heard Defendant's Motion to Quash the Jury Panel. The Court is of the opinion that said motion should be, and is hereby, overruled. It is ordered that Defendant shall be afforded the opportunity to offer evidence in support of his allegations in this motion upon a hearing of Defendant's Motion to Quash the Indictment.

Judge Presiding

(File endorsement omitted.)

[fol. 9] IN DISTRICT COURT OF JACKSON COUNTY

[Title Omitted]

ORDER OVERRULING MOTION TO QUASH THE INDICTMENT

October 4, 1951

On this the 4th day of October, 1951, came on to be heard the motion of the defendant, Pete Hernandez, to quash the indictment in this cause, and came into open court the defendant in person and his counsel and the District Attorney appeared for the State, and all parties announced ready, whereupon the evidence was presented by both sides and thereafter the Court heard the argument of counsel on such motion, and, after due consideration, the Court is of the opinion that such motion should be in all things overruled.

Therefore, it is hereby ordered and decreed by the Court on this the 4th day of October 1951, that defendant's motion to quash the indictment in this case be, and the same is hereby, in all things overruled. To which ruling of the Court the Defendant then and there in open court excepted.

Frank W. Martin, Judge Presiding.

[fol. 10] IN DISTRICT COURT OF JACKSON COUNTY

[Title omitted]

MOTION TO QUASH JURY PANEL—UNITL SEPTEMBER 24, 1951

Now comes Pete Hernandez, Defendant in the above-styled and numbered cause and files this, his motion to quash the entire panel of petit jurors selected by the Jury Commissioners for the following reasons:

I

The said panel was improperly selected in that from said Grand Jury Commissioners all persons were excluded who are of Mexican or Latin American descent or belonging to a class known as "Mexicans". That the Defendant herein is of Mexican descent and that persons of his national origin or class have been systematically, intentionally and deliberately excluded from Jury Commission and Grand Juries.

That there are persons of the Defendant's national origin or class who are citizens of Jackson County, Texas, and are qualified to serve as Jury Commissioners but they have never been given an opportunity to do so and that the Defendant has been denied and is being denied the equal protection of the laws.

II

In support of the foregoing Defendant would show the Court that people of his national origin or class are, on the whole, of a low economic level and considered members of a distinct race, separate and apart from the other citizens of Jackson County and that by reason of this fact Defendant is not afforded a trial by jury of his peers, and is deprived of his constitutional rights guaranteed by the Fourteenth Amendment to the Federal Constitution.

III

Defendant would further show the Court that not only are persons of Mexican descent excluded from the Jury Commission but that they are otherwise treated as members of an inferior race, are denied services in many public places [fol.11] in Jackson County and for many years children of said national origin or class were segregated in the public schools of Jackson County, just as if they were members of a different race.

IV

Defendant would further show the Court that he has not heretofore had an opportunity to challenge the selection of the Jury Commissioners or the Jury Panel by them selected because said Commissioner and the Jury Panel were named anterior to the Commission of the alleged offense charged in the Indictment.

Gus C. Garcia. Attorney for Defendant. 433 International Building. San Antonio, Texas.

10-4-51. Overruled. Deft Excepts, Frank W. Martin, Judge.

ORDER OVERRULING MOTION TO QUASH JURY PANEL

On this the 24th day of September, A.D. 1951, came on to be heard Defendant's Motion to Quash the Jury Panel. The Court is of the opinion that said motion should be, and is hereby, overruled. It is ordered that Defendant shall be afforded the opportunity to offer evidence in support of his allegations in this motion upon a hearing of Defendant's Motion to Quash the Indictment.

(File endorsement omitted.)——, Judge Presiding.

[fol. 12] IN THE DISTRICT COURT OF JACKSON COUNTY

[Title Omitted]

ORDER OVERRULING MOTION TO QUASH JURY PANEL AND SPECIAL VENIRE—October 4, 1951

On this 4th day of October, 1951 came on to be heard the motion of the defendant, Pete Hernandez, to quash the jury panel and special venire ordered in this cause, and came into open court the defendant in person and his counsel and the District Attorney appeared for the State, and all parties announced ready, whereupon the evidence was presented by both sides and thereafter the Court heard the argument of counsel on such motion, and, after due consideration, the Court is of the opinion that such motion should be in all things overruled. Therefore, it is hereby Ordered and Decreed by the Court on this the 4th day of October, 1951, that defendant's motion to quash the jury panel and special venire in this cause be, and the same is hereby, in all things overruled. To which ruling of the Court the Defendant then and there in open court excepted.

Frank W. Martin, Judge Presiding.

[fol. 13] IN THE DISTRICT COURT OF JACKSON COUNTY

[Title omitted]

APPLICATION FOR SUSPENDED SENTENCE—filed October 8, 1951

Offense—Murder

To the Hon. Frank Martin, Judge of said Court: Now comes the defendant in the above styled and numbered cause, and show to the Court: That he stands charged by indictment with a felony, to wit: Murder which is one of the felonies to which the suspended sentence act applies. He further shows to the Court that he has never heretofore been convicted of a felony in this or any other State. Therefore defendant respectfully requests the Court to submit the issue of suspended sentence to the Jury, and allow the introduction of evidence of the facts herein alleged, and of the character of the defendant. If the Jury finds defendant guilty of the offense with which he is charged, and assesses his punishment at confinement in the penitentiary for five years or less, and further find that he has never heretofore been convicted of felony in this or any other state, and recommend the suspension of such sentence, that said sentence be suspended.

Pete Hernandez, Defendant.

Duly sworn to by Pete Hernandez. Jurat omitted in printing.

[fol. 14] (File endorsement omitted.)

[fol. 15] IN THE DISTRICT COURT OF JACKSON COUNTY
[Title omitted]
CHARGE OF THE COURT - FILED OCTOBER 11, 1951

Gentlemen of the Jury: (1) The defendant, Pete Hernandez, stands charged by indictment with the offense of murder of Joe Espinosa, alleged to have been committed in Jackson County, Texas, on or about the 4th day August, 1951. (2) To this charge the defendant has pleaded "not guilty". (3) As to the law of the case I charge you as follows: (4) Whoever shall voluntarily kill any person within this State shall be guilty of murder. Murder shall be distinguished from every other species of homicide by the absence of circumstances which reduce the offense to negligent homicide or which excuse or justify the killing. (5) Murder, as above defined, may be committed either with or without malice aforethought. When murder is committed with malice aforethought the punishment for such murder shall be death or confinement in the penitentiary for life or for any term of years not less than two. When murder is committed, but not with malice aforethought, the punishment for such murder is by confinement in the penitentiary for not less than two nor more than five years. (6) "Malice aforethought" is the voluntary and intentional doing of an unlawful act by one of sound memory and discretion with the purpose, means and ability to commit the reasonable and probable consequences of the act. It is a condition of the mind which shows a heart regardless of social duty and fatally bent on mischief, the existence of which is inferred from acts committed or words spoken. (7) "Malice", in its legal sense, denotes a wrongful act done intentionally and without just cause or excuse.

[fol.16] (8) A "deadly weapon" is a weapon which, from the manner used, is calculated or likely to produce death or serious bodily injury. (9) Now, if you believe from the evidence beyond a reasonable doubt that the defendant, Pete Hernandez, in Jackson County, Texas, on or about August 4, 1951 with malice aforethought, as that term has heretofore been defined, and with the intent then and there to kill the said Joe Espinosa, did unlawfully and voluntarily kill Joe Espinosa by then and there shooting him, the said Joe Espinosa, with a gun, which, from the manner used, was calculated or likely to produce death or serious bodily injury, and as alleged in the indictment, then you will find the defendant guilty of murder with malice aforethought and so state in your verdict, and assess his punishment at death or at confinement in the penitentiary for life or for any term of years not less than two. (10) You are instructed that should you find the defendant guilty of murder, yet unless you believe from all the facts and circumstances in evidence beyond a reasonable doubt that the defendant in killing the deceased, if he did kill him, acted with malice aforethought, then you cannot assess any punishment against the defendant for a longer period than five years in the penitentiary.

(11) If you find from the evidence beyond a reasonable doubt that the defendant under the instructions given in this charge and under the facts and circumstances in evidence is guilty of murder, but should you have a reasonable doubt as to whether the defendant, in committing the offense, was prompted by malice afterthought, you should resolve that reasonable doubt in favor of the defendant, and in such case the punishment assessed by you for such offense, if any, cannot be for a longer period than five years in the penitentiary. (12) And in this connection you are instructed that murder without malice is a voluntary homicide committed without justification or excuse under the immediate influence of a sudden passion arising from an adequate cause, by which it is meant such cause as would commonly produce [fol.17] a degree of anger, rage, resentment or terror in a person of ordinary temper sufficient to render the mind incapable of cool reflection. (13) Now, if you believe from the evidence beyond a reasonable doubt that the defendant, Pete Hernandez, on or about August 4, 1951, in Jackson County, Texas, with the intent then and there to kill Joe Espinosa, did unlawfully and voluntarily kill the said Joe Espinosa by shooting him with a gun which from the manner used was calculated or likely to produce death or serious bodily injury and as alleged in the indictment, but if you believe from the evidence, or if you have a reasonable doubt thereof, that at the time the defendant killed the deceased, if you find he did kill him, the defendant was laboring under the immediate influence of a sudden passion, such as anger, rage, resentment or terror, which rendered his mind incapable of cool reflection, and that such condition of his mind, if any, was brought about by circumstances or conditions which would commonly produce such a state of mind in a person of ordinary temper, then you will find the defendant guilty of murder without malice and so state in your verdict, and assess his punishment at confinement in the penitentiary for not less than two nor more than five years. (14) And unless you believe from the evidence beyond a reasonable doubt that the defendant is guilty of murder as hereinbefore explained and defined to you, then you will acquit the defendant. (15) You are instructed that when a person is unlawfully attacked or threatened with attack by another and there is thereby creat-

ed in the mind of the person attacked or threatened with an attack from the words, acts or conduct of the one making or threatening such unlawful attack a reasonable expectation or fear of death or serious bodily injury, as viewed from his standpoint at the time, then the law excuses or justifies such person in resorting to any means at his command to prevent his assailant from taking his life or from inflicting upon him any serious bodily [fol. 18] injury, and it is not necessary that there should be actual danger, as a person has the right to defend his life and person from apparent danger as fully and to the same extent as he would had the danger been real, provided he acted upon a reasonable apprehension of danger as it appeared to him from his standpoint at the time, and in such case the person acting under real or apparent danger is in no event bound to retreat in order to avoid the necessity of killing his assailant, but may stand his ground and defend himself by any means at his command. (16) Now, if you believe from the evidence beyond a reasonable doubt that the defendant, Pete Hernandez, killed the deceased, Joe Espinosa, by shooting him with a gun, but if you believe from the evidence, or if you have a reasonable doubt thereof, that at such time the deceased, Joe Espinosa, was making or about to make what appeared to the defendant, as viewed from his standpoint at the time, taking into consideration the relative sizes and strength of the parties and defendant's knowledge or belief of the character or disposition of the deceased, and any other fact and circumstance in evidence, to be an unlawful attack upon him, the defendant, producing a reasonable belief in the defendant's mind from the words, acts or conduct of the said Joe Espinosa at the time that he, the defendant, was in danger of losing his life or suffering serious bodily injury at the hands of the said Joe Espinosa, and if you find that the defendant killed the deceased under such circumstances, or if you have a reasonable doubt thereof, then you will acquit the defendant. (17) You are further instructed when there is more than one assailant, the slayer has the right to act upon the hostile demonstration of either one or all of them and to kill either one or all of them, if it reasonably appears to him that they are present for the purpose of acting together to take his life or to do him serious bodily injury. (18) You are further instructed that if you believe from the evidence, or if you have a reasonable doubt thereof, [fol.19] that at the time of the difficulty between the parties here involved and prior to the shooting of Joe Espinosa by the defendant, if you find that Joe Espinosa was shot by the defendant, Henry Cruz was making or about to make what appeared to the defendant, as viewed from his standpoint at the time, taking into consideration the relative sizes and strength of the parties and the defendant's knowledge or belief of the character or disposition of Henry Cruz, to be an unlawful attack upon him, the said defendant, producing a reasonable belief in the defendant's mind from the words, acts or conduct of the said Henry Cruz at the time that he, the said defendant, was in danger of losing his life or suffering serious bodily injury at the hands of the said Henry Cruz, and that while the said Henry Cruz was making or about to make what appeared to the defendant, as viewed from his standpoint at the time, to be said unlawful attack or threatened attack, Joe Espinosa joined in what appeared to the defendant, viewed from his standpoint at the time, to be said attack or threatened attack, then the defendant had a right to defend himself against such attacks of the said Henry Cruz and Joe Espinosa, or either of them, and had a right under such circumstances to kill the said Joe Espinosa, and if you find from the evidence, or if you have a reasonable doubt thereof, that Joe Espinosa was killed under such circumstances, then you will acquit the defendant. (19) The defendant in this case has filed an affidavit with the Court among other things stating that he has never been convicted of a felony in this State, or any other State, and in the event of his conviction, he prays that you will recommend a suspension of his sentence. (20) Our statue provides that where a person is charged with the offense of murder and the jury finds him guilty and assesses the punishment at imprisonment in the penitentiary for any term not more than five years, and they further find that the defendant has never been convicted of a felony in this State or any other State, the jury may cause the sentence to be suspended during the good behavior [fol. 20] of the defendant. (21) Now, if you find the defendant guilty of murder and the punishment assessed by you is for not more than five years, and you further find that he has never been convicted of a felony in this State or any other State, you may, in your discretion, cause the sentence to be suspended during the good behavior of the defendant, and in case you desire to suspend the sentence of this defendant let your verdict show that you find the defendant has never been convicted of a felony in this State or any other State, and further show that you recommend the suspension of the sentence. You are instructed that the plea for suspended sentence filed herein is no evidence of defendant's guilt, and you must not consider same as evidence of his guilt. (22) The indictment in this case is no evidence of defendant's guilt, and you will not consider the indictment nor the fact that defendant has been indicted as any evidence in the case, but you will wholly disregard the same, and pass upon the guilt or innocence of the defendant wholly and solely from the evidence given before you in the trial of this case, and the law as given in the Court's charge. (23) In all criminal cases the burden of proof is upon the State. (24) The defendant is presumed to be innocent until his guilt is established by legal evidence beyond a reasonable doubt: and in case you have a reasonable doubt as to the defendant's guilt you will acquit him, and say by your verdict "not guilty". (25) You are the exclusive judges of the facts proved, of the credibility of the witnesses, and of the weight to be given their testimony, but you are bound to receive the law from the Court, which is herein given you, and be governed thereby.

Frank W. Martin. Judge Presiding.

You will find attached hereto for your convenience every [fol. 21] possible form of verdict which you can render under the evidence and law of this case. However, these forms are submitted purely and solely for your use and convenience in the event you reach a verdict, and shall not be considered or used by you for any other purpose. In the event you use one of these forms in returning your verdict, have your foreman sign on the line at the bottom of the form which you use and scratch a line through all the remaining forms which you do not use.

Frank W. Martin, Judge Presiding. 24th District Court of Jackson County, Texas.

We, the jury, find the defendant, Pete Hernandez, not guilty.——, Foreman.

We, the jury, find the defendant, Pete Hernandez, guilty of murder without malice as charged in the indictment, and assess his punishment at—years in the State Penitentiary.——, Foreman.

We, the jury, find the defendant, Pete Hernandez, guilty of murder with malice aforethought as charged in the indictment, and assess his punishment at—years in the State Penitentiary.——, Foreman.

We, the jury find, the defendant, Pete Hernandez, guilty of murder with malice aforethought as charged in the indictment and assess his punishment at imprisonment in the State Penitentiary for life.——, Foreman.

We, the jury, find the defendant, Pete Hernandez, guilty of murder with malice aforethought as charged in the indictment and assess his punishment at death.——, Foreman.

We, the jury, find the defendant, Pete Hernandez, [fol. 22] guilty of murder without malice and assess his punishment at years in the penitentiary. We further find that the defendant has never been convicted of a felony in this or any other State, and recommend his sentence be suspended.——, Foreman.

We, the jury, find the defendant, Pete Hernandez, guilty of murder with malice aforethought and assess his punishment at—years in the penitentiary. We further find that the defendant has never been convicted of a felony in this or any other State, and recommend his sentence be suspended.——, Foreman.

(File endorsement omitted.)

[fol. 23] IN DISTRICT COURT OF JACKSON COUNTY

[Title omitted]

NOTATION ON JUDGE'S TRIAL DOCKET

9-24-51. Case set for trial at 9:00 A.M. Monday, October 8, 1951. Clerk instructed to draw special venire of 130 men to be summoned by mail to appear in Court in Edna at 10:00 o'clock A.M. Monday, October 8, 1951. Writ returnable Thursday, October 4, 1951, at 12:00 o'clock noon.

10-4-51. Defendant & State announce ready on all motions. Defendant presents motions to quash indictment and special venire. Court hears testimony on motions. Motion by defendant to change venue offered—both sides present evidence. Motion to quash venire overruled. Motion to quash indictment overruled. Motion to change venue overruled.

10-8-51. Case called, both sides announce ready. Begin voir dire examination jurors 1:30 P.M.

10-9-51. Special venire exhausted 5 P.M. Sheriff ordered to summon 12 talesman to complete panel.

10-11-51. Evidence completed both sides rest at 11 A.M.

10-11-51. Charge read to jury 1:15 P.M.

10-11-51. Argument commenced 1:25 P.M.

10-11-51. Jury received case at 4:30 P.M.

10-11-51. Verdict received at 8 P.M. Jury Discharged.

12-15-51. Defendant files amended motion for new trial with leave of Court Motion new trial heard & overruled deft excepts gives notice of Appeal to Court of Criminal Appeals at Austin, Tex.

[fol. 24] IN DISTRICT COURT OF JACKSON COUNTY

[Title omitted]

VERDICT OF THE JURY—Filed October 11, 1951

(4) We, the jury, find the defendant, Pete Hernandez, guilty of murder with malice aforethought as charged in the indictment and assess his punishment at imprisonment in the State Penitentiary for life.

H.S. Woodland, Foreman. (File endorsement omitted)

[fol. 25] IN THE DISTRICT COURT, 24TH JUDICIAL DISTRICT JACKSON COUNTY, TEXAS
No.2091
THE STATE OF TEXAS
vs.
PETE HERNANDEZ
Charge: Murder

JUDGEMENT—October 8, 1951 [sic]

This day, October 8, 1951, this cause was called for trial, and the state appeared by her District Attorney, Wayne L. Hartman, the County Attorney, Cullen B. Vance, and the employed Counsel, Wm. H. Hamblen, and the Defendant. Pete Hernandez, appeared in person, in open Court his Counsel Gus C. Garcia and John J. Herrera, also being present, and both parties announced ready for trial, and the Defendant, Pete Hernandez, being duly arraigned in open Court, pleaded not guilty to the charge contained in the indictment herein, to-wit murder with malice: thereupon a jury, of good and lawful men, to-wit, H. S. Woodland and eleven others, was duly selected, impaneled, and sworn, who, having heard the indictment read, and the defendant's plea of not guilty thereto, and having heard the evidence submitted, and having been duly charged by the Court, retired on October 11, 1951, in charge of the proper officer to consider of their verdict, and afterward, on the same day, October 11, 1951, were brought into open court by the proper officer, the defendant and his counsel being present, and being asked if they had agreed upon a verdict, answered they had, and returned to the court a verdict which was read aloud by the clerk: and thereupon the defendant asked that the jury be polled, and the name of each juror was then separately called, and each juror as his name was called was asked by the Court if the said verdict was his name was called was asked by the court if the said verdict was his verdict and each of said jurors answered in the affirmative: whereupon the said verdict was received by the court and is here now entered upon the minutes as follows: "We, the jury, find the defendant, Pete Hernandez, guilty of murder with malice aforethought as charged in the indictment, and assess his punishment at imprisonment in the State Penitentiary for life. H.S. Woodland, Foreman."

[fol. 26] It is therefore considered and adjudged by the court that the defendant, Pete Hernandez, is guilty of the offense of Murder, with malice aforethought, as found by the jury, and that he be punished as has been determined by the jury, by confinement in the penitentiary for a term of his natural life, and that the State of Texas do have and recover of the said defendant, Pete Hernandez, all costs in this prosecution expended, for which execution will issue; and that the said defendant be remanded to jail to await the further order of this court herein.

[fol. 27] IN DISTRICT COURT OF JACKSON COUNTY
[Title omitted]

MOTION FOR NEW TRIAL—Filed October 11, 1951

Now comes Pete Hernandez, Defendant, and files this his Original Motion for New Trial, on the following grounds:

The verdict is against the law.

The verdict is against the evidence.

Gus C. Garcia. Attorney for Defendant. (File endorsement omitted.)

[fol. 28] IN DISTRICT COURT OF JACKSON COUNTY

[Title Omitted]

. . . New trial leave of Court having been first had and obtained, and says that the Court erred in overruling the following motions filed and urged by Defendant herein:

1. Motion to Quash Jury Panel

Now comes Pete Hernandez, Defendant in the above—styled and numbered cause and files this, his motion to quash the entire panel of petit jurors selected by the Jury Commissioners for the following reasons:

I

The said panel was improperly selected in that from said Grand Jury Commissioners all persons were excluded who are of Mexican or Latin American descent or belonging to a class known as "Mexicans". That the defendant herein is of Mexican descent and that persons of his national origin or class have been systematically, intentionally and deliberately excluded from Jury Commissions and Grand Juries. That there are persons of the Defendant's national origin or class who are citizens of Jackson County, Texas and are qualified to serve as Jury Commissioners but they have never been given an opportunity to do so and that the Defendant has been denied and is being denied the equal protection of the law.

II

In support of the foregoing Defendant would show the Court that people of his national origin or class are, on the whole, of a low economic level and considered members of a distinct race, separate and apart from the other citizens of Jackson County and that by reason of this fact Defendant is not afforded a trial by jury of his peers, and is deprived of his constitutional rights guaranteed by [fol. 29] the Fourteenth Amendment to the Federal Constitution.

III

Defendant would further show the Court that not only are persons of Mexican descent excluded from the Jury Commission but that they are otherwise treated as members of an inferior race, are denied services in many public places in Jackson County and for many years children of said national origin or class were segregated in the public schools of Jackson County, just as if they were members of a different race.

IV

Defendant would further show the Court that he has not heretofore had an opportunity to challenge the selection of the Jury Commissioners or the Jury Panel by them selected because said Commissioner—and the Jury Panel were named anterior to the Commission of the alleged offense charged in the Indictment.

(S.) Gus C. Garcia, Attorney for Defendant, 433 International Building, San Antonio, Texas.

II. Motion to Quash Indictment

Now comes Pete Hernandez, Defendant, and moves the Court to set aside the Indictment in the above-styled and numbered cause for the following reasons:

1. In the selection of the Grand Jury Commissioners who subsequently appointed the Grand Jurors who returned this Indictment, Defendant was deprived of his Constitutional rights and denied the equal protection of the law as guaranteed by the Fourteenth Amendment to the Constitution of the United States.

2. In the selection of the Grand Jurors who returned this Indictment Defendant was likewise deprived of his Constitutional rights and the equal protection of the laws as guaranteed by the Fourteenth Amendment to the Constitution of the United States.

In substantiation of the foregoing grounds, Defendant embodies in this Motion the allegations heretofore set out [fol. 30] in his Motion to Quash the Jury Panel, a copy of which is attached hereto and made a part hereof.

3. Defendant further states that there are persons permanently residing in Jackson County, Texas listed on the Tax rolls and Poll Tax rolls of said County for the year 1951 who are qualified for Jury Commission and Grand Jury Service.

4. Defendant further states that approximately twenty-five per cent (25 per cent) of the population of Jackson County consists of persons of Mexican descent who are members of Defendant's class and of the same national origin and who are considered as members of a separate race by the other residents and citizens of said Jackson County.

5. Defendant further states that this is the first opportunity that he has had to raise the issue of his Constitutional rights as to the selection of the members of Jury Commission and the members of the Grand Jury because both the Jury Commissioners and said Grand Jury have been selected prior to the Commission of the alleged offense averred in this Indictment.

(S.) Gus C. Garcia, Attorney for Defendant.

Wherefore, Defendant prays that he be granted a new trial.

Gus C. Garcia, Attorney for Defendant, 433 International Building, San Antonio, Texas.

A copy of this Amended Motion for a New Trial has been mailed to Honorable Wayne Hartman, District Attorney, Cuero, Texas.

(File endorsement omitted.)

[fol. 31] IN THE DISTRICT COURT OF JACKSON COUNTY
[Title omitted]
ORDER OF COURT OVERRULING AMENDED MOTION TO GRANT A NEW TRIAL

This the 15th day of December, 1951, came on to be heard the amended motion of the defendant, Pete Hernandez, to set aside the verdict and judgment herein rendered, and grant him a new trial of this cause; and the State being present in court by her District Attorney, and the defendant, Pete Hernandez, and also his attorney of record, John J. Herrera, being present in court in person, and the Court having heard the said motion is of the opinion that same should be refused.

It is, therefore, Considered, Ordered and Adjudged by the Court that the said amended motion for a new trial herein be and the same is refused, and in all things overruled. Whereupon the defendant, Pete Hernandez, in open court, excepted to such judgment and gave notice of an appeal herein to the Court of Criminal Appeals of the State of Texas, sitting at Austin, Texas, which said notice is here now entered of record. Defendant shall have the time prescribed by law for filing bills of exception and Statement of facts in the lower court. Duly entered this the 15th day of December, A.D. 1951. Frank W. Martin, Acting Judge, 24th Judicial District of Texas.

[fol. 32] IN DISTRICT COURT OF JACKSON COUNTY

[Title omitted]

SENTENCE - December 15, 1951

Charge: Murder

This day, December 15, 1951, this cause being again called, the State appeared by her District Attorney, and the Defendant, Pete Hernandez, was brought into open Court, in person, in charge of the Sheriff, and his counsel also being present, for the purpose of having the sentence of the law pronounced in accordance with the verdict and judgment herein rendered and entered against him on the 11th day of October, A. D. 1951. And thereupon the Defendant, Pete Hernandez, was asked by the Court whether he had anything to say why said sentence should not be pronounced against him, and he answered nothing in bar thereof. Whereupon the Court proceeded, in the presence of said Defendant, Pete Hernandez, to pronounce sentence against him as follows: It is the order of the Court that the Defendant, Pete Hernandez, who has been adjudged to be guilty of Murder with malice aforethought, be delivered by the Sheriff of Jackson County, Texas, immediately to the Superintendent of Penitentiaries or other persons authorized to receive such convicts, and the said Pete Hernandez shall be confined in the said Penitentiary for a term of not less than two years nor more than his natural life, in accordance with the provisions of the law governing the Penitentiaries of this State, and the said Pete Hernandez is remanded to Jail until said Sheriff can obey the directions of this Sentence. But the defendant, Pete Hernandez, having this 15th day of December, 1951 excepted to the Order of the Court in overruling his First Amended Motion for a new trial, and having given notice of appeal to the Court of Criminal Appeals of the State of Texas, this sentence is ordered suspended and held in abeyance until said appeal has been decided, and until the mandate of the Court of Criminal Appeals of the State of Texas has been received and filed in this Court.

[fol. 33] IN THE DISTRICT COURT OF JACKSON COUNTY

Copy of Letter Written By Frank W. Martin, Judge, 135th District Court to Mr. Gus C. Garcia—Filed January 17, 1952

Frank W. Martin

District Judge

135th Judicial District

Goliad, Texas

January 16, 1952

Counties

Calhoun

De Witt

Goliad

Jackson
Refugio
Victoria
Mr. Gus C. Garcia,
C/o Garcia and Cadena,
432 International Building,
San Antonio, Texas.
Dear Mr. Garcia:
You called me a few days ago with reference to the Pete Hernandez case at Edna. I have since communicated with Mr. Otto Kehrer, the reporter, and he advised me that he has not received an order for a statement of facts. I presume that you will want a statement of facts. I presume that you will want a statement of facts of some of the testimony anyway, and in that connection I call your attention to the Session Laws of the 52nd Legislature providing that the attorney for the appellant shall file within 15 days after notice of appeal is given and request is made of the official court reporter for the preparation of transcript of all or any part of the evidence desired, and shall specify the portions desired in narrative form, if any, and the portions desired in question and answer form, if any, and the portions that are desired to be omitted. In view of the fact that Mr. Kehrer stays very busy he is not always able to get up a statement of facts within a few days, and if you desire a statement of facts in the cause mentioned above, I would suggest that you now make satisfactory arrangements with Mr. Kehrer for the statement of facts to be furnished, and this particularly in view of the fact that over 30 days has now elapsed since the motion for new trial was overruled.
Yours very truly, Frank W. Martin, Judge, 135th District Court.
FWM/ph.
cc: Miss Gena Lee Lawrence, Clerk, District Court, Edna, Texas; Mr. Otto Kehrer, Victoria, Texas.
Dear Mrs. Lawrence: Please file the copy of this letter in the papers of the Pete Hernandez case upon the date received by you.
FWM.
(File endorsement omitted.)

[fol. 34] IN DISTRICT COURT OF JACKSON COUNTY
COPY OF LETTER WRITTEN BY O.G. KEHRER TO MR. GUS C. GARCIA—
filed March 10, 1952
Victoria, Texas, January 30, 1952
Via Registered Mail—Return Receipt Requested
Mr. Gus C. Garcia,
Attorney at Law,
432 International Building,
San Antonio, Texas.
Dear Mr. Garcia:
Re: Cause No. 2091, The State of Texas versus Pete Hernandez, In the 24th District Court of Jackson County, Texas.

In compliance with your request by long distance telephone on the afternoon of January 18, 1952, that I prepare statement of facts, in question and answer form, in the above numbered and entitled cause in so far only as it relates to (1) Defendant's Motion to Quash Indictment, (2) Defendant's Motion to Quash Jury Panel, and (3) Defendant's Motion to Quash the Talesmen after Special Venire was Exhausted, I have prepared and enclose same herewith. In view of the fact that some of the proceedings were had in connection with hearing on defendant's motions on October 4, 1951, and still other proceedings were had in connection with the trial of the cause on the merits beginning October 8, 1951, after announcement of ready, I have prepared two statements of fact. I enclose herewith my bill for services in the sum of $51. Thanking you and with kind regards, I am,

Very truly yours, (S.) O.G. Kehrer, Court Reporter, 2207 North De Leon Street, Victoria, Texas.

(File endorsement omitted.)

[fols. 35-37] Clerk's Certificate to foregoing transcript omitted in printing.

[fol. 38] IN DISTRICT COURT OF JACKSON COUNTY
[Title omitted]
TRANSCRIPT OF HEARING ON MOTION TO QUASH JURY PANEL AND MOTION TO QUASH THE INDICTMENT—October 4, 1951
APPEARANCES:

Mr. Wayne L. Hartman, District Attorney in and for the 24th Judicial District of Texas, Cuero, Texas;

Mr. Cullen B. Vance, Country Attorney, Jackson County, Edna, Texas;

Mr. Wm. H. Hamblen, Special Prosecutor, Edna, Texas; Appearing for the State of Texas;

Mr. Gus C. Garcia, 432 International Building, San Antonio, Texas;

Appearing for the Defendant.

[fol. 39] Whereupon, in said cause the following proceedings were had, to-wit:

Court: Which motion are you presenting first? Mr. Garcia: I am offering the Motion to Quash the Jury Panel and the Motion to Quash the Indictment.

DEFENDANT'S TESTIMONY IN CHIEF

Mrs. Gena Lee Lawrence, called as a witness on behalf of the defendant, having been first duly cautioned and sworn to testify the truth, the whole truth, and nothing but the truth, testified as follows:

Direct examination.
By Mr. Garcia:

Q. What is your name?

A. Gena Lee Lawrence.

Q. What official position do you hold in Jackson County?

A. District Clerk.

Q. How long have you held that official position?

A. Fifteen years.

Q. As part of your official duty do you have the responsibility of taking care of the lists of jury commissioners and grand jurors and petit jurors?

A. I take care of the list that the jury commissioners [fol. 40] select of grand jurors and petit jurors.

Q. In the course of your official duties do you get to see the names of the jury commissioners as they are appointed from time to time?

A. If the Judge gives me the authority to open the lists.

Q. And also the names of the grand jurors and petit jurors?

A. Yes, sir.

Q. During the time you have served in that official capacity have you known of a person of so-called Mexican or Latin American descent to be appointed a member of a jury commission in this Country?

A. I don't think so; I don't recall that there ever was.

Q. Have you ever heard of a person of Latin American or Mexican descent being appointed as a member of a grand jury in this County?

A. I don't recall having heard of it.

Q. Have you ever seen or heard of a person of Mexican or Latin American descent being drawn on a venire for a petit jury?

A. I don't think so.

Q. I am going to ask you if you would be kind enough to make an investigation of your records and in the event you find there have been some that you did not recall, will it be-

Mr. Garcia: What I want to establish is the fact that the statement I just made is not contradicted. I want her to look over the records of her office to see if in reality there [fol. 41] ever has been in the last twenty-five years a person of Mexican or Latin American descent on a jury commission or grand jury or petit jury in this County.

Mr. Hartman: So far as the State is concerned it has no objection to Mrs. Lawrence doing that and no objection to counsel for the defendant introducing from the witness stand any testimony he might have after having done so, but we don't want it arbitrarily inserted in the record without an opportunity of cross-examination.

Court: No, sir. (Addressing the witness) Do you have the records available?

Witness: I can look in the minutes.

Court: Look and see what you can find.

Witness: I can look on the minutes.

Court: Mrs. Lawrence will look at the records she has.

Q. Are you a native of this County?

A. Yes, sir.

Q. I will ask you whether it is not a fact that in this County the people of the so-called Mexican or Latin American descent are looked upon as actually of a different race?

A. I don't think so.

Q. Isn't the expression "Mexican" and "white person" rather common in this community?

A. What was the question?

Q. Are not people of Mexican descent commonly referred [fol. 42] to as "Mexicans" or "Latin Americans" and people of other national origins referred to as "white people"?

A. I think we all understand that the Latin Americans are considered as white people.

Q. Isn't it a common expression in this community, the expression "Mexican" or "Latin American" in contrast with that of "white person" or "White man" or "white woman"?

A. I don't know but what it is—"Latin Americans".

A. Are you familiar with the service rendered to people of Mexican descent by public establishments in this community? Do you know anything about whether some business places do not serve people of Mexican origin?

A. No, sir.

Q. Do you know what the approximate percentage of the population of Jackson County consists of Mexican or Latin American origin?

A. No, sir.

Q. I will ask you whether or not it is a fact that persons of Mexican or Latin American origin appear on the tax rolls who would be eligible for jury commissioners or grand jury or petit jury service?

Mr. Hartman: Object to that because he has not established that she is qualified to know what the qualifications are for service on the grand jury and on the petit jury, and until we know she is qualified in this respect we do not believe she is qualified. [fol. 43] Court: If she knows, she can answer.

Q. Do you know what the qualifications are for service on a jury commission and grand jury and petit jury?

A. Yes, sir.

Q. You do know?

A. Yes, sir.

Q. Based on the knowledge, I will repeat my question, and that is: Isn't it a fact that there are persons of Latin American or Mexican descent in Jackson County who are eligible for service on jury commissioners and grand juries and petit juries?

A. I think I would have to say the Tax Collector would know that—whether they have paid their poll taxes.

Q. You don't know of your own knowledge whether any people of Mexican or Latin American descent have paid their poll taxes?

A. I don't know of my own knowledge. I could not tell you who had paid.

Q. You don't know of a single instance?

A. No, sir; I could not give you a single name just offhand.

Q. If you know, isn't it a fact that, generally speaking, people of Mexican descent are of rather low economic status in this County?

A. I guess, generally speaking, it is true.

Mr. Garcia: That is all.

[fol. 44] Cross examination
By Mr. Hartman:

Q. Mrs. Lawrence, you stated while ago that during your service as District Clerk of Jackson County you did not know of your own knowledge of any person of Mexican of Latin American descent having served as jury commissioner?

A. Yes, sir.

Q It is or not possible - Are you undertaking to say that they have not?

A. No, sir. I don't know.

Q. Isn't it possible that some one of them may have served without your knowledge?

Mr. Garcia: I don't think that question is phrased properly.

The Court: Objection overruled.

Q. Is it or not possible?

A. Yes, sir, it is possible.

Q. Now, when you undertake to say in your knowledge no person of Latin American or Mexican descent has served on a jury commission, do you base that on name alone or do you undertake to say no one of Latin American or Mexican blood has served on a jury commission during the ten years so far as you know?

A. I take it by names. I don't know; some of them might have been Latin American.

[fol. 45] Q. It is highly possible some or many of them might have had Latin American blood to a certain degree and not have a Latin American name, is that right?

A. Yes, sir.

Q. Now, I will ask you whether or not the same is true in regard to service on grand juries?

A. Yes, sir.

Q. It is possible that Mexicans or Latin Americans may have served on grand juries without your knowledge?

A. Yes, sir.

Q. And it is possible that people with Latin American or Mexican blood with English or Polish or some other national name might have served on grand juries?

A. Yes, sir.

Q. And I will ask you whether or not the same is true in regard to jury panels generally?

A. Yes, sir.

Q. Now, you stated while ago that people of Mexican or Latin American descent were often referred to as "Mexicans" in Jackson County?

A. I said usually "Latin Americans".

Q. Ma'am?

A. I think usually as "Latin Americans".

Q. They refer to them as "Latin Americans-?

A. Yes, sir, and sometimes they are referred to as "Mexicans".

[fol. 46] Q. Isn't it also true sometimes Bohemians are referred to as "Bohemians"?

A. Yes, sir.

Q. And Polish people as "Polanders"?

A. Yes, sir.

Q. And Germans as "Germans"?

A. Yes, sir.

Q. And on down the line?

A. Yes, sir.

Q. Have you or not during the time that you have served as District Clerk at any time seen any evidence of discrimination against the Mexican or Latin American nationality or Mexican or Latin American people in any of your official functions in the courthouse?

A. No, sir.

Mr. Garcia: Object to that as calling for conclusion.

Court: Objection overruled.

A. I have not.

Q. Have you ever heard the Court say anything in your presence which would indicate that he had discriminated in any way against the Mexican or Latin American people?

A. No, sir, I have not.

Q. Now, Mrs. Lawrence, you stated while ago you lived in Jackson County?

A. Yes, sir

[fol. 47] Q. And you are native of Jackson County?

A. Yes, sir.

Q. Isn't it a fact that the children of Mexican or Latin American descent had the same schools as those of all other nationalities?

A. Yes, sir.

Q. And isn't it a fact that the Mexican and Latin American children play on the football teams we have?

A. It is a fact.

Q. And that the Mexican and Latin American parents belong to the Parent-Teacher Association?

A. Yes, sir.

Q. And the Mexicans or Latin Americans attend our theaters here in Jackson County?

A. Yes sir.

Q. Have you as District Clerk in any of your official duties ever discriminated in any way against a Mexican or Latin American person or nationality?

A. I have not.

Re-direct examination
By Mr. Garcia:

Q. You say that on occassions you have heard Polish people to refer to as "Poles" and Germans as "Germans" is that right?

A. I have.

Q. But in all those instances people of Polish or German [fol. 48] descent never referred to as anything but "white" and so on?

A. They were speaking of them as a different nationality.

Q. But never heard a person of Bohemian descent referred to as anything but "white", while you have heard people of Mexican descent called "Mexican", the distinction made between "whites" and "Bohemians" that you say is made on occasion between "Mexican" and "white"?

Court: Will you break that down?

Mr. Garcia: I withdraw the question.

Q. Have you heard anyone referred to as a German and a white man?

A. No, sir, I don't think so.

Q. Have you ever heard anyone say "Bohemian" and "white man"?

A. No, sir.

Q. But you have heard people say "Mexican" and "white man" in contrast?

A. Yes sir, I have heard that.

Q. And when you were questioned by the District Attorney you stated it was possible that people of Mexican or Latin American descent with an Anglo name might have served on juries?

A. Yes, sir

Q. Can you give me the name of a single person in Jackson County who is considered of Mexican or Latin American descent who has an Anglo name?

A. What is the question?

[fol. 49] Q. That is considered a Mexican but bears an Anglo American name?

Mr. Hartman: Object to that because she is not qualified to say who is considered a Mexican.

Q. Can you give me a single person who is a resident citizen of Jackson County who is of Mexican or Latin American blood but who bears an Anglo American name?

A. I don't recall any.

Q. Do you recall any Spanish named person ever appearing on the petit juries or grand juries or jury commission rolls of this county?

A. I don't recall any.

Q. With reference to school attendance, do you know how long the children of Mexican parents and the children of American parents have been going together here to school?

A. No, sir: but it has been several years.

Q. You would not say it was since the year 1948?

A. I would not say what year.

Q. And in answer to the District Attorney's question you stated that to your knowledge parents of Mexican children are members of Parent—Teacher Association along with parents of Anglo American children?

A. Yes, sir.

Q. Is that true of service clubs like the Lions, Kiwanis and Optimists, or anything like that?

A. I could not tell you.

[fol. 50] Q. Do you know of any person of Mexican ancestry belonging to the Chamber of Commerce in this community?

A. I can say that I think there are members, but I could not tell their names.

STIPULATION

Mr. Hartman: The State will stipulate that for the last twenty-five years there is no record of any person with a Mexican or Latin American name having served on a jury commission, grand jury or petit jury in Jackson County.

Court: That stipulation was made by both parties in open court and is approved by the Court.

CLAUDIUS BRANCH, called as a witness on behalf of the defendant, having been first duly cautioned and sworn to testify the truth, the whole truth, and nothing but the truth, testified as follows:

Direct examination.

By Mr. Garcia:

Q. Will you please state your name?

A. Claudius Branch.

Q. What official position do you hold in Jackson County?

A. County Tax Assessor and Collector.

Q. In the discharge of your duties in that position do you have charge of the assessment of property and tax rendition rolls of this County?

[fol. 51] A. Yes, sir.

Q. That includes the poll tax rolls?

A. Yes, sir.

Q. Are you a native of this County?

A. Yes, sir.

Q. Do you know the population of Jackson County?

A. I hate to say off-hand. It has changed in the last two or three years—something like 18,000.

Q. Approximately 18,000?

A. Yes, sir.

Q. Will you tell us approximately what percentage of that population consists of people of Mexican or Latin American descent?

A. That is an awful hard question. Roughly, I would say something——

Mr. Hartman: We don't want any rough estimate. We would like to have the facts.

Court: He is just estimating it.

A. (continued) I judge around 15 per cent.

Q. Now, do you have Spanish named persons on your property tax rolls in this County?

A. Yes, sir.

Q. Do you have Spanish named persons on your poll tax rolls?

A. Yes, sir.

Q. Do you have Spanish named persons, who are either natives or naturalized citizens of the United States, who [fol.52] own property *property* and pay their poll taxes in this County?

A. Yes, sir.

Q. You would not be able to give us any idea how many?

A. No. I would have to check the tax rolls. The question has never came up before.

Q. You are familiar with the legal prerequisites for service as a member of a jury commission and grand jury and petit jury?

A. Yes, sir.

Q. Based upon that knowledge and the information in your office, would it be your testimony that there are persons with Spanish names who are eligible for service on a jury commission, grand jury and petit jury in this County?

A. I presume so.

Q. How is a special venire formed in this County? How is it drawn? I am not trying to trick you. I don't know.

A. A jury commission is appointed and that jury commission goes over the tax rolls. After they go over the tax rolls then they go to the certified poll tax list furnished by my office showing that these tax payers are eligible for voting, and the list is taken from the lists that they are furnished.

Q. How long did you say you served in that capacity?

A. I took over January 1, 1946.

Q. During the time you have been in office have you ever known of a grand jury commission selecting a Spanish named person to serve on the venire?

A. I have not had any reason to check it.

[fol. 53] Q. You are, of course, in charge of the poll tax rolls and tax rolls for 1951?

A. Yes, sir.

Q. And there are Spanish named persons on both rolls?

A. Yes, sir.

Q. Based upon your knowledge of the requirements and prerequisites for service on grand juries, jury commissions and petit juries, and from the information that you have in your office affecting tax rolls and poll tax rolls, would you say there are persons with Spanish names who are eligible for service here as jury commissioners or grand jurors or petit jurors in the year 1951?

A. Yes, sir.

Cross examination.
By Mr. Hartman

Q. You don't normally keep track in your office yourself of the grand jury list and jury commission lists and petit jury lists?

A. No, sir.

Q. You are not qualified to say whether they have served or not?

A. No, sir.

Q. Now, you stated while ago in your opinion there were approximately 15 per cent Mexicans or Latin Americans in Jackson County?

A. That is a wild guess.

[fol. 54] Q. Can you or not state whether 15 percent of the taxpayers are Mexicans or 10 per cent Bohemians? Does that same rule apply to others?

A. No, sir.

Q. You are not prepared to say how many freeholders of Mexican or Latin American descent were on your tax rolls?

A. No, sir, but, a rough estimate, I would say something like probably 6 or 7 per cent.

Q. You are not prepared to say how many householders are of Mexican or Latin American descent?

A. No, sir. I would not think—

Q And you are not undertaking to say how many of the people of Mexican or Latin American descent in Jackson County can read and write the English language?

A. No, sir, I could not.

Q. And you are not undertaking to say how many are women?

A. No, sir.

Q. From your experience in the Tax Collector's Office since 1946 have you at any time seen anybody in any way discriminate against a Mexican or Latin American because of his nationality?

A. No, sir. We carry them on the tax rolls as whites, I mean on the poll tax rolls.

Q. And they are looked upon in your office as "whites", just the same as a German or Pole or Bohemian?

A. Yes, sir.

[fol. 55] Re-direct examination.
By Mr. Garcia

Q Have they always been carried in your office as "whites"?

A. To the best of my knowledge, yes, sir.

Q. Of course, you are not in position to say whether other people in this County look upon them as "whites"?

A. No, sir.

Re-cross examination.
By Mr. Hartman;

Q. They have been carried on your rolls as "white" ever since you have been in office?

A. Yes, sir.

LEWIS WATSON, called as a witness on behalf of the defendant, having been first duly cautioned and sworn to testify the truth, the whole truth, and nothing but the truth, testified as follows:

Direct examination.

By Mr. Garcia:

Q. What is your name?

A. Lewis Watson.

Q. Mr. Watson, you are the Sheriff of Jackson County?

A. Yes, sir.

Q. How long have you been serving in that capacity?

A. Approximately ten years.

[fol. 56] Q. Are you a native of Jackson County?

A. Yes, sir.

Q. Are you familiar, Mr. Watson, with the service or lack of service offered to people of so-called Mexican or Latin American descent in this community in public places?

A. Yes, sir.

Q. Do all restaurants in this community serve people of Mexican of Latin American descent?

A. We have one here in town that does not.

Q. Can you tell us where that is located?

A. In the east end of town—Mr. Winn's cafe.

Q. Is that the one that has a sign on the outside?

A. Yes, sir.

Q. When was that sign "No Mexicans Served" removed?

A. I don't know when it was removed. I just saw it up there a couple or three weeks ago, or a month ago, but I see it is not there now.

Q. Have you endeavored in your position as Sheriff to practically improve relations between Latin Americans and Americans?

Mr. Hartman: That is irrelevant and immaterial.

Court: Sustain the objection.

Mr. Garcia: I withdraw the question.

Q. Do you know of any other places at the present time or in the last few years that have refused to serve people because of their Mexican or Latin American descent?

[fol. 57] Q. You don't know about the other restaurants on Main Street, right across from the courthouse square?

A. No, sir. They feed them I understand—both of them.

Q. When I asked that question, I mean assuming that the person is otherwise acceptable to the person, that he is not disorderly and not unclean. I mean solely on the basis of ancestry. On that basis, do you know of any other places that have refused to serve them in years past?

A. No, sir.

Q. The words "white man" or "white men" as distinguished from "Mexican" or "Latin American" are used rather commonly in this County?

A. I have heard it, yes, sir.

Q. With no particular disparagement, it is just a usage, custom and practice?

A. Yes, sir.

Q. As members of a group or a class, isn't it true that actually in this County you have three groups or classes: Anglo American, or "whites", also the people called Mexicans or Latin Americans, and the third class Negroes, isn't that true, in most affairs of the County?

A. Well, the Latin Americans are white and the Negro is a Negro.

Cross examination.

By Mr. Hartman:

Q. Mr. Watson, you stated while ago that there is one [fol. 58] cafe in Edna which had a sign for a time on it. What did that sign say?

A. "No Mexicans Served" I believe is the way it was.

Q. There was never any trouble over that?

A. No, sir.

Q. You state that the sign is not there now?

A. I don't think it is. Unless they put it back. I noticed it was moved.

Q. Neither you or anyone that you know of told him to take that sign down recently?

A. No, sir.

Q. And that is the only place you know of that did not at that time serve them?

A. That is right.

Q. Do you know whether they serve them now or not?

A. I don't know, because I have not been in there. In fact, it has been three weeks since I have been in the place.

Q. Isn't it true, Mr. Watson, that the citizens of Jackson County are composed of a number of nationalities?

A. Yes, sir.

Q. There is a large Bohemian population in Jackson County?

A. Yes, sir.

Q. And there is probably a large English population?

A. Yes, sir.

Q. And there are some Mexicans or Latin Americans?

[fol. 59] A. Yes, sir.

Q. Now, has it not been your experience that in social affairs the various nationalities more or less are inclined to stick together when they associate with one another?

A. Yes, sir.

Q. Is it LaWard that has quite a large Bohemian population?

A. Ganado and LaSalle.

Q. And they are more or less inclined to stick together?

A. Yes, sir.

Q. They are not excluded from anything anywhere?

A. No, sir.

Q. And isn't the same thing true of Mexican people?

A. Yes, sir.

Q. Isn't it true that most of them, or at least a large portion of them, speak Mexican or Spanish as their day-to-day tongue?

A. They do.

Q. And has it not been your experience that they are more or less inclined to stick together because of language?

A. Yes, sir.

Q. The same way with the Bohemians?

A. Yes, sir.

Q. And the same way with some of the Germans?

A. Yes, sir.

Q. You have a son here playing on the Edna High School football team?

[fol. 60] A. He played the last four years.

Q. Are there members of the Mexican or Latin American nationality on this football team?

A. Yes, sir.

Q. Playing with him?

A. Yes, sir.

Q. Side by side?

A. Yes, sir.

Q. On the first string?

A. Yes, sir.

Q. Now, then, have you or any member of your Department ever in any way discriminated against a person of Mexican or Latin American nationality simply because of that nationality?

A. We have not, no, sir.

Q. Isn't it a fact that in the Jackson County jail, when you had prisoners in there, you make no distinction between Latin Americans and any other nationality when it comes time to put them in jail?

A. No, sir. I put Latin Americans, Whites, Bohemians, Germans all on one side, and the Negroes on the other side.

Q. Have you during your term as Sheriff here ever heard of the Court or any other court officer do or say anything that would indicate to you that he was discriminating against the Mexican or Latin American nationality because of their ancestry or nationality?

[fol. 61] Mr. Garcia: I think that is asking for a conclusion.

Court: Sustain the objection.

Re-direct examination.
By Mr. Garcia:

Q. Have you ever seen a sign "No Bohemians Allowed" or "No Bohemians Served"?

A. No, sir, I have not.

Q. Have you ever seen a sign "No Germans Served" or "No Germans Allowed"?

A. No, sir.

Q. Have you ever seen a sign "No Englishman served" or "No Englishman Allowed"?

A. No, sir.

Q. But you have seen a sign "No Mexicans Served"?

A. At one place.

Q. And that sign was on the outside?

A. Yes, sir.

Q. In large letters?

A. Yes, sir.

Q. You have heard people referred to as "Bohemians" or as "English"?

A. Yes, sir.

Q. But you have never heard anyone say "This is a Bohemian" and "This is a white man"?

A. Yes, sir, I have heard them say that; I sure have.

Q. But it was not a Bohemian saying that?

[fol. 62]A. Yes, sir, I have heard Bohemians say that.

Q. You have heard Bohemians say that?

A. I have heard Bohemians call one another "Bohemian".

Q. The question I was asking was this: Whether you heard the words "white man" used as distinguished from "Bohemian"?

A. Yes, sir, I have heard them talking and say, "I am white and you are a Bohemian." I have heard Bohemians say, "I am a Bohemian and you are white".

Q. You have never heard anyone use that in seriousness, more or less in jest?

A. Yes, sir, I guess so.

Re-cross examination.
By Mr. Hartman:

Q. Isn't it a fact from your experience with people generally as Sheriff and as an official in the County that it is customary when a particular nationality sticks to its native tongue and carries on most of its conversations in its native tongue that they are then referred to by nationality much more so than when they all speak the English language?

Mr. Garcia: That is predicated upon a hypothesis that has not been established?

Court: Objection overruled.

A. Yes, sir, I have heard that, and seen it.

Q. When a German speaks German as his customary tongue, he is more readily referred to as a "German" than [fol. 63] a German who speaks English regularly?

A. Yes, sir.

Q. And the same is true with the other nationalities?

A. Yes, sir.

Q. And the same is true when they stick to their native Spanish?

A. Yes, sir.

Q. As Sheriff of Jackson County you have sat with many grand juries?

A. Yes, sir.

Q. Isn't it a fact that based upon your experience with those grand juries that every grand jury you have met with has given the same attention when the case under consideration involved people of Mexican or Latin American nationality as they have people of any other nationality?

Mr. Garcia: Objection to that because it calls for a conclusion.

Court : Objection overruled.

Mr. Garcia: Note our exception.

A. Yes, sir, they did.

Q. And has not it been your experience that the courts here in Jackson County—District Court, County Court, Justice Court—have given the same consideration?

A. Yes, sir.

Mr. Garcia: Same objection.

Court: Same ruling.

Mr. Garcia: Note our exception.

[fol. 64] Q. As they have of other nationalities?

A. Yes, sir.

Q. And the same has been true with you and the employees in your Department?

A. Yes, sir.

Oscar Bounds, called as a witness on behalf of the defendant, having been first duly cautioned and sworn to testify the truth, the whole truth, and nothing but the truth, testified as follows:

Direct examination.
By Mr. Garcia:

Q. What is your name?

A. Oscar Bounds.

Q. What is your position with the School District.

A. I am Superintendent of Schools.

Q; Is that Superintendent of the Edna Independent School District?

A. Yes, sir.

Q How long have you held that position?

A. A year in August.

Q Are you familiar with the policy or policies of the Edna Independent School District or System prior to your becoming Superintendent?

A; I was employed here prior to that.

Q. Mr. Bounds, can you tell us what year it was that *that* [fol.65] the separate school for children of Mexican parents was abandoned by the Edna District?

A. No, sir; I did not have anything to do with that.

Q. You don't know what year?

A. I know it was approximately three or four years ago.

Q. Would you say it was before or after the Federal Court decision prohibiting the segregation?

A. I would not say.

Q. At any rate until it was abandoned it was another school?

A. I don't think 100 per cent for children of Mexican descent, no, sir.

Q. What we are asking, that was about—

A. It was Latin American, but it was not 100 per cent for Latin Americans.

Q. Why was it called the Mexican school?

A. Because it was chiefly for Latin American children that had language difficulties. If a child was able to speak the English language they were not required to go to the Mexican school. Some children left before finishing the 4th grade.

Q. How many years were they taught in this school?

A. Four.

Q. Were children given language tests before they were sent to this school?

A. I am not sure.

Q. You say that some children left that school before finishing [fol. 66] the 4th grade?

A. Yes, sir.

Q. About how many children a year?

A. I don't know.

Q. Would you say it would be a few or many?

A. I would say it would be few.

Q. After they taught them a year, would you say that there were few or many that left in the same year?

A. I don't know. I would not say.

Q. Where would you draw the line of demarcation? Why was it four years?

A. On the basis that if the teacher felt the child was ready and had become familiar with the English language then they were permitted to go.

Q. Were there Latin American children who were permitted to go to the other school from the very beginning?

A. I don't know about that either.

Q. You don't recall of any instance?

A. I am not positive. I believe it was after the teacher had them a while.

Q. And this school was maintained in a separate building from the other school?

A. That is right.

Q. Where the other children attended?

A. Yes, sir.

[fol. 67] Q. The Latin American school was separate and apart?

A. Yes, sir.

Q. Was it on the same campus?

A. No, sir; different location.

Q. That school is no longer maintained?

A. That is right.

Q. It was abandoned altogether?

A. Yes, sir.

Q. The building is no longer used?

A. It is being used for "Farmers' Ag" for the White High School.

Q. When it was abandoned and the children were permitted to go to the other school, what other school was it?

A. We had Sam Houston and Austin Elementary.

Q, When you abandoned the use of the Latin American school, I will not say "use", but permitted the children to go either to the Sam Houston or Austin Elementary School regardless nationality origin?

A. That is right.

Q. And regardless of whether they had any language handicap?

A. Yes, sir.

Q. You decided your theory had been wrong about language handicap?

A. I did not make that decision.

Q. That was made prior to your becoming Superintendent?

A. Yes, sir.

Q. Mr. Bounds, does the Edna Independent School District [fol. 68] take care of out-lying sections?

A. Yes, sir.

Q. It covers more than the City of Edna?

A. Yes, sir.

Q. Can you tell us in approximate figures what the scholastic population of this County?

A. The County or the District?

Q. The District?

A. Around 1555.

Q. Can you tell us in approximate figures what percentage of this scholastic population consists of children of Mexican or Latin American descent?

A. I could not.

Q. You would not be able to give us any idea at all?

A. No, sir.

Q. Perhaps I phrased it wrong. Say, of Spanish named children?

A. I still would not be able to give it to you.

Q. Would you say that the bulk of the Latin American children that attend school are in the first 4 grades?

A. Yes. Sir—I would say 5th or 6th grade.

Q. Generally speaking, that is about as high as they go?

A. The larger percent drop out around the 6th grade.

Q. Do you have any idea what the "casualties" would be?

A. No, sir.

Q. But the larger percent do drop out?

[fol. 69] A. I say a large per rent. I will not say the larger per cent.

Q. Do you know anyone that could give us the approximate figures of the scholastic population as to Latin American children?

A. I don't know of anyone that could give it to you.

Q. Of Spanish named children—on the basis of surnames?

A. No, sir, I don't know of anyone that could give you that.

Q. I presume you have all your school children listed on a roll?

A. We have a census roll you could check, but we don't break it down as to Latin American or Irish or French names, and so forth.

Q. Who in the System is in charge of keeping the rolls?

A. I have a copy of last year's roll. No one has a roll this year. It has not been sent out.

Q. Could you make that roll available for us?

A. Certainly.

Mr. Garcia: Your Honor. I would like to ask leave of the Court to get a copy of the roll and offer it in evidence for the purpose of showing the number of Spanish named children on the school census rolls of this District.

Court (Addressing the witness): You will furnish him copy of this roll by 1 or 1:15 o'clock?

Witness: Yes, sir.

Cross examination.
Question by Mr. Hartman:

Q. You have been connected with the Edna Independent [fol. 70] School District for some time?

A. Since 1938.

Q. And you started with them as a teacher?

A. That is right—elementary school principal—teacher.

Q. And you have been with them ever since 1938?

A. Yes, sir.

Q. You have been Superintendent for how long?

A. One year.

Q. That was last year?

A. That was the last scholastic year and so far this year.

Q. Now, then, you were here then before the elementary school which you referred to -while ago was abandoned?

A. Yes, sir.

Q. The one in which students were placed who had language difficulties?

A. Yes, sir.

Q. Was it or not solely because of their language difficulties that they were placed in this other school here?

A. Yes, sir.

Q. Not because the School System and its teachers were discriminating against them because they were of Mexican or Latin American descent?

A. I don't think there was any discrimination. I don't know the basis back of the initial point. I don't know when it was started or how long it was in existence.

[fol. 71] Q. Do you know who started it?

A. No, sir.

Q. The purpose of the school, so far as you know, was to better teach children of Latin American descent who could not speak English?

A. That to the best of my knowledge, was the purpose.

Q. Did you ever have any indication there was because any were being discriminated against and were not given the consideration they gave other children?

A. I never had any evidence of that.

Q. You stated that after the 5th or 6th grade some of these students of Latin American or Mexican descent dropped out of school?

A. Yes, sir.

Q. It is true that some other nationalities dropped out of school too along about that time?

A. Yes, sir.

Q. They did not all finish?

A. No, sir.

Q. And you don't undertake to say why they dropped out of school?

A. I don't really know the reason why.

Q. And I believe you stated -while ago when a child of Mexican or Latin American descent was placed in that elementary school it was kept there just so long as it was necessary for it to overcome the language difficulty?

[fol. 72] A. Yes, sir.

Q. And after that it was transferred to the other school?

A. At any time the teacher that was teaching the child felt—into the regular class it was brought over.

Q. Do you know of any instance where a child was placed in that school and after becoming ready to transfer was refused the right to transfer simply because of its nationality?

A. I do not.

Q. I believe you said that this elementary school has since been abandoned and is now used us an Agricultural School by the white High School. How many High Schools do you have in the District?

A. Two.

Q. The White and the Negro?

A. Yes, sir.

Q. And this Vocational School is for the "White" High school and not for the Negro High School?

A. Yes, sir.

Q. You have quite a few students of Latin American descent that go all through and finish high School, don't you?

A. I could not say how many.

Q. You have some?

A. Yes, sir.

Q. It is not unusual for one of them to finish?

A. I would not say about that.

[fol. 73] Q. Do you or not when they get into the regular school discriminate against them in any way in the school just because of their nationality?

A. Certainly not.

Q. They attend the same classes and sit in the same seats and use the same restrooms and play on the football team—there is no discrimination at all?

A. No, sir.

Re-direct examination.
Question by Mr. Garcia:

Q. You testified a moment ago that the reason for the maintenance of that Latin American elementary school was strictly one of language handicap or difficulty?

A. Did what?

Q. You testified a moment ago that the only reason that the Latin American school was maintained was because of the language handicap?

A. Yes, sir.

Q. I believe you testified in answer to my question you did not know why it was maintained or when it was started?

A. I told you I did not know why it was started. The only thing I told you is that when the child proved he had gotten to know the English language he was permitted to enter that group and use the English language.

Q. Who set up the standard for that?

[fol. 74] A. I don't know.

Q. Was it left entirely to the discretion of the particular teacher?

A. To the best of my knowledge the teacher recommended that that child go into another group and was permitted to do so.

Q. In answer to a question put to you by the District Attorney about that you stated you did not know of any instance where a child was refused admittance to the other school if he proved himself eligible from a language standpoint?

A. Yes, sir.

Q. Do you know of any specific instance where such a change took place before the child finished the 4th grade in the Latin American school?

A. Yes, sir.

Q. How many cases do you know.

A. I know of one specific one.

Q. And you have been with the School System since 1938?

A. Yes, sir. I said I know one definitely. I would have to check back and see. I am very familiar with the child.

Q. Would you say that such an event was unusual for a child to get transferred to the other school?

A. I would say it was a small percentage.

Q. Now, if that school was maintained in order to overcome the child's language handicap, I assume you had special techniques or methods that were used that you did not [fol. 75] have in the other school?

A. I don't know anything about the technique. I did not have supervision of that.

Q. Do you know of anything in that school that was different from the other school?

A. I do know they concentrated more on the use of English speaking and devoted more time to developing that phase than they did in the other school.

Q. I presume the building where these children were housed—and I am speaking of the Latin American school—was the same as Sam Houston and Austin buildings?

A. No.

Q. What was the difference?

A. These were stone structure and this other was frame structure.

Q. And I presume that substantially the same facilities were provided in the Latin American school as in the other?

A. To the best of my knowledge, yes, sir.

Q. How many rooms did the Latin American school have?

A. Two I believe.

Q. Two rooms and four grades?

A. Yes, sir.

Q. And two teachers?

A. Yes, sir.

Q. Each teacher taught two classes I presume?

A. I am not positive, but I imagine.

[fol. 76] Q. And to your knowledge it was the theory of the Edna Independent School District by having two teachers for four grades, each teaching two grades, that would be the best way to overcome the language handicap?

A. That was the theory back of it.

Q. Do you have two grades to a teacher in either Austin or Sam Houston School?

A. Yes, sir.

Q. Which one?

A. Sam Houston School.

Q. How many cases like that?

A. I don't know, but I do know there were some.

Q. But most of the time in the other school you had one teacher to a grade?

A. All departmentalized.

Q. Do you have any idea what the teachers' load was in the Latin American school?

A. No, I don't know.

Q. Have you any idea what the average teacher's load was in the other schools?

A. No, sir.

Q. Do you know how long that frame building had been standing there that was used for a Latin American school? When was it built?

A. I don't know, but it was a relatively new building.

Mr. Hartman: I don't see the relevancy of these questions.

[fol. 77] Mr. Garcia: I was trying to clarify some point.

Court: Go ahead.

Q. Do you have any children whose native tongue is Bohemian attending your System?

A. I would imagine, but I never hear any of them speaking Bohemian.

Q. To your knowledge has a separate school been maintained to overcome language handicap for any other nationality than Latin American in the Edna Independent School District?

A. Not to my knowledge.

Q. How many High School graduates did you have last year?

A. 63.

Q. How many of those were Latin America?

A. I don't know.

Q. Were there some?

A. Yes, I am positive there were some.

Q. But you do not know how many?

A. No, sir.

Q. When you get the census rolls, will you be kind enough to provide for me the list of names of the graduates?

A. I think I can.

Re-cross examination.
Questions by Mr. Hartman:

Now, Mr. Bounds, Mr. Garcia asked you -while ago who it was that recommended or decided when these children in [fol. 78] the Latin American elementary school were ready to go to the other school, and you stated that the teacher did. Isn't it true that the development of any child in school and the rate of development is left more or less in the teacher's hands?

A. Yes, sir.

Q. And isn't it true she is the one that decides when a child is promoted from one grade to another?

A. Yes, sir.

Q. And you stated you do not know of any instance where a child was denied the right of advancing once it was ready?

A. Yes, sir.

Q. You stated yourself you knew of only one case where a child was advanced before finishing the four years?

A. I said I definitely know of one.

Q. You are not undertaking to say that is the only one?

A. No, sir.

Q. Is it your belief there were more?

A. I don't know.

Q. The object in this elementary school was to teach the child English along with the other subjects, but was not the emphasis on teaching English?

A. Yes, sir.

Q. Speaking, reading and writing the English language?

A. Yes, sir.

Q. And approximately how long does it take to teach a [fol. 79] child the English language?

Mr. Garcia: I want him qualified on that, and if he is an expert on it then I will take him on voir dire.

Mr. Hartman: I withdraw the question.

Q. Do you from your experience in public school work as a teacher, as Superinten-dent, do you or not know approximately how long it takes to teach the average Latin American student to speak the English language?

A. No, sir. That would vary and depend on how much assistance from home. Many things enter into that. I don't have any idea.

Q. Do you know whether there were any students who remained in this elementary school for 4 years and still had language difficulty?

A. I don't know about that.

Q. Isn't it a fact that many small schools, country schools, various country schools, only have one or two rooms in them?

A. Yes, sir.

Q. And isn't it a fact that one or two teachers take care of every grade in those schools?

A. That is right.

Q. And those students, if they pass their work, are qualified to go on to High School?

A. Yes sir.

Q. From your experience in the schools which nationality [fol. 80] of children has the most language difficulty, the Bohemians, Germans, or Mexicans or Latin Amer-icans?

A. The one I have by experience is Latin Americans.

Q. They have the most language difficulty?

A. Yes sir.

Q. And you stated so far as you know you did not have any Bohemian students who could not speak English?

A. That is right.

Q. And do you or not know of any instance where a German child started elemen-tary school without being able to speak English?

A. No, sir, I don't know of any.

Q. You no longer maintain the school for language difficulty?

A. No, sir.

Q. You stated to Mr. Garcia you don't know how many member of the Mexican or Latin American nationality were in your graduation class last year?

A. Yes, sir.

Q. Isn't it a fact that all Latin American students were given the same opportunities to graduate from school as those children of any other nationality?

A. That is right.

Re-direct examination.
Question by Mr. Garcia:

Q. From your experience as a teacher would you state that it is easier to teach a child a foreign language by segregating [fol. 81] that child with other children who speak only that language at the age of 6 or 7 or that it would be easier to teach them by let-ting them mix freely with children who do speak that language all right?

A. I have never taught any language. I don't know.

Q. You are not vouching for the system or rather the policy pursued by the Edna Independent School District prior to the abandonment of the school?

A. As far as whether they learn English quicker when in contact with others who speak English constantly, I don't know.

Q. Do you have any idea what the solution for a 6-year old child is?

A. No, sir. That will vary with each child.

Q. Would you say for a teacher teaching two grades in one room, altogether in one room, would be conducive to the rapid learning of a foreign language by those children?

A. Certainly it is.

Q. You do that in all grades in Sam Houston or Austin?

A. No, sir, not all grades.

Q. For a teacher to have two grades in either Austin or Sam Houston was the exception rather than the rule?

A. I believe that is pretty well true.

Q. But it was the rule and not the exception in the Latin American school?

A. I believe that is true.

[fol. 82] STIPULATION

Mr. Garcia: It is stipulated by counsel for the State and counsel for the defendant that there are some male persons of Mexican or Latin American descent in Jackson County who, by virtue of being citizens, householders, or freeholders, and having all other legal prerequisites to jury service, are eligible to serve as members of a jury commission, grand jury and/or petit jury.

Mr. Garcia: I have nothing further, except getting the percentage of names on the rolls and the percentage of High School graduates.

STATE'S TESTIMONY IN CHIEF

L. S. HORTON, called as a witness on behalf of the State, having been first duly cautioned and sworn to testify the truth, the whole truth, and nothing but the truth, testified as follows:

Direct examination.
Questions by Mr. Hartman:

Q. You are L. S. Horton?

A. Yes, sir.

Q. Where do you live?

 [fol. 83] A. Ganado.

Q. What business are you in?

A. I am supposed to be retired. I am working now for the Mauritz Rice Storage Company.

Q. You are a citizen of Jackson County?

A. Yes, sir.

Q. I will ask you to state whether or not you were recently appointed a jury commissioner for Jackson County?

A. Yes, sir.

Q. And by whom were you appointed?

A. I guess the District Judge. Mr. Watson notified me to come.

Q. And you were then appointed and sworn in by the District Judge, Howard P. Green?

A. Yes, sir.

Q. And you did serve in that capacity?

A. Yes, sir.

Q. Did you or not in company with other jury commissioners select the Grand Jury Panel for the present term of the District Court, 24th District, in Jackson County?

A. We did.

Q. I will ask you, Mr. Horton, whether or not in making your selections on this Grand Jury Panel you or any of the other Jury commissioners in your presence at any time discriminated against persons of Mexican or Latin American descent in forming that Grand Jury Panel?

[fol. 84] Mr. Garcia: The word "discrimination" called for a conclusion. I want to know what counsel is asking, what he means by "discrimination".

Mr. Hartman: Withdraw the question.

 Q. How did you go about selecting the men to serve on the Grand Jury Panel?

A. The District Judge gave us each instructions as to what they would be; they had to have a poll tax receipt, and be a freeholder, and a householder in the County.

Q. Did you or not then select for service on this Panel the men in Jackson County who were qualified and whom you thought to be best qualified for that service?

A. Yes, sir.

Q. Did you in selecting the man to serve on that Grand Jury Panel in any way discriminate against any person otherwise eligible simply because of the fact that he was of Mexican or Latin American descent?

A. We did not.

Q. Did you purposely leave off of that panel any man who was otherwise qualified simply because he was of Mexican or Latin American descent?

A. No, sir.

Q. Did you receive any instructions from the Court which would have indicated to you it was his desire that you leave anyone off of the Grand Jury Panel simply because such [fol. 85] person was of Mexican or Latin American descent?

A. We did not.

Cross examination.
Questions by Mr. Garcia:

Q. You are a native of this County?

A. I have been here almost 33 years.

Q. You know, of course, there is a certain percentage of people of Mexican or Latin American descent that are residents of Jackson County?

A. Yes, sir.

Q. By the same token matters that come before the Grand Jury often they affect people of Mexican or Latin American descent?

A. As I said, we find all nationalities have misdemeanors or felonies and disobey the law.

Q. No particular racial or nationality group has a monopoly?

A. That is right.

Q. However, because of the fact that Spanish is the native tongue of these people wouldn't it occur to you that possibly having a person who speaks Spanish on the Grand Jury would be of benefit?

A. Well, to my knowledge, that was not discussed.

Q. You do know, of course, there are many people of Mexican or Latin American descent in this County who don't speak any English at all?

A. Yes, sir. In fact, I know quite a few myself that don't [fol.86] understand English.

Q. There was a likelihood that non-English speaking people would come before the Grand Jury?

A. It is possible.

Q. But the matter was never discussed in selecting members of the Grand Jury?

A. No, sir.

Q. It was not discussed either way?

A. No, sir.

Q. And it was your testimony you simply selected the people who were best qualified to serve on the Grand Jury?

A. Yes, sir.

Re-direct examination.
Questions by Mr. Hartman:

Q. While giving you instructions as jury commissioners, isn't it a fact that the District Judge told you a legal requirement for service on the Grand Jury is the ability to read and write the English language?

A. Yes, sir.

Re-cross examination.
Questions by Mr. Garcia:

Q. And you made no effort to ascertain whether or not a person or persons of Mexican descent were eligible to serve on the Grand Jury?

A. No, sir.

[fol. 87] Redirect examination.
By Mr. Hartman:

Q. That matter was not discussed?

A. There was no racial discrimination discussed. We selected them irrespective of nationality. We did not turn this man down because he was a Bohemian, or this man because he was a Pole, or this one because he was a Negro, or this one because he was Spanish. We selected good, levelheaded men that are outstanding for good common sense for our Grand Jury.

Q. And the men that were on that panel were the ones you selected?

A. Yes, sir.

Re-cross examination.
By Mr. Garcia:

Q. In addition to selecting the Grand Jury here, did you have a Petit Jury Panel?

A. Yes, sir.

Q. How many people did you select for the Petit Juries?

A. As well as I recall we selected 250—for 5 weeks at 50 each.

Q. And with reference to that you followed the same procedure, in selecting the 250 Petit Jurors, that you did with reference to the Grand Jury?

A. Yes, sir. In other words, we did not want to have an ex-horse thief as a juror.

Q. And you made those efforts to determine whether [fol. 88] there were any ex-horse thieves?

A. We did not pay any attention to what nationality he was. We selected the man, not the nationality.

Q. And in carrying out that policy, you just did not have to select any people of Mexican descent on your jury panel?

A. That is right.

Q. And I believe you answered my question while ago you made no particular effort to determine whether there were any people of Mexican descent eligible to serve?

A. We had a roll and that was what we used. We never discussed it.

Re-direct examination.
By Mr. Hartman:

Q. And you did not leave any off simply because of his nationality?

A. No, sir.

Re-cross examination.
By Mr. Garcia:

Q. It just is not customary for people of Mexican descent to serve on Grand Juries?

A. I could not say about that.

Mrs. SHIRLEY SCHROEDER, called as a witness on behalf of the State, having been first duly cautioned and sworn to testify the truth, the whole truth, and nothing but the truth, testified as follows:

[fol. 89] Direct examination.
By Mr. Hartman:

Q. What is your name?

A. Mrs. Shirley Schroeder.

Q. You live in Edna?

A. Yes, sir.

Q. In Jackson County?

A. Yes, sir.

Q. How long have you lived here?

A. Six years in October.

Q. What is your business?

A. I am the Secretary of the Jackson County Chamber of Commerce.

Q. How long have you held that position?

A. We have just organized the Jackson County Chamber of Commerce on July 1st, of this year, and I assumed that position at that time. This present Chamber of Commerce is the outgrowth of the Edna Chamber of Commerce and it is now a County-wide organization, and I had served with the previous organization.

Q. As Secretary?

A. Yes, sir.

Q. There is another thing: Has the Edna Chamber of Commerce merged into and become a part of the Jackson County Chamber of Commerce?

A. Yes, sir.

[fol. 90] Q. I will ask you to state whether or not you are familiar with the membership of the present Jackson County Chamber of Commerce?

A. Generally so, yes, sir.

Q. Are there or not members of your organization who are of Latin American or Mexican descent?

A. Well, I believe right now we only have one. We have several on our potential membership list that we are hoping will come in, but they have not sent in their memberships yet.

Q. Does that or not mean that you are soliciting their membership into your organization?

A. Yes, sir. I might explain: In the Edna Chamber of Commerce we had a list of members and we had several Latin Americans on the list and when we organized countywide we, naturally, solicited all of our old members for membership in the countywide organization.

Q. There is nothing in your charter or your by-laws which prohibits a person of Mexican or Latin American descent to belong?

A. Definitely not.

Q. As a matter of fact, they are welcome?

A. They are invited.

Q. Do you know whether or not any person of Mexican or Latin American descent has ever sat on the Board of Directors of the Edna Chamber of Commerce before merging [fol. 91] into the countywide organization?

A. Yes, sir. In the year 1949-1950 we had two Latin Americans on the Board of Directors, and 1950-1951 we had two Latin Americans on the Board of Directors.

Cross examination.
By Mr. Garcia:

Q. Do you recall approximately how many members you had in the old Edna Chamber of Commerce, before it merged with the County Chamber of Commerce?

A. I believe it was about 170.

Q. And about how many were Latin Americans?

A. I could not—I don't know exactly.

Q. Would you say fewer than 10 or more than 10?

A. I would say it would be fewer than 10.

Q. Would you say about 5?

A. Without checking my rolls I would not say, but I would say it was less than 10.

Q. And at present you say you have two on the rolls of the Jackson County Chamber of Commerce?

A. I believe that is right. We are just getting organized and our membership, I don't remember it exactly.

Q. As Secretary of the Chamber of Commerce I take it you have had occasion to observe the activities and functions of the service clubs, like Kiwanis Club, Lions Club, Rotary Club, and so on?

[fol. 92] A. In a general way, yes, sir.

Q. How many service clubs do you have here?

A. We have the Rotary and Lions and recently organized a Junior Chamber of Commerce, which I think is classified as a service club.

Q. Do you know of any Latin Americans who have ever been members of the Rotary or Lions?

A. I would not be in position to know.

Q. You don't know either way?

A. No, sir.

Q. How about the Junior Chamber of Commerce?

A. I would not know.

Q. Are you a native of Jackson County?

A. No, sir. I have lived here since 1945.

W.C. SIMONS, called as a witness on behalf of the State, having been first duly cautioned and sworn to testify the truth, the whole truth, and nothing but the truth, testified as follows:

Direct examination.
By Mr. Hartman:

Q. Your name is W.C. Simons?

A. Yes, sir.

Q. Where do you live?

A. Vanderbilt.

[fol. 93] Q. What business are you in?

A. Ranching.

Q. How long have you lived in Vanderbilt?

A. I have been living there about 10 years.

Q. How long have you lived in Jackson County?

A. All my life.

Q. Mr. Simons, you were appointed by the District Court of Jackson County to serve as a Jury Commissioner for this term of court?

A. Yes, sir.

Q. Did you or not serve in that capacity?

A. Yes, sir.

Q. And you, along with the other members of the Commission, selected our Grand Jury Panel for this term of Court and the Petit Jury Panel?

A. Yes, sir.

Q. I will ask you whether or not, when you were sworn in as Jury Commissioner by the District Court—Who swore you in?

A. Judge Green.

Q. Judge Howard P. Green?

A. Yes, sir.

Q. Judge of the 24th Judicial District of Texas?

A. Yes, sir.

Q. Did he at that time say anything to that Jury Commission in regard to discriminating in any way against any person or persons of a nationality?

[fol. 94] A. None whatsoever.

Q. Did he or not say anything in his instructions to you in regard to discriminating against anyone of Mexican or Latin American descent in selection of the Grand Jury Panel or the Petit Jury Panel?

A. No, sir.

Q. There were five members on your Commission?

A. Yes, sir.

Q. And you all five concurred in the selection made, consulted on them and concurred in them?

A. Yes, sir.

Q. State whether or not you as a member or whether any of the other members of the Commission in your presence failed to place anyone on the Grand Jury Panel or Petit Jury Panel because of his nationality?

A. No, sir.

Q. Was any distinction made in anyway in any of those selections because of nationality?

A. No, sir.

Q. Was the matter of nationality even discussed?

A. No, sir; it was not discussed.

Q. And when you and the other members of the Jury Commission appointed the members of the Grand Jury Panel, did you or not follow the Court's instructions and select the men whom you thought were the best qualified for the job?

[fol. 95] A. That is what we tried to do.

Q. And did you do the same in regard to the Petit Jury Panel?

A. Yes, sir.

Q. Did you or not in any way at any time during your service on the Jury Commission discriminate against any such person where he was of Mexican or Latin American descent?

A. No, sir.

Mr. Hartman: That is all.

Mr. Garcia: No questions.

W. J. SMITH, called as a witness on behalf of the State, having been first duly cautioned and sworn to testify the truth, the whole truth, and nothing but the truth, testified as follows:

Direct examination.
By Mr. Hartman:

Q. You are Mr. W. J. Smith?

A. Yes, sir.

Q. Where do you live?

A. At Marbro.

Q. In Jackson County?

A. Yes, sir.

Q. What is your business?

A. In the oil field.

Q. How long have you lived in Jackson County?

[fol. 96] A. Eight years.

Q. You were appointed by the District Court of Jackson County to serve as Jury Commissioner for this term of court?

A. Yes, sir.

Q. You were sworn in as such and then served as such?

A. I did.

Q. Were you or not sworn in by Judge Howard P. Green, Judge of the 24th District Court of Jackson County, Texas?

A. I was.

Q. I will ask you to state whether or not at that time Judge Green, the Court, gave you any instructions in regard to discriminating in any way against any person because of his nationality in making your selections on that panel?

A. No, sir.

Q. He gave you no such instructions, is that right?

A. That is right.

Q. And he did not mention it?

A. No, sir.

Q. And when you served on the Jury Commission along with the other four members and when you made your selections for the Grand Jury Panel and the Petit Jury Panel, did you or any one of the other Commissioners at any time fail to place anybody on either of those Panels simply because of their nationality?

A. We did not.

Q. Did you fail to place anyone on there because be was of [fol. 97] Mexican or Latin American descent?

A. We did not.

Q. Was any type of discrimination discussed by you?

A. No, sir.

Q. And when those selections were made, did you appoint men whom you and the other Jury Commissioners thought best qualified?

A. To the best of our ability we did.

Mr. Hartman: That is all

Mr. Garcia: No questions.

FLOYD LARKIN, called as a witness on behalf of the State, having been first duly cautioned and sworn to testify the truth, the whole truth, and nothing but the truth, testified as follows:

Direct examination.
By Mr. Hartman:

Q. You are Floyd Larkin?

A. Yes, sir.

Q. You live our at Coredele?

A. Yes, sir.

Q. What business are you in?

A. Farming.

Q. How long have you lived in Jackson County?

A. All my life—37 years.

Q. You were appointed by the District Court of Jackson [fol. 98] County as a Jury Commissioner for this term of court?

A. Yes, sir.

Q. And you were sworn in as such by Judge Howard P. Green, judge of that Court?

A. Yes, sir.

Q. In his instructions to you, did the Court tell you anything to indicate to you he wanted you or the other Jury Commissioners to in any way discriminate against anybody by reason of their nationality?

A. No, sir.

Q. Did he tell you or anybody on the Commission to leave anybody off of the Grand Jury Panel or Petit Jury Panel because he was a Mexican or Latin American or because he was any other nationality?

A. No, sir.

Q. And when you and the other Jury Commissioners selected the Grand Jury Panel for this term and the Petit Jury Panel for this term, did you or any of the other Commissioners leave anybody off of those Panels by reason of their nationality?

A. No, sir.

Q. Did you leave anyone off because he was a Latin American or Mexican?

A. No, sir.

Q. Did you or not make appointments of men whom you and the other Jury Commissioners thought were best qualified for the job?

[fol. 99] A. Yes, sir, we did.

Mr. Hartman: That is all.

Mr. Garcia: No questions.

C. D. WINSTEAD, called as a witness on behalf of the State, having been first duly cautioned and sworn to testify the truth, the whole truth, and nothing but the truth, testified as follows:

Direct examination.
By Mr. Hartman:

Q. What is your name?

A. C. D. Winstead.

Q. You live in Ganado?

A. Yes, sir.

Q. Jackson County?

A. Yes, sir.

Q. How long have you lived in Ganado, Jackson County?

A. About 10 years.

Q. How long have you lived in Jackson County?

A. About 10 years.

Q. What is your business?

A. I am Tax Collector for the School District.

Q. Are you or not familiar with the students who go to the Ganado Independent School District?

A. Yes, sir.

[fol.100] Q. Are you familiar with the students who go to the Ganado School?

A. Yes, sir. I have taught there, taught vocation and I have coached football there.

Q. Please state whether or not during your experience with the Ganado School there have been students of Latin American descent who have played on the football team?

A. Yes, sir, there have been.

Q. And have been members of the chief squad?

A. Ycs, sir.

Q. State whether or not in your experience any student of Latin American descent has ever been discriminated against simply because of nationality?

A. Not to my knowledge since I have been there.

Q. Now, arc you a member of any service organization?

A. Yes, sir.

Q. Which one?

A. The Rotary.

Q. Do you hold any office?

A. I was President last year.

Q. I will ask you to state whether or not any of the members of the Rotary are of Latin American descent?

A. Yes, sir.

Q. How many?

A. I recall only one. There might be others.

[fol. 101]Q. Is he still a member?

A. He is not.

Q. Why not?

A. He left town.

Q. He is not a member of your Club, but so far as you know he is still a member of Rotary International?

A. I don't know. However, he was a member when he was there.

Q. And a member when he left?

A. Yes, sir.

Q. Was he a member in good standing?

Λ. Vcry good standing.

Q. Met with you regularly?

A. Yes, sir.

Q. And took part in your service organization?

A. Yes, sir.

Cross examination.
By Mr. Garcia:

Q. Mr. Winstead, you testified you were Superintendent?

A. No, sir. Tax Collector.

Q. You are familiar with the operation of the Ganado Independent School District?

A. Yes, sir.

Q. How many schools does your District consist of?

A. Only one.

Q. Do you know the approximate enrollment in your school?

[fol. 102] A. Yes, sir.

Q. How many?

A. A little less than 800.

Q. As I understand then it is one building and the children go to school from the first grade through to the high school?

A. Yes, sir.

Q. Now, can you tell me approximately what percentage of those pupils are of Mexican or Latin American descent?

A. I don't know.

Q. Can you tell me what the approximate percentage of the residents of the Ganado Independent School District or patrons of that District are of Mexican or Latin American descent?

A. I don't know.

Q. You would not have any idea from your tax collections?

A. No, sir.

Q. Can you tell us approximately how many graduated last year?

A. I believe there were 30.

Q. Can you tell me how many of those were of Mexican or Latin American descent?

A. No, sir.

Q. Do you recall any of them being of Mexican or Latin American descent?

A. I do not.

Q. Do you have any affirmative recollection of any Latin American graduating from your High School?

A. Yes, sir.

[fol. 103] Q. But you don't recall that to have been last year?

A. No, sir.

Q. You have no affirmative recollection?

A. The only recollection I have is when I was connected with the school teaching and had boys playing on the football team. I knew when those boys graduated and I knew they were of Latin American descent.

Q. You knew what they were?

A. Yes, sir.

Q. As far as you know, there has never been more than one school building in that District?

A. Yes, sir; there have been several.

Q. In recent years?

A. Well, since 1946 there were more than two and as recently as 1948 there were more than two.

Q. Were any of those schools Latin American?

A. No, sir.

Q. There has never been any segregation in your System?

A. Not that I know of.

Q. And you were connected with the system how many years?

A. I lived in Ganado 10 years.

Q. I take it then all other buildings, schools, were consolidated in one building, school building?

A. Yes, sir.

Q. And as far as you know, there has never been any [fol. 104] separate school for persons of Mexican or Latin American descent?

A. Not that I know of. They all attended the same school.

Q. Regardless of whether or not they spoke English when they first came to school?

A. That is my recollection.

Re-direct examination.
By Mr. Hartman:

Q. Mr. Winstead, Ganado is in Jackson County?

A. Yes, sir.

Q. How far is it from Edna?

A. About 9 miles.

LON R. DRUSHEL, called as a witness on behalf of the State, having been first duly cautioned and sworn to testify the truth, the whole truth, and nothing but the truth, testified as follows:

Direct examination.
By Mr. Hartman:

Q. What is your name?

A. Lon R. Drushel.

Q. You live in Edna, Jackson County?

A. Yes, sir.

Q. What business are you in?

A. I am in the banking business.

Q. In the Jackson County State Bank?

A. Yes, sir.

[fol. 105] Q. Have you lived in Jackson County all your life?

A. Yes, sir.

Q. You were appointed by the District Court of this County as a Jury Commissioner to serve at this term of the District Court?

A. Yes, sir.

Q. And you were, accordingly, sworn in as a Jury Commissioner by Judge Howard P. Green, District Judge—

A. Yes, sir.

Q.—24th Judicial District of Texas?

A. Yes, sir.

Q. I will ask you to state whether or not at the time that Judge Green swore you in or at any other time while he was informing or instructing the Jury Commissioners he made any statement to you or any of the other members of the Jury Commission which would indicate that he wanted you to discriminate against anybody in making your selections on the Grand Jury Panel and Petit Jury Panel?

A. No, sir, he did not.

Q. Was anything like that said by the Court at all?

A. Not that I can recall. I am sure there was not.

Q. And after you had been sworn in and you and the other members of the Jury Commission were making your selections for the Grand Jury Panel and Petit Jury Panel for this term did you or any other member leave anybody off of either of those lists simply because of their nationality?

[fol. 106] A. No, sir.

Q. Did you or any other member of the Jury Commission discriminate against the Mexican or Latin American nationality in any way in making those selections?

A. Not that I can think of.

Q. Did you or not when you made those selections select the men whom you thought best qualified?

A. That is what we did.

Q. Irrespective of nationality?

A. Yes,

Cross examination.
By Mr. Garcia:

Q. It never occurred to you any person of Mexican or Latin American descent might be eligible for Grand Jury work, did it?

A. Well, I am sure there are. I understood they were eligible.

Q. How about your Petit Jury list? Did it occur to you there might be some who might be eligible?

A. I am sure we probably have some. It was quite a list. I don't recall just who was on it, but I am sure we probably have some. I don't know without looking them over.

Q. It just is not customary for Grand Jury Commissioners to appoint people of Mexican or Latin American descent on Grand Jury Panels and Petit Jury Panels?

A. I don't know about that. I think that we tried to pick [fol.107] the men best qualified.

Re-direct examination.
By Mr. Hartman:

Q. As far as your knowledge?

A. I think possibly we did.

Q. And the Petit Jury list?

A. Yes, sir.

DEFENDANT'S REBUTTAL

JOHN J. HERRERA, called as a witness on behalf of the defendant, having been first duly cautioned and sworn to testify the truth, the whole truth, and nothing but the truth, testified as follows:

Direct examination.
By Mr. Garcia:

Q. What is your name?

A. John J. Herrera.

Q. Are you a member of the Texas Bar?

A. I am.

Q. Where do you practice?

A. I practice all over the State of Texas.

Q. Mr. Herrera, I will ask you whether you examined a list that I handed you with some 63 names that has been handed to me from the Edna Independent School District [fol. 108] showing the graduates for the term 1951 from the Edna High School. I will ask you whether you examined that list?

A. I did.

Q. Is Spanish your native tongue?

A. Yes, sir.

Q. Did you learn it simultaneously with English or before you learned English?

A. Yes, sir.

Q. At home did you ordinarily speak Spanish?

A. Yes, sir.

Q. Will you say you are well versed with the Spanish language?

A. Yes, I would say so.

Q. Are you bilingual?

A. Yes; and I can read and write them too.

Q. Are you familiar with surnames that can be considered Spanish or Hispanic?

A. Yes, I am.

Q. Names like Garcia and Herrera, and so on?

A. Yes, sir.

Q. Did you find on that list of 63 graduates any Spanish names?

A. Yes, I did.

Q. How many?

A. Two.

Q. Do you recall what those names were?

A. One was Victor Rudriguez. I believe the last name [fol. 109] was more or less misspelled. The correct spelling would be R-o-d-r-i-g-u-e-z. I believe on the list the last name was that. And the other name was Chris Rosas.

Q. You found no other Spanish names?

A. No, sir.

Q. During the noon recess I will ask you if you had occasion to go back here to a public privy, right in the back of the courthouse square?

A. Yes, sir.

Q. The one designated for men?

A. Yes, sir.

Q. Now did you find one toilet there or more?

A. I found two.

Q. Did the one on the right have any lettering on it?

A No, sir.

Q. Did the one on the left have any lettering on it?

A. Yes, it did.

Q. What did it have?

A. It had the lettering "Colored Men" and right under 'Colored Men" it had two Spanish words.

Q. What were those words?

A. The first word was "Hombres".

Q. What does that mean?

A. That means "Men".

Q. And the second one?

[fol. 110] A. "Aqui", meaning "Here".

Q. Right under the words "Colored Men" was "Hombres Aqui" in Spanish, which means "Men Here"?

A. Yes, sir.

Cross examination.
By Mr. Hartman:

Q. What list was that you were talking about while ago?

A. The list I believe Mr. Winstead gave to Mr. Garcia and Mr. Garcia handed it to me.

Q. I am sorry. I did not understand.

Q. I think a gentleman by the name of Winstead handed it to Mr. Garcia and Mr. Garcia handed it to me.

Q. What was the list, supposed to be?

A. Reported to me as being the list of the last senior graduation class of the High School in Jackson County.

Q. And you state there were two Spanish names on that list?

A. Yes, sir. I should say there were only two names that could be interpreted as being Hispanic or Mexican origin. There might have been more. Of course, sometimes they inter-marry.

Q. You are not undertaking to say that there were only two of those graduates of Latin American descent, but only two had Spanish names?

A. Yes, sir.

Q. And, of course, you are not undertaking to say there was any discrimination against any other Latin American [fol. 111] pupils so that they could not have graduated?

A. No, sir.

Q. You are just down here on a visit?

A. Yes, sir.

Q. There was not a lock on this unmarked door to the privy?

A. No, sir.

Q. It was open to the public?

A. They were both open to the public, yes, sir.

Q. And didn't have on it "For Americans Only", or "For English Only", or "For Whites Only"?

A. No, sir.

Q. Did you undertake to use either one of these toilets while you were down here?

A. I did feel like it, but the feeling went away when I saw the sign.

Q. So you did not?

A. No, sir, I did not.

Q. But you are not telling the Court you could not have used the unmarked toilet simply because your name is Herrera?

A. No, sir.

Re-direct examination.
By Mr. Garcia:

Q. Neither can you tell the Court that you were invited to use the one on the right?

A. No, sir.

[fol. 112] Q. And the one on the left that had the lettering "Colored Men" and "Hombres Aqui" you did not see a sign "For Whites Only", or "For English Only", or "For Americans Only"?

A. No, sir.

Q. Only "Colored Men" and "Hombres Aqui"?

A. Yes, sir.

JAMES DE ANDA, called as a witness on behalf of the Defendant, having been first duly cautioned and sworn to testify the truth, the whole truth, and nothing but the truth, testified as follows:

Direct examination.
By Mr. Garcia:

Q. What is your name?

A. James De Anda.

Q. Mr. De Anda, what is your business or occupation?

A. I am an attorney.

Q. Where do you live?

A. In Houston, Harris County, Texas.

Q. Are you now engaged in active practice?

A. Yes, sir.

Q. Mr. De Anda, I will ask you to identify the documentary instrument you have in your hands.

A. This is a census roll for Jackson County, the School District.

Q. I handed you that instrument?

[fol. 113] A. Yes, sir.

Court: We will let the record show that is the one that Mr. Bounds delivered to Mr. Garcia.

Mr. Hartman: That is correct.

Q. What else does that say?

A. This is the white, apparently white children; it is dated 1950 to 1951.

Q. And the heading is "Consolidated Census Roll"?

A. Yes, sir.

Q. Mr. De Anda, will ask you whether or not you counted the number of names on that consolidated census roll?

A. I did, yes, sir.

Q. How many names did you find on that roll?

A. I found 1184 names.

Q. In all?

A. Yes, sir.

Q. Now, Mr. De Anda, are you familiar with Spanish or Hispanic names?

A. Yes, I am.

Q. You are familiar with the Spanish language?

A. Yes, sir. I speak Spanish.

Q. Do you also read and write Spanish?

A. To a limited extent.

Q. Do you recognize common Spanish and Hispanic names?

A. Yes, I do.

[fol. 114] Q. At my request did you peruse this list for the purpose of obtaining the Spanish or Hispanic names thereon?

A. Yes, sir.

Q. Did you make a record of each of those names?

A. Yes, I did. I computed the numbers.

Q. You testified you found 1184 names on that list?

A. Yes, sir.

Q. Of the 1184 scholastics in the Edna Independent School District of Jackson County, how many have Spanish or Hispanic names?

A. 211.

Q. 211?

A. Yes, sir.

Q. I will ask you whether or not you found that certain names on the roll bad been struck?

A: Yes, sir. You could still read the names, but for some reason there had been lines drawn through them. I did not count those names.

Q. Did you observe whether or not those names that were struck out were Spanish or Hispanic?

A. I would say the large majority were Spanish names.

Q. You don't know why they were struck out?

A. No, sir, but I assume they were not on the roll and did not include them.

Q. But those were struck after you found 211 out of 1184 [fol. 115] to be Spanish names?

A. Yes, sir.

Q. Did you make a computation of the percentages?

A. No, sir, but 211 out of 1184 would be between 15 and 20 per cent. I don't know exactly right off-hand.

Examination.
By the Court:

Q. Is that for 1950?

A. It says 1950-1951. I suppose it is from 1950 through 1951. It is probably from September of 1950 through June of 1951.

Continuation of direct examination.
By Mr. Garcia:

Q. You assume that is on the basis of the scholastics at the time?

A. Yes, sir.

Cross examination.
By Mr. Hartman:

Q. This list you just now computed from or referred to made no distinction between Latin American children and children of other nationalities?

A. No, sir.

Q. It is designated the list of white students?

A. Yes, sir.

Q. And Latin American or Mexican children are on that list too?

A. Yes, sir.

Q. You don't know, of course, how many Negro scholastics there are?

A. No, sir.

[fol. 116] Re-direct examination.
By Mr. Garcia:

Q. Do you know what the purpose of the census roll is?

A. To compute the number of children going to school in the School District.

Q. To be sent to Austin, if you know?

A. Well, I suppose the State does have the State list, but I don't know what it is for.

[fols.117-118] Reporter's Certificate to foregoing transcript omitted in printing.

[fols. 119-121] IN DISTRICT COURT OF JACKSON COUNTY
AGEEMENT OF COUNSEL
[Title omitted]

We, the undersigned, attorneys of record for the State of Texas and the Defendant in the above numbered and entitled cause, do hereby agree that the foregoing pages numbered from 1 through 79 constitute a full, true and correct transcript of all the evidence adduced and proceedings had in connection with the hearing on motions presented by the defense on October 4, 1951, in such cause in so far only as the same relative to (1) Defendant's Motion to Quash the Indictment and (2) Defendant's Motion to Quash the Jury Panel, together with all the objections to the admission or exclusion of evidence, and the rulings of the Court on such objections; and we do further agree that said pages numbered from 1 through 79 may be filed as the State-ment of Facts, in question and answer form, in connection with such hearing in so far only as the same relatives to the Motions enumerated above.

Dated this the 13th day of March, A. D. 1952.

(S.) Wayne L. Hartman, Counsel for the State of Texas; Gus C. Garcia, Counsel for Defendant.

[fol. 122] DISTRICT COURT OF JACKSON COUNTY
[Title omitted]

TRANSCRIPT OP HEARING ON MOTION TO QUASH THE INDICTMENT, MOTION TO QUASH JURY PANEL, AND MOTION TO QUASH THE TALES-MEN AFTER SPECIAL VENIRE WAS EXHAUSTED—October 8, 1951

APPEARANCES:

Mr. Wayne L. Hartman, District Attorney, 24th Judicial District of Texas, Cuero, Texas,

Mr. Cullen B. Vance, County Attorney, Jackson County, Edna, Texas,

Mr. Wm. H. Hamblen, Special Prosecutor, Edna, Texas, Appearing for The State of Texas;

Mr. Gus C. Garcia, 432 International Building, San Antonio, Texas,

Mr. John J. Herrera, 710 Scanlan Building, Houston, Texas,

Appearing for the Defendant.

[fol. 123] Whereupon, in said cause the following, among other, proceedings were had in the absence of the jury, to-wit:

COLLOQUY

Mr. Garcia: At this time I should like to dictate a motion to quash the indictment first based on the same grounds as I set out in my motion to quash the indictment and my motion to quash the entire jury panel.

Court: Overruled.

Mr. Garcia: Note our exception.

Mr. Garcia: I want to introduce a photograph of the sign at the privy alluded to.

Court: All right.

Court; I am calling the case of The State of Texas versus Pete Hernandez. What does the State say?

Mr. Hartman: The State is ready.

Court: What does the defense say?

Mr. Garcia: The defendant is ready.

[fol. 124] Reporter's Note: At this point the Court administered the following oath to the special veniremen: "You, and each of you, solemnly swear that you will make true answers to such questions as may be propounded to you by the Court, or under its direction, touching your service and qualification as a juror, so help you God."

Court (Addressing counsel for the respective parties):

Are you ready to proceed with the examination?

Mr. Hartman: Yes, sir.

Mr. Garcia: Yes, sir.

Reporter's Note: Thereupon each special venireman was examined by counsel for the respective parties separate and apart from the other special veniremen, and when such examination was concluded late on October 9, 1951, only 11 jurors had been obtained. The Court thereupon administered the appropriate oath to the Sheriff, Mr. Lewis Watson, and his Deputy, Mr.—Gabrysh, and instructed them to summon 12 talesmen to report at 9 o'clock A.M. on October 10, 1951.

Mr. Garcia: In order to preserve the record, I would like to object to this method of obtaining talesmen to supplement the regular special venire drawn by the Court.

Court: Objection overruled, and let the record show [fol. 125] that all of the jurors who were drawn were here examined, except those excused by consent, and we have only 11 jurors at this time.

The following proceedings, among others, were had in the absence of the jury, to-wit:

Reporter's Note: Counsel for each of the respective parties was furnished a list of the 12 talesmen summoned by the Sheriff and his Deputy in accordance with instructions from the Court.

Mr. Garcia: Defendant challenges the array of talesmen and moves that they be dismissed on the same grounds stated with reference to the manner in which they have been selected, which previous motion was overruled by this Honorable Court. The grounds are that it is not permissible for additional veriremen to be obtained in the manner that these talesmen have been obtained, but that they should and must be drawn from the regular panel appointed by the Jury Commissioners.

Court: Well, now, the Court will overrule the motion to quash the panel for the reasons that the Sheriff and his Deputy who summoned the additional talesmen prior to summoning such talesmen were duly sworn under Article 2119, Revised Civil Statutes, and such officers were cautioned [fol. 126] to summon qualified jurors and to obtain jurors from over the County generally and not in one particular locality and obtain jurors, so far as possible, who were free of bias or prejudice in the case, and the list of jurors on the special venire having been exhausted and gone through and additional talesmen being necessary to complete the jury in the case, there having been only 11 jurors taken and sworn in when the additional talesmen were ordered to be summoned.

Mr. Garcia: Note our exception.

STIPULATION

It is stipulated by counsel for the State and counsel for defendant that there is no person of Mexican or other Latin American descent or blood on the list of talesmen.

MOTION TO QUASH THE ARRAY

Mr. Garcia: Defendant further challenges the array of talesmen and moves that said array be quashed and that they be dismissed on the ground that by virtue of the fact that no person of Mexican descent or other Latin American origin was summoned as a talesman. This constitutes additional evidence of the custom, usage and practice in Jackson County, Texas, of discriminating against persons of Mexican descent, and of classing them as a group separate and apart from groups of other races or national origins [fol. 127] in that by virtue of that fact defendant, who is a person of Mexican descent, is being deprived of his Constitutional rights, particularly those guaranteed him by the 14th Amendment of the United States Constitution. In connection with this motion defendant incorporates and embodies all the allegations heretofore set out in his motion to quash the jury panel and his motion to quash the indictment and makes them a part hereof for all purposes. As additional support of this motion to establish the custom, usage and practice of discrimination against persons of Mexican descent in Jackson County defendant offers the witness, Mrs. Chris Rosas.

MRS. CHRIS ROSAS, a witness called on behalf of the defendant, having been first duly cautioned and sworn to testify the truth, the whole truth, and nothing but the truth, testified as follows:

Direct examination.
By Mr. Garcia:

Q. Your name is Mrs. Chris Rosas?

A. Yes, sir.

Q. You are a resident of Edna?

A. For 20 years.

Q. Are you a native born citizen of the United States?

[fol. 128]A. In Victoria County, 20 miles on the other side of Victoria—McFaddin.

Q. Are you married to a resident of Edna?

A. Yes, sir.

Q. Do you have any children?

A. I have three.

Q. What are their names?

A. Chris Rosas, Jr.; Esther Rosas; Alfred Rosas.

Q. And their ages?

A. Chris is 19; Esther is 17, and Alfred is 14.

Q. In addition to your three children you have an adopted child?

A. Yes, sir.

Q. What is her name and age?

A. Mary Elizabeth Rosas, 8 months.

Q. Are you the owner of land in this community?

A. Yes, sir.

Q. You own real estate?

A. Real estate.

Q. Do you have a business in this community?

A. Yes, sir.

Q. A cafe?

A. Yes, sir.

Q. Is this Chris Rosas the same Chris Rosas who graduated from High School in Edna this year?

A. Yes, sir.

[fol. 129]Q. In June, 1951?

A. Yes, sir.

Q. You speak English fluently yourself?

A. Yes, sir.

Q. Did you teach your children English at home or not?

A. I have spoken English to them since they were babies.

Q. Did you teach them English before you taught them Spanish or not?

A. We teached them both. I usually talk English and Spanish.

Q. I will ask you whether or not you attempted to enroll one or more of your children in the school in which only Anglo Americans went?

A. I attempted to enroll Chris, Jr., in that school, but they would not accept him.

Q. When you say "they", who did you talk to?

A. I talked to Mr. Hays.

Q. Who was be?

A. He was the Superintendent.

Q. What year was that approximately?

A. The first year he went to school.

Q. How old was he?

A. Six.

Q. I will ask you whether or not Chris spoke English at the time.

A. He did.

Q. Did you tell the Superintendent your son spoke English?

[fol. 130]A. I did.

Q. And what did he tell you?

A. He told me that they did not accept any Latin Americans in that school.

Q. Where did you send your boy to school?

A. I sent him to the Latin American school and to the Academy.

Q. Why?

A. Because I did not want my boy to go to school in one room for those four years.

Q. At that time you say the school consisted of one room and one teacher teaching four grades?

A. Yes, sir. The teacher was Miss Lucille Linberg.

Q. Mrs. Roses, do you know approximately how many children were in that one room school house?

A. No, I really don't.

Q. I will ask you, if you know, was the majority of the Latin American boys and girls enrolled in the first four grades?

A. Yes, sir.

Q. The majority of the Latin American children in Edna?

A. Yes, sir.

Q. Did you attempt to enroll any other of your children in that school?

A. The girl.

Q. What is her name?

A. Esther.

[fol. 131] Q. How old was she?

A. She was 6.

Q. How old is she now?

A. She is 17.

Q. What luck did you have with her?

A. They did not accept her either.

Q. Whom did you talk to?

A. I talked to Mr. Hays.

Q. He was still the Superintendent?

A. Yes, sir.

Q. At that time did they still have a house for four grades?

A. Yes, sir.

Q. Now, were any particular difficulties involved in getting the children into this one-room school house?

Mr. Hartman: I object. That is too general.

Court: I sustain the objection.

Q. Will you describe what the condition of this one-room school house was?

A. They did not have any conveniences inside the school house, and they have a wood stove in there, and when it rained the kids did not get in the school and the teacher usually dismissed them when it rained because the water was so bad they could not get in the school.

Q. Did the Edna Independent School District provide [fol. 132] transportation for children of Mexican descent?

A. They not have ride. Those that came in the bus they did not accept them.

Q. I did not understand you.

A. I mean they hauled them in the—

Q. They made him ride on a separate trip from the Anglo American children and did not let them ride together?

A. Yes, that is what I mean.

Q. Now, you say you talked to Mr. Hays about getting your daughter in? I will ask you whether or not your daughter spoke English?

A. She did.

Q. When you talked to Mr. Hays what did he say?

A. He just said they did not allow Latin American kids in the school and they had a separate school until they reached the fourth grade.

Q. Do you recall when the school became a two-room school house?

A. I really don't, because I don't remember, because from then on I never did try to-

Q. Now, did you send your daughter to Victoria?

A. Victoria Academy—that is a convent.

Q. How far did she attend the Victoria Academy?

A. Until she was in the 6th grade.

Q. Did you then send her to school here?

A. Yes, sir.

Q. You mean to Edna?

[fol. 133] A. Yes, sir.

Q. You say Mr. Hays told you Latin American children were not permitted to attend this same school with Anglo American children?

A. Yes, sir; Mr. Hays told me Latin American kids were not allowed in the school until they were in the 4th grade.

Q. Do you know when the Latin American school was abolished?

A. No, I really don't know.

Examination.
By the Court:

Q. Mrs. Rosas, these occasions you are talking about when your two children started to school that you testified about, when was that? How long back was that?

A. Well, my oldest boy is 19.

Q. And when did he start school?

A. When he was 6 years old.

Q. That would be about 13 years ago?

A. Yes, sir.

Q. And about 12 years ago for the girl?

A. Yes, sir.

Q. When was that that you talked to Mr. Hays that you testified he told you your children could not attend?

A. When I started the boy to school.

Q. That was 12 or 13 years ago?

A. When he started to school.

Q. The boy?

[fol. 134] A. When he started to school.

Q. The boy?

A. The boy.

Mr. Hartman: We object to this testimony and ask that it be stricken for the reason that it is too remote in point of time in the present case that is on trial.

Court: I will refuse the motion and I will let it go in for whatever it is worth.

Cross examination.
By Mr. Vance:

Q. Mrs. Rosas, was there any question about teaching or your son by anybody?

A. Yes, sir.

Q. Was there any question about qualification?

A. She was not qualified, because she did not teach them all the time.

Q. Did she meet the State requirements?

A. She did, but they never—I don't know if the State did or not. She just teached them some things.

Q. Her qualifications in this respect never were questioned?

A. I could not tell you, because my children did not go to school here.

Q. Didn't the students in the Latin American school get the same course of instruction as the children in the other school?

A. I could not tell you.

[fol. 135] Q. You just don't know about that?

A. No.

By Mr. Hartman:

Q. You are not undertaking to say that there was any discrimination against a person of Latin American or Mexican descent in the case we are trying?

A. I think there was discrimination.

Q. Who?

A. The town.

Q. Who?

A. The town.

Q. The whole town?

A. Yes, sir; they discriminated, the town.

Q. Who in the town? Can you give us any names?

A. I could not name any one.

Court: Are there any more questions?

Mr. Hartman: The State has no more questions.

Mr. Garcia: That is all for the defendant.

Mr. Hartman: The state has nothing further.

MOTION OVERRULED

Court: I am overruling this motion and, in doing so, I am taking into consideration the testimony that has been heretofore offered by the State in making my ruling. I am taking into consideration all the testimony offered by both [fol. 136] sides in this matter. I think it would naturally go to the merits of the motion.

[fols.137-138] Reporter's Certificate to foregoing transcript omitted in printing.

[fols. 139] IN THE DISTRICT COURT OF JACKSON COUNTY
[Title omitted]
AGREEMENT OF COUNSEL

We, the undersigned, attorneys of record for the State of Texas and the Defendant in the above numbered and entitled cause, do hereby agree that the forgoing pages numbered from 1 through 15 constitute a full, true and correct transcript of all the evidence adduced and proceedings had upon the trial of said cause on the merits beginning on October 8, 1951, in so far only as the same relate to (1) Defendant's Motion to Quash the Indictment, (2) Defendants' Motion to Quash the Jury Panel, and (3) Defendant's motion to Quash the Talesmen after the Special Venire was exhausted, together with all the objections to the admission or exclusion of evidence, and the rulings of the Court on such objections: and we do further agree that said pages numbered from 1 through 15 may be filed as the Statement of Facts, in question and answer form, in said cause only in so far as the same relate to the Motions enumerated above.

Dated this the 13TH day of March, A.D. 1952.

(S.) Wayne L. Hartman, Counsel for the State of Texas; Gus C. Garcia, Counsel for the Defendant.

[fols. 140-166] IN THE DISTRICT COURT OF JACKSON COUNTY
[Title omitted]
JUDGE'S CERTIFICATE

I hereby approve the foregoing pages numbered from 1 through 15 as a full, true and correct statement of all the evidence adduced and proceedings had upon the trial of said cause on the merits beginning on October 8, 1951, in so far only as the same relate to (1) Defendant's Motion to Quash the Indictment, (2) Defendant's Motion to Quash the Jury Panel, and (3) Defendant's Motion to Quash the Talesmen after the Special Venire was Exhausted, and order the same filed as the Statement of Facts, in question and answer form, in so far only as the same relates to the Motions enumerated above, on this the—day of—A.D. 1952.

_ _, Judge Presiding, 24th Judicial District of Texas

[fol. 167] (File endorsement omitted)

[fol. 168] IN THE COURT OF CRIMINAL APPEALS OF TEXAS
No. 25,816
PETE HERNANDEZ, APPELLANT
v.
THE STATE OF TEXAS, APPELLEE
APPEAL FROM JACKSON COUNTY
OPINION—filed June 18,1952

Murder is the offense, with the punishment assessed at life imprisonment in the penitentiary.

Appellant is a Mexican, or Latin American. He claims that he was discriminated against upon the trial of this case because members of the Mexican nationality were deliberately, systematically, and willfully excluded from the grand jury that found and returned the indictment in this case and from the petit jury panel from which was selected the petit jury that tried the case. He sought, for said reasons, to quash the indictment and petit jury panel, claiming he had thereby been deprived of equal protection. The action of the court in overruling the two motions presents the sole question for review. In support of his contention appellant relies upon the so-called rule of exclusion as announced by the Supreme Court of the United States—that is, that the long and continued failure to call members of the Negro race for jury service, where it is shown that members of that race were available and qualified for jury service, grand or petit, constitutes a violation of due process and equal protection against members of that race. The rule appears to have been first announced in Norris v. Alabama, 294 U.S. 587, 55 S. Ct. 579, 79 L. Ed. 1074, and since then followed. See Smith v. Texas, 311 U.S. 128, 61 S. Ct. 164, 85 L. Ed. 84, Hill v. Texas, 316 U.S. 400, 62 S. Ct. 1159, 85 L. Ed. 1559; Cassell v. Texas, 339 U.S. 282, 70 S. Ct. 629, 94 L. Ed. 839, and Ross v. Texas, 341 U.S. 91, 71 S. Ct. 742, 95 L. Ed. 1352. Appellant would have the above rule to extend to and apply to members of different nationalities—particularly to Mexicans. [fol. 169] Much testimony was introduced by which appellant sought to show the systematic exclusion of Mexicans from jury service and that there were members of that nationality qualified and available for such service in Jackson County. The facts proven, however, were of no greater probative force than those stipulated by the state and the appellant which we quote as follows: "The State will stipulate that for the last twenty-five years there is no record of any person with Mexican or Latin American name having served on a jury commission, grand jury or petit jury in Jackson County." "It is stipulated by counsel for the State and counsel for the defendant that there are some male persons of Mexican or Latin American descent in Jackson County who, by virtue of being citizens, householders, or freeholders, and having all other legal prerequisites to jury service, are eligible to serve as members of a jury commission, grand jury and or petit jury." With reference to the petit jury, we quote the following:

"It is stipulated by counsel for the State and counsel for defendant that there is no person of Mexican or other Latin American descent or blood on the list of talesmen." These stipulations of necessity included the ability to read and speak the English language. It was shown that Jackson County had a population of approximately 18,000, 15 per cent of which—a witness estimated as a "wild guess"—were Mexicans. The same witness also testified as a "rough estimate" that 6 or 7 per cent of that 15 per cent were freeholders upon the tax rolls of the country. It was shown, also, that the population of Jackson County was composed also of Bohemians, Germans, Anglo-Americans and Negroes. The relative percentages of these, however, were not estimated. It may be said, therefore, that the facts relied upon by the appellant to bring this case within the rule of systematic exclusion are that at the time the grand jury was selected and at the time of the trial of this case there were "some male persons of Mexican or Latin American descent in Jackson County" who possessed the qualifications requisite to service as grand or petit jurors, and that [fol. 170] no Mexican had been called for jury service in that county for a period of twenty-five years. There is an absence of any testimony here suggesting express or factual discrimination against appellant or other Mexicans in the selection, organization, or empaneling of the grand or petit jury in this case. To sustain his claim of discrimination, appellant relies only upon an application of the rule of exclusion mentioned. In so far as this court is concerned, the question here presented was determined adversely to appellant's contention in the case of Sanchez v. State, 147 Tex. Cr. R. 436, 181 S.W. 2d 87, where we said: "In the absence of a holding by the Supreme Court of the United States that nationality and race bear the same relation, within the meaning of the constitutional provision (Fourteenth Amendment) mentioned, we shall continue to hold that the statue law of this State furnishes the guide for the selection of juries in the State, and that, in the absence of proof showing express discrimina-

tion by administrators of the law, a jury so selected in accordance therewith is valid."
(Parentheses supplied)

Within our knowledge, no decision of the Supreme Court of the United States has been rendered which would change the conclusion just expressed. The validity of laws of this state providing for the selection of grand or petit jurors (Arts. 333-350, C.C.P.) has never been seriously challenged. Indeed, the Supreme Court of the United ed States, in Smith v. Texas, 311 U.S. 128, 61 S. Ct. 164, 85 L. Ed. 84, recognized the validity thereof when it said: "Here, the Texas statutory scheme is not in itself unfair: it is capable of being carried out with no racial discrimination whatsoever."

It was with this statement in mind that we said, in effect, that, in the absence of express discrimination, a jury, grand or petit, drawn in accordance with the statute law of this state was valid. Appellant challenges the correctness of our conclusions [fol. 171] and charges that by such holding we have extended special benefits to members of the Negro race which are denied to Mexicans, thereby violating equal protection to them. Such contention calls, of necessity, for a construction of the equal protection clause of the Fourteenth Amendment to the Federal Constitution with reference to the selection of juries in the state court trials and the decisions of the Supreme Court of the United States relative thereto.

The Fourteenth Amendment to the Federal Constitution in relation to equal protection* was adopted to secure to members of the Negro race, then recently emancipated, the full enjoyment of their freedom. Nixon v. Herndon, 273 U.S. 536, 71 L. 597, 47 S. Ct. 446; Buchanan v. Warley, 245 U.S. 60, 62 L. Ed. 149, 38 S. Ct. 16; Neal v. Delaware, 103 U.S. 370, 26 L. Ed. 567; Strauder v. West Virginia, 100*

"Section 1. All persons born or naturalized in the United States, and subject to the Jurisdiction thereof, are citizens of the United States and of the States wherein they reside. No state shall make or enforce any law which shall abridge the privileges or immunities of citizens of the United States: nor shall any State deprive any person of life, liberty, or property, without due process of law: nor deny to any person within its jurisdiction the equal protection of the laws."

U.S. 303, 25 L. Ed. 664; Slaughter—House cases, 16 Wall (U.S.) 36, 21 L. Ed. 394. While the Supreme Court of the United States had before it the question of race discrimination under the Fourteenth Amendment in the Slaughter—House cases, it appears that it was not until the case of Strauder v. West Virginia that the court had occasion to determine that race discriminated in jury organization was prohibited by the Fourteenth Amendment. In the latter case a statute of West Virginia limited jury service to white male persons. This statute was held as discriminatory against members of the Negro race and, therefore, violative of equal protection.

Following the Strauder case, the question of race discrimination in the selection of juries was before the Court [fol. 172] upon several occasions.

In Carter v. Texas, 177 U.S. 442, 44 L. Ed. 839, 20 S. Ct. 687, the rule was stated as follows: " Whatever by name any action of the State, whether through its legislature, through its courts, or through its executive or administrative officers, all persons of the African race are excluded, solely because of their race or color, from serving as grand jurors in the criminal prosecution of a person of the African race, the equal protection of the laws is denied to him, contrary to the Fourteenth Amendment of the

Constitution of the United States. Strauder v. West Virginia, 100 U.S. 303, 25 L. Ed. 664; Neal v. Delaware 103 U.S. 370, 397, 26 L. Ed. 567, 574: Gibson v. Mississippi, 162 U.S. 565, 40 L. Ed. 1075, 16 S. Ct. 904."

The rule, as thus established, applies equally to petit jury selection. For a time, and until the case of Norris v. Alabama, 294 U.S. 587, 55 S. Ct. 579, 79 L. Ed. 1074, establishment of discrimination rested upon facts showing actual or express discrimination against members of the Negro race. In the Norris case, however, the so-called rule of exclusion was announced in the following language, viz: "We think that the evidence that for a generation or longer no Negro had been called for service on any jury in Jackson County, that there were Negroes qualified for jury service, that according to the practice of the jury commission their names would normally appear on the preliminary list of male citizens of the requisite age but that no names of Negroes were placed on the jury roll, and the testimony with respect to the lack of appropriate consideration of the qualifications of Negroes established the discrimination which the Constitution forbids."

In succeeding cases this rule of exclusion was followed or adverted to in the cases of Smith v. Texas, 311 U.S. 128, 85 L. Ed. 84, 61 S. Ct. 164; Hill v. Texas, 316 U.S. 400, 86 L. Ed. 1559, 62 S. Ct. 1159; and Akins v. Texas, 325 U.S. 398, 89 L. Ed. 1692, 65 S. Ct. 1276.

The effect of the rule of exclusion is to furnish means by which proof of discrimination may be accomplished. In the Akins case, the idea of proportional representation of races on a jury as a constitutional requisite was rejected. The basis of such rejection was pointed out in Cassell [fol. 173] v. Texas, 339 U.S. 282, 70 S. Ct. 629, 94 L. Ed.839, as follows: "We have recently written why proportional representation of races on a jury is not a constitutional requisite. Succinctly stated, our reason was that the Constitution requires only a fair jury selected without regard to race. Obviously, the number of races and nationalities appearing in the ancestry of our citizens would make it impossible to meet a requirement of proportional representation." The conclusion of race discrimination expressed in the Cassell case, which is one of the latest expressions by the Supreme Court of the United States upon the subject, appears not to have been based upon the so-called rule of the exclusion above mentioned but upon the conclusion that the jury commissioners appointed to select the list of names from which the grand jury was to be selected did not "familiarize themselves fairly with the qualifications of the eligible jurors of the county without regard to race and color. They did not do so here, and the result has been racial discrimination." In addition to that conclusion, the Cassell case also announced the rule that discrimination may be shown by inclusion as well as exclusion, on account of race, in jury selection. To our minds, it is conclusive that, in so far a the question of discrimination in the organization of juries in state courts is concerned, the equal protection clause of the Fourteenth Amendment contemplated and recognized only two classes as coming within that guarantee: the white race, comprising one class and the Negro race, comprising the other class. We said in Sanchez v. State, 243 S. W. 2d 700, that "Mexican people are not a separate race but are white people of Spanish descent." In contemplation of the Fourteenth Amendment, Mexicans are therefore members of and within the classification of the white race, as distinguished from members of the Negro race. In so far as we are advised, no member of the Mexican nationality challenges that statement. Appellant does not here do so. [fol. 174] It is apparent, therefore that appellant seeks to have this court recognize and classify Mexicans as a special class within the white race and to recognize that special class as entitled to special privileges in the organization of grand and petit juries in this state. To so hold would constitute a violation of equal protection, because it would be extending to members of a class special privileges not accorded to all others of that class similarly situated. Moreover, it must be remembered that no man, or set of men, has the right to require that a member of his race be a member of the grand jury that indicts him or of the petit jury that tries him. All that the Constitution, State or Federal, guarantees in that connection is that in the organization of such juries he be not discriminated against by reason of his race or color. Thomas v. Texas, 212 U.S. 278, 26 S. Ct. 338, 53 L. Ed. 512; Martin v. Texas, 200 U.S. 316, 26 S. Ct. 66, 50 L. Ed. 497; Carter v. Texas, 177 U.S. 442, 20 S. Ct. 686, 44 L. Ed. 839.

To say that members of the various nationalities and groups composing the white race must be represented upon grand and petit juries would destroy our jury system, for it would be impossible to meet such requirement. Such also, would destroy the rule above stated and would be tantamount to authorizing an accused to demand that a member of his nationality be upon the jury that indicts and tries him. In addition, to so hold would write into the equal protection clause proportional representation not only of races but of nationalities, which the Supreme Court of the United States has expressly rejected. Mexicans are white people, and are entitled at the hands of the state to all the rights, privileges, and immunities guaranteed under the Fourteenth Amendment. So long as they are so treated, the guarantee of equal protection has been accorded to them. [fols. 175-176] The grand jury that indicted appellant and the petit jury that tried him being composed of members of his race, it can be said, in the absence of proof of actual discrimination, that appellant has been discriminated against in the organizations of such juries and thereby denied equal protection of the laws.

The judgment is affirmed.

Davidson, Judge.

(Delivered June 18, 1952)

Opinion approved by the court.

[fol. 177] IN THE COURT OF CRIMINAL APPEALS OF THE STATE OF TEXAS

[Title omitted]

APPELLANT'S MOTION FOR REHERSING—filed July 2, 1952

Appellant, Pete Hernandez, moves this Court to set aside [its] judgment heretofore rendered herein and to enter a judgment reversing appellant's convictions in the court below and ordering the prosecution dismissed. As this Court will remember, appellant was convicted of murder in the District Court of Jackson County, Texas, and sentenced to life imprisonment. His appeal is based solely [fol. 178] on the fact that he, a person of Mexican descent, has been denied the equal protection of the laws and deprived of liberty without due process because persons of Mexican descent were intentionally, arbitrarily and systematically excluded from service on the grand jury which indicted him and the petit jury which convicted him. This Court rejected appellant's contentions. Appellant bases this motion for rehearing upon the following grounds:

FIRST

The refusal of this Court to apply the rule of exclusion announced in Norris v. Alabama constitutes "State Action" depriving appellant of his liberty without due process of law and denying him the equal protection of the laws. It is clear from the Court's opinion in this case that it has reaffirmed the position taken in Sanchez v. State, 147 Tex. Cr. R. 436, 181 S. W. 2d 87 (1944), to the effect that, "in the absence of proof showing express discrimination by administrators of the law," it cannot be said that appellant has been discriminated against in the selection of grand and petit jurors. Appellant admits, of course, that, as the Supreme Court of the United States observes in Smith v. Texas, 311 U.S. 128 (1941), the Texas statutes governing the organization of grand and petit juries are "capable of being carried out" with no discrimination. However, the fact that the statutory scheme is not itself unfair is no insurance that it will be fairly administered. This Court well knows that the statutory scheme is capable of being, and in fact has been, administered in a discriminatory manner. Indeed, the State of Texas is more than adequately represented in [fol. 179] the roll call of cases in which the Supreme Court has condemned the discriminatory administration of laws which are "capable of being carried out" without discrimination if only those who administer them are willing to perform their duties fairly and impartially. Ross v. Texas, 341 U.S. 918 (1951): Cassel v. Texas, 339 U.S. 282 (1950): Akins v. Texas, 325 U.S. 389 (1945); Hill v. Texas, 316 U.S. 400 (1942): Smith v. Texas, supra; Thomas v. Texas, 212 U.S. 278 (1909): Martin v. Texas, 200 U.S. 316 (1906); Carter v. Texas, 177 U.S. 442 (1900). It thus appears that, in spite of the fair nature of the Texas statutes, jury commissioners in the various counties have, for more than half a century, made zealous efforts to administer them in a discriminatory manner and would have succeeded but for the watchful attitude of the Supreme Court of the United States. Therefore, it cannot be said that if appellant has shown a discriminatory administration of the Texas statutes, his appeal to the protective clauses of the Fourteenth Amendment can be defeated by the fact that the Texas statutory scheme is non—discriminatory in form. In effect, this Court has held that appellant has not shown such discriminatory administration. It clearly appears from this Court's opinion that, had appellant been a Negro, the exclusion rule announced in Norris v. Alabama, 249 U.S. 587 (1935), would have been applied. But there is no need to rely on implications which are latent in the language of this Court. We have an express statement by the Supreme Court which leaves no doubt concerning the sufficiency of the testimony in this case, were [fol. 180] appellant a Negro. In Patton v. Mississippi, 332 U.S. 463 (1947), the evidence showed that there were only 12 or 13 Negroes in the county available for jury service, as against 5,000 whites. The Supreme Court said: "Whatever the precise number of qualified colored electors in the county, there were some; and if it can possibly be conceived that all of them were disqualified for jury service . . . we do not doubt that the State could have proved it." 332 U.S. at 468.

Even were the Supreme Court bound, as it is not, by this Court's interpretation of the facts, the evidence here is stronger than that in the Patton case. Here there is no need for a court to demonstrate an unwillingness to presume that all of the persons of Mexican descent in Jackson County are disqualified. In this case the State stipulated, as set out on page 2 of this Court's opinion, that there were some persons of Mexican descent in the county who possessed all necessary qualifications for jury service. The result of this Court's holding in this case, and in prior cases involving persons of Mexican descent, can be simply stated. There exist, in the State of Texas, one rule of evidence for Negroes, and a different rule for persons of Mexican descent. From certain facts, this Court will conclude, in accordance with the Norris case, that there has been arbitrary, intentional and systematic exclusion of Negroes. Given the same facts, but changing the color of the appellant, this Court refuses to find that there has been an arbitrary, intentional and systematic exclusion of persons of Mexican descent. It requires the latter to show express discrimination, and it states frankly that persons [fol. 181] of Mexican descent must bear this more onerous burden solely because they are not Negroes; i.e., because they are white. If a Negro shows certain facts, the burden of proving absence of discrimination shifts to the State; that is, certain facts give rise to a presumption of discrimination. A showing of the same facts by a person of Mexican descent does not impose any burden of proof of absence of discrimination on the State; that is, no presumption of discrimination arises. As this Court points out on page 5 of its opinion, the rule of the Norris case, in effect, furnishes "means by which proof of discrimination may be accomplished." Thus, it becomes patent that this Court has denied to this appellant a means of proving discrimination which is available to Negroes: and that this denial is based solely, exclusively and expressly on the fact that appellant is not a Negro. To put it in simpler terms, this Court has set up a classification based solely, exclusively and expressly on race. Let us suppose that a Legislature enacted a statute to the effect that proof of certain facts by a Negro should give rise to certain presumptions favorable to the Negro, but that proof of the same facts by a white person should give rise to no such presumptions in favor of the white person. Can there be any doubt concerning the invalidity of such a statute? If doubt there is, even a casual reading of Oyama v. California, 332 U.S. 633 (1948), will dispel it. In the opinion delivered in this case, this Court does not discuss the validity of its judicially imposed racial classification in the light of the Oyama decision. Even should appellant admit, as he does not, that the [fol. 182] Fourteenth Amendment, insofar as discrimination in the organization of juries is concerned, recognizes only two groups—whites and Negroes—it does not follow that, for the purpose of formulating rules of evidence, this Court may discriminate against white persons by making the sufficiency of evidence depend on the color of the person presenting it. The Fourteenth Amendment forbids discrimination against whites, as well as against Negroes. Buchanan v. Warley, 245 U.S. 60 (1917). Appellant would also point out that the litigant injured by the discriminatory rule of evidence in the Oyama case was not a Negro. Thus, it cannot be said that, insofar as the validity of rules of evidence based solely on racial grounds is concerned, the Fourteenth Amendment recognizes only two classes, white and Negroes. And even if this untenable proposition be admitted for the purpose of argument, it does not follow that the Amendment sanctions discrimination against white persons by rules which impose upon them a burden more onerous than that placed on Negroes. Appellant submits, therefore, that the action of this Court in establishing a rule of evidence which imposes a greater burden on appellant that is imposed on a Negro, and which does so solely, exclusively and expressly because of appellant's race, is "state action" in violation of the Fourteenth Amendment. A classification based on race is not beyond the Constitutional prohibitions merely because it is a judicial tribunal, rather than a legislature or administrative agency, which has seen fit to make race the determining factor in selection of the rules which it applies. This is mere hornbook law.

[fol. 183] Appellant insists that, insofar as proof of the fact of intentional and systematic exclusion of persons of Mexican descent from jury service is concerned, this Court cannot, consistently with the provisions of the Fourteenth Amendment, hold that appellant has not shown such exclusion. Nor can it require that appellant bear a more onerous burden of proof than that which is borne by Negroes.

SECOND

Intentional, arbitrary and systematic exclusion of persons of Mexican descent from jury service, as shown in this case, deprives appellant of liberty without due process of law and denies to him the equal protection of the laws.

This Court's opinion is based on the fact that, even if persons of Mexican descent are excluded from juries, such exclusion does not violate the provisions of the Fourteenth Amendment. Appellant suggests to this Court that such a view is based on a misinterpretation of the Fourteenth Amendment, and that some of the reasons given in support of the Court's conclusion constitute a misconception of the contentions made by appellant. Appellant believes and insists that the facts in this case show a violation of the due process and equal protection clauses of the Fourteenth Amendment.

A. Denial of Due Process

As this Court points out, the Texas statutory scheme is fair on his face. It contains no provisions excluding person of Mexican descent from jury service. The exclusion results solely from the activities of those citizens of Jackson County who were entrusted with the solemn duty of administering statutes which are capable of being enforced without [fol.184] discrimination. These jury commissioners of Jackson County who have decided that our statutes are inadequate since, if administered as written, such legislation would allow persons of Mexican descent to sit on juries. In view of what apparently was constructed by them as a lack of legislative wisdom and foresight, these gentle citizens of Jackson County have courageously volunteered to plug the leak in the dike and to exclude persons of Mexican descent from Jackson County juries. Can there be any doubt that such action is a violation of the due process clause of the Fourteenth Amendment. Can such doubt still linger in view of the following language by the Ninth Circuit Court of Appeals? ". . . the acts of respondents were and are without authority of California law. . . . Therefore, conceding for the sake of argument that California could legally enact a law authorizing the segregation as practiced, the fact stands out unchallengeable that California has not done so. . . . By enforcing the segregation of school children of Mexican descent . . . respondents . . . have violated . . . the Fourteenth Amendment by depriving them of liberty and property without due process of the law . . ." Westminster School District v. Mendez, 161 F. 2d 774, 780-781 (9th Cir. 1947).

The court in the Mendez case observed that it was "aware of no authority justifying any segregation fiat by any administrative or executive decree." 161 F. 2d at 780. Does this Court know of any authority justifying the exclusionary fiat by the jury commissioners of Jackson County?

B. *Denial of Equal Protection of the Laws*

Appellant cannot agree with this Court's observation that "it is conclusive that, in so far as the question of discrimination in the organization of juries is concerned, the equal [fol. 185] protection clause of the Fourteenth Amendment contemplated and recognized only two classes as coming within that guarantee: the white race, comprising on class, and the Negro race, comprising the other class." Appellant has found no decision by the Supreme Court, by the lower Federal courts, or by the courts of the other states which support such a statement. In State v. Guirlando, 152 La. 570, 93 So. 796 (1922), the Louisiana court indicated that the exclusion of persons of Italian descent from jury service would violate the Fourteenth Amendment. However, appellant does not believe that such an observation can be constructed as furnishing even slight support for this Court's position.

The amendment itself, of course, does not mention juries. Nor does it contain any language from which it can be inferred, either inductively or deductively, that in jury cases it "contemplated and recognized only two classes . . . : the white race . . . and the Negro race." The language of the equal protection clause is simple and direct. It provides that no State shall "deny to any person within its jurisdiction the equal protection of the laws." The word "person" is neither preceded nor followed by any qualifying or restrictive term. In fact, this very Court has not construed the equal protection clause in the manner indicated in its opinion in this case. In Juarez v. State, 102 Tex. Cr. R. 297, 277 S.W. 1091 (1925), this Court held that systematic exclusion or Roman Catholics from juries is proscribed by the Fourteenth Amendment. Although appellant's brief called the Juarez case to the Court's attention, it was not discussed in the Court's opinion in this case. No attempt [fol. 186] was made to explain the obvious incompatibility of this Court's holding in the Juarez case with the "two classes" theory upon which the Court bases its decision in this case. A careful reading of the Juarez opinion has elicited no facts even tending to show that the appellant there was a Negro Roman Catholic. How explain the Juarez case in view of this Court's language in the instant case? This Court's "two classes" theory is squarely opposed to what is believed to be the only expression by the Supreme Court on the subject. In Strauder v. West Virginia, 100 U.S. 303 (1879), the Supreme Court said:

"Nor, if a law be passed excluding all naturalized Celtic Irishmen, would there be any doubt of its inconsistency with the spirit of the Amendment." 100 U.S. at 308.

Appellant readily admits that the above statement is dictum, but it is not believed that that fact can be used to give such language the character of authority for this Court's conclusion. Perhaps this Court's "two classes" theory is based on the fact that all jury cases which have been considered by the Supreme Court have involved Negroes. But this fact cannot serve as an adequate foundation for the structure which this Court has sought to erect upon it. With but one exception, all the cases involving discrimination in the field of education which have reached the Supreme Court have involved Negroes. And, in the lone exception, the Chinese claimant was unsuccessful. Gong Lum v. Rice, 275 U.S. 78 (1927). Would this Court then extend its "two classes" theory to cases involving discrimination in the public [fol. 187] schools? The Federal courts have not reached such a conclusion. They have held that segregation of children of Mexican descent in the public schools is a denial of equal protection. Gonzales v. Sheely, 96 F. Supp. 1004 (D.C. Ariz. 1951); Mendez v. Westminster School District 64 F. Supp. 544 (S.D. Cal.1946), aff'd., 161 F. 2d 774 (9th Cir. 1947). Before these cases were decided, a Texas court stated that arbitrary segregation of children of Mexican descent in the public schools, if shown, would be unconstitutional. Del Rio Independent School District v. Salvatierra, 33 S.W. 2d 790 (Tex. Civ. App, 1930). The only Supreme Court pronouncements concerning the unconstitutionality of judicial enforcement of racial restrictive convenants are to be found in cases involving Negroes. Would this lead this Court to extend its "two classes" theory to these cases? A Texas court has decided otherwise. In Clifton v. Puente, 218 S.W. 2d 272 (Tex Civ. App., 1949, err. ref'd. n. r. e.), its was held that a covenant prohibiting sale of land to persons of Mexican descent could not be enforced by Texas courts. What, then, is peculiar about discrimination in the organization of juries that this Court can read into the Fourteenth Amendment a limitation which the Supreme Court has stated, in the Strauder case, is not there? What is so peculiar about discrimination in the organization of juries that this Court will read into the Fourteenth Amendment a limitation which the lower Federal courts, in the field of education, have held is not there, and which a Texas court has indicated is not there? What is so peculiar about discrimination in the organization of the juries that this Court [fol. 188] can read into the Fourteenth Amendment a limitation which a Texas court has held, concerning judicial enforcement of racial restrictive covenants, is not there? What is so sacred about discrimination in the organization of juries that prompts this Court to shield it against the reach of the Fourteenth Amendment? What is so desirable about discrimination in the organization of juries that this Court is not impressed by the statement in Yick Wo v. Hopkins, 118 U.S. 356, 369 (1886), to the effect that the provisions of the Fourteenth Amendment "are universal in their application, to all persons under the territorial jurisdiction, without regard to any differences of race, or color, or of nationality"? What is so peculiar, so sacred, so desirable about discrimination in the selection and organization of juries that this Court will uphold the right of grand jury commissioners to exclude persons of Mexican descent, in the face of the fact that the Supreme Court has struck down an attempt by a state legislature to exclude a white Austrian from employment? Truax v. Raich, 239 U.S. 33 (1915). Appellant admits that the Fourteenth Amendment does not require proportional representation. But to condemn the exclusion here shown is not to impose proportional representation. The fact that Negroes have succeeded in their fight against exclusion from juries has not imposed proportional representation of Negroes. The fact that this Court has decreed that Roman Catholics may not be excluded has not imposed proportional representation of Roman Catholics. Appellant does not contend that any percentage of jurors [fol. 189] must be persons of

Mexican descent. He does not contend that he has a right to demand that a person of Mexican descent sit on the jury which indicted him or the jury which convicted him. To uphold appellant is not tantamount to giving him such rights. Upholding the right of the Negro against discrimination in the organization of juries has not given them such rights. Upholding the right of Roman Catholics against discrimination in the organization of juries has not given them such rights. Why would the extension of equal protection to appellant bring about consequences which did not result from the extension of equal protection to Negroes and Roman Catholics? Appellant does not seek proportional representation: he does not demand that persons of Mexican descent sit on any particular grand or petit jury. He merely asks that they not be systematically excluded from all juries. This can be achieved without destroying our jury system and without overruling the Supreme Court. It has been achieved in cases involving Negroes and Roman Catholics, and our jury system has not been destroyed. Does this Court believe that, in every county in the State of Texas, 25 years go by without seeing a person of Mexican descent called for jury service? Does this Court, in brief, feel that the Jackson County pattern is the general pattern in Texas? Of course not. Does this Court have any information showing that in counties where "Mexicans" are allowed to sit on juries the practice has led to the destruction of our jury system? Of course not. In all humility, appellant submits that in speaking of proportional representation and of giving a person the right [fol. 190] to demand that a person of his group be on a particular jury, this Court has done no more than to demolish a straw man of its own creation. On page 7 of its opinion, this Court quotes the following language from Cassel v. Texas, 339 U.S. 282, 287: "Obviously, the number of races and nationalities appearing in the ancestry of our citizens would make it impossible to meet a requirement of proportional representation." The correctness of appellant's contention is implicit in such language. How could the number of "nationalities appearing in the ancestry of our citizens" make proportional representation impossible if, as, this Court holds, persons may be excluded because of national origin? If this Court's "two classes" theory is correct, the number of nationalities found in the ancestry of our citizens is altogether irrelevant. It can present no problem, since they may be completely excluded. On page 7 of its opinion this Court says that appellant seeks to have this Court classify "Mexicans as a special class," and to grant them "special privileges." This, the Court says, would violate the Fourteenth Amendment by "extending to members of a class special privileges not accorded to all of that class similarly situated." What is this "special privilege" which appellant seeks? The right not to be discriminated against in the selection of jurors. Is that a special privilege, or is it a constitutional right? Appellant believes that it is latter. Does this court truly believe that, in Jackson County Texas, this is a right which is not enjoyed by other members of the white race? Does this Court believe that, in Jackson County, Texas, only Negroes are allowed to serve as jurors? Does [fol. 191] this Court feel that if persons of Mexican descent were to be allowed to serve as jurors in Jackson County, Texas, they would be enjoying a "special privilege" which other white citizens in that county do not enjoy. Just what white citizens of Jackson County does this Court have in mind when it speaks of "all others of that class similarly situated" who do not have the right to sit on juries?

Unless this Court takes the position that only Negroes serve on Jackson County juries, it must conclude that white persons are allowed to serve on juries. Therefore, it follows that some white persons in Jackson County have a right which the jury commissioners have denied to persons of Mexican descent. Under such circumstances, who is enjoying a right which is not extended to "all other members of that class similarly situated" in Jackson County? Can the denial to persons of Mexican descent of a right enjoyed by other white persons be defended by references to special privileges? Perhaps Ross v. Texas, 341 U.S. 918 (1951), represents the last attempt to deny Negroes the "special privilege" of sitting on juries. Are other members of the white race excluded? This court has considered cases involving exclusions of two groups other than Negroes : Roman Catholics and persons of Mexican descent. It has accorded the "special privilege" to Roman Catholics. Why? Because they are Roman Catholics? Is this Court saying that persons of Mexican descent may be excluded because they are not Roman Catholics? Is it establishing a classification based on religious belief? If X cannot be excluded because he is a Roman Catholic, may Y be excluded because he is not? Has [fol. 192] this Court's "two classes" theory, through some process of a sexual inbreeding, conceived and given birth to a third class? In conclusion, let us assume that a legislature passed a law excluding persons of Mexican descent from jury service. Would such a statute be valid? Can the jury commissioners of Jackson County do what the legislature cannot do? Appellant thinks not. Does this Court think they can?

Wherefore, appellant prays that this motion be granted, that the opinion heretofore rendered by this Court in this case be withdrawn and the prior judgment of this court be set aside, and that the judgment of the trial court be reversed and the prosecution be ordered dismissed.

Respectfully submitted, (S.) Carlos C. Cadena, 112 College Street, San Antonio, Texas; Gus C. Garcia, International Building, San Antonio, Texas.

[fol. 193] IN CLERK'S OFFICE, COURT OF CRIMINAL APPEALS, AUSTIN, TEXAS
CERTIFICATION TO ORDER OVERRULING MOTION FOR REHEARING
October 22, 1952

I, Glen Haynes, Clerk of the Court of Criminal Appeals of Texas, at Austin, do herby certify that Appellant's Motion for Rehearing in Cause No. 25,816

PETE HERNANDEZ
vs.
THE STATE OF TEXAS

was, on October 22, 1952, overruled without written opinion. Witness my hand and seal of said Court, this 17th day of January, A.D. 1953.

Glenn Haynes, Clerk, Court of Criminal Appeals.

[fol. 194] IN THE COURT OF CRIMINAL APPEALS OF TEXAS
[Title omitted]
MINUTE ENTRIES OF OPINION AND ORDER OVERRULING MOTION FOR REHEARING
OPINION OF AFFIRMANCE BY JUDGE DAVIDSON—June 18, 1952

This cause came on to be heard on the transcript of the record of the court below, and the same being inspected, because it is the opinion of the Court that there was no error in the judgment, it is ordered, adjudged, and decreed by this Court that the judgment be in all things affirmed, and that the appellant pay all costs in this behalf expended, and that this decision be certified below for observance.

MOTION FOR REHEARING OVERRULED WITHOUT WRITTEN OPINION—October 22, 1952

This cause came on to be heard on Appellant's Motion for Rehearing, and the same being considered, it is ordered, adjudged and decreed by the Court that said motion be and the same is hereby in all things overruled.

Clerk's Certificate to foregoing papers omitted in printing.

[fol. 195] Clerk's certificate to foregoing transcript omitted in printing.

[fol. 196] SUPREME COURT OF THE UNITED STATES, OCTOBER TERM, 1953
No. 2, Misc.
PETE HERNANDEZ, PETITIONER
vs.
STATE OF TEXAS
ORDERING ALLOWING CERTIORARI—filed October 12, 1953

The petition herein for a writ of certiorari to the Court of Criminal Appeals of the State of Texas is granted, and the case is transferred to the appellate docket.

And it is further ordered that the duly certified copy of the transcript of the proceedings below which accompanied the petition shall be treated as though filed in response to such writ.

The Chief Justice took no part in the consideration or decision of this application.

Appendix VI

Brief of Petitioner
I
INDEX

III.
LIST OF AUTHORITIES
Cases

IV.
LIST OF AUTHORITIES—(Continued)

Statutes

V.
LIST OF AUTHORITIES—(Continued)
Textbooks

Articles

Miscellaneous

VI.
STATEMENT DISCLOSING BASIS OF
JURISDICTION

1. Jurisdiction is invoked under 28 U. S. C. Sec. 1257(3).
2. The judgment of the Court of Criminal Appeals of the State of Texas, court of last resort in criminal matters, was entered June 18, 1952. (R. p. 91). Motion for rehearing, timely filed, was overruled on October 22, 1952, (R. p. 111).
3. Petitioner was indicted for murder by a grand jury of Jackson County, Texas. (R. p. 1). He moved to quash the indictment because persons of his national origin were intentionally, arbitrarily and systematically excluded from service as jury commissioners and as grand jurors. (R. p. 2). Petitioner also moved to quash the jury panel because persons of Mexican descent were intentionally, arbitrarily and systematically excluded from service on all petit juries, including the one which was summoned to try petitioner. (R. p. 5). Both motions were overruled by the trial court. (R. pp. 5, 7). Petitioner was convicted and sentenced to life imprisonment. (R. p. 17). Motion for new trial was timely filed and overruled. (R. p. 21). In affirming the conviction, the Texas Court of Criminal Appeals held that petitioner had not shown intentional, arbitrary and systematic exclusion of persons of Mexican descent from jury service, and that a defendant of Mexican descent is not denied due process or equal protec-

tion of the law by the intentional, arbitrary and systematic exclusion of persons of Mexican descent from the grand

VII.

jury which indicted him and from the petit jury which convicted him. (R. pp. 91-98).
4. The conclusion of the Texas Court of Criminal Appeals presents a substantial question concerning the extent and scope of the due process and equal protection clauses of the Fourteenth Amendment to the Constitution of the United States. The Texas Court of Criminal Appeals has denied to petitioner a right specially set up and claimed by petitioner under the Fourteenth Amendment to the Constitution of the United States.
5. Petition for writ of certiorari was filed in this Court on January 21, 1953 and was granted October 12, 1953. (R. p. 111).
6. The following cases sustain jurisdiction:
Strauder v. West Virginia, 100 U. S. 303 (1879).
Neal v. Delaware, 108 U. S. 370 (1880).
Norris v. Alabama, 294 U. S. 587 (1935).
Smith v. Texas, 311 U. S. 128 (1941)
Truax v. Raich, 239 U. S. 33 (1915).
Westminster School District v. Mendez, 161 F. 2d 774 (1947).

REPORT OF CASE BELOW

The opinion of the Texas Court of Criminal Appeals is reported, sub nom. Hernandez v. State, in 251 S. W. 2d 531.

IN THE
SUPREME COURT OF THE UNITED STATES

October Term, 1953
No. 406
PETE HERNANDEZ, Petitioner
VS.
THE STATE OF TEXAS, Respondent

BRIEF FOR PETITIONER

ON WRIT OF CERTIORARI TO THE COURT OF CRIMINAL APPEALS OF
THE STATE OF TEXAS

QUESTIONS PRESENTED

1. Whether, in criminal proceedings against petitioner, a person of Mexican descent, the arbitrary and systematic exclusion of persons of Mexican descent from service as grand jurors and petit jurors deprives petitioner of liberty without due process of law and/or denies to him the equal protection of the laws guaranteed by the Fourteenth Amendment to the Constitution of the United States. 2. Whether the Court of

Criminal Appeals of the State of Texas, in denying to petitioner the benefit of the rule of exclusion announced by the Supreme Court of the United States in Norris v. Alabama, 294 U. S. 587 (1935), and in requiring petitioner, because he is not a Negro, to show express discrimination in the selection of grand jurors and petit jurors, deprived petitioner of liberty without due process and/or denied to petitioner the equal protection of the laws guaranteed by the Fourteenth Amendment to the Constitution of the United States.

NATURE OF THE CASE

Petitioner, a person of Mexican descent, was indicted for murder by a grand jury of Jackson County, Texas. (R., p. 1) Prior to a trial on the merits, petitioner moved to quash the indictment because persons of Mexican descent were systematically and arbitrarily excluded from service on the jury commission which selected the grand jury which indicted petitioner, and from service on such grand jury. (R., p. 2) Petitioner also filed a motion to quash the petit jury panel called for service in petitioner's case because persons of Mexican descent were arbitrarily and systematically excluded from service on such petit jury. (R., p. 3) Both of these motions were overruled by the trial court. (R., pp. 3-5). An appeal was perfected to the Court of Criminal Appeals of the State of Texas, the state court of last resort in criminal cases. The Court of Criminal Appeals affirmed the conviction. 251 S.W. 2d 531. The sentence assessed was life imprisonment. (R., p. 22) As reflected by the opinion of the state court, the action of the trial court in overruling the two motions above mentioned was the sole question presented to that court for review. (R., p. 91).

SUMMARY OF ARGUMENT
I.

The Fourteenth Amendment to the Constitution of the United States forbids the arbitrary and systematic exclusion of persons of Mexican descent from jury service. There is no basis for the theory advanced by the Texas Court of Criminal Appeals that "in so far as the question of discrimination in the organization of juries in the state courts is concerned, the equal protection clause of the Fourteenth Amendment contemplated and recognized only two classes as coming within that guarantee: the white race, comprising one class, and the Negro race, comprising the other." In demanding the right to participate fully in the government of their state by serving on juries, persons of Mexican descent are not demanding what the Texas court described as recognition "as a special class" which is entitled "to special privileges in the organization of grand and petit juries in the State of Texas." Petitioner merely demands a right which is accorded to all: the right to a trial by a fair and impartial jury from which persons of his national origin are not arbitrarily and systematically excluded. The recognition of petitioner's constitutional right will not, as the Texas court fears, "destroy our jury system"; nor will such recognition write into the equal protection clause "the proportional representation . . . of nationalities."

II.

In Norris v. Alabama, 294 U. S. 587 (1935), this Court held that the unexplained absence of Negroes from juries over a long period of time, when there were in the county Negroes eligible for jury service, constituted proof of discrimination in the selection of juries. Petitioner presented such proof with reference to persons of Mexican descent in Jackson County, Texas. By refusing to give to petitioner, solely because he is not a Negro, the benefit of the evidentiary rule which operates in favor of Negroes upon the establishment of similar facts, the Texas court has established a rule of evidence which imposes on petitioner a more onerous burden of proof than is imposed on Negroes, and which does so solely, expressly and exclusively because petitioner is not a Negro. The promulgation of an evidentiary rule founded exclusively on a classification based on race deprives petitioner of his liberty without due process of law and deprives him of the equal protection of the laws.

ARGUMENT
I.

INTENTIONAL, ARBITRARY AND SYSTEMATIC EXCLUSION OF PERSONS OF MEXICAN DESCENT FROM JURY SERVICE DEPRIVES PETITIONER OF LIBERTY WITHOUT DUE PROCESS OF LAW AND DENIES TO HIM THE EQUAL PROTECTION OF THE LAWS.

The Texas Court of Criminal Appeals is firmly committed to the view that exclusion of persons of Mexican descent from jury service does not violate the provisions of the Fourteenth Amendment. One of the earlier enunciations of this view is to be found in Salazar v. State, 149 Tex. Crim. Rep. 260, 193 S. W. 2d 211 (1946). In that case, the Texas court said: "The complaint is made of discrimination against nationality, not race. The Mexican people are of the same race as the grand jurors. We see no question presented for our decision under the Fourteenth Amendment." 193 S. W. 2d 211, 212. This position was reaffirmed in 1951, when the Texas court held that exclusion of persons of Mexican descent raised no constitutional question, since they "are not a separate race, but are white people of Spanish descent." Sanchez v. State, 243 S. W. 2d 700, 701. In the case now before this Court, the Texas court said: "In contemplation of the Fourteenth Amendment . . . Mexicans are members of and within the classification of the white race, as distinguished from members of the Negro race." 251 S. W. 2d 531, 535. (R., p. 97). Again: "It is apparent, therefore, that appellant seeks to have this court recognize and classify Mexicans as a special class within the white race and to recognize that special class as entitled to special privileges in the organization of grand and petit juries in this state." 251 S. W. 2d 531, 535. (R., p. 97). And again: "To our minds, it is conclusive that, in so far as the question of discrimination in the organization of juries in state courts is concerned, the equal protection clause of the Fourteenth Amendment contemplated and recognized only two classes as coming within that guarantee: the white race, comprising one class, and the Negro race, comprising the other class." 251 S. W. 2d 531, 535. (R., p. 97). There can be no doubt that, as far as the Texas court is concerned, the Fourteenth Amendment does not prohibit discrimination in the selection of juries because of national origin or, as the Texas court calls it, "nationality."[1] Applications of this view are to be found in the following cases, each of which involved exclusion of persons of Mexican descent: Ramirez v. State, 119 Tex. Crim. Rep. 362, 40 S. W. 2d 138 (1931), cert. denied, 284 U. S. 659 (1931); Carrasco v. State, 130 Tex. Crim. Rep. 392, 95 S. W. 2d 433 (1936); Sanchez v. State, 147 Tex. Crim. Rep. 436, 181 S. W. 2d 87 (1944) ; Bulsillos v. State, 152 Tex. Crim. Rep. 275, 213 S. W. 2d 837 (1948). Petitioner submits that the view of the Texas court rests upon a misinterpretation of the Fourteenth Amendment, and that some of the reasons given by the state court in support of its conclusions in this case constitute a misconception of the contentions made by petitioner. Petitioner believes and insists that intentional, systematic and arbitrary exclusion of persons of Mexican descent from jury service violates the due process and equal protection clauses of the Fourteenth Amendment.

A. Denial of Due Process.

As this Court has pointed out, the Texas statutory scheme governing the organization of juries in state courts is fair on its face and is capable of being carried out with no discrimination whatever. Smith v. Texas, 311 U. S. 128 (1941). The exclusion of persons of Mexican descent from jury service in this case results solely from the actions of those citizens of Jackson County, Texas, who were entrusted with the solemn duty of administering, in a fair and impartial manner, statutes which are capable of being administered without discrimination. The jury commissioners of Jackson County have taken it upon themselves to exclude persons of Mexican descent from juries. That such action is a violation of the due process clause of the Fourteenth Amendment becomes apparent when it is examined in the light of the following language by the Court of Appeals for the Ninth Circuit: " . . . The acts of respondents were and are without authority of California law . . . Therefore, conceding for the sake of argument that California could legally enact a law authorizing the segregation as practiced, the fact stands out unchallengeable that California has not done so . . . By enforcing the segregation of school children of Mexican descent . . . respondents . . . have violated . . . the Fourteenth Amendment by depriving them of liberty and property without due process of law . . ." Westminster School District v. Mendez, 161 F. 2d 774, 780-781. The court in the Mendez case observed that it was "aware of no authority justifying any segregation fiat by any administrative or executive decree." 161 F. 2d at 780. Is there any authority justifying the exclusionary fiat by the jury commissioners of Jackson County?

B. Denial of Equal Protection of the Laws.

Petitioner cannot agree with the view of the Texas court that, insofar as the organization of juries in state courts is concerned, "the equal protection clause of the Fourteenth Amendment contemplated and recognized two classes as coming within that guarantee: the white race, comprising one class, and the Negro race, comprising the other class." Petitioner has found no decision by this Court, by the lower Federal courts, or by the courts of any other state which will support such a conclusion. The

---

[1]The use of the term 'nationality" by the Texas court is questionable usage. Petitioner does not contend that Mexican citizens have the right to sit on Texas juries. The use of the term "Mexicans" is also incorrect from the point of view of citizenship. Except when quoting the Texas court, the term "persons of Mexican descent" is used throughout this brief.

conclusion of the Texas Court is supported only by its own decisions. Petitioner has found no decision by this Court dealing with the exclusion of persons from juries because of national origin. With but one exception,[2] all decisions by this Court concerning the exclusion of ethnic groups from jury service have involved the exclusion of Negroes. Apparently, all of the cases considering the question of exclusion because of national origin in which a definitive decision has been made have arisen in Texas and have involved exclusion of persons of Mexican descent.[3] The only expression by this Court dealing with exclusion from juries because of national origin seems to be the following dictum uttered in Strauder v. West Virginia, 100 U. S. 303, 308 (1879): "Nor, if a law be passed excluding all naturalized Celtic Irishmen, would there be any doubt of its inconsistency with the spirit of the amendment."

The Texas court's "two classes" theory is obviously inconsistent with this Court's statement to the effect that the provisions of the Fourteenth Amendment "are universal in their application, to all persons under the territorial jurisdiction, without regard to any differences of race, of color, or of nationality." Yick Wo v. Hopkins, 118 U. S. 336, 369 (1886). And how would the "two classes" theory explain the direct holding by this Court that a state statute which imposed discrimination in employment against a white Austrian violated the Fourteenth Amendment? Traux v. Raich, 239 U. S. 33 (1915). The plain truth is that, in announcing its "two classes" theory, the Texas court is reading into the Fourteenth Amendment a limitation which is not there. In fact, the Texas court has not uniformly construed the equal protection clause of the Fourteenth Amendment in the manner indicated by its opinion in this case. In Juarez v. State, 102 Tex. Crim. Rep. 297, 277 S. W. 1091 (1925), the Texas court held that systematic exclusion of Roman Catholics from juries is proscribed by the Fourteenth Amendment. A careful reading of the opinion in the Juarez case has uncovered no facts even tending to show that the defendant in that case was a Negro Roman Catholic. The Juarez case, although called to the attention of the Texas court by petitioner in his brief filed in that court, is not discussed in the Texas court's opinion in this case. No attempt was made by the Texas court to explain the obvious incompatibility of the holding in the Juarez case with the decision in this case. In order to explain the Juarez decision, the "two classes" theory, through some process of asexual inbreeding, must give birth to a third class. Would the "two classes" theory be extended to cases involving discrimination in the field of education? The lower Federal courts have held that segregation of school children of Mexican descent violates the Fourteenth Amendment. Gonzalez v. Sheely, 96 F. Supp. 1004 (D. C. Ariz., 1951); Mendez v. Westminster School District, 64 F. Supp. 544 (S. D. Cal., 1946), aff'd., 161 F. 2d 774 (9th Cir. 1947). Before these cases were decided, a Texas court stated that arbitrary segregation of children of Mexican descent in public schools, if shown, would violate the Fourteenth Amendment. Del Rio Indepen-

---

[2]In the lone exception a person of Japanese descent complained that members of his race were not allowed to serve as jurors. But there the exclusion was because of citizenship, and not because of race or National origin. In re Shibuya Jugiro, 140 U. S. 291 (1891).

[3]In State v. Guirlando, 152 La. 570, 93 So. 796, the Louisiana court indicated that the intentional exclusion of persons of Italian descent from jury service would be unconstitutional.

dent School District v. Salvatierra, 33 S. W. 2d 790 (Tex. Civ. App., 1930). Would the "two classes" theory be extended to cases involving judicial enforcement of covenants restricting sale of land to members of certain ethnic groups? A Texas court has held that the Fourteenth Amendment forbids judicial enforcement of a covenant prohibiting sale of land to persons of Mexican descent. Clifton v. Puente, 218 S. W. 2d 272 (Tex. Civ. App., 1949, err. ref'd.). To petitioner's knowledge, the "two classes" theory has not been applied in any type of case involving discrimination or segregation except by the Texas Court of Criminal Appeals in cases involving exclusion of persons of Mexican descent from jury service. True, the Texas court limits its unique theory to cases involving discrimination in the organization of juries in state courts. But there is no apparent reason for the application of a unique rule in the jury exclusion cases. The Fourteenth Amendment itself does not mention juries. The language of the equal protection clause is simple and direct. It provides that no state "shall deny to any person within its jurisdiction the equal protection of the laws." The word "person" is neither preceded nor followed by any restrictive adjective. What is so sacred about discrimination in the organization of juries which requires a reading into the Fourteenth Amendment of a limitation which this Court said, in the Strauder case, is not there? What is so desirable about discrimination in the organization of juries which would prompt a court into reading into the Fourteenth Amendment a limitation which the lower Federal courts have held, in the field of education, is not there, and which a Texas court has said is not there? What is so peculiar about discrimination in the organization of juries which requires a court to read into the Fourteenth Amendment a limitation which a Texas court, concerning the enforcement of restrictive covenants, has held is not there? What is so sacred, so desirable and so peculiar about such discrimination that the Texas court is moved to ignore the statement by this Court in Yick Wo v. Hopkins that the provisions of the Fourteenth Amendment "are universal in their application . . . without regard to any differences of . . . nationality"? 118 U. S. at 369. Further illustration of the unsoundness of the "two classes" theory is to be found in the cases holding that exclusion of members of defendant's political party, or faction thereof, constitutes discrimination. Kentucky v. Powers, 139 Fed. 452 (C. C. E. D. Ky., 1905), rev'd on another ground, 201 U. S. 1 (1906); State v. McCarthy, 76 N. J. L. 295, 69 Atl. 1075 (Sup. Ct., 1908). In both of these cases the decision was based on the equal protection clause of the Fourteenth Amendment. This Court has held that the exclusion of daily wage earn ers from petit jurors in Federal courts was reversible error. Thiel v. Southern Pacific Co., 328 U. S. 217 (1946). And in Ballard v. United States, 329 U. S. 187 (1946), this Court held that where women were qualified to serve on juries under state law, they could not be excluded from juries in Federal courts. Petitioner admits that in those cases the decisions were based on the fact that the exclusions shown amounted to an improper administration of justice. But in both cases this Court was concerned with upholding the tradition that trial by jury contemplates an impartial jury from a cross section of the community. The following language from the Thiel case is significant: "The American tradition of trial by jury . . . necessarily contemplates an impartial jury drawn from a cross-section of the community . . . This does not mean, of course, that every jury must contain representatives of all the economic, social, religious, racial, political and geographical groups of the community . . . But it does mean that prospective jurors should be selected by court officials without systematic and intentional exclusion of any of these groups. Jury competence is an individual rather than a class matter. That fact lies at the very heart of the jury system. To disregard it is to open the door to class distinctions and discriminations which are abhorrent to the democratic ideals of trial by jury." 328 U. S. at 220. Certainly, the Fourteenth Amendment requires that the criminal procedure of the state be such as to assure to a defendant a fair trial. For example, a defendant is denied his constitutional rights if he is tried by a prejudiced judge. Tumey v. Ohio, 273 U. S. 510 (1927). The requirement of an impartial jury is closely analogous. See Ex parte Wallace, 24 Cal. 2d 933, 152 P. 2d 1 (1944). Can it be said that in a county where, over a period of 25 years, no persons of Mexican descent have been called for jury service, a person of such descent is afforded a trial by a fair and impartial jury? This Court must bear in mind that, until shortly before petitioner's trial, several places catering to the public displayed signs reading: "No Mexicans." This Court cannot overlook the fact that in the county in which petitioner was tried up to three or four years before this trial, children of Mexican descent were segregated in the public schools. Perhaps there is some significance in the fact that in the court house of Jackson County, Texas, judicious use of a sign in the Spanish language was calculated to direct persons of Mexican descent to the public rest room facilities furnished for Negroes. (R., pp. 38, 44, 75). The blunt truth is that in Texas, persons of Mexican descent occupy a definite minority status. They are subject to discrimination in employment. Marden, Minorities in American Society, 140 (1952). In an estimated 50 Texas counties with a large population of persons of Mexican descent, persons of Mexican descent have never been known to be called for jury service. Kibbe, Latin-Americans in Texas, 229 (1946). They are frequently denied access to public places and facilities. McDonagh & Richards, Ethnic Relations in the United States, 179 (1953). Children of Mexican descent have been segregated in the public schools. The recent end of this practice in Jackson County, Texas, is perhaps explainable by the fact that in 1948 a Federal District Court in Texas ruled that such segregation violated the Fourteenth Amendment.[4] As late as May 8, 1950, the Texas State Board of Education found it necessary to issue an order specifically directing compliance with this ruling throughout the state. Marden, Minorities in American Society, 149. It is against this background that this Court should consider the statement by the Texas court that petitioner seeks to have "Mexicans" recognized as a "special class within the white race" which is "entitled to special privileges" in the organization of juries. This "special privilege" of which the Texas court speaks is the right to be free from discrimination in the selection of juries. To eliminate such discrimination, according to the Texas court, would violate the Fourteenth Amendment by "extending to members of a class special privileges not accorded to all others of that class similarly situated." 251 S. W. 2d 531, 535. The "class" of which the court speaks is composed of members of the white race. The Texas court is apparently under the impression

---

[4]Delgado v. Bastrop Ind. School Dist., Civ. Cause No. 338 (W. D. Tex., 1948). The court's judgment in this unreported ease is reprinted in Sanchez, Concerning Segregation of Spanish-Speaking Children, 72-73 (IX Inter-American Education Occasional Papers, University of Texas, 1951).

that, in Jackson County, Texas, only Negroes are allowed to serve as jurors. Unless the Texas Court of Criminal Appeals thinks that only Negroes are allowed to serve as jurors in Jackson County, it is impossible to see how elimination of discrimination against persons of Mexican descent would give to this "special class" any "special privileges" which are not enjoyed by other members of the white race in Jackson County. Can the denial to persons of Mexican descent of a right enjoyed by "all others of that class similarly situated" be defended by reference to imaginary "special privileges"? Petitioner readily admits that the Fourteenth Amendment does not require proportional representation of the component ethnic groups of a community on juries. But to condemn the exclusion shown in this case is not tantamount to imposing proportional representation. The fact that Negroes have succeeded in their fight against exclusion from juries has not imposed proportional representation of Negroes. The fact that the Texas court has held that Roman Catholics may not be systematically excluded has not imposed proportional representation of Roman Catholics. Petitioner does not contend that any proportion of jurors must be persons of Mexican descent. He does not contend that he has a right to demand that persons of Mexican descent should sit as members of the grand jury which indicted him, or of the petit jury which convicted him. Upholding the rights of Negroes and Roman Catholics to sit on juries has not given these groups any such rights. To uphold petitioner in this case would not give such rights to persons of Mexican descent. No reason is given why the extension of equal protection to petitioner would bring about consequences which did not result from the extension of equal protection to Negroes and Roman Catholics. Petitioner does not demand that persons of Mexican descent sit on any particular jury. He merely asks that they not be systematically excluded from all juries. This can be achieved without destroying our jury system and without violating the Fourteenth Amendment. It has been achieved in Texas in cases involving Negroes and Roman Catholics, and the jury system has not been destroyed. With all due deference to the Texas court, petitioner submits that, in talking of proportional representation and of giving to petitioner the right to demand that a person of Mexican descent be on a particular jury, the Texas court was demolishing a straw man of its own creation. In view of the undoubted minority status of persons of Mexican descent in Texas, it is at least mildly ironic for the Texas court to uphold the discriminatory practice of which petitioner complains by pointing out that, after all, persons of Mexican descent are members of the dominant "class" in Texas. (See Appendix B). Petitioner believes that the following language, in Cassel v. Texas, 339 U. S. 282, 287 (1950), is pertinent: "Obviously, the number of races and nationalities appearing in the ancestry of our citizens would make it impossible to meet a requirement of proportional representation." The correctness of petitioner's contention is implicit in such language. How could the "number of . . . nationalities appearing in the ancestry of our citizens . . . make it impossible to meet a requirement of proportional representation" if, as the Texas court holds, persons may be excluded from jury service because of national origin? If the Texas court's "two classes" theory is correct, the number of nationalities appearing in the ancestry of our citizens is altogether irrelevant. It can present no problem, since persons may be systematically excluded from jury service because of their national origin. Finally, let us assume that the Texas legislature passed a statute excluding persons of Mexican descent from jury service. Would such legislation be constitutional? Obviously not. Can the jury commissioners of Jackson County, Texas, do what the state legislature cannot do? Petitioner thinks not.

II

WHERE IT IS SHOWN THAT, OVER A PERIOD OF TWENTY-FIVE YEARS, NO PERSONS OF MEXICAN DESCENT HAVE BEEN CALLED FOR JURY SERVICE, ALTHOUGH MEMBERS OF SUCH ETHNIC GROUP WERE AVAILABLE AND QUALIFIED FOR JURY SERVICE, SUCH EVIDENCE ESTABLISHES THE INTENTIONAL, ARBITRARY AND SYSTEMATIC EXCLUSION OF PERSONS OF MEXICAN DESCENT, AND THE FAILURE OF THE TEXAS COURT OF CRIMINAL APPEALS TO APPLY THE "RULE OF EXCLUSION" ANNOUNCED BY THE SUPREME COURT OF THE UNITED STATES IN NORRIS V. ALABAMA, 294 U. S. 587 (1935), DEPRIVES PETITIONER OF HIS LIBERTY WITHOUT DUE PROCESS OF LAW AND DENIES TO HIM THE EQUAL PROTECTION OF THE LAWS.

THE EVIDENCE

The Texas Court of Criminal Appeals summarizes the evidence relied on by petitioner as follows: "It may be said, therefore, that the facts relied upon by the appellant to bring this case within the rule of systematic exclusion is that at the time of the trial of this case there were 'some male persons of Mexican or Latin-American descent in Jackson County' who possessed the qualifications requisite to service as grand or petit jurors, and that no Mexican had been called for jury service in that county for a period of twenty-five years." 251 S. W. 2d 531. (R., p. 93).

Since 1930, The United States Bureau of the Census has not used the classification "Mexican" in compiling populations statistics. However, the 1950 census contains statistics concerning "persons of Spanish surname" The 1950 census figures for Jackson County, Texas, show the following facts: 1. The total population of Jackson County is 12,916.[5] Persons of Spanish surname total 1,865, of whom 1,738 are native-born citizens, and 65 are naturalized citizens.[6] Persons with Spanish surnames thus constitute about 14% of the total population of Jackson County. 2. The number of males in Jackson County aged 21 or over is 3,754.[7] Of these, 408, or approximately 11%, have Spanish surnames.[8] 3. While no separate figures are given relative to the educational attainments of males of Spanish surname, the census shows that of 645 such persons aged 25 or over, 245 have completed from 1 to 4 years of elementary schooling; 85 have completed the fifth and sixth years; 35 have completed 7 years of elementary schooling; 15 have completed 8 years; 60 have completed from one to three years of high school; 5 have completed 4 years of high school; and 5 are college graduates. 9 For 20 such persons, no educational information was available.

---

[5]U.S. Census, 1950, Vol. II, Part 43, p. 180.
[6]Id., Vol. IV, Part 3, Ch. C, p. 45.
[7]Id., Vol. II. Part 43, p. 180.
[8]Id., Vol. IV, Part 3, Ch. C, p. 67.

PRESCRIBED QUALIFICATIONS FOR JURY SERVICE.

A. Grand Jury. (See Appendix "A")
In order to be eligible for service on Texas grand juries, a person must be a male citizen who is qualified to vote; he must be a freeholder in the state or a householder in the county; he must be of sound mind and good moral character and able to read and write; and he must not have been convicted of a felony or be under indictment for theft or any felony. Tex. Code Crim. Proc., Art. 339. While no age requirement is specified, the voting qualification impliedly limits grand jury service to persons 21 years of age or more. Hill v. State, 99 Tex. Crim. Rep., 290, 269 S. W. 90 (1925). There is no property qualification, since a "householder" is any person who is the head of a family." Lane v. State, 29 Tex. Crim. App. 310, 15 S. W. 827 (1890).
B. Petit Jury. (See Appendix "A")
In order to qualify as a petit juror, a person must be a male citizen, 21 years of age, who is qualified to vote and who is of sound mind, able to read and write, and either a householder in the county or a freeholder in the state. Tex. Code Crim. Proc., Arts. 612, 616. The possession of a poll tax is not a prerequisite for eligibility for service on petit juries. Tex. Code Crim. Proc., Art. 579. Oddly enough, the statutes do not require that a prospective petit juror in a criminal case be of good moral character.

ARGUMENT

In 1935, this Court announced that the long and continued failure to call members of the Negro race for jury service, where it is shown that Negroes were available and qualified for jury service, was sufficient to make out a case of discriminatory exclusion. Norris v. Alabama, 294 U. S. 587. This holding has been consistently followed by this Court. Cassel v. Texas, 339 U.S. 282 (1950); Hill v. Texas, 316 U. S. 400 (1942); Smith v. Texas, 311 U. S. 128 (1941).
A. This Case Comes within the Rule of Norris v. Alabama.
In cases involving the exclusion of Negroes, this Court has held that evidence establishing the following facts made out a case of discriminatory exclusion:
In a county where 1/6 of the population was colored, no Negro had served as a juror for many years. Hale v. Kentucky, 303 U. S. 613 (1938). In a county having a population of 36,881, including 2,688 Negroes, no Negro had been called for jury service in a generation, although at least 30 Negroes in the county qualified for jury service. Norris v. Alabama, 294 U. S. 587 (1935). No Negro had been called for jury service in a generation, although Negroes made up 1/6 of the population. Norris v. Alabama, supra. In this case, as shown above, about 14% of the population of Jackson County consisted of persons of Mexican descent. In view of the census figures pertaining to the number of male citizens 21 years of age or more, and in view of the figures concerning the number of school years completed by persons of Mexican descent 25 years of age or over, it is obvious that in Jackson County there were, at the very least, 30 persons of Mexican descent qualified to serve as jurors. Cf. Norris v. Alabama, supra. While there are no figures concerning the number of poll taxes held by persons of Mexican descent, this fact is altogether irrelevant in determining qualification for service on petit juries. And yet, for a period of twenty-five years, no

person of Mexican descent has served on a Jackson County jury. In Patton v. Mississippi, 332 U. S. 463 (1947), the evidence showed that there were only 12 or 13 Negroes available for jury service in the county, as against 5,000 whites. This Court said: "Whatever the precise number of qualified colored electors in the county; there were some; and if it can possibly be conceived that all of them were disqualified for jury service . . . we do not doubt that the State could have proved it." 332 U. S. at 648. To use the very language of the Texas court in this case, the facts established that there were "some male persons of Mexican descent" in Jackson County who possessed the qualifications requisite to service as jurors. 251 S. W. 2d 531, 533. Further, here there is no need for this Court to demonstrate an unwillingness to presume that all persons of Mexican descent in Jackson County are disqualified. In this case the State stipulated that there were some persons of Mexican descent who possessed all necessary qualifications for jury service. 251 S. W. 2d 531,533.

B. Refusal to Decide This Case under the Rule of Norris v. Alabama Denies to Petitioner the Equal Protection of the Laws. From the foregoing, it appears conclusively that, were petitioner a Negro, the Texas court would have been bound to reverse the conviction and order the indictment dismissed. The question in this case, then, is simply this: Does the rule of Norris v. Alabama apply to a case involving exclusion of persons of Mexican descent from jury service? The Texas court refused to apply the aforementioned rule. Quoting from its previous decision in Sanchez v. State, 147 Tex. Crim. Rep. 436, 181 S.W. 87 (1944), the Texas court said: "'In the absence of a holding by the Supreme Court of the United States that nationality and race bear the same relation within the meaning of the constitutional provision (Fourteenth Amendment) mentioned, we shall continue to hold that the statute law of this State furnishes the guide for the selection of juries in this State, and that, in the absence of proof showing express discrimination by administrators of the law, a jury so selected in accordance therewith is valid.'"251 S. W. 2d 531, 533. In the concluding sentence of its opinion, the Texas court reiterated its position by saying that "in the absence of proof of actual discrimination," it cannot be said that petitioner was discriminated against in the selection of juries and thereby denied equal protection of the laws.

The rule of Norris v. Alabama is nothing more nor less than a rule of evidence. It creates a presumption which arises upon the showing of certain facts. As the Texas court pointed out, "the effect of the rule of exclusion is to furnish means by which proof of discrimination may be accomplished." 251 S. W. 2d 531, 535. The effect of the Texas court's holding in this case, and in previous cases involving persons of Mexican descent is simply this: In the State of Texas, there is one rule of evidence for Negroes, and a different rule for persons of Mexican descent. From certain facts, the Texas court will conclude, in accordance with the Norris case, that there has been an arbitrary, intentional and systematic exclusion of Negroes. Given the same facts, but changing the color of the accused, the Texas court refuses to find that there has been an arbitrary, intentional and systematic exclusion of persons of Mexican descent. The Texas court requires a person of Mexican descent to show express discrimination, and it states frankly that persons of Mexican descent must bear this more onerous burden of proof solely and simply because they are not Negroes. It is patent, therefore, that the Texas court has denied to this petitioner a means of proving discrimination which is available to Negroes; and no effort is made to disguise the fact that this denial is based solely and exclusively on the fact that this petitioner is not a Negro. To put it bluntly, the Texas court has set up a classification based solely, exclusively and expressly on race. Let us suppose that the legislature of the State of Texas enacted a statute to the effect that proof of certain facts by a Negro should give rise to certain presumptions favorable to a Negro, but that proof of the same facts by a white person should give rise to no such presumptions in favor of the white person. Or, to bring the matter closer to the case at hand, suppose that the legislature of the State of Texas, by statute, provided that proof of long-continued absence of Negroes from juries where it is shown that there are qualified Negroes should give rise to a presumption of intentional exclusion of Negroes, but that proof of long-continued absence of persons of Mexican descent from juries should not be sufficient to overcome the presumption that the jury-selecting officials acted fairly and without prejudice. Can there be any doubt concerning the invalidity of such a statute? If doubt there is, even a casual reading of Oyama v. California, 332 U. S. 633 (1948), will dispel it.

Although a thorough search of the cases has been made, no case has been found which furnishes even the semblance of support for the astounding proposition that a state court may make the outcome of litigation depend upon the race of a litigant. By making the outcome of a case depend on the applicability of a rule of evidence, and by making the applicability of the rule of evidence depend on the race or color of a litigant, the Texas court has made the outcome of a case depend on the race of the accused. The conviction in this case would have been reversed were petitioner a Negro. The conviction is affirmed because petitioner is a person of Mexican descent. Can any person sincerely believe that, as the Texas court says, the equal protection clause of the Fourteenth Amendment not only permits, but compels such an incongruous rule of law? Even should petitioner admit, as he does not, that the Fourteenth Amendment, insofar as discrimination in the organization of state juries is concerned, contemplated only two classes—whites and Negroes—it does not follow that, in the formulation of rules of evidence, the Texas court may discriminate against white persons by making the sufficiency of the evidence depend on the color of the person presenting it. The Fourteenth Amendment prohibits discrimination against whites as well as against Negroes. Buchanan v. Warley, 245 U. S. 360 (1917). Petitioner would also point out that the litigant injured by the discriminatory rule of evidence in the Oyama case was not a Negro. Thus, it cannot be said that, insofar as the validity of rules of evidence is concerned, the Fourteenth Amendment recognizes only two classes—Negroes and whites. And even if this untenable proposition be admitted for the purpose of argument, it does not follow that the Amendment sanctions discrimination against white persons by rules of evidence which imposes upon them a burden more onerous than that which is placed on Negroes. A classification based on race is not beyond the reach of the Constitutional prohibitions merely because it is a judicial tribunal, rather than a legislature or administrative agency, which has seen fit to make race the determining factor in selecting the rules which it will apply. As this Court said in Strauder v. West Virginia, 100 U. S. 303 (1879): "A state may act through different agencies—either by its legislative, its executive or its judicial authorities, and the prohibitions of the amendment extend to all action of the state denying equal protection of the laws, whether it be action by one of these agencies or by another." 100 U. S. at 318. More recently, the late Chief Justice Vinson said: "That the action of state courts and of judicial officers in their official capacities is to be regarded as action of the State within the meaning of the Fourteenth Amendment is a proposition which has long been established by the decisions of this Court." Shelley v. Kraemer, 334 U. S. 1, 14 (1948). Petitioner, therefore, submits that, insofar as proof of the fact of intentional and systematic exclusion of persons of Mexican descent from jury service is concerned, the Texas court cannot, consistently with the provisions of the Fourteenth Amendment, hold that petitioner has not shown such exclusion. It cannot do so without denying to petitioner the equal protection of the laws. The unconstitutional basis for the decision of the Texas court in this case can find no justification in the fact that that court's denial of petitioner's right to the equal protection of the laws had as its objective the upholding of the unconstitutional discriminatory acts of the jury commissioners of Jackson County, Texas. A state court cannot, by adopting a discriminatory rule of evidence, weave a protective cloak behind which local jury commissioners can continue to disregard the plain mandates of the Fourteenth Amendment.

CONCLUSION

Petitioner submits that the evidence in this case establishes beyond any doubt that the jury commissioners of Jackson County, Texas, have, for at least 25 years, consciously and deliberately excluded persons of Mexican descent from jury service. To attribute the complete absence of persons of petitioner's national origin from Jackson County juries to coincidence strains all credulity. Such uniformity of result betrays the existence of a master plan. If my name appears on 14% of the lots from which repeated drawings are made over a period of 25 years, and my name is never drawn a single time, I would be more than justified in suspecting that the person doing the drawing was cheating. By engaging in such practices, the jury commissioners have violated the constitutional rights of this petitioner. They have denied to petitioner, and to all other persons of Mexican descent, the right to a trial by a fair and impartial jury. The Texas court's "two classes" theory is without foundation in reason; it is without support in the decisions of this or any other court. All courts which have considered the question have held that the Fourteenth Amendment forbids discrimination because of national origin. Such a theory, itself without foundation, cannot support the heavy weight of the discriminatory practices which it is forced to uphold in this case, if the decision of the Texas court is to stand. The invalidity of the "two classes" theory becomes apparent when it is examined in the light of the minority status of persons of Mexican descent in Texas. They occupy an inferior social and economic position. The increase in the number of cases in which the Texas court has given its sanction to the practice of excluding them from jury service shows that they also occupy an inferior legal status. The Texas court has announced that it will continue to hold them in such inferior legal status until this Court compels it to do otherwise. While the Texas court elaborates on its "two classes" theory, in Jackson County, and in other areas in Texas, persons of Mexican descent are treated as a third class—a notch above the Negroes, perhaps, but several notches below the rest of the population. They are segregated in schools, they are denied service in public places, they are discouraged from using non-Negro rest rooms. They are excluded from juries, and a Texas court upholds their exclusion by a paternal reminder that they are members of the dominant white class. As members of the dominant class, they are chided by the Texas court for seeking "special privileges." They are told that they are assured of a fair trial at the hands of persons who do not want to go to school with them, who do not want to give them service in public places, who do not want to sit on juries with them, and who would prefer not to share rest room facilities with them, not even at the Jackson County court house. Finally, to insure that they do not succeed in their selfish demand for "special privileges," the Texas court formulates a special rule of evidence for them so that they may never gain admission to the jury box. That the Texas statutory scheme for the selection of juries is not in itself discriminatory is recognized by petitioner. The Texas statutes do not exclude persons of Mexican descent from jury service. But this Court well knows that the Texas statutory scheme is capable of being and, in fact, has been, used in a discriminatory manner. Indeed, the State of Texas is more than proportionately represented in the roll call of cases in which this Court has condemned discriminatory administration of laws which are capable of being carried out without discrimination if only those who administer them are willing to perform their duties fairly and impartially. Petitioner agrees with the Texas court when it says that a jury selected in accordance with the Texas statutory scheme presents no cause for complaint. If the inherent fairness of the Texas jury statutes had been accepted and applied by the jury commissioners of Jackson County, petitioner would not be asking this Court to aid him in securing his rights. If Texas jury commissioners had seen fit to administer non-discriminatory statutes in a non-discriminatory manner, the "two classes" theory would never have been concocted. The language of the Fourteenth Amendment is clear and direct. It states that no state "shall deny to any person within its jurisdiction the equal protection of the laws." The words "any person within its jurisdiction" clearly includes persons of Mexican descent. The Amendment guarantees to persons of Mexican descent the right to sit on juries. "If this could be refused solely on the ground of race or nationality, the prohibition of the denial to any person of the equal protection of the laws would be a barren form of words." Truax v. Raich, 229 U. S. 33, 41 (1915). All of the talk about "two classes"; all of the verbal pointing with alarm at a "special class" which seeks "special privileges" cannot obscure one very simple fact which stands out in bold relief: the Texas law points in one direction for persons of Mexican descent, like petitioner, and in another for Negroes. Cf. Oyama v. California, 332 U. S. 633, 641 (1947). Under such circumstances, can it be said that the State of Texas has accorded to petitioner the protection of equal laws? Distinctions negate equality, and "distinctions between citizens solely because of their ancestry are by their very nature odious to a free people whose institutions are founded upon the doctrine of equality." Hirabayashi v. United States, 320 U. S. 81, 100 (1943).

PRAYER

Petitioner, therefore, prays that the judgments of the trial court and of the Texas Court of Criminal Appeals be reversed, and that the indictment against petitioner be ordered dismissed.

Respectfully submitted,
CARLOS C. CADENA
112 College Street
San Antonio 5, Texas
GUS C. GARCIA
403 N. Flores Street
San Antonio, Texas
Attorneys for Petitioner
MAURY MAVERICK, JR.
San Antonio, Texas
JOHN J. HERRERA
Houston, Texas
JAMES DE ANDA
CHRIS ALDRETE
Of Counsel
By: Carlos C. Cadena

APPENDIX "A" STATUTORY APPENDIX TEXAS CODE OF CRIMINAL PROCEDURE

Organization of the Grand Jury.

Art. 333. The district judge shall, at each term of the district court, appoint three persons to perform the duties of jury commissioners who shall possess the following qualifications:

1. Be intelligent citizens of the county and able to read and write.
2. Be qualified jurors and freeholders in the county.
3. Be residents of different portions of the county.
4. Have no suit in court which requires the intervention of a jury.

Art. 338. The jury commissioners shall select sixteen men from the citizens of different portions of the county to be summoned as grand jurors for the next term of court.

Art. 339. No person shall be selected to serve as a grand juror who does not possess the following qualifications:

He must be a citizen of the State, and of the county in which he is to serve, and qualified under the Constitution and laws to vote in said county; but whenever it is made to appear that the requisite number of jurors who have paid their poll taxes cannot be found within the county, the court shall not regard the payment of poll taxes as a qualification for services as a juror.

2. He must be a freeholder within the State, or a householder in the county.

3. He must be of sound mind and of good moral character.

4. He must be able to read and write.

5. He must not have been convicted of any felony.

6. He must not be under indictment or other legal accusation for theft or any felony.

Art. 344. Within thirty days of the next terms of the district court and not before, the clerk shall open the envelope containing the list of grand jurors, make out a copy of the names of those selected as grand jurors, certify it under his official seal, and deliver it to the sheriff.

Art. 345. The sheriff shall summon the persons named in the list at least three days, exclusive of the day of service, prior to the first day of the term of court at which they are to serve, by giving personal notice to each juror of the time and place when and where he is to attend as a grand juror, or by leaving at his place of residence with a member of his family over sixteen years old a written notice to such juror that he has been selected as a grand juror, and the time and place when and where he is to attend.

Art. 352. When as many as twelve men summoned to serve as grand jurors are in attendance upon the court, it shall proceed to test their qualifications as such.

Art. 354. In trying the qualifications of any person to serve as grand juror, he shall be asked: 1. Are you a citizen of this State and county, and qualified to vote in this county, under the Constitution and laws of this State? 2. Are you a freeholder in this state or a householder in this county? 3. Are you able to read and write?

Art. 355. When, by the answer of the person, it appears to the court that he is a qualified juror, he shall be accepted as such, unless it be shown that he is not of sound mind or of good moral character, or unless it be shown that he is not in fact qualified to serve as a grand juror. Qualifications for Serving as Petit Jurors in Criminal cases. Texas Code of Criminal Procedure:

Art. 616. A challenge for cause is an objection made to a particular juror alleging some fact which renders him incapable or unfit to serve on the jury. It may be made for any one of the following causes:

1. That he is not a qualified voter in the State and county, under the Constitution and laws of the State.

2. That he is neither householder in the county nor a freeholder in the State.

3. That he has been convicted of theft or any felony.

4. That he is under indictment or other legal accusation for theft or any felony.

5. That he is insane, or has such defect in the organs of seeing, feeling, or hearing, or such bodily or mental defect or disease as to render him unfit for jury service.

6. That he is a witness in the case.

7. That he served on the grand jury which found the indictment.

8. That he served on a petit jury in a former trial of the same case.

9. That he is related within the third degree of consanguinity or affinity to the defendant.

10. That he is related within the third degree of consanguinity or affinity to the person injured by the commission of the offense, or to the special prosecutor, if there be one.

11. That the juror has conscientious scruples in regard to the infliction of the punishment of death for crime.

12. That he has a bias or prejudice in favor of or against the accused.

13. That from hearsay or otherwise there is established in the mind of the juror such a conclusion as to the guilt or innocence of the defendant as will influence him in his action in finding a verdict.

14. That he cannot read and write. This cause of challenge shall not be sustained when it appears to the court that the requisite number of jurors who are able to read and write cannot be found in the county.

Art. 616, of course, has reference to the formation of petit juries in capital cases. But Art. 632 of the Code of Criminal Procedure provides: "Challenges for cause in all criminal cases are the same as provided in capital cases in Art. 616, except cause 11 in said article."

Art. 579. Failure to pay poll tax shall not disqualify any person from jury service.

APPENDIX "B" STATUS OF PERSONS OF MEXICAN DESCENT IN TEXAS

The Spanish-Mexican people have been in the Southwest for more than 300 years. During the Spanish-colonial period their numbers were small, and they were thinly distributed from the Gulf Coast of Texas to the Pacific. The brief period during which the Southwest was a part of the Mexican republic did little to change either the isolation, the cultural outlook, or the numbers of these people. It was the Mexican War, and the transfer of the Southwest to the United States, that made drastic changes in their way of life.[9] In Texas, the war for independence aroused antagonisms that still descent. "Mexican" became a term of opprobrium, and barriers began to be built up between those of Mexican descent and the so-called Anglos. Those barriers led to the establishment of a status for "Mexicans" like that assigned by the dominant group to the Negro.[10] The great movement into the United States of people from Mexico during 1870-1920 accentuated these natio-racial distinctions. Today there are some 1,500,000 persons of Mexican descent in Texas, the majority of whom are citizens of the United States. There are 30 counties whose populations are more than 40% of Mexican descent.[11] Being largely of Indian blood, the Mexican immigrant was literally and sociologically highly visible. That visibility became the peg upon which to hang the stereotype of the "Mexican"; and, once stereotyped, the immigrant acquired burdens which augmented his socio-economic problems and increased his sociological visibility. Thus, he fell into a vicious circle out of which he has been trying to break with only meager success.[12] It still is not unusual to find in Texas segregated schools for "Mexican" children.[13] Often, they are barred from swimming pools, cafes, movie theatres, and even public parks.[14] In some communi-

[9]Carey McWilliams, NORTH FROM MEXICO, Lippincott, 1949.
[10]Pauline Kibbe, LATIN AMERICANS IN TEXAS, U. of N. Mex. Press, 1946.
[11]Lyle Saunders, THE SPANISH-SPEAKING POPULATION OF TEXAS, U. of Texas Press, 1949.
[12]Eli Ginzberg and Douglas W. Bray, THE UNEDUCATED, Columbia U. Press, 1953 (Chapter 4).
[13]George I. Sanchez, CONCERNING SEGREGATION OF SPANISH-SPEAKING CHILDREN IN THE PUBLIC SCHOOLS, U. of Texas Press, 1951.
[14]George I. Sánchez, "Pachucos in the Making," COMMON GROUND, Autumn, 1943.

ties there are separate American Legion Posts for "whites" and "Mexicans." Restrictive covenants limit the areas in which a person of Mexican descent may buy or rent a home.[15] These practices have been so prevalent that the Texas legislature on several occasions has considered the passage of laws prohibiting discrimination against persons of Mexican descent. Only the fear that such protection would have to be extended to Negroes also has prevented the passage of such legislation! While legally white (anthropologically he is predominantly Indian)[16] frequently the term "white" excludes the "Mexican" and is reserved for the rest of the non-Negro population. Official forms sometimes call for the "racial" classification of "White-Negro-Mexican." Even Selective Service, during World War II, indulged in this practice for a period, and the Texas Department of Public Health still uses those classifications in at least one official form. It is so well recognized that Mexican-Americans are a class apart that the United States Bureau of the Census, since 1930, has been collecting data that distinguish between the two segments of the white population in Texas and the rest of the Southwest. That Bureau, as part of the 1950 Census of Population, has issued a special report, Persons of Spanish Surname.[17] In its 1950 United States Census of Housing, that Bureau presents a special tabulation for people of Spanish surname.[18] The under-privileged status of this population group is quickly evidenced by these Census reports. Not only is the Mexican-American commonly regarded as a class apart, but by every objective measurement—from biological makeup to deaths from tuberculosis and from infantile diarrhea—he is a class apart. The professional literature is replete with data supporting the statement that the Mexican-American is regarded as, and is, a class apart. From the pioneer surveys of Professor Paul S. Taylor, of the University of California Department of Economics, a quarter of a century ago,[19] to graduate theses written within the last year or two at the University of Texas, all evidence bears this out. The attitude of the non-professional on the subject is well exemplified by the common practice in the Texas press of "race-labelling" this population group, just as the Negro is race-labelled. This attitude is also evidenced by the previously mentioned segregation of "Mexicans" in public schools—a practice responding not to pedagogical considerations but to the attitude of the dominant group in the community.[20] Because of the widespread discrimination against persons of Mexican descent, Mexico at one time "blacklisted" the entire State of Texas (i.e., refused to permit Mexican contract workers to enter the State of Texas for employment). The State of Texas officially recognized the widespread mistreatment of persons of Mexican descent, citizens and aliens alike, by establishing the Texas Good Neighbor Commission in 1943.[21] The Commission was

[15]See Clifton v. Puente, 218 S. W. 2d 272 (Tex. Civ. App., 1949).

[16](Mexico) Secretaria de la Economia Nacional, MEXICO EN CIFRAS (ATLAS ESTADISTICO), 1934. See also: George I. Sánchez, MEXICO, A REVOLUTION BY EDUCATION, Viking 1936.

[17]U. S. Department of Commerce, Bureau of the Census, SPECIAL REPORT P-E NO. 3C.

[18]U. S. Department of Commerce. Bureau of the Census,. BULLETIN H-A 43.

[19]Paul S. Taylor, AN AMERICAN-MEXICAN FRONTIER, U. of N. Carolina Press, 1932. See also: Herschel T. Manuel. THE EDUCATION OF MEXICAN AND SPANISH-SPEAKING CHILDREN IN TEXAS, U. of Texas Press, 1930.

[20]Virgil Strickland and George I. Sanchez "Spanish Name Spells Discrimination," THE NATION'S SCHOOLS, January, 1948.

[21]McWilliams, op. cit., especially pp. 270-275.

established by the State to seek to improve the relations between the two clearly recognized classes of its white population—"Anglos" and "Latins." It was hoped that, by taking this step, the State would be removed from Mexico's "blacklist." That the action was not fully successful is shown by the fact that Mexico still "blacklists" many areas in Texas and refuses to allow braceros (Mexican contract workers brought in under the terms of the international agreement with the United States) to work there. It seems significant, indeed, that not only do both professional and nonprofessional workers in Texas recognize that persons of Mexican descent are, and are treated as, a class apart, but the State of Texas, too, concurs in that recognition. Some ten years ago the Governor issued a proclamation, and the Legislature adopted a joint resolution, recognizing that this minority group was being subject to discrimination. That the Good Neighbor Commission has not fulfilled its mission, and that persons of Mexican descent are still subjected to widespread discrimination as a class, was recognized by the present governor of Texas when he named the Texas Council on Human Relations (now defunct) to attempt to do unofficially and with private support, what the Good Neighbor Commission could not do as an official and publicly-supported agency of the State.

Appendix VII

SUPREME COURT OF THE UNITED STATES
OCTOBER TERM, 1953
No. 406
PETE HERNANDEZ,
Petitioner,
v.
THE STATE OF TEXAS,
Respondent.
BRIEF IN OPPOSITION
JOHN BEN SHEPPERD
Attorney General of Texas
RUDY G. RICE
Assistant
MILTON RICHARDSON
Assistant
HORACE WIMBERLY
Assistant
Capitol Station
Austin, Texas
Attorneys for Respondent

SUBJECT INDEX

INDEX OF AUTHORITIES
(Other than cited in the quoted Opinion below)

IN THE
SUPREME COURT OF THE UNITED STATES
OCTOBER TERM, 1953
No.406
PETE HERNANDEZ,
Petitioner,

v.

THE STATE OF TEXAS,
Respondent.
BRIEF IN OPPOSITION
OPINION BELOW
The opinion below of the Texas Court of Criminal
Appeals (R. 91) is reported at 251 S.W. 2d 531.
(Tex. Crim. 1952.)

JURISDICTION
As admitted by Petitioner on page 2 of his petition under his statement pertaining to jurisdiction, his petition for rehearing in the Texas Court of Criminal Appeals was denied October 22, 1952. Not counting that date, the 90-day period thereafter ended on January 20, 1953, but petition herein was not filed during that time nor was an extension of time had, but the petition was filed on January 21, 1953. Late filing denied Petitioner jurisdiction in this matter. Furthermore, Respondent has not had served on it a printed copy of the petition. By making this response, Respondent does not waive any rule or requirement with which Petitioner should have heretofore or should now or should here-after comply. Respondent submits that this Court should not be required to take cognizance of this matter because same is of no importance beyond its own particular facts and has been correctly decided on adequate state grounds irrespective of any federal questions discussed.

ARGUMENT AND AUTHORITIES
Petitioner far over estimates the evidence in this case and thereupon vainly reaches for conclusions unwarranted by the facts. In the wording of his Questions Presented, Petitioner has assumed that he presented what would be considered enough evidence to show systematic exclusion from jury service. The evidence is strongly contrary to such an assumption. In the hearing on Defendant's Motion to Quash the Indictment and Defendant's Motion to Quash the Jury Panel, some seventy-nine (79) pages of testimony were produced, wherein defendant offered six witnesses and the State of Texas offered seven witnesses, all being subjected to full cross-examination as desired by Counsel. Much of Petitioner's testimony was about former school procedures and matters not pertinent to this inquiry. His witnesses in no instance showed that any plan had been worked nor purpose pursued toward keeping those white persons characterized by him as Mexican or Latin American from serving on juries in Jackson County, Texas. The State produced as witnesses all five members of the Jury Commission who had selected the Grand Jury and Petit Jury panels involved in this inquiry. Each Commissioner positively testified under

oath that no discrimination was allowed in selecting the jury lists (R. 57-73). This shows full performance of all legal duties imposed by our law on these Commissioners. They are not shown to have been acting like the Commissioners in the Cassell case, 339 U.S. 282 (1949) who were not in that instance fulfilling their duty. The Respondent, the State of Texas, does not condone discrimination against persons of Latin American origin as to serving on Jury Commissions, grand juries, or Petit juries. The Respondent's position in this case is that the record does not disclose systematic exclusion from jury service of Latin Americans so as to deprive Petitioner of his constitutional right of due process and equal protection of law. Now, if in picking out 250 men from a list of seven thousand, we can get men whose education, varied business experiences, constant contact with the public and clear understanding of human nature will best fit them for service on grand jury or petit jury so as to be impartial in their decisions, yet able to understand the intricacies of various situations presented to them as jurors, as has been done in Jackson County, Texas, we have done great and good service to this fundamental institution, trial by jury. The defendant in this case is a white man. The jury was composed of white men. No actual exclusion of the white race or any other race therefrom is shown. No discrimination against the white race or based on race or color is shown. If we are to divide the white race into small segments such as blondes and brunettes, or redheads and others, or left handers and right handers, or Protestant and Catholic and Jew, or by economic classification, or by Irish origin, German origin, etc., then try and force our State to see that proportional or other representation of each such classification is on each trial and grand jury, we have but so encumbered the jury system as to utterly ruin it and nullify any good which might be expected from it. No jury could be perfect, except perhaps the particular jury which acquits a man will have that standing in that man's individual views. Any jury which convicts is subject to the censure of the criminal who appeared before it. Your decision in Brown v. Allen, 344 U.S. 470 (1953) has shown that this Honorable Court will not lightly upset State procedure and make forever uncertain and perplexing what rights our courts and jury system have in the administration of justice. Certainly Petitioner has not shown one iota of discrimination against himself in the matters he tries to urge upon this Court. The jury list was from a source which reasonably reflects a cross-section of the population of Jackson County having upon it men suitable in character and intelligence for that duty, some more capable than others. We wish to now quote the opinion of the Texas Court of Criminal Appeals rendered in this very case and reported in Vol. 251, S.W. 2d 531:

OPINION

"Murder is the offense, with punishment assessed at life imprisonment in the penitentiary. "Appellant is a Mexican, or Latin American. He claims that he was discriminated against upon the trial of this case because members of the Mexican nationality were deliberately, systematically and willfully excluded from the grand jury that found and returned the indictment in this case and from the petit jury panel from which was selected the petit jury that tried . . . for said reasons, to quash . . . petit jury panel, claiming . . . been deprived of equal protection . . . court in overruling the two . . . the sole question for review. In support of his contention, appellant relies upon the so-called rule of exclusion as announced by the Supreme Court of the United States-that is, that the long and continued failure to call members of the Negro race for jury service, where it is shown that members of that race were available and qualified for jury service, grand or petit, constitutes a violation of due process and equal protection against members of that race.

"The rule appears to have been first announced in Norris v. Alabama, 294 U. S. 587, 55 S. Ct. 579, 79 L. Ed. 1074, and since then followed. See Smith v. Texas, 311 U. S. 128, 61 S. Ct. 164, 85 L. Ed. 84; Hill v. Texas, 316 U. S. 400, 62 S. Ct. 1159, 86 L. Ed. 1559; Cassell v. Texas, 339 U. S. 282, 70 S. Ct. 629, 94 L. Ed. 839; and Ross v. Texas, 341, U.S. 918, 71 S. Ct. 742, 95 L. Ed. 1352."

"Appellant would have the above rule to extend to and apply to members of different nationalities—particularly to Mexicans. "Much testimony was introduced by which appellant sought to show the systematic exclusion of Mexicans from jury service and that there were members of that nationality qualified and available for such service in Jackson County. The facts proven, however, were of no greater probative force than those stipulated by the state and the appellant, which we quote as follows: "'The State will stipulate that for the last twenty-five years there is no record of any person with a Mexican or Latin American name having served on a jury commission, grand jury or petit jury in Jackson County.' "'It is stipulated by counsel for the State and counsel for the defendant that there are some male persons of Mexican or Latin American descent in Jackson County who, by virtue of being citizens, householders, or free-holders, and having all other legal prerequisites to jury service, are eligible to serve as members of a jury commission, grand jury and/or petit jury.' "With reference to the petit jury, we quote the following: "It is stipulated by counsel for the State and counsel for defendant that there is no person of Mexican or other Latin American descent or blood on the list of talesmen.' "These stipulations of necessity included the ability to read and speak the English language. "It was shown that Jackson County had a population of approximately 18,000, 15% of which—a witness estimated as a 'wild guess'—were Mexicans. The same witness also testified as a 'rough estimate' that 6 or 7% of that 15% were freeholders upon the tax rolls of the county. It was shown, also, that the population of Jackson County was composed also of Bohemians, Germans, Anglo-Americans, and Negroes. The relative percentages of these, however, were not estimated. "It may be said, therefore, that the facts relied upon by the appellant to bring this case within the rule of systematic exclusion are that at the time the grand jury was selected and at the time of the trial of this case there were 'some male persons of Mexican or Latin American descent in Jackson County' who possessed the qualifications requisite to service as grand or petit jurors, and that no Mexican had been called for jury service in that county for a period of twenty-five years. "There is an absence of any testimony here suggesting express or factual discrimination against appellant or other Mexicans in the selection, organization, or empaneling of the grand or petit jury in this case. To sustain his claim of discrimination, appellant relies only upon an application of the rule of exclusion mentioned. "In so far as this court is concerned, the question here presented was determined adversely to appellant's contention in the case of Sanchez

v. State, 147 Tex. Cr. R. 436, 181 S. W. 2d 87, where we said: "'In the absence of a holding by the Supreme Court of the United States that nationality and race bear the same relation, within the meaning of the constitutional provision (Fourteenth Amendment) mentioned, we shall continue to hold that the statute law of this State furnishes the guide for the selection of juries in the State, and that, in the absence of proof showing express discrimination by administrators of the law, a jury so select- ed in accordance therewith is valid.' (Parentheses supplied) "Within our knowledge, no decision of the Supreme Court of the United States has been rendered which would change the conclusion just expressed. "The validity of laws of this state pro- viding for the selection of grand or petit jurors (Arts. 333-360, C. C. P.) has never been seriously challenged. Indeed, the Supreme Court of the United States, in Smith v. Texas, 311 U. S. 128, 61 S. Ct. 164, 85 L. Ed. 84, recognized the validity thereof when it said: "'Here, the Texas statutory scheme is not in itself unfair; it is capable of being carried cut with no racial discrimination whatsoever.'

'It was with this statement in mind that we said, in effect, that, in the absence of express discrimination, a jury, grand or petit, drawn in accordance with the statute law of this state was valid. "Appellant challenges the correctness of our conclusion and charges that by such holding we have extended special benefits to members of the Negro race which are denied to Mexicans, thereby violating equal protection to them. Such contention calls, of necessity, for a construction of the equal protection clause of the Fourteenth Amendment to the Federal Constitution with reference to the selection of juries in state court trials and the decisions of the Supreme Court of the United States relative thereto. "The Fourteenth Amendment to the Federal Con- stitution in relation to equal protection was adopted to secure to members of the Negro race, then recently emancipated, the full enjoyment of their freedom. Nixon v. Herndon, 273 U. S. 536, 71 L. 579 47 S. Ct. 446; Buchanan v. Warley, 245 U. S. 60, 62 L. Ed. 149, 38 S. Ct. 16; Neal v. Delaware, 103 U. S. 370, 26 L. Ed. 567; Strauder v. West Virginia, 100 U. S. 303, 25 L. Ed. 664; Slaughter-House cases, 16 Wall (U.S.) 36, 21 L. Ed. 394." 'Section 1. All persons born or naturalized in the United States, and subject to the jurisdiction thereof, are citizens of the United States and of the State wherein they reside. No State shall make or enforce any law which shall abridge the privileges or immunities of citizens of the United States; nor shall any State deprive any person of life, liberty, or property, without due process of law; nor deny to any person within its jurisdiction the equal protection of the laws.' "While the Supreme Court of the United States had before it the question of race dis- crimination under the Fourteenth Amendment in the Slaughter-House cases, it appears that it was not until the case of Strauder v. West Virginia that the court had occasion to determine that race discrimination in jury organization was prohibited by the Fourteenth Amendment. In the latter case a statute of West Virginia limited jury service to white male persons. This statute was held as discriminatory against mem- bers of the Negro race and, therefore, violative of equal protection. "Following the Strauder case, the question of race discrimination in the selection of juries was before the court upon several occasions. "In Carter v. Texas, 177 U.S. 442, 44 L. Ed. 839, 20 S. Ct. 687, the rule was stated as follows:

"'Whenever by any action of a State, whether through its legislature, through its courts, or through its executive or administrative officers, all persons of the African race are excluded, solely because of their race or color, from serving as grand jurors in the criminal prosecution of a person of the African race, the equal protection of the laws is denied to him, contrary to the Fourteenth Amendment of the Constitution of the United States. Strauder v. West Virginia, 100 U. S. 303, 25 L. Ed. 664; Neal v. Delaware, 103 U.S. 370, 397, 26 L. Ed. 567, 574; Gibson v. Mississippi, 162 U. S. 565, 40 L. Ed. 1075, 16 S. Ct. 904.' "'The rule, as thus established, applies equally to petit jury selection. "For a time and until the case of Norris v. Alabama, 294 U. S. 587, 55 S. Ct. 579, 79 L. Ed. 1074, establishment of discrimination rested upon facts showing actual or express discrimination against members of the Negro race. In the Norris case, however, the so-called rule of exclusion was announced in the following language, viz. "'We think that the evidence that for a generation or longer no Negro had been called for service on any jury in Jackson County, that there were Negroes qualified for jury service, that according to the practice of the jury commission their names would normally appear on the preliminary list of male citizens of the requisite age but that no names of Negroes were placed on the jury roll, and the testimony with respect to the lack of appropriate consideration of the qualifications of Negroes established the discrimination which the Constitution forbids.' "In succeeding cases this rule of exclusion was followed or adverted to in the cases of Smith v. Texas, 311 U. S. 128, 85 L. Ed. 84, 61 S. Ct. 164; Hill v. Texas, 316 U. S. 400, 86 L. Ed. 1559, 62 S. Ct. 1159; and Akins v. Texas, 325 U. S. 398, 89 L. Ed. 1692, 65 S. Ct. 1276. "The effect of the rule of exclusion is to furnish means by which proof of discrimination may be accomplished. "In the Akins case, the idea of proportional representation of races on a jury as a constitutional requisite was rejected. The basis of such rejection was pointed out in Cassell v. Texas, 339 U.S. 282, 70 S. Ct. 629; 94 L. Ed. 839, as follows: "'We have recently written why proportional representation of races on a jury is not a constitutional requisite. Succinctly stated, our reason was that the Constitution requires only a fair jury selected without regard to race. Obviously, the number of races and nationalities appearing in the ancestry of our citizens would make it impossible to meet a requirement of proportional representation.' "The conclusion of race discrimination expressed in the Cassell case, which is one of the latest expressions by the Supreme Court of the United States upon the subject, appears not to have been based upon the so-called rule of exclusion above mentioned but upon the conclusion that the jury commissioners appointed to select the list of names from which the grand jury was to be selected did not 'familiarize themselves fairly with the qualifications of the eligible jurors of the county without regard to race and color. They did not do so here, and the result has been racial discrimination.' "In addition to that conclusion, the Cassell case also announced the rule that discrimination may be shown by inclusion as well as exclusion, on account of race, in jury selection. "To our minds, it is conclusive that, in so far as the question of discrimination in the organization of juries in state courts is concerned, the equal protection clause of the Fourteenth Amendment contemplated and recognized only two classes as coming within that guarantee: the white race, comprising one class, and the Negro race comprising the other class. "We said in

Sanchez v. State, 243 S. W. 2d 700, that 'Mexican people are not a separate race but are white people of Spanish descent.' In contemplation of the Fourteenth Amendment, Mexicans are therefore members of and within the classification of the white race, as distinguished from members of the Negro race. In so far as we are advised, no member of the Mexican nationality challenges that statement. Appellant does not here do so. "It is apparent, therefore, that appellant seeks to have this court recognize and classify Mexicans as a special class within the white race and to recognize that special class as entitled to special privileges in the organization of grand and petit juries in this state. "To so hold would constitute a violation of equal protection, because it would be extending to members of a class special privileges not accorded to all others of that class similarly situated. Moreover, it must be remembered that no man, or set of men, has the right to require that a member of his race be a member of the grand jury that indicts him or of the petit jury that tries him. All that the Constitution, State or Federal, guarantees in that connection is that in he organization of such juries he be not discriminated against by reason of his race or color. Thomas v. Texas, 212 U. S. 278, 26 S. Ct. 388, 53 L. Ed. 512; Martin v. Texas, 200 U. S. 316, 26 S. Ct. 66, 50 L. Ed. 497; Carter v. Texas, 177 U. S. 442, . . . S. Ct. 686, 44 L. Ed. 889.

"To say that members of the various nationalities and groups composing the white race must be represented upon grand and petit juries would destroy our jury system, for it would be impossible to meet such requirement. Such, also, would destroy the role above stated and would be tantamount to authorizing an accused to demand that a member of his nationality be upon the jury that indicts and tries him. In addition, to so hold would write into the equal protection clause proportional representation not only of races but of nationalities, which the Supreme Court of the United States has expressly rejected. "Mexicans are white people, and are entitled at the hands of the state to all the rights, privileges, and immunities guaranteed under the Fourteenth Amendment. So long as they are so treated, the guarantee of equal protection has been accorded to them. "The grand jury that indicted appellant and the petit jury that tried him being composed of members of his race, it cannot be said, in the absence of proof of actual discrimination, that appellant has been discriminated against in the organization of such juries and thereby denied equal protection of the laws.

"The judgment is affirmed.

"Davidson, Judge

"(Delivered June 18, 1952)

"Opinion approved by the court."

SPECIAL POINTS

Respondent herein specially points out that Petitioner Pete Hernandez with malice aforethought murdered Joe Espinosa (Indictment, R. 1) which shows both the murderer and the murdered to be of the Latin American origin as per names and that no denial of equal protection of law is shown by the record in this case, as might be otherwise vaguely inferred if the victim had been of some other national origin. Reference to "Mexican or Latin American name" in stipulations is invalid as proof of absence of persons of Mexican or Latin American blood since it is common knowledge that many persons in the area of Texas including Jackson County, Texas, who have names other than Mexican or Latin American names are nevertheless of Mexican or Latin American blood.

CONCLUSION

The Petition for Writ of Certiorari should be denied.

Respectfully submitted,

JOHN BEN SHEPPERD
Attorney General of Texas
RUDY G. RICE
Assistant
MILTON RICHARDSON
Assistant
HORACE WIMBERLY
Assistant
Capitol Station
Austin, Texas
Attorneys for Respondent

Appendix VIII

A Cotton Picker Finds Justice!
THE SAGA OF THE *HERNANDEZ* CASE
Compiled by
RUBEN MUNGUIA

IN MEMORIAM

On the day preceding his admission to the hospital, where he was to pass away a few days later, Maury Maverick finished the Foreword which appears in this pamphlet. Thus we of Mexican and Hispanic heritage, for whom Maury did so much, were destined to be the recipients of the product of his last intellectual efforts. Maury Maverick needs no monument of mortar, steel, or stone. The memory of this amazing individual is instilled in the hearts of men and women, reared during the Depression, who have splendid physiques instead of bodies crippled by rickets; it is reflected in the eyes of those who gaze upon the unique beauty of the San Antonio River; it is echoed in the ears of people who listen to exotic melodies at La Villita. Maury Maverick will live forever in the minds of those who have decent housing instead of shacks and lean-to's; in the spirit of all who believe in giving a tangible meaning to such ideals as progress and equality and opportunity, and those two much misunderstood though often-quoted expressions: civil liberties and the American way of life. No, Maury Maverick's monument is not pedestrian—it is not even mundane. It can only be described as something found in the souls of men. It is unfortunate that the span of life of this remarkable being was so short; it is sad that this international figure did not rise even higher than he did, nor help determine even more what the future of mankind shall be; it is tragic that, like other great men before him, he was so often forced to waste his brilliance jousting with pygmies. We humbly and reverently dedicate this little publication to Maury—who carried an already famous name to immortality.

-30-
—Gustavo C. Garcia
June, 1954.

Foreword [by Maury Maverick]

Society, composed of human beings of all kinds, all over the world, ceaselessly marches on. Now and then in this ceaseless march, occur events which are true mile posts. "The Hernandez Case" is such a mile post, and represents a climax of long years of struggle of Mexican-American people for first-class citizenship. It is not boastful to say that this case is even of world importance.

Of course, the Mexican-American people are Americans: they are not "hyphenated" Americans. This segregating hyphen was stuck in between them by others, in spite of the fact that in every war for liberty they have always shed more than their required proportion of blood. Excellent doctors, lawyers, engineers, and businessmen have developed among these people—just as with English, or French or German-Americans, and it is rather patronizing to even say this because everybody knows it.

In the Hernandez case, which went to the Supreme Court of the United States, the rights of people—all people—were protected. The attorneys were No. 1 in brains

356

and courage—Carlos Cadena, Gus Garcia and Johnny Herrera. They attacked the principle of excluding people of Mexican ancestry from grand juries, petit juries and jury commissions. They won a unanimous decision that exclusion of people of Mexican ancestry was unconstitutional. These attorneys made a substantial, dignified and creditable showing for their people before the Highest Court of our land. The unanimous decision upheld these lawyers' viewpoint, and it was a victory for dignity and equality for every breathing soul in the United States. In writing this it is important that not only people in Texas but that people all over the world understand. In World War II, I was in Washington and subscribed to the San Antonio papers: the casualty list ran far higher with Latin American names than with Anglo names like my own. The papers told the same story during the Korean War. By actual count, the Latins from Texas in the Armed Forces—defending a democratic world whose blessings they did not always share—outnumbered the Anglos 2 to 1.

Now—returning from World War II—the Mexican-Americans found that the same prejudices existed as when they left, and in some instances their services were not at all appreciated. Some places wouldn't even bury a "Mexican" veteran killed overseas. Their children were segregated in many public schools. In some Texas counties well qualified persons of Mexican blood who didn't even know how to talk Spanish were kept off jury service. Such men could have decent incomes, be university graduates, and live honorably, but the Spanish name was a bar.

Personalities must be injected throughout this because many bright Mexican names will appear. Gus García met Professor George Sánchez, who had written several books on problems of the Southwest. They decided to bring together a lot of people to lay the ground work for a test case on school segregation. Various groups decided that they would not be held back in their contribution to the posterity of America. They marked education as Number One and Required, on their future Calendar of Progress. John D. Rockefeller III and a committee from the Rockefeller Foundation came down. They could not believe the sordid conditions that existed. They soon saw that the "Mexican" schools were a disgrace. Then came Dr. Lyle Saunders and with the help of the Rockefeller Foundation and Dr George Sánchez's graduate students they put together convincing statistical data and all kinds of facts for the success of the test cases. Some of their matter resulted in the victory in the *Delgado* Case in which United States District Judge Ben H. Rice, Jr., held that the segregation of children of Mexican descent was a violation of the 14th Amendment of our Constitution. He prohibited the school board defendants from engaging in the practice of segregation. He enjoined the State Superintendent of Public Instruction from participating in segregation in any way. I write for people who don't necessarily know our Texas jargon. So let us stop and get various organizations in our minds before we go any farther: The LULACS and the American G.I. Forum. LULAC stands for League of United Latin American Citizens. The G.I. Forum is another organization, younger and under the vigorous leadership of Dr. Hector García. Both organizations sent out instructions and regulations to all school systems telling of the court decision in the *Delgado* case. Some school boards were recalcitrant—that is, either they bogged down, or put on the slow down. But the organizations and different individuals fought on, and segregation has practically ceased to exist throughout Texas. It can be reported, also that the spirit of co-operation and fellowship among so-called Anglo and Latin Americans seems natural and pleasant. The second court battle saw an humble man by the name of Puente, represented by his attorneys, Carlos C. Cadena and Alonso S. Perales, battle against restrictive covenants in real estate which prevented persons of his national origin from buying property where they chose. In this case, the courts of the State of Texas, in the wake of a United States Supreme Court decision on the subject, upheld Puente's contention. The Texas state courts outlawed restrictive covenants and even went farther than the Supreme Court of the United States.

Third came the *Hernandez* case. It is the climax case, and is principally dealt with here. Ever since the county started, Jackson County had never let anybody with a Latin name serve on any kind of jury. Hernandez was convicted of a crime. The conviction was reversed unanimously by the Supreme Court of the United States. It was notice and public advertisement to all the world that America stood for equality and freedom. It was an order putting the Declaration of Independence and the Constitution into effect. Besides these court battles, we can think of work by various dedicated leaders which they did in other fields. 1. "Wetbacks". For those who don't know a wetback is a man who swam the Rio Grande illegally, or walked across a dry spot, but is still a wetback. The leaders of the LULAC and G.I. Forum went out and did battle on the wetback menace. They spoke to President Truman (I know—I got an appointment for Gus Garcia with the man from Independence), and I imagine they will talk to President Eisenhower, about the evils of permitting the wholesale influx of illegal immigrants, which is no good for the immigrant, who is inevitably persecuted, and no good for the U.S.A. Not much has been done by Washington, but the lawyer watch-dogs are watching and fighting and some day the problem will be solved. The Immigration Department itself admits 800,000 wetbacks who came in during 1953. 2. These leaders have battled with backward state officials for improvement in conditions and to see that Mexican Americans get representation in state-appointed positions and on boards and commissions. Where there is bad treatment for their people which was entirely uncorrected, these leaders have retired with dignity and decorum such as when Dr. George Sánchez and Gus Garcia resigned in 1952 from the "Texas Commission on Human Relations" (a stuffed shirt outfit). This withdrawal had its effect and the people at least knew the Mexican Americans were not getting a fair deal. 3. These leaders have spurred their own people to get up and improve themselves, to speak English, to become better Americans, pay their poll tax (and vote!), to support public health programs. Results in all these fields have been good, I should say excellent. 4. They fought for a Civil Rights Act submitted to the Texas Legislature to stop discrimination of all kinds in public places. 5. They have spent numberless thousands of dollars of their own on traveling, wiring and telephoning, and they have, in a good old-styled American fashion, hollered and yelled, pleaded, cajoled and demanded whenever or wherever an issue arose. Now, I know the Latin-American groups have been accused of self-segregating themselves. Well, they came out of World War II and out of the Korean War and got booted around like their fathers and grandfathers had been. Even in many regular Veterans' Posts they suffered segregation and neglect. So I can understand and most people can understand why Americans of Mexican extraction formed their organizations. The

American G.I. Forum got rolling under Dr. Hector P. García of Corpus Christi and Ed Idar of Austin. This organization has spread to neighboring states. LULAC started over a quarter of century ago. It seems to me some of their policies are rather conservative. Nevertheless that organization and G.I. Forum together are both necessary and both do essential work. As I said in the beginning, brilliant, well-educated men have developed out of this welter of humanity. Anyhow, they are dedicated men. I will give the names of only a few:

DR. GEORGE SÁNCHEZ

I first met him when I was in Congress. He lived in New Mexico then. Methodical and courageous, and having a brain to think with, he's a Number One planner and peace maker. Among my Latin American brethren he soothes what we Anglos (I resent that word "Anglo") call the "clashing personalities" and what I secretly call ("don't quote me") prima donnas like the volatile Garcias (of San Antonio and Corpus).

DR. HECTOR P. GARCÍA

Here is a capable, smooth, able, well-educated physician of the highest order. With patients he has the bedside manner and his patients swear by him. Outside, he is an able fighter, a capable man who started rough and tough, and who is mellowing down now to a great leader. He can talk to people in their own language as well as any man I ever knew.

ED IDAR

Ed belongs to a family that believes in education. His deceased father was persecuted and his late uncle was national Vice President of the American Federation of Labor in the darkest days. Both inspired him. Ed works to improve everybody else— and himself. Working eight hours every day and helping other people four hours each day, he also spends part of his time at the University of Texas studying law. When he sleeps, I do not know.

CARLOS C. CADENA

Here is a subtle fellow, possessor of a profound legal mind. He is the scholarly kind of man like Cardozo, who sat on the Supreme Court of the United States. He has an obsession for anonymity and is sometimes overlooked.

GUS GARCIA

Now comes Garcia. He either carried the Message to Garcia or he got the Message or something, maybe from the Lord, though when need be it is said he consults with the Devil. A brilliant and eloquent man, he is forceful and dramatic. Chances are, he would have made just as great a flamenco dancer or bullfighter as he has a trial lawyer. Some people say (again "don't quote me") he's a sort of neuropsychiatric, but he's all the good things they say, too. He needs no brightening up. If we can just get him dulled down a little bit there will be a man for you. The message that we want to send to this Garcia is to get rid of his phobias and frustrations, but maybe he is number 1 of all; he surely will be if we can knock off some of his edges.

R.A. CORTEZ

Raoul is another highly controversial figure, who, nevertheless had what amounted to three years of policy making for the LULACS. First, he was regional governor of Texas. Then he was twice-elected National President. It was under his administration that the groundwork was laid for some of the more recent accomplishments and that the historical school segregation case was carried to a successful conclusion. Except that I demand the use of English, I would say, Viva Raoul! Let it be said in his behalf that he was always ready to back up the judgment of his advisors like Dr. Sánchez and Gus Garcia and a definite stand was taken on every important issue that arose. There is no doubt about it, Raoul was instrumental in making LULAC a great national organization.

JOHN J. HERRERA

Johnny is best known for the fact that his great, great grandfather, Col. Francisco Ruiz, was one of the two native Texans who signed the Texas Declaration of Independence alongside my own ancestor, Samuel Maverick. As a matter of fact, however, it not necessary for Johnny to have to depend on ancestral background for recognition because he can stand on his own two feet. Both as a National President of LULAC and as a soldier in the ranks, he has been ready any time of any day or night to render whatever service he could when his assistance was needed.

They are not rich, these men. Money is lost, not made, by people who work on civil rights cases. These men are not opportunists—nor are they saints. They are not personally powerful—these men. They cannot be compared to the influential political figures of South Texas who have amassed wealth and domination in their respective bailiwicks. But these men and others like them are the ones making history for the Spanish-speaking people, that is, for all American people—for the world. It is they who have changed the complex of the Latin American problem from a purely sectional issue to a national disgrace. Their pleas have reached the ears of responsible and great men in high places. They have fought like sensible men, not like toreros, and they will be remembered long after wealthier and more powerful men have been forgotten.

Maury Maverick
May 1954

GARCIA

A nimble brain and a sharp tongue set the pace throughout the case.

CADENA

A great legal mind came to the aid of the people.

AN INFORMAL REPORT TO THE PEOPLE
By Gustavo C. Garcia

At the risk of being boresome, I am submitting this report in connection with Cause No. 406, *Hernandez vs. The State of Texas*, before the Supreme Court of the United States, submitted on January 11, 1954. (Opinion announced May 3, 1954).

At the outset, I shall apologize for my verbosity. Having reached the ripe old age of 38 years, however, I feel that any information that we submit to the people should be in writing, lest our feeble words be wafted away into thin air and future generations not know of the battles that have been waged in behalf of what, next to the Navajoes, constitutes the most unfortunate minority group in the United States. In order to present the background of the *Hernandez* case, perhaps we had better follow it in its proper chronological sequence, so that all persons, be they laymen or professionals, understand the issues fully. In September 1951, I agreed to defend one Pete Hernandez, laborer and cotton picker, charged by indictment with murder with malice in Jackson County, Texas. Located in East Texas, Jackson adjoins Wharton County, which, in 1945, gained dubious fame when a man by the name of Macario Garcia, winner of the Congressional Medal of Honor, wearing his uniform and all his ribbons, was denied service in a restaurant, beaten about the head, and driven out of the place because he was a "Mexican." Obviously, the migrant-labor family of the defendant Hernandez could not raise a fee commensurate with the responsibility, effort, and time required by the case. Nevertheless, I accepted employment because, first, I could not resist the tearful pleadings of the defendant's mother, who knew that the authorities in Jackson County were determined to do their utmost to send her 26-year-old boy to the electric chair; and, secondly, because, after a preliminary investigation, I decided that we had an excellent opportunity to make a test case on the issue of the systematic exclusion of persons of Mexican and other Latin American descent from service as jury commissioners, grand jurors, and petit jurors. As all lawyers will understand, in order to lay the proper predicate, it was necessary to file certain motions, raising the "exclusion" issue under the Fourteenth Amendment to the Constitution of the United States. This was done. Then it was necessary to present evidence to prove the allegations in these motions. This, also, was done at a hearing prior to the trial of the case on its merits. At this hearing, much to my dismay, I found no one in the courtroom on our side, or even mildly sympathetic towards us. I learned that in that county, "Mexicans" apparently did not attend court sessions, and furthermore, that there was much hostility against my client, both on the part of the Anglo Americans and the Latin Americans, because he had killed a well-liked and respected citizen. My usual aplomb somewhat jarred, I decided to contact the only man I knew who could possibly help me, namely, John J. Herrera of Houston, who, at that time, was the first National Vice-President of LULAC. I explained the situation to him. I told him that I was jittery and that I was in desperate need of help. He didn't ask if there were any fees involved. He didn't even ask if there was money for expenses. He cancelled a trip which he was about to take with the Houston Chamber of Commerce to Mexico City and immediately drove to Edna, the county seat of Jackson County, bringing with him his very capable young associate, Attorney James de Anda. Not only did Messrs. Herrera and de Anda assist the writer as counsel in the hearing on the motions and in the trial of the case on its merits, but they even served as witnesses.[1] In the course of the hearing on our motion to quash

---

[1]Mr. de Anda checked school census rolls, court records, and other official documents for pertinent information and rendered testimony as to his findings. Mr. Herrera accidentally discovered and subsequently testified as to the lettering on the doors of the public restroom in the court house square, to which Mr. Chief Justice Warren makes such pointed reference in his opinion.

the indictment and to quash the venire, we established the three essential elements to sustain our proposition that there was a systematic exclusion of persons of Mexican and other Latin American descent from jury service:

(1) That no persons of Mexican or other Latin American descent had served in any capacity as jurors or jury commissioners, or had been called for such jury service, in at least 25 years.

(2) That there were persons of Mexican decent qualified to serve as jurors and jury commissioners.

(3) That discrimination and segregation were a common practice in Jackson County and in the County seat, Edna, and, therefore, persons of Mexican descent were actually treated as a "race," class, or group apart from all other persons. It might be said in passing, that it was necessary for us to travel a hundred miles to and from Houston each morning and evening to attend Court because, for obvious reasons, it would have been ill advised to stay overnight in Edna, even if adequate accommodations had been available. Let it be said to the credit of some very fine people, however, namely District Judge Frank Martin, District Attorney Wayne L. Hartman, Sheriff Lewis W. Watson, District Clerk Gena L. Lawrence, and all the other officials that we were treated with kindness respect and utmost courtesy.[2] Unfortunately, Johnny Herrera and I were sandwiched in between the arguments of the handsome young District Attorney, a dynamic and eloquent speaker, Mr. Wm. H. Hamblen, a Special Prosecutor employed by the family of the victim, who is an orator of the old school, and the very capable then County Attorney Mr. Cullen B. Vance. Needless to say we were buffeted about pretty badly. The verdict: Guilty! The punishment assessed was life imprisonment. Before preparing a motion for new trial, I discussed the matter at length with the defendant and the members of his family. I pointed out to them that even if the case were reversed; it would have to be tried all over again with all attendant risks. Hernandez insisted that the homicide was justifiable and that I file my motion at once. His family, likewise, was adamant in this regard. My ethical duty discharged, I proceeded to comply with their instructions. The motion for new trial was filed in due time. It was urged by the indefatigable Mr. Herrera. By then, our original fee had been exhausted on expenses and we were beginning to put money out of our pockets. Subsequently, an appeal was perfected to the Texas Court of Criminal Appeals in Austin, which is the Supreme Court in criminal matters in our state, or as the lawyers say, "the court of last resort". Incidentally, I would like to express my gratitude to Mr. William Maldonado, Sr., San Antonio labor leader and liberal thinker, who picked up the undersigned from a sick bed and drove him to Jackson County to file the Statement of Facts, and the Tran-

---

[2]Judge Martin, a former ace prosecutor himself, and Mr. Hartman are such able lawyers that in our opinion, nothing even resembling reversible error on procedure or substantive law could be found in the record. As all trial lawyers desperately sweating out a capital case with one eye cocked on the appellate court are wont to do, I tried every trick in the book—not to mention a few improvised ones of doubtful ethical vintage—in a vain attempt to a goad them into some ruling, word, or action that would give me a peg on which to hang my appellate sombrero. But it was no use. The excellent shape of the case, from the state's standpoint, plus the shortage of funds required for a lengthy record, explain why the only question raised on appeal was the strictly constitutional issue of the systematic exclusion of persons of Mexican descent—an issue upon which Judge Martin had ruled correctly in accordance with the case law then prevailing in Texas.

script on the last day permissible. Full credit for the work on appeal, both before the Texas Court of Criminal Appeals and the Supreme Court of the United States, should be given to Professor Carlos C. Cadena of San Antonio, my former law partner and now on the staff of St. Mary's School of Law. Intellectually speaking, I can accurately describe Professor Cadena as the best brain of my generation. There are no adequate words, however, which can do justice to his greatness of spirit and profound love for his less fortunate fellowmen. Shy, reserved, and retiring, he is often overlooked by newspapermen and orators who sing the praises of less worthy, though perhaps more flamboyant, individuals. Nevertheless, those of us who know "Carlitos" Cadena for his true merit will always cherish his friendship and will be ever grateful for his selflessness and devotion to the defense of human rights. The people of Mexican ancestry can feel fortunate that his genius was given to us during such a critical period in our history. What more can I say, except that when my second child turned out to be another girl, and I could not name her Carlos, she was baptized by Professor Cadena as "Carlita." Having drifted far a field from our original theme, we should return to the scene at the Court of Criminal Appeals in Austin, which rejected our briefs and oral arguments and ruled, quite in keeping with the precedents previously established by that same Court, that the Fourteenth Amendment could not be applied in the case at bar. In order to preserve our right of appeal to the United States Supreme Court, it was necessary to file a motion for a rehearing. This was done and it, too, was overruled. After that came much soul searching and numerous discussions with some of our friends who had advised us in the past with reference to our civil rights cases. Harboring many misgivings, we finally filed an application for a Writ of Certiorari with the Supreme Court of the United States on January 19, 1953, the last day allowable. This application was typewritten because there was no money to cover expenses of printing. We had little hope that it would be approved because every year hundreds of applications are submitted but only a few are granted. Much to our surprise, our petition received favorable consideration on Oct. 12, 1954, Columbus Day, or better known throughout Latin America and Spain as "El Día de La Raza". Our elation was dimmed somewhat by the fact that immediately after receipt of this notification, we were served with a telegram from the Clerk of the Court, collect, requesting the additional sum of $900.00 at once, to cover court costs.[3]

---

[3]We have been severely taken to task by some of our guard-house lawyers and Monday-morning quarterbacks—specially among the San Antonio Lulacs—because we failed to go up to the Supreme Court on a pauper's oath. "Look at the Rosenberg's," they cry. "They perfected a score of appeals that way". In the first place, I would hardly call the ultimate conclusion in the Rosenberg cases successful from the standpoint of the defense. Secondly, surely, we felt, the 3 million persons of Mexican descent in the United States, or at least the noisy well-heeled clowns and poseurs who are constantly seeking publicity as "civic leaders", should be able to provide for court costs and bare expenses in the first case to come before that august tribunal. Have we, because we are in a sense a conquered people, lost all sense of pride? G.I. Forums, LULAC, Texas Good Relations Association, and private individuals as best they could, considering the apathy of the general public, raised some $3,000 all told for all purposes. Contrast this with the experienoo of Negro attorneys. Expenditures on the part of the National Association for the Advancement of Colored People have ranged from—$45,000.00 to over $100,000.00, for each of their important victories in the civil liberties field. This is not to detract from the merits or the self-sacrifice of the barristers who have so ably handled this litigation; they could probably be millionaires if they specialized in such fields as corporation law. But at least they receive some compensation for their efforts—and considerably less criticism from birdbrained contemporaries.

In desperation, we turned to local sources, and let it be said to the eternal credit of San Antonio Lulac Council No. 2 that, undoubtedly in violation of established procedure and regulations, the sum of $900.00 was promptly advanced from the scholarship fund to cover this expense. This money should be replaced by the National Office because it was borrowed from the scholarship fund and, furthermore, there is no reason why San Antonio should have to bear the brunt of the expenses for printing and court costs. After all, the case is national and even international in scope.[4]

In connection with this $900.00 item, we should point out the fact that through the intervention of pioneer Lulacker Alonso Perales, and that grand old man who feared not the Texas Rangers, Judge J.T. Canales of Brownsville, the sum of $900.00 was sent to San Antonio by the Texas Good Relations Association, some 48 hours after the local LULAC Committee had voted that amount. The delay was occasioned by the unfortunate illness of the President, Dr. Carlos C. Castaneda, professor at the University of Texas. The check was returned to Dr. Castañeda, but we will always remember their great gesture. The following country bumpkins went to Washington:

Attorneys (1) Cadena, (2) Herrera and (3) Garcia participated in this case before the Supreme Court of the U.S. Messrs. Cadena and Garcia "presented the oral arguments, and Mr. Herrera, sitting at counsel table, assisted in the organization of the arguments and the preparation of the notes, made suggestions and rendered memoes as the case progressed before the Court. (4) Mr. Abel Cisneros, courageous radio commentator of Wharton, Texas, who went along because the substantial sum contributed by his hometown was conditioned upon his accompanying Mr. Herrera. He took copious notes and, after he came home, rendered a lengthy report over the radio to the people of East Texas. (5) Mr. Manuel B. Lopez of San Antonio, a graduate attorney, who is at present serving his hitch in the Army in Virginia, was very helpful to us, guiding us around Washington, and faithfully carrying out all the duties of an all-round "leg man." (6) Mr. Anthony (Tony) Garcia, Director of Municipal Markets of San Antonio, attended as an observer for the Lulacs, on his vacation time and at his own personal expense. His moral support, his encouragement, and his timely suggestions were invaluable to us. (7) Mr. Chris Aldrete, Chairman of the American G.I. Forum. Though too recent a law graduate to be presented to the Court, he, too, was very helpful. We all stayed at the Mayflower Hotel, which is neither higher nor cheaper than any other first class hospice in Washington. The average rate per person is $10.00 a day. After Tony Garcia, Johnny Herrera, and Abel Cisneros arrived, the writer moved into a suite with them, which cost us $36.00 per day. The undersigned slept on a couch in the living room, which, however, was far more comfortable and luxurious than many a bed in which he has slept in his day. Tony Garcia stretched out his hefty frame on a roll-away bed. By obtaining this suite, we actually saved at least a dollar per person per day and at the same time had a decent place

---

[4]We use the term "international in scope" because we made certain that all motions included the words "Mexican and/or Latin American descent". We also interspersed the term "Spanish-speaking". This means that anyone considered "Mexican", "Latin American", "Hispanic", "Spanish-speaking", (even Portuguese-speaking Brazilians!), etc., can claim his rights under the Fourteenth Amendment if he is tried in a county where persons considered as members of that "class" are denied the right to serve on jury commissions, grand juries or petit juries. The citizenship of the accused person does not matter.

to hold meetings among ourselves, with members of the press, and with some friends from Washington, who guided us and assisted us, and who deserve our sincerest thanks. Among them are a young lawyer, formerly from Texas, by the name of Harvey Rosenberg; our great and good friend the Honorable Dennis Chavez, senior Senator from New Mexico; Dennis, Jr., his brilliant son, their entire staff, consisting among others of some very beauteous creatures, who are as pretty as they are competent; Jake Jacobson, from Senator Price Daniels' office; Senator Price Daniels, who left a committee meeting to introduce us to the Supreme Court; Senator Lyndon B. Johnson, and Sam Houston, and Tony Martinez, out of Senator Chavez' office and Attorney Al Wirin of California. To all these splendid people we say: gracias, muchas gracias. Special commendation should go to Sarah McClendon, charming and brilliant newspaper woman. Eventually, it came to pass that we appeared before the Supreme Court of the United States. As far as the presentation of the case is concerned, the news releases were as accurate as could be expected, except for the fact that our case was heard about one hour earlier than had been anticipated; consequently, the newspaper reporters were not present when Carlos Cadena made his historical opening argument and he did not receive the full credit due him. By the same token, John J. Herrera, who juggled the notes, the points, and the suggestions, was hardly mentioned, in spite of the fact that it was he who kept our heads level when we were bombarded by questions from some of the justices, particularly the Honorable Tom C. Clark.[5]

We took advantage of our stay in Washington to contact several senators and some of the more prominent congressmen to lay our problems before them. We wailed about the wetback situation. We pointed out to them that there are virtually no Spanish-speaking persons in the American embassies in Latin America. We called their attention to the fact that even though we are now catering to Generalissimo Franco's Spain, there is not a single person of Spanish descent with our military mission there. I hardly think that our politically minded friends in Washington will worry about this very insignificant pressure group, namely, the "Mexicans", but, nevertheless, the least we could do was to explain, suggest and protest: you simply cannot let things be lost by default. Regretfully, because of the lack of time and the thinness of the pocket book, we did not participate in the gaiety that is supposed to pervade Washington after sundown. After temporarily concluding our work there

---

[5]The remarks attributed to the writer in the newspapers to the effect that General Sam Houston was only a wetback from Tennessee were not as bad as might appear at first blush. Actually this was said in a jocular vein, of course, although, in a sense, all Anglo Americans who settled in Texas were looked upon as uncouth foreigners, Johnny-come-lately's, and impecunious adventurers by the rather snobbish Spanish-speaking families (like mine) who had colonized Texas between 1720 and 1800. Nothing delights me more than to speak deprecatingly about some of my stuffy, society-conscious relatives as bankrupt Mexican blue bloods. The truth of the matter is that this writer has always had a soft spot in his heart for two Anglos, in particular, who participated in the Texas revolutionary movement: Sam Houston and Jim Bowie. I admire them for many reasons, but I suspect mainly because (1) these two charming swashbucklers were bon vivants, raconteurs, and devout worshipers at the altar of Bacchus; (2) they demonstrated in the most emphatic manner possible that they harbored no notions of racial superiority: Houston, to use the vernacular, shacked up with an Indian squaw for several years after his extremely brief and disastrous marital venture with Tennessee Anglo aristocracy, while Bowie became a Catholic and married the cultured and distinguished daughter of the Mexican vice governor, Señorita Ursula de Veramendi. Unfortunately she and their two children perished in Mexico during an epidemic, and the inconsolable Bowie went on a protracted binge which ended only a short time before the clash at the Alamo, where he died as the brave and reckless man that he had always been.

(Professor Cadena having returned immediately after the case to resume his teaching duties at St. Mary's Law School), Tony Garcia and I went to New York with certain specific missions in mind. Dennis Chavez, Jr., accompanied us. Unfortunately Mr. Herrera was unable to go with us because he suffered a severe fall on an icy sidewalk while strutting around Washington in his high-heeled boots, and had to return to Houston for examination and treatment. In New York, Mr. Tony Garcia and I were together only one day. According to press reports, he returned to San Antonio because of the illness of his one and only son. For historical purposes, however, let the record show that he read over my shoulder that the temperature would go down to a flat zero that night—and immediately contacted Eastern Airlines. After working for some 48 hours, I had a relapse of the intestinal flu that I had carried with me from San Antonio. For three days, I did no good to anyone except the hotel, running up room, doctor's, and drug bills. I shall always be grateful, to my good friends Jaime Escobar of the Mexican delegation to the United Nations and Rafael Carvajal of the Voice of America. They mothered me and held my hand during my illness and worried about me more than I did. The only satisfaction I got of this whole deal was the fact that I discovered I am not allergic to penicillin. Eventually, I braved the seven degree weather to visit such organizations as the American Civil Liberties Union, the National Association for the Advancement of Colored people, the Anti-Defamation League of B'nai Braith, the Japanese-American Citizens League, the Rockefeller Foundation, the Marshall Trust Foundation, the National offices of the American Federation of Labor, the National offices of the C.I.O., and other organizations, which, in the past, have shown an interest in our plight and our problems. All of these people in these institutions were unanimous in their opinion that what we need is a powerful, rich national organization to fight our battles, with a lobbyist in Washington and each state capital where we constitute a substantial portion of the population. They said that it would be a simple matter for every person of our ethnic group to contribute a pittance to the "cause" and that, in that manner, we would amass a great fund. I smiled and told them that they didn't know Mexicans.[6] I regret to say that while in New York I saw more of the darkness of the subway (taxi fares being prohibitive for people of small means like me) than anything else. I took in no shows, not even the free television performances. I finally returned to Washington on a coach and stood up all night because there was no other means of transportation available. I had to go back to see what had happened to some of the things that we had left pending there. Eventually, on one good Sunday in January, after a delay because of bad weather and some three weeks after my departure from the Alamo City, I flew back to San Antonio, where I was greeted, under a gloriously sunny sky, by my loving wife and a somewhat skeptical elder daughter—aged three—who thought I was the milkman.

  If the reader will consider the cost of traveling, of lodging, cabs in Washington (there is no subway), tips (which are a must) "handouts", etc., he may well under-

---

[6]These seemingly unimportant details are set out for two purposes: (1) to demonstrate that leaders of our organizations need to cultivate contacts with national figures and institutions; (2) to give the reader an idea of the multitude of details and intricate weaving, dodging and doubling-back necessary to carry out an effective minority group program.

stand why civil rights lawyers don't get rich. And now what of Pete Hernandez? He seems to have been forgotten in the hubbub of headlines, constitutional issues, and uninhibited celebration. He is still languishing behind prison bars. He has been confined either in jail or the penitentiary for over three years. A new charge has already been filed, and the District Attorney has indicated that he will press for an early trial after a re-indictment (undoubtedly with some "Mexicans" on the jury) is returned next September. So we shall start our heartbreaking task all over again, as far as he an individual is concerned. But his welfare is, and should properly be, our primary concern. His rights, are paramount—and he is not a guinea pig to be discarded after the experiment has succeeded. All that we can hope for is that we can get some public support, both moral and financial, in his behalf. His family, unfortunately, is virtually destitute. To conclude, I would like to make some observations as to the social significance of this case and a few suggestions as to what the pattern of our future course of action should be. In the first place, this lawsuit marks the end of legal relief for our basic social ills. I do not mean to say that there will be no further litigation; on the contrary, many cases will undoubtedly be appealed under this and other rulings, specially where local authorities attempt to give us mere "token" representation in our jury system. But the foundation has been laid here, as it was in the Mendez[7] and Delgado cases on the issue of school segregation and the Puente[8] case on restrictive covenants in real estate. This was the last major issue left for the courts to decide. No court decision on civil rights has any worthwhile significance, however, unless translated into positive, constructive, and practical every day action. What our people must do on a local basis is to become familiar with the state of the law, keep abreast of the times, and notify organizations like LULAC and the G.I. Forum of the violation or attempted circumvention of court rulings, laws, or constitutional provisions. After all, we—lawyers, professors, and just plain crusaders—who are rapidly approaching middle age, or have already reached it, and who find ourselves without any semblance of security, cannot spend the rest of our lives pulling Mexican chestnuts out of the fire for "the people". We have a living to make for our families, and furthermore we have been quite disillusioned to discover (though we should have known it all along) that the public, for the most part, is not only a forgetful and ungrateful, but actually a sadistic, creature. As to our future conduct: I trust the reader will forgive me if I indulge in what our younger generation would unhesitatingly classify as corny preaching on the part of an old square. But I think I am entitled to at least this one whimsey, to which most of us Mexicans fall victim after devoting a number of years to "do-gooding". Somehow we all begin to conceive the ridiculous notion that we have become olive-skinned versions of Bernard Baruch.

At any rate, here it is: It has always been my contention that social discrimination is the least of our worries. If little Adelita is not asked to pledge that exclusive sorority—worry not. She's probably a lot better off anyway. If we are denied service in one restaurant, we can always find another where the tinkling of coins means more than the teachings of Mein Kampf. In our society, regretfully enough, the most

---

[7]Westminster School Dist. vs. Mendez, 161 Fed. (2d) 774 (1946).
[8]Clifton vs. Puente, 218 S.W. (2d) 272 (1949).

effective means of reaching the hearts of men is through their pocketbooks. Further-more, I have no desire to go where I am not wanted. And personally I deem it my constitutional right to keep anyone who is to me persona non grata out of my home, my office, or my place of business. The principle of Civil Rights, you know, is not a one-way street. These views do not apply, of course, in the case of public places or facilities constructed or maintained with tax funds to which all the people contribute. That, to translate freely an ancient Spanish axiom, "is flour from another barrel." I do ask the reader to take this free legal advice for whatever it is worth—with apolo-gies to my more practical brethren in the profession who charge for such services— and that is: in Texas, at least, there is no law which requires the owner of a public establishment to serve you, even if you appear in morning frock and are driven up to the door by a liveried chauffeur in a plush-lined, air-conditioned limousine. So stop worrying about it. Education and social pressure -on both sides of the fence—will take care of these odious distinctions. Unfortunately, it is often the least important incidents which result in the splashing of the goriest headlines and cause the great-est amount of harm to Anglo-Latin relations. We are not passing through anything different from that endured at one time or another by other unassimilated population groups: the Irish in Boston (damned micks, they were derisively called); the Polish in the Detroit area (their designation was bohunks and polackers); the Italians in New York (referred to as stinking little wops, dagoes and guineas); the Germans in many sections of the country (called dumb square heads and krauts); and our much maligned friends of the Jewish faith, who have been persecuted even here, in the land of the free, because to the bigoted they were just "lousy kikes."

The point to remember is this: all these other ethnic and religious groups have managed to overcome the same obstacles now besetting our path and, in spite of lan-guage handicaps, ignorance, and old-world superstitions, they have all contributed materially to the development of their community, state, and nation. I grant that the problem is somewhat more difficult for us because of the close proximity of the mother country—actually the cultural umbilical cord has not yet been completely severed—and because of unfortunate historical wounds which some nitwits delight in reopening year after year. ("Remember the Alamo!"). But eventually we can over-come all these difficulties—make no mistake about that.

Using Texas as a barometer, we discover for example, that, projecting our pres-ent fantastic birth rate into the future, by 1970 we shall actually be a majority of the population in this state. Proportionately, the same thing holds true in all other states with a heavy "Mexican" population. Thus, in spite of infant diarrhea, tuberculosis, and other diseases which would seem to decimate our ranks, we are rapidly being swept forward to a position which will call for more responsible leadership and for more effective participation in the every day affairs of our society. That is precisely why I have been so deeply concerned about educational problems among our peo-ple, specially the children of migrant workers. Let's face it: in Texas, which is no bet-ter and no worse than other southwestern states in this respect, if you pick out at ran-dom any day of the school year, and make a check of school attendance, you will discover that over one-half of school-aged children of Mexican descent will not be found in any grade in any school. The number of pupils, who reach high school is infinitesimal. As I have often said, we are still producing generation after generation of illiterates, semi-literates, and cotton pickers. The percentage of draftees of Mexican ancestry rejected for illiteracy during World War II was disgraceful. This is a problem which can be solved only by an intelligent program on the part of our organizations as well as by a more enthusiastic application of worthwhile methods by the state educational authorities. A final word of caution: do not place on a pedestal those whose fate it has been to fight your battles. We are not little tin gods. A truly great statesman—an Irishman named Parnell who, but for personal scandal, might have led his people to an early freedom—whispered to his beloved Katie O'Shea on his deathbed that, alas, alas, all mortals have feet of clay. Crusaders, at best or at worst, depending on your point of view, are simply ordinary folk with little quirks and an inflated social conscience—and, perhaps, a Messiah complex. Most of all, try to remember this last bit of advice, which I express while having to resort to that moth—eaten cliché about don't—do-as-I-do-but-do-as-I-say: the right to occupy a respected place in our social strata can never be demanded; it must, of necessity, be earned.

Legal Ramifications of the Hernandez Case

A THUMBNAIL SKETCH
By Carlos C. Cadena

The first case involving discrimination against persons of Mexican descent from jury service in Texas was decided by the State Court of Criminal Appeals in 1931. Since that year, in a number of decisions the Texas Court of Criminal Appeals clung firmly to the theory that discrimination in the selection of juries because of national origin was not forbidden by the Constitution of the United States. In taking and maintaining this position, the State Courts evolved the novel theory that the Fourteenth Amendment recognized only two classes as coming within the guarantee of equal protection of the laws: "the White race comprising one class, and the Negro race, comprising the other." Since, according to this Court, persons of Mexican descent were members of the white race, and since white Anglos sat on all juries, "Mexicans" had no cause for complaint. On June 18, 1952, the Texas Court of Criminal Appeals indignantly informed Pete Hernandez that his brazen attempt to seek the protection of the Fourteenth Amendment was merely an effort to have that court "recognize and classify Mexicans as a special class within the white race and to recognize that special class as entitled to special privileges."[9] Thus, in a hand-dusting fashion seldom seen in law books, the court rebuffed Hernandez by patronizingly reminding him that, whether he liked it or not, and whether the Anglo-Americans in Jackson County believed it or not, he was a member of the superior Caucasian race and, presumably, must endure all hardships as part of the "white man's burden."

---

[9]The writer is reminded of the story told by the great Judge Leibowitz, who, on a postman's holiday in Florida, saw a number of Negroes on the jury panel. He approached a young lawyer and commented that he was surprised that Negroes should be serving on juries in this state, which, in spite of a civilized Spanish colonial background, is notorious for its bigotry. The youthful barrister replied: "Well, we wouldn't have any of these niggers except that a sonofabitch by the name of Leibowitz forced them on us in the Scottsboro case." It appears that some Anglos will say the same thing in the Southwest about lesser lights like Garcia, Cadena and Herrera.

While some may argue that exclusion from jury service because of national origin is a matter of minor importance, since most citizens (white, brown and black) go to great lengths to evade it, the basic issue involved was of great moment.[10] The Texas Court of Criminal Appeals, by adopting a unique "two classes" theory, was greatly restricting the reach of the protective arm of the Fourteenth Amendment. Such a theory, having no basis in the decisions of any other court in the land, could severely curtail the rights of persons of Mexican descent in Texas. Even if exclusion from jury service were a minor matter,—and it is not—a theory which placed us beyond the shelter of the Fourteenth Amendment had to be attacked and exploded as a myth resting upon a gross misinterpretation of that amendment. Without attempting to become melodramatic, we can state that dire consequences were implicit in the acceptance of the "two classes" theory. Persons of Mexican descent could be segregated in schools, parks, and all other public places, and any objection could be met with the bland statement that there was no ground for complaint since "Mexicans" are white and by being restricted to associating with each other, they were not being discriminated against because of race. Cities could enact zoning ordinances forcing persons of Mexican origin to live in segregated ghettoes, and the "two classes" theory blindfold would hide and protect the discriminatory practices. Naturally it stands to reason that the Honorable Court of Criminal Appeals did not foresee the potentially sinister implications of its "two classes" theory. Evidently it saw no distinction between this theory and its own decision in the Juarez case* in which it held that the systematic exclusion of Roman Catholics violated the provisions of the Fourteenth Amendment. To Judge Davidson, who wrote the opinion for the Court, the Juarez decision did not even merit an allusion to it, in spite of the pleas by counsel for the defendant Hernandez in the case at bar that some explanation be given for this obvious conflict. Perhaps it was the dangers inherent in such an unorthodox theory that impelled the Supreme Court to grant a Writ of Cerciorati against the Court of Criminal Appeals of Texas. The objective sought by the attorneys for the defendant Hernandez was the destruction and eradication of such a dangerous and insupportable legal fallacy. That objective was achieved. The Supreme Court bluntly stated that the exclusion from jury service solely because of their ancestry and/or national origin is discrimination prohibited by the Fourteenth Amendment. Paying particular attention to the "two classes" theory, Mr. Chief Justice Warren observed simply that the Fourteenth Amendment is not directed "solely against a discrimination due to a 'two classes' theory—that is, based upon differences between 'whites' and Negroes." Thus, the Supreme Court refused to read into the Fourteenth Amendment a limitation which is not there. It clearly and explicitly recognized that when the existence of a distinct class is shown and it appears that the laws as written or applied "single out that class for different treatment, not based on some reasonable classification, the guarantees of the Constitution have been violated." The notion that the Constitution prohibits discrimination because of national origin is not new. As early as 1879, the Supreme Court had observed that the exclusion of naturalized Irishmen from jury service would violate the Fourteenth Amendment. One immediate result is that in

---

[10]See Hernandez vs. State 251 S.W. (2d) 531. Juarez vs. State 277 S.W. 1091.

any county of the United States (including the parishes of Louisiana) or its territorial jurisdictions where the Jackson County procedure has been followed in selecting juries, all pending indictments against persons of Mexican descent are void. The rejection of the "two classes" theory guarantees that all ethnic groups in our nation are assured of equality before the law and are protected against discrimination because of their ancestry or national origin. So, too, a Protestant in a predominantly Catholic community would certainly be protected against "different treatment" by governmental officials due solely to his religious beliefs. It must be remembered that this decision is based strictly on a question of national origin—not race. Those of Mexican descent who decry it as classifying "our people" as non-white should keep this in mind. For that matter "Mexicans" should be proud to be identified with other minority groups, including the ultra-progressive Negro-Americans, instead of attempting to build a cultural fence around themselves and live in a vacuum. Strangely enough, it seems to be the dark-complexioned Mexicans who are the most sensitive. Beyond this we can only speculate. What effect does the Hernandez decision have on the Texas constitutional provision excluding women from jury service? It is deceptively easy to read into a judicial opinion much that is not there by failing to limit the general language employed by the Court to the particular facts involved in the case. It is, of course, evident that, as opposed to men, women are a "distinct class." With reference to jury service, the Texas Constitution singles them out for "different treatment." Is such different treatment based on some "reasonable classification?" ¿Quién sabe?

HERRERA
a pioneer Texan helped write a new chapter in Texas history.
The United States LAW WEEK
22 LW 4237

The petitioner met the burden of proof imposed in Norris v. Alabama, supra. To rebut the strong prima facie case of the denial of the equal protection of the laws guaranteed by the Constitution thus established, the State offered the testimony of five jury commissioners that they had not discriminated against persons of Mexican or Latin American descent in selecting jurors. They stated that their only objective had been to select those whom they thought were best qualified. This testimony is not enough to overcome the petitioner's case. As the Court said in Norris v. Alabama: "That showing as to the long-continued exclusion of negroes from jury service, and as to the many negroes qualified for that service, could not be met by mere generalities. If, in the presence of such testimony as defendant adduced, the mere general assertions by officials of their performance of duty were to be accepted as an adequate justification for the complete exclusion of Negroes from jury service, the constitutional provision . . . would be but a vain and illusory requirement."[11] The same reasoning is applicable to these facts. Circumstances or chance may well dictate that no persons in a certain class will serve on a particular jury or during some particular period. But it taxes our credulity to say that mere chance resulted in there

---

[11]294 U.S., at 598.

being no members of this class among the over six thousand jurors called in the past 25 years. The result bespeaks discrimination, whether or not it was a conscious decision on the part of any individual jury commissioner. The judgment of conviction must be reversed. To say that this decision revives the rejected contention that the Fourteenth Amendment requires proportional representation of all the component ethnic groups of the community on every jury[12] ignores the facts. The petitioner did not seek proportional representation, nor did he claim a right to have persons of Mexican descent sit on the particular juries which he faced.[13] His only claim is the right to he indicted and tried by juries from which all members of his class are not systematically excluded—juries selected from among all qualified persons regardless of national origin or descent. To this much, he is entitled by the Constitution. Reversed.

Each item of each stipulation was amply supported by the testimony adduced at the hearing.

---

[12]See Akins v. Texas, 325 U. S. 398, 403; Cassell v. Texas, 339 U. S. 282, 286–287.

[13]See Akins v. Texas, supra, note 16, at 403. CARLOS C. CADENA and GUS C. GARCIA (MAURY MAVERICK, JR., JOHN J. HERRERA, JAMES DE ANDA, and CHRIS ALDRETE with them on the brief) for petitioner; HORACE WIMBERLY, Assistant Attorney General of Texas (JOHN BEN SHEPPERD, Attorney General, RUDY G. RICE and MILTON RICHARDSON, Assistant Attorneys General, with him on the brief) for respondent. 5.4.54 The United States LAW WEEK (Top of Page).

Appendix IX

GREGORIO CORTEZ'S TRIAL.

Motion for a Change of Venue Being Heard.

SPECIAL TO THE NEWS.

Karnes City, Tex., Oct. 4.—The case of the State vs. Gregorio Cortez, who stands charged in the District Court of Karnes County with the murder of Sheriff W. T. Morris, was called for trial on the 2d instant. The attorneys for the defendant immediately filed a motion to quash the indictment, alleging in the motion that the defendant was discriminated against in the selection of the Grand Jury which found the bill of indictment against him, and that the Mexican race was generally discriminated against in the selection of the Grand and Petit Juries in this county on account of the prejudice existing against that particular race.

Judge Wilson, after hearing the evidence in support of the motion, overruled it. The defendant then, through his attorneys, asked for a change of venue of the case, alleging in his application that it would be impossible for him to obtain a fair and impartial trial in this county on account of the feeling existing against him here, and further alleging that there was a dangerous combination of influential citizens of this county working against him, and by reason of this fact he could not expect a fair trial. The court has been engaged for the last two days in hearing the evidence in support of this motion and it will probably consume all of tomorrow to dispose of same, the special venire of eighty men drawn in this case having been discharged until next Monday. There are numerous officers from different parts of the State in attendance upon court. There is perfect quiet here and everybody seems to be of the opinion that he can have a fair trial in this county.

Dallas Morning News, October 5, 1901, p. 9.